REASSESSING THE PRESIDENCY

THE RISE OF THE EXECUTIVE STATE
AND THE DECLINE OF FREEDOM

REASSESSING THE PRESIDENCY

THE RISE OF THE EXECUTIVE STATE AND THE DECLINE OF FREEDOM

JOHN V. DENSON, ED.

MISES
INSTITUTE

DEDICATION

To H.L. Mencken, the brilliant classical-liberal journalist and staunch critic of the *imperial* American presidents, especially Woodrow Wilson and the two Roosevelts.

ACKNOWLEDGMENTS

First, there are many people associated with the Ludwig von Mises Institute in Auburn, Alabama, to thank, including the supporters and contributors who have made this book possible. Also, thanks go to Lew Rockwell, the president and founder of the Mises Institute; Pat Barnett, who handled the Institute conference at Callaway Gardens, Georgia, where the authors in this book first presented their papers; and Judy Thommesen, Kathy White, and Jamie Creamer, who performed the Herculean task of proofreading, checking all quotations, getting permission to quote, and generally putting the book together.

I want to give special thanks to my legal secretary, Donna Moreman, who worked many extra hours in addition to her regular duties to type many drafts of my chapters and introduction, as well as keeping track of all of the other chapters which I had to read and comment upon. Also, many thanks to Dr. Ward Allen of Auburn, tax historian Charles Adams, and Patrick Reid, in my office, who all read my chapters, as well as others in the book, and gave many helpful comments.

CONTENTS

INTRODUCTION

JOHN V. DENSON

There are already many books analyzing the American presidency, that unique political institution created by our eighteenth-century Founders. Two of the most popular books on this subject are *The Imperial Presidency*, by Arthur M. Schlesinger, Jr.,[1] and *The American Presidency*, by Forrest McDonald.[2] These books are well-researched, and both authors are competent scholars who express their ideas through excellent prose. So why another book on this subject? The main reason is to express various viewpoints in the long tradition of classical liberalism which are not contained in any other books on the presidency with which I am familiar. Schlesinger essentially states the viewpoint of *modern* liberals, and McDonald states basically that of the conservatives. Also, the viewpoints expressed in this volume are very different from the perspectives of most of the professional historians whose polls are studied in the first essay herein by professors Richard Vedder and Lowell Gallaway. In every published poll taken of selected groups of professional historians since 1948, Presidents Abraham Lincoln and Franklin Roosevelt have been rated as two of the three "greatest," compared with the judgment expressed in this book which rates them as the two "worst" presidents.[3] Therefore, we need to begin with an explanation of the term *classical liberalism* and distinguish it from *conservatism* and *modern liberalism*.

Ralph Raico, a classical liberal and a professional historian who has an excellent chapter on President Truman in this volume, has correctly stated that, "Classical liberalism—or simply liberalism, as it was called until around the turn of the century—

[1] Arthur M. Schlesinger, Jr., *The Imperial Presidency* (Boston: Houghton Mifflin, 1973).

[2] Forrest McDonald, *The American Presidency: An Intellectual History* (Lawrence: University Press of Kansas, 1994).

[3] President Washington is invariably ranked with Lincoln and Franklin Roosevelt as the three greatest presidents in these polls of the professional historians, which speaks volumes about the political persuasion of a large part of this profession.

is the signature political philosophy of Western civilization."[4] He is referring to the political philosophy of a limited, constitutional government which follows an economic policy of the free market and a foreign policy of noninterventionism, all ideas which were very popular and influential in America in the eighteenth and early nineteenth centuries. He is not praising the philosophy of big government associated with the term "liberal—" which today signifies a belief in a central government designed to promote egalitarianism, with a regulated, highly taxed economy and an interventionist foreign policy appropriately described, in my opinion, as "globaloney." These modern liberals, who were calling themselves "progressives" or "socialists" in the early part of the twentieth century, later adopted the term "liberal" for the same reasons that the American Whig Party adopted the venerable term "Whig" from the British in the nineteenth century. American Whigs believed in big government and the British Whigs believed in limited government. The adoption of the terms "liberal" and "Whig" were done to confuse the American people about the true intentions of the advocates of big government. Felix Morley described this shell game of labels in 1951 as follows:

> Those who urge the progressive intervention of government in business were once accurately and dispassionately known as "Socialists." But most American Socialists now describe themselves as "liberals," although that designation for a believer in State planning is directly opposite to the historic meaning of the word. There is no doubt that this type of semantic duplicity, or double-talk, has been politically influential.[5]

However, today the political label "liberal" has become such an opprobrious word of political baggage to a significant number of the general public that many modern liberals have retreated to their previous label of "progressives." The modern liberal wants to bring about his plan of the welfare state through the democratic process, or "social democracy," a term born during the French Revolution. The egalitarian ideas of the

---

[4]Ralph Raico, "The Rise, Fall, and Renaissance of Classical Liberalism—Part I" *Freedom Daily* (August 1992): 11.

[5]Felix Morley, *The Foreign Policy of the United States* (New York: Alfred A. Knopf, 1951), p. 4.

French Revolution inspired the socialist movement in the nineteenth century, which filtered into the American political system at the end of that century through the "progressive" movement. As progressives became the dominant political force in the early part of the twentieth century, they changed their label to "liberals."[6]

The word "classical" is defined by the dictionary as "not new and experimental; as, classical political science."[7] In an excellent recent book entitled *Classical Liberalism: The Unvanquished Ideal*, the British political philosopher David Conway points out that the term "liberalism," as used today to describe a political philosophy, must be further defined as either modern liberalism or classical liberalism. He points out that these terms have an opposite meaning, primarily as they relate to the size, power, and purpose of the central government. This is especially true in regard to the role of government as it relates to the economy.[8] We also learn from Conway's book, and as indicated in its subtitle, that classical liberalism is an "unvanquished ideal" which has been almost completely discarded in the twentieth century, primarily as a result of World War I.

Conway traces the historical development of classical liberalism back as far as the seventeenth century, although its roots can actually be traced to ancient Greece, and he states,

> After falling into almost complete intellectual disrepute toward the end of the nineteenth century, classical liberalism was rescued from oblivion and revived in the twentieth century by such notable thinkers as Ludwig von Mises and Friedrich Hayek.[9]

---

[6]This was first noted in two popular magazines at the time, the *New Republic* and *Nation* which both supported their ideas. See Dwight D. Murphey, *Liberalism in Contemporary America* (McLean, Va.: Council for Social and Economic Studies, 1992).

[7]*Webster's New Universal Unabridged Dictionary*, deluxe 2nd ed. (New York: New World Dictionaries/Simon and Schuster, 1979), p. 334.

[8]David Conway, *Classical Liberalism: The Unvanquished Ideal* (New York: St. Martin's Press, 1995); see also another excellent history and analysis of classical liberalism in *Great Thinkers in Classical Liberalism*, vol. 1, *The Locke–Smith Review*, Amy H. Sturgis, ed. (Nashville, Tenn.: LockeSmith Institute, 1994).

[9]Conway, *Classical Liberalism*, p. 8.

Later, Conway comments on the importance of this philosophy:

> No society has ever fully exemplified that form which classi-
> cal liberals maintain is best. Classical-liberal ideas greatly
> influenced the founding fathers of the U.S.A. in their design of
> its constitution. They also inspired much reform in Britain in
> the nineteenth century. However, today, neither society comes
> close to being a liberal polity as classical liberals conceive of
> one. Both contain far too much legislation and regulation
> restrictive of the liberty of members.[10]

Conway reviews the ideas of some of the principal advocates
of classical liberalism, such as John Locke in the seventeenth
century, Adam Smith and David Hume in the eighteenth century, and John Stuart Mill in the nineteenth century.

Ludwig von Mises, one of the two most prominent classical
liberals identified by Conway in the twentieth century, is mainly
known today as an economist, but he expressed many of his
political ideas in 1927 in a book entitled *Liberalism*. He had to
change the title in subsequent editions to distinguish classical
liberalism from the term "liberal" that is used today. The title of
a later edition of the same book was *Liberalism: In the Classical
Tradition*.[11] The other classical liberal identified by Conway,
Friedrich A. Hayek, who is also known mainly as an economist,
was a student of Mises and attended his famous seminars presented in Vienna. Hayek won the Nobel Prize for economics in
1974, though his views on classical liberalism can be seen in his
influential books, *The Road to Serfdom* and *The Constitution of Liberty*.

At the probable risk of justified criticism for oversimplifica-
tion, I will give a brief statement of the ideas and differences of
the three main political philosophies which are important for
readers of this book. Probably the main issue which distin-
guishes classical liberalism from both modern liberalism and
conservatism is the recognition by the classical liberal that a
citizen's own government is more likely to be a threat to his

---

[10]Ibid., p. 25.

[11]Ludwig von Mises, *Liberalism: In the Classical Tradition* (Irvington-on-
Hudson, N.Y.: Foundation for Economic Education and San Francisco: Cob-
den Press, 1985).

liberty than any foreign government or domestic criminal.[12] Therefore, the classical liberal is sensitive to the issue of big government and wants it to be limited to a very narrow range of powers to which it is best suited and otherwise restrained by a constitution from violating the citizens' rights. Therefore, the issue of "liberty versus power" is the essential reference point for the classical liberal regarding government.[13] The American Founding Fathers were very sensitive to this issue of their own government taking away their freedom because of their experience as subjects of the British Empire. They primarily designed the American government through the Constitution and the Bill of Rights, to protect citizens from their own central or federal government by preventing the concentration of too much power into the hands of that government and by letting most of the political power remain with the States and the people. This was made explicit in the Ninth and Tenth Amendments.

On the other hand, *modern* liberals and conservatives both want a larger, more powerful federal government, but each wants this for different purposes. The modern liberals want a big government to regulate the economy and for the egalitarian purposes of the welfare state, so that tax money can be redistributed by central planners and bureaucrats to various groups. Conservatives want a large and powerful government, although usually not as big as the modern liberals, primarily for "national defense," including the CIA, and for "law and order," including the FBI and the Bureau of Alcohol, Tobacco, and Firearms. Also, conservatives believe that government should be in partnership with business and grant it certain favors such as subsidies, tariffs, and protection for its economic interests, both at home and abroad.

Conservatives believe in private enterprise, but classical liberals believe in free enterprise with no partnership or help from the federal government and with virtually no controls or regulations by the federal government over the economy. Both modern liberals and conservatives supported big government during the cold war to fight communism, and they have continued their support in recent times to allow America to become the world's policeman. Classical liberalism believes in free-market global

---

[12]See the classic work by Albert Jay Nock, *Our Enemy, The State* (New York: Free Life Editions, 1973).

[13]See Joan Kennedy Taylor, ed., *Liberty Against Power: Essays by Roy A. Childs, Jr.* (San Francisco: Fox and Wilkes, 1994).

trade but also believes that business and banking interests should engage in foreign trade at their own risk without government aid and that America should not be the world's policeman. This is the classical-liberal idea of a noninterventionist foreign policy.

As Conway states, classical liberalism had a dominant influence at the time of the formation of the American government. Among the Founders, Thomas Jefferson is usually identified as the person most representative of classical liberalism and is most often quoted for his belief "That government governs best which governs the least."[14] Jefferson applied this general idea specifically to the American government: "The policy of the American government is to leave their citizens free, neither restraining *nor aiding them in their pursuits*."[15] Alexander Hamilton, among the Founders, is usually designated as the best representative of conservatism. Christopher Hollis, in his excellent work on American history, summarizes the Jefferson–Hamilton conflict as follows:

> Hamilton was content to support the Constitution because he was confident that, once a central government was established, it would be able at each crisis, or pretended crisis, to filch from the States such powers as might seem to it convenient. In this he has been proved disastrously right. Jefferson, also foreseeing the danger, thought to guard the liberty of the individual by the addition to the Constitution of a series of Amendments [the first Ten Amendments, known as the Bill of Rights]. Many others doubted and were induced to support ratification only by the argument that there could be no danger in giving the Constitution a trial, since any state could always secede again if it wished to do so. What a sorry joke have their descendants made of poor Jefferson and his friends. How Alexander Hamilton must grin from his grave![16]

Both Jefferson and Hamilton served in the first cabinet of President George Washington. Washington is not usually remembered as an intellectual, and he probably favored more of Hamilton's views than Jefferson's concerning the size and power

[14]Charles T. Sprading, ed., *Liberty and the Great Libertarians: Anthology on Liberty, A Handbook of Freedom* (New York: Arno Press and *The New York Times*, 1972), p. 82.

[15]Antony Jay, ed., *The Oxford Dictionary of Political Quotations* (New York and Oxford: Oxford University Press, 1996), p. 193 (emphasis added).

[16]Christopher Hollis, *The American Heresy* (New York: Minton, Balch, 1930), p. 38.

of the federal government. Clearly he did so in regard to the issue of central banking. Nevertheless, Washington was definitely influenced by the classical-liberal ideas which pervaded the eighteenth century and expressed one of the principal classical-liberal viewpoints about government: "Government is not reason, it is not eloquence—it is force! Like fire it is a dangerous servant and a fearful master; Never for a moment should it be left to irresponsible action."[17] Ludwig von Mises went into more detail in describing the danger of government in general, or "the state," by expressing the following classical-liberal idea in his excellent book on politics entitled *Omnipotent Government: The Rise of the Total State and Total War*:

> The state is essentially an apparatus of compulsion and coercion. The characteristic feature of its activities is to compel people through the application or the threat of force to behave otherwise than they would like to behave. . . .
>
> The state is, if properly administered, the foundation of society, of human cooperation and civilization. It is the most beneficial and most useful instrument in the endeavors of man to promote human happiness and welfare. But it is a tool and a means only, not the ultimate goal. It is not God. It is simply compulsion and coercion; it is the police power. . . .
>
> The state is a human institution, not a super human being. He who says "state" means coercion and compulsion. He who says: There should be a law concerning this matter, means: The armed men of government should force people to do what they do not want to do, or not to do what they like. . . . The worship of the state is the worship of force. There is no more dangerous menace to civilization than a government of incompetent, corrupt, or vile men. The worst evils which mankind ever had to endure were inflicted by bad governments. The state can be and has often been in the course of history the main source of mischief and disaster. . . .
>
> The essential characteristic features of state and government do not depend on their particular structure and constitution. They are present both in despotic and in democratic governments. Democracy too is not divine. We shall later deal with the benefits that society derives from democratic government.

---

[17]Sprading, ed., *Liberty and the Great Libertarians*, p. 53.

> But great as these advantages are, it should never be forgotten that majorities are no less exposed to error and frustration than kings and dictators. That a fact is deemed true by the majority does not prove its truth. That a policy is deemed expedient by the majority does not prove its expediency. The individuals who form the majority are not gods, and their joint conclusions are not necessarily godlike.[18]

The danger of democracy to liberty was an important point considered by the American framers, who were as concerned about the dangers to liberty from the majority as from a monarchy. They often referred to the danger of "King Numbers" or "Mobocracy" as a severe threat to liberty, and, therefore, they designed the Constitution, especially the Bill of Rights, to protect citizens' rights from majority rule. Today, most conservatives and modern liberals speak of "protecting democracy" at home or "spreading democracy" abroad, but rarely do they speak of "protecting liberty" or "spreading liberty." As pointed out by Mises, democracy does not necessarily promote liberty and it may even become despotic to a substantial minority.

A couple of aphorisms serve to describe the general philosophy of classical liberalism, which believes in trying to solve social and economic problems primarily through private, voluntary action and in the market economy rather than turning to government. One of these was often expressed by President Ronald Reagan during his campaigns, but, unfortunately, he did not—or was not allowed to—put the idea into practice during either of his two administrations. His campaign slogan was "Government is not the answer, it is the problem." Another which captures the essence of classical liberalism was made by an obscure lyric poet in Germany who died in 1843. He stated, "What has made the State a hell on earth has been that man has tried to make it his heaven."[19]

There have been many reforms, especially in the twentieth century, beginning with the "progressives" and coming up to the

---

[18]Ludwig von Mises, *Omnipotent Government: The Rise of the Total State and Total War* (New Rochelle, N.Y.: Arlington House, 1969), pp. 46–47.

[19]Yohann Christian Friedrich Hölderlin as quoted by F.A. Hayek in *The Collected Works of F.A. Hayek*, vol. 10, *Socialism and War: Essays, Documents, Reviews*, Bruce Caldwell, ed. (Chicago: University of Chicago Press, 1997), p. 175.

modern liberals today who want specific and good social programs. To accomplish their ends, they pass laws to force the program onto everyone and to force all of the taxpayers to pay for it. It is this constant increase in taxation and the power of government in order to create "good" government programs that has been one of the major causes of government becoming a "Leviathan," which then becomes a threat to the liberty of all the citizens.

As noted earlier, the ideas of conservatism and classical liberalism were dominant in American politics at the beginning of the Republic. The battle over what the proper role and power of the federal government should be continued up until the time of the American Civil War. Those individuals who controlled the American government during and at the end of the Civil War believed in a strong central government with a high or protective tariff, which amounted to a partnership between big business and big government. These were the basic ideas of Alexander Hamilton and conservatism at that time. The ideas of Thomas Jefferson and of limited government and states' rights were largely discarded after this war.

One of the principal goals and great achievements of classical liberalism was the abolition of slavery—which occurred throughout Western civilization in the nineteenth century—without war being necessary—except for the revolt in Haiti—despite the fact that slavery had been a significant, well-accepted, worldwide institution for thousands of years. The great tragedy for classical liberalism, and for American political thought, was that the ideas of limited government and states' rights, which were the classical-liberal ideas adopted by the South, became intertwined with the idea of slavery, which classical liberalism opposed. Even though the Civil War was not waged by the North for the purpose of the abolition of slavery, as will be shown in my essay on Lincoln herein, slavery was abolished after the war through the Thirteenth Amendment. However, the war also had the unfortunate effect of destroying the classical-liberal ideas of states' rights and limited government at the same time because they were all advocated by the South. Big government advocates stated, then and now, that states' rights and slavery went hand in hand. Big government advocates, even today, often claim that the abolition of slavery was their great achievement in spite of the fact that big government and slavery had been joined together for many centuries and were the twin evils classical liberalism always opposed.

Immediately after the Civil War, the famous historian of liberty, Lord Acton, wrote to General Robert E. Lee and asked what the result of the Civil War was in Lee's opinion. Lee replied in a letter dated December 15, 1866, and, in part, stated:

> [T]he consolidation of the states into one vast republic, [is] sure to be aggressive abroad and despotic at home . . . [and] will be the certain precursor of that ruin which has overwhelmed all those [governments] that have preceded it.[20]

At the end of the nineteenth century in America the political battle was no longer between classical liberalism and conservatism. It was between two advocates of big government, but for different purposes: one was conservatism, which favored big government and a partnership with big business, and the other was "progressivism," which wanted big government to regulate or control the economy and move toward egalitarianism and the welfare state.[21]

Turning now to the American presidency as viewed by classical liberals, one of my favorite presidents is not covered in this book. He was the first president after the Civil War who attempted to revive the ideas of Jefferson and classical liberalism; unfortunately, however, he was also the last. Grover Cleveland, in my opinion, is the last good president from a classical-liberal perspective, and a few illustrations of his actions while in office will show that classical liberalism does not advocate a "do-nothing" president or one that is weak. Classical liberalism believes that the president should use his power to promote and protect individual liberty rather than to increase the power of the federal

---

[20]John V. Denson, ed., *The Costs of War: America's Pyrrhic Victories*, 2nd ed. (New Brunswick, N.J.: Transaction Publishers, 1999), app. 1, p. 496; see also *Essays in the History of Liberty: Selected Writings of Lord Acton*, J. Rufus Fears, ed. (Indianapolis, Ind.: Liberty Classics, 1985), p. 365.

[21]See Christopher Hollis, *The American Heresy*, cited earlier. This is an excellent study of American history which concludes that the Jeffersonian theory of a limited central government and States' rights ended with the Civil War and was replaced by Hamilton's ideas of big government in partnership with big business, which was solidified into place by Woodrow Wilson who led America into World War I.

government. Cleveland stood for sound money and the gold standard,[22] and he was opposed to the protective tariff.[23] He advocated the increased respect and sovereignty of the States as a check and balance on the power of the central government.[24] Cleveland generally supported the ideas of a limited federal government and the strict construction of the Constitution, a free-market economy, and the separation of banking from the government.[25]

Two good examples of Grover Cleveland acting as a strong president, trying to protect individual liberty rather than promoting power in the federal government, will illustrate my point. The first relates to a domestic issue regarding a rather meager attempt by Congress to create a welfare system—which Cleveland fought because of his belief that the federal government should not be involved in any welfare program, not only because it increased the power of the federal government, but also because it decreased the liberty and the moral character of the people who might become dependent upon it. This political principle in no way meant he was opposed to private charity, which of course he supported. Cleveland used the power of the presidency to veto a federal welfare program of only $10,000 for drought relief in Texas, and he stated:

> I do not believe that the power and duty of the general Government ought to be extended to the relief of individual suffering. . . . A prevalent tendency to disregard the limited mission of this power should, I think, be steadfastly resisted, to the end that the lesson should be constantly enforced that though the people support the Government the Government should not support the people. . . . Federal aid in such cases encourages the expectation of paternal care on the part of the Government and weakens the sturdiness of our National character.[26]

[22]Richard E. Welch, Jr., *The Presidencies of Grover Cleveland* (Lawrence: University Press of Kansas, 1988), pp. 118, 129.

[23]Ibid., pp. 83, 88, 93.

[24]Ibid., p. 147.

[25]Ibid., pp. 147, 207.

[26]Garet Garrett, "The Revolution Was" in *The People's Pottage* (Caldwell, Idaho: Caxton Printers, [1953] 1993), p. 55.

Garet Garrett notes that Cleveland's veto was: "[O]ne way of saying a hard truth that was implicit in the American way of thinking, namely, that when people support the government they control government, but when the government supports the people it will control them."[27] Modern liberalism completely supports government welfare as a principle, and although most conservatives condone the practice, they mainly oppose the amount of tax money for the program and want it to be smaller, rather than opposing the principle of government welfare altogether.

The second example of Cleveland's use of presidential power to promote liberty was his restraint on Congress in regard to the declaration of war which prevented the Spanish–American War during his presidency. Louis Fisher, in his excellent book on the presidential war power, relates the following account of President Cleveland's confrontation with several congressmen:

> Some members of Congress itched for war. An associate of President Cleveland was once present when a delegation from Congress arrived at the White House to announce, "We have about decided to declare war against Spain over the Cuban question. Conditions are intolerable." Cleveland responded bluntly, "There will be no war with Spain over Cuba while I am President." A member of Congress protested that the Constitution gave Congress the right to declare war, but Cleveland countered by saying that the Constitution also made him Commander in Chief and "I will not mobilize the army." Cleveland said that the United States could buy Cuba from Spain for $100 million, whereas a war "will cost vastly more than that and will entail another long list of pensioners. It will be an outrage to declare war." This standoff raises the intriguing possibility that a President, presented with a declaration of war from Congress, could veto it on the ground that intelligence obtained from diplomatic sources demonstrated that war was unnecessary. In such situations, one would assume that this information would be shared with Congress and derail efforts to declare war.[28]

---

[27]Ibid.

[28]Louis Fisher, *Presidential War Power* (Lawrence: University Press of Kansas, 1995), p. 42.

However, Congress later had a willing president to go along with their efforts to abandon the ideas of the Founders, especially George Washington's ideas in his famous *Farewell Address* wherein he promoted a noninterventionist foreign policy. It was President McKinley, who led America into its first imperialistic war by using the lie that the battleship USS *Maine* was sunk by the Spanish.[29] America made its tragic mistake of forgetting its heritage of liberty and by seeking power with the conquest of the Philippines in Asia. The new foreign policy of imperialism was thus born in America.

I had a discussion with Jeffrey Hummel regarding his selection of Van Buren as the best example of a good classical-liberal president, and I asked him if he had considered Grover Cleveland. He stated that while he ranked him very high in most respects, he did not rate him above Van Buren because of Cleveland's use of federal troops to break up the Pullman strike. This action by Cleveland certainly increased the power of the central government over the States. One of his biographers, Richard E. Welch, Jr., sums up this mistake by Cleveland, who severely violated one of the main principles of federalism that was inherent in the Constitution, as it was originally conceived:

> Cleveland was not the first American president to send federal troops to maintain law and order during a railroad strike; Hayes had done so during the "Great Strike" of 1877. Cleveland was, however, the first president to do so at his own initiative and not at the application of a state governor. Not only did the governor of Illinois not request the dispatch of federal troops, he objected publicly and often. Cleveland insisted that under Section 5298 of the Revised Statutes, he possessed the unrestricted authority to dispatch federal troops wherever there was a threat to life and property. [Governor] Altgeld insisted that police powers were reserved exclusively for the states; in time of peace, federal troops could only intervene if invited to do so by a state legislature or governor. Altgeld wrote angry letters to the president and received equally angry replies. Cleveland argued that the troops had been sent only after he had received conclusive evidence from the judicial officers of the United States "that the process of the Federal courts could not be executed through the ordinary means, and upon

---

[29]H.D. Rickover, *How the Battleship* Maine *was Destroyed* (Washington, D.C.: U.S. Department of Navy, 1976), p. 91.

competent proof that the conspiracies existed against commerce between the States."[30]

Welch further elaborates on this use of federal troops by
Cleveland and his evolving stance regarding the authority of the
president:

> For a student of the American presidency, the most interesting
> feature of Cleveland's actions during the Pullman strike is the
> witness they offer to his evolving conception of presidential
> authority. In the campaign of 1884, Cleveland had run on a
> Democratic platform calling for renewed respect for the rights
> and sovereignty of the individual states, and for many years
> thereafter he had given periodic warning against undue cen-
> tralization of power in the federal government. In 1894 he
> claimed for the chief executive of the national government the
> authority to supersede the state of Illinois as the protector of
> law and order within its boundaries. Brushing aside the objec-
> tions of Governor Altgeld, Cleveland assumed the police pow-
> ers traditionally reserved to state and local governments as he
> authorized the use of federal military power in a labor–man-
> agement dispute. Like his hero Andrew Jackson, Cleveland
> could simultaneously speak against the centralization of
> power in the federal government and expand the power of the
> federal executive. Cleveland's interpretation of the traditions of
> the Democratic Party was, at least, flexible. He quoted Jeffer-
> son when denouncing federal interference in local elections,
> but he acted like Jackson when he overrode Governor Altgeld
> and claimed supremacy for the federal government and its
> chief executive during the Chicago railroad strike.[31]

I think Jeffrey Hummel is probably right to downgrade
Cleveland's status because of his action in the Pullman strike,
but I want to relate another example about Grover Cleveland
which shows him to be a person of sound political principles
rather than simply a person loyal to his political party regardless of its principles. This occurred in the presidential election in
1896, when Cleveland refused to vote for William Jennings
Bryan, who was the Democratic Party nominee, and he also
refused to vote for William McKinley, who was the Republican

---

[30]Welch, *The Presidencies of Grover Cleveland*, p. 145.
[31]Ibid., p. 147.

nominee. Instead he voted for a third-party candidate, Senator John M. Palmer. His biographer, Welch, states:

> Here perhaps, he could be indicted for party recusancy, if not treason. Cleveland, however, believed that the Democratic Party under Bryan was no longer the party of Jefferson and Jackson. The Bryan Democrats were Populists, and the Gold Democrats who were running as a third party were the true heirs of the Founding Fathers of Democracy.[32]

There is still much to admire about President Cleveland from a classical-liberal viewpoint.

David Conway's book, as mentioned earlier, states that classical liberalism is the "unvanquished ideal." It is true that these ideas have never been proven wrong or defeated but were simply discarded after the American Civil War. With the exception of the two terms of Grover Cleveland, classical liberalism never again became a major influence in American politics, in my opinion.[33] Some might argue that the administrations of Presidents Harding and Coolidge demonstrate a rebirth of classical liberalism, but I question this. They certainly did not seem to have the commitment to classical liberalism that Cleveland did, and they were greatly affected by the results of President Wilson's war and his despotic domestic policy during the war confirming Robert E. Lee's prediction that the consolidated federal government would become "aggressive abroad and despotic at home." The successive Harding and Coolidge administrations attempted to return America to "normalcy" after the war was over, but while they both stood for the principle of reducing government spending, as well as the excessive rates of Wilson's income tax, they were still "good" Republicans who advocated a higher protective tariff to help business. They also were caught up in the ideas of the "Progressive Era" and supported much government regulation of industry, like the radio, so long as government also remained in a partnership with industry.[34]

---

[32]Ibid., p. 211.

[33]For the same opinion, see David T. Beito and Linda Royster Beito, "Gold Democrats and the Decline of Classical Liberalism, 1896–1900," *The Independent Review: A Journal of Political Economy* vol. 4, no. 4 (Spring 2000): 555–71.

[34]The interested student may want to consult the following works analyzing the Harding and Coolidge administrations: Eugene P. Trani and

My study of constitutional history indicates that the Founders intended for the legislative branch of Congress, composed of both the House and Senate, to be the dominant branch of the federal government, which was then very limited in scope and power. Today the executive has become, by far, the dominant branch of government, even to the point that it is the main threat to the liberty and freedom of American citizens. Arthur Schlesinger, Jr., a modern liberal, admits and comments on this fact as follows:

> The Imperial Presidency was essentially the creation of foreign policy. A combination of doctrines and emotions—belief in permanent and universal crisis, fear of communism, faith in the duty, and the right of the United States to intervene swiftly in every part of the world—had brought about the unprecedented centralization of decisions over war and peace in the Presidency. With this came an unprecedented exclusion of the rest of the executive branch, of Congress, of the press and of public opinion in general from these decisions. Prolonged war in Vietnam strengthened the tendencies toward both centralization and exclusion. So the imperial Presidency grew at the expense of the constitutional order. Like the cowbird, it hatched its own eggs and pushed the others out of the nest. And, as it overwhelmed the traditional separation of powers in foreign affairs, it began to aspire toward an equivalent centralization of power in the domestic polity.
>
> We saw in the case of Franklin D. Roosevelt and the New Deal that extraordinary power flowing into the Presidency to meet domestic problems by no means enlarged presidential authority in foreign affairs. But we also saw in the case of FDR and the Second World War and Harry S. Truman and the steel seizure that extraordinary power flowing into the Presidency to meet international problems could easily encourage Presidents to extend their unilateral claims at home.[35]

Schlesinger continues:

> The imperial Presidency, born in the 1940s and 1950s to save the outer world from perdition, thus began in the 1960s and

---

David L. Wilson, *The Presidency of Warren G. Harding* (Lawrence: University Press of Kansas, 1977) and Robert Sobel, *Coolidge: An American Enigma* (Washington, D.C.: Regnery Publishing, 1998).

[35]Schlesinger, *The Imperial Presidency*, p. 208.

1970s to find nurture at home. Foreign policy had given the President the command of peace and war. Now the decay of the parties left him in command of the political scene, and the Keynesian revelation placed him in command of the economy. At this extraordinary historical moment, when foreign and domestic lines of force converged, much depended on whether the occupant of the White House was moved to ride the new tendencies of power or to resist them.[36]

Of course, we know that all the occupants of the White House after Franklin Roosevelt rode this vast presidential power over foreign and domestic matters, although at different paces, rather than resisting it.

Another competent observer of this phenomenon of the shift of power to the presidency during the Franklin Roosevelt era is Dean E. Blythe Stason of the University of Michigan Law School, who stated that the years immediately prior to and during World War II caused a "shift in constitutional dominance over the affairs of the nation from the legislative and judicial supremacy of bygone years to the ascendancy of the executive branch of government."[37] Constitutional scholar E.S. Corwin agrees with Schlesinger and Stason that presidential power was greatly increased by war, but he traces the origin of the dangerous "war powers" doctrine back to President Lincoln, who drastically increased the powers of his office and the federal government in general during the Civil War. Corwin states:

> The sudden emergence of the "Commander-in-Chief" clause as one of the most highly charged provisions of the Constitution occurred almost overnight in consequence of Lincoln's wedding it to the clause that makes it the duty of the President "to take care that the laws be faithfully executed." From these two clauses thus united, Lincoln proceeded to derive what he termed the "war power," to justify the series of extraordinary measures that he took in the interval between the fall of Fort Sumter and the convening of Congress in the special session on July 4, 1861.[38]

[36]Ibid., p. 212.

[37]Edward S. Corwin, *Total War and the Constitution* (New York: Alfred A. Knopf, 1947), p. vii.

[38]Ibid., p. 16.

Another knowledgeable observer of the phenomenon of the increased powers of the federal government, and especially the power of the presidency because of war, all at the expense of liberty, was Charles Evans Hughes.[39] As a result of World War I, and on June 21, 1920, Hughes expressed his fear for the future of the country with the following words: "We may well wonder in view of the precedents now established whether constitutional government as hitherto maintained in this Republic could survive another great war *even victoriously waged.*"[40]

Another dangerous expansion of the power of the presidency is commented upon by Dean Blythe Stason. He shows that the executive branch received vastly increased powers through the regulatory legislation of the administrative bodies to which Congress unconstitutionally delegated its lawmaking powers. He states:

> [H]ow far can we continue to progress in the direction of conferring upon administrative officials more and more virtually unreviewable discretionary power over the lives and activities of men without finally reaching a state of absolutism that can no longer be called a liberal democracy.[41]

He continues by stating that:

> [W]e are confronted by the uncomfortable fact that the experience of history has not yet shown us how constitutional democratic institutions can be preserved in the presence and under the control of ever-increasing administrative discretion.[42]

The process of the general increase in the power of the federal government from the Civil War to the present is a good demonstration of the "ratchet effect" made famous in Robert Higgs's excellent book *Crisis and Leviathan*. In the Civil War, Lincoln vastly increased the power of the presidency, and after his

---

[39]Hughes served in numerous public offices including Governor of New York, Associate Justice of the U.S. Supreme Court, Secretary of State and as Chief Justice of the U.S. Supreme Court from 1930 to 1941. Woodrow Wilson barely defeated him for the presidency in 1916.

[40]Corwin, *Total War and the Constitution*, p. 2; see also Schlesinger, *The Imperial Presidency*, p. 93 (emphasis added).

[41]Corwin, *Total War and the Constitution*, pp. vii and viii.

[42]Ibid., p. viii.

death Congress reacted and tried to assert its supremacy. Finally, the Supreme Court stepped in to assert its power over Congress and the presidency. The McKinley and Wilson administrations then reacted on behalf of the presidency through the "war powers" established by Lincoln and asserted the supremacy again of the presidency. The net effect of the three branches jockeying for positions of power, which has continued throughout the remainder of the twentieth century, has increased the power of the federal government in general. However, as Schlesinger stated, the "Imperial Presidency" is the main problem today and it was created primarily by Franklin Roosevelt. The Constitution, as written by our Founders, is now in shreds and all but forgotten. No longer do presidents go to Congress to ask for a declaration of war. They simply send troops where and when they please throughout the world. Rarely does the Supreme Court hold acts of Congress unconstitutional because they cannot find in the Constitution where Congress has been given specific authority to legislate. Congress simply does what it wants and the Supreme Court turns its head. The Supreme Court no longer merely interprets the law, it makes laws, a power granted in the Constitution only to Congress.

It is because of this vast increase in the power of the presidency to its present "imperial" status that the Mises Institute decided to hold a conference at Callaway Gardens in Pine Mountain, Georgia, to study this threat to our liberty. The Mises Institute was formed in 1982 by Lew Rockwell to promote the ideas of Ludwig von Mises, which fit comfortably within the long tradition of classical liberalism and the ideas of the American Founding Fathers. If America is ever to regain its greatness and again become the best example of individual freedom and liberty in the world, as envisioned by our Founders, we must investigate how, where, and when we abandoned those ideas. The conference and this book have attempted to do this. The chapters on the presidencies of Thomas Jefferson and Andrew Johnson and the Jacksonian era were not part of the conference but were vital to the scope and role of the present-day "imperial presidency." Jefferson was the first classical-liberal president, and while Andrew Johnson was not a classical liberal, he was a Jacksonian Democrat who opposed a strong centralized government. During Johnson's administration, immediately following that of Lincoln, he took a courageous stand against a runaway

Congress which sought to impose on the South the most aggressive and dictatorial government in American history.

The chapters in this volume are arranged generally in the chronological order of the presidents they discuss. The first, by Richard Vedder and Lowell Gallaway, sets the stage for all of the other chapters and shows the ratings by the professional historians, and other polls, which differ greatly from the assessment of the presidents made by the classical-liberal viewpoint of the authors herein. Vedder and Gallaway attempted to rate the presidents through an objective standard by determining the growth of the central government during their respective terms since the size and power of the central government is a key factor for classical liberals. While this objective standard is useful, it certainly has its problems, as Vedder and Gallaway admit, since it rates Andrew Johnson and Harry Truman as two of the best. This result follows mainly because Johnson and Truman followed presidents who greatly expanded the federal government, and therefore the Johnson and Truman administrations looked very good by comparison as they both attempted to reduce, in some fashion, the size and power of the federal government. This was especially true of Andrew Johnson, as Scott Trask's chapter demonstrates. However, as Ralph Raico points out later, Harry Truman certainly is not rated highly from a classical-liberal viewpoint. Vedder–Gallaway show ratings by establishment historians or "court historians" over the years and then place the polls beside their objectively-created standard. The reader will see that other authors herein differ at times and to some degree from the Vedder–Gallaway objective rating insofar as whether a president is "good" or "bad" from a classical-liberal viewpoint.

David Gordon shows that President Washington has been rated as one of the three greatest presidents by most historians' polls, as well as the general public opinion, because of his unquestionable integrity rather than his philosophy of government or his actions during his two terms as president. Scott Trask covers the two administrations of Thomas Jefferson and shows the difficulty of working within the framework of the Constitution to accomplish goals which the president feels are "right," such as the Louisiana Purchase. Trask also refers to the problems of Jefferson and the Barbary pirates. Modern advocates of the idea that the Constitution does not require a declaration of war by Congress to enable the president to send troops abroad often point to the experience of Presidents Jefferson and Madison in dealing with these pirates without a declaration of war. Therefore, they argue that modern presidents need no declaration of war by Congress. Louis Fisher comments about this modern position and replies specifically to historian Arthur Schlesinger, Jr., as follows:

> Harking back to Jefferson's use of ships to repel the Barbary pirates, Schlesinger claimed that American Presidents "have repeatedly committed American armed forces abroad without prior Congressional consultation or approval."
>
> Schlesinger neglected to point out that Jefferson told Congress he was "unauthorized by the Constitution, without the sanction of Congress, to go beyond the line of defense." It was the prerogative of Congress to authorize "measures of offense also." Congress enacted ten statutes authorizing action by Presidents Jefferson and Madison in the Barbary wars.[43]

Marshall DeRosa points out that the Supreme Court has been an accomplice to the rise of executive power, and while this is true throughout the presidency, and especially during the term of President Franklin Roosevelt, most of his emphasis relates to the period of time from 1812 to 1826, and therefore showcases Jefferson. He emphasizes that the attack on states' rights by the Supreme Court in the early Republic weakened the checks and balances intended by the Founders on the power of the central government. Randall Holcombe's chapter on the electoral college centers mainly on its evolution from the time of President Washington to the election of President Jackson, with special emphasis on the administration of Jackson. He points out correctly that the framers of the Constitution had a great fear that democracy would destroy liberty if left unchecked and unrestrained, therefore the electoral college was designed to prevent "King Numbers" from selecting the president. He further points out that Andrew Jackson had an unrealistic confidence in democracy and failed to see the wisdom of the Founding Fathers. The demise of the electoral college, as it was envisioned by the Founders, has contributed greatly to the decline in the quality of presidents, especially in the twentieth century.

Clyde Wilson relates the problem of political parties as it may affect the presidency, and while this theme is applicable to

---

[43]Fisher, *Presidential War Power*, p. 90.

all of the presidents, he concentrates mainly on the Jacksonian era, and for that reason, I have put his essay at this point. The title of Wilson's chapter, "The American President: From Cincinnatus to Caesar," could have served as the title of this book.

The Founders looked to the example of the ancient Roman Republic and its leaders for much of their inspiration in creating the American Republic. One of the heroes of the Roman Republic was the legendary general and statesman Cincinnatus who was chosen by the Senate and called from his farm in 458 B.C. to lead Rome and its army in order to save the Republic. Upon achieving victory he immediately relinquished all of his political and military powers and returned to his plow on his four-acre farm. In fact, George Washington became the first president of The Society of Cincinnati in America because of his relinquishment of military and political power and retirement to his home at Mt. Vernon.[44]

The main theme of the book traces the progression of power exercised by American presidents from the early American Republic, which compared favorably with the laudatory ideal of Cincinnatus, up to the eventual reality of the power-hungry Caesars which later appeared as presidents in American history. The history of Rome is very similar in this respect to the history of America. The question inherent in our study of the American presidency created by our Founders is to determine how it degenerated into the office of American Caesar. Did the character of the man who held the office corrupt it, or did the power of the office, as it evolved, corrupt the man? Or was it a combination of the two? Was there too much latent power in the original creation of the office as the Anti-Federalists claimed? Or was the power externally created and added to the position by corrupt or misguided men?

Jeffrey Hummel's chapter on Martin Van Buren asserts that he is our best example of a "good" classical-liberal president and compares him to the British statesman and classical liberal, William Gladstone. Hummel shows that during Van Buren's one term, he was primarily concerned with protecting individual liberty in both his domestic and foreign policies and resisted the temptation to enlarge the powers of the central government when given the opportunity to do so. Presidents must be

---

[44]See Garry Wills, *Cincinnatus: George Washington and the Enlightenment, Images of Power in Early America* (Garden City, N.Y.: Doubleday, 1984).

judged on their "greatness" when they had the levers of power in their hands. While Jefferson, by most measurements, would be considered a "great" man and maybe the greatest to serve as president, Van Buren may have been a "better" president because of the actions he took when he had the power to do so. The reader will see in a footnote to Clyde Wilson's chapter that he nominates John Tyler as one of the great classical-liberal presidents, placing him possibly above Van Buren.

Tom DiLorenzo and I team up on the critique of Abraham Lincoln, who is generally considered by most professional historians and the general public as one of the three "greatest" presidents in American history. DiLorenzo concentrates on Lincoln's economic policies, and specifically the protective tariff and mercantilism, which were major causes of the American Civil War. I also show the importance of the protective tariff and other political pressures which motivated Lincoln to wage war against the South and examine in detail his masterful political trick of maneuvering the South into firing the first shot at Fort Sumter, rallying what had been weak support in the North into a strong force to preserve the Union. Lincoln's war resulted in a victory for the economic policies of mercantilism and the political idea of a strong centralized government which destroyed the idea of states' rights thereby changing the course of American history by 180 degrees.

Scott Trask and Carey Roberts cover the amazing administration of President Andrew Johnson. Johnson took a courageous stand against the Radical Republicans in Congress, who wanted to impose military rule and conquest of the South in order to perpetuate the new, regional Republican Party. The period of Andrew Johnson's administration and the several which followed it are known as the Reconstruction era, one of the most neglected periods of study. It is also one of the most important in order to understand the purpose and result of the Civil War as demonstrated by the increase of power into the central government and general decline of states' rights and individual liberty. Generally, modern professional historians have not been kind to Andrew Johnson. John F. Kennedy, in his excellent book, *Profiles in Courage*, tells the interesting and courageous story of Senator Edmund G. Ross of Kansas, who, along with six other senators, voted not guilty at the impeachment trial of President Andrew Johnson, and thus destroyed their own political careers while supporting the Constitution. Kennedy could have easily just written about the political courage of Andrew Johnson.[45]

Joseph Stromberg addresses the next major change in American history which occurred during the administration of President McKinley, which carried America into foreign imperialism by acquiring an Asian empire. The abandonment of the 100-year-old tradition of noninterventionism was largely the result of big government joining with big business. Thomas Woods examines the presidency of Theodore Roosevelt and shows how he enjoyed the exercise of power and openly advocated the "Imperial Presidency," which would later be consummated by his cousin, Franklin. Theodore Roosevelt completely turned the ideas of the Founders upside down by assuming that, as president, he had the power to act unless specifically prohibited from doing so by the Constitution. He is truly an excellent example of the beginning of the modern American Imperial Presidency. George Bittlingmayer's chapter on the presidential use and abuse of the Sherman Antitrust Act from Cleveland to Clinton is inserted at this point because much of the history he examines relates to the actions of Presidents Theodore Roosevelt and William H. Taft during the "Trust Busting Era." The Sherman Act became the principal weapon in the battle of the economic titans as the House of Morgan battled the Rockefeller interests. This Act made winning the presidency a major economic factor since the executive branch included the Justice Department which administered this Act, and it could be used as a weapon against one's economic enemies. William Marina examines William Howard Taft, who was first the administrator of McKinley's colonial empire in Asia. Marina addresses the question of whether Taft supported imperialism or was a reluctant imperialist and examines the bureaucracy that he created.

Richard Gamble's assessment of Woodrow Wilson's administration is very timely since America, under President Clinton, reinstituted Wilson's policy of "humanitarian" wars. President

---

[45] John F. Kennedy, *Profiles in Courage* (New York: HarperPerennial, 1964), pp. 132–58. Also for a very favorable and thorough analysis of the amazing career of Andrew Johnson, including his presidency and his subsequent return to the U.S. Senate, see Lloyd Paul Stryker, *Andrew Johnson: A Study in Courage* (New York: Macmillan, 1929).

George Washington, in his *Farewell Address*, strongly warned against America becoming involved in the constant wars of Europe. Woodrow Wilson explicitly repudiated that advice and launched America into World War I, which has drastically changed both American and European history. It was primarily Wilson's war which caused the great ideas of classical liberalism to be abandoned for the remainder of the twentieth century.

Tom DiLorenzo and I again team up on the president who firmly established the Imperial Presidency, Franklin Roosevelt. DiLorenzo covers his New Deal economic policies and I cover the story of Pearl Harbor and show how he followed Lincoln's example by causing the "enemy" to fire the first shot, thereby unifying a reluctant American people into waging a war by deceitfully making them believe that Japan was the aggressor.

Barry Dean Simpson and Yuri Maltsev team up to show how Josef Stalin and Franklin Roosevelt joined forces to cause despotism to be a dominant factor following World War II. Maltsev was an economic adviser to the Soviet leader Mikhail Gorbachev and he has a unique perspective in viewing Franklin Roosevelt as a world leader who had the bloody dictator Stalin as his "partner in crime."[46]

Paul Gottfried examines the original ideas of the framers who designed the Constitution to allow the legislative branch to lead the American Republic, but today it is the presidency which is dominant and the main danger to individual liberty. Ralph Raico shows how President Truman exercised the imperial powers established primarily by his predecessor in office in both foreign and domestic affairs and openly proclaimed for the first time in American history that a president can declare war and may ignore the Constitution which clearly provides that only Congress can declare war. Truman said he could simply send troops to Asia without Congressional authority or approval. Raico's article, which covers Truman's foreign and domestic policies, demonstrates clearly that Truman does not deserve, from a classical-liberal viewpoint, to be rated highly, as the Vedder–Gallaway objective test rated him.

---

[46]For an excellent analysis of the disastrous consequences of Franklin Roosevelt's alliance with the bloody dictator Josef Stalin, see Amos Perlmutter, *FDR and Stalin: A Not So Grand Alliance, 1943–1945* (Columbia: University of Missouri Press, 1993).

Michael Levin examines the presidency in the role of social engineer over the American people, and he discusses mostly the presidencies of Truman, Lyndon Johnson, and Nixon. Joseph Salerno examines the presidential mismanagement of the economy, and in particular the monetary policies of John Kennedy and Richard Nixon.

The final chapter is by Hans-Hermann Hoppe, who states his objections to the Constitution in the same spirit as such notable Anti-Federalists as Patrick Henry and George Mason did when the Constitution was being written and ratified. Patrick Henry refused to go to the Constitutional Convention because he "smelled a rat," and George Mason refused to sign the Constitution as a delegate because of the strong centralization of power into the federal government which the document provided. Patrick Henry and George Mason have been proven correct by American history and Hoppe believes that the fatal error was to give the central government the power to tax and legislate, even though the original Constitution placed much limitation on these powers. It took a Constitutional amendment in 1913 during the administration of Woodrow Wilson to allow the income tax, and Congress now legislates on almost all issues, not just those involving powers delegated to the central government by the Constitution. Federalism and the Ninth and Tenth Amendments have very little, if any, meaning to any of the three branches of government today. Hoppe suggests that we may have reached a point of no return with our present Constitution and that a new "American Revolution" in political thought may be needed in order to protect individual liberty.

Appendix A contains the courageous speech by Congressman Clement Vallandigham of Ohio, and it cost him dearly. He was later arrested and tried by a military court in Ohio which convicted him for the expression of his political opinions and exiled him from the United States—a rare and unconstitutional sentence. He condemned the dictatorial conduct of President Lincoln who virtually destroyed the Constitutional limitations on the power of the president through his concept of the "war powers." Lincoln's actions during the Civil War were the greatest usurpations of power by any president in American history and set a harmful example which had tremendous influence on such twentieth-century presidents as Woodrow Wilson and Franklin Roosevelt.

Appendix B contains the outstanding speech by U.S. Senator Robert M. La Follette, Sr., opposing President Woodrow Wilson's request for a declaration of war against Germany for World War I. The Senator has been proven correct. America's entry into that war was probably the greatest error in American history. America's entry into the war led to the Treaty of Versailles, which was so unfair to Germany that it created conditions which allowed Hitler to assume power by advocating the repeal or overthrow of the treaty. Senator La Follette has been proven correct in his opposition to entering World War I, signing the Treaty of Versailles, and joining the League of Nations. The League of Nations proved to be simply a vehicle by which England and France tried to enforce the unfair and vindictive Versailles treaty.

1

RATING PRESIDENTIAL PERFORMANCE

RICHARD VEDDER AND LOWELL GALLAWAY

Politicians crave to be president of the United States for a variety of reasons. Presidents are guaranteed a comfortable life of moderate affluence, as they usually are able to command a lifetime income of millions of dollars in book royalties, lecture, and corporate director fees after leaving office. A president has a great deal of power and derives satisfaction from being the most important person in the country, if not the world. Yet there is a third form of compensation that is particularly alluring: the chances of receiving eternal recognition in the history books. The reputation of chief executives with historians, political scientists, and other presidential scholars is important in defining a president's long-term legacy. Thus several presidents have taped their office conversations with a view of improving their post-presidential standing. Dick Morris, sometime adviser to President Bill Clinton, suggested in his lively account of his years advising Clinton that the president was particularly attentive and interested in discussions of his longer-term historical reputation.[1] In their conversations with aides and friends, presidents as diverse as Harry Truman and Richard Nixon made frequent references to the presidency in a historical context.[2] Like his predecessors, Bill Clinton thought of his role in

---

[1]Dick Morris, *Behind the Oval Office: Winning the Presidency in the Nineties* (New York: Random House, 1997).

[2]Richard Nixon liked to discuss presidential leadership with world leaders. For example, he had a lengthy conversation about Lincoln and his greatness with Chou En-lai during his first China visit. See Richard Nixon, *The Memoirs of Richard Nixon* (New York: Grosset and Dunlap, 1978), pp. 577–78. Discussions of the relative performance of past leaders, both in the U.S. and in the world, were common with key staff personnel. See, for example, H.R. Haldeman, *The Haldeman Diaries: Inside the Nixon White House* (New York: G.P. Putnam's Sons, 1994), p. 227. Harry Truman was an amateur historian who ruminated considerably on the performance of his predecessors.

history with nearly every move he made, and in that he was hardly unique.

STATIST BEHAVIOR AND PRESIDENTIAL REPUTATION: A HYPOTHESIS

Thus modern presidents not only try to appeal to voters, but to the constituency of historians and other presidential scholars who are influential in interpreting the presidency in future years. It is our thesis that these scholars generally are dependent on government for their income and tend to be sympathetic to an expansive role for the state. Most are politically liberal in the modern American sense of that word. To persons with this perspective, a "good" president is one who actively uses the powers of the American federal government, while a president who curtails the state and allows markets greater primacy in the allocation of resources and the distribution and creation of income is considered lackluster or mediocre.

This hypothesis is to some extent testable. There have been a number of surveys of presidential scholars asking them to rank the presidents. These give a good guide to the reputations of former heads of state among the group who write the history books and biographies which ultimately impact on popular opinion. Also, there is some imperfect but useful information about the relative size of American government. Budgetary data are available for the U.S. government since the Washington administration, and scholars have likewise estimated the size of the national output back to the beginning of the Republic. Accordingly, it is possible to calculate federal government expenditures as a percent of the national output throughout history.

It is reasonable to assume that government's share of total output will grow with activist presidents, and that it will fall with

---

See Harry S. Truman, *Memoirs By Harry S. Truman*, vol. 2, *Years of Trial and Hope* (Garden City, N.Y.: Doubleday, 1956), pp. 191–204. No one takes a back seat to Lyndon Johnson in being absorbed by his role in history. As Michael Beschloss says,

> So seized was Johnson by the historical and managerial importance of secretly recording his conversations that on his first night as president, despite all his other worries, he apparently had the presence of mind to ensure that his first conversations in his new job were captured on a . . . taping system. (*Taking Charge: The Johnson White House Tapes, 1963–64* [New York: Simon and Schuster, 1997], p. 548)

presidents who are skeptical of the ability of the government to positively promote the common welfare. If presidential scholars on balance have a bias toward activism, we would hypothesize that there would be a positive relationship between the growth of the relative size of government during a presidency and the reputation of that president with the presidential scholars.

Austrian scholars tend to be cautious about the use of quantitative measures, and with good reason. Several caveats are in order before we proceed. First, the gross national product (GNP) or gross domestic product (GDP) is a statistic that is profoundly difficult to calculate with any reasonable degree of accuracy in the best of circumstances. To cite just two problems, there is much market activity that is excluded (illegal services, intra-family transactions, etc.), and governmental output is valued at the prices government paid for inputs, which often is considerably more than the amount that consumers of governmental services value the output. The problem is compounded for earlier eras, for which data are limited.[3]

In addition, while government expenditures are but one measure of the command that the state has over the citizenry, it is not a perfect one. For example, government can establish regulatory mandates that impose enormous costs on the public but involve only modest government expenditures. A case in point: Consumers probably spend billions of dollars annually buying air bags for their cars that they otherwise would not spend. Consequently, government spending as a percent of GNP or GDP does not fully capture the impact of this mandate on our lives.

Despite these caveats (and others not mentioned), government spending as a percent of total output is probably a reasonably good proxy for government activism. If government spending as a percent of GNP is rising, government in some sense is becoming more important in our lives and is intervening in some sense to a greater extent in our economy. If such spending falls as a percent of total output, there is a strong likelihood that governmental influence in our lives is declining.

---

[3]See, for example, Richard Vedder, "Statistical Malfeasance and Interpreting Economic Phenomena," *Review of Austrian Economics* 10, no. 2 (1997): 77–89.

RANKING THE PRESIDENTS
FROM A CLASSICAL-LIBERAL–AUSTRIAN PERSPECTIVE

We took data on governmental expenditures by fiscal years, as reported in *Historical Statistics of the United States* and other documents, and related them to estimates of total output reported by the Department of Commerce for modern times, by Simon Kuznets for a few decades around the beginning of this century, and by Thomas Senior Berry for the century between the beginning of constitutional government and 1889.[4] We have calculated federal expenditures as a percent of GNP or GDP for the entire period.[5] Figure 1 shows that there have been significant fluctuations in that statistic, with a generally strong upward trend.

We then calculated the *change* in government spending as a percent of GDP during the administration of each president, comparing the year prior to the inauguration of the president with the president's last year in office. Thus in his last full year in office, 1980, Jimmy Carter presided over a government that spent 21.22 percent of the nation's total output, compared with 20.44 percent in 1976, the year before he assumed office. Subtracting the latter figure from the former, we conclude that the federal government absorbed 0.78 percent more of the gross domestic product during the Carter presidency. Two presidents, William Henry Harrison and James Garfield, served as presidents for only a fraction of a year, and thus are excluded from our analysis.

From a classical-liberal or Austrian perspective, increases in government's share of total output would likely be considered bad or intrusive on personal liberty, while decreases would be considered good. In Table 1, we rank the presidents solely using

---

[4]Our output data were obtained from Thomas S. Berry, *Production and Population Since 1789: Revised GNP Series in Constant Dollars* (Richmond, Va.: The Bostwick Press, 1988), U.S. Department of Commerce, Bureau of the Census, *Historical Statistics of the United States, Colonial Times to 1970* (Washington, D.C.: U.S. Government Printing Office, 1975), and the *Economic Report of the President*, various years.

[5]Before 1929, the measure of output used is gross national product. From 1929 to the present, the U.S. Department of Commerce has calculated gross domestic product, which we use. The difference between GNP and GDP is typically very small, less than 1 percent.

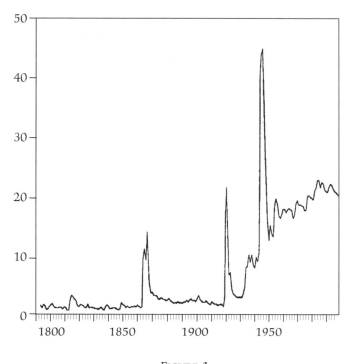

FIGURE 1
FEDERAL GOVERNMENT SPENDING
AS A PERCENT OF TOTAL OUTPUT, 1792–1997

such a criterion, ignoring any other factor that might be used to evaluate the president. We also indicate what the ranking of the presidents was using the broadest of the conventional presidential scholar assessments, namely that conducted by Murray and Blessing, as well as a *Chicago Tribune* ranking compiled by Steve Neal.[6] These ratings end with President Carter. The Murray–Blessing survey involved 846 American historians belonging to the American Historical Association; the Neal study involved a self-selected group of 49 rather distinguished presidential scholars.[7] Finally, we include another recent large survey

[6]Robert K. Murray and Tim H. Blessing, *Greatness in the White House: Rating the Presidents, Washington Through Carter* (University Park: Pennsylvania State University Press, 1988) and Steve Neal, "Our Best and Worst Presidents," *Chicago Tribune Magazine* (January 10, 1982).

[7]The original ranking of presidents was conducted by Arthur M. Schlesinger, Sr. His last poll appeared as "Our Presidents: A Ranking by 75

Table 1
Four Rankings of Presidential Performance
(Ranked from Best [no. 1] to Worst)

Vedder–Gallaway	Murray–Blessing	Steve Neal	Ridings–McIver
1. Truman	1. Lincoln	1. Lincoln	1. Lincoln
2. A. Johnson	2. F. Roosevelt	2. Washington	2. F. Roosevelt
3. Harding	3. Washington	3. F. Roosevelt	3. Washington
4. Clinton	4. Jefferson	4. T. Roosevelt	4. Jefferson
5. Nixon	5. T. Roosevelt	5. Jefferson	5. T. Roosevelt
6. Coolidge	6. Wilson	6. Wilson	6. Wilson
7. Grant	7. Jackson	7. Jackson	7. Truman
8. Eisenhower	8. Truman	8. Truman	8. Jackson
9. Washington	9. J. Adams	9. Eisenhower	9. Eisenhower
10. Monroe	10. L. Johnson	10. Polk	10. Madison
11. J.Q. Adams	11. Eisenhower	11. McKinley	11. Polk
12. Jefferson	12. Polk	12. L. Johnson	12. L. Johnson
13. Taft	13. Kennedy	13. Cleveland	13. Monroe
14. Taylor	14. Madison	14. Kennedy	14. J. Adams
15. Arthur	15. Monroe	15. J. Adams	15. Kennedy
16. T. Roosevelt	16. J.Q. Adams	16. Monroe	16. Cleveland
17. Van Buren	17. Cleveland	17. Madison	17. McKinley
18. Hayes	18. McKinley	18. Van Buren	18. J.Q. Adams
19. Buchanan	19. Taft	19. J.Q. Adams	19. Carter
20. Reagan	20. Van Buren	20. Taft	20. Taft
21. Cleveland	21. Hoover	21. Hoover	21. Van Buren
22. Tyler	22. Hayes	22. Hayes	22. G.H.W. Bush
23. Fillmore	23. Arthur	23. Ford	23. Clinton
24. Jackson	24. Ford	24. Arthur	24. Hoover
25. McKinley	25. Carter	25. B. Harrison	25. Hayes
26. Pierce	26. B. Harrison	26. Taylor	26. Reagan
27. B. Harrison	27. Taylor	27. Carter	27. Ford
28. Kennedy	28. Tyler	28. Tyler	28. Arthur
29. Carter	29. Fillmore	29. Coolidge	29. Taylor
30. Polk	30. Coolidge	30. A. Johnson	30. Garfield
31. J. Adams	31. Pierce	31. Fillmore	31. B. Harrison
32. Madison	32. A. Johnson	32. Grant	32. Nixon
33. G.H.W. Bush	33. Buchanan	33. Pierce	33. Coolidge
34. L. Johnson	34. Nixon	34. Buchanan	34. Tyler
35. Ford	35. Grant	35. Nixon	35. W.H. Harrison
36. Hoover	36. Harding	36. Harding	36. Fillmore
37. Wilson			37. Pierce
38. Lincoln			38. Grant
39. F. Roosevelt			39. A. Johnson
			40. Buchanan
			41. Harding

(Ridings–McIver) of about 700 political scientists which extends up to Bill Clinton.[8]

Before going into the specifics of the rankings, we calculated the correlation coefficient between our libertarian-oriented ratings and those involving historians and presidential scholars. The correlation coefficient between our ranking and the Murray–Blessing assessment was -0.35 and was statistically significant at the 5-percent level. The correlation between our ranking and the *Chicago Tribune* and Ridings–McIver rankings was a bit lower, -0.31 and -0.30, respectively. The negative correlation coefficient is interesting. Since our ranking is solely determined by the relative size of government, the results support our initial hypothesis that, other things equal, presidential historians prefer presidents who expand the relative size of the public sector. Within the presidential scholar community, there seems to be great agreement, as the correlation coefficients between the various "mainstream" rankings above is between +0.964 and +0.977.

The Founding Fathers (Washington, John Adams, Jefferson, and Madison) rank very well among presidential scholars, all above average, with Washington and Jefferson consistently in the top five. While both Washington and Jefferson rank in the top third of presidents in our initial rankings, John Adams and James Madison rank in the bottom third of presidents, as government spending expanded significantly in their administrations, with Madison presiding over the War of 1812, one of the least glorious moments in American military history by any reckoning.

Looking at the antebellum presidents (Monroe through Buchanan), our assessment of Monroe and John Quincy Adams is moderately more favorable than the scholars, but we rank Andrew Jackson sharply lower than the other scholars (see Table 1). Jackson is something of an enigma to libertarians or Austrians, who like his suspicion of central power and his successful efforts to rid America of central banking but dislike his expansionist view of the federal government and his increased

---

Historians," *New York Times Magazine* (July 29, 1962). The poll stops with President Eisenhower and thus is viewed as too dated for discussion here.

[8]William J. Ridings and Stuart B. McIver, *Rating the Presidents: A Ranking of U.S. Leaders, from the Great and Honorable to the Dishonest and Incompetent* (Secaucus, N.J.: Carol Publishing Group, 1997).

spending, among other things. Our assessment of Van Buren and Tyler does not deviate radically from the presidential scholars, but that is not the case with James Polk, who consistently ranks in the top third of presidents among the scholars but makes it into our bottom ten. Again, he is an expansionist president. We rate Zachary Taylor and Millard Fillmore higher than the scholars, but share with them a generally mediocre evaluation of Franklin Pierce. Finally, we find Buchanan to be a rather average president who presided over a slight decline in government spending relative to total output, whereas the presidential scholars all view Buchanan as one of our five worst presidents.

Abraham Lincoln is revered by presidential scholars and, by most Americans, is considered the greatest president in all the surveys mentioned above, greater even than such giants as George Washington and Thomas Jefferson. In our "black box" calculations, however, Lincoln appears as America's second *worst* president. Under Lincoln, the government's role in American economic life grew to what were, up to then, unprecedented levels. The country was subjected to hyperinflation, ended links of the currency to precious metals, and introduced an income tax, as well as such nonlibertarian phenomena as military conscription and the suspension of *habeas corpus* rights. More importantly, it endured a massive civil war that killed more Americans than any other conflict. The robust rate of economic growth prevailing in the 1840s and 1850s ground to a halt for several years, and it took the South over a century to regain its relative economic standing. To Austrians, this is a nightmare. On moral grounds as well as the grounds of promoting free markets for labor services, Lincoln can be championed for ending slavery, but such subjective considerations did not enter into our rankings, which were purely based on the statistical evidence relating to the size of government.

Looking at the postbellum nineteenth-century presidents (Andrew Johnson through McKinley), we diverge sharply from presidential scholars with respect to the first two, Andrew Johnson and U.S. Grant, whom the scholars view as being among the worst presidents, but whom we evaluated very highly.[9] In a

---

[9]Another surprising admirer of Andrew Johnson was Harry S. Truman, who referred to him as "one of the most mistreated of all Presidents." See his *Memoirs*, vol. 2, p. 197.

sense, both presidents were in the right place at the right time from the standpoint of our approach to evaluating greatness, as they presided over dismantling most of the governmental apparatus that existed during the Civil War. While government spending as a percent of total output fell sharply under both Johnson and Grant, the decline was only about two-thirds of the increase in government's share of output that occurred during the Lincoln years. This is consistent with the notion of Robert Higgs that "crises" lead to a ratchet effect, whereby government spending rises dramatically, then declines only modestly during the subsequent return to normalcy.[10] We will return to this later. We generally like Rutherford B. Hayes and Chester A. Arthur a bit more than the presidential scholars, and Grover Cleveland and William McKinley a bit less. We are in agreement with their mediocre evaluation of Benjamin Harrison.

Turning to the first third of the twentieth century, we diverge sharply from the presidential scholars with respect to virtually every president. Theodore Roosevelt is always on the presidential scholars top-five list, but we put him near the middle. His type of activist "progressive" regulatory policies and foreign policy initiatives do not endear him to Austrian libertarian types, but do to statist-oriented presidential scholars. We like William Howard Taft a good deal more than the other scholars, but our divergence here is nothing like that in the case of Woodrow Wilson. Wilson ranked sixth in all the cited polls, but third from the bottom in our list. On his watch the income tax was enshrined in the American Constitution, the Federal Reserve was established, and more militant government intervention ensued in the private sphere (for example, new antitrust laws). And, from the standpoint of rankings, the most important fact was that the United States became embroiled in World War I, beginning the era of extensive American involvement in foreign disputes.

We evaluated Harding and Coolidge highly, placing them in the top ten. Naturally, they both are in the bottom ten in the lists of the presidential scholars, with Harding ranking dead last. While Harding's administration was mired in scandals, they appear to be modest relative to those of the Clinton era. Moreover,

---

[10]Robert Higgs, *Crisis and Leviathan: Critical Episodes in the Growth of American Government* (New York: Oxford University Press, 1987).

taxes were slashed, and industrial production during Harding's tragically short tenure rose over 60 percent. Furthermore, Harding let markets work to end the 1920–1921 depression. Playing golf and poker and drinking whiskey, Harding allowed the price mechanism to lower unemployment from double-digit levels when he assumed office to less than 4 percent when he died. Yet, returning to Higgs's ratchet effects, the combined exertions of Harding and Coolidge in reducing government, while commendable, did not return us to the prewar norm. Herbert Hoover is a horse of a different color. No one seems to like Hoover, but we like him even less than the presidential scholars, putting him on our short list of worst presidents. Aside from being a pre-Keynesian big spender, Hoover interfered in major ways in labor markets, setting the stage for the Great Depression.[11] He was a meddling interventionist, a Franklin D. Roosevelt without the charisma.

In the large presidential surveys, Franklin D. Roosevelt ranks above George Washington, right behind Abraham Lincoln. In our objective evaluations, he was absolutely the worst American president. Roosevelt, more than any other man, set the stage for the modern American welfare state. We are today still grappling with problems that are part of the Roosevelt legacy, ranging from Social Security to anachronistic laws regulating labor and financial markets. Whether Roosevelt could have kept America out of World War II may be debatable, but Roosevelt's statist legacy is significant independent of the war effort. To mainstream scholars, Roosevelt's activism is something to be admired. Ignored are the facts that America took longer to get out of the Great Depression than any other nation, and that the median annual unemployment rate during Roosevelt's twelve years in office exceeded 17 percent.

Turning to the postwar presidents, Harry Truman is another example of someone whose ranking benefitted from his predecessor's profligacy. Truman is on everyone's top-ten list, including

---

[11]See Murray N. Rothbard, *America's Great Depression* (Auburn, Ala.: Mises Institute, 2000), especially chaps. 7 and 8, or Richard Vedder and Lowell Gallaway, *Out of Work: Unemployment and Government in Twentieth-Century America*, updated ed. (New York: New York University Press, 1997), especially chap. 5. Government spending as a percent of GDP rose dramatically during the Hoover administration, far more than during the first two (prewar) terms of Franklin D. Roosevelt.

ours. Truman presided over a sharp decline in government spending—but to nowhere near the levels relative to output prevailing in the prewar era. Truman's reduction in government spending as a percent of total output ranks first, but that occurred despite his basic interventionist instincts. We return to this point later.

The same thing can be said for Eisenhower, whom we rank highly, similar to the mainstream scholars. His good ranking comes from the end of the Korean War. We think the scholars seriously overrate John F. Kennedy, but our divergencies regarding Lyndon Johnson and Richard Nixon are even greater. The historians think Lyndon Johnson was a very good president, no doubt because of his Great Society, which essentially is the reason we reach the opposite conclusion, ranking him, along with Gerald Ford, as the worst postwar president. Nixon, on the other hand, gets high marks from us and very low marks in the other surveys. Many presidential scholars were born and raised as Nixon-haters. Our high evaluation relates to some modest reduction in the public sector as a consequence of the end to the Vietnam War. Spending soared during Gerald Ford's brief tenure, as he went along with a Democratic Congress's spending spree, ostensibly to get the nation out of a severe recession.

Our ranking of Jimmy Carter is similar to that of Murray–Blessing and Steve Neal—a below-average president. Carter is rising in the rankings over time, however, and actually is slightly above the average in the Ridings–McIver poll, no doubt reflecting both Carter's postpresidential efforts at winning popularity and the statist orientation of political scientists. Ronald Reagan is right in the middle in our rankings. While his antigovernment rhetoric was good, the actual reduction in governmental spending as a percent of GDP was extremely small. Unsurprisingly, the Ridings–McIver poll ranks Reagan well below average. George H.W. Bush ranks lower in our estimation than in the Ridings-McIver poll. Government spending grew significantly in the Bush years, as well as such other interventions as the Americans with Disabilities Act, a law raising the minimum wage, expanded civil rights legislation, and so forth.

Any evaluation of Bill Clinton must be tentative. Based on his first five years of performance, however, Clinton ranks high. Government spending as a percent of GDP has declined noticeably during his administration, although more credit probably goes to the antistatist Republican Congress elected in 1994 than to the president, a man who tried to foist a major expansion in government (the Clinton healthcare proposal) onto the American people. Interestingly, the Ridings–McIver poll gives Clinton a mediocre ranking, far below ours.

ALTERNATIVE WAYS OF RANKING PRESIDENTS

Our rankings based on changes in government spending relative to total output can be criticized on a number of grounds, some of which we mentioned above. To begin, a shift in, say, one-half of 1 percent of the national output away from government today is not a dramatic change in the role of government in our society—after all, federal spending exceeds 20 percent of GDP. Yet in the early nineteenth century, a reduction in government spending from 2 to 1.5 percent of GDP involved a very significant relative downsizing of government. Perhaps we should evaluate presidents by the *percentage change* in the proportion of national output absorbed by the federal government. For example, if government spending falls from 2.0 to 1.5 percent of GDP, we would consider that a 25 percent decline (1.5 is 25 percent less than 2 percent), while a reduction from 20 percent to 19.5 percent of GDP, precisely the same absolute change, is a change of only 2.5 percent—one-tenth as much. Accordingly, in Table 2, we offer a variant of the original rankings based on percentage changes in the government spending—GDP ratio.

Another problem arises because some presidents inherit a government swollen in size by a recent crisis (most often a war) and despite interventionist tendencies manage to reduce it in size. Harry Truman is the classic case in point. Accordingly, we used a different statistical approach to a third variant of presidential rankings. With ordinary least squares regression analysis, we used as our dependent variable annual government spending as a percent of GDP for the years 1792 to 1997, and introduced the inherited size of government for each president as an independent variable in the analysis, along with "dummy" variables for each president, referenced on Bill Clinton. We derived our rankings from the coefficients for the dummy variables.

The alternative approaches to presidential assessment have little impact on the rankings at the extremes. Harry Truman, Andrew Johnson, and Warren G. Harding are at the top in all

Table 2
Alternative Presidential Rankings Based on Government Size

Percent Change in the Federal Government's Share of GDP	Regression Model With Inherited Status and Dummy Variable
1. A. Johnson	1. Truman
2. Truman	2. A. Johnson
3. Harding	3. Harding
4. Washington	4. Taylor
5. Coolidge	5. Van Buren
6. Grant	6. Grant
7. J.Q. Adams	7. Washington
8. Taylor	8. Monroe
9. Taft	9. Tyler
10. Jefferson	10. Cleveland
11. Monroe	11. Jefferson
12. Van Buren	12. Fillmore
13. Arthur	13. Jackson
14. T. Roosevelt	14. Madison
15. Buchanan	15. J. Adams
16. Hayes	16. B. Harrison
17. Tyler	17. J.Q. Adams
18. Clinton	18. Arthur
19. Nixon	19. Pierce
20. Eisenhower	20. Polk
21. Cleveland	21. Eisenhower
22. Reagan	22. Hayes
23. Kennedy	23. T. Roosevelt
24. Carter	24. McKinley
25. McKinley	25. Buchanan
26. Jackson	26. Coolidge
27. Fillmore	27. Taft
28. G.H.W. Bush	28. Clinton
29. L. Johnson	29. L. Johnson
30. Pierce	30. Nixon
31. Ford	31. Kennedy
32. B. Harrison	32. Reagan
33. Madison	33. Carter
34. Polk	34. G.H.W. Bush
35. Adams	35. Wilson
36. Hoover	36. Ford
37. Wilson	37. Hoover
38. F. Roosevelt	38. Lincoln
39. Lincoln	39. F. Roosevelt

variants. Likewise, Franklin D. Roosevelt, Abraham Lincoln, Herbert Hoover, and Woodrow Wilson rank in the bottom five in all rankings. Most of the modern presidents rank lower in the alternative rankings. Bill Clinton goes from 4th to 18th or 28th, for example, and Richard Nixon from 5th to 19th or 30th, that is from above average to about average (in the first variant) or into the bottom third of the presidents (second variant). Dwight Eisenhower goes from 8th to 20th or 21st in the rankings. Our own sense is these are probably more accurate statements of the contributions of these presidents from the standpoint of human liberty. Several modern presidents (for example, Gerald Ford, Lyndon Johnson, John F. Kennedy, George H.W. Bush) are viewed poorly in all variants of the rankings. In one ranking (the regression model), Ronald Reagan falls into the bottom third of all presidents, which strikes us as somewhat too harsh, as he ranks below Nixon and Lyndon Johnson.

John Adams and James Madison are viewed as bad presidents in two of our models, but slightly above average using the regression model. Andrew Jackson, who is ranked 24th and 26th in the spending models, moves up to the bottom of the top third (13th) in the regression model. Moving up even more is Martin Van Buren, who goes from a so-so 17th in the original estimation to 12th in the percentage change model to 5th in the regression model. Similar movements occur for John Tyler and Zachary Taylor, with the latter being among the top ten by either of the two alternative variant models. The regression model likewise moves Millard Fillmore into the top third of American presidents. Other presidents move less dramatically.

In the postbellum era, U.S. Grant is highly rated in all rankings, Rutherford B. Hayes is consistently in the middle, Chester A. Arthur a bit above the middle, and William McKinley consistently below the middle. In the regression model, Grover Cleveland moves from just below the median to the bottom of the top ten.

Turning to the twentieth century, the historians consistently rank Theodore Roosevelt high, while we consistently rank him in the middle third of presidents. The regression model moves Taft down out of the top third of the presidents where our other estimates put him. The nonregression spending models consistently put Coolidge in the top ten, but the regression model drops him to the bottom of the middle third of presidents.

COMPOSITE RANKINGS: SPENDING-BASED MODELS
AND THE MAINSTREAM SCHOLARS

There are arguments for and against any set of our rankings, or, for that matter, those of the mainstream scholars. In Table 3, we present a composite of both our and the mainstream rankings, ordering the presidents from best to worst by summing our three rankings shown in Tables 1 and 2 above, and by combining the rankings shown in the three polls of mainstream scholars.

The differences in the two sets of rankings are profound. For sake of discussion, let us assert that the top thirteen (or one-third) of the presidents (excluding William Henry Harrison and James Garfield) were "good," that the middle thirteen were "average" and that the bottom thirteen were "poor." Using that taxonomy, a *majority of the presidents considered good by us using government size as the measurement of assessment were considered poor by mainstream scholars*. Specifically, we are speaking of Andrew Johnson, Warren G. Harding, U.S. Grant, Zachary Taylor, Calvin Coolidge, John Tyler, and Chester A. Arthur. Almost half (six) of the presidents that the mainstream scholars considered good, we assessed as being poor: Abraham Lincoln, Franklin D. Roosevelt, Woodrow Wilson, James Polk, Lyndon B. Johnson, and James Madison. All six of these presidents by any definition were highly activist chief executives. Others on their "good" list, such as Andrew Jackson and Theodore Roosevelt, also were known for their aggressive use of presidential authority. Thus the "good" presidents as evaluated by mainstream scholars were mostly highly activist, while their "poor" president list was dominated by relative laissez-faire types such as Arthur, Taylor, Coolidge, and Harding.

Another way in which we differ from the mainstream scholars is that we tend to find most of the good presidents in the early decades of the Republic, while we evaluate the more recent presidents far less favorably. For analytical purposes, let us divide the history of the U.S. into three periods of roughly equal length: the early period encompassing the first thirteen presidents, Washington through Pierce; a middle period encompassing thirteen presidents from Buchanan through Harding; and a modern period encompassing the thirteen presidents since Calvin Coolidge.

A majority (seven) of the thirteen presidents on our "good" list came from the early period, while only two came from the modern (Coolidge and after) era. By contrast, a majority (seven) of the bad presidents came from the modern era, compared with

Table 3
Composite Rankings: Vedder–Gallaway and "Experts"

Vedder–Gallaway	Mainstream "Experts"
1. Truman	1. Lincoln
2. A. Johnson	2. F. Roosevelt
3. Harding	3. Washington
4. Grant	4. Jefferson
5. Washington	5. T. Roosevelt
6. Taylor	6. Wilson
7. Monroe	7. Jackson
8. Jefferson	8. Truman
9. Van Buren	9. Eisenhower
10. J.Q. Adams	10. Polk
11. Coolidge	11. L. Johnson
12. Tyler	12. J. Adams
Arthur	13. Madison
14. Eisenhower	14. Kennedy
15. Taft	15. Monroe
Clinton	16. Cleveland
17. J. Adams	McKinley
18. Cleveland	18. J.Q. Adams
19. T. Roosevelt	19. Van Buren
20. Nixon	Taft
21. Hayes	21. Hoover
22. Buchanan	G.H.W. Bush
23. Fillmore	23. Hayes
24. Jackson	Clinton
25. McKinley	25. Carter
Reagan	26. Ford
27. Pierce	27. Arthur
B. Harrison	28. Reagan
29. Madison	29. B. Harrison
30. Polk	30. Taylor
Kennedy	31. Tyler
32. Carter	Pierce
33. L. Johnson	33. Coolidge
34. G.H.W. Bush	34. Fillmore
35. Ford	35. A. Johnson
36. Hoover	36. Nixon
Wilson	37. Grant
38. Lincoln	38. Buchanan
39. F. Roosevelt	39. Harding

three each in the early and middle periods. Why? In the modern era, government spending has tended to grow fairly consistently as a share of gross domestic product, and the most conservative and laissez-faire of presidents (Ronald Reagan in particular comes to mind) have done relatively little about it. In the early years of the Republic, this strong upward trend in government spending was not apparent.

Our time preference (to use an Austrian expression) for the earlier period was not shared as enthusiastically by the conventional historians and political scientists. They find modern presidents to be far better than we do. For example, they believe four of the good presidents come from the modern period, compared with two for us. We believe seven of the bad presidents come in the modern era, compared with their three.

TAKING INFLATION INTO ACCOUNT: FINAL RANKINGS

Any mechanistic procedures for evaluating presidents based on a single, albeit important, criterion is bound to have deficiencies. We do not really believe, for example, that Harry Truman is the best of all presidents, although we would agree that such presidents as Franklin D. Roosevelt and Woodrow Wilson are probably about as bad as the rankings indicate. One important factor that is not included in the above rankings is measurable, however; namely price stability. While we have made the equivalent of a respectable, if modest, scholarly career out of pointing out deficiencies in price indices, they nonetheless crudely approximate changes in the purchasing power of currency. Most economists, and virtually all free-market oriented ones, would argue that price inflation is typically a bad thing. Five percent inflation annually is worse than 1 percent inflation, which in turn is worse than overall price stability.

The institutional arrangements governing our monetary system have varied substantially over time, and with that the president's ability to effect stability. Over a majority of the history of the nation, some form of central bank (for example, the Second Bank of the United States, the Federal Reserve System) has played a significant role in the creation of money, and that bank usually has had a fair amount of independence from the president. Nonetheless, the central bank itself is a creation of the government, and typically the president has made key appointments of personnel to the bank (for example, the chairman and members of the Board of Governors of the Federal Reserve System). Moreover, the president has been influential in other ways in influencing prices, such as Lincoln's support of the issuance of greenbacks (fiat paper money) during the Civil War, or through their policies on the role of gold and silver in the monetary system. For example, both Franklin D. Roosevelt and Richard Nixon took steps to essentially eliminate gold as a medium of exchange.

While most economists with an appreciation of the powers of markets in allocating resources would agree that inflation is bad, there is some division of opinion on what is the optimal policy regarding the purchasing power of money. Austrians tend to look with great disdain on the discretionary creation of money by central banks, even if that creation is associated with price stability as measured by price indices. To Austrians, such increases in the supply of money lead to a divergence of money interest rates from the true rate of time preference, or of what Wicksell called the "natural rate" of interest. The classic case of inappropriate monetary manipulation occurring within an environment of measured price stability was in the 1920s.[12]

From that perspective, a zero rate of reported inflation is not necessarily good. Austrians would probably in general applaud the moderately deflationary monetary record of the last third of the nineteenth century during the heyday of the classical gold standard, for example, and would have condemned a "stable price" monetary policy in that period that augmented monetary growth induced by increased gold stocks with paper money creation in order to maintain price stability in some version of the consumer price index. In our "variant 1" in Table 4, a negative rate of inflation is considered good, and the more negative the inflation rate, the better.[13]

In variant 2 in Table 4, we assume that the "optimal" amount of measured inflation is zero, and that ideally the nation is best served by having currency that maintains its purchasing

---

[12]See Rothbard, *America's Great Depression*, chap. 4.

[13]Another approach would have been to look at some measure of monetary aggregates, or of paper money created by government fiat, or bank credit expansion. Unfortunately, good monetary statistics are not available for the earlier decades under examination.

Table 4
Rankings Based on Size of Government and Inflation*

Variant 1	Variant 2
1. Harding	1. J.Q. Adams
2. A. Johnson	2. Jefferson
3. Grant	3. Taylor
4. Monroe	4. J. Adams
5. Van Buren	Coolidge
6. Taylor	6. Buchanan
7. Jefferson	7. Fillmore
8. Arthur	8. Jackson
9. Tyler	9. Grant
10. J.Q. Adams	Cleveland
11. Hayes	11. Tyler
12. Cleveland	12. A. Johnson
13. Coolidge	McKinley
Truman	Eisenhower
15. J. Adams	15. Arthur
16. Polk	16. Van Buren
Buchanan	17. B. Harrison
Hoover	T. Roosevelt
19. Eisenhower	19. Truman
20. Fillmore	20. Taft
21. Jackson	21. Monroe
22. Washington	22. Madison
23. T. Roosevelt	23. Washington
24. Taft	24. Clinton
25. McKinley	25. Hayes
26. B. Harrison	26. Kennedy
27. Clinton	27. Pierce
28. Madison	28. Harding
29. Nixon	29. Polk
30. Pierce	30. Nixon
Kennedy	31. Reagan
32. Reagan	32. L. Johnson
33. L. Johnson	33. F. Roosevelt
34. G.H.W. Bush	34. G.H.W. Bush
35. F. Roosevelt	35. Ford
36. Carter	Carter
37. Ford	37. Wilson
38. Wilson	38. Hoover
39. Lincoln	39. Lincoln

*See text for explanation; both variants based one-half on size of government considerations and one-half on price stability–inflation considerations.

power at a constant rate over time.[14] It can be argued that information costs of understanding the signals generated by markets are lower during periods of aggregate price stability. Under this scenario, the "best" presidents from a monetary policy perspective are the ones who maintain price stability, and 5 percent annual deflation (which occurred, for example, under Herbert Hoover) is as bad as 5 percent annual inflation (which occurred, for example, under Ronald Reagan). Since negative rates of inflation occurred during thirteen presidencies, these alternative views on appropriate monetary policy lead to somewhat different results.

Before presenting the rankings, several caveats must be stated. Aggregating price changes into an index is an exercise fraught with peril. It is doubly a problem in the earlier era when systematic price data were not collected by a small army of bureaucrats as is the case today. Problems of quality change, weighting, changing relative price effects, and other issues make it prudent to treat any findings with caution.[15] Nonetheless, as indicated earlier, these price indices are probably roughly right—they report huge inflation during the administrations of Lincoln, Wilson, and Truman, for example, and even the most orthodox Austrian would agree that such inflation in fact did occur, despite deficiencies in price indices.

In Table 4, we report our rankings of presidents with an inflation adjustment. We took the rankings in Table 3, added the numerical rank based on the rate of inflation, and then ranked the presidents based on the numeric sum of the two numbers (the lower the number, the better the perceived performance). Implicitly, we are putting an equal weight on size-of-government

---

[14]Still another option would be to look at the variations in the rate of inflation, taking the view that any given inflation, if highly predictable, will be anticipated by economic agents, reducing if not eliminating most of the adverse effects of the inflation.

[15]A special problem exists for the Washington and Adams administrations. We used the consumer price index (CPI) as reported by the Bureau of Labor Statistics, U.S. Department of Labor. That index starts in 1800. We correlated the Warren–Pearson index of wholesale prices against the aforementioned CPI for the years 1800 through 1830, and then used that regression to predict values of the CPI for the years 1788 through 1799, which we then used in our rankings. Data used were obtained in *Historical Statistics* and the *1997 Economic Report of the President.*

and price stability considerations. As discussed above, variant 1 assumes that measured deflation is preferable to perfect price stability, while variant 2 considers perfect price stability as optimal.

Turning to the variant 1 (which we suspect many Austrians would find preferable), six presidents move at least ten ranks from that reported in our rankings based on the size-of-government consideration alone (Table 3). Harry Truman goes from 1st (which we are subjectively uncomfortable with) to tied for 13th. Because of the lifting of World War II price controls in 1946, the reported inflation rate is probably too high for Truman, and too low (because of the price controls) for Roosevelt.[16] Two other presidents fall dramatically on the basis of high reported inflation: George Washington goes from 5th to 22nd, which may be very unfair given the particularly dubious quality of the data in that era, and Bill Clinton goes from being tied for 15th to 27th, which we subjectively view as very fair indeed. Three presidents move up in the rankings substantially. James Polk goes from being tied for 30th to being tied for 16th, that is, from being clearly in the list of "bad" presidents to being one that might be called roughly average. The same thing happens even more dramatically to Herbert Hoover, who moves from 36th to 18th. The high recorded deflation of the Hoover era is viewed as a sign of a highly inspired monetary policy, a view that to our knowledge is actually espoused by no economist, living or dead. Even with this decidedly pro-Hoover interpretation, he barely is above the median for all presidents. Last, the moderate deflation of the Hayes presidency helps him move from 21st to 11th in our rankings.

In variant 2, monetary greatness depends on achieving price stability. Compared with our rankings in Table 3, fully thirteen (one-third) of the presidents move dramatically in the rankings. John Quincy Adams moves from 10th to 1st. Others moving up importantly include John Adams (17th to 4th), Millard Fillmore (23rd to 7th), James Buchanan (23rd to 7th), Andrew Jackson

---

[16]Truman wanted to continue price controls and vetoed the bill continuing them on the grounds that it was too weak. This left the nation with no price-control law. Repressed inflation came out into the open in 1946. Correcting for this problem, however, would not dramatically change the rankings of Truman or Roosevelt.

(24th to 8th), William McKinley (tied for 25th to 12th), and Benjamin Harrison (27th to 17th). Moving down in the rankings in a significant fashion are Washington (5th to 23rd), Harding (3rd to 28th), Andrew Johnson (2nd to 12th), Harry Truman (first to 19th), James Monroe (7th to 21st), and Richard Nixon (20th to 30th).

With either set of inflation-related rankings, the modern presidents fare poorly. Using variant 1, eight of the thirteen worst presidents are from the modern era (defined as from Coolidge to the present); in variant 2, seven of the worst come from this period. None of the top ten presidents in either list is from the modern era. The inflation associated with the era of Keynesian economics leads to relatively low evaluations of modern presidents.

Comparing the two variations of the inflation adjustment, most of the bad presidents are the same in both cases. Looking at the best presidents, four are in the top ten in both lists: Thomas Jefferson, John Quincy Adams, Zachary Taylor, and U.S. Grant. Warren Harding, James Monroe, Martin Van Buren, and Andrew Johnson drop sharply in rankings in the second variant that evaluates deflation negatively. In the first variation, Herbert Hoover is slightly above average; in the second variation, he is America's second worst president.

PRESIDENTIAL PERFORMANCE
AND POLITICAL AFFILIATION

The mainstream scholars are largely liberal and probably mostly vote for Democratic Party candidates for president. Conventional wisdom suggests that Republican candidates tend to favor smaller government and sound money, so our classical-liberal rankings should be expected to give higher assessments of Republican presidents than Democrats. Examining the presidents since 1860, when the first Republican was elected (Lincoln), we can look at the party affiliation of the twenty-four presidents who were Republicans or Democrats. (Andrew Johnson was not a member of either party at the time of his election to the vice presidency in 1864.)

Looking first at the mainstream scholar evaluations (from Table 3), let us arbitrarily give the grade of A to the top eight ranked, B to the second eight, etc. The mainstream scholars give three Democrats As (Franklin D. Roosevelt, Wilson, and

Truman), three Bs (Lyndon Johnson, John F. Kennedy, and Grover Cleveland), one C (Clinton) and one D (Carter), for a cumulative grade point average (on a 4.0 scale) of 3.0, or a B average.

The mainstream evaluation of Republicans is far more negative. The only As go to activists Lincoln and Theodore Roosevelt. Eisenhower, Arthur, and McKinley get Bs, while Hayes, Taft, Hoover, and G.H.W. Bush get Cs. The experts give three Ds, to Ford, Reagan, and Benjamin Harrison. While no Democrats are considered failures, four Republicans are: Coolidge, Nixon, Grant, and Harding. The cumulative average is 1.75, about a C–, dramatically below the B average given Democrats. The Democratic-interventionist bias of the so-called experts seems confirmed.

In Figure 2, we show our distribution of grades (using the same grading scale as above) for Republican and Democratic presidents, using variant 1 of Table 4 (taking into account inflation) as our measure. Our distribution of grades of Republicans is almost even across the board, with three at every level except D. As go to Harding, Grant, and Arthur; Bs to Hayes, Coolidge, and Hoover; Cs to Eisenhower, Theodore Roosevelt, and Taft; Ds to McKinley, Benjamin Harrison, Nixon, and Reagan; and Fs to G.H.W. Bush, Ford, and Lincoln. The cumulative grade point average is a lowly 1.93, a little below a C average, and below the average of all presidents (including the antebellum ones before the modern two-party system is fully established). So much for the possible pro-Republican bias of our rankings. Indeed, the evidence here seems to show that Republicans are not overwhelmingly supportive of principles of small government and sound money, their rhetoric notwithstanding. No Republican in the past two-thirds century received a grade above C.

At the same time, however, our assessment of the Democrats is even more scathing, as Figure 2 shows. There are no As, Cleveland and Truman getting B. While Clinton and Kennedy eked out passing grades (Ds), fully four presidents were given failing grades: Lyndon Johnson, Franklin Roosevelt, Jimmy Carter, and Woodrow Wilson. The cumulative average is 1.0, or a D. While it is true that we find the Republicans on average to be better than the Democrats, modern presidents of either political affiliation have tended to be mediocre, Democrats somewhat more so than Republicans.

REPUBLICAN PRESIDENTS

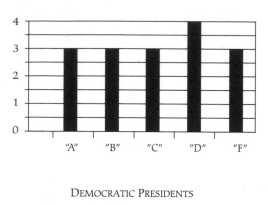

DEMOCRATIC PRESIDENTS

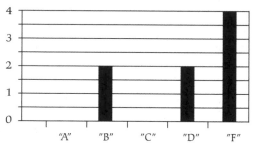

FIGURE 2
VEDDER–GALLAWAY "GRADES" FOR PRESIDENTS,
BY POLITICAL PARTY, BASED ON TABLE 4, VARIANT 1

ADDITIONAL OBSERVATIONS

The rankings above are based on the size of government and, in Table 4, on the presence of inflationary or deflationary conditions. There are numerous other things that could be used to evaluate presidents—for example, the growth in real income per capita or the level of tariffs. Unfortunately, the data on these (and most other possible additional variables) are not available in a reliable enough form for us to feel comfortable with their use over the entire two-century sweep of American history.

The purpose of these rankings is to call into doubt the subjective evaluations of so-called experts on the presidency, a group dominated by individuals with a bias toward state intervention. From the standpoint of the philosophy that "the best government is the one that governs least," conventional wisdom is severely wanting. That wisdom considers Warren G. Harding, U.S. Grant, and Chester A. Arthur to be mediocre or bad presidents. Our assessment (using variant 1 of Table 4) evaluates these men as very good presidents. Conventional wisdom suggests that Lincoln, Franklin D. Roosevelt, Woodrow Wilson, and Lyndon Johnson were very good or great presidents; our rankings puts these activist chief executives in the bottom ten.

At the same time, we do not consider these rankings infallible. The performance of presidents depends on factors other than government expenditure size and inflationary trends. There are issues of integrity and character, adeptness in foreign policy, and so forth. Our own subjective evaluations, while highly correlated in a positive direction with those reported in either Table 3 or Table 4, are somewhat different than those reported. We believe, for example, that Ronald Reagan was a better president than Richard Nixon or Bill Clinton, the quantitative evidence cited above notwithstanding. We do not think the totality of evidence suggests that Lincoln is about our worst president or, using Table 4, that George Washington was a mediocre one.

One thing that is striking, looking at the evidence: *It takes several good presidents to undo the damage caused by one bad one.* The Higgs spending ratchet, cited earlier and visually observable in Figure 1, is a very powerful force in American history. The first ratchet effect occurs with James Madison and the War of 1812. Federal spending goes from 1.23 percent of total output in 1811 (the lowest level ever recorded) to 3.87 percent two years later—more than a tripling. We *never* returned to the 1811 level, and it took eighteen years and three presidents to get us more than 90 percent of the way back in 1831. In 1860, spending was 1.59 percent of GDP, more than quintupling during the war (and our statistics understate the total, since Confederate spending is not included). In 1912—fifty-two years after the previous trough—spending had returned about 97 percent of the way back to that trough, to 1.75 percent of GDP. We never completely returned to the antebellum spending norm, and it took decades to even approach it.

The second decade of the twentieth century is often underrated in terms of the destructive impact that it had on human liberty in the United States. Spending as a percent of GDP rose from 1.75 percent of GDP in 1912 to over 19 percent in fiscal year 1919. While it fell back to slightly over 3 percent in the Coolidge administration (over 90 percent of the way back to the prewar trough), again it never quite reached the prewar level (and it took a decade to even partially recover). The Hoover–Roosevelt surge in spending, the next great ratchet, was followed by some decline in the Truman era, but, unlike after earlier ratchets, the drop was nowhere near 90 percent or more of the way back to the prewar trough. While some may blame this on the cold war, the rise in nondefense spending and the modern welfare state is the chief culprit. Fifty years ago, in 1948, federal government spending was less than 12.7 percent of GDP—now it is around 20 percent. The downward drift in the federal spending–output ratio, present during most of peacetime history, seems to have disappeared. The modest drop in that ratio since 1982 is tepid indeed in terms of returning to the postwar (1948) level. The decline in fiscal restraint associated with the breakdown in the unwritten fiscal constitution of balanced budgets existing in the pre-Keynesian era has assisted in the erosion of individual liberty.[17]

There is also some evidence of an *inflationary* ratchet effect in the post-Keynesian era. Beginning in 1933, prices have risen rather consistently, never falling for more than two consecutive years. While there has been some healthy popular revulsion developing in recent years against the use of inflationary fiscal and monetary stimulus, we have not had a single year of stable prices in any presidential administration since John F. Kennedy, even allowing for possible distortion in the consumer price index.

FURTHER EVIDENCE ON THE HIGGS RATCHET EFFECT

The phenomenon of the Higgs ratchet deserves a more in-depth treatment. We have performed an econometric analysis to determine the impact of previous peak levels of federal government spending on the current volume of outlays. The overall results are consistent with the Higgs hypothesis. On average, federal government spending is ratcheted upward by almost 40 percent of the previous peak level of spending. Thus, the long-term effects of a surge in federal spending to new heights are indeed profound. We have also explored the individual impacts

---

[17]On this point, see James M. Buchanan and Richard E. Wagner, *Democracy in Deficit: The Political Legacy of Lord Keynes* (New York: Academic Press, 1977).

of the spending peaks reached in specific presidencies. Six presidents established new highs for federal spending: Washington (since he was the first president), John Adams, Madison, Lincoln, Wilson, and Franklin Roosevelt. The ratchet effects of the first two of these, Washington and Adams, are not statistically significant. However, the last four are, and they provide some revealing insights into the impact of extremely high levels of federal government spending.

Table 5 provides summary statistics concerning the four significant ratchets. The econometric analysis allows us to calculate the permanent effects of these four presidents on the level of federal government spending. The Madison ratchet contributes 0.81 percentage points, Lincoln 2.39, Wilson 4.72, and Franklin Roosevelt 9.93. Collectively, the impact of these four presidents amounts to 17.85 percent of national output, over 88 percent of the 1997 level of spending. This is the permanent legacy of the profligacy of the past. It is remarkable to note that, though he died over fifty years ago, to this day Franklin Roosevelt is still appropriating one dollar of every ten dollars of national output to be used by the federal government establishment. In a sense, all of us tithe to the memory of this man.

War and Peace

A clear pattern emerges from the discussion of the ratchet effects. The four statistically significant ones are associated with the phenomenon of war, in sequence, the War of 1812, the Civil War, and the two world wars. Further, there is a pronounced association between major wars and the presidential rankings offered by both the mainstream experts and us. The average expert ranking of the four presidents associated with the war-induced ratchets is 5.5, with Madison being the lowest, ranked at 13th. On the other hand, we rank these four on average at 35.6. More generally, the mainstream scholars liked virtually all war presidents, including ones presiding over other wars, such as James Polk, William McKinley, and Lyndon Johnson. Indeed, the experts universally ranked high all the presidents in office during what might be called the high cold war, from 1945 to about 1968.

To the extent that presidents try to maximize their perceived historical legacy, the prowar bias of the conventional historians and political scientists suggests that at the margin some wars

Table 5
Selected Statistics Relating to Impact of Previous
Peak Federal Spending Levels Established During
Administrations of Four Presidents

Statistic	President under Whom Ratchet is Established			
	Madison	Lincoln	Wilson	Franklin Roosevelt
Number of Years Ratchet in Effect	50	56	25	54
Mean Federal Spending During Ratchet	2.00%	3.41%	9.03%	20.36%
Mean Value of Ratchet Variable	3.84%	11.55%	21.80%	46.02%
Recovery Factor	39%	69%	54%	59%
Long-Term Impact on Federal Spending*	+ 0.81	+ 2.39	+ 4.72	+ 9.93

Source: Authors' Calculations
* Measured in percentage points.

may be fought to enhance presidential reputation rather than to right wrongs or maximize the national interest.[18] In making a cost–benefit calculation whether to engage in war, presidents might consider the private benefit they receive from a probable

[18]This does not only apply to recent presidents. James Polk seemed to want a little war with Mexico to enhance his standing, but instead ended up with a bigger conflict than he expected. See Paul Johnson, *A History of the American People* (New York: HarperCollins, 1997), p. 380, for more details.

enhancement in their presidential reputation. Wars make presidents look heroic, and everyone loves a hero. Indeed, wars are responsible for the election of many presidents, beginning with George Washington, and including Zachary Taylor, U.S. Grant, and, more recently, Dwight Eisenhower.

Should the experts exalt wartime leaders or should we denigrate them? We think the weight of the evidence on this issue is on our side. While it may be inappropriate to assign complete responsibility for the advent of war to the nation's chief executive when hostilities occur, neither is treating the onset of war as a random event warranted. War does not occur in a vacuum. It is the culmination of a series of public-policy positions either avowed or pursued prior to its outbreak. In the case of the American Civil War, for example, the very *persona* of the newly elected president, Abraham Lincoln, was a contributing factor in accounting for the commencement of hostilities. As to World War I, a significant degree of responsibility for our entry into that conflict has to be assigned to the president who campaigned for reelection in the summer and fall of 1916 invoking the slogan, "He kept us out of war," and then, in a remarkable about-face, some five months after the election stood before the Congress asking for a declaration of war against Germany.

Things are not as clear-cut in the case of World War II, but the Japanese attack on the naval base at Pearl Harbor did follow a series of policy initiatives that escalated tension between Japan and the United States, a set of circumstances for which Franklin Roosevelt does bear the responsibility.[19]

Of course, war impacts on our presidential rankings by increasing the level of federal spending. However, such surges in spending are not permanent. Or are they? Whatever the reason for government spending, it diverts resources from the private sector of the economy. In the process, the public must become accustomed to a lower level of private consumption. Customarily, this is regarded as acceptable in the name of patriotism or some other civic virtue. At the conclusion of hostilities, this period of public sacrifice is over and there exists what has come to be

---

[19]Even mainstream historians criticize the Roosevelt administration for failing to heed signals that Japan was ready to attack the United States. See, for example, Gordon W. Prange, *At Dawn We Slept: The Untold Story of Pearl Harbor* (New York: McGraw-Hill, 1981).

called a "peace dividend" that may be "spent." The operative word here is "spent." The simplest thing to do with a peace dividend is to return it to the public to be used in the pursuit of its private consumption. However, once resources have passed under the control of the central government, it is often difficult to retrieve them. To be sure, some of the peace dividend will be returned to the private sector. But much of it will be retained in the public arena to do "good works"; that is, to enhance social spending. A large pool of public resources is an irresistible attraction for what Mancur Olson has called the "distributional coalitions" in a society.[20] To the extent they are able to capture a portion of the peace dividend for their special-interest purposes, the volume of public spending will be maintained at levels that are greater than the prewar ones.[21] This is the Higgs ratchet.

The phenomenon of the ratchet disguises the permanence of the impact of war by transforming military spending into social outlays. Thus, the ratchet effects attributable to the Madison, Lincoln, Wilson, and Franklin Roosevelt presidencies are still with us today in the form of higher taxes, either explicit or implicit, that have funded a remarkable expansion of social programs. Therefore, our downgrading of the presidential performance of those who were wartime leaders would seem to be appropriate. To illustrate the magnitude of these effects, Figure 3 shows the contributions of the four wars that produced significant ratchet effects to current levels of federal government spending, which amounted to slightly over 20 percent of GDP in 1997. This figure dramatically demonstrates the long-term costs of war to a society.[22]

[20]See Mancur Olson, *The Rise and Decline of Nations* (New Haven, Conn.: Yale University Press, 1982), for a more extended discussion of this point.

[21]For a more extended discussion of the peace dividend, and the historical experience relating to the ending of wars, see Dwight Lee and Richard Vedder, "The Political Economy of the Peace Dividend," *Public Choice* 88 (1996): 29–42.

[22]For an excellent extended discussion of the cost of wars to American society, see John V. Denson, ed., *The Costs of War: America's Pyrrhic Victories* (New Brunswick, N.J.: Transaction Publishers, 1997).

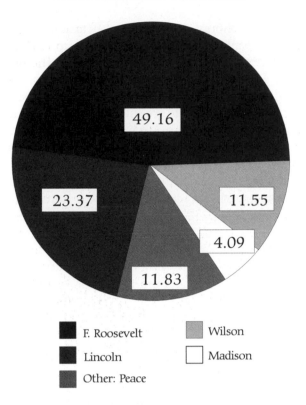

FIGURE 3
WAR AND PEACE
PERCENT OF FEDERAL SPENDING ATTRIBUTABLE TO WAR PRESIDENTS

CONCLUSIONS

Individual happiness is not created in large part through the actions of political leaders. The dynamic, chaotic market processes of individual human economic actions have had far more to do with America's material prosperity and happiness than the behavior of any president. Yet bad political leaders can have lasting negative consequences. The half-life of the adverse consequences of ill-considered political activism is long.

Classical-liberal scholars should ponder why this is so. Why cannot or did not, say, a Ronald Reagan do much to roll back government? Why has the seemingly promising laissez-faire behavior of the 94th Republican Congress (1995–1996) not been followed by a really substantial retreat of government, rather than the tepid (although still welcome) amounts observed to date? Insights by Austrian and public-choice scholars on the nature of government, bureaucracies, special interest groups, and so forth help us pave the way to finding answers to these questions.[23] One of the "special interest groups" is academia, and its government-funded prointerventionist bias, as demonstrated in the mainstream presidential performance polls. It contributes to the reluctance of presidents to be decisive in reducing the federal role in our affairs. In striving to please the academic mandarins evaluating the presidency, modern chief executives have stimulated the growth of Leviathan and the nanny state.

[23]See, for example, Ludwig von Mises, *Bureaucracy* (New Rochelle, N.Y.: Arlington House, 1969); William Niskanen, *Bureaucracy and Public Economics* (Brookfield, Vt.: Edward Elgar, 1994); and Thomas E. Borcherding, ed., *Budgets and Bureaucrats: The Sources of Government Growth* (Durham, N.C.: Duke University Press, 1977).

2

GEORGE WASHINGTON: AN IMAGE AND ITS INFLUENCE

DAVID GORDON

George Washington took office as president in 1789 with an asset of inestimable value. People viewed him as the hero of the American Revolution who, disdaining power, had like the Roman general Cincinnatus returned home to his farm. When he allowed himself, with great reluctance, to be nominated as chief executive, his prestige was unparalleled. Indeed, his reputation was worldwide. When he died,

> Napoleon Bonaparte decreed that the standards and flags of the French army be dressed in mourning crepe. The flags of the British Channel Fleet were lowered to half-mast to honor the fallen hero. Talleyrand, the French minister of foreign affairs, . . . [called] for a statue of Washington to be erected in Paris.[1]

Poets likewise sang his praises.

> Washington achieved mythic status in his own lifetime, receiving poetic encomia from English poets as different as William Blake and Byron, who contrasted Washington favorably with the despotic Napoleon. . . . His contemporaries were impressed by the fact that the general who led a successful revolution did not establish a personal dictatorship.[2]

Were the effects of the influence that accompanied this prestige good or bad for liberty? This chapter shall endeavor to show that in two instances, these effects were bad; in one case, though, Washington's fame led to fortunate consequences for individual

---

[1]Matthew Spalding and Patrick J. Garrity, *A Sacred Union of Citizens* (Lanham, Md.: Rowman and Littlefield, 1996), p. 189.

[2]Michael Lind, ed., *Hamilton's Republic* (New York: The Free Press, 1997), p. 99.

freedom. Washington, though not a principal author of the Constitution, supported calling a convention to revise the Articles of Confederation. At the convention itself, he strongly backed Madison's plans for centralized control.

On assuming power, Washington soon faced a division of opinion in his cabinet. Secretary of the Treasury Alexander Hamilton was not satisfied with the centralization already achieved by the Constitution. He called for a national bank and a governmentally directed program of industrial development. Thomas Jefferson raised a decisive objection to Hamilton's proposal: Did it not entirely exceed the bounds of power granted the central government by the new Constitution? The constitutional issue did not faze Hamilton, who produced an analysis that granted the central government broad power to do whatever Hamilton thought best. In this conflict, Washington once again weighed in on the side of the centralizers.

In his *Farewell Address*, though, Washington at least partially redeemed himself, from a classical-liberal standpoint. He cautioned against America's involvement in European power politics, with which the United States had no concern. His warning against permanent alliances guided much of American foreign policy in the nineteenth century; and, in the twentieth, opponents of the bellicose policies of Woodrow Wilson and Franklin Roosevelt appealed to it. Washington's prestige for once had beneficial results.

We have spoken of whether Washington's influence was "good" or "bad" for liberty. By what standard are these judgments made? This author writes from a classical-liberal perspective, in which the growth of government is viewed as an unmitigated disaster and expansionist foreign policy is resolutely opposed. Thus, "states' rights" receive support as against increases in federal authority, and wars, except in cases of exercising self-determination or repelling direct invasion, are opposed.[3]

One might object to the proposed criterion in this way. The goal of classical liberalism is to promote individual liberty. Why then tie it down to the specific policies indicated?

---

[3]A classical-liberal analysis of just wars has been well set forth by Murray Rothbard in "America's Two Just Wars: 1775 and 1861" in *The Costs of War*, John V. Denson, ed., 2nd ed. (New Brunswick, N.J.: Transaction Publishers, 1999), pp. 119–33.

In certain cases, may not the federal government serve better to protect the individual than the states?[4] Further, even if local control is in ideal circumstances best, may not a decentralized polity prove no match for a strong opponent? Along the same lines, why must a realistic foreign policy be confined to defense of the national territory? In some cases, may not the best defense be to strike at a prospective enemy first?[5]

These worries cannot be addressed in detail here. Suffice it to say that a good rule-utilitarian case can be constructed for spurning federal interventions that allegedly aim at promoting liberty. In like fashion, aggressive war shackles us with devastation and restriction of liberty in order to combat speculative dangers.[6]

These remarks have at least the appearance of dogmatism, and they are advanced rather to indicate a viewpoint than to make a case. One illustration of how such a case would proceed is taken from Murray Rothbard. The Articles of Confederation established a much less centralized system than the Constitution. Yet because ratification by all the states was required for the Articles to come into effect, most of the American Revolution was fought with no written structure of authority over the states at all. As Rothbard notes,

> The Articles were not exactly received with huzzahs; rather, they were greeted quietly and dutifully, as a needed part of the war effort against Britain. One of the keenest critiques of the Articles, as might be expected, came from Thomas Burke, who warned that, under cover of the war emergency, eager power-seekers were trying to impose a central government upon the states. . . . [t]he Articles of Confederation were not to be ratified

---

[4]For a defense of this position, see Clint Bolick, *The Affirmative Action Fraud* (Washington, D.C.: The Cato Institute, 1996). See also my criticisms in *The Mises Review* 2, no. 2 (Summer 1996): 13–17.

[5]Walter Lippmann opposed "isolationist" policy during the 1930s, charging it with unrealistically ignoring the increasing power of Germany. For a criticism of his views, see my "A Common Design: Propaganda and World War" in *The Costs of War*, John V. Denson, ed., 2nd ed. (New Brunswick, N.J.: Transaction Publishers, 1999), pp. 312–19.

[6]For a strong historical case showing that war has led to growth in government, see Robert Higgs, *Crisis and Leviathan* (New York: Oxford University Press, 1987).

and go into effect until 1781, when the Revolutionary War would be all but over.[7]

So much for the supposed necessity for a strong central government to combat other nations.

However much supporters of localism might view even the Articles as going too far in the wrong direction, Washington held a decidedly different view. In 1783, he wrote to Alexander Hamilton: "It is clearly my opinion, unless Congress have powers competent to all general purposes, that the distresses we have encountered, the expense we have incurred, and the blood we have spilt, will avail nothing."[8]

Among the "distresses" of which Washington spoke, one may speculate that personal considerations loomed large. Throughout his adult life, Washington avidly sought land. "His family had first speculated in Ohio Valley land decades ago [before the 1780s], and Washington owned nearly sixty thousand acres."[9]

A project that aroused his interest offered a chance to appreciate greatly the value of his land. "If a canal could be pushed over the mountains to link up with the Allegheny river system, then all the future produce of the Ohio Valley could flow through Virginia land, (not coincidentally, past Mount Vernon)."[10]

A crucial obstacle confronted Washington's hopes for a Potomac Canal. Under the Articles of Confederation, a state had the right to levy fees on the use of waterways that passed through its boundaries. If the states bordering the Potomac were to do so, the proposed canal might generate no profit for him. One can readily see why the great general was "distressed." As

---

[7]Murray N. Rothbard, *Conceived in Liberty*, vol. 4, *The Revolutionary War, 1775–1784* (Auburn, Ala.: The Mises Institute, 1999), pp. 255–56. Donald W. Livingston argues that David Hume saw a confederation of small republics as the solution to the defense problem. Further, Livingston argues that Hume influenced the American founders. See his *Philosophical Melancholy and Delirium* (Chicago: University of Chicago Press, 1998), pp. 317–32.

[8]W.E. Woodward, *George Washington: The Image and the Man* (New York: Horace Liveright, 1962), p. 411.

[9]Richard Brookhiser, *Founding Father: Rediscovering George Washington* (New York: The Free Press, 1996), p. 49.

[10]Ibid., p. 48.

one observer notes, "[h]e was drawn to the plan by important private and public interests, and the political steps he took to fulfill it led directly to the Constitutional Convention, if not a canal."[11] A strong central government would remove the threat of interstate taxation.

This is not to suggest that Washington's economic interests determined his support for a stronger central government. To do so would be to fall into the fallacy that wrecked Charles Beard's *An Economic Interpretation of the Constitution*. Nevertheless, personal interest cannot be neglected in an explanation of Washington's policy.

Regardless of Washington's motives, the fact that someone of his probity and reputation advocated a Constitutional Convention eased the doubts of those who feared centralization. How could one suspect the proposed convention of aims destructive of liberty if Washington, the Cincinnatus who had spurned dictatorship, endorsed the call for it? Was not the case for the good intentions of the proposed convention conclusively made once it became known that Washington himself had agreed to serve as a delegate to it? Richard Brookhiser puts the essential point well:

> Much of the political class was happy with the current arrangements. . . . Supporters of change would have to make the case that a new government would not threaten liberty. . . . Washington's presence would help immeasurably to make that case. He had already held more power than any man in America, and after eight and half years, he had surrendered it. He was the most conspicuous example of moderation and disinterestedness that the nation could supply.[12]

At the convention, Washington's primary aim was not to enact a particular plan of government. The need rather was to act immediately, so that centralization could be secured as fast as possible.

> During the constitutional debates, Washington insisted that the Articles of Confederation be overhauled quickly. "Otherwise," he wrote, "like a house on fire, whilst the most regular mode of extinguishing it is contended for, the building is

[11]Ibid., p. 49.
[12]Ibid., p. 56.

reduced to ashes." What was needed, Washington thought, was any solid national government.[13]

Washington was quite willing to push his argument to extremes. So essential did he deem centralization that he contemplated a monarchy for America, should the Constitutional Convention fail. He was not himself a monarchist—far from it. But a letter of March 31, 1787, to James Madison shows that conceivable circumstances might change him into one.

In his definitive study of James Madison's political thought, Lance Banning summarizes Washington's thoughts in this vital letter:

> No one could deny the indispensability of a complete reform of the existing system, which he hoped the Constitutional Convention would attempt. But only if complete reform were tried, and the resulting system still proved inefficient, would a belief in the necessity of greater change begin to spread "among all classes of the people. Then, and not till then is my [Washington's] opinion, can it [monarchy] be attempted without involving all the evils of civil discord."[14]

One wonders how those whose fears of the convention had been calmed by Washington's endorsement would have reacted had they known of this letter. But of course the convention, by its own lights, did not fail; and the fact that Washington contemplated monarchy remained hidden.

Any centralized form of government, Washington held, was desirable so long as it could be quickly established. But it does not follow from this that Washington was indifferent to the type of centralized government established. He soon fell in with the radical nationalism of Madison's Virginia Plan.

To Madison, Washington's presence at the convention was essential: It was "an invitation to the most select characters

---

[13]Russell Hardin, *Liberalism, Constitutionalism, and Democracy* (New York: Oxford University Press, 1999), p. 273, citing a letter from Washington to Henry Knox, February 3, 1787.

[14]Lance Banning, *The Sacred Fire of Liberty: James Madison and the Founding of the Federal Republic* (Ithaca, N.Y.: Cornell University Press, 1995), p. 123, citing a letter from Washington to Madison, March 31, 1787.

from every part of the Confederacy."[15] Madison reported that Washington arrived at the Philadelphia convention "amidst the acclamations of the people, as more sober marks of the affection and veneration which continue to be felt for his character."[16]

With Washington present, Madison hoped to achieve his aims. One political theorist, a disciple of Leo Strauss, summarizes these aims in this way: Washington's presence and the presence of "lesser figures of impeccable republican credentials allowed the convention to rebut the charge of being an aristocratic conspiracy while conferring on it the opportunity to behave like one."[17]

Strong words, but the details of Madison's plans bear out the interpretation that the Straussian Gary Rosen has advanced. Madison and other extreme nationalists sought to eviscerate entirely the power of the states to thwart the will of the nation.

Under the Virginia Plan, which Madison submitted to Washington before the convention opened, Congress could veto any law enacted by a state legislature that it deemed unconstitutional.

> It called, as Washington's summary of Madison's draft put it, for a "due supremacy of the national authority," including "local authorities [only] whenever they can be subordinately useful." . . . Madison had originally called for an even more sweeping national power over state laws, a "negative in all cases whatever."[18]

In fairness to Washington, he did not vote in favor of Madison's radical proposal of an unlimited congressional veto. But neither did he oppose the plan. Madison noted that

> Gen. W. was "not consulted." How could he not have been consulted? He never missed a session. Most probably, Gen. W. had been consulted privately, and the result of the consultation

---

[15]Gary Rosen, *American Compact: James Madison and the Problem of Founding* (Lawrence: University Press of Kansas, 1999), p. 85, citing a letter from Madison to Washington, December 7, 1786.

[16]Ibid., p. 86, citing a letter from Madison to Thomas Jefferson, May 15, 1787.

[17]Ibid.

[18]Brookhiser, *Founding Father*, p. 63.

was that, since Madison had the voters anyway, Washington chose not to take a public stand on an inflamed issue.[19]

It seems quite clear that opposition by Washington would have at once ended so far-reaching a plan, but it was not forthcoming. Surely then he cannot have been very strongly against it. Had he been, he need only have spoken a word. But why speculate on Washington's private opinion of Madison's proposal? Its importance for our purposes is this: Many of those who feared that the convention would strike a fatal blow at states' rights were reassured by Washington's presence. But, unknown to them, he was at least a fellow traveler of radical centralism. His image as a Cincinnatus averse to power led many into error. It did not follow from Washington's personal reluctance to hold office that he was not an opponent of states' rights, as this concept was understood in the 1780s.

Fortunately, for those opposed to centralism, no version of the congressional veto survived into the Constitution's final draft. But the Constitution, even without it, was far more centralizing than the Articles; and Washington's image once again proved useful when the Constitution came up for ratification. Just as before, skeptics could be reassured: Would Washington support a regime inimical to liberty? Thus, in Virginia, opposition to the Constitution was in part disarmed by Washington's prestige. "Few, if any of Virginia's revolutionary leaders questioned Madison's republican credentials. All, no doubt, were comforted by their awareness that George Washington would head the federal government if it were put into effect."[20]

By no means is this meant to suggest a monocausal view, in which Washington's image sufficed to quell all opposition to the new document. Quite the contrary, in the very passage just cited, Lance Banning maintains that Madison's skill at argument was needed to win over the recalcitrant. Confidence in Washington was not enough because in 1788, "quite unlike today, few believed that the executive would set the federal government's directions."[21] Nevertheless, the importance of the "Washington-image factor" cannot be gainsaid.

[19]Ibid., p. 64.
[20]Banning, *The Sacred Fire of Liberty*, p. 253.
[21]Ibid.

The Constitution did not in all respects settle the nature of the American system. What sort of government would result from it? Would its provisions be interpreted loosely, to enable the central government to seize as much power from the states as possible? Two conflicting approaches to government split Washington's cabinet, one favored by Alexander Hamilton and the other by Thomas Jefferson.

These divergent views have been ably summarized by Forrest McDonald.

> In Federalist Essay number 70, Hamilton had said that "energy in the executive is a leading ingredient in the definition of good government." . . . In essays 71 and 73, he made his position clearer: "It is one thing," he said, for the executive "to be subordinate to the laws, and another to be dependent on the legislative body." In other words, the executive authority must operate independently and with a wide range of discretion in its field, the Constitution and laws providing only broad guidelines and rules.[22]

Jefferson and his followers saw matters entirely otherwise.

> In Jefferson's view, and that of most Republicans, such discretionary authority was inherently dangerous and smacked of monarchy. . . . A society would grow better . . . by stripping social and governmental institutions to the bare minimum so that the natural aristocracy might rise to the top.[23]

The differences between Hamilton and Jefferson were not confined to abstract argument, but quietly became manifest in practical affairs. Although Hamilton considered himself a student of economics, his views embodied the discredited doctrines of mercantilism.

> One of the duties of the federal government, according to the Hamilton philosophy, is the active promotion of a dynamic industrial capitalist economy . . . by establishment of sound public finance, public investment in infrastructure, and promotion of new industrial sectors unlikely to be profitable in their early stages.

---

[22]Forrest McDonald, *The Presidency of George Washington* (Lawrence: University Press of Kansas, 1974), pp. 94–95.

[23]Ibid., pp. 95–96.

As Hamilton wrote in *The Report on Manufactures*:

> Capital is wayward and timid in leading itself to new under-
> takings, and the state ought to excite the confidence of capi-
> talists, who are ever cautious and sagacious, by aiding them to
> overcome the obstacles that lie in the way of all experiments.[24]

Where the State would acquire the requisite understanding
to direct the economy, Hamilton neglected to inform his readers;
and Jefferson and his followers were reluctant to take the matter on faith. In particular, the Jeffersonians rejected Hamilton's
plan, as part of reforming public finance, to establish a national
bank.

In this opposition they had a seemingly irrefutable argument. Hamilton's plan for a bank clearly violated the Constitution. Nowhere does that document give Congress the power to
charter a national bank. So small a matter did not deter Hamilton from avid pursuit of his scheme.

In response to a request by Washington, Hamilton delivered
a "Defense of the Constitutionality of the Bank" to him on February 23, 1791.

> The well-known part of the defense spelled out the "loose con-
> structionist" doctrine of the Constitution. The Constitution,
> said Hamilton, defined only in general terms the broad pur-
> poses for which the federal government was created. . . . If
> Congress determined to achieve an end authorized by the Con-
> stitution, it was empowered by the final clause in Article I,
> Section 8 [the "necessary and proper" clause] . . . to use any
> means that were not prohibited by the Constitution.[25]

Hamilton's argument by far exceeded in importance the
matter of the bank, though that in itself was no small thing. If
Hamilton's views were accepted, little of limited government
could remain. Given the vaguest aims, for example, the promotion of "the general welfare," the government had the power,
Hamilton alleged, to do whatever it thought was needed to attain
them.

Faced with so blatant a challenge to constitutional rule,
what did Washington do? He accepted Hamilton's opinion,

---

[24]Lind, ed., *Hamilton's Republic*, p. 5, quoting Hamilton's Report.
[25]McDonald, *The Presidency of George Washington*, p. 77.

refusing Madison's advance to veto the bank bill. Hamilton's "defense convinced Washington, and on February 25 [1791], he signed the bank bill into law."[26]

Once again Washington lent his prestige and authority to the cause of a strong central state. From a classical-liberal perspective, his course of action was a disastrous blunder.

But the record is not all black. So far Washington has been presented as an opponent of the libertarian tradition. He used his fame to secure unwarranted credence for a convention that aimed to strengthen the central government. At that convention, he gave the most extreme centralizers at least tacit support. And, as we have just seen, he accepted an argument that freed the government from all constitutional restraint. Nevertheless, from the classical-liberal perspective, Washington almost redeemed himself.

In his *Farewell Address*, Washington set forward principles of foreign policy that, if followed, would virtually immunize America from involvement in foreign wars. (The *Address* was not delivered as a speech. It was a circular published in *The American Daily Advertiser*, September 19, 1796.)[27]

In the *Address*, Washington sharply separated European affairs from those of the United States.

> Europe has a set of primary interests, which to us have none or a very remote relation. Hence she must be engaged in frequent controversies, the causes of which are essentially foreign to our concerns. Hence therefore it must be unwise in us to implicate ourselves, by artificialities, in . . . the ordinary combinations and collisions of her friendships, or enmities.[28]

But, interventionists such as Walter Lippmann were later to object, does not the argument of the *Address* wrongly take for granted that European politics do not concern America? What if a single power dominated the continent? Would this not threaten us? If so, should we not be concerned actively to prevent such domination?

---

[26]Ibid., p. 26.

[27]Spalding and Garrity, *A Sacred Union of Citizens*, p. 57. For the controversy about Hamilton's role in drafting the *Address*, see pp. 55ff.

[28]Ibid., p. 186, quoting the text of the *Address*.

Washington rejected this contention in advance.

> Our detached and distant situation invites and enables us to pursue a different course. If we remain in one People, under an efficient government, the period is not far off, when we may defy material injury from external annoyance. . . . Why forego the advantages of so peculiar a situation? Why quit our own to stand upon foreign ground.[29]

Here Washington adopts the much maligned Fortress America stance so derided by critics of isolation. Given the manifest perils of war, will not a classical-liberal system take advantage of a favorable geographic position to steer clear of foreign entanglements? Such, at any rate, was Washington's argument; and for once, his immense prestige aided the cause of liberty.[30]

Opponents of American entry into the world wars frequently appealed to the *Address*. If they were ultimately unsuccessful, at least the fame of the *Address* and its author helped slow the race toward war and statism.

[29]Ibid.

[30]For a contemporary defense of the soundness of the foreign policy prescriptions of the *Address*, see Eric Nordlinger, *Isolationism Reconfigured* (Princeton, N.J.: Princeton University Press, 1995).

3

THOMAS JEFFERSON: CLASSICAL-LIBERAL STATESMAN OF THE OLD REPUBLIC

H. ARTHUR SCOTT TRASK

Was Thomas Jefferson a great president? One's answer to that question depends on how one defines "greatness." If we define greatness as how far a president leads the United States down its historically determined path toward the centralized interventionist state, then Jefferson fails to qualify. On the other hand, if we define greatness as how well a president defended the true and original principles of the federal Constitution and the economic and civil liberties for which Americans had fought the Revolution, then Jefferson deserves to be ranked among the better presidents. Yet he also deserves to be ranked as one of the most disappointing, since there was so much that he could have done, was expected to do, but did not do.

As we survey his presidency, it will be useful to keep in mind three questions. First, did Jefferson's election to the presidency and the Republican capture of Congress in 1800 constitute "a revolution in the principles of our government as that of 1776," as Jefferson himself contended ten years after he had retired to Monticello?[1] Second, was Jefferson a true and consistent classical republican statesman whose policies were consistent with his professed political and economic philosophy of small government, strict construction, states' rights, low taxes, free trade, non-involvement in foreign affairs, and peace? And third, does his presidency constitute a model for future leaders of a classical-liberal and constitutional-federalist persuasion to follow? The short answers to these questions are that Jefferson failed to carry through a revolution which he himself had helped to

---

[1]Jefferson to Spencer Roane, September 6, 1819, *Thomas Jefferson: Writings* (New York: Library of America, 1984), p. 1425.

originate, that he was consistent in many ways but inconsistent in others, and that his presidency constitutes a useful model but also a warning.

THE ELECTION OF 1800

Although the Federalists had controlled Congress and the presidency for twelve successive years, their policies had not been popular. If the Judiciary Act of 1789, the funding of the national debt, the assumption of the states' debts, the national bank, the system of internal taxation, Jay's Treaty with Great Britain (1794), and the creation of a professional standing army and navy had been submitted to a popular referendum, probably none of them would have been approved, nor would the federal Constitution have been ratified in the first place. Early Federalist political success in passing their program and holding on to power can be attributed to three factors: the lack of an organized political opposition until the late 1790s, the success of the new political system in thwarting the popular will, and General Washington's tremendous popularity and prestige. If the president had been elected directly by the people, Jefferson would have given his first inaugural address in 1797 instead of in 1801. However, the popular memory is short, and the Republicans could not hope to ride to power simply on the basis of the unpopularity of Federalist measures in the early 1790s. They finally triumphed in 1800 because the internal tax system provided a regular reminder that the Federalists believed in an intrusive and energetic government, and the quasi-war with France in 1798 demonstrated beyond any doubt that the Federalists were inveterate Anglophiles—Jefferson called them "Anglomen"— who wanted to build an expensive professional war machine to go to war against Spain and France in alliance with England.

The Republicans were right to believe that the Federalists wanted to turn the American confederation of states into an empire mightier than the British empire and one with a perpetual public debt, high domestic taxes, a large standing army, a navy with ships-of-the-line, large manufacturing establishments subsidized by government, a permanent civil bureaucracy, a strong executive, an irresponsible political judiciary, the consolidation of political power in the federal government, and financial corruption of the federal legislature. Jefferson could speak of his election as a "revolution" because he believed that the people of the states had rejected the Federalist theory and program of government, which were British, neomercantilist, centralizing, and statist, in favor of the agrarian, decentralist, libertarian, and republican principles which had been dominant during the Revolution and were once again ascendant.

As president, Jefferson set out to reverse the Federalist program, to restore the federal government to its constitutional role (that is, protecting the confederacy and its trade from foreign enemies and managing relations between the states), and to ensure that the people of the states were left alone to regulate their own private pursuits in a state of freedom. He hoped to gradually break the alliance between the government and the monied elite which had already been forged by the Federalists. According to Albert Jay Nock, Jefferson "was for control of government by the producing class; that is to say, by the immense majority which in every society actually applies labor and capital to natural resources for the production of wealth," and that he opposed Federalist efforts to forge a neomercantilistic alliance between the general government and "the exploiting classes," that is, bankers, bondholders, and officeholders.[2]

FEDERAL SPENDING UNDER JEFFERSON

In a 1799 letter to a Massachusetts Republican, Jefferson summarized what would be the fiscal policies of his administration, if he were elected:

> I am for a government rigorously frugal and simple, applying all the possible savings of the public revenue to the discharge of the national debt; and not for a multiplication of officers and salaries merely to make partisans, and for increasing, by every device, the public debt, on the principle of its being a public blessing.[3]

In his first inaugural address Jefferson explained that for him, "the sum of good government" was a "wise and frugal" one "which shall restrain men from injuring one another, [but] shall leave them otherwise free to regulate their own pursuits of

[2]Albert Jay Nock, *Mr. Jefferson* (Tampa, Fla.: Hallberg Publishing [1926] 1983), p. 116.

[3]Jefferson to Elbridge Gerry, January 26, 1799, *Thomas Jefferson: Writings*, p. 1056; see also, Jefferson to Gideon Granger, August 13, 1800, ibid., pp. 1078–79.

industry and improvement, and shall not take from the mouth of labour the bread it has earned."[4]

Jefferson opposed all but the most minimal taxes because he believed that taxes diminished public happiness by depriving individuals of a portion of their hard-earned money and hence of the means of supporting their families and improving their estates. He warned that "the general tendency" of the government party was "to increase expense[s] to the ultimate term of burden which the citizen can bear" and leave "to labor the smallest portion of its earnings on which it can subsist," so that "government shall itself consume the residue of what it was instituted to guard."[5]

Jefferson also was determined to pay off the national debt. He opposed public borrowing on a number of grounds. First of all, by enabling the government to increase its expenditures without calling on the people for increased taxes, it minimized public opposition to increased spending. Second, public borrowing shifted the burden of payment to posterity. Jefferson believed that imposing financial burden on future generations in order to pay for the profligacy of the present generation was a profoundly unrepublican and immoral act. Third, public borrowing created a class of bondholders who had a vested interest in funding and increasing the debt and opposing its discharge. Last, a public debt created a justification for keeping up taxes to pay the interest.[6]

Thus Jefferson and his Swiss-born secretary of the Treasury, Albert Gallatin, set out to reduce federal expenditures and federal taxes and pay off a considerable portion of the federal debt. Although the second goal appears to be in conflict with the third, Jefferson and Gallatin hoped that reductions in spending would compensate for the reduction in federal tax revenue.

In the State Department, Jefferson reduced the number of foreign missions to three—London, Paris, and Spain—one for each of the three great world powers. In the Treasury Department, he dismissed all of the collectors and inspectors of the internal revenue. This change alone reduced the number of federal

[4]Jefferson, "First Inaugural Address," March 4, 1801, ibid., p. 494.
[5]Jefferson, "First Annual Message," December 8, 1801, ibid., pp. 504–05.
[6]Jefferson to Madison, September 6, 1789, ibid., pp. 959–64.

employees by more than one-third. However, Jefferson and Gallatin planned on saving the most money in the War and Navy Departments. By early 1802, Jefferson had reduced the size of the regular army by almost half, from 6,000 men when he took office to 3,312. Federalist expenditures on the War Department averaged $1.9 million from 1793 through 1800. Jefferson reduced them to an average of $1.3 million for 1801 through 1808, which was a reduction of almost $600,000 a year. Federalist expenditures on the Navy Department had averaged $1.3 million a year from 1794 (the first year of the navy) through 1800. Jefferson actually spent a little more, averaging $1.5 million a year for his two terms. However, if one compares his naval expenditures to those of his immediate predecessor, John Adams, who averaged $2 million a year, Jefferson managed to reduce them by an average of almost $500,000 a year. He accomplished this by laying-up seven of the thirteen frigates built by the Federalists. Through such measures of economy, Jefferson managed to reduce government expenditures, minus interest and debt reduction, from $7.5 million for fiscal year 1800 to less than $5 million for 1801 and to an average of $4 million for the years 1802–1804. However, increased military expenditures after 1804 significantly raised overall spending during his second term. All in all, while Federalist expenditures averaged $7.1 million from 1793 through 1800, Republican expenditures actually averaged $8.7 million, an increase under Jefferson of $1.6 million a year.[7]

FEDERAL TAXATION UNDER JEFFERSON

The federal government had three sources of revenue in 1800: public land sales, customs duties, and internal taxes. Tariffs averaged only 13 percent ad valorem, although specific duties on sugar, tea, coffee, and salt ranged from 50 percent to 100 percent. The Federalists had imposed internal taxes on whiskey stills, domestic liquor sales, auction sales, carriages, and legal documents. These taxes produced $1 million in federal revenue in 1800, four-fifths of which came from the excises on whiskey and distilled spirits. When Jefferson recommended repealing these taxes, the Federalists replied that import duties

[7]Davis R. Dewey, *Financial History of the United States* (New York: Longmans, Green, 1903), pp. 111, 120, 124.

on such "necessities" as coffee, tea, and sugar should be reduced instead. They argued that reducing the duties on tropical commodities would be of more benefit to the people than reducing the whiskey excise. The Federalists knew what they were about. They wanted to retain the internal revenue system with its host of revenue officers, collectors, and inspectors. They understood that a reduction in import duties could always be reversed by a future congress, but that while it would be much more difficult to re-impose internal taxes and recreate a machinery of domestic tax collection after both had been repealed and abolished. They remembered well that the first attempt in 1794 to impose an excise on whiskey produced a tax revolt in the American backcountry.[8] A future Federalist administration might face even greater domestic resistance in trying to bring back the excise than they faced in imposing it. For the same reasons, Jefferson and his Republican allies were determined to repeal altogether, not just reduce, the internal taxes and to abolish the inspectors and collectors of the revenue. They were successful. Jefferson signed the reform bill into law in March 1802. Jefferson next set his sights on repealing the duty on imported salt which brought in over $500,000 in revenue annually. Jefferson began to push for its repeal in 1806. His party abolished the salt duty early the next year.[9]

In his Second Inaugural Address, Jefferson noted with triumph and satisfaction that federal taxes were "being collected on our seaboards and frontiers only, and incorporated with the transactions of our mercantile citizens." Thus, "it may be the pleasure and pride of an American to ask, what farmer, what mechanic, what laborer ever sees a tax-gatherer of the United States."[10]

If federal expenditures on the whole were not reduced under President Jefferson and if taxes were twice reduced, then why did the Treasury Department run a surplus each year from 1801

---

[8]Thomas P. Slaughter, *The Whiskey Rebellion: Frontier Epilogue to the American Revolution* (New York: Oxford University Press, 1986).

[9]Dewey, *Financial History*, pp. 120, 122; Paul Studenski and Herman E. Krooss, *Financial History of the United States: Fiscal, Monetary, Banking, and Tariff* (New York: McGraw-Hill, 1952), p. 67; Alexander Balinky, *Albert Gallatin: Fiscal Theories and Policies* (New Brunswick, N.J.: Rutgers University Press, 1958), pp. 116–19, 122–25.

[10]Jefferson, "Second Inaugural Address," March 5, 1805, *Thomas Jefferson: Writings*, p. 519.

to 1808? There are two reasons. First, Jefferson raised taxes. In early 1804, Gallatin and Jefferson proposed increasing the tariff duties by 2.5 percent and by adding an additional duty of 10 percent on all goods imported via foreign vessels. The change would have increased the average tariff rate to 16 percent ad valorem. Because its ostensible purpose was to finance the unexpected expenses arising from the Tripolitan war, it became known as the "Mediterranean Fund." The Republican majority promptly passed the measure. The additional duties brought in about $1 million of increased revenue a year, thus compensating for the loss of revenue due to the repeal of the internal taxes. Both Gallatin and the Republican congressional leaders promised that the increased tariff would be only a temporary measure. Their bill required that the tariff be brought back to its previous level three months after the close of hostilities with the Barbary powers. However, the Republicans renewed the tax in 1807 despite the cessation of hostilities the previous year. The renewal was due also to the increase in the customs revenue during the 1800s. The increase was created by growing imports, the profitable carrying trade, and the acquisition of the port of New Orleans under the Louisiana treaty. Under the carrying trade, American vessels brought Spanish and French colonial goods to an American port, paid a duty, and then reexported them to Europe. The volume of this trade was enormous in 1801 and 1805–1807.[11]

FEDERAL DEBT REDUCTION UNDER JEFFERSON

Jefferson and Gallatin inherited a national debt of $83 million. Annual interest payments on the debt averaged about $3.1 million a year under President Adams, thus accounting for about 42 percent of all federal expenditures during those years. Jefferson and Gallatin believed that continuing to discharge these high interest payments just to maintain the debt diminished their flexibility in spending money on legitimate national purposes, such as buying foreign territory, and created upward pressure on federal taxes. They also believed that having a large outstanding debt would be a serious financial handicap should the country go to war in defense of its territory or citizens.

[11]Dewey, *Financial History*, p. 121; Studenski and Krooss, *Financial History*, p. 68; Balinky, *Gallatin*, pp. 116, 120–21.

Interest payments for the previous debt would still have to be made, the principal would be further augmented by new borrowing, and many sources of loanable capital already would be invested in government stock.

Accordingly, Jefferson and Gallatin proposed creating an annual sinking fund of $7.3 million to be used for the dual purpose of paying interest on the debt and reducing the principal by retiring maturing bonds and buying still outstanding bonds in the market. If this plan were adhered to by Jefferson and his successors, and if no new debt were created, the national debt would be retired in sixteen years. Congress passed this measure in April 1802.

Jefferson's purchase of Louisiana from France in 1803 for $15 million threatened his debt reduction program. However, federal revenue was so great that he and Gallatin had little difficulty paying for the purchase, all the while maintaining their debt reduction plan. Gallatin proposed to pay for the purchase by selling $11.25 million in new 6-percent federal stock, which 6 percent was added to the long-term federal debt; by borrowing $1.75 million in a temporary loan, to be paid from future Treasury surpluses; and by appropriating $2 million in cash from the current Treasury surplus. In the immediate aftermath of the purchase of Louisiana, the administration decided to increase the sinking fund to $8 million a year. In eight years, Jefferson and Gallatin managed to redeem $37.2 million of the principal of the federal debt and bring the total amount outstanding down from $83 million in 1800 to $57 million at the end of 1808.[12]

FOREIGN POLICY AND MILITARY SPENDING: THE FIRST TERM

Jefferson believed that the happiness of his countrymen would be promoted best by a policy of "peace, commerce, and friendship with all nations, entangling alliances with none." He envisioned his country as a peaceful, agrarian–commercial federal republic of self-sufficient farmers and mechanics slowly spreading across space to fill in the beautiful and bountiful land vouchsafed them by Providence. Possessing "a wide and fruitful land," "with room enough for our descendants to the thousandth and thousandth generation," and "kindly separated by

---

[12]Dewey, *Financial History*, pp. 124–26; Studenski and Krooss, *Financial History*, pp. 69–71; Balinky, *Gallatin*, pp. 90, 107.

nature and a wide ocean from the exterminating havoc of one quarter of the globe."[13] America, Jefferson believed, had the blessed opportunity to keep itself free from the incessant rivalries, jealousies, and conflicts of the Old World. For Jefferson, the wise and patriotic statesman would take advantage of his country's fortunate geography and situation by defending a policy of national independence, neutrality, and noninvolvement in European affairs.

Jefferson's defense policy was to maintain a peacetime military establishment composed of a small standing army (about 3,000 men) to defend the frontier against hostile Indians and possible Spanish incursions from the Floridas and a small naval squadron to protect American commerce from the depredations of third–rate powers, such as the Barbary states of North Africa. Jefferson possessed a classical republican aversion to large military and naval establishments both for their expense (which required either taxes or debt to maintain) and their potential threat to the liberties of the people.

Far from being idealistic or utopian, Jefferson's vision and policies were based on a realistic understanding of America's geopolitical situation in the Atlantic world. He believed that it would be pure folly and extravagance to build a large ocean-going fleet, composed of hundreds of frigates and ships-of-the-line. He rightly surmised that building such a fleet would alarm the British and encourage a preemptive strike by their navy in the event of hostilities. Thus, building a fleet could actually increase the possibility of war with England. Jefferson did not believe that his country could be seriously threatened by the armies of either England, France, or Spain, the three great world powers. Although both England and Spain possessed territory contiguous to the borders of the young republic, both would have to transport large forces across the Atlantic and would be forced to fight on hostile territory far from their base of supplies. On the other hand, the Americans could mobilize hundreds of thousands of able-bodied militia to fight for their homeland. Not one of the great powers had the resources to send sufficient troops to conquer the American states. Jefferson rejected the Federalist axiom that in order to have peace one must prepare for war—the theory being that the more powerful a country was in

---

[13]Jefferson, "First Inaugural Address," *Thomas Jefferson: Writings*, p. 494.

armaments the less likely it was to be attacked. Jefferson doubted both the wisdom of this theory and Federalist sincerity in invoking it. He believed that history demonstrated that the more a country prepared for war, the more likely it was to go to war. First, having a powerful military force offered a temptation to rulers to engage in wars for conquest and glory.[14] And second, far from deterring aggression, a powerful navy and army often frightened other nations into building up their own forces and forming hostile alliances, tempting them to instigate hostilities for the purpose of gaining a strategic advantage or weakening their rival.

Jefferson believed that the Federalists, far from wishing to avoid war, actually welcomed war. In 1798 and 1799, the Federalists were eager to convert an undeclared naval confrontation with France into a full-scale war in order to obtain a formal military alliance with Great Britain. In the end, the only thing that kept the country out of a large war was President Adams's last-minute decision to reach an agreement with France. Jefferson was convinced that the Federalist leaders favored a war with France or Spain as a means to strengthen the federal government, increase the national debt, raise taxes, and place themselves in power.[15]

Early in his first term, Jefferson was faced with the question of whether he should use the naval force inherited from the Federalists to protect American trade in the Mediterranean. The pasha of Tripoli, the leader of one of the four Barbary powers on the northern coast of Africa (the others being Morocco, Algiers, and Tunis), demanded additional tribute from the United States as the price for allowing American shipping to trade in the Mediterranean free of piratical raids by his navy. The Barbary powers had been long extorting payments from the European

---

[14]Ibid., p. 503.

> [S]ound principles will not justify our taxing the industry of our fellow citizens to accumulate treasure for wars to happen we know not when, and which might not perhaps but from the temptations offered by that treasure.

[15]Jefferson to Thomas Lomax, March 12, 1799, ibid., p. 1063; Jefferson to the Special Envoy to France (Monroe), January 13, 1803, ibid., p. 1111; Jefferson to Barnabas Bidwell, July 5, 1806, ibid., p. 1164; Jefferson to Dr. Thomas Leib, June 23, 1808, ibid., p. 1188.

states for the "privilege" of trading with them and for the freedom to navigate the sea without attack. Rather than combining to suppress these piratical powers, the Europeans decided to pay them off, either in cash or in the form of ships, arms, or military supplies. The Washington and Adams administrations had followed the established custom and made treaties with Algeria in 1795, Tripoli in 1796, and Tunis in 1797; in ten years, the Federalists had paid these powers more than $2 million in tribute. When Jefferson assumed the presidency and was faced with the demand for more money from the pasha of Tripoli, he refused.

Jefferson's moral nature was no doubt offended by the prospect of paying for the privilege of not being robbed, but even more he must have seen this system of sordid bribery and intrigue as an impediment to his hopes for establishing free trade between the American republic and all the world, as well as an affront to the code of republican honor.

The pasha responded by taking down the American flag—a tacit declaration of war—and dispatching his warships to attack and capture American merchant vessels in the Mediterranean. In the spring of 1801, Jefferson dispatched three frigates and an armed schooner to the Mediterranean to protect American commerce and to intimidate Tripoli into honoring the 1796 treaty. Upon reaching Gibraltar in the late summer, the naval squadron found two Tripolitan cruisers on blockade duty awaiting American vessels. The American squadron chased off the two cruisers; the schooner *Enterprise* engaged one of them in battle and captured it; and the squadron proceeded to Tripoli where it blockaded the harbor. Thus, for the second time in only four years, the United States found itself in an undeclared naval war.

Jefferson sent additional forces to the Mediterranean each year until, by the summer of 1805, almost the entire American navy was deployed off the shores of Tripoli. In addition to escorting American merchant vessels and blockading Tripoli (in 1801 and 1803–1805), the American fleet bombarded Tripoli five times in August and September of 1804. By the early summer of 1805, facing a renewed and even more destructive series of bombardments from the American navy, and hearing of the fall of the town of Derbe to a land force composed of Americans, Greeks, and Tripolitan exiles commanded by William Eaton (the former American consul at Tunis), the pasha sued for peace and signed a treaty ending the war. The June 1805 treaty abolished annual payments from the United States to Tripoli and provided for the payment of a $60,000 ransom for more than two hundred American captives, mostly sailors from the U.S. frigate *Philadelphia* that had been captured after running aground off Tripoli in 1803.

Was this war for free trade and national honor consistent with Jefferson's stated policy of strict construction, peace, and economy in the public expenditure? Two things are clear. The pasha of Tripoli was the aggressor in this conflict, and Jefferson was committing armed forces to protect American lives and property from aggression. Yet because he failed to obtain a declaration of war from Congress, Jefferson was soon waging an undeclared war in violation of the Constitution. He thus set a dangerous precedent for future, more militaristic, presidents.

The Tripolitan war naturally resulted in greater naval expenditures and higher annual federal spending than Gallatin had planned. Not only did Jefferson shelve his plans to lay up all the American frigates in dry dock, but he even constructed five new brigs. Jefferson continued to pay tribute to the other Barbary States through the end of his second term. (Madison would continue making payments until 1816.)

When he assumed office Jefferson's major foreign policy objective was to purchase the city of New Orleans from France and the two provinces of Florida from Spain. The commercial importance of New Orleans was immense, for it was the major port through which Americans who lived west of the Appalachians sold their agricultural products abroad. Because it could at any time close the port to American commerce, the power that controlled New Orleans possessed tremendous leverage against the United States.

West Florida was important for similar reasons. It contained the port of Mobile, and it controlled the outlet for the rivers which drained the fertile Mississippi territory. The Floridas were strategically important, for they provided Spain, one of the three great world powers, with a foothold contiguous to the southern border of the United States. By acquiring them, Jefferson not only hoped to provide more territory for American settlement but to secure the southeastern border against Spain without having to build forts and deploy regiments of regulars in Georgia and Mississippi. It would also lessen the potential of conflict between Spain and the U.S. Such an acquisition, provided it could be accomplished without war, would be fully consistent with his policy of economy, peace, strategic isolation, and a small military establishment. In 1806, after Napoleon's conquests reduced Spain to the status of a French vassal state, Jefferson had his Secretary of State, James Madison, instruct the American ambassador to France to offer Napoleon $5 million for the Floridas and Texas.

THE LOUISIANA PURCHASE

Arguably the greatest accomplishment of Jefferson's presidency was the acquisition of Louisiana, bought from France for $15 million. The province was enormous at 828,000 square miles, and it contained some of the richest farmland in the world. Louisiana was comprised of New Orleans, a bustling city, St. Louis, a small city; a few isolated French settlements along the Mississippi; and some scattered Indian tribes. Other than that it was virtually uninhabited.

The story of its acquisition is a familiar one to most students of American history. After hearing of the Spanish retrocession of Louisiana to France, Jefferson instructed the American minister to France, Robert R. Livingston, to negotiate for West Florida and New Orleans. If that failed, he was to try to acquire some land on the lower Mississippi for an American port; and if that failed, he was to seek a French guarantee for free navigation of the Mississippi and the right of deposit at New Orleans.

In January 1803, Jefferson named James Monroe as minister plenipotentiary to France and sent him to Paris prepared to offer $10 million for New Orleans and West Florida. Just as Monroe was arriving in Paris, Talleyrand shocked Livingston by offering to sell not only New Orleans but the whole of Louisiana to the United States. Recognizing the advantages of such a purchase, Livingston negotiated a treaty. Both Livingston and Monroe signed the treaty and sent it to Jefferson.

When news of the Louisiana treaty reached Jefferson and Madison, they were exultant. Not only did the cession obtain New Orleans, but it secured the free navigation of the Mississippi River, removed a potentially hostile power from the west bank of the Mississippi, and provided a seemingly inexhaustible reserve of land for American settlement. It was fully in accord with Jefferson's policy of making the country secure without resorting to war or funding an expensive military and naval establishment. They also believed that it would help preserve the agrarian character of the American confederation for generations to come.

How much credit does Jefferson deserve for acquiring Louisiana? Many Federalists charged that he deserved none at all, that he just happened to be president when Napoleon made his unexpected offer. While that is true, it is also true that Napoleon would never have offered the province to a pro-British Federalist administration. Napoleon regarded the Republicans as anti-British and in basic sympathy with his country. Napoleon hoped to cement ties of friendship with the Americans, to increase their debt of gratitude, and to entice them into joining France in a military alliance against the British Empire. Jefferson's policy of neutrality and his well-known French sympathies created an environment in which Napoleon could feel safe in parting with Louisiana and could even hope to gain from it.

The Federalists opposed the purchase on two grounds. First, they warned that such a vast enlargement of territory would endanger the cohesion and the existence of the union. Jefferson responded by arguing that the confederal nature of the American republic made expansion safe.

> Who can limit the extent to which the federative principle may operate effectively? The larger our association, the less will it be shaken by local passions; and in any view, is it not better that the opposite bank of the Mississippi should be settled by our own brethren and children, than by strangers of another family? With which shall we be most likely to live in harmony and friendly intercourse?[16]

The "federative principle" was the principle of divided, or decentralized, power between the national and the state governments, under which the former was "charged with the external and mutual relations only of these states" while "the states themselves have principal care of our persons, our property, and our reputation."[17] Jefferson was asking why, given such a decentralized and flexible system, the union could not be doubled or even tripled in size? And in addition, the acquisition actually made it easier for the federal government to fulfill its constitutional responsibility of providing for the common defense.

[16] Jefferson, "Second Inaugural Address," *Thomas Jefferson: Writings*, p. 519.
[17] Jefferson, "First Annual Message," December 8, 1801, ibid., p. 504.

The Federalists also objected that the treaty was unconstitutional. After all, the Constitution conferred no power on the federal government to acquire foreign territory and incorporate it into the Union. On this point, Jefferson reluctantly concurred. He believed that the Louisiana treaty required not only Senate ratification but additional constitutional authorization through an amendment. In fact, soon after receiving news of the treaty on June 30, he drew up an amendment which stated that "the province of Louisiana is incorporated with the United States and made part thereof," and he distributed it to his cabinet.[18] His cabinet did not seem to think that an amendment was necessary. His attorney general, Levi Lincoln, was indecisive; so was Madison; and Gallatin was emphatic that it was not needed at all. Earlier in the year, the latter had written Jefferson explaining that "the United States as a nation have an inherent right to acquire territory," and "Congress have the power either of admitting into the Union as a new State, or annexing to a State with the consent of that State."[19]

Jefferson, however, remained convinced that an amendment was both necessary and prudent.

> There is a difficulty in this acquisition which presents a handle to the malcontents among us, though they have not yet discovered it. Our confederation is certainly confined to the limits established by the revolution. The general government has no powers but such as the constitution has given it; and it has not given it a power of holding foreign territory and still less of incorporating it into the Union. An amendment of the constitution seems necessary for this. In the meantime we must ratify and pay our money, as we have treated, for a thing beyond the constitution, and rely on the nation to sanction an act done for its great good, without its previous authority.[20]

---

[18]Henry Adams, *History of the United States of America During the Administrations of Thomas Jefferson and James Madison*, 2 vols. (New York: Library of America, 1986), vol. 1, p. 358.

[19]On Levi Lincoln's opinion, see Dumas Malone, *Jefferson the President: First Term, 1801–1805* (Boston: Little, Brown, 1970), pp. 312 and 321; Gallatin to Jefferson, January 13, 1803, quoted in Everett S. Brown, *Constitutional History of the Louisiana Purchase* (Berkeley: University of California Press, 1920), pp. 20–22.

[20]Jefferson to John Dickinson, quoted in ibid., pp. 23–24.

This passage from an August letter to John Dickinson represented Jefferson's settled opinion on the matter, which he had arrived at after conferring with his chief constitutional advisers—Madison, Gallatin, and Lincoln. He expressed the same idea in a letter to his friend John Breckinridge of Kentucky but added that an amendment adopted after the treaty had been ratified and paid for would constitute a popular endorsement of the acquisition and actually "confirm and not weaken the Constitution, by more strongly marking out its lines."[21]

Upon receiving a warning from Livingston in Paris that Napoleon might change his mind, Jefferson urged his cabinet and political associates to keep quiet for a time about the constitutional question so as not to give Napoleon a pretext for withdrawing his offer. Jefferson wanted the treaty ratified as soon as possible. However, he still thought it wise and necessary to adopt an amendment sanctioning the treaty. The draft amendment he distributed to members of his cabinet stated that

> Louisiana as ceded by France to United States is made a part of the United States. Its white inhabitants shall be citizens, and stand, as to their rights and obligations, on the same footing with other citizens of the United States.[22]

His draft also authorized the incorporation of Florida into the United States "whenever it may be rightfully obtained."

Jefferson found himself almost alone in insisting that the Constitution did not sanction the acquisition of new territory, whether through conquest, purchase, or treaty. Not only was his cabinet not behind him, neither were his chief congressional supporters. The stalwart John Randolph, the Republican majority leader in the House, saw no constitutional difficulty in the purchase. Neither did Senator Breckinridge of Kentucky, nor Representatives Joseph Nicholson of Maryland or Caesar Rodney of Delaware.[23] Jefferson's friend and political supporter Senator Wilson Cary Nicholas even wrote the president, urging him to drop his constitutional scruples. He warned that if Jefferson's opinion were made public, it could produce mischief by creating

---

[21]Jefferson to John C. Breckinridge, August 12, 1803, *Thomas Jefferson: Writings*, p. 1139.

[22]Adams, *History of the United States*, vol. 2, pp. 360–61.

[23]Brown, *Constitutional History*, pp. 62–65.

a precedent for future infractions and giving the Federalists an issue with which to assail the administration. But creating a precedent was exactly Jefferson's fear, and he did not think it a proper solution to pretend that they were not subjecting the Constitution to a very liberal reading when that was exactly what they would be doing. Nicholas argued that the Constitution already authorized incorporating new territory outside the territorial limits of the U.S. in 1783. Jefferson's reply is one of the most cogent and eloquent expressions of the doctrine of strict construction ever penned.

> I do not believe it was meant that they might receive England, Ireland, Holland, etc. into it, which would be the case on your construction. When an instrument admits two constructions, the one safe, the other dangerous, the one precise, the other indefinite, I prefer that which is safe and precise. I had rather ask an enlargement of power from the nation, where it is found necessary, than to assume it by a construction which would make our powers boundless. Our peculiar security is in the possession of a written Constitution. Let us not make it a blank paper by construction. I say the same as to the opinion of those who consider the grant of the treaty making power as boundless. If it is, then we have no Constitution. If it has bounds, they can be no others than the definitions of the powers which that instrument gives. It specifies and delineates the operations permitted to the federal government, and gives all the powers necessary to carry these into execution. . . . Nothing is more likely than that their enumeration of powers is defective. This is the ordinary case of all human works. Let us go on then perfecting it, by adding, by way of amendment to the Constitution, those powers which time and trial show are still wanting. . . . I confess, then, I think it important, in the present case, to set an example against broad construction, by appealing for new power to the people.[24]

However, Jefferson conceded that he would not insist on his view but would acquiesce in the prevailing opinion of the Republican Party, for he trusted "that the good sense of our country will correct the evil of construction when it shall produce ill effects."[25] Jefferson's concession would prove to be a

---

[24]Jefferson to Wilson Cary Nicholas, September 7, 1803, *Thomas Jefferson: Writings*, pp. 1140–41.

[25]Ibid., p. 1141.

fatal one, for the evils of broad construction would begin to work their mischief under Jefferson's successor, James Madison, and "the good sense of the country" on this question would fall silent.

Henry Adams argued that "the Louisiana treaty gave a fatal wound to 'strict construction,' and the Jeffersonian theories never again received general support."[26] This is simply not true. The "Jeffersonian theories" continued for sixty years to be the heart and soul of American political culture, and strict construction was by no means dead. Yet even if the wound were not fatal, it was serious; for the idea was planted that legislation for the good of the country should not be obstructed by an overly scrupulous adherence to the terms of the compact. Although he fails to note that the Federalists were the first to commit a serious breach of the Constitution when they chartered the first National Bank, the historian Henry Cabot Lodge understood the damage that the Jeffersonians had done.

Thus the first example was given of both the will and desire to violate the Constitution, if the popular feeling would sustain the executive and legislature in so doing; and in this fact lies the pernicious and crying evil of the Louisiana Purchase. It was the first lesson that taught Americans that numerical majority was superior to the Constitution and was a safe protection against it when violated, and that when policy approved the necessity of change, it was easier to break than to legally and regularly amend the provisions of our charter.[27]

It is also true that the easy ratification of the treaty without even a discussion of an amendment made the Republicans seem inconsistent and hypocritical and provided ammunition for those consolidationists who saw the Constitution as an impediment to their dreams of national greatness. John Quincy Adams declared that the purchase of Louisiana represented

> an assumption of implied power greater in itself and more comprehensive in its consequences, than all the assumptions of implied power in the twelve years of the Washington and Adams administrations put together. . . . After this, to nibble at a bank, a road, a canal, the mere mint and cumin of the law was but glorious inconsistency.[28]

---

[26]Adams, *History of the United States*, vol. 2, p. 363.

[27]Quoted in Brown, *Constitutional History*, p. 32.

[28]From John Quincy Adams, *Memoirs*, vol. 5, pp. 364–65, 401, quoted in ibid., p. 30.

Jefferson acquiesced when he should have stood firm. While party leaders were not supportive, he still could have appealed directly to the people by penning a special message imploring them to ratify a new amendment specifying which territories could be incorporated in the Union and spelling out the exact procedure for admitting them as new states. Jefferson failed to understand that the Constitution was written to protect the people from themselves and that to rely on those very people to correct defects in the Constitution, only when those defects had been already exploited for ulterior purposes, was foolish indeed.

CONSTITUTIONAL PHILOSOPHY, JUDICIAL REFORM, AND THE SUPREME COURT

When Jefferson ran for president in 1800, he made it clear that he supported strict construction, original intent jurisprudence, federalism, and states' rights.

I do then, with sincere zeal, wish an inviolable preservation of our present federal Constitution, according to the true sense in which it was adopted by the States. . . . I am for preserving to the States the powers not yielded by them to the Union, and to the legislature of the Union its constitutional share in the division of powers; and I am not for transferring all the powers of the States to the General Government, and all those of that government to the executive branch.[29]

He confessed to his friend and political ally from Connecticut, Gideon Granger, that he was sincerely

attached to the preservation of the federal Constitution according to its obvious principles, and those on which it was known to be received; attached equally to the preservation to the States of those rights unquestionably remaining with them.[30]

He warned his friend that

[29] Jefferson to Elbridge Gerry, January 26, 1799, *Thomas Jefferson: Writings*, p. 1056.
[30] Jefferson to Gideon Granger, August 13, 1800, ibid., p. 1078.

"[o]ur country is too large to have all its affairs directed by a single government" and if ever the powers of the state governments should become concentrated in the general government "it would become the most corrupt government on the earth."[31]

In his first annual message to Congress, Jefferson charged that

this government is charged with the external and mutual relations only of these states; [and] that the states themselves have principal care of our persons, our property, and our reputation, constituting the great field of human concerns.[32]

He promised that his consistent objective as president would be "to preserve the general and State governments in their constitutional form and equilibrium."[33]

When the Federalists began to develop their theory of federal judicial review in the aftermath of their crushing political defeat in 1800, Jefferson quickly denounced it as unrepublican and contrary to the intent of the framers and the state ratifying conventions. Jefferson argued that such a power would violate the separation of powers and make the least republican of the three branches of government the most powerful, thus striking a blow against "the vital principle of republics," which was "absolute acquiescence in the decisions of the majority" on all matters entrusted to them by the Constitution.[34] Chief Justice Marshall asserted in his *Marbury* decision that the federal courts had the final right to decide questions of disputed constitutionality and the authority to set aside federal laws which they thought contrary to the Constitution. Jefferson argued that an alternative doctrine, concurrent review, was closer to the intentions of the framers and the ratifying conventions. According to Jefferson, each branch of the federal government, plus the state governments, had the right to interpret the Constitution for itself, and none had the right to bind the others by its decision. Jefferson explained this doctrine in a private letter written while he was president.

[31]Jefferson to Gideon Granger, August 13, 1800, ibid., p. 1079.

[32]Jefferson, "First Annual Message," ibid., p. 504.

[33]Ibid., p. 509.

[34]Jefferson, "First Inaugural," ibid., p. 495.

> The judges, believing the law [the Sedition Act] constitutional, had a right to pass a sentence of fine and imprisonment, because that power was placed in their hands by the constitution. But the Executive [Jefferson], believing the law to be unconstitutional, was bound to remit the execution of it; because that power has been confided to him by the constitution. That instrument meant that its co-ordinate branches should be checks on each other. But the opinion [Marshall's] which gives to the judges the right to decide what laws are constitutional, and what not, not only for themselves in their own sphere of action, but for the legislative and executive also in their spheres, would make the judiciary a despotic branch.[35]

Dumas Malone, Jefferson's biographer, concedes that "jurists of our day" may find Jefferson's doctrine of constitutional interpretation "vague and remote." However, he points out that in Jefferson's

> own day . . . and for some decades thereafter it approximated the actualities of the government situation. . . . [T]he legislature and the executive continued to determine for themselves whether or not they were acting within the bounds of the Constitution.[36]

It must be kept in mind that Marshall and his allies did not formulate their novel doctrine of judicial review to restrain the power of government or to protect the rights of the people, but to protect governmental measures and institutions already enacted by the Federalists and believed to be threatened by the Republicans, such as the Judiciary Acts of 1789 and 1801, the national bank, the navy, and the internal tax system. In other words, for the Federalists, judicial review was a pro-government measure designed to prevent democratic majorities from shrinking the size or reducing the powers of government. The Federalists, after all, were the party of active government and liberal construction of the Constitution. Two modern constitutional historians have made the case that concurrent review "favors limited government" by making it more difficult for

---

[35] Jefferson to Abigail Adams, September 11, 1804, quoted in Dumas Malone's *Jefferson the President: First Term, 1801–1805* (Boston: Little, Brown, 1970), p. 155.

[36] Ibid., p. 156; Malone offers a good discussion of this whole issue, pp. 152–56.

the federal government to embark on a new area of legislation or regulation.[37] While this is true, Jefferson's primary concern was to prevent the will of the majority from being subverted or thwarted by the federal courts. Under concurrent review, the courts could pronounce a law unconstitutional, but they could not bind the other two branches; they could render an opinion, but they could not enforce it. The president would be free to block the execution of a law whose constitutionality he disputed, or to continue to execute a law even though it had been declared unconstitutional by the courts.

Concurrent review also applied to the several states. Jefferson did not believe that the states were bound to submit in all cases to the Supreme Court, to presidential decree, or even to federal law. As he put it in his draft of the 1798 Kentucky Resolutions,

> the government created by this compact was not made the exclusive or final judge of the extent of the powers delegated to itself; since that would have made its discretion, and not the Constitution, the measure of its powers; but that, as in all other cases of compact among powers having no common judge, each party has an equal right to judge for itself, as well of infractions as of mode and measure of redress.[38]

Jefferson understood that the true meaning of the supremacy clause was to render the Constitution itself the supreme law of the land; federal law was to be considered supreme and binding on all only when it was consistent with the Constitution. The clause reads: "The Constitution, and the laws of the United States which shall be made in Pursuance thereof; . . . shall be the supreme Law of the Land."[39]

Although he was himself a nationalist, Henry Adams understood perfectly the issue that was at stake when Jefferson and his party assumed power in 1801: namely, whether the Republican "revolution" would be truly revolutionary. In other words, would they make the kind of fundamental reforms that would last beyond their time in power? Adams wrote:

---

[37]William J. Quirk and R. Randall Bridwell, *Judicial Dictatorship* (New Brunswick, N.J.: Transaction Publishers, 1995), pp. 10–15.

[38]Jefferson, "Draft of Kentucky Resolutions," *Thomas Jefferson: Writings*, p. 449.

[39]*The Constitution of the United States (1788)*, Art. VI, 2nd par.

The essence of Virginia republicanism lay in a single maxim: THE GOVERNMENT SHALL NOT BE THE FINAL JUDGE OF ITS OWN POWERS. The liberties of America, as the Republican party believed, rested in this nutshell; for if the Government, either in its legislative, executive, or judicial departments, or in any combination of them, could define its own powers in the last resort, then its will, and not the letter of the Constitution, was law. To this axiom of republicanism the Federalist Judiciary opposed what amounted to a flat negative. Chief-Justice Marshall and his colleagues meant to interpret the Constitution as seemed to them right, and they admitted no appeal from their decision. . . . The question how to deal with the Judiciary was, therefore, the only revolutionary issue before the people to be met or abandoned; and if abandoned then, it must be forever. No party could claim the right to ignore its principles at will, or imagine that theories once dropped could be resumed with equal chance of success. If the revolution of 1800 was to endure, it must control the Supreme Court. The object might be reached by constitutional amendment, by impeachment, or by increasing the number of judges.[40]

Just days before Jefferson was to be sworn in as the third president, the lingering Federalist majority passed, and President Adams signed into law, the Judiciary Act of 1801. It reduced the number of Supreme Court justices from six to five (to deprive Jefferson of an early appointment when the next justice retired), abolished the existing federal circuit courts, created six new circuit courts, and divided the latter into twenty-three districts presided over by sixteen new federal circuit judges. These became known as "the midnight judges," since President Adams appointed Federalists to all the new positions.

The act also added to the number of federal marshals, district attorneys, and law clerks. Most ominously for the Republicans, it vested jurisdiction of all "federal questions" in the circuit courts. A federal question referred to those areas of law over which the Constitution had vested jurisdiction in the Supreme Court and in such inferior courts as Congress might establish. The Constitution defined federal questions as "all cases, in law and equity, arising under this Constitution, the laws of the United States, and treaties made, or which shall be made."[41] The

---

[40]Adams, *History of the United States*, vol. 1, pp. 174–75.

[41]Quoted in Malone, *Jefferson the President: First Term*, p. 119.

Judiciary Act of 1789, which had established the federal court system, had wisely left the question of federal jurisdiction to the state courts, but it had allowed appeals of state supreme court decisions to be heard before a federal circuit court. Clearly, the Judiciary Act of 1801 was a last-minute effort by the Federalists to erect some kind of judicial barrier against the feared revolutionary measures of the incoming administration.

The creation of patronage positions for Federalist lawyers was an incidental benefit. Jefferson described the new judicial establishment as "a parasitical plant engrafted at the last session on the judiciary body."[42] The Federalists, he wrote, "have retired into the Judiciary as a stronghold. There the remains of federalism are to be preserved and fed from the Treasury; and from that battery all the works of republicanism are to be beaten down and erased."[43] He regarded the act as a moral nullity, since it was passed by a party that had already been repudiated by the majority and was on the verge of surrendering power. For these reasons, he and his party were determined to repeal it at the earliest opportunity. After taking care of more pressing matters having to do with federal taxation, spending, and debt, the Jeffersonians, in December 1801, turned their attention to repeal. After a long and bitter debate, the Republicans passed the Repeal Act on March 8, 1802. It restored the old judicial system and abolished the new judgeships and federal district attorneys. Henry Adams estimated that the repeal saved $30,000 a year.[44] A month later, the Republicans passed the Judiciary Act of 1802, which restored to six the number of Supreme Court justices, created six circuit courts, and fixed one term annually for the high court.

The question now was what would Jefferson do about the Judiciary Act of 1789, which had created a three-tiered federal judicial structure. The top of the structure was a six-member Supreme Court staffed by a chief justice and five associate justices. The middle tier was made up of three circuit courts to be staffed only twice a year by a district judge and two itinerant

[42]Quoted in Dumas Malone, *Jefferson the President: Second Term, 1805–1809* (Boston: Little, Brown, 1974), p. 119.

[43]Jefferson to John Dickinson, December 19, 1801, quoted in Adams, *History of the United States*, vol. 1, p. 175.

[44]Ibid., p. 187.

Supreme Court justices. On the bottom were district courts presided over by a district judge; each state had one district court, except Virginia and Massachusetts, each of which had two. Henry Adams described this act as "a triumph of Federalist centralization," for it "had conferred on the Supreme Court jurisdiction over the final judgment of State courts in cases where the powers of the general government had been 'drawn in question' [that is, federal questions] and the decision was unfavorable to them."[45] As Adams pointed out, defenders of states' rights feared that this act eventually would "make the state judiciaries inferior courts of the central government," for "the powers of the general government might be 'drawn in question' in many ways and on many occasions . . . until the national courts should draw to themselves all litigation of importance, leaving the State courts without character or credit."[46]

At the time, Senator Richard Henry Lee of Virginia had proposed creating a single appellate federal supreme court with no other federal courts at all, except for a few admiralty courts. All cases arising under federal jurisdiction would be tried before state courts and only on appeal would they be brought before the supreme court. Other Republicans proposed a larger supreme court that would travel about the country to hear all federal cases. The Federalist-controlled Congress rejected both options and chose the more centralist and elaborate judicial system proposed by Senator Oliver Ellsworth of Connecticut.[47]

Jefferson and the Republicans had two available models with which they could have replaced the Judiciary Act of 1789. Yet they made no effort to repeal it. What is more, with the important exception of trying the remedy of judicial impeachments, they made no effort to enact any other kind of judicial or constitutional reform.

According to Henry Adams, Jefferson's biggest failure (next to the embargo) was his unwillingness to take advantage of the momentum and prestige of victory and his overwhelming

[45]Ibid., p. 177.

[46]Ibid., p. 187.

[47]Wythe Holt, "The Judiciary Act of 1789," in *The Oxford Companion to the Supreme Court of the United States*, Kermit L. Hall, ed. (New York: Oxford University Press, 1992), pp. 472–74.

Republican majority in Congress to enact fundamental judicial and constitutional reform. As he correctly points out, "loopholes for the admission of European sovereignty into the citadel of American liberty were seen in 1800 as clearly as [in 1860]."[48] While Adams is in no way sympathetic to Old Republican political and constitutional theories, he is undoubtedly right to point to the significance of Jefferson's failure to institutionalize his revolution. With the single exception of impeachments, Jefferson did not even try to enact constitutional safeguards against the dangers posed by national centralism and neomercantilism. Why he did not do so remains something of a mystery. Jefferson was certainly aware of Federalist plans for a more "energetic" government. And he was not ignorant of possible reforms, for a prominent Virginia Republican had proposed a set of them in October 1801. Judge Edmund Pendleton, head of the Virginia Court of Appeals, published an influential article in the *Richmond Enquirer* entitled "The Danger Not Over." The article was soon reprinted in the administration newspaper, the Washington *National Intelligencer*.[49] Pendleton's article was a classical-republican manifesto full of negative references to the dangers posed to American liberty by standing armies, undeclared war, executive influence, government debt, excessive civil offices, legislative corruption, judicial irresponsibility, and consolidated central power. Pendleton warned that Americans should not be complacent simply because faithful Republicans were now holding the reigns of power, for men were "fallible," new men of uncertain principles inevitably would succeed them, and experience had already shown that "much mischief may be done under an unwise administration, and that even the most valuable parts of the Constitution, may be evaded or violated."[50] As a result, he urged them to take advantage of the opportunity provided by the temporary overthrow of Federalist men and principles "to erect new barriers against folly, fraud and ambition; and to explain such parts of the Constitution, as have been

---

[48]Adams, *History of the United States*, vol. 1, pp. 174–75.

[49]Edmund Pendleton, "The Danger Not Over," October 5, 1801, reprinted in *Life and Letters of Edmund Pendleton, 1734–1803*, David John Mays, ed. (Charlottesville: University Press of Virginia, 1967), pp. 695–99.

[50]Ibid., p. 698.

already, or may be interpreted contrary to the intention of those who adopted it."[51]

Pendleton suggested the following constitutional amendments to correct several notable "defects" in the Constitution. As he believed the presidency was too powerful, he proposed that the president be ineligible for a second term, and his power of appointing federal judges and ambassadors be transferred to the House of Representatives. He also believed the federal Senate was too powerful, and he recommended either shortening senators' terms of service or making them removable by the state legislatures, and depriving them of their "executive" powers (the power to ratify treaties and confirm appointments), which presumably would be transferred to the House.

Pendleton saw a defect in the irresponsibility of the federal judiciary. He proposed that by a concurring vote of both houses, Congress could remove federal judges and Supreme Court justices from office. He believed there to be a lack of restrictions on the power of the federal government to borrow money and go into debt. Pendleton suggested "some check" on this power, although he did not specify what kind. He was also worried about the lack of precision in certain areas and the existence of some general phrases in the Constitution which provided opportunities for mischievous constructions. He recommended "defining prohibited powers so explicitly, as to defy the wiles of construction." He recommended that the Constitution should state explicitly that the common law of England was not a part of the law of the United States, and that the crime of treason was "confined to the cases stated in the Constitution" and could not be extended further by law or construction. He also believed that there existed too much uncertainty about the exact boundaries between the federal and state spheres of authority. Therefore, he suggested that "the distinct powers of the General and State Governments" should be "marked out with more precision." He closed his article by quoting from an unnamed classical-republican author who had observed "that of men advanced to power, more are inclined to destroy liberty, than to defend it." He urged them not to let this propitious opportunity be lost before forming

[51]Ibid., p. 695.

"new barriers to counteract recent encroachments on their rights."[52]

Adams himself wondered why Jefferson never pushed for an amendment to excise "certain phrases in the Constitution [which] had been shown by experience to be full of perils, and were so well-established by precedent in their dangerous meaning," such as the necessary and proper clause. He wondered why Jefferson did not try to limit constitutionally the war- and treaty-making powers "with their undefined and therefore unlimited consequences."[53] He also asked why Jefferson did not ask Congress "to confirm the action of Virginia and Kentucky by declaring the Alien and Sedition Laws to be unconstitutional and null as legislative precedents." After all, as Adams points out, John Taylor and other Virginia Republicans at the time thought that Congress should have formally repealed those laws instead of merely allowing them to expire according to statute.[54]

Jefferson also did nothing to erase what has since proved to be the fatal precedent established by *Marbury*, that the Supreme Court had the authority to strike down a state or federal law whose constitutionality it disputed. Jefferson could have asked Congress for an amendment to reverse Marshall's opinion in *Marbury* and formally declare that the Supreme Court did not have the power of judicial review. Jefferson believed that since Marshall's opinion was issued *obiter dictum* (an incidental opinion having no bearing on the case in question, and hence not binding) and had no historical precedent, it was therefore null and void. He was right, but that did not prevent future justices from citing it. Last, Jefferson erred by deciding against pushing for an amendment to authorize the Louisiana Purchase and to answer the questions raised by territorial expansion—namely, which other North American territories could be incorporated in the Union, how could they be incorporated lawfully, what powers exactly did Congress and the president have over the territories, and what would be the exact procedure for forming new states out of them and admitting them to the Union.

Jefferson also failed to appoint a states'-rights Republican to the Supreme Court who could rival John Marshall in erudition,

---

[52]Ibid., pp. 698–99.

[53]Adams, *History of the United States*, vol. 1, pp. 173–74.

[54]Ibid., p. 177.

strength of personality, and determination to uphold a consistent constitutional philosophy. Jefferson had three Supreme Court appointments. He appointed William Johnson of South Carolina in 1804, Henry Brockholst Livingston of New York in 1806, and Thomas Todd of Kentucky in 1807. Although all three were Republicans, none of them consistently upheld the compact theory of the Constitution, or what was then known as the Virginia school of constitutionalism. Johnson, who was the most republican of the three, cited *Marbury* as a precedent and concurred in Marshall's major centralizing opinions (*McCulloch v. Maryland*; *Martin v. Hunter*; *Gibbons v. Ogden*; and *Dartmouth College v. Woodward*). Livingston was an even greater disappointment than Johnson. Instead of helping to form a Jeffersonian phalanx on the court, he quickly fell under Marshall's influence and voted with the nationalist majority on all major cases. Thomas Todd, whom Jefferson appointed to fill a newly created sixth associate justice position, turned out to be a non-entity, a mere rubber stamp for Marshall and Story.

Historians have little or nothing to say about Jefferson's Supreme Court appointments. Neither Henry Adams nor Dumas Malone even discuss them. Yet here was Jefferson's best chance to counter John Marshall. With three strong Republican appointments, Jefferson could have reduced Marshall's majority to a bare 4–3 by 1807. With just one more solid appointment in 1811, Jefferson's hand-picked successor, Madison, could have ended the Marshall Court and begun a Jeffersonian Court with strict constructionist, states'-rights jurists in the majority. In the meantime, vigorous dissenting opinions issued by Jeffersonian jurists could have weakened the force of Marshall's opinions and added legitimacy to future reversals. Because Marshall's most seminal nationalist decisions, apart from *Marbury* in 1803, came after the War of 1812, Jefferson could have changed the whole course of constitutional history.

Why did Jefferson make such weak appointments? It was not because there were no intellectually formidable jurists committed to states' rights and strict construction. Actually, there were many available, including two prominent Virginians with whom Jefferson corresponded. Judge Spencer Roane (1762–1822) had been on the Virginia Court of Appeals since 1794, and after the death of Edmund Pendleton in 1803 became its recognized leader. President-elect Jefferson was apparently considering appointing him to the position of chief justice of the

Supreme Court before Adams appointed Marshall just six weeks before he was to leave office. Why Jefferson at the first opportunity did not appoint Roane to the court as a check upon Marshall is not clear. Another formidable Virginia jurist who shared Jefferson's constitutional and judicial philosophy was St. George Tucker (1752–1827). Tucker had been a judge of the general court of Virginia for twelve years, and a professor of law at the college of William and Mary from 1800–1803, and he was elected to the state court of appeals in 1803 to fill the vacancy created by the death of Pendleton. In the same year, he published a five-volume annotated edition of William Blackstone's *Commentaries of the Laws of England*. Tucker suffused his "republicanized" version of Blackstone with the doctrines of states' rights, strict construction, and the compact theory.[55] There is no doubt that Roane and Tucker were the intellectual and scholarly equals, and possibly superiors, of Marshall and that they would have challenged his centralizing and nationalistic opinions at every opportunity. If Jefferson had appointed these two men to the court and favored a true Republican, instead of Madison, to be his successor, it is very likely that the Marshall Court would have come to an end in 1811; and historians would now be writing about a Roane or a Tucker Court during the 1810s and 1820s.

Jefferson did try the experiment of whether Congress's power of impeachment could be used as a means of disciplining or checking the power of federal judges and Supreme Court justices. In February 1803, Jefferson recommended to the House that they consider the impeachment of Federal District Judge John Pickering of New Hampshire. Jefferson charged that Pickering's habitual drunkenness rendered him unfit to perform his duties and that such dereliction constituted a misdemeanor which was legal grounds for impeachment. On March 3, 1803, the House voted 45–8 to impeach Pickering. A year later, on March 12, 1804, the Senate found Pickering guilty of a misdemeanor and ordered him removed from office.[56]

---

[55]For an excellent short discussion of Tucker and his edition of Blackstone, see *St. George Tucker, View of the Constitution of the United States: With Selected Writings*, Clyde Wilson, ed. (Indianapolis, Ind.: Liberty Fund, 1999), pp. vii–xvii.

[56]Adams, *History of the United States*, vol. 2, pp. 398–99.

Jefferson was certainly pleased with Pickering's impeachment, but it was two other events in the late winter and spring of 1803 that finally motivated him to recommend to his chief supporters in Congress the impeachment of a Supreme Court justice. On February 24, 1803, John Marshall rendered his gratuitous and bold assertion of judicial power in *Marbury v. Madison*. Jefferson was alarmed and angered by the decision. Then, on May 2, Associate Justice Samuel Chase of the Supreme Court delivered a political harangue before a grand jury in Baltimore. Chase denounced the Republican's repeal of the Judiciary Act of 1801, the recent adoption of universal manhood suffrage by the state of Maryland, and "the modern doctrines of our late reformers [the Jeffersonians], that all men in a state of society are entitled to enjoy equal liberty and equal rights." Chase warned the jury that unless these changes were reversed and the doctrines behind them repudiated, the government would become "a mobocracy . . . and peace and order, freedom and property, shall be destroyed."[57] Jefferson was infuriated. He considered Chase's comments to be "seditious," constituting an "official attack on the principles of our Constitution and the proceedings of a State." Consequently, just ten days later, he wrote a letter urging one of his chief supporters in the House to begin impeachment proceedings against Chase.[58] For Jefferson, the time had arrived to humble the power and pretensions of the Federalist-controlled Supreme Court and at the same time to see if impeachment could function as an effectual legislative check upon the judiciary. On March 12, 1804, the House voted to impeach Chase by a vote of 73–32. The Senate trial would begin a year later. The chief House managers at the Senate trial were John Randolph of Virginia, Joseph Nicholson of Maryland, and George W. Campbell of Tennessee.

Samuel Chase was an arch-Federalist of imperious habits who had allowed his own political partisanship to influence his official duties as an associate justice of the Supreme Court. Chase had favored the government prosecution in his handling of two important sedition trials in Baltimore in 1800; he had left the bench without a quorum in order to campaign for John Adams

---

[57]Quoted in ibid., vol. 2, pp. 401–02.

[58]Ibid., pp. 402–03.

the same year; he was also given to harassing Republican lawyers and delivering political diatribes while on the bench. The House managers brought eight articles of impeachment against Chase. The most serious charges were that during the sedition trial of John Fries, Chase had denied the defendant the right to counsel and had treated him in an "arbitrary, oppressive, and unjust" manner; during the libel trial of James Callender, Chase had failed to excuse a prejudiced juror and had refused to hear an important witness for the defense; after a federal grand jury in Newcastle, Delaware, had finished its business, Chase kept it in session and urged it to inspect a local paper for evidence of sedition; and Chase had delivered a political speech before the grand jury in Baltimore.[59]

The chief issue before the Senate was what were the proper grounds for judicial impeachment. The Federalists and some Northern Republicans contended that a justice could be impeached only for actual violations of the law (criminal impeachment). The Southern Republicans, led by John Randolph and William Branch Giles, contended that a justice could be impeached for misconduct, partisanship, and abuses of judicial power (political impeachment). The latter was Jefferson's opinion. On March 1, 1805, the Senate began voting on the eight articles of impeachment. In order to convict Chase, two-thirds of the senators present (twenty-three) would have to vote to convict him on at least one article. The most votes to convict were nineteen on article eight and eighteen on articles three and four. Chase was acquitted. Although Randolph has often been blamed for botching the trial, the real reason for the failure to convict was that five Northern Republicans and one Southern Republican voted to acquit Chase on all eight articles.[60]

Thus, to Jefferson's and Randolph's great disappointment, the issue of whether impeachment could be used to check a politicized and consolidationist judiciary had been settled in the negative. Right after the acquittal, John Randolph introduced a resolution that the House should pass and submit to the states an amendment to the Constitution providing that "the judges of the

---

[59]M.E. Bradford, "Samuel Chase: Maryland Vesuvius," in *Against the Barbarians and Other Reflections on Familiar Themes* (Columbia: University of Missouri Press, 1992), pp. 110–12.

[60]Adams, *History of the United States*, vol. 2, pp. 451–66.

Supreme and all other courts of the United States shall be removed by the President on the joint address of both houses of Congress."[61]

Joseph Nicholson of Maryland pushed for an amendment empowering the legislature of any state to recall one of their senators and vacate his seat. The House voted to refer both resolutions to the next Congress.[62] Jefferson gave neither amendment any support. Writing just two years later during the Burr treason trial, Jefferson admitted to one of his chief supporters in the Senate that "impeachment is a farce which will not be tried again." He observed with alarm that "one of the great coordinate branches of the government [the judiciary]" had set "itself in opposition to the other two and to the common sense of the nation." He suggested that if Burr were acquitted due to the obstructions placed in the way of conviction by Chief Justice Marshall, who was presiding over the trial, that the people "will see then and amend the error in our Constitution, which makes any branch independent of the nation."[63]

Once again Jefferson did nothing. He even sounded as if the president had no power or influence in proposing a constitutional amendment which would have limited the powers of the federal court and made its justices, as well as other federal judges, removable for misconduct. He had many ways of making such a recommendation: he could have drafted a special message to Congress; he could have included it in his upcoming annual message; and he could have suggested it to his chief supporters in Congress. But he did none of these things. Jefferson should have known better. He should have realized that political power in a republic is ephemeral and that the temptations to abuse power were so great that future administrations and congresses would be sure to seize the forbidden fruit, which was all the more reason to erect as many dikes and moats and eliminate as many unguarded passages to the throne of arbitrary power as was possible. Years later, when Jefferson himself admitted that the enemy was in the camp, he could not say that he had not been warned; his fellow Virginian Republicans, Edmund Pendleton, John Randolph, and John Taylor, had warned him.

[61]Ibid., p. 463.

[62]Ibid.

[63]Jefferson to William Branch Giles, April 20, 1807, *Thomas Jefferson: Writings*, p. 1175.

Henry Adams suggested four reasons why Jefferson did not push for constitutional revision and reform. First, Jefferson found some federal powers useful for his policy of territorial expansion, such as the treaty-making power. Second, his majority in the Senate was too small; he needed two-thirds to pass an amendment. Third, he could not count on the support of his Northern political allies. Adams contended that while the "Southern Republicans" were strongly committed to limited government, states' rights, and strict construction, the "Northern democrats" were more interested in making the federal government responsive to the wishes of the people than in restricting its power. Fourth,

> Jefferson wished to overthrow the Federalists and annihilate the last opposition before attempting radical reforms. Confident that States-rights were safe in his hands, he saw no occasion to alarm the people with legislation directed against past rather than future dangers.[64]

Adams was right. Early in his presidency, Jefferson made a fateful decision to safeguard the Republican revolution by political rather than constitutional means. His strategy was to draw away the great body of the Federalist voters, most of whom he believed were republican at heart, from their ambitious and unprincipled leaders. Once that had been done, the republic would be safe and fundamental reforms could be enacted. He admitted to a correspondent very early in his presidency that

> some things may perhaps be left undone from motives of compromise for a time, and not to alarm by too sudden reformation, but with a view to be resumed at another time. . . . What is practicable must often controul [sic] what is pure theory; and the habits of the governed determine in a great degree what is practicable.[65]

In the meantime, he hoped "by degrees to introduce sound principles and make them habitual." In other words, he feared

---

[64]Adams, *History of the United States*, vol. 1, pp. 174, 176, 178.

[65]Jefferson to P.S. Dupont de Nemours, January 18, 1802, *Thomas Jefferson: Writings*, pp. 1099–1101.

that radical measures would alarm many moderate Federalists and new Republican voters, thus driving them back into the arms of the Hamiltonians and the High Federalists of New England.

Many of Jefferson's early policy decisions can be explained only by a desire to placate and win over the bulk of the Federalists to the Republican Party. Why else was he so reluctant to remove any but the most partisan or incompetent Federalists from office? Why did he decide only to reduce, instead of abolish, the navy when the latter had been his initial intention and the fond wish of so many of his Southern supporters? Why did he decide to send the fleet to the Mediterranean to fight the pasha of Tripoli when he needed only to sign a new treaty with an increased tribute? After all, Jefferson continued throughout his presidency to pay tribute to the other Barbary powers. Jefferson knew that the navy was popular in the Eastern states, the region of his weakest strength, and he knew that most navy officers were Federalists. Why did Jefferson support a compromise settlement for the shameful Yazoo bribery scandal, if not to win over New England Federalists who were personally interested in that sordid financial transaction?

There are numerous references in Jefferson's letters during the course of his presidency indicating how important it was to him that the Republican majority grow and the Federalist minority shrink.[66] Moreover, there are indications that Jefferson was not simply postponing constitutional reform to a later day when the Republicans were stronger, but that he actually regarded such reforms as secondary in importance to winning over the Federalist minority to republicanism:

> [S]hould the whole body of New England continue in opposition to these principles of government, either knowingly or through delusion, our government will be a very uneasy one. It can never be harmonious and solid, while so respectable a portion of its citizens support principles which go directly to change of the federal Constitution, to sink the State governments, consolidate them into one, and to monarchize that.[67]

---

[66]Jefferson to Elbridge Gerry, March 29, 1801, ibid., pp. 1088–89; Jefferson to C.F. de C. Volney, February 8, 1805, ibid., p. 1158; Jefferson to Barnabas Bidwell, July 5, 1806, ibid., p. 1163.

[67]Jefferson to Gideon Granger, August 13, 1800, ibid., p. 1078.

In other words, Jefferson understood that constitutional prohibitions alone would not deter or prevent a determined faction from subverting a government in which they did not believe. By his policies, Jefferson placed stronger emphasis on restoring harmony and unity to the country and on bringing back the great body of the Federalists to their "ancient principles," "the principles of '76," than he did on constitutional reform. Jefferson simply refused to believe that the majority could not be relied upon to defend the Constitution and the cause of liberty. He was sure that while they might stray from sound principles on occasion they would always return to their senses before it was too late.

INTERNAL IMPROVEMENTS AND A MILITARY ACADEMY

During Jefferson's Second Inaugural Address, he suggested for the first time that federal funds be applied in the future "to rivers, canals, roads, arts, manufactures, education, and other great objects within each state."[68] On the basis of this passage, many historians have rushed to the conclusion that Jefferson in his second term became an advocate of public works programs, government spending as an engine of prosperity, and expansive federal powers. They are wrong, for Jefferson was merely suggesting one way in which surplus federal funds could be spent after the federal debt had been fully retired. He also made it clear that an amendment to the Constitution would have to be obtained in order to authorize such spending.

He brought up the subject again in his Sixth Annual Message. He explained to his countrymen that federal revenues were increasing at such a rate that there would be very soon a surplus beyond what was required to pay the interest and the sinking fund on the federal debt. He pointed out that there were two things that could be done. Congress could reduce the impost, or it could apply the funds to "public education, roads, rivers, canals, and other such objects of public improvement as it may be thought proper to add to the constitutional enumeration of federal powers."[69] Once again, he stressed the need for an amendment to the Constitution, for "the objects now recommended are

---

[68] Jefferson, "Second Inaugural Address," ibid., p. 519.
[69] Jefferson, "Sixth Annual Message," December 2, 1806, ibid., p. 529.

not among those enumerated in the constitution, and to which it permits the public moneys to be applied."[70] As the impost was low, and as it was applied mainly to "foreign luxuries," he recommended spending the surplus on objects of public improvement. Jefferson was not suggesting that an empowered federal government take up the responsibility of funding and supervising educational institutions all over the country; rather, he was suggesting merely that Congress should consider founding a "national establishment for education," or a national university:

> Education is here placed among the articles of public care, not that it would be proposed to take its ordinary branches out of the hands of private enterprise, which manages so much better all the concerns to which it is equal; but a public institution can alone supply those sciences which, though rarely called for, are necessary to complete the circle, all the parts of which contribute to the improvement of the country.[71]

That he had thought through this subject is evident from the fact that earlier in the year he had discussed the issue with his friend Joel Barlow and had sent him a draft of a "bill for the establishment of a National Academy & University at the city of Washington."[72] However, Jefferson refused to propose such a bill to Congress until the latter had obtained constitutional authorization by passing an amendment. Jefferson again brought the subject up in his last annual message to Congress. He asked:

> Shall [the surplus] lie unproductive in the public vaults? Shall the revenue be reduced? Or shall it rather be appropriated to the improvement of roads, canals, rivers, education, and other great foundations of prosperity and union, *under the powers which Congress may already possess*, or such amendment of the constitution as may be approved by the States?[73]

---

[70]Ibid., p. 530.

[71]Ibid.

[72]Jefferson to Joel Barlow, February 24, 1806, ibid., p. 1160.

[73]Jefferson, "Eighth Annual Message," November 8, 1808, ibid., p. 549 (emphasis added).

Here Jefferson for the first time equivocated on this issue. Just four months before he would be stepping down as president, he suggested that maybe Congress already had the power to fund internal improvements: "While uncertain of the course of things, the time may be advantageously employed in obtaining the powers necessary for a system of improvement, should that be thought best."[74] Jefferson had run into the same problem he had encountered with the Louisiana treaty. He was finding himself alone in defending strict construction.

Jefferson himself was fairly consistent in not undertaking unconstitutional improvement projects. In March 1802, he signed a bill which authorized him to establish a military academy at West Point, New York. The law limited the academy to twenty officers and men. Establishing an institution for the training of military officers, particularly engineers, certainly fell within Congress's powers to "provide for the common Defense" and "raise and support Armies."[75] Jefferson's one slight inconsistency in this area was his approval of the Cumberland Road bill in March 1806. Under its terms, Congress appropriated $30,000 and authorized the president to appoint three commissioners and surveyors to survey and lay out a national road connecting Cumberland, Maryland, on the Potomac River with Wheeling, Virginia, on the Ohio River. The president was also required to get the approval of Maryland, Pennsylvania, and Virginia, states through which the road would pass. Jefferson fulfilled the terms of the law. However, construction did not begin nor were any funds appropriated for that purpose under Jefferson's presidency.[76] President James Madison began construction of the road in 1811; Monroe completed it in 1818.

FOREIGN POLICY AND THE EMBARGO: THE SECOND TERM

Jefferson's second term was marked by the growing controversy with Great Britain over the latter's increasing restrictions on and seizures of American commerce and impressments of American seamen. These began and steadily increased after the

---

[74]Jefferson, "Eighth Annual Message," ibid., p. 549.

[75]Malone, *Jefferson the President: Second Term, 1805–1809*, p. 510; Adams, *History of the United States*, vol. 1, p. 205.

[76]Malone, *Jefferson the President: Second Term*, p. 556.

resumption of war between Great Britain and France in 1803. The two chief points of controversy were the right of the Americans to transport the products of the French and Spanish West Indies to ports on the continent controlled by these two powers (the neutral trade), and the status of ex-British seamen who were now serving on American merchant ships and even on American naval vessels. The neutral trade not only was profitable for American merchants, but it was swelling the federal customs revenue, thus helping Jefferson and Gallatin pay off the federal debt.

The neutral trade was strongly supported by the New England commercial interests, the Federalist Party, and some Northern Republicans. After the resumption of war, the British Royal Navy had quickly swept the Atlantic Ocean of French and Spanish vessels. The British hoped to weaken Napoleon by depriving him of the rich exports from the French West Indies. Obviously, American neutral carriers frustrated their plans. Thus, in July 1805, a British judge rendered the infamous Essex decision, which declared that trade forbidden in peace could not be legal during war. In other words, since the peacetime navigation laws of France and Spain forbade American or British vessels from carrying French or Spanish colonial produce to the continent, then such laws could not be relaxed or disregarded in time of war. The judicial decision was nakedly political and of doubtful legality. Nevertheless, it provided the British Ministry the pretext it sought, and soon the Royal Navy was interdicting American commerce and seizing those ships that were carrying French or Spanish property. British naval vessels would take captured American ships to a British port where a British judge would rule that the cargo was now British property. Then a British merchant vessel or warship would transport it to London where it would be sold and often shipped to a European port. The Americans were right to suspect that British seizures had as much to do with driving American mercantile competition from the ocean and making money than it did with national security. (Throughout the war, Napoleon purchased the uniforms for his soldiers from British textile firms.)

By 1806, the British Navy had established a cordon around every American port on the Atlantic seaboard. No American ship could leave port without the likelihood of being stopped and searched for ex-British seamen or Caribbean goods. As for the ex-British seamen, some had actually deserted from the Royal

Navy, either by jumping ship in an American port or simply walking away while on shore leave; many had left British commercial vessels; and a few had simply migrated to America. Americans were quick to grant citizenship to the seamen, for they needed them to fill their growing merchant marine. The British were alarmed at the growing desertions of experienced sailors, for it was weakening both their navy and their merchant marine. Not surprisingly, as Napoleon went from victory to victory on land, gradually gaining mastery of the whole continent, the Royal Navy stepped up its impressments of British–American sailors, whom they considered as still British subjects. In June 1807, the British escalated the conflict when the Royal Navy frigate *Leopard* fired on, boarded, and removed four British deserters from the American navy frigate *Chesapeake* a few miles off Norfolk, Virginia. Americans regarded this act as an insult to American honor and national independence. The British regarded American employment of their seamen as a threat to their national security and an insult to their national honor.

Jefferson had five foreign policy options. At one extreme, he could go to war with Great Britain. Jefferson knew that this would be a risky endeavor. New England was strongly opposed to a war with England and would give it little support. The country was vulnerable to British attack. The British could launch raids, shell cities, land an invasion force anywhere they wanted along the coast, launch a ground invasion from Canada, and blockade the Atlantic ports. To defend the country, his administration would have to fortify the Atlantic cities, arm and train the militia, increase the size of the navy, and raise a larger standing army, all of which would be an expensive endeavor requiring taxes and borrowing. In short, war meant the overthrow of his fiscal program of economy, tax reduction, and debt reduction. Not surprisingly, Jefferson rejected this option out of hand.

At the other extreme was the option of a British alliance, whether formal or informal. The minimal terms of such an alliance would require the United States to cease trading directly with France or her allies on the Continent. Instead, all American vessels, whether their cargo were American exports or French and Spanish re-exports, would have to land in London and pay a duty before proceeding to a Continental port. The Americans would have to cease accepting British seamen for service on their ships. In return, the British would cease their seizures of American commerce. Apart from some New England Federalists, virtually no Americans favored such an alliance. Jefferson regarded this option as a dishonorable and disgraceful submission to the edicts of an imperious and predatory military commercial empire, as well as a compromise of the republic's independence.

Jefferson had three other options. First, he could continue his policy of strict neutrality and commercial engagement. It would avoid war, keep down military expenditures, and keep up the customs revenue. American shipping increasingly suffered from British seizures and some French seizures as well, but the New England and middle-state merchants decided that the profit to be made from completed voyages in the neutral trade and the regular export trade outweighed the losses they were sustaining. Jefferson followed this course until the end of 1807, right before the last year of his presidency. Second, he could authorize the arming of merchant vessels and issue letters of marque, authorizing private vessels to attack and seize foreign commercial vessels. Third, he could adopt a policy of commercial coercion by either restricting or banning all trade with European powers on the theory that they so needed the American market, American foodstuffs, and American neutral carriers that they would be forced to revoke their restrictions and depredations on American commerce. Jefferson believed that peaceful coercion was the perfect republican solution to the worsening commercial crisis. It would avoid war and entangling alliances, keep down military expenditures along with debt and taxes, vindicate the national honor, defend vital interests, and preserve the country's independence.

Jefferson felt his hand being forced by the British in 1807. First, in January, there was an Order in Council issued which prohibited neutral—that is, American—shipping from the North American coasting trade. (American ships could make only one stop and then had to return.) Next, in June, there was the *Chesapeake* incident, an act of war which had infuriated the American public and created the strongest anti-British sentiment since the Revolution. Finally, in December, news reached Washington of a new Orders in Council (November 11) which prohibited all neutral, or American, trade with any European port from which the British flag was excluded (which was most of them). It also prohibited the export of cotton to France. Only ships that first landed in a British port, paid a customs duty, and bought a

license could proceed to ports on the French-controlled Continent. By these new orders, the British were no longer simply
claiming the right to interdict the American carrying trade; they
were claiming the right to interdict the American regular export
trade (cotton, rice, tobacco, beef, fish, grains, etc.). The Americans would now have to pay the British for the privilege of
being allowed to trade. Jefferson believed that the British had
finally pressed his country to the point where they had only two
options: submission or resistance.

Jefferson decided it was time to try the experiment of
"peaceable coercion." His Republican allies promptly reinvoked
the Non-Importation Act that had passed in April 1806 and had
been suspended in December 1806, which prohibited the importation of English manufactures which could be produced in the
United States, and passed the Embargo Act (December 22, 1807),
which forbade any U.S. vessels from leaving for a foreign port,
or for any foreign vessel to depart from a U.S. port carrying
American merchandise. The act required all registered sea-letter
vessels to post bonds of double the value of the ship and cargo
before embarking on voyages to other American ports. All ships
were required to obtain clearance papers and show a manifest of
the cargo before departing and to produce a certificate proving
that they had landed in a foreign port. Just one week after the
embargo went into operation, Congress passed a supplementary
measure, the Second Embargo Act (January 8, 1808), in order to
prevent vessels licensed only for the coasting trade from secretly
sailing to a Canadian or West Indian port. The act required all
coasting vessels, as well as whalers and fishing boats, to post
bonds. Although it was ostensibly designed for their benefit, the
embargo was not a popular measure among the American mercantile class, and they soon found loopholes and ways of evad-
ing the provisions of the law. For instance, American merchants
began a brisk trade with Canada across the northern border and
to a lesser extent with the Spanish Floridas. As a result, Congress
passed the Third Embargo Act (March 12, 1808) forbidding
trade by land or inland waterway between the U.S., Canada, and
Florida. But massive evasions of the law continued. Smuggling
along the northern border continued, and American ships and
vessels began to engage in an illicit trade with British ships off
the Atlantic coast, often with the active assistance and participation of the British navy. One of the most notorious smuggling
routes was Lake Champlain. New Yorkers and Vermonters

openly transported products on large rafts and boats across to Canada.

On April 19, 1808, Jefferson proclaimed the existence of an "insurrection" along the northern border "too powerful to be suppressed by the ordinary course of judicial proceedings."[77] He called on the governors of Vermont and New York to call out their militia to suppress the illicit traffic. Jefferson and Gallatin soon realized that if the embargo were to be successful, a strict enforcement act was going to be necessary. Congress passed the Fourth Embargo Act, also known as the Enforcement Act, in late April 1808. Under its terms, no ship or coasting vessel could depart for a port or district *adjacent to foreign territory* without the express permission of the president; collectors in districts *adjacent to foreign territory* could seize merchandise on shore they suspected was intended for eventual export and detain it until the owner would pay a bond guaranteeing that it would be transported to a domestic port; federal revenue cutters and naval vessels could stop, search, and bring back to port any American ship on mere suspicion that it might be carrying goods for export; and collectors could detain suspicious vessels in harbor until the president personally sanctioned their release. In authorizing searches, seizures, and detentions of ships and merchandise, the law made no mention of such constitutional requirements as search warrants and judicial due process. Yet despite this new measure, smuggling and illicit trading continued.

To enforce the embargo against a recalcitrant public, Jefferson early on resorted to regular army and navy forces to assist the customs service. The First Embargo Act authorized the navy to interdict ocean-going vessels headed for foreign ports. Without legislative authority, Jefferson, in February 1808, directed Secretary of the Navy Robert Smith to send naval gunboats to intercept American merchantmen trading with the British off the Delaware coast. The Enforcement Act authorized naval vessels to stop, search, and detain any ship or boat suspected of engaging in unlawful commerce, whether at sea, along the coast, sailing an inland waterway, or still in harbor. In July, Jefferson directed Smith to place his ships at the disposal of Secretary of Treasury Gallatin, whom Jefferson had made the chief enforcement

---

[77] Jefferson, "Proclamation of April 19, 1808, *Annals of Congress (1808-09)*, p. 580.

officer for the embargo. Thus, by late summer of 1808, revenue cutters, naval gunboats, brigs, and frigates were patrolling the Atlantic coastline as well as every harbor, bay, inlet, inland waterway, and bordering Canada, lakes Ontario and Champlain. In July, Jefferson ordered Secretary of War Henry Dearborn to send regular army units to the Lake Champlain area to assist the local militia in interdicting smuggling. In August, after Governor Tompkins of New York ordered five hundred state militia to his northern border, Jefferson ordered Dearborn to station regulars in upper New York at key points along Lake Ontario and the St. Lawrence River. Thus, by the late summer of 1808, Jefferson had deployed a military and naval cordon around the United States from Lake Ontario in the north to New Orleans in the south.

However, widespread and systematic evasions of the law continued into the fall, and Jefferson and Gallatin decided that an even more rigorous enforcement measure was needed. In early January 1809, Congress passed the Second Enforcement Act. It gave the president and anyone under his authority (collectors, federal marshals) the authority to employ the army and naval forces of the United States to assist them in their duties whenever and wherever they thought it necessary. It also granted collectors and marshals even greater latitude in their searches, seizures, and detentions. Federal officers were now authorized to search any vehicles of transportation or warehouses and to seize and hold specie or other articles of domestic growth, produce, or manufacture which they suspected were intended for export at any port or location in the Union, not just at ports or locations adjacent to foreign territory. To obtain their release, owners had to give bonds to the full value of the articles. Coasting vessels now had to give bonds amounting to six times the value of the vessel and cargo. Once again, Jefferson, his administration, and the Republican-controlled Congress ignored the protections afforded by the Fourth, Fifth, and Sixth Amendments to the Constitution.

In deciding for an embargo, Jefferson made the biggest mistake of his presidency. Commercial coercion failed utterly to achieve its object of forcing Great Britain and France to respect neutral rights. Despite fifteen months of embargo, the Royal Navy continued to impress American seamen, and the British ministry did not revoke their Orders in Council. Jefferson overestimated the effect an embargo would have on the British economy. While British manufacturing suffered, farmers benefitted from a higher price for their crops, British shipping filled the vacuum created by the removal of American competition, and British merchants turned to South America as a new export market and source of imports. In addition, with the active cooperation of the Royal Navy at sea and the British army in Canada, British merchants engaged in a brisk smuggling trade with Americans who were determined to keep on trading in defiance of the law.

In pursuing an embargo policy, Jefferson did serious damage to the Republican cause for which he was the recognized national leader, and he violated many of the Republican principles for which he had contended in the 1790s. First of all, the enforcement provisions of the embargo acts were in clear violation of the Fourth and Fifth Amendments, for they authorized revenue officers, custom collectors, federal marshals, and naval officers to conduct searches and seizures without judicial warrants or any kind of due process. Furthermore, Jefferson and his Republican allies assumed a power of doubtful constitutional legitimacy. As John Randolph contended in the House, the Constitution granted the federal government the power to "regulate" commerce with foreign nations, but it did not grant it the power to prohibit it altogether. To concede that the power of prohibition is implied in that of regulation could only add legitimacy to the Federalist doctrine of implied powers.

Jefferson understood as well as Randolph that the assumption of a doubtful power would establish a precedent for others and that the doctrine of implication once conceded eventually would render the Constitution ineffectual as a check upon government power. However, unlike the Louisiana question, Jefferson never seemed to consider the constitutional implications of his embargo and enforcement measures. Perhaps his dislike of the British and also of New Englanders rendered him temporarily blind. But whatever the reason, there is no doubt that Jefferson had become the author of a major enhancement in unconstitutional federal power.

There was great irony in the fact that the major judicial decision upholding the constitutionality of the embargo was rendered by a New England Federalist, Judge John Davis of the federal district court for Massachusetts.[78] Judge Davis's opinion (September 1808) drew on all the expansive constitutional doctrines first advanced by Alexander Hamilton in the early 1790s. He spoke of the "discretion of the national government" with regard to locating the proper bounds of the commerce power; he cited the "necessary and proper clause" as authorization for the power to lay an embargo; he invoked the doctrine of "inherent sovereignty," which was simply the doctrine of implied powers by another name; and he even denied the federated and limited nature of the American confederation. In a sentence which should have sent Jefferson rushing to repeal his experiment in peaceable coercion, Davis wrote that "in our national system, as in all modern sovereignties, it [the commerce power] is also to be considered as an instrument for other purposes of general policy and interest."[79]

Judge Davis clearly knew what he was about. Instead of bowing to the shortsighted wishes of his mercantile friends and fellow Federalists in striking down the hated embargo, he saw an opportunity to lay a foundation stone for the nationalist-centralist theory of the Constitution which was favored by the neomercantilists and empire-builders in the Federalist party. Even better, in defending the constitutionality of a Republican measure, he could make the nationalist theory appear nonpartisan and render his centralizing opinion unassailable by the Republicans. For if the latter attacked his reasoning, they would be all but admitting that Jefferson had transgressed the bounds of the Constitution.

The embargo also violated the classical-liberal principles that Jefferson had defended in the 1790s and had consistently respected as president. In a letter written to a Massachusetts supporter in 1800, Jefferson promised to limit "the general government . . . to foreign concerns only" and to leave "commerce, which the merchants will manage the better, the more they are left free to manage for themselves," alone.[80]

---

[78]Adams, *History of the United States*, vol. 2, pp. 1111–13.

[79]Ibid., pp. 1112–13.

[80]Jefferson to Gideon Granger, August 13, 1800, *Thomas Jefferson: Writings*, p. 1079.

Seven years later, Gallatin wrote to Jefferson warning him that the embargo would have many negative consequences, including "privations, sufferings, [loss of] revenue," and a strengthening of the Federalists, and would be of doubtful effect in swaying the British to change their hostile policy. Gallatin described hopes for the latter as altogether "groundless." He urged that the embargo should be of short duration, that it should not be pressed too hard upon their countrymen, and that they should be prepared to retract it at the first signs that it was doing more harm than good. Gallatin concluded his argument with a beautiful statement of laissez-faire principles:

> Government prohibitions do always more mischief than had been calculated; and it is not without much hesitation that a statesman should hazard to regulate the concerns of individuals, as if he could do it better than themselves.[81]

Jefferson should have heeded Gallatin's advice, for the latter's warnings and predictions were vindicated by events. Yet Jefferson pressed on despite mounting evidence that the embargo was proving a disaster. It is difficult to defend the embargo as a policy of national defense or honor, for those who were chiefly suffering at the hands of the British navy (the Northern mercantile classes) were the embargo's most vigorous opponents. No one was forcing them to continue trading in the Atlantic market in face of mounting British and French restrictions, seizures, and confiscations. In fact, despite the steady loss of cargo, sailors, and ships, they were still making a sizeable profit, still finding a market for American produce, and still bringing in record sums for the federal treasury through customs. Years later, Condy Raguet of Philadelphia, perhaps the most influential classical-liberal political economist of the 1830s, dated the republic's first and fateful departure from its original free-trade policies to Jefferson's 1807 embargo. As Raguet pointed out, the embargo was followed by the nonintercourse acts, the War of 1812, and the protective tariffs of 1816, 1820, 1824, and 1828.[82]

---

[81]Gallatin to Jefferson, December 18, 1807, quoted in Adams, *History of Jefferson's Second Administration*, vol. 2, pp. 1043–44.

[82]Condy Raguet, "On the Principles of Free Trade," *Free Trade Advocate* (January 1829): 2.

The economic effects of the embargo were calamitous for the commercial and navigating interests of New England and the middle states. Despite smuggling, trade was crippled: sailors and mechanics could not find work; ships languished in dock; many merchants and shipbuilders were ruined, all suffering diminished business. Nor was the distress limited to the Eastern states. The South suffered grievously by losing the market for their tobacco, cotton, rice, indigo, wheat, and corn.

John Randolph would lament years later that the embargo and the economic restrictions were the beginning of ruin for many planters in Virginia. That Jefferson would cause such misfortune through a policy which was intended to vindicate the cause of free trade is the supreme irony and is yet more proof that an activist government invariably does more harm than good to its intended beneficiaries.

Other unintended consequences of the embargo were an increase in sectional animosity and distrust between the Eastern and Southern states, a revival of Federalist political strength in New England, and the sanction lent by the Jeffersonians to the precedent of using the army and navy to enforce an unpopular law on American citizens.

There was a bitter irony for Federalists and dissident Republicans in that the chief use of Jefferson's gunboat flotilla and additional army regiments turned out not to defend the country against British invasion but to enforce the terms of an unpopular federal law upon the citizens of the states. The political party that rose in opposition to a standing army and navy on the grounds that they posed a threat to the liberties of the citizens was now using those very forces to deprive Americans of their right to trade with foreign countries. The historian Henry Adams summed up well the damage done by Jefferson to his own cause by his policy of "peaceful" coercion:

> The embargo and the Louisiana purchase taken together were more destructive to the theory and practice of a Virginia republic than any foreign war was likely to be. Personal liberties and rights of property were more directly curtailed in the United States by embargo than in Great Britain by centuries of almost continuous foreign war.[83]

---

[83]Adams, *History of the United States*, vol. 2, p. 1116.

MILITARY POLICY: THE SECOND TERM

As tensions with Great Britain increased during his second term, Jefferson thought it prudent to make some defensive preparations. At first these involved modest appropriations. In 1806, the Republican Congress authorized $250,000 for the construction of fifty gunboats and $150,000 to increase the fortifications at some key harbors. Jefferson believed that gunboats were the answer to the American dilemma of how to defend the large country from the threat posed by the British navy without having to spend a fortune building ships-of-the-line, heavy frigates, and brigs.

Jefferson knew that British naval supremacy was so great that their ships could crush whatever fledgling fleet the Americans could build and put out to sea. What is more, the very building of such a fleet would be seen as a threat and might provoke them into launching a preemptive strike to destroy the new ships and shipyards before they would become large enough to challenge the British navy. The British destruction of the Danish fleet as it lay at anchor in Copenhagen—Denmark was a neutral power and not at war with Britain at the time—was proof that they would not let the technicality of American neutrality stop them from sailing up the Chesapeake in force to destroy the Norfolk and Washington shipyards.

The Americans had nothing but a handful of frigates, brigs, and schooners, how could they defend their coastline from British depredations in the event of a war? For Jefferson, gunboats were the answer. Gunboats were basically floating barges with lots of guns. They were relatively cheap to build; they did not pose a threat to the British fleet on the ocean; and they were thought to be effective in battling larger warships in the close quarters of harbors, bays, and inland waterways. In other words, Jefferson saw them as the perfect defensive weapon to guard against British invasion.

Jefferson also decided to augment the size of the standing army and to arm the state militias. In February 1808, Jefferson had Dearborn request authorization to add eight regiments to the regular army since war loomed with Great Britain. The Republicans promptly passed a bill authorizing the increase. Just ten years previously, when the country was engaged in an undeclared naval war with France, the Republicans had vetoed an Adams administration measure to create twelve new army regiments. John Randolph was one of the few Republicans in the House to remain consistent with his classical-republican opposition to standing armies and commercial wars. He voted against the eight regiment bill, just as he had voted against the twelve regiment bill in 1798.

In the last year of his presidency, Jefferson doubled the size of the regular army, thus making it larger than it had been when he took office. Nor was that all. At the president's urging, Congress passed other military measures including $850,000 for 188 gunboats, $1 million for harbor fortifications, authorization for the president to sell surplus muskets to the states, $200,000 to arm and equip the state militias, authority for the president to require the state governors to organize, arm, and equip 100,000 state militia, and the authority for the president to call all, or part, of those forces for six months of federal service.[84]

The question of Jefferson's motivation in making preparations for war, even while embarking on a policy of peaceable coercion, is important. There are three possibilities for this. First, he may have believed that defensive preparations on top of the embargo would induce the British to repeal their Orders in Council and cease their impressments for fear of a war with the United States. This explanation is consistent with his earlier diplomacy in which he repeatedly dropped hints to one of the three great powers that he was considering making an offensive alliance with one of their rivals. Second, he may have already foreseen the need for new gunboats and army regiments to enforce his embargo. Jefferson knew that the mercantile classes, especially in New England, did not favor the embargo and that they had a long tradition of resisting commercial restrictions by smuggling. Third, Jefferson may have been seriously contemplating an eventual war with Great Britain. While Jefferson sincerely wanted peace and understood that a war would bring in its train taxes and debt, he also knew that a successful war would offer one splendid prize—Canada.

The Republicans had long coveted Canada, and it was taken for granted that in the event of a second war with Great Britain, the Americans would invade and add it to the confederation.

---

[84]Adams, *History of the United States*, vol. 2, p. 1081; Malone, *Jefferson the President: Second Term*, pp. 512, 515.

During the war fever produced by the British attack on the American frigate *Chesapeake*, Jefferson and his cabinet discussed the feasibility of invading Canada during the winter of 1808–1809. Gallatin even prepared a memorandum for Jefferson outlining possible military operations against their northern neighbor; he estimated that its conquest would require 30,000 soldiers.[85]

Jefferson believed that acquiring Canada would bring the same kind of benefits as had acquiring Louisiana—land, security on the cheap, and independence from Europe. He understood that the more territory his countrymen controlled on the North American continent, the less need they would have of a regular army, the more secure they would be from invasion, and the more insulated they would be from the incessant wars and political entanglements of the Old World. Throughout his career, Jefferson often expressed his wish "that there were an ocean of fire between us and the Old World."[86]

An important contrast should be kept in mind. Jefferson and his party were willing to consider war only if it were in the national interest; the Federalists, on the other hand, sought war for the incidental benefits it would bring—taxes, debt, centralization of power, patronage, glory—and seemed not to care a whit for the good of the country. For instance, it is hard to see what benefits (land, increased security, or commercial wealth) a military alliance with Great Britain would have brought the people.

Whatever Jefferson's initial intentions in increasing military expenditures and making war preparations, by June 1808, he

---

[85]John Randolph referred to the Republican desire to incorporate Canada during his famous speech on Gregg's Resolutions in March 1806, quoted in Russell Kirk, *John Randolph of Roanoke* (Indianapolis, Ind.: Liberty Press, 1978), p. 326; see also Malone, *Jefferson the President: Second Term*, pp. 427, 508–09. Ten days after the United States Congress declared war on Great Britain, Jefferson expressed the hope that his countrymen would invade and conquer Canada and thus "strip her [Great Britain] of all her possessions on this continent." Jefferson to General Thaddeus Kosiusko, June 28, 1812, *Thomas Jefferson: Writings*, p. 1265. A year and a half later, he repeated his desire that the American army would "remove them [the British] fully and finally from our continent." Jefferson to Madame de Tesse, December 8, 1813, ibid., p. 1316.

[86]Jefferson to Elbridge Gerry, May 13, 1797, ibid., p. 1044.

was already considering the possibility that the embargo would fail and his country would have to go to war with England.

But if this is before the repeal of the Orders of Council, we must abandon it only for a state of war. "The day is not distant, when that will be preferable to a longer continuance of the embargo. But we can never remove that, and let our vessels go out and be taken under these orders, without making reprisal."[87]

Reprisal meant issuing letters of marque and arming merchant ships, both of which Jefferson knew would lead to war with Great Britain. By late 1808, most of the new gunboats and army regiments were employed trying to prevent Americans from trading with the British, and the latter showed no sign of wanting to negotiate or make concessions. What is more, opposition to the embargo in the Eastern states was steadily increasing. Jefferson's response was to intensify the enforcement effort and prepare for war. Jefferson and his cabinet agreed that the proper policy to pursue was to tighten the enforcement of the embargo, increase war preparations, and set a date in the early summer of 1809 when, unless the British and French repealed their restrictions on American commerce, Congress would declare war against one or both powers.

In early December, at the recommendation of Gallatin (and hence Jefferson) Senator William Branch Giles introduced the Second Enforcement Act in Congress. Later in the month, at the recommendation of Dearborn (and hence Jefferson), the House began debating a bill to raise, train, and equip 50,000 volunteers at the cost of $2.1 million. The volunteers would serve one month annually for a period of two years, and they could be called into active service by the president at any time during that period. If this bill were to pass on top of the 9,000 regulars already serving and the president's new authority to call up 100,000 militia at any time, President Madison would be able to deploy 160,000 troops for an invasion of Canada, the defense of the coastline, and perhaps an invasion of Florida as well.

Jefferson's program was only partly enacted. On January 6, Congress passed the Second Enforcement Act. On January 20, the House passed a bill calling for an early or extra session of Congress to meet on May 22, the purpose of which would be to

---

[87] Jefferson to Dr. Thomas Leib, June 23, 1808, ibid., pp. 1188–89.

end the embargo and declare war. On January 30, Jefferson's close ally Wilson Cary Nicholas introduced a measure declaring that if Great Britain and France had not repealed their orders and edicts directed against America's neutral commerce before June 1, then the embargo would cease and letters of marque and reprisal would be issued against those two powers. Everyone knew that the issue of such letters would initiate hostilities and be followed by war.[88]

In a series of votes in early February 1809, Congress stepped back from enacting Jefferson's and Madison's war program. First, it rejected the Nicholas bill and voted to end the embargo on March 4; second, it voted for a mild nonintercourse act; and third, it refrained from passing the bill for 50,000 volunteers. The Northern Republicans, especially those from New York and New England, had turned against the administration's measures because they decided that neither they nor their constituents wanted war. When the bulk of the Northern Republicans joined the antiwar, antiembargo coalition of Federalists and Old Republicans, Jefferson's party lost its majority and the embargo was doomed. Bowing to the inevitable, Jefferson signed the bill repealing the embargo on March 1, just three days before he retired from the presidency.

---

[88]Jefferson remarked thus on his program:

> The course the Legislature means to pursue, may be inferred from the act now passed for a meeting in May, and a proposition before them for repealing the embargo in June, and then resuming and maintaining by force our right of navigation. [Should France and Great Britain not relent in the spring], we must again take the tented field, as we did in 1776 under more inauspicious circumstances. (Jefferson to Colonel James Monroe, January 28, 1809, *Thomas Jefferson: Writings*, p. 1199)

After Nicholas's resolution was defeated, Jefferson wrote in evident disappointment:

> I thought Congress had taken their ground firmly for continuing their embargo till June, and then war. But a sudden and unaccountable revolution of opinion took place the last week, chiefly among the New England and New York members, and in a kind of panic they voted the 4th of March for removing the embargo, and by such a majority as gave all reason to believe they would not agree either to war or non-intercourse. (Jefferson to Thomas Mann Randolph, February 7, 1809, quoted in Adams, *History of the United States*, vol. 2, pp. 1230–31)

What saved the country from war in 1809 was the activity and defiance of the New England Federalists, acting in the same spirit and on the same principles as the Republicans had done in 1798–1799. By late 1808, prominent New England Federalists were taking the preliminary steps to calling a convention of the five New England states and New York to protest the embargo and to adopt measures of cooperation in resisting its enforcement. The chief leaders of this movement were U.S. Senators Timothy Pickering of Massachusetts and James Hillhouse of Connecticut, Massachusetts Senate leader Harrison Gray Otis, and Connecticut Governor Jonathan Trumbull.[89]

The first public manifestation of this well-organized and well-orchestrated movement was the holding of town meetings all across Massachusetts in January 1809. Resolutions passed by these meetings challenged the constitutionality of the embargo, vowed cooperation among the towns in resisting the second Enforcement Act, and promised to oppose any future war with Great Britain.[90] The Boston town meeting appealed to the General Court for its "interposition" to protect the "liberties and property" of the people of the state from the oppressive embargo system.[91] Soon thereafter, the Massachusetts legislature passed a series of antiwar, antiembargo resolutions. They promised to "co-operate" with their "sister States" "in measures to rescue our common country from impending ruin," including the adoption of amendments to the Constitution designed to defend the rights of commerce; "to give to the commercial States fair and just consideration in the government of the Union"; and to afford "permanent security, as well as present relief, from the oppressive measures under which they now suffer."[92] The Connecticut legislature soon followed Massachusetts's example and passed similar resolutions. Governor Trumbull publicly invoked the doctrine of state interposition in his opening speech to the Connecticut legislature:

[89]Adams, ibid., pp. 1204–07.
[90]See Adams's summary of these meetings, ibid., pp. 1209–13.
[91]Ibid., pp. 1210–11.
[92]Ibid., pp. 1213–14.

> Whenever our national legislature is led to overleap the pre-
> scribed bounds of their constitutional powers, on the State leg-
> islatures in great emergencies devolves the arduous task—it is
> their right, it becomes their duty—to interpose their protect-
> ing shield between the rights and liberties of the people and the
> assumed power of the general government.[93]

Trumbull was not just blowing smoke. When War Secretary Dearborn requested him to select militia officers on whom the collectors might call for military assistance in enforcing the embargo, he refused to lend his cooperation. Trumbull reasoned that the Second Enforcement Act was "unconstitutional in many of its provisions, interfering with the State sovereignties, and subversive of the rights, privileges, and immunities of the citizens of the United States."[94] The New England states had made their intent plain: Not only would they not cooperate in the Republican policy of embargo followed by war but they would actively resist it by collective measures, including the calling of a New England convention.

Jefferson and his cabinet were faced with a grim dilemma. Not only was the embargo not working, but they feared that were it to be persisted in, it might provoke the Eastern states to secede. If they opted for war, they could not count on New England troops to help in the invasion of Canada; what was worse, war might well drive those states to secession and common cause with England. If they chose to abandon the embargo, they would be admitting a costly and humiliating failure of policy. Ultimately, members of their own party forced their hand. When the state resistance of New England was coupled with the growing defection of Northern Republicans from the embargo and quasi-war policy, Jefferson and his cabinet had no choice but to surrender their experiment of commercial coercion and their preparations for war. Years later, he would write:

> I felt the foundations of the government shaken under my feet
> by the New England townships. . . . [a]nd although the whole
> of the other States were known to be in favor of the measure,

---

[93]Ibid., p. 1215.
[94]Ibid., pp. 1214–15.

yet the organization of this little selfish minority enabled it to overrule the Union.[95]

Jefferson was bitter about this denouement. He long believed that at a time when the nation's independence and honor was at stake, the Federalists of New England could think only of their pocketbooks.

If the irony of the political situation was palpable, so was the opportunism and hypocrisy of many New England Federalists who only eight years previously had been hard-core consolidationists and advocates of federal over state authority. Nevertheless, the New England Federalist's invocation of the principles of '98 gave added weight to Jefferson's own core belief that states' rights were "the surest bulwarks against anti-Republican tendencies."[96] Jefferson's belief that the decentralized and extensive nature of the federal Union was the best security for popular liberties had now been confirmed twice by experience. Although Jefferson never admitted it, Massachusetts and Connecticut in 1809 had served the cause of constitutional liberty much as Virginia and Kentucky had done in 1798 when

> by a part of the Union having held on to the principles of the Constitution, time has been given to the States to recover from the temporary frenzy into which they had been decoyed, to rally round the Constitution, and to rescue it from the destruction with which it had been threatened even at their own hands.[97]

CONCLUSION

When assessing Jefferson's presidency, it is worthwhile to reconsider what his old rival, Alexander Hamilton, said of him seven weeks before he took office:

> Nor is it true that Jefferson is zealot enough to do anything in pursuance of his principles which will contravene his popularity or his interest. He is as likely as any man I know to temporize, to calculate what will be likely to promote his own

---

[95] Jefferson to Joseph C. Cabell, February 2, 1816, *Thomas Jefferson: Writings*, p. 1381.

[96] Jefferson, "First Inaugural Address," ibid., p. 494.

[97] Jefferson to Gideon Granger, August 13, 1800, ibid., pp. 1079–80.

> reputation and advantage; and the probable result of such a
> temper is the preservation of systems, though originally
> opposed, which, being once established, could not be over-
> turned without danger to the person who did it. To my mind,
> a true estimate of a temporizing rather than a violent sys-
> tem.[98]

While slightly overdrawn, Hamilton's prophecy is a fairly accurate prediction of the course of Jefferson's presidency, and it offers a plausible explanation of why Jefferson would shrink from truly revolutionary measures. It certainly helps to explain why Jefferson never tried to repeal the Judiciary Act of 1789, repeal the charter of the national bank, or abolish the navy. The Old Republicans were certainly disappointed that Jefferson did not go further in reversing Federalist innovations and creating safeguards against future encroachments by a government con-trolled by consolidationists and neomercantilists. John Taylor of Virginia summed up Jefferson's presidency in 1810:

> There were a number of people who soon thought and said to
> one another that Mr. Jefferson did many good things, but neg-
> lected some better things; and who now view his policy as
> very like compromise with Mr. Hamilton's. . . . Federalism,
> indeed, having been defeated, has gained a new footing by
> being taken into partnership with republicanism. It was this
> project which divided the Republican party by changing its
> principles from real to nominal.[99]

That was harsh, but it was also true. The "good things" to which Taylor was referring were undoubtedly the repeal of the Judiciary Act of 1801, the abolishment of the internal taxes, the reduction in the number of federal officials, the reduction of the regular army, the shrinking of the navy, the paying down of the national debt, and the addition of New Orleans and Louisiana to the Union. These were real and solid accomplishments. However, as Taylor pointed out, Jefferson "neglected some better things."

---

[98]Hamilton to Bayard, January 15, 1801, quoted in Adams, *History of the United States*, vol. 1, pp. 188–89.

[99]John Taylor to James Monroe, October 26, 1810, quoted in Richard Ellis, *Jeffersonian Crisis: Courts and Politics in the Young Republic* (New York: Oxford University Press, 1971), p. 235.

He did not try to repeal the Judiciary Act of 1789 or revoke the charter of the national bank. He left most of the ocean-going navy in service. He did not appoint a Spencer Roane or a St. George Tucker, both intellectually powerful and consistent states'-rights' Republicans, to the Supreme Court. And worst of all, he did not push for constitutional reform in the form of amendments that would have checked the power of the federal judiciary by negating the power of judicial review and making federal judges removable by Congress and by inhibiting the ability of the federal government to make use of general phrases in the Constitution to expand its powers at the expense of the states.

Jefferson's compromises with Federalism were as follows: the retention of the navy and the national bank; the appointment of quasi-Federalists to the Supreme Court; his administration's broad reading of the treaty-making power; and perhaps worst of all, his choice of the neo-Federalist James Madison to be his successor. Another Old Republican from Virginia, John Randolph, was equally harsh in his assessment of Jefferson's presidency:

> It had my hearty approbation for one-half of its career. As to my opinion of the remainder of it, it has been no secret. The lean kine of Pharaoh devoured the fat kine. The last four years, with the embargo in their train, ate up the rich harvest of the first four, and, if we had not some Joseph to step in, and change the state of things, what would have been now the condition of the country? I repeat it; never has there been any administration which went out of office and left the country in a state so deplorable and calamitous as the last.[100]

While most of Jefferson's sins were those of omission, the embargo was his one great sin of commission. It led to other sins: the tripling of the standing army in 1808, the precedent of turning the regular army and navy against American citizens to enforce an unpopular law of dubious constitutionality, and the violations of the Fourth, Fifth, and Sixth Amendments under the enforcement acts—not a record of which any president claiming to be a Republican can be proud. In fact, as Taylor pointed out, Jefferson's adoption of increasingly harsh measures to enforce

---

[100]Quoted in Kirk, *John Randolph of Roanoke*, p. 92.

his embargo policy recalled the Federalist excesses of the 1790s: Washington's calling out of the militia in 1794 to crush the "whiskey insurrection," the Alien and Sedition Acts of 1798, and Adams's calling out militia and regulars to suppress "Fries rebellion" in 1799.

Ultimately, Jefferson's failure to institutionalize his "revolution" was due to his misplaced faith in the good sense of the people. He simply could not believe that they would ever discard the federal Constitution and its restraints on power for the allure of an energetic state that could accomplish "great" things. He was wrong. Jefferson's faith in self-government turned out to be stronger than his faith in constitutionalism or liberty, to the long-term detriment of all three.

After two hundred years, what can we conclude about Jefferson's presidency? He advanced the cause of liberty in many concrete ways, and his state papers include some of the most eloquent defenses of federalism, constitutionalism, and liberty in our political literature.

However, he did little for the cause of constitutionalism, and he may even have harmed it. He had an opportunity to perfect America's federal constitutional order, but through a misplaced faith in the wisdom and watchfulness of the people, he let it pass by. The lesson by now should be clear to all: In the long run, democracy cannot be relied upon to protect liberty and the rule of law.

4

SUPREME COURT AS ACCOMPLICE: JUDICIAL BACKING FOR A DESPOTIC PRESIDENCY

MARSHALL L. DEROSA

COMMENCING DEMAGOGUES, ENDING TYRANTS

Despotism was a paramount concern of the framers of the U.S. Constitution, particularly executive despotism. In their minds, it was a phenomenon that would surely become manifest if favorable circumstances were to arise; hence, their distrust of a unitary democracy headed by a strong chief executive. Publius acknowledged that the "road to the introduction of despotism" is constructed by men who begin their careers "by paying an obsequious court to the people, commencing demagogues and ending tyrants." The framers, especially the Anti-Federalists, were very prescient. The concentration of national power has the commensurate effect of heightening the probability of presidential despotism, a despotism adept at "overturning the liberties of republics," that is, the states.[1]

To the extent that power is usurped from the American republics (that is, the states in their corporate and collective identities) by the national government, the nation is moved further down the road to presidential despotism. Constitutional liberalism[2] is supposedly the bulwark against the emergence of

---

[1]Alexander Hamilton, James Madison, and John Jay, *The Federalist Papers* No. 1, Clinton Rossiter, ed. (New York: Mentor, 1961), p. 35.

[2]My working definition of constitutional liberalism is the distribution of political power in such a manner that it is both fragmented and competitively self-checking. It is essentially the original Madisonian model in which "ambition is made to counteract ambition" and the interests of the officeholders (for example, national and state legislators, executives, judges) are integrally connected to their respective offices and to identifiable constituencies. See *The Federalist Papers* Nos. 10 and 51; my working definition of despotism is the illegitimate utilization of governmental powers against the fundamental rights of the governed within their respective states, especially the fundamental right to be self-governing.

national despotism. As is evidenced by the framers' commitment to limited government via separation of powers, checks and balances, and states' rights federalism, political power was to be decentralized:

> But the great security against a gradual concentration of the several powers in the same department consist in giving to those who administer each department the necessary constitutional means and personal motives to resist encroachments of the others. . . . Ambition must be made to counteract ambition. . . . [And in] the compound republic of America, the power surrendered by the people is first divided between two distinct governments, and then the portion allotted to each subdivided among distinct and separate departments. Hence a double security arises to the rights of the people. The different governments will control each other, at the same time that each will be controlled by itself.[3]

But this scheme, for all intents and purposes, is failing. Power is steadily flowing from the states to the national center. The rights of the people in the collective national sense and the requisite national power to enforce those rights—states' rights police powers notwithstanding—constitute the foundation of presidential despotism. To the extent that the national government is the arbiter of rights, to that same extent the "double security to the rights of the people" is diminished. The formula is quite elementary: The greater the national government's policy prerogatives regarding rights is combined with increased presidential policy implementation responsibilities to ensure those rights, equals enhanced opportunities for presidential despotism.

The promise of the original constitutional system of separation of powers and federalism notwithstanding, constitutional liberalism contains the seeds of its own destruction and the inherent development of presidential powers which feed off tensions between states' rights and national government hegemony.[4] This

---

[3]Hamilton, Madison, and Jay, *The Federalist Papers* No. 51, p. 323.

[4]The original federal arrangement divided political power between the national and state governments; the states delegated to the national government certain powers, while reserving the remaining powers. The distinction between reserved and delegated powers, as articulated by the U.S. Supreme Court, has been—and continues to be—the crux of case law controversy and, as will be discussed, the fundamental failure of American republicanism.

does not mean that states' rights and nationalism are inherently incompatible. If states have an exit from overbearing national power—for example, interposition of national policy within the state's jurisdiction or, ultimately, state secession—the states would have the wherewithal to forestall presidential despotism.[5] But in the absence of genuine (that is, interposition or secession) states' rights, the U.S. presidency has become the repository of horrendously extensive national powers. This is not to imply that the U.S. Congress, the courts, the states, or elections do not actually and potentially place checks on presidential powers. However, it does imply that when the national branches act pursuant to a common policy objective, and the president is the "chief executive" of that policy objective, limits on presidential powers are amorphous at best. It is also not meant to imply that despotism at the state level, with the state governor as the despot, is impossible; less probable, yes, but not impossible. If citizens are genuinely politically virtuous and capable of self-government, their liberties are more secure at the state level due to the proximity of the government to the governed. For a variety of reasons, the former can more effectively be held accountable to the governed.

The absence of presidential accountability to the governed and the president's reliance on coercion are key to understanding the despotic nature of presidential powers. Policy-sanctioned—in contradistinction to authentic constitutionally-sanctioned—presidential coercion against regional or numerical minorities is tantamount to despotism, perhaps soft in one instance and hard in another, but despotism nonetheless.

In the American political tradition, constitutional liberalism is premised upon several key tenets: the rule of law; the institutional—legislative, executive, judicial—separation of powers; and states' rights. The rule of law and separation of powers were theoretically and historically the weakest bulwarks against the emergence of unitary national powers and have steadily collapsed under the weight of Supreme Court endorsed nationalism.[6] States' rights was the strongest bulwark and required the

[5] John C. Calhoun has written the theoretical *tour de force* on this topic; see his "The Disquisition On Government and Discourse On The Constitution of the United States" in *Union and Liberty: The Political Philosophy of John C. Calhoun*, Ross M. Lence, ed. (Indianapolis, Ind.: Liberty Fund Press, 1992), pp. 3–78.

[6] If the rule of law is contingent upon U.S. Supreme Court judicial review, and the court is accountable—albeit remotely at times but in the end

most persistently coercive efforts to extinguish liberty's last refuge from the omnipotence.[7]

This is not hyperbole. The reality of presidential despotism need not be consciously experienced by the governed in order to be validated. Moreover, one should not expect a servile, inattentive, or hyper-nationalistic people to either care about or object to a soft and presumably benevolent presidential despotism. But it is not the purpose here to quibble over whether an American president acted despotically, either occasionally (the War between the States was undoubtedly presidential despotism on a large scale) or continuously (many of the regulatory policies of national bureaucracies are likely manifestations of presidential despotic powers).

However, if it can be substantiated that the constitutional foundation has been laid for presidential despotism, that in and of itself is a significant cause for concern. More to the point, within current American constitutionalism one finds circumstances not only conducive to, but necessitating, presidential despotism. Such being the case, perhaps the only effective response is the reactionary imperative of states' rights.

The utilization of states' rights is not to be confused with minimal discretionary powers of states in a more or less unitary national government. The term ultimately involves the bond which ties the states collectively together in an associational Union that is administered by the national government as the agent of the states. The nature of the bond is critical to understanding the nature of the Union and the legitimate powers of the national government in relation to the association of states. Within the scheme of republicanism, it is significant if the bond maintaining the association of states is primarily consensual or coercive. It is a self-evident truth—one that no intellectually honest person can deny—that the Constitution of 1787 would not have been ratified had the document specified that the Union would be coercively maintained against the will of one or more

---

accountable—to national politics, judicial review is a political process and case law its public policy output. (See John C. Calhoun, "Fort Hill Address, 1831," and "Discourse On The Constitution Of The United States" in *Union and Liberty: The Political Philosophy of John C. Calhoun*, Ross M. Lence, ed., pp. 79–284, 367–400.)

[7]See Bertrand de Jouvenel, *On Power: The Natural History of Its Growth* (Liberty Fund Press, 1993), pp. 120–21.

states. The prospect of applying coercion against a state or states was anathema to the political culture upon which the national government was crafted, and for good reason. The framers were focused upon holding the national government accountable to the member states, in contradistinction to a unitary model of individual Americans. They realized that the latter would be an easy target for national oppression, whereas quasi-autonomous states would be much more formidable obstacles to nationally generated despotism. The transition from a states' rights federalism to a unitary nationalism with an actual or potential presidential despot at its head was the most significant development in American politics. This transition is manifested in American case law, and at the core of the relevant case law are the confluent themes of fundamental rights and governmental uniformity.

CONFEDERATE REPUBLIC

It is somewhat awkward to refer to Publius as partial to states' rights; but whether out of political necessity or theoretical conviction, Publius articulated a states'–rights position, especially when contrasted to post-World War II standards. Not wavering in his advocacy that "A firm Union will be of the utmost moment to the peace and liberty of the states," he equated the proposed Constitution with a *confederate republic*:

> The definition of a *confederate republic* seems simply to be "an assemblage of societies," or an association of two or more states into one state. The extent, modifications, and objects of federal authority are mere matters of discretion. So long as the separate organization of the members be not abolished; so long as it exists, by a constitutional necessity, for local purposes; though it should be in perfect subordination to the general authority of the union, it would still be, in fact and in theory, an association of states, or a confederacy. The proposed Constitution, so far from implying an abolition of state governments, makes them constituent parts of the national sovereignty, by allowing them a direct representation in the Senate, *and leaves in their possession certain exclusive and very important portions of sovereign power*. This fully corresponds, in every rational import of the terms, with the idea of a federal government.[8]

[8]Hamilton, Madison, and Jay, *The Federalist Papers* No. 9, p. 76.

As a consequence of the successful American Revolution (1776–1783), the relations between rulers and ruled finalized the devolution of political power from the British Crown and Parliament to the states. The final paragraph of the Declaration of Independence and Article II of the Articles of Confederation confirmed the sovereign and independent status of the states.[9] Of course, the relationship between rulers and ruled underwent another transformation in 1789, when the U.S. Constitution was ratified.

The movement from the Articles of Confederation to the U.S. Constitution was theoretically sloppy, perhaps necessarily so. Ambiguity was requisite to ratification. If, for example, the Constitution specified the scope of congressional commerce powers, the Anti-Federalists probably would have prevailed in the ratification struggle. The significant substantive questions regarding the scope of congressional commerce powers was only authoritatively answered by the Supreme Court subsequent to ratification. Thus, the ambiguity of the U.S. Constitution not only has profoundly empowered the Supreme Court as the self-proclaimed official expounder, but, more significantly, has left the essence of the Constitution—the locus of sovereignty conjoined with the rule of law—a spectacle to unfold in the rough-and-tumble of partisan politics.

Publius's model of federalism juxtaposes the states "for local purposes" with "perfect subordination to the general authority of the union." The juxtaposition is not problematical, providing there is a clear and consensual partition of policy prerogatives. But herein lies the rub. It was quite obvious that disputes between the states and national authorities over policy jurisdictions would arise. If the states were to be "constituent parts of the national sovereignty," then perfect subordination to general authority would be realized by such disputes being resolved by national authority, with the latter having the authority to

---

[9]The last paragraph of the Declaration maintains the *"free and independent states . . .* and that as *free and independent states,* they have full Power to levy War, conclude Peace, contract Alliances, establish Commerce, and do all other Acts and Things which *independent states* may of right do." Article II of the Articles of Confederation stipulates that "Each state retains its sovereignty, freedom and independence, and every Power, Jurisdiction and right, which is not by this confederation expressly delegated to the United States, in Congress assembled."

abrogate a state's independence by controlling its internal affairs on the grounds of general authority. Even though Publius's version of federalism sanctions perfect subordination of a state and a regional minority of states to a national majority, it also leaves intact substantial policy functions for the states. National supremacy was constrained by the constitutional distinction between delegated and reserved powers. Of course, there would be "perfect state subordination" to the constitutional exercise of delegated powers. But neither the 1787 Constitutional Convention nor the state ratifying conventions resolved that there would be or should be perfect state subordination to the *unconstitutional* exercise of power or that the U.S. Supreme Court was authorized to provide *constitutional* legitimacy to what a state deemed to be the unconstitutional national usurpation of the state's reserved powers.

As important as the more conspicuous nineteenth-century landmark cases regarding national supremacy are,[10] they did not strip the states of the institutional wherewithal to administer their respective internal affairs *vis-à-vis* the national government; moreover, they did not deprive the states of adjudicating disputes regarding the terms of their association with the national sovereign. And even though the ambiguous distinction between local and general authority regarding commerce was substantially expounded upon to the benefit of national supremacy, states' rights was still left largely intact by those cases. Most importantly, as long as state supreme courts were co-equal with the U.S. Supreme Court in delineating the ambiguities of the U.S. Constitution, the states retained an important measure of security against national coercion and constitutionally suspect intrusions into their internal affairs. But once the U.S. Supreme Court extended its jurisdiction to the point of subordinating state supreme courts to the U.S. Supreme Court, a major bulwark of the federal component of checks and balances was compromised. In the words of Justice Benjamin Curtis—a Whig nationalist—"Let it be remembered, also, for just now we may be in some danger of forgetting it, that questions

---

[10]*Marbury v. Madison*, 1 Cranch (5 US) 137 (1803), *McCulloch v. Maryland*, 4 Wheat (17 US) 316 (1819), and *Gibbons v. Ogden*, 9 Wheat (22 US) 1 (1824), and *Cooley v. The Board of Wardens*, 53 U.S. (12 How.) 299 (1851).

of jurisdiction were questions of power as between the United States and the several states."[11]

The transition from states' rights federalism to unitary nationalism is manifested in American case law, and at the center of the transition is the issue of judicial jurisdiction. Even if it is to be assumed that the fluidity is attributable to a circumstantial delegation of power from the states to the national government, with the latter exercising more extensive policy functions to keep pace with developing economic and social circumstances, it does not necessarily follow that legal disputes stemming from ever-expanding national policy functions must be ultimately adjudicated in national—in contradistinction to state—courts. The landmark case *McCulloch v. Maryland* (1819) established national public policy supremacy *vis-à-vis* state reserved powers; but *McCulloch* was not as significant a decision as the extension of U.S. Supreme Court jurisdictional supremacy over state courts, an effect that was sealed by the landmark case *Martin v. Hunter's Lessee* (1816). *Martin* deprived the states of the jurisprudential wherewithal to challenge national government usurpation of their reserved powers and thereby removed a significant check on presidential despotism.

VIRGINIA'S JURIDICAL INTERPOSITION

U.S. Supreme Court supremacy over its state court counterparts rests on a weak ideological reed, in contradistinction to constitutional principle. The facts behind *Martin v. Hunter* are complex and intricately tied to the earlier case of *Fairfax's Devisee v. Hunter's Lessee* (1812).[12] Both cases involved Virginia's obligations under the 1783 Treaty of Paris and the 1794 Jay's Treaty; the treaties protected British Loyalists' landholdings from state confiscation. The relevant provisions are:

> Article IV—It is agreed that creditors on either side shall meet with no lawful impediment to the recovery of full value in sterling money, of all *bona fide* debts heretofore contracted. Article V—It is agreed that the Congress shall earnestly recommend it to the legislatures of the respective states, to provide for the

---

[11]Charles Alan Wright, *Law of Federal Courts* (St. Paul, Minn.: West Publishing, 1983), pp. 1–2.

[12]*Fairfax's Devisee v. Hunter's Lessee*, 11 (US) (7 Cranch) 1816, 603–32.

restitution of all estates, rights and properties which have been confiscated, belonging to real British subjects, and also of estates, rights, and properties of persons resident in districts in the possession of His Majesties arms, and who have not borne arms against the United states. . . . Article VI—That there shall be no future confiscations made, nor any prosecutions commenced against any person or persons for, or by reason of the part which he or they may have taken in the present war; and that no person shall, on that account, suffer any future loss or damage, either in his person, liberty or property; and that those who may be in confinement on such charges, at the time of the ratification of the treaty in America, shall be immediately set at liberty, and the prosecution so commenced be discontinued.[13]

In October 1783 (the treaty dates from September 1783) Virginia enacted the following:

Whereas it is stipulated, the sixth article of the treaty of peace between the United states and the King of Great Britain, that there shall be no future confiscations made; Be it enacted, That no future confiscations shall be made, any law to the contrary notwithstanding; provided, that this act shall not extend to any suit, pending in any Court, which was commenced prior to the ratification of the treaty of peace.[14]

According to Virginia, seizure of the disputed land was initiated prior to 1783 and therefore was not affected by the 1783 and 1794 treaties.[15] The legal issues were: (1) Did the treaty of peace release the confiscation? (2) Could a subsequent state act affect the terms of the treaty? And (3) there was the overriding question of jurisdiction: Did the U.S. Supreme Court have jurisdiction to decide this case and on what constitutional grounds? Our focus will be on the third issue.

[13]Henry Steele Commager, *Documents of American History* (New York: F.S. Crofts, 1943), pp. 118–19.

[14]*Fairfax v. Hunter*, 608–09.

[15]"An act concerning escheats and forfeitures from British subjects," May 1779, chap. 14; "An act to amend the foregoing," Oct. 1779, chap. 18; and "An act concerning escheators," May 1779, chap. 45; see *Fairfax v. Hunter*, 609–10.

First and foremost, much has been made of the supremacy clause in Article VI: This Constitution, and the Laws of the United States which shall be made in Pursuance thereof; and all Treaties made, or which shall be made, under the Authority of the United States, shall be the supreme Law of the Land; and the Judges in every state shall be bound thereby, any Thing in the Constitution or Laws of any state to the Contrary notwithstanding.

The wording clearly stipulates that if state laws or constitutional provisions are repugnant to a U.S. treaty, the state laws and constitutional provisions are to be of no effect. The wording, however, does not establish which high court, U.S. or state, is the court of last resort in determining what is or is not pursuant to the U.S. Constitution. As a matter of fact, the supremacy clause instructs state judges how to rule when state laws or constitutions are repugnant to the U.S. Constitution, laws, or treaties.

Nevertheless, section 25 of the 1789 Judiciary Act did grant appellate jurisdiction from state high courts to the U.S. Supreme Court. But Virginia held section 25 to be unconstitutional, on the grounds that it is inconsistent with the "genius, spirit, and tenor of the constitution."[16] Upon receipt of the writ of error to the Virginia Court of Appeals to obey the mandate issued as a result of *Fairfax v. Hunter*, the Virginia court issued the judgment that

the court is unanimously of the opinion that the appellate power of the Supreme Court of the United States does not extend to this court under a sound construction of the constitution of the United States; that so much of the 25th section of the act of Congress, to establish judicial courts of the United States, as extends the appellate jurisdiction of the Supreme Court to this court, is not in pursuance of the constitution of the United States. That the writ of error in this cause was improvidently allowed under the authority of that act; that the proceedings thereon in the Supreme Court were *coram non judice* [judgment void due to a lack of jurisdiction] in relation to this court, and that obedience to its mandate be declined by the court.[17]

16*Martin v. Hunter*, 314.
17Ibid., 303.

The pertinent element of this case is the role of the courts in the enforceability of a treaty upon a reluctant state. Publius realized the magnitude of this question. On the one hand he acknowledged the role of coercion in sanctioning the enforcement of laws. In the context of American federalism, the operation of national laws affects individuals, bypassing the states; this innovation was considered to be a substantial improvement over the Articles of Confederation. However, a Supreme Court mandate directed against a state high court pitted the national government against a state. According to Publius,

> In an association where the general authority is confined to collective bodies of the communities [that is, states] that compose it, every breach of the laws must involve a state of war; and military execution must become the only instrument of civil obedience. Such a state of things can certainly not deserve the name of government, nor would any prudent man choose to commit his happiness to it.[18]

But Publius also conceded that state court cases that are appealed to the U.S. Supreme Court involve the "collective bodies of the communities," state and national, and potentially involve a "state of war" if presidential coercion is utilized to give effect to a U.S. Supreme Court ruling:

> The difference between a federal and national government, as it relates to the *operation of the government* . . . that in the former the powers operate on the political bodies composing the confederacy in their political capacities; in the latter, on individual citizens composing the nation in their individual capacities. On trying the Constitution by this criterion, it falls under the *national*, not the *federal* character; though perhaps not so completely as has been understood. *In several cases, and particularly in the trial of controversies to which states may be parties, they must be viewed and proceeded against in their collective and political capacities only.*[19]

Publius's quest for national harmony is especially evidenced by his reluctance to leave the jurisdiction of the U.S. Supreme Court strictly to those types of controversies found in Article III;

[18]Hamilton, Madison, and Jay, *The Federalist Papers* No.15, p. 110.

[19]Hamilton, Madison, and Jay, *The Federalist Papers* No. 39, pp. 244–45 (emphasis added).

its jurisdiction was also to include all controversies "in which the state tribunals cannot be supposed to be impartial or unbiased."[20] Was Publius sanctioning a "state of war" and military execution of the laws by the U.S. president against a state if its high court refused to comply with a U.S. Supreme Court ruling? Yes, if "every breach of the laws must involve a state of war" and "military execution the only instrument of civil obedience."[21]

Due to the role of the courts in the articulation of what the law is and the adjudication of disputes accordingly, the centrality of the relation between the U.S. Supreme Court and the states' counterparts is inescapable. That relation is a remnant of the old Articles of Confederation, because it potentially pits the national government against a state in its corporate capacity. Publius sighed that the

> great and radical vice in the construction of the existing Confederation is in the principle of *legislation* for *states* or *governments*, in their *corporate* or *collective capacities*, and as contradistinguished from the *individuals* of whom they consist. . . . The consequence of this is that though in theory their resolutions concerning those objects are laws constitutionally binding on the members of the Union, yet in practice they are mere recommendations which the states observe or disregard at their option.[22]

This was precisely the scenario presented to Justice Story by Virginia's refusal to acknowledge the Supreme Court's jurisdiction over its highest court. Should Virginia prevail, American constitutional development would have taken a sharp turn in the direction of states' rights. Both Justices Story and Johnson realized the stakes and were quite determined in their reaffirmation of nationalism and, if necessary, presidential military execution of a writ of the U.S. Supreme Court against a state.

A STORIED NATIONALISM

Justice Story was perceptive in realizing the implications of Virginia's position. His response to Virginia's recalcitrance was

---

[20]Hamilton, Madison, and Jay, *The Federalist Papers* No. 80, p. 475.
[21]Hamilton, Madison, and Jay, *The Federalist Papers* No. 15, p. 110.
[22]Ibid., p. 108.

threefold: First, Virginia lacked authority to challenge the jurisdiction of the U.S. Supreme Court on this issue.[23] Virginia lacked authority because sovereignty on this issue was strictly national. According to Justice Story, "The constitution of the United States was ordained and established, not by the states in their sovereign capacities, but emphatically, as the preamble of the Constitution declares, by 'the people of the United States.'"[24] It was the American people who authorized the Congress to enact the 25th section of the Judiciary Act; it was the American people who subordinated Virginia's courts to the Supreme Court. Upon ratification of the Constitution, Virginia acquiesced. Second, the power to subordinate Virginia's courts need not be explicit. Due to the "inscrutable purposes of Providence," the national Congress may "adopt its own means to effectuate legitimate objects, and to mold and model the exercise of its powers, as its own wisdom and the public interests should require."[25] Third, although the Constitution does not explicitly extend national court jurisdiction over the state high courts, based upon the necessity of national supremacy, the American people authorized the Congress to do so. The 1789 Judiciary Act

> is the voice of the American people solemnly declared, in establishing one great department [the Congress] of that government which was, in many respects, national, and in all supreme. It is a part of the very same instrument which was to act not merely upon individuals, but upon states; and to deprive them altogether of the exercise of some powers of sovereignty, and to restrain and regulate them in the exercise of others.[26]

[23]The Virginia Court of Appeals concluded that

> the appellate power of the Supreme court . . . does not extend to this court . . . that so much of the 25th section [of the 1789 Judiciary Act] is not in pursuance of the Constitution . . . that the writ of error in this cause was improvidently allowed under the authority of that act; that the proceedings thereon were, *coram non judice*, in relation to this court, and that obedience to its mandate be declined by the court. (*Martin v. Hunter*, 322)

[24]Story's position is both ahistorical and politically motivated; however, to address this point is beyond the scope of our present purposes. See Forrest McDonald, *States' Rights and the Union: Imperium in Imperio, 1776–1876* (Lawrence: University Press of Kansas, 2000), pp. 19–22.

[25]*Martin v. Hunter*, 326.

[26]Ibid., 326.

According to *Martin v. Hunter*, Virginia's refusal to acknowledge the U.S. Supreme Court's jurisdiction jeopardized case law uniformity and national safety. Consequently, the U.S. Supreme Court's "original or appellate jurisdiction ought not, therefore, to be restrained, but should be commensurate with the mischiefs intended to be remedied, and, of course, should extend to all cases whatsoever."[27] Operating under this rule of construction, whatever the Supreme Court deems to be the "supreme law of the land," state court judges have an "imperative obligation in their official, and not merely in their private, capacities," to give effect to the Supreme Court ruling.[28] Clarifying the national government's "imperative obligation," in the concurring opinion Justice Johnson sanctioned the use of force against state courts that failed to comply with Supreme Court mandates.[29]

Conspicuously absent from Story's majority opinion are serious concerns for popular control or popular consent over national public policy and the integral role of American federalism—the context into which American jurisprudence was to be lodged. He dismissed Virginia's claim that extending Supreme Court appellate jurisdiction over state high courts would be "inconsistent with the genius of our government and the spirit of the constitution" by reiterating his claim that Virginia lacks sovereignty over those delegated (expansively defined) national powers. Moreover, he made the peculiar claim that "It is always a doubtful course to argue against the use or existence of a power, from the possibility of its abuse."[30] Story willingly jettisoned a fundamental axiom of the constitutional order: that checks and balances, the rule of law, separation of powers, federalism, and frequent elections, are premised upon the potential abuse of power by those who wield power. Moreover, one is reminded of the linchpin of Chief Justice Marshall's specious opinion in *McCulloch v. Maryland* (1819) that states lack the power to tax agents of the national government (such as a branch of the Bank of the U.S.), because the power to tax is the power to destroy; in other words, it would constitute "the possibility of

---

[27]*Martin v. Hunter*, 346, 334.

[28]Ibid., 338.

[29]Ibid., 363.

[30]Ibid., 342.

abuse." It is also antithetical to Publius's admonition regarding factions that

> If the impulse and the opportunity be suffered to coincide, we well know that neither moral nor religious motives can be relied on as an adequate control. They are not found to be such on the injustice of individuals, and lose their efficacy in proportion to the number combined together, that is, in proportion as their efficacy becomes needful.[31]

Martin v. Hunter laid the foundation for national judicial supremacy. Consequently, an important component of American federalism—a sort of judicial parity between the U.S. and state courts—was displaced and along with it an important check on the emergence of presidential despotism.

IDEOLOGICAL BLUEPRINT

Judicial review is not devoid of ideological conduct and not, as political mythology would leave us to believe, above politics. It may appear to be merely a matter of interpreting the Constitution and statutes and to be more remote from the factional politics than the elected branches of government. But judicial review is politics to the extent that it is ideological, and that extent has grown to be very great. Because the bases of judicial review are the Justices' respective ideologies (for example, originalism versus nonoriginalism, interpretivism versus noninterpretivism), judicial review by necessity is policy-oriented. According to Oakeshott,

> political ideology purports to be an abstract principle, or set of related abstract principles, which has been independently premeditated. It supplies in advance of the activity of attending to the arrangements of society a formulated end to be pursued, and in so doing it provides a means of distinguishing between those desires which ought to be encouraged and those which ought to be suppressed or redirected.[32]

It would be difficult to substantiate the existence of a politics without a policy, or a policy not premised upon an ideology. To

[31]*The Federalist Papers* No. 10.

[32]Michael Oakeshott, *Rationalism in Politics and Other Essays* (Indianapolis, Ind.: Liberty Press, 1991), p. 48.

be politically motivated requires an ideology, simply defined as "knowledge of the ends to be pursued," a knowledge of what is to be done.[33] Significantly, political ideology is neither an "independently acquired knowledge of the ends to be pursued," nor a purely empirical activity." Rather, ideology is the product of political activity:

> It is supposed that a political ideology is the product of intellectual premeditation and that, because it is a body of principles not itself in debt to the activity of attending to the arrangements of a society, it is able to determine and guide the direction of that activity. If, however, we consider more closely the character of a political ideology, we find at once that this supposition is falsified. So far from a political ideology being the quasi-divine parent of political activity, it turns out to be its earthly stepchild. Instead of an independently premeditated scheme of ends to be pursued, it is a system of ideas abstracted from the manner in which people have been accustomed to go about the business of attending to the arrangements of their societies. . . . In short, political activity comes first and a political ideology follows after.[34]

As Oakeshott points out, political ideology "cannot be premeditated in advance of a manner of attending to the arrangements of a society." Political ideology "no more existed in advance of political practice than a cookery book exists in advance of knowing how to cook."[35] Similarly, judicial review is not the product of independent inquiries of the constitutional text and precedent, but rather political recipes for particular occasions. Supreme Court decisions are ideological statements "attending to the arrangements of society." Even a contemporary hard-core originalist has essentially adopted the politics of the framers, that is, their preferred arrangements of society.

Moreover, abstractions derived from concrete political activity—the building blocks of ideology—whether the terminology is natural rights or universal human rights or nationalism or states' rights or social justice, are always inadequate, because the abstractions fail to capture the nuances and complexities of the concrete activity. In the words of Oakeshott, "the important

[33]Ibid., p. 49.
[34]Ibid., pp. 50–51.
[35]Ibid., pp. 52–53.

point is that, at most, an ideology is an abbreviation of some manner of concrete activity."[36] Abstractions may vary by degrees the manner and extent to which they approximate concrete activities, but all fall short. The concrete political activity, imperfections included, is complete, but when contrasted to an idealized abstraction that is in and of itself incomplete but assumed to be complete, the political concrete activity is mistakenly considered to be ideologically remediable. Such being the case, Justice Story's national judicial supremacy is *carte blanche* for ideological pursuit of incorporating a majority of the Justices' ideological dreams into American case law; that is, American public policy. Unfortunately the nationalistic utopian dreams of the justices will prove to be the nightmares of the people living under the yoke of presidential despotism. Because state supreme courts have been mostly stripped of the capacity to check nationally, or for that matter internationally, ideological political pursuits—and thanks to Presidents Jackson and Lincoln the states lack the peaceful alternatives of interposition and secession—the stage has been set for the president, with a wink and a nod from the U.S. Congress and Supreme Court, to rearrange society as he deems appropriate.

THE HUMAN FAMILY'S PRESIDENT

The U.S. president, in his role of chief executive, is instrumental in the enforcement of coercive policies far removed from the framers' vision of popular control and popular consent. The negation of popular control is all the more difficult to discern because a major bulwark against the implementation of policies independent of popular control was torn down early on in the republic's development—a viable and meaningful judicial federalism. The originalist judicial federalism manifested in Virginia's position in *Martin v. Hunter* is so alien to contemporary perspectives regarding national and the emerging international judicial supremacy, that parity between the U.S. and state supreme courts is rejected *prima facie*.

This is especially troublesome in light of the fact that treaties and international agreements provide the Supreme Court with the requisite raw juridical materials to incorporate internationally-generated public policies into U.S. case law. The Supreme

[36]Ibid., p. 54.

Court's evolved relevance to the rule of law poses a special problem to the popular control embodied in states' rights. The shift from state-based popular control to nationally- and even internationally-generated public policies facilitates a type of elitism anathema to a federal system in which

> The powers of the general government and of the state, although both exist and are exercised within the same territorial limits, are yet separate and distinct sovereignties, acting separately and independently of each other, within their respective spheres.[37]

A meaningful judicial federalism would contribute to the national and state governments "acting separately and independently of each other" when separateness and independence are constitutionally sanctioned; and that determination is not the exclusive prerogative of the U.S. Supreme Court.

Obviously, jurisdictional disputes between the U.S. and state supreme courts will arise and the relationship between the two court systems will, at times, be confrontational. But judicial uniformity resting upon community self-determination is not by default inferior to judicial efficiency that procures coercively enforced national standards, or more specifically, what the framers would have recognized as despotism. Moreover, uniformity does not necessarily originate within or stop at national boundaries. For example, the United Nations Charter; the U.N. Declaration of Human Rights, the International Covenant on Economic, Social, and Cultural Rights (ICESCR); and the International Covenant on Civil and Political Rights (ICCPR) potentially constitute the incorporation of internationally generated policies into national standards. This juridical process has precedence, such as Fourteenth Amendment incorporation developments, but now the supremacy clause of Article 6 may prove to be the primary conduit of national uniformity. Like ticking time bombs, these international documents are ripe for detonation by future U.S. Supreme Court justices if they should decide to level the few remaining pillars of states' rights judicial federalism. A brief overview will suffice.

Revealing the preference for increasingly larger political jurisdictions, the preamble to the 1948 United Nations Declaration of

---

[37]*Abelman v. Booth*, 62 U.S. (21 How.) 506 (1859).

Human Rights is applicable to "all members of the human family . . . the aspiration of the common people" and "the peoples of the United Nations."[38] The significance of a U.N. that is representative of the "human family" in contradistinction to exclusively representing nations, is that the former constitutes mandates superseding national standards. Nations that deviate from acceptable universal norms by violating the rights of members of the human family will be held accountable. From a juridical perspective the supremacy of universal standards over nation-based standards could be rationalized on the grounds that nations have been lawfully integrated by these U.N. documents into the "human family," an emerging political unit in its own right.

There is precedent for judicially integrating sovereign political units (the states) into a more encompassing unitary political unit (the nation). As early as 1793 Justice Wilson addressed a similar issue:

> This is a case of uncommon magnitude. One of the parties to it is a state; certainly respectable, claiming to be sovereign. The question to be determined is whether this state, so respectable, and whose claim soars so high, is amenable to the jurisdiction of the supreme court [sic] of the United States? The question, important in itself, will depend on others, more important still; and, may, perhaps, be ultimately resolved into one, no less radical than this—do the people of the United States form a nation?

Relying on the "We the People" phrase of the preamble, Justice Wilson answered with an emphatic yes.[39] Chief Justice Marshall, in the case that established legislative national supremacy over the states, deduced from the preamble's "We the People" that the national "government proceeds directly from the people and is ordained and established in the name of the people."[40] As the people of the states were integrated into the people of the United States—essentially a gradual transfer of sovereignty from the states to the nation—the people of the nation could be integrated into the U.N.'s human family—once again, a merging of sovereignties into a sovereignty by judicial fiat.

[38]*The International Covenant on Human Rights and Optional Protocol* (New York: U.N. Office of Public Information, 1976), p. 1.

[38]See *Chisholm v. Georgia*, 1 L.Ed. 440 (1793).

[39]See *McCulloch v. Maryland*, 4 L.Ed. 579 (1819).

The march toward integration took a major step in 1976 via the ICESCR, the ICCPR, and The Optional Protocol. These U.N. agreements supplement the "moral force" of the 1948 Declaration with "legal obligations."[41] Nevertheless, the 1948 Declaration is the central document with subsequent documents functioning as clarifications and implementation guidelines.[42]

The ICCPR most directly subsumes national and state identities into that of the "human family." The document proclaims that "the equal and inalienable rights of all members of the human family is the foundation of freedom, justice, and peace in the world." The potential impact for the U.S. is the shifting of sovereignty away from the states and nation to the U.N.—the governing unit representing the human family and determining what is a universal fundamental right and providing remedies for violations thereof. When those rights have been violated, the nations are primarily responsible for providing effective remedies, but not exclusively. The fact that a remedy is an inherent right of the claimant, domestic law notwithstanding, is a significant development, because the claimant need not be a citizen of the nation against which the claim is filed. Article 2 stipulates that

> Each state Party to the present Covenant undertakes to respect and to ensure to *all individuals within its territory and subject to its jurisdiction* the rights recognized in the present Covenant, without distinction of any kind, such as race, color, sex, language, religion, political or other opinions, *national or social origin*, property, birth or other status.[43]

---

[41]See *The International Covenants on Human Rights and Optional Protocol*, 1976), p. 1. The imprint declares that "Having proclaimed this Universal Declaration [1948], the U.N. turned to an even more difficult task: transforming the principles into treaty provisions which established the legal obligations on the part of each ratifying state" (ibid.). The U.S. Senate ratified the ICCPR and Optional Protocol in 1992. To date, the ICESCR has not been ratified by the Senate; however, pending ratification does not preclude its terms from influencing American jurisprudence as components of the customary law of nations.

[42]See Imre Szabo, "The Historical Foundations of Human Rights and Subsequent Developments," in *The International Dimensions of Human Rights*, Karol Vasak, ed., vol. 1 (Westport, Conn.: Greenwood Press, 1982), p. 23.

[43]International Covenant on Civil and Political Rights (ICCPR), pp. 13, 14 (emphasis added).

To remove any ambiguity that citizens of a country may enjoy rights and privileges denied to noncitizens but nevertheless citizens of the human family, Article 26 of the ICCPR stipulates that

> *All persons* are equal before the law and are entitled without any discrimination to the equal protection of the law. In this respect, the law shall prohibit any discrimination and guarantee to all persons equal and effective protection against discrimination on any ground such as race, color, sex, language, religion, political or other opinion, national, or social origin, property, birth, or other status.[44]

Part V of the ICCPR established the Human Rights Committee and procedures for an *ad hoc* Conciliation Commission. The committee consists of eighteen nationals, who "shall serve in their personal capacity," national allegiances notwithstanding.[45] To wit, "Every member of the Committee shall, before taking up his duties, make a solemn declaration in open committee that he will perform his functions impartially and conscientiously." The Committee serves as a court of last resort after it has "ascertained that all domestic remedies have been invoked and exhausted."[46]

Following similar rules of procedure—excepting the closed sessions—nations that acceded to the Optional Protocol to the ICCPR are open to claims by "individuals subject to its jurisdiction who claim to be victims of human rights violations."[47] In the absence of the Optional Protocol, an individual was dependent on another nation to file a claim on his behalf. For example, a noncitizen inhabitant of the U.S. seeking protection against a state for rights violations would have to secure the assistance of a second nation to file a complaint. But under the Optional Protocol, the individual may directly file his claim before the Human Rights Committee.[48] This is a major departure from traditional international law that governed relations between

---

[44]Ibid., p. 22 (emphasis added).

[45]The term *national* in this context is broader than the term *citizen*; see *Brassert v. Biddle*, D.C. Conn., 59 F. Supp. 457, 462 (*Black's Law Dictionary*, 6th ed. [St. Paul, Minn.: West Publishing, 1990]).

[46]ICCPR, Arts. 28, 38, and 41.

[47]Optional Protocol to the ICCPR, Art. 1.

[48]See Part IV of the ICCPR.

nations. This departure is the "real test of the effectiveness of a system of international protection for human rights." Traditionally, the individual had no *locus standi* within the context of international law. But that traditional rule was premised upon the relevance of sovereign nation–states, a relevance no longer sustainable in a world where "a common standard of achievement for all peoples and all nations is the goal."[49]

INTERNATIONAL REMEDIES FOR DOMESTIC DISPUTES

Several points need to be emphasized. First, the guarantees against discrimination include public and private, governmental and nongovernmental. Second, the reliance on the word "persons" is a direct link to the human family without the intermediate nation–states. Third, the American federal system of reserved powers to the states are negated theoretically and technically, as is evidenced by Articles 28, 50, and 10 of the ICESCR, ICCPR, and Optional Protocol respectively, which stipulate that "The provisions of the present Covenant shall extend to all parts of federal states without any limitations or exceptions", such as the Tenth Amendment to the U.S. Constitution. Nonetheless, the more immediate threat to sovereignty in the U.S. is the U.S. Supreme Court. The current prevailing political reality precludes any U.N. tribunal (whether the International Court of Justice or the Human Rights Commission) from directly implementing its "human family" agenda.[50] But this is not to say that the U.S.

[49]A.H. Robertson, "The Implementation System: International Measures," in *The International Bill of Rights: The Covenant on Civil and Political Rights*, Louis Henkin, ed. (New York: Columbia University Press, 1981), pp. 357 and 365.

[50]For example, the ICESCR delineates the fundamental rights that members must respect, including: the right of all people to self-determination (Art. 1); the equal right of men and women to the enjoyment of all economic, social, and cultural rights (Art. 2); the right to work and the right to freely choose or accept the work one does (Art. 6); the right to favorable working conditions, fair wages, leisure, and paid holidays (Art. 7); the right of everyone to form a trade union, the right of trade unions to form national federations, the right of national federations to form international trade-union organizations, the right to strike (Art. 8); the right of everyone to social security and social insurance (Art. 9); the right of everyone to an adequate standard of living and the fundamental right to be free from hunger (Art. 11); the right of everyone to the "enjoyment of the highest attainable standard of physical and mental health" (Art. 12); and "the right of everyone to education" (Art. 13).

does not have certain legal obligations as a consequence of ratifying these U.N. agreements, obligations enforceable in U.S. courts. The ICCPR stipulates that

> To ensure that any person whose rights or freedoms as herein recognized are violated shall have an effective remedy . . . by competent judicial, administrative or legislative authorities, or by any other competent authority provided by the legal system of the state [nation], and to develop the possibilities of judicial remedies.[51]

It was the clear intent of the drafters of the ICCPR and the Optional Protocol to ensure injunctive relief through domestic courts first and foremost, leaving open the option of international remedies if domestic legal systems were to fail.[52] In 1985 this intent was formalized by the U.N. General Assembly when it adopted the Basic Principles on the Independence of the Judiciary, thereby stipulating that

> Whereas the ICESCR and on ICCPR both guarantee the exercise of those rights. . . . Whereas frequently there still exists a gap between the vision underlying those principles and the actual situation, Whereas the organization and administration of justice in every country should be inspired by those principles, and efforts should be undertaken to translate them fully into reality, Whereas rules concerning the exercise of judicial office should aim at enabling judges to act in accordance with those principles, Whereas judges are charged with the ultimate decision over life, freedoms, rights, duties and property.

Former U.N. General Secretary Boutros Boutros-Ghali stated the importance of nationally based judiciaries as the essential and inevitable part of the "historical synthesis resulting from a long historical process" when he maintained:

> [T]o move from identifying inequality to rebelling against injustice is only possible in the context of a universal affirmation of the idea of human rights. Ultimately, it is this idea which allows us to move from ethical to legal considerations,

---

[51]ICCPR, Art. 2.

[52]See Oscar Schachter, "The Obligation to Implement the Covenant in Domestic Law," in *The International Bill of Rights*, p. 325.

and *to impose* value judgments and *judicial constraints* on human activity.[53]

National sovereignty will be transformed when the basic norms of national legal orders are substantively qualified by international legal norms. The complex relation between national and international systems is evolving toward hegemony of the latter over the former. Just as Fourteenth Amendment selective incorporation doctrine substantively altered state constitutional orders, the incorporation of international legal norms will similarly impact the U.S. constitutional order.[54] Ian Brownlie explains developments regarding the links between international and domestic laws. Brownlie acknowledges that Article 2, paragraph 7, of the U.N. Charter restates the "classical rule" of international law:

> Nothing contained in the present Charter shall authorize the United Nations to intervene in matters which are essentially within the domestic jurisdiction of any State or shall require the Members to submit such matters to settlement under the present Charter . . .

Summarizing commentaries on the relevance of Article 2's domestic jurisdiction reservation, Brownlie explains how the Article 2 reservation will be negated on three fronts: First, the reservation applies to specific organs of the U.N., and not with the rule of general international law already operative in nation–states; second, the reservation is inoperative when a treaty is involved; and third, human rights obligations, which in 1947 were hortatory, have subsequently been construed by the U.N. "as presenting definite and active legal obligations" on nation–states.[55]

Articles 55 and 56 of the Charter, the 1976 ICESCR, the ICCPR, and The Optional Protocol are the "teeth" that Brownlie suspects

---

[53]Boutros Boutros-Ghali, "Address" at World Conference on Human Rights, Vienna, 14 June 1993, *The United Nations and Human Rights, 1945–1995* (New York: U.N. Office of Public Information, 1995), pp. 442, 443 (emphasis added).

[54]International law terminology varies, using incorporation, adoption, and transformation when describing what is essentially the same effect; see Ian Brownlie, *Principles of Public International Law*, 5th ed. (Oxford: Oxford University Press, 1998), pp. 42, 55–56.

[55]Brownlie, pp. 557–58. The parallels between Art. 2, par. 7, and the Tenth Amendment are obvious.

will make the substance of Article 2, paragraph 7, "disappear."[56] These U.N. agreements supplement the "moral force" of the 1948 declaration with "legal obligations."[57] Nevertheless, the 1948 Declaration is the central document with subsequent documents functioning as clarifications and implementation guidelines.[58]

MISSOURI DUCKS

When ideology and opportunity converge, the development of public policy is affected accordingly—the niceties of constitutional barriers not necessarily withstanding. Opportunities will be utilized in the implementation of ideologically-derived policy objectives. The American constitutional order is premised upon this postulate, as is the traditional American rule of law.[59] Significantly, nontraditional articulation of human rights has very few checks and very little balance and the rule of law is readily malleable into cover for government by an unaccountable elite with a U.S. president as its CEO.[60] Consequently, when

---

[56]Brownlie, pp. 558, 573–74.

[57]See *The International Covenants on Human Rights and Optional Protocol* (New York: The U.N. Office of Public Information, 1976), p. 1. The imprint declares that "Having proclaimed this Universal Declaration [1948], the U.N. turned to an even more difficult task: transforming the principles into treaty provisions which established the legal obligations on the part of each ratifying State" (ibid., p. 1). The U.S. Senate ratified the ICCPR and Optional Protocol in 1992. To date the ICESCR has not been ratified by the Senate; however, that does not preclude its terms from influencing American jurisprudence as components of the customary law of nations.

[58]See Szabo, "The Historical Foundations of Human Rights and Subsequent Developments," p. 23.

[59]See *The Federalist Papers* No.10.

> If the impulse and opportunity be suffered to coincide, we well know that neither moral nor religious motives can be relied on as an adequate control. They are not found to be such on the injustice of individuals, and lose their efficacy in proportion to the number combined together, that is, in proportion as their efficacy becomes needful.

[60]What is meant by the traditional rule of law cannot be easily explained, but only appreciated; in other words, it is less abstraction and more procedure. For example, the rule of law does not necessarily require that a U.S. president serve a four-year term instead of a five-year term. Article V of the Constitution allows for the change from four- to five-year terms.

the judicial and the chief executive elite share the same ideological objectives, the end result will very well be the unconstitutional exercise of despotic presidential powers.

From a practical viewpoint, it appears to be quite a stretch to link the idealistic language of U.N. documents to U.S. public policy; but there are theoretical and historical justifications for doing so. Just as nineteenth-century case law precedent established national supremacy over the states—"the laws must be faithfully executed"—twentieth-century precedent has established a form of supranational supremacy over the states that has resulted in making the nation itself vulnerable to presidential powers grounded in "external sovereignty."[61]

The first significant precedent case law that stripped the states of their prerogatives *vis-à-vis* external sovereignty was the 1920 case, *Missouri v. Holland*. At issue was the constitutionality of the 1916 treaty between the U.S. and Great Britain and the Migratory Bird Treaty Act of 1918, the purpose of which was to execute the terms of the treaty. The state of Missouri maintained that the treaty and the statute were repugnant to the Tenth Amendment. Counsel for Missouri argued that

> The treaty-making power conferred on the president and senate does not include the right to regulate and control the property and property rights of an individual state, held in its quasi-sovereign capacity. . . . The lack of legislative power in Congress to divest a state of its property right and control over the wild game within its borders cannot be supplied by making a treaty with Great Britain. . . . The treaty-making power of the national government is limited by other provisions of the Constitution, including the 10th Amendment. It cannot, therefore, devest [sic] a state of its police power, or take away its ownership or control of its wild game.[62]

The essential legal issue was, can a treaty validate an otherwise unconstitutional congressional statute? For the court, Justice Holmes provided an emphatic yes. He maintained that in

---

Rather the rule of law requires that the length of the term be determined by constitutional procedures, such as the amendment process and not congressional statute of judicial decree.

[61] This term was used by Justice Sutherland, to be discussed below.

[62] *Missouri v. Holland*, 64 L.Ed. 641 (1920), 645.

those instances when the national interests are at stake, and in those matters that require national action, the power to secure those interests and execute the necessary action must reside somewhere. Because the states are incompetent to individually secure national interests, the power by necessity is conferred upon the national government, not necessarily by the Constitution but by the Court. He wrote:

> With regard to that [the 1916 treaty], we may add that when we are dealing with words that also are a constituent act, like the Constitution of the United States, we must realize that they have called into life a being the development of which could not have been foreseen completely by the most gifted of its begetters. It was enough for them to realize or to hope that they have created an organism; it has taken a century and has cost their successors much sweat and blood to prove they created a nation. The case before us must be considered in light of our whole experience, and not merely in that of what was said a hundred years ago. The treaty in question does not contravene any prohibitory words to be found in the Constitution. The only question is whether it is forbidden by some invisible radiation from the general terms of the Tenth Amendment. We must consider what this country has become in deciding what that amendment has reserved.[63]

These few lines represent a jurisprudence that will prove to have a profound impact on the American constitutional order and presidential power within that order. The tenets of that jurisprudence are: (1) statutory and fundamental laws are organic in nature; (2) the Constitution and laws are to be circumstantially interpreted; (3) the Tenth Amendment is subject to a juridical sliding scale, whereby the reserved powers of the states are circumstantially contracted as those of "superior" governments are expanded; (4) the U.S. Supreme Court is empowered to keep the organism growing and healthy; and (5) presidential powers are circumstantially open-ended. The expansion of presidential powers is part and parcel of that growth, due to the president's indispensable role in policy formulation and implementation. And who would have been responsible for the enforcement of the 1918 act if Missouri had resisted? President Wilson, of course, with the Supreme Court's blessing.

[63]Ibid., 648.

The significance of the U.S. president as the enforcer of U.N. mandates is a natural outgrowth of his power as the enforcer of chief for national mandates and long-standing international norms. nation–states in international law require four conditions: (1) there must be a people in the aggregate who live together in a community; (2) there must be a country with a recognized territory; (3) there must be a recognizable government exercising authority; and (4) there must be a sovereign "independent of any other earthly authority."[64] The juridical logic of *Missouri v. Holland* complements these four conditions, whereas the original constitutional order with its limitations on the president and deference to the states does not. For example, under the original American constitutional order there is not, in the strict sense, "a people in the aggregate who live together in a community." There are, however, distinct peoples living in state-based communities. Collectively the states form a national community, of sorts. But each is governed by recognizable governments exercising reserved and delegated powers within recognized jurisdictions. Neither the national nor the state sovereigns are completely independent of each other. Even the arch-nationalist Chief Justice Salmon Chase remarked, "The Constitution, in all its provisions, looks to an indestructible Union, composed of indestructible states."[65] Indestructible states are not reducible to the status of administrative agents of the national government, but exercise meaningful sovereignty over designated areas of public policy.[66] According to *Missouri v. Holland*, however, the demarcation between reserved state powers and delegated national powers is circumstantially arbitrary, or more precisely, ideological. Thus, the sovereignty of the states over their purely internal affairs is not contingent upon the rule of law, but upon the rule of national political expediency; especially when "a national interest of very nearly the first magnitude is involved," as presumably was the case in protecting Canadian migratory birds from Missouri duck hunters.

[64]These four conditions are a slight variation of those found in L. Oppenheim's *International Law: A Treatise*, I.H. Lauterpacht, ed., vol. 1 (New York: David McKay, 1962), pp. 118–19.

[65]*Texas v. White*, 19 L.Ed. 227 (1869).

[66]"The powers not delegated to the United States by the Constitution, nor prohibited by it to the states, are reserved to the states respectively, or to the people" (Tenth Amendment to the Constitution of the United States).

CIRCUMVENT THE CONGRESS

Significantly, the most state-based branch of the national government, the Congress, can be bypassed by the president and Supreme Court. The constitutional implications of *Missouri v. Holland* were shortly thereafter expanded in *U.S. v. Curtiss-Wright* (1936). At issue was the constitutionality of the law-making powers to the U.S. president and the separation of powers. Can the president constitutionally make laws? If the law-making function falls exclusively within the category of internal affairs, it would be unconstitutional in the absence of congressional delegation of such powers to the president.[67] However, if it falls within the category of external affairs, the delegation of presidential law-making powers is not open to successful constitutional challenge.[68] Grounding his majority opinion not in the "provisions of the Constitution, but in the law of nations," Justice Sutherland ruled that "the investment of the federal government with the powers of external sovereignty did not depend upon the affirmative grants of the Constitution."[69] The powers of external sovereignty passed from the Crown, that is King George III, to the government of the United States, and then onto the office of the president of the United States.

Stemming from a twisted interpretation of American history, particularly the Declaration of Independence, Sutherland maintained that the states never were independent or free and that the American people existed only in the national aggregate. Sutherland maintained that

> Rulers come and go; governments end and forms of governments change; but sovereignty survives. A political society cannot endure without a supreme will somewhere. Sovereignty is never held in suspense. When, therefore, the external sovereignty of Great Britain in respect to the colonies ceased, it immediately passed to the Union. . . . The Union existed before the Constitution . . . [it] was the sole possessor of

[67]For example, in the Youngstown case, President Truman's seizure of the steel mills was declared to be unconstitutional due to Congress's specific refusal in the Taft-Hartley Act to yield such power to the president; see Justice Black's court opinion in *Youngstown Sheet & Tube Co. v. Sawyer* (343 U.S. 579 [1952]).

[68]*U.S. v. Curtiss-Wright*, 299 U.S. (1936), 315–16.

[69]Ibid., 303.

external sovereignty. . . . Otherwise, the United States is not completely sovereign.[70]

But to make the U.S. completely sovereign, Justice Sutherland had to rewrite a good portion of American political history along the Hobbesean model of government. Once again, ideology masquerading as explication of the U.S. Constitution.

But this was precisely the point! The U.S. was not designed to be "completely" sovereign; nor was it designed to confer King George-like powers on the president of the U.S. Nevertheless, *Missouri v. Holland* and *U.S. v. Curtiss-Wright* constitutionally sanction presidential tyranny, if the 1776 American revolutionaries are to be believed and King George III was in possession of tyrannical powers.[71]

And one year after the Curtiss-Wright decision, the Court took another step and freed the treaty-making powers of the presidency from Senate ratification. In *U.S. v. Belmont* the Court elevated international executive agreements to the same Article VI "supreme law of the land" legal standing as treaties.[72]

---

[70]Ibid., 302–03.

[71]See the Declaration of Independence and *The Federalist Papers* No. 1.

[72]*U.S. v. Belmont*, 301 U.S. 324 (1937). The legislative response to this decision was headed by U.S. Senator John Bricker, a conservative Republican from Ohio. Senator Bricker unsuccessfully proposed a series of constitutional amendments, the last one in 1956. It stipulated:

Section 1. A provision of a treaty or other international agreement not made in pursuance of this Constitution shall have no force or effect. This section shall not apply to treaties made prior to the effective date of this Constitution. Section 2. A treaty or other international agreement shall have legislative effect within the United States as a law thereof only through legislation, except to the extent that the Senate shall provide affirmatively, in its resolution advising and consenting to a treaty, that the treaty shall have legislative effect. Section 3. An international agreement other than a treaty shall have legislative effect within the United States as a law thereof only through legislation valid in the absence of such an international agreement. Section 4. On the question of advising and consenting to a treaty, the vote shall be determined by yeas and nays, and the names of the Senators voting for and against shall be entered on the Journal of the Senate. (Duane

Depending upon the circumstances, a president may make and enforce laws, the reserved powers of the states notwithstanding. When considering the mounting international commitments and the attending interest group politics attached thereto, the opportunities for domestic presidential tyranny are ripe.[73]

CONCLUSION

Quite frankly, the U.S. Supreme Court has failed and is failing in its constitutional responsibility to check the expansion of presidential power to despotic limits. This failure is to be expected. To be effective, the power to check the expansion must be lodged with those who have the most to lose: the states. Nevertheless, because the expansion has been and continues to be incremental and at times barely discernible, the judicial federalism bulwark against the growth of despotic national powers has been effectively dismantled, and the American people effectively socialized to the legitimacy and merits of that dismantlement.

As American jurisprudence is the mother's milk of legitimizing the ever-expanding presidential power, the American presidency is increasingly acquiring greater prerogative powers. It is a certainty that American presidents, with their international counterparts, will be increasingly responsible for the so-called global interests of the human family. This does not bode well for genuine community self-determination within the context of the rule of law, either for states officially within the United States or its imperial colonies. As Justice Story conceded, it is the necessity of "uniformity" that justifies centralization.[74] Uniformity toward *what* objective is the open-ended question.

Tannanbaum, *The Bricker Amendment Controversy: A Test Of Eisenhower's Political Leadership* [Ithaca, N.Y.: Cornell University Press, 1988], p. 227)

[73]Could the case be made that presidential tyranny against non-Americans has been actualized for some time? Consider President Clinton's military adventures in Iraq, Sudan, Pakistan, and Yugoslavia. By the stroke of his presidential pen he has sent cruise missiles and sorties into civilian and military targets; he can issue a naval blockade, trade sanctions, or deny "most favored nations" status. An interesting question, but beyond the scope here.

[74]*Martin v. Hunter*, 346.

For Justice Story, it was the American empire; for contemporaries, both here and abroad, it is centralization toward the human family—that is, the global empire legitimated and held together by judicial decrees. There may soon be no room for individual freedom and community self-determination within the context of the "American" rule of law in the house that Justice Story and other Supreme Court nationalists helped to construct. Ironically, is it too far-fetched that the American nation may face the fate of the Confederate South at the hands of some modern-day Lincoln progeny: compliance with international judicial norms at the point of a bayonet? To dismiss, mock, or ignore the question is to answer it.

5

THE ELECTORAL COLLEGE AS A RESTRAINT ON AMERICAN DEMOCRACY: ITS EVOLUTION FROM WASHINGTON TO JACKSON

RANDALL G. HOLCOMBE

When the American colonies declared their independence from Britain in 1776, the fundamental principle underlying the new government they created was the principle of liberty. To the Founders, liberty meant freedom from government oppression, because at that time, government was the primary threat to the liberty of individuals. The Declaration of Independence contains a long list of grievances that the colonists had against the King of England to document how King George had infringed upon the liberty of the colonists, and those grievances provided their justification for creating a new government, independent of Britain. At that time, the concept of liberty was a relatively new and truly revolutionary idea, and it provided the fundamental principle for the design of the new American government. Two centuries later, the principle of liberty has been replaced by the principle of democracy, and most Americans at the end of the twentieth century surely would view the fundamental principle of American government to be democracy, not liberty.

The modern principle of democracy holds that public policy should be determined by the views of the nation's citizens, as aggregated through electoral and other political institutions. The government should do what the people want. But the Founders went to great lengths to insulate the activities of their new government from democratic pressures. One of the ways that they tried to limit their government from democracy was by selecting the nation's chief executive through the use of an electoral college, rather than through direct democratic election. The electoral college never worked as planned, however, and by 1828, when Andrew Jackson was elected president, the method of electing the president had almost completely metamorphized into the democratic system that still exists at the beginning of the twenty-first century.

This metamorphosis of the electoral college mirrors changes that have occurred more generally in American government during its first two centuries. At its founding, American citizens believed that their government was created to protect their liberty, and the government was designed to be limited in scope. The Constitution was written to protect the rights of individuals and limit the powers of government. In other words, it was intended to preserve liberty. Not only did the Founders not intend for public policy to be determined democratically, they actively tried to design their new government to prevent public policy from being directed by the demands of its citizens. They recognized that liberty could be compromised by democracy, and that the will of the majority had the potential to be just as tyrannical as a king or dictator. Yet over the centuries, the principle of liberty that the Founders fought for became less of a priority for American citizens, and the principle of democracy became more significant. At the end of the twentieth century, the term *liberty* had an almost quaint sound to it, while trying to encourage the spread of American-style democracy around the world had become a significant part of American foreign policy.

The Founders tried to prevent the formation of a democratic government. It sounds almost anti-American to question the principle of democracy, at least as the term *democracy* is understood today. The electoral college was an important part of their attempt to limit the influence of democracy on American government. The evolution of the electoral college is, in one sense, only a small part of the story of the transformation of the fundamental principle of American government from liberty to democracy. Yet it is an important part of the story, because it was one of the earliest manifestations of this transformation. Within a few decades of the nation's founding, one of the most significant checks that the Founders tried to enact to control democracy had been eliminated.

Liberty, Democracy, and the U.S. Constitution

The hundred years preceding the American Revolution saw a major change in the way that people viewed the rights of individuals and the relationships between citizens and their governments.

When Thomas Hobbes wrote *Leviathan* in 1651,[1] he argued that without government, life would be a war of all against all, and that to maintain an orderly society, people had to pledge their allegiance to the sovereign, and to follow the sovereign's rules. The rules of the sovereign amounted to a social contract, Hobbes argued, and the government was justified in killing those who did not accept the sovereign's rules. Only a few decades later, John Locke, in his *Second Treatise of Government*,[2] offered a radically different vision of the social contract. People did not get their rights from government, as Hobbes suggested. Rather, people naturally had rights, and it was the role of the government to protect those natural rights. The social contract as Locke envisioned it was an agreement among citizens to respect each others' rights, not a contract between the government and the people, as Hobbes had described it. The government of the United States was established to preserve this Lockean notion of rights.

The ideas of Locke and other European Enlightenment writers became popularized by the mass media. One prominent example was a series of newspaper columns written in the *London Journal* in the 1720s by John Trenchard and Thomas Gordon, using the pen name Cato. Cato's letters were collected and widely reprinted.[3] These ideas found their way to the American colonies, where newspaper columnists and pamphleteers incorporated this new concept of liberty into their writing, spreading the idea of liberty to the general public and transforming the way that citizens viewed their governments.[4] The idea that governments should serve their citizens, rather than the other way around, was a radical new idea in the 1700s, but one that laid the intellectual foundation for the American Revolution. The Revolution was fought to secure the liberty of the new nation's citizens, and the Founders firmly believed that the main threat to liberty was the power of government. Thus, their challenge

[1]Thomas Hobbes, *Leviathan* (New York: E.P. Dutton, [1651] 1950).

[2]John Locke, *Two Treatises of Government* (Cambridge: Cambridge University Press, [1690] 1967).

[3]John Trenchard and Thomas Gordon, *Cato's Letters, or, Essays on Liberty, Civil and Religious, and Other Important Subjects* (Indianapolis, Ind.: Liberty Fund, 1995).

[4]For a discussion of the influence of pamphleteers on the ideas behind the American Revolution, see Bernard Bailyn, *The Ideological Origins of the American Revolution*, enlarged ed. (Cambridge, Mass.: Belknap, 1992).

was to create a government that had the power to protect the liberty of its citizens but that was constrained from violating those rights it was designed to protect.

The new nation's first constitution was the Articles of Confederation, which were approved by the states in 1781. Under the Articles, the United States was run by a unicameral legislature and had no executive or judicial branches of government. It had no powers of direct taxation, but rather had to requisition the state governments for funds. State governments had a substantial amount of control over the federal government under the Articles. Following the philosophy of liberty, the Articles of Confederation guaranteed the rights of Americans and strictly limited the powers of the federal government.[5] Indeed, by the mid-1880s many of the Founders believed that the Articles too severely limited the powers of the federal government, to the extent that it had insufficient power to protect the liberty of its citizens. Thus, in 1787 Congress called for a convention to amend the Articles of Confederation in order to create a stronger federal government. The result was the United States Constitution. The Constitution represented a major change in both the structure of the federal government and in the powers of the federal government. Still, it was designed to protect the liberty of its citizens and to prevent decisions from being made democratically.

A limited amount of democratic decision-making is called for in the Constitution, but only to undertake the enumerated powers of the federal government. The government was deliberately designed to be limited in scope. In the event of any remaining uncertainty, the Tenth Amendment to the Constitution—a part of the original Bill of Rights that was ratified along with the Constitution—reads, "The powers not delegated to the United States by the Constitution, nor prohibited by it to the States, are reserved to the States respectively, or to the people." In short, unless the Constitution says that the federal government can undertake a certain activity, the Constitution prohibits the federal government from undertaking it. During the nineteenth

---

[5]A discussion of the provisions of the Articles of Confederation, and a comparison between government under the Articles and government under the U.S. Constitution, is found in Randall G. Holcombe, "Constitutions as Constraints: A Case Study of Three American Constitutions," *Constitutional Political Economy* 2, no. 3 (Fall 1991): 303–28.

century this idea was taken seriously, and Congress would routinely debate whether specific proposals were within the powers enumerated by the Constitution. In the twentieth century the idea increasingly fell by the wayside, and the limits of public policy became determined by the popular opinion of the electorate rather than by the limits specified in the Constitution. Why this happened is well beyond the present scope[6]; for present purposes, the point is that the transformation of the electoral college was an early step in the process.

The Constitution specifies that the government itself arrive at decisions by a democratic process. Legislation must be approved by both houses of Congress and then approved by the president, for example. Presidential vetoes can be overridden by a two-thirds vote, and a two-thirds vote is required to impeach a president. Legislative and executive responsibilities are constitutionally separated, and they remain separated as interpreted by the Supreme Court at the end of the twentieth century. Thus, even within the government, decisions are not simply made by democratic voting. Rather, there are procedures and a division of power that are established by the Constitution, and the powers of government were intended to be limited only to those enumerated by the Constitution. The Constitution was designed with democracy as a means to an end, as a tool of governmental decision-making. The Constitution was also designed with a system of checks and balances so that the three branches of government would each check the power of the others as a method of limiting the scope of governmental activity. The Founders actively tried to prevent creating a government that would undertake whatever actions met with a consensus of approval of those who were in charge and actively tried to insulate the decisions of those who were in charge from the demands of the citizenry.

THE ELECTORATE AND THEIR GOVERNMENT

The notion of three branches of government, each with roughly equal power, checking each other, is a part of the fundamental design of American government. At the end of the twentieth century, Americans had the idea that their government

---

[6]I consider the issue in detail in my forthcoming book, *From Liberty to Democracy: The Transformation of American Government* (Ann Arbor: University of Michigan Press, 2002).

should be accountable to the electorate, but the Founders had very different ideas, as is evident simply by looking at the design of the Constitution. Consider each of the three branches.

The legislative branch was intended to be most accountable to the electorate in the Founders' design, because members of the House of Representatives were chosen in popular elections. Senators, however, were originally chosen by their state legislatures, and this system continued until 1913, when the Seventeenth Amendment to the Constitution was ratified, specifying that senators were to be chosen by a direct vote of the electorate. But for more than a century, and for more than half of the nation's history (as this is being written), senators were chosen by their state legislatures, not by popular vote. The logic of that system is straightforward. The House of Representatives already represents the views of the nation's citizens. To have a Senate elected by those same citizens means that legislation must meet the approval of two bodies who represent the same population and the same interests. As the Founders designed it, legislation had to meet the approval of the representatives of the citizens in the House of Representatives, and the representatives of the state governments in the Senate, which is a much more stringent test.[7] The Seventeenth Amendment that mandated direct election of senators was yet another step in the transformation of American government from liberty to democracy. In the Constitution as originally written, senators were not democratically elected, but were chosen by other government officials, and this deliberately insulated senators from the democratic pressures of American citizens.

Thus, looking at the legislative branch of government, only half of it was originally democratically elected by the citizens. The other half was chosen by people in government. Furthermore, the Constitution did not specify who had the right to vote for members of the House of Representatives. It said only that the voters "shall have the Qualifications requisite for Electors of the most numerous branch of the State Legislature." The qualifications for voting were determined by the states themselves and differed from state to state, but the Constitution, as originally written,

---

[7]This logic of bicameralism is discussed in James M. Buchanan and Gordon Tullock, *The Calculus of Consent* (Ann Arbor: University of Michigan Press, 1962).

gave nobody the explicit right to vote in federal elections. Several constitutional amendments have since changed that. People had the right to vote in federal elections only if their states gave it to them. In the original Constitution, democratic input by citizens was very limited, even in the legislative branch of government.

The judicial branch of government is overseen by the Supreme Court, and justices are still appointed by the president and confirmed by Congress. There has never been any direct accountability of Supreme Court justices to the electorate. Similarly, the Constitution specified that the president would be selected by an electoral college, or by the House of Representatives if no candidate got votes from a majority of the electors. The Constitution never has specified how a state's electors are chosen, and the Founders tried to insulate the election of the president from popular democratic pressures, too.

Looking at the three branches of government as originally designed by the Founders, only members of half of one branch were to be chosen democratically. If each branch was designed to have roughly equal power, as would have to be the case if the branches were designed to check and balance each other, the federal government was designed to be only one-sixth democratic, and even there, it allowed the states to determine who could vote for members of the House of Representatives. Senators were chosen by their state legislatures, the president was chosen by an electoral college, and Supreme Court justices were appointed by the president. The government was not designed to be democratic, and the Founders had no intention of allowing citizens to directly select the individuals who ran the government. Rather, various mechanisms were established for selecting federal officials such that no faction would be able to maintain control over who would hold positions of power. The electoral college was one of those mechanisms designed to prevent the government from becoming democratic.

THE ELECTORAL COLLEGE

The Constitution was designed so a group of highly qualified experts would be designated to select the president and vice president. Article II, Section 1, states,

> Each State shall appoint, in such a Manner as the Legislature thereof may direct, a Number of Electors, equal to the whole

Number of Senators and Representatives to which the State may be entitled in the Congress; but no Senator or Representative, or Person holding an Office of Trust or Profit under the United States, shall be appointed as an Elector.

Constitutional amendments have changed some aspects of the process by which the president is elected, but this provision remains unchanged.

It is apparent from the wording of this provision of the Constitution that the Founders did not intend for electors to be democratically elected (although they did not rule out the possibility) and is even more apparent that however the electors were chosen, they did not intend the method of choice to dictate how the electors would cast their ballots. Otherwise, why would the Constitution rule out federal officials as electors? Article II, Section 1 of the Constitution continues, "The Electors shall meet in their respective States, and vote by Ballot for two Persons, of whom one at least shall not be an Inhabitant of the same State with themselves." The person receiving the most votes would then become president if that person received votes from a majority of the electors, and the person with the second-highest number of votes would become vice president. This provision was changed slightly by the Twelfth Amendment in 1804 so that the president and vice president were voted on separately, but the electoral college system remained essentially unchanged otherwise. The Constitution has never bound electors to vote for specific candidates, and the Constitution makes it clear that the Founders envisioned electors using their discretion to select the candidates they viewed as best-qualified. That system remains intact at the beginning of the twenty-first century, and even though electors are associated with specific candidates, it has not been uncommon for an occasional elector to break ranks and vote for someone other than the candidate chosen by the state's voters.[8]

In practice, most presidents have won election by receiving a majority of the electoral votes, but at the time the Constitution was written, the Founders anticipated that in most cases no candidate would receive votes from a majority of the electors.[9]

---

[8]For example, in 1972, 1976, and 1988 electors cast votes for candidates other than those chosen by the voters of their states.

[9]Forrest McDonald, *The American Presidency* (Lawrence: University Press of Kansas, 1994), pp. 177–78, discusses this aspect of the Constitution.

The Founders reasoned that most electors would prefer candidates from their own states, so the typical elector would vote for one candidate from his own state and a candidate from another state, following the constitutional requirement, and it would be unlikely that voting along state lines would produce any candidate with a majority of votes. This state bias is reinforced by the fact that these electors are constitutionally charged to meet in their states and then forward their votes to the president of the Senate to be counted. There is much less of an opportunity for consensus under this system than if the electors from all of the states gathered together in a common location, making it even more likely that no candidate would receive a majority.

Today, it is common for people to conjecture that electors were to meet in their own states rather than gather in a central location because transportation was much more difficult then. Yet it is apparent that the system of having electors meet in their own states rather than all together as one group serves another purpose: It makes it more difficult for the electoral college to arrive at a consensus when there is in fact no consensus candidate. Article II, Section 1 of the Constitution specifies that "if no Person [has] a Majority, then from the five highest on the List the said House shall in like Manner chuse [sic] the president." The Founders envisioned that in most cases no candidate would end up receiving votes from a majority of the electors, so the president would end up being chosen by the House of Representatives from the list of the five top electoral-vote recipients.

As it has evolved, the actual practice of electing a president is quite different from the way that the Founders intended. The Founders intended electoral votes to be cast by electors who would be more knowledgeable than the general public, rather than by popular mandate, and the Founders envisioned that in most cases the final decision would be made by the House of Representatives rather than the electors anyway. Furthermore, there was no indication that the number of electoral votes actually received should carry any weight besides creating a list of the top five candidates. The House could then use its discretion to determine who on that list would make the best president. Quite clearly, the process was not intended to be democratic, although it has evolved that way despite the fact that the constitutional provisions for selecting a president remain essentially unchanged. As specified in the Constitution, the election process should resemble the way that a search committee might serve to locate a high-ranking corporate (or government, or academic) administrator. The committee, like the electoral college, would develop a list of candidates, and the CEO (or bureau chief, or university president) would then select his or her most preferred candidate from the list. As it actually has evolved, this multi-step process has been set aside in favor of popular elections.

The electoral college system envisioned by the Founders was designed to select a chief executive for the nation from a candidate pool composed of an elite group. Successful candidates would have to be well-known and viewed as highly qualified in many states to get enough electoral votes to make the final list and would have to have enough respect from within the House of Representatives to be chosen from a list of five finalists. Those involved in the selection process would be an elite group of Americans, and the process was engineered in order to produce a president who came from the upper echelons of the American elite. The process was not intended to be democratic.

THE SELECTION OF PRESIDENTIAL ELECTORS

The current selection of electors is by a restricted general ticket, which allows voters only to vote for a bloc of electors who represent a specific candidate, but this method of election was not well-established until at least three decades after presidential elections began. The most common method for selecting electors early in the nation's history was to have state legislatures do it. In the first presidential election, only two states, Pennsylvania and Maryland, used general-ticket elections to select their presidential electors. In the second presidential election in 1792, there were fifteen states, and three used general-ticket elections, ten chose their electors in the state legislature, and two had district elections for electors. In the election of 1800, which elected Thomas Jefferson for his first term, there were sixteen states, and only one used general-ticket election while ten had their state legislatures choose their electors.

The selection of electors by state legislatures remained common through 1820, when James Monroe was elected to his second term of office. In that election, nine out of twenty-four states chose their electors in the state legislature, while eight used general-ticket elections. After 1820 the selection of electors through general ticket elections became rapidly more common. In 1824, twelve of the twenty-four states used general-ticket elections, and only six selected electors in their state legislatures. By 1828, eighteen of twenty-four states used general-ticket elections and only two chose electors in the legislature, and by 1832, only South Carolina chose their electors in the legislature; one state had district elections; and the other twenty-two used general-ticket elections. In 1836 all states but South Carolina used general-ticket elections. South Carolinians did not vote directly for their electors until after the Civil War.[10]

The movement toward democratic elections for president in the nation's early history is striking. States used a variety of methods for selecting their electors, but through 1820, the most common method of selecting electors was through the state legislature, without direct voting. By 1832, just twelve years later, direct voting was used almost nationwide. The design of the Constitution makes it apparent that the Founders did not intend to have the president elected by direct vote, but they left it up to the states to determine exactly how presidential electors would be chosen. The result was that, despite the retention of the electoral college, the president is effectively chosen by direct vote and has been since the 1820s. The movement toward the democratic election of the president also corresponds with a more democratic notion of the office itself, beginning in the 1820s.

THE ELITE PRESIDENCY: 1789–1829

When the office of the president was being designed by the Founders at the Constitutional Convention, one factor underlying the discussion was the assumption that George Washington would be elected the first president. Washington, revered today, also commanded a huge amount of respect after the revolution, and the office was designed in part with the thought that Washington would set the precedent for the details of the office that were left out of the Constitution.[11] Design of the government would have been more difficult, and might have proceeded along different lines, had there not been such an obvious and popular candidate to become the first president.

The Founders were wary of the potential for tyranny that majorities could exert in a democratic government and tried to

[10]Data on the methods of selecting electors is from *Historical Statistics of the United States, Colonial Times to 1970* (Washington, D.C.: Bureau of the Census, 1975), p. 1071.

[11]See McDonald, *The American Presidency*, pp. 5, 143, and chap. 9.

guard against the exploitation of a minority by a majority in several ways. The role of democratic decision-making was severely limited both by insulating the new government from direct voting and by constitutionally limiting the scope of the government. In addition, the Founders wanted to guard against the emergence of factions to prevent citizens from viewing their interests as being represented by one group of political candidates rather than another. Especially with regard to the presidency, the system was designed to select the most qualified individual to head the executive branch of government, rather than to select a candidate who represented some citizens more than others.

The Constitution makes no reference to political parties, and the methods of selecting federal officials were designed to prevent them from playing a major role. Modern sources tend to cite party affiliations for all past presidents, but political parties in the modern sense did not assume any importance in presidential elections until 1828, when Andrew Jackson was elected. Candidates for the office came from a political elite, and because of widespread selection of electors by state legislatures, candidates needed to win the support of others in the political elite in order to win the office. Despite the rapid emergence of factions in American government, prior to 1828 parties did not campaign for presidential candidates.

George Washington and John Adams, the first two presidents, are associated with the Federalist Party, a distinction which became crucial during Adams's term as president. Washington remained unchallenged as head of state during his two terms as president and had a solid enough following that his vice president, John Adams, was elected president when Washington chose not to serve a third term. But while Washington was not seriously challenged during his two elections, Adams won his election by a margin of only two electoral votes over Thomas Jefferson, a member of the Democratic–Republican Party, who then, following the rules of the original Constitution, became vice president.

By the time of Adams's election in 1796, there had developed some serious philosophical differences regarding the way that the federal government should evolve. At the center of much of the controversy was Alexander Hamilton, Washington's secretary of the Treasury. Hamilton served as much more than just the secretary of the Treasury during Washington's administration;

indeed, one historian referred to him as effectively being the "prime minister," partly because the Treasury Department was so large compared to the rest of the government at that time, and partly because Hamilton took it upon himself to strengthen the position of the federal government whenever the opportunity presented itself.[12] One of the issues that created a considerable amount of controversy was the creation of the first Bank of the United States as a federally chartered corporation. As Treasury secretary, this was Hamilton's project, but among its significant opponents were James Madison and Thomas Jefferson. Despite opposition, in 1791 the first Bank of the United States was given a twenty-year charter.

The Bank of the United States was but a part of Hamilton's broader vision of the role of the United States government. At the Constitutional Convention, Hamilton had argued that all communities can be divided into the few who are rich and well-born, and the remaining mass of people. Their interests are often at odds, but the masses are seldom good judges of what is right. Thus, Hamilton wanted a Constitution that would ensure the "rich and well-born their distinct, permanent share in the government."[13] As secretary of Treasury, he tried to design a government that would protect and promote industry. Hamilton's "Report on Manufactures," written while he was secretary of Treasury, promoted government policy that encouraged government protection of industry, and Hamilton advocated an internal improvements program that would spend enough to maintain the national debt. Hamilton viewed the debt as creating a tie among the interests of financial groups, businesses, and creditors with the federal government. "A national debt, if not excessive, will be to us a national blessing," Hamilton said.[14]

James Madison, who had strongly opposed parties and factions in *The Federalist Papers* No. 10, revised his opinion as a

---

[12]McDonald, *The American Presidency*, p. 230, refers to Hamilton as "prime minister" (quotations in the original), and discusses Hamilton's role in the Washington administration at greater length in pp. 225–43.

[13]Quoted from Arthur M. Schlesinger, Jr., *The Age of Jackson* (Boston: Little, Brown, 1945), p. 10. Schlesinger writes, "The rock on which Alexander Hamilton built his church was the deep-seated conviction that society would be governed best by an aristocracy, and that an aristocracy was based most properly and enduringly on property" (p. 12).

[14]Ibid., p. 11.

reaction to the Hamiltonian expansion of the scope of government and, along with Thomas Jefferson created the Democratic–Republican Party to try to counter the growing power of the federal government that they viewed was occurring in the Washington administration. After Washington stepped down, his vice president, John Adams, was elected president in a close election. Thomas Jefferson's electoral vote total was almost equal to that of Adams's, and he was able to create an unpleasant political environment for Adams, who was the first one-term president and was unseated by Jefferson in the election of 1800. The problems created by having a president and vice president from different parties laid the foundation for the Twelfth Amendment, which created separate electoral balloting for the offices of president and vice president.

Jefferson's two terms were followed by his fellow Democratic–Republicans, Madison and Monroe. While their political alignments originally arose in opposition to Hamilton's vision of a United States government that would promote elite commercial and business interests, their policies drifted toward Hamilton's. Interestingly enough, despite Madison's leadership in the opposition to the First Bank of the United States, whose charter ran out in 1811, the Second Bank of the United States was chartered in 1816, also for twenty years, during Madison's presidency. Madison had decided that a nationally chartered bank was not such a bad idea after all. As Arthur Schlesinger, Jr., noted,

> The approval of the Second Bank of the United States in 1816 by the man who twenty-five years before had been the ablest opponent of the First Bank was an appropriate commentary on the breakdown of the Jeffersonian idyl.[15]

What appeared to be a fissure between factions that created the Democratic–Republican Party in hindsight did not result in a great division, especially in comparison to the political divisions that would appear within a few decades.

The first six presidents were members of America's political elite, chosen by America's political elite. After a close election for his first term, Jefferson received 162 out of 176 electoral votes to win his second term in the first election where the vice president was selected from a separate ballot. Madison and Monroe, the

[15]Ibid., p. 19.

fourth and fifth presidents, each won two terms in office with electoral landslides, making the elite nature of the office uncontroversial. Outside of George Washington, Monroe might lay claim to the title of the least partisan of all American presidents.[16] But controversy erupted in the election of 1824, when John Quincy Adams was selected by the House of Representatives to be the nation's sixth president.

Four candidates received electoral voters for president in 1824. Andrew Jackson received the highest number of electoral votes with 99, followed by John Quincy Adams with 84, William H. Crawford with 41, and Henry Clay with 37. Because no candidate had a majority, following the rules modified by the Twelfth Amendment, the House of Representatives was to choose the president from the top three vote recipients. Rather than choose Jackson, a war hero but a political outsider, the House chose Adams, the son of the nation's second president and a member of the political elite. Adams's election followed the rules, but Jackson's supporters were outraged by the choice, believing that Adams was chosen only because of a "corrupt bargain" between Adams and Henry Clay in which Clay was appointed secretary of state in exchange for Clay's support of Adams's candidacy.

THE ELECTORAL COLLEGE BEFORE JACKSON'S PRESIDENCY

The history of the election of 1824 tends to emphasize the collusion between John Quincy Adams and Henry Clay that eventually delivered Adams the presidency. But a neglected underlying factor in the historical controversy was the evolution of the electoral college in the nation's first few decades. Adams's election followed the constitutional rules exactly, and even followed the intent of the Founders. No candidate received votes from a majority of the electors, so the House was to select the candidate it preferred, which it did. Neither the Founders nor the Constitution intended to give any preference to the top electoral vote-getter or to take into account the number of electoral votes each candidate received. And even if they had, the electoral vote counts of Adams and Jackson were very close

---

[16]This is the evaluation of Ralph Ketcham, *Presidents Above Party: The First American Presidency, 1789–1829* (Chapel Hill: University of North Carolina Press, 1984), p. 124.

anyway. Members of the House simply undertook their constitutional responsibility to choose a president following exactly the constitutional rules and the intentions of the Founders. So why were Jackson's supporters so upset? They were upset because the actual practice of presidential elections had deviated significantly from the Founders' intent in the decades preceding the 1824 election, and if the actual practice at the time had been followed, rather than the literal rules of the Constitution, Jackson's supporters believed that he would have been elected president.

The Founders intended for the electoral college to be composed of knowledgeable electors, as a kind of search committee to forward a list of the top candidates for the presidency to the House, which would then choose the president except in cases where there was a consensus among electors. But the system had never worked that way. John Quincy Adams was the first president who did not receive an electoral majority, meaning that the nation had selected presidents for more than three decades without ever having a president selected in the House. Over those decades, the methods that states used to select their electors had changed so that rather than having state legislatures choose them, they were chosen by the electorate directly. Furthermore, electors represented specific candidates instead of being chosen for their ability to select good candidates. Thus, in effect, there was popular voting for president despite the process specified in the Constitution, and if the president was in fact elected by popular vote, Jackson's supporters believed that he should have been selected as president in 1824.

Another factor was that after the election of 1800, when Jefferson narrowly edged out Adams, there was not a close election again until 1824, and with nearly a quarter of a century of consensus choices, Americans became accustomed to the idea that the popular vote-winner became president. When almost all states had adopted general-ticket voting for electors, the notion that the nation's chief executive was chosen by popular vote was reinforced. The Constitution has always specified, and still specifies, that the presidential electors cast votes for president. Despite what the document says, and despite what the Founders intended, by 1824 the nation had gone to popular voting for president. Jackson's supporters felt cheated because Jackson was denied the presidency despite the fact that he got the most votes.

THE FORMATION OF THE DEMOCRATIC PARTY

The dissatisfaction of Jackson's supporters was consistent with the increasing democratization of American government. Presidential elections were increasingly being decided by popular vote, with the big transition occurring in the 1820s. In the election of 1820, nine states still chose their electors in their state legislatures, but by 1824, when John Quincy Adams was elected, only six did. In 1828, when Andrew Jackson unseated Adams to become president, only two states had their legislatures choose their electors. The increasingly democratic election methods came along with the formation of the Democratic Party, which was organized for the specific purpose of electing Andrew Jackson to the presidency. Jackson's supporters, led by Martin Van Buren, formed the Democratic Party after the election of 1824 to ensure that, in the next election, Jackson would get a majority of the electoral votes and so could not be denied the presidency by an elitist House of Representatives.

Van Buren's efforts would undoubtedly have gone in a different direction had the electoral college actually functioned as the Founders intended. The formation of a political party to get popular support made a great deal of sense under the new system in which the president was chosen by popular vote but would have made no sense a few decades before, when most electors were chosen by their state legislatures. The formation of the Democratic Party was a significant event in American politics, but the party was formed only because of the transformation of the electoral college.

Van Buren's efforts to form the Democratic Party began even before John Quincy Adams was inaugurated as president. Although Adams's bargain to appoint Clay as secretary of state seemed reasonable to Adams, and there was no doubt that Clay was eminently qualified, Van Buren was quick to paint Adams as undertaking partisan activity. In contrast to presidents over the previous two decades, Adams had a very narrow base of political support, which in itself created political opposition and enhanced the appearance of factionalism. Adams could only appeal to his supporters in order to accomplish anything while in office, enhancing the appearance of governance by a political elite. Although the "corrupt bargain" between Adams and Clay gave Adams the immediate reward of the presidency, it also initiated the process that unseated him four years later, gave rise to the party system that has dominated American politics since, and greatly accelerated the movement of the United States toward democracy as its fundamental principle.[17]

Well-defined factions had existed within American government for decades. It was in George Washington's administration, after all, that Jefferson and Madison had begun their political party to oppose what they viewed as an unwarranted expansion of government power. In contrast to the elitist notion of party that had characterized American politics and that had placed John Quincy Adams in the White House, Van Buren began to promote a new and more positive view of political parties. Van Buren's idea was that "Parties should be democratic associations, run by the majority of the membership."[18]

Van Buren was well aware of the American tradition opposing political parties, tracing its origins back through *The Federalist Papers* No. 10, and supported in word by all six of the first presidents but Van Buren, a senator from New York, perceived legitimate political differences among politicians that could be expressed along party lines. More significantly, he viewed the opposition of incumbents to organized parties as support for the continuance of political dominance by America's aristocratic elite. Without organized opposition, the elite could continue to dominate American government indefinitely. Parties served the legitimate interest of organizing political opposition, resisting the concentration of power in an elite group and providing a broader representation of the political views of most Americans.

Van Buren did not misperceive the role that his new Democratic Party would play. Indeed, the Founders tried to insulate the federal government from democratic control for what they believed were good reasons and had no notion that the president would be chosen by the popular vote of American citizens. Yet the Democratic Party had formed to do just that. The efforts of Van Buren and the Democrats were an unqualified success, and Jackson won the presidency in 1828, defeating the incumbent president by an electoral total of 178 to 83. The modern party

[17]Robert V. Remini, *The Legacy of Andrew Jackson* (Baton Rouge: Louisiana State University Press, 1988), p. 14.

[18]Quoted from Ketcham, *Presidents Above Party*, p. 141.

system was born, as both the Democrats and their opponents recognized that after Jackson's election, a party organization would be necessary to win the presidency. After Jackson's two terms as president, Van Buren was elected president for one term and was unseated by his Whig challenger William Henry Harrison in 1840. The American two-party system has evolved since then, but fundamentally it has not changed.

JACKSONIAN POLICY

Jackson campaigned for the presidency based on a platform of liberty. Jackson viewed himself as following a Jeffersonian tradition, both in opposing the *status quo* of the previous administration and of trying to limit the powers of the federal government and loosen the grip of the political elite over American government. The federal government remained relatively limited in scope, but under Jackson's predecessors its power had been slowly but steadily growing and was controlled by elites, allowing the broader population little say in the operation of their government. Jackson wanted to limit the powers of the federal government, and he believed that the way to do so was to move from government by elites to government by democracy. The Founders had intended for the federal government to be controlled by elites rather than responding to the masses, placing Jackson's populist ideas at odds with his predecessors, but the Founders just as clearly intended for the federal government to be strictly limited in scope, making Jackson's ideas in this area more in harmony with the Founders.

One of the most visible issues that Jackson pursued was the Second Bank of the United States, which he opposed as an institution that centralized power and shackled the growth of the American economy. Jackson believed that the policies of the Second Bank perpetuated monopoly in the banking industry, giving privilege to the few at the expense of the many. Despite an attempt by Congress to extend the bank's charter, Jackson was able to veto the bank, and it passed out of existence in 1836, the last year of Jackson's second term.[19] Jackson's philosophy of

---

[19]Schlesinger, *The Age of Jackson*, pp. 74–114, discusses Jackson's battle with those who supported the Second Bank in detail. Robert V. Remini, *The Life of Andrew Jackson* (New York: Harper and Row, 1988), p. 143, notes

government came from a group of successful businessmen who pushed laissez-faire ideas.[20] While monopolistic business practices could prove harmful, the Jacksonians, following Adam Smith, believed that government was more often the source of monopolistic business practices than the solution.[21] Rather than try to get the government involved in the economy, Jackson attempted to pull back, in the case of the Second Bank and in the case of government regulation and support of the economy more generally.

Jackson wanted to dilute the economic power wielded by America's business elite, and he viewed that much of that power was driven by government policy, including policies of incorporation. In Jackson's day, banks were the corporations that wielded the most economic power, and Jackson wanted to eliminate bank notes and move to a system of hard money to remove some of the power of banks. Banks were only a part of the incorporation problem, however. Often, corporate charters were granted for projects that conveyed some monopoly power, such as the building of toll roads and bridges, and Jackson wanted to extend the ability to incorporate so that anybody would be allowed to create a corporation following general laws, rather than having to specifically be granted a corporate charter. General incorporation laws at the state level, following the Jacksonian idea, began to spread prior to the War Between the States, and became universal after the war. Corporate forms of business are so common today that it is difficult to imagine business without it, but the modern corporate form is "a direct legacy from Jacksonian democracy."[22]

---

that Jackson, along with many others, viewed that corruption within the Second Bank was responsible for initiating the panic of 1819 and the resulting economic collapse.

[20]Jackson's advice often came from a group of "counsellors" who were paid well by the federal government, but were not officially appointed to cabinet positions, thus giving rise to the term Kitchen Cabinet. See Marquis James, *Andrew Jackson: Portrait of a President* (New York: Grosset and Dunlap, 1937), p. 191.

[21]Schlesinger, *The Age of Jackson*, pp. 314–17, notes the influence of Adam Smith's *The Wealth of Nations* on the Jacksonian philosophy.

[22]Schlesinger, *The Age of Jackson*, p. 337.

Another important issue was the federal funding of internal improvements. Jackson was against it, not just as a matter of policy, but as a Constitutional issue. Jackson saw no allowance within the Constitution for the federal government to engage in public works and believed that if the people wanted the government involved, they should either petition their state governments to undertake the projects they desired or amend the Constitution.[23] This was an issue in which Jackson stood in stark contrast with John Quincy Adams, who in his first State of the Union address proposed a stunning array of public works, including roads and canals, a national university, and federal support for the exploration of the western territories.[24] These activities should be undertaken for the good of the nation, regardless of popular opinion, Adams argued. Adams inadvertently gave Jackson two issues that clearly differentiated the two and created a clear contrast for the presidential election of 1828. The first issue was directly related to the federal government's involvement in public works, but the second larger issue was the role of popular opinion as a check on government power.

Jackson's first major move against public works was his Maysville veto in 1828, against a bill that would have provided federal funding for a road that was to be entirely within Kentucky. The bill's supporters argued that the road would be an important link in the federal transportation system, but Jackson viewed this argument as irrelevant. The federal government had no constitutional authority to finance internal improvements, whether or not they were national in character, Jackson argued.[25]

Jackson also believed that the courts, and the law itself, were too inaccessible to most citizens, and the favored codification and simplification of law to remove some of the power of the courts.[26] Jackson would not have prevented the courts from interpreting the law, but the believed the Supreme Court was substantially overstepping its constitutional bounds whenever it

[23]Remini, *The Legacy of Andrew Jackson*, p. 11.

[24]Remini, *The Life of Andrew Jackson*, p. 159.

[25]Donald B. Cole, *The Presidency of Andrew Jackson* (Lawrence: University Press of Kansas, 1993), pp. 63–65.

[26]Schlesinger, *The Age of Jackson*, pp. 329–31.

attempted to divine the true meaning of ambiguous parts of the Constitution.[27] To do so made the actions of the other branches of government subordinate to the interpretations of the judiciary, which was contrary to Jackson's vision of the Constitution's design.

In contrast to Alexander Hamilton's view, Jackson opposed the national debt and by 1835 had retired it entirely, an accomplishment in which he took pride.[28] He also wanted the federal government to give up its ownership of public lands.[29] Jackson claimed to be a Jeffersonian Republican, committed to the idea of limited government and determined to turn around what he viewed as the expansion of federal government power under his predecessors. His policies were consistently laissez-faire, and he left his mark on the nation by successfully limiting the scope of government in many ways. At the same time, Jackson viewed the federal government as a necessary check on the power of state governments and believed that this balance was necessary to preserve liberty.[30] When South Carolina threatened secession in 1833, Jackson made it perfectly clear that he would use military force if necessary to preserve the Union, setting a precedent upon which Lincoln called less than three decades later.[31]

In most respects, Jackson's ideas on public policy were very libertarian, recalling the Founders' own ideas that the purpose of the federal government was to preserve the liberty of its citizens. He was opposed to federal involvement in public works, in banking and monetary policy, and in giving privileges such as corporate charters to some that were not available to all, and he was opposed to the public debt. But he believed that the federal government was essential to further this goal, so he opposed state nullification of federal laws and opposed the secession of states from the Union. He was also opposed to governance by a privileged elite, and believed that the population as a whole should

---

[27]See William Graham Sumner, *Andrew Jackson* (Boston: Houghton, Mifflin, 1899), pp. 218–19, and Remini, *The Life of Andrew Jackson*, pp. 305–06.

[28]Ibid., p. 295.

[29]Sumner, *Andrew Jackson*, pp. 229–36.

[30]Ibid., pp. 246–64, discusses the nullification issue in detail. Some Southern states wanted to establish their power to nullify federal laws, to which Jackson strenuously objected.

[31]Remini, *The Life of Andrew Jackson*, pp. 244–51.

have more control over their government, as a check on the power of the elite.

JACKSONIAN DEMOCRACY

The public policy positions taken by Jackson were consistently aimed at the goal of reducing the scope and power of the federal government, but in addition to these policy ends, Jackson also believed in democracy as a means to control the federal government. The top officials in the government should be elected directly, Jackson believed, including senators and the president, in order to make them more accountable to the people, and once elected, they should heed the wishes of the electorate. Because popular election would give voters a direct method of removing from office officials who did not further the will of the electorate, popular elections would create an incentive structure that would hold elected officials more accountable to the demands of the voters. Through democracy, Jackson wanted to remove the federal government from the control of the political elite that had overseen it since the approval of the new Constitution. As it happens, his ideas on democracy have had a more lasting impact on the nation than his Jeffersonian ideas of limited government.

As an outsider, a war hero, and a person who had worked his way up to national prominence rather than having been born into privilege, Jackson found a sympathetic audience in the electorate. As one historian put it,

> it was much in Jackson's favor that he was an ignorant man, fully as devoid as the average citizen could be of all the training, through books or practice, which had theretofore been commonly regarded as constituting the odious superior qualifications of a detestable upper class.[32]

In short, Jackson's ideas were not the product of thoughtful scholarship and an in-depth understanding of political theory, but rather were a reaction to his perception that a government established to protect the liberty of its citizens had been accumulating power in the hands of a political elite. Democracy was the mechanism Jackson favored for redistributing power away from this elite and returning it to the people.

---

[32]John T. Morse, Jr., p. viii, in the introduction to Sumner, *Andrew Jackson.*

What Jackson did not anticipate was that by making government officials more accountable to the general public, they would be more inclined to make decisions that pandered to popular opinion rather than sticking to the guidelines of the Constitution. The Founders had good reason for trying to insulate the actions of the federal government from the demands of popular opinion, but Jackson wanted to remove that insulation, making the federal government more accountable to the electorate. Jackson was successful, and his most lasting legacy is that he made the federal government more democratic and thus more oriented toward satisfying the demands of the voters than protecting their liberty. Of course, Jackson would not have been able to do so had the electoral college functioned as the Founders originally envisioned. Given the changes in presidential elections that occurred prior to 1828, it was inevitable that somebody would come along who would mobilize popular opinion, and that person happened to be Andrew Jackson. But Jacksonian democracy was as much a product of the evolution of the electoral college as it was of Jackson himself.

THE TWO-PARTY SYSTEM

The creation of the Democratic Party directly led to the creation of America's two-party system. With the Democrats explicitly organized to get their candidate into the White House, any opposing candidate would need a similar organization in order to mount a plausible opposition. Thus, the Whig Party developed a similar organization in order to mount an opposition to the Democrats. Eventually they succeeded. Jackson was a very popular president, and after he served two terms, Democratic nominee Martin Van Buren, who had been instrumental in forming the party, was elected to the presidency. Van Buren proved less popular than Jackson, however, and served only one term before being displaced by Whig William Henry Harrison. Thus, the two-party system was born.

The American electoral system naturally lends itself to two parties, but no more. Politicians tend to be viewed as being somewhere on a political spectrum from left to right, and voters tend to favor the candidate that is closest to their own views on that left-right continuum. Thus, in the typical election one candidate gains most of the votes of the people on the right while the other gets most of the votes of the people on the left.

In order to win, the candidate must get the votes of people in the middle, and this causes most successful candidates to pull their platforms toward the center of the political spectrum. If a third party were to arise and gain strength, it would tend to take votes from one or the other party, making two of the three parties unviable. They would either have to merge or one would fade away, perhaps after adopting some of the views of the party it was closest to. This idea is well-established as a part of political theory, and the reason for bringing it up here is to show how the emergence of the Democratic Party coupled with the quick transformation of the presidential election system into a winner-take-all popular vote contest inevitably, and rapidly, led to the creation of a two-party system.[33]

The Constitution says nothing about political parties, and the Founders did not anticipate that they would play a major role in presidential elections. However, the nation has had a two-party system since the creation of Jackson's Democratic Party. The Whigs were the first challengers to the Democrats, but once the Republicans gained strength, the Whig Party disappeared, maintaining the two-party system. This would not have happened without the creation of the Democratic Party to elect Jackson, but perhaps it was inevitable that the two-party system would emerge eventually once the Founder's vision of the electoral college was phased out in favor of popular voting for electors. Because of that, organized presidential campaigns to gain popular support could pay big dividends in a way that would not be possible if the electoral college had actually functioned as a group of well-informed electors who would forward a slate of candidates to the House for final selection.

Thus, the transformation of the electoral college directly led to the creation of the modern two-party system.[34] Had the system worked as the Founders originally envisioned, states rather than

---

[33]See Anthony Downs, *An Economic Theory of Democracy* (New York: Harper and Row, 1957), for a frequently cited exposition of these ideas.

[34]It is perhaps worth remarking that the reason other nations can support more than two parties (Germany is a good example) is because parties are elected to their legislatures in proportion to the votes the parties get. Thus, in Germany, a party that gets 20 percent of the votes gets 20 percent of the seats. In the United States, a candidate who gets 20 percent of the votes gets defeated.

political parties would have been the nucleus of political support. There would have been room for more political parties, on the one hand, but on the other hand, parties would have served a much smaller purpose in presidential elections. If the electoral college was composed of a group of people who knew the candidates and could judge their strengths and weaknesses personally, party affiliation would have been secondary to the political views and personal qualities of the candidates, so there would have been less of an incentive for candidates to affiliate with parties. The modern two-party system in the United States is a direct result of the evolution of the electoral college early in the nineteenth century.

INTERESTS IN JACKSON'S ADMINISTRATION

Within the context of the growth of federal government power, Andrew Jackson's presidency had two opposing effects. As noted earlier, Jackson favored a smaller federal government with less power and with less oversight over the activities of state governments. This return to Jeffersonian principles had the immediate effect of reducing the scope and power of the federal government. Pulling in the other direction, however, was Jackson's desire for more democratic representation in the federal government and Jackson's assigning of federal government positions based on political patronage. The fledgling civil service system that existed when he was elected was done away with by Jackson. Prior to Jackson's administration, there was the notion that as long as civil servants performed their duties well, they were entitled to keep their jobs. Jackson saw things differently. He believed that the jobs were not so demanding that people of reasonable intelligence could not perform them, and he argued that more was lost by giving people a guarantee of continuing employment than was gained by retaining an experienced workforce. Thus, Jackson replaced many government workers after his election.[35]

Jackson's argument about giving government workers an incentive to perform has some merit and found a sympathetic hearing in his day, but one by-product of Jackson's actions was

[35]See Ketcham, *Presidents Above Party*, pp. 151–52, for a discussion. Also, Remini, *The Life of Andrew Jackson*, pp. 185–86, explains Jackson's point of view.

the transformation of government jobs into political patronage awards. Jackson's political supporters ended up getting government jobs and had an incentive to continue supporting Jackson if they wanted to keep their jobs. Political appointments have a certain logic behind them, because if government workers perform poorly, incumbent politicians are more likely to lose the next election and those workers are likely to lose their jobs. Thus, political appointees have an incentive to make the government look good. But it was also apparent that many government employees had their jobs only because they supported the Democratic Party.

This aspect of political parties is almost inevitable, although civil service reform that began at the end of the nineteenth century has curbed the process somewhat. When presidents were selected by political elites from a group of political elites, they did not accumulate political debts and were not compelled to act in a partisan fashion. But when a president is elected because of the support of a political party, the president owes his election to the party and is pressured to repay the favor by giving benefits to his political supporters. With a limited federal government early in the nineteenth century, the major kind of benefit that could be tendered was government employment. Thus, Jacksonian democracy brought with it political patronage and reinforced the idea that in a political competition, to the victor belongs the spoils. The nation had taken another step away from liberty and another step toward democracy.[36]

The tariff was a major issue of the time, and while Jackson was philosophically in favor of lower tariffs, he also wanted to keep tariff revenue flowing in order to retire the federal debt. In 1828, Jackson sought to maintain political support by adjusting tariff rates on different goods, producing a tariff with so many different rates tailored to special interests that it has since been called the "tariff of abominations."[37] Federal tariff policy became one of the issues over which the Southern states argued they should secede from the union. In 1832, most of the "abominations" were eliminated from the tariff in a new bill that reduced rates. Still,

---

[36]Sumner, *Andrew Jackson*, pp. 188–92, discusses Jackson's use of "the spoils system," noting that while it had previously been employed at the state level, Jackson deserves the credit for bringing it to the federal level.

[37]Ibid., pp. 243–46.

the tariff was one of the earliest issues in which interest groups became involved in distributive politics.[38]

While Jackson viewed himself as aligned with Jeffersonian political ideals, his election campaign had little to do with issues and everything to do with personalities. The Democratic Party was formed to elect Jackson, and for that, Jackson owed a debt to those who supported him. Jackson repaid his supporters with federal government positions. Jackson's avowed motives were in line with the tenets of his Democratic Party. He viewed that replacing a complacent elite group of federal employees with a new group of citizens would enhance the democratic nature of government and would improve the efficiency of its operation. The result was to establish political patronage as a method of rewarding those who support victorious politicians—to the victor belongs the spoils. In fact, during the first eighteen months of his administration, Jackson only replaced 919 people out of 10,093 on the federal payroll, but he did so in a more deliberate manner than his predecessors.[39] As Arthur Schlesinger, Jr., notes, "Jackson ousted no greater a proportion of officeholders than Jefferson, though his administration certainly established the spoils system in national politics."[40]

The spoils system and the beginning of interest-group politics came directly from the fact that Jackson relied on his party to get him elected. The strategy of forming a party to elect a candidate, in turn, was a result of the changes in the method of presidential elections. Thus, there is a direct connection between interest-group politics and the transformation of the electoral college. With little imagination, one can envision how American politics would be different today if the president were chosen by a search committee of knowledgeable electors not committed to any candidate, rather than by popular voting.

THE ELECTORAL COLLEGE AND AMERICAN DEMOCRACY

The Founders intended for the president to be selected by a very different process than actually occurred. The process differed even in the very first presidential elections, and the electoral college never worked as the Founders had envisioned. Yet because

---

[38]See Cole, *The Presidency of Andrew Jackson*, pp. 106–08.

[39]Remini, *The Life of Andrew Jackson*, p. 185.

[40]Schlesinger, *The Age of Jackson*, p. 47.

there was substantial consensus regarding the candidates elected to the presidency in the early 1800s, the fact that the process differed from what the Founders intended was not fully exposed until the election of 1824, when the House selected John Quincy Adams over Andrew Jackson. The original idea was to insulate the presidential selection process from popular opinion, but by 1828, the current system of popular voting for president was firmly in place. That election also marked the first time that a president was elected because of the support of a political party, and it marked the first time that the president did not come from America's political elite.

Jackson's presidency brought with it a number of other changes, largely as a result of the way in which he was elected. Political appointments were made as a reward for political support, with no apologies from Jackson, and interest groups that had supported Jackson's candidacy expected to be rewarded once Jackson took office. Thus, Jackson's election brought with it interest-group politics and created America's two-party system. Jackson's election had a huge impact on American democracy, partly because of Jackson and his policies, but also largely because of Jackson's reliance on a political party to get elected. That strategy, in turn, was feasible only because the electoral college had rapidly evolved into a system of popular voting for president.

Andrew Jackson's Democratic Party was appropriately named, for Jackson believed that liberty could be protected only by allowing the people to govern through majority rule.[41] The increased scope of democracy over American government was something Andrew Jackson favored. He favored direct election of the president and senators and even favored democratic oversight of the Supreme Court.[42] Jackson saw democracy and liberty as self-reinforcing, because democratic oversight of the government would guard against its being taken over by a political elite and would prevent the elite government from pursuing policies that would benefit the elite few at the expense of the masses. The Founders felt otherwise, for two reasons. First, they did not believe that most people had the capacity to make thoughtful and informed decisions about their government.

[41]Remini, *The Legacy of Andrew Jackson*, p. 26.
[42]Ibid., pp. 32–33.

Second, they believed that rule by majority could be just as tyrannical as rule by a king, or rule by any elite group. Thus, they designed the government to be run by a political elite, constrained in its actions by the Constitution.

Jackson fought for democracy as a method of limiting the scope and power of the federal government, but ironically, the result of his making the nation's government more democratic has been to increase the scope and power of government in response to popular demands for government programs. This was the result the Founders foresaw and tried to guard against by limiting the role of democracy in their new government. Jackson was a strong president and was able to accomplish many of his immediate goals while he was in office, but the results of his presidency do not look as good, judged by his own goals, over a longer time horizon. Although Jackson wanted to limit the powers of the federal government and succeeded in doing so during his own administration, the more democratic government that he created laid the foundation for future government growth. The growth of government as a direct result of Jacksonian democracy, after Jackson left office, more than offset the reductions in the scope of government that Jackson presided over during his eight years in the White House.

Andrew Jackson's presidency was pivotal in the development of American democracy, but its lasting impact was largely a result of changes in the electoral college prior to his election. Had the electoral college functioned as the Founders intended, Jackson would have been an unlikely presidential candidate because he was not a member of the political elite. But more significantly, there would have been no point in creating a broad-based political party like the Democratic Party, because popular support for a candidate would have had little impact on a presidential election. In response, the Whig Party was formed, and because of the winner-take-all nature of the presidential contests, the two-party system was born as a direct result of the changes that occurred in the electoral college. Political parties, in turn, have led to the creation of factions and interests in American politics, which the Founders explicitly tried to prevent.

When one analyzes the changes associated with Andrew Jackson's presidency in the context of the earlier changes in the electoral college, one can see that the most lasting changes brought by Jackson were a result of the electoral college rather than Jackson himself. The growth of political parties and interest group politics, and the promotion of democracy as a fundamental principle of American government, all came as a result of the move to popular voting for president. Jackson's ideas for limiting the scope of the federal government were completely undone by the growth of democracy in America. Indeed, had Jackson not been so successful in promoting democracy, the cause of liberty would have been better served. But even this gives Jackson too much credit, because by the time he was elected, the incentives in presidential politics had changed, making parties and interest-group politics inevitable. The Founders envisioned a system of presidential elections that would have curbed this, but they left too much discretion to the states. If they had clearly specified the nondemocratic procedure they had envisioned for presidential elections, that would have gone a great way toward insulating the presidency from the demands of popular opinion and would have furthered the cause of liberty that they tried so hard to embody in the Constitution.

6

MARTIN VAN BUREN:
THE AMERICAN GLADSTONE

JEFFREY ROGERS HUMMEL

President Martin Van Buren does not usually receive high marks from historians. Born of humble Dutch ancestry in December 1782 in the small upstate New York village of Kinderhook, Van Buren gained admittance to the bar in 1803 without benefit of higher education. Building upon a successful, country legal practice, he became one of the Empire State's most influential and prominent politicians, during the very period when the state was surging ahead as the country's most populous and wealthy. After election to the United States Senate in 1821, this consummate backroom strategist helped mastermind a reemergence of ideologically distinct political organizations out of the corrupt and faction-ridden interlude of single-party rule—euphemistically labeled "The Era of Good Feelings"—that had followed the War of 1812. A new Democratic Party resuscitated the old Jeffersonian alliance between planters of the South and plain Republicans of the North, united behind the charismatic hero of the West, General Andrew Jackson.

Jackson was elected to the White House in 1828, and Van Buren succeeded to the presidency as Old Hickory's heir-apparent on March 4, 1837. This triumphant fulfillment of a lustrous career would prove short-lived, however. The eighth U.S. president was soundly defeated for reelection in 1840, initiating a new series of single-term chief executives. Four years later, the democracy rejected its venerable architect as presidential nominee, and Van Buren's 1848 candidacy as standard bearer for the Free Soilers, an antislavery third party, failed to carry a single state. The elderly New Yorker survived long enough to witness the outbreak of Civil War but passed away in July 1862, at the age of seventy-nine.

Van Buren was a lawyer–president who represented a new breed of professional politician. His opponents denounced him during his life for subtle intrigue, scheming pragmatism, and indecisive "non-commitalism." These charges were reflected in such popular nicknames as the Little Magician, the Red Fox of Kinderhook, and the American Talleyrand. The ideologically compatible but personally acerbic John Randolph of Roanoke once observed that "he rowed to his objective with muffled oars," faulting Van Buren as "an adroit, dapper, little managing man," who "can't inspire respect."[1] Van Buren's demeanor reinforced these impressions. Appearing shorter than his five feet and six inches, he was stout and balding by the time of his inauguration, his formerly red sideburns now gray and framing a large head with a prominent brow and calculating blue eyes. Always fashionably dressed, charmingly witty, and imperturbably amiable, Van Buren never let political differences master his emotions or cloud his social relations. He was not a daring, original intellect in the mold of John C. Calhoun of South Carolina, and his ability to draw out the views of others often masked his pious devotion to orthodox Jeffersonianism.

Even sympathetic historians tend to slight Van Buren's term in office as the third Jackson administration. Arthur M. Schlesinger, Jr., concludes that, while president, "Van Buren was weak in the very respect in which he might have been expected to excel—as a politician." Except during the last year in office, his management was "negligent and maladroit" and showed very little "executive energy."[2] On the other hand, modern advocates of decentralization and states' rights are often more taken with Van Buren's better known rival, Calhoun, and his doctrine of nullification. Van Buren admittedly would not go to the lengths of a John Randolph in sacrificing political success for ideological purity. Yet the New Yorker's career overall displayed far more consistency in opposing government power at all levels than the many twists and turns of the swaggering opportunist from South Carolina. Van Buren was also better attuned to Old Republican antistatism than the irascible, impulsive, and militaristic Old Hickory, as strikingly illustrated by Van Buren's

---

[1]As quoted in William Cabell Bruce, *John Randolph of Roanoke, 1773–1833: A Biography Based Largely on New Material* (New York: G.P. Putnam's Sons, 1922), vol. 2, p. 203; and John Niven, *Martin Van Buren: The Romantic Age of American Politics* (New York: Oxford University Press, 1983), p. 358.

[2]Arthur M. Schlesinger, Jr., *The Age of Jackson* (Boston: Little, Brown, 1945), p. 263.

more conciliatory rejection of nullification, in spite of bitter personal differences with Calhoun. Above all, in sharp contrast to his political mentor, Thomas Jefferson, the Little Magician managed to hew more closely to principle while occupying the White House than outside of it. Indeed, a close examination of Van Buren's four years in office reveals that historians have grossly underrated his many remarkable accomplishments against heavy odds. These, in my opinion, rank Martin Van Buren as the greatest president in American history.[3]

I

Greatness must be measured against some standard. Let us begin our examination with foreign policy, the area where a president's individual traits probably can make the most difference in history's trajectory. Conventional historians tend to have a nationalist bias that makes them appreciate a strong executive who lastingly contributes to the growth of central authority. They thus have a particular weakness for wartime presidents. Unless the commander-in-chief turns out to be

---

[3]Three older biographies of Van Buren are Edward M. Shepard, *Martin Van Buren*, rev. ed. (Boston: Houghton, Mifflin, 1899), Denis Tilden Lynch, *An Epoch and a Man: Martin Van Buren and His Times* (New York: Horace Liveright, 1929), and Holmes Alexander, *The American Talleyrand: The Career and Contemporaries of Martin Van Buren, Eighth President* (New York: Harper and Brothers, 1935)—all of which give little space to his presidency. A more recent biography, John Niven's *Martin Van Buren* (Oxford: Oxford University Press, 1983), is detailed and sympathetic. But Niven likewise races through the presidential years, and his treatment of ideological issues is often sparse or nonexistent. More attentive to ideas, although harsher in its judgments, is Donald B. Cole's political biography, *Martin Van Buren and the American Political System* (Princeton, N.J.: Princeton University Press, 1984). The best book on the Little Magician, however, is Major L. Wilson's magnificent *The Presidency of Martin Van Buren* (Lawrence: University Press of Kansas, 1984). Another volume devoted exclusively to Van Buren's presidency, James C. Curtis, *The Fox at Bay: Martin Van Buren and the Presidency, 1837–1841* (Lexington: University Press of Kentucky, 1970), is more focused on politics than on analyzing economics. For Van Buren's earlier years, Robert V. Remini's *Martin Van Buren and the Making of the Democratic Party* (New York: W.W. Norton, 1959) is indispensable. Unfortunately, "The Autobiography of Martin Van Buren," *Annual Report of the American Historical Association for the Year 1918*, vol. 2, John C. Fitzpatrick, ed. (Washington, D.C.: U.S. Government Printing Office, 1920), cuts off before the presidential years.

utterly inept, war allows him to show off forceful, dynamic leadership. In a 1961 collection of scholarly articles on *America's Ten Greatest Presidents*, for instance, half the subjects were presidents who had dragged the country into war. And when the collection was revised ten years later to make it *America's Eleven Greatest Presidents*, the additional chapter was on Harry Truman, a president whose reign spread over two hot wars plus a cold war.[4]

In contrast, presidents merit recognition for keeping the United States out of war, and Van Buren has the unique distinction of keeping the U.S. out of two: one with Mexico and another with Britain. Van Buren's deep commitment to peace and neutrality was evident even before he assumed the highest office. He was instrumental, as Jackson's first secretary of state, in negotiating the opening of direct trade with the British West Indies, a long-standing American goal that the previous administration of John Quincy Adams had completely botched. In the midst of Old Hickory's second term, while Van Buren was serving as vice president, the president's hot temper almost provoked conflict with France over spoilation claims arising out of depredations on American commerce during the Napoleonic Wars. The vice president, fortunately,

---

[4]Morton Borden, ed., *America's Ten Greatest Presidents* (Chicago: Rand McNally, 1961), and Borden, ed., *America's Eleven Greatest Presidents*, 2nd ed. (Chicago: Rand McNally, 1971). The chosen ten (with asterisks indicating the wartime presidents) were Washington, Adams,* Jefferson, Jackson, Polk,* Lincoln,* Cleveland, T. Roosevelt, Wilson,* and F.D. Roosevelt.* Two others from this list might be considered wartime presidents as well, because the war with the Barbary pirates occurred during Jefferson's first term, and the U.S. was still suppressing the Filipino insurrection when Theodore Roosevelt assumed office. Borden based his initial choices on a 1948 poll of fifty-five historians, conducted by Arthur M. Schlesinger, Sr., and published in *Life Magazine*. Subsequent presidential ratings appear in Thomas A. Bailey, *Presidential Greatness: The Image and the Man from George Washington to the Present* (New York: Appleton-Century, 1966); Steve Neal, "Our Best and Worst Presidents," *Chicago Tribune Magazine* 135 (January 10, 1982): 9–18; and Robert K. Murray and Tim H. Blessing, *Greatness in the White House: Rating the Presidents from George Washington through Ronald Reagan*, 2nd ed. (University Park: Pennsylvania State University Press, 1994). Most recently, Arthur M. Schlesinger, Jr., reported on a recent presidential poll of historians in "The Ultimate Approval Rating," *New York Times Magazine* 146 (December 15, 1996): 46–51. The predominance of wartime presidents remains unaltered throughout all these efforts.

helped moderate Jackson's belligerence and bring the dispute to an amicable settlement.

Jackson's closing policies, however, handed the president-elect another potential conflict. The hero of New Orleans had looked on with pleasure as American settlers in the Mexican province of Texas declared independence in 1836 and staged a successful revolt. Popular expectations ran high on both sides of the southwest border that the fledgling Texas Republic would soon join the United States. But Mexico refused to recognize the new nation, and the Texas constitution sanctioned slavery, setting off a hue and cry among American abolitionists about the "Slave Powers'" latest expansion into new territory. Any annexation by the United States threatened both a foreign war and domestic political controversy between Southerners and Northerners. Although the Little Magician helped to delay formal U.S. recognition of Texas independence until after safely winning the 1836 presidential election, the retiring Jackson menacingly pressed American claims against the Mexican government for monetary damages.

But the new president, unlike his predecessor, was not eager for war in the southwest. On top of his sincere desire for friendly relations with all foreign powers, Van Buren correctly foresaw that territorial expansion might split Democratic ranks. He therefore deftly rebuffed Texas overtures, and Secretary of State John Forsyth of Georgia announced on August 25, 1837, formal rejection of the offer of annexation. Over the next two years, Van Buren's diplomatic skill and patience got the Mexican government to accept arbitration of U.S. claims by a commission made up of two members from each country and one designated by the King of Prussia.

The eighth president's hope for peace endured well after he left office. Machinations on the part of President John Tyler of Virginia and none other than John C. Calhoun subsequently catapulted Texas annexation into the midst of the 1844 presidential campaign. Van Buren was then frontrunner for the Democratic nomination. Yet he issued a public statement favoring annexation only if it could be accomplished without upsetting U.S. relations with Mexico, despite his full knowledge that this qualification would cost him politically. "We have a character among the nations of the earth to maintain," Van Buren avowed. While "the lust of power, with fraud and violence in the train, has led other and differently constituted governments to aggression and conquest, our movements in these respects have always been regulated by reason and justice."[5] An increasing number of Southern Democrats turned away from the New Yorker, including Jackson himself—dying but still influential. The Little Magician held support from a majority of delegates as the party's convention opened in Baltimore, but the convention rules required a two-thirds vote to nominate. After eight dead-locked ballots, the delegates settled on the first dark-horse candidate in American history: James Knox Polk of Tennessee, an ardent expansionist. Polk would win a slim victory at the presidential polls and then conduct the very war that Van Buren had tried so hard to prevent.[6]

President Van Buren also could have had a war over Canada. The United States had twice mounted military expeditions to conquer its Northern neighbor, first during the American Revolution and again during the War of 1812. At other times, annexation was under consideration, sometimes to the point of encouraging insurgencies similar to those that helped swallow up Florida and Texas. Van Buren was in office less than a year when rebellions broke out in both Lower and Upper Canada. Americans lent support to the rebel "patriots" with recruits and provisions, and although Canadian authorities easily dispersed any organized resistance, border incidents kept anti-British feelings at fever pitch, especially in the president's home state. A raiding party of Canadian militia in December 1837 violated U.S. territory near Buffalo, New York, in order to burn a small steamship, the *Caroline*, that was transporting supplies to the rebels, killing one U.S. citizen. In retaliation, a group of Americans

---

[5]As quoted by Charles Sellers, *The Market Revolution: Jacksonian America, 1815–1846* (New York: Oxford University Press, 1991), p. 415.

[6]Both Curtis, *The Fox at Bay*, pp. 152–88, and Wilson, *The Presidency of Martin Van Buren*, pp. 147–69, provide excellent coverage of Van Buren's foreign policy. For additional details on Texas and Mexico, consult Justin H. Smith, *The War with Mexico*, 2 vols. (New York: Macmillan, 1919); Smith, *The Annexation of Texas*, corrected ed. (New York: Barnes and Noble, 1941); Frederick W. Merk, *Slavery and the Annexation of Texas* (New York: Alfred A. Knopf, 1972); David M. Pletcher, *The Diplomacy of Annexation: Texas, Oregon, and the Mexican War* (Columbia: University of Missouri Press, 1973); and Jennifer Roback Morse, "Constitutional Rules, Political Accidents, and the Course of History: New Light on the Annexation of Texas," *Independent Review* 2 (Fall 1997): 173–200.

boarded and burned the Canadian steamer, *Sir Robert Peel*, on the St. Lawrence in May 1838.

Any one of these incidents might have led to a declaration of war, had Washington and London wanted a fight. The president responded to the crisis by issuing two strong proclamations of neutrality, by calling out the militias of New York and Vermont to enforce the proclamations, and by sending General Winfield Scott on a mediatory mission. Scott was a member of the opposition Whig Party but a loyal subordinate. A giant man, he traveled up and down the eight hundred-mile frontier in full dress uniform using little more than his personal influence to calm inflamed passions.

No sooner had the one crisis subsided than another, even more dangerous one flared up. The boundary between Maine and New Brunswick since 1783 had left twelve thousand square miles in dispute. Canadian lumberjacks took up timber operations in the disputed region along the Aroostook River during the winter of 1838–1839. When the Canadians refused an order of the Maine legislature to leave, the state militia marched to the river and nervously faced New Brunswick troops in a confrontation that became known as the Aroostook War. Democratic Governor John Fairfield of Maine warned Van Buren that "should you go *against* us upon this occasion—or not espouse our cause with *warmth* and *earnestness* and with a true *American feeling*, God only knows what the result will be *politically*."[7] Realizing that a single diplomatic misstep could cause tensions in either country to erupt into bloodshed, the president emphatically supported Maine's claim but warned Governor Fairfield that the federal government would not tolerate the state unilaterally drawing it into open hostilities. As Congress authorized fifty thousand volunteers, extended militia drafts from three to six months, and appropriated $10 million for war, Van Buren again dispatched General Scott to the trouble spot. Together they negotiated a truce in which both sides withdrew their forces in March 1839.[8]

---

[7]As quoted in Curtis, *The Fox at Bay*, p. 185.

[8]Again, Curtis and Wilson are fine accounts of Van Buren's diplomacy. Albert B. Corey's older work on *The Crisis of 1830–1842 in Canadian-American Relations* (New Haven, Conn.: Yale University Press, 1941) can be somewhat unreliable on Van Buren's role. The best treatment of the disputes with Canada is Howard Jones, *To the Webster–Ashburton Treaty: A*

None of the outstanding issues between the United States and Canada had been resolved fully when the New Yorker stepped down in 1841. The Maine boundary was still unsettled, the United States was still demanding an apology for the *Caroline* incident, and the British government was vigorously protesting New York state's murder trial of a Canadian deputy sheriff, Alexander McLeod, for his participation in the *Caroline* raid. Nonetheless, the Little Magician's astute and unruffled diplomacy had preserved the peace, leaving final settlements to a future administration. In this case, President Tyler followed Van Buren's lead by negotiating the Webster–Ashburton Treaty of 1842 with Britain, bringing all major questions to a mutually satisfactory conclusion. What makes President Van Buren's peaceable determination all the more exemplary was its political cost. During his reelection bid in 1840, Whig victories in the normally Democratic northern tier of New York counties cost him that state, and it was the only time the Whig Party ever carried Maine and Michigan in a presidential race. Indeed, a few of the Red Fox's closest political advisers had privately urged him to start a foreign war in order to distract public attention from the administration's domestic difficulties.[9]

II

With respect to domestic policies, Martin Van Buren would have been quite pleased to let his time in office become a placid addendum to the tumultuous eight years of President Jackson. One historian, Major L. Wilson, has characterized Van Buren's inaugural address as "essentially a charter for inaction."[10] It

---

Study in Anglo-American Relations, 1783–1843 (Chapel Hill: University of North Carolina Press, 1977). Also helpful are Henry S. Burrage, *Maine in the Northeastern Boundary Controversy* (Portland, Me.: Marks, 1919), pp. 231–311; Charles Winslow Elliott, *Winfield Scott: The Soldier and the Man* (New York: Macmillan, 1937), pp. 335–44, 356–66; Oscar A. Kinchen, *The Rise and Fall of the Patriot Hunters* (New York: Bookman Associates, 1956); John S.D. Eisenhower, *Agent of Destiny: The Life and Times of General Winfield Scott* (New York: Free Press, 1997), pp. 176–83, 195–203; and Kenneth R. Stevens, *Border Diplomacy: The* Caroline *and* McLeod *Affairs in Anglo-American Relations, 1837–1842* (Tuscaloosa: University of Alabama Press, 1989).

[9]Wilson, *The Presidency of Martin Van Buren*, pp. 100, 145.

[10]Ibid., p. 39.

contained nothing more innovative than calls for "strict adherence to the letter and spirit of the Constitution" and for "friendship of all nations as the condition most compatible with our welfare and the principles of our Government."[11] But fate ironically intervened. Only two months after the inauguration, a major financial panic engulfed the country's eight hundred banks, forcing all but six to cease redeeming their bank notes and deposits for specie (gold or silver coins).

The preceding Jackson presidency had slowly and painfully brought ideological definition to the Democratic Party. Van Buren, for instance, had persuaded Old Hickory to veto appropriations for the Maysville Road, eventually making opposition to nationally-funded internal improvements part of the Democratic canon. Although the Little Magician once had supported protective tariffs in an effort to enlist Northern votes for Jackson's election, whereas the General himself had been evasive, the nullification crisis put the Democracy solidly behind tariff reduction. But the controversy that came to eclipse all others in drawing new party lines was the "Bank War." The hardening disposition of President Jackson and his western advisers against a nationally-chartered bank escalated from Jackson's resounding veto of the bill to recharter the Second Bank of the United States in 1832 into a crusade to destroy what they called "the Monster." The Treasury gradually transferred its sizeable deposits from the Second Bank into an assorted group of state-chartered banks, and then in July 1836, Old Hickory issued a "Specie Circular," requiring payment for public land in only gold or silver, rather than bank notes.

By the time of Van Buren's elevation to the White House, hostility to any new national bank unified all Democrats. Within this consensus, however, two factions had arisen. The less numerous but more radical group, epitomized by Senator Thomas Hart Benton of Missouri and the Locofoco contingent of New York City Democrats, advocated a complete "divorce" of the national government from dealings with all banks in an effort to promote hard money. The majority, led by Senators Nathaniel P. Tallmadge of New York and William C. Rives of Virginia, who would soon style themselves "conservatives," believed that the

[11]James D. Richardson, ed., *A Compilation of the Messages and Papers of the Presidents* (New York: Bureau of National Literature, 1922), vol. 2, pp. 1536–37.

"credit system" promoted economic growth and wanted to maintain the intimate relationship between the government and state-chartered deposit banks. They had gone so far as to join with the opposition in Congress to repeal Jackson's Specie Circular, only to have the general pocket veto the bill.

Van Buren at first tried to reconcile the two factions, as befit his personality and past record. On the one hand, when serving in the New York legislature, he had voted against all bank charters, save one for war-ravaged Buffalo, and as early as 1817, he had advocated throwing banking open to unrestricted competition, a radical proposal two decades ahead of its time. On the other hand, as the Empire State's governor in 1829, he had sponsored creation of the Safety Fund, a system of government-mandated bank note insurance. The panic of 1837, however, pushed the Little Magician, along with many other wavering members of his party, unequivocally into the radical camp. If the national government did not sever its relationship with the suspended state banks—with their unredeemable, depreciating paper currency—then it would be in the same position as at the close of the War of 1812, when financial chaos had provided the impetus for chartering the Second Bank.

Holding firm against mounting pressure to revoke the Specie Circular, the president called an emergency session of Congress to convene at the beginning of September 1837. His message to this first special legislative session since the presidency of James Madison was a bold and acute program to meet the depression with government retrenchment. "All communities are apt to look to government for too much," warned Van Buren. "Even in our own country, where its powers and duties are so strictly limited, we are prone to do so, especially at periods of sudden embarrassment and distress."[12] To yield to this temptation, however, would be a mistake, because "[a]ll former attempts on the part of the Government" to "assume the management of domestic or foreign exchange" had in his opinion "proved injurious." What was needed was a "system founded on private interest, enterprise, and competition, without the aid of legislative grants or regulations by law,"[13] one that embodied the Jeffersonian maxim "that the less government interferes with private pursuits the better for the general prosperity." The president

[12]Ibid., p. 1561.
[13]Ibid., p. 1547.

therefore refrained "from suggesting to Congress any specific plan for regulating the exchanges of the country, relieving mercantile embarrassments, or interfering with the ordinary operation of foreign or domestic commerce," because "their adoption would not promote the real and permanent welfare of those they might be designed to aid."[14]

Daniel Webster, Whig senator from Massachusetts, denounced the president's message for "leaving the people to shift for themselves."[15] The lone exception to Van Buren's rejection of government activism was a proposal for a new bankruptcy law that would allow the national government to shut down any bank that too long suspended specie payments. The Twenty-fifth Congress refused even to consider this measure. But it quickly enacted the president's suggestion of granting importers a six-month moratorium on payment of customhouse bonds. What makes this tax relief significant is the fact that tariffs were the national government's only source of revenue at the time, outside of the sale of public lands. Of still greater import was the legislature's willingness to go along with Van Buren's insistence on halting distribution of federal money to the state governments. Senator Henry Clay of Kentucky and his neo-Hamiltonian Whigs had saddled the previous administration with this nineteenth-century version of modern revenue sharing after the national debt had been paid off for the first and only time in American history. General Jackson, "with a repugnance of feeling and a recoil of judgment" according to "Old

---

[14]Ibid., pp. 1561–62. Van Buren also discussed the causes of the panic, in probably the most economically sophisticated presidential address ever penned. His explanation combined a rudimentary version of the Austrian trade cycle theory and a discerning presentation of the real-bills doctrine, along with an emphasis on the international factors that cliometricians have recently demonstrated to be decisive. On top of all that, the message made an objection to a national bank that remains still unanswered:

> In Great Britain where it has been seen the same causes have been attended with the same effects, a national bank possessing powers far greater than are asked for by the warmest advocates of such an institution here has also proved unable to prevent an undue expansion of credit and the evils that flow from it. (pp. 1545–46)

[15]*Congressional Globe*, 25th Cong., 2nd sess. (January 31,1838) app. p. 606.

Bullion" Benton, had signed off on the distribution of the surplus because John C. Calhoun had incorporated it into a bill regulating the Treasury's dealings with the deposit banks.[16] But
after the panic, federal revenues declined, and there was no
longer any surplus revenue to hand out. Along with ending distribution, Congress accepted Van Buren's preference to finance
the reappearing national debt with $10 million worth of short-
term Treasury notes rather than long-term loans.

But the centerpiece of the Little Magician's special message
was his courageous call for a total separation of bank and state
through an Independent Treasury. The Independent Treasury
was an idea that could assume several forms and accommodate
differing views on currency and banking, but its most fundamental requirement was that the government hold all monetary
balances in the form of specie, rather than bank notes or
deposits. Either existing Treasury officials or newly established
subtreasuries could serve this function. Some versions
restricted to specie all payments received by the government as
well, whereas others let the Treasury accept notes from specie-
paying banks so long as they were speedily redeemed or paid
back out. Such ultra-bullionists as Senator Benton hoped that

---

[16]Thomas Hart Benton, *Thirty Years' View: Or a History of the Working of the
American Government for Thirty Years, From 1820 to 1850* (New York: D.
Appleton, 1854–56), vol. 1, p. 657. Calhoun's role in putting distribution
into the Deposit–Distribution Act of 1836 is revealed in John M. McFaul, *The
Politics of Jacksonian Finance* (Ithaca, N.Y.: Cornell University Press, 1972),
pp. 132–34, and Charles M. Wiltse, *John C. Calhoun: Nullifier, 1829–1839*
(Indianapolis, Ind.: Bobbs-Merrill, 1949), vol. 2, pp. 257–58, 265–67.
Although Jackson himself had earlier toyed with the idea of distribution, his
preferred plan was to eliminate the surplus by reducing tariffs and land prices,
whereas the Democrats in Congress had proposed investing the surplus in
state bonds. See Robert V. Remini, *Andrew Jackson and the Course of American
Democracy, 1833–1845* (New York: Harper and Row, 1984), pp. 322–25;
Charles Grier Sellers, Jr., *James K. Polk: Jacksonian, 1795–1843* (Princeton,
N.J.: Princeton University Press, 1957), pp. 223–33; Edward G. Bourne, *The
History of the Surplus Revenue of 1837: Being an Account of Its Origin, Its Dis-
tribution Among the States, and the Uses to Which It Was Applied* (New York:
G.P. Putnam's Sons, 1885); and Richard H. Timberlake, Jr., "The Specie Cir-
cular and Distribution of the Surplus," *Journal of Political Economy* 68 (April
1960): 109–17, which was revised and reprinted as chap. 5 of Timberlake,
Monetary Policy in the United States: An Intellectual and Institutional History
(Chicago: University of Chicago Press, 1993).

the Independent Treasury, by eliminating government support for bank notes, would ultimately drive them out of circulation and return the entire economy to an exclusive hard-money currency. Supporters of unregulated banking, among them Dr. John Brockenbrough, president of the Bank of Virginia, realized that the national government's finances were too small relative to the economy to effect this result and hoped in contrast that a divorce would be good for the state banks. Still others, including Secretary of the Treasury Levi Woodbury of New Hampshire, wanted to supplement the Independent Treasury with some federal regulation of banking, such as restrictions on bank notes of small denominations. And some proponents went so far as Senator James Buchanan of Pennsylvania in favoring a government-issued paper money, anticipating the Greenbacks and gold certificates of the Civil War.[17]

Administration spokesman Silas Wright of New York introduced into the Senate an Independent Treasury bill that simply assigned the keeping of funds to existing officials and was silent on how payments could be made. Calhoun then startled members of both parties with another one of his sudden but inept political reversals. Abandoning his Whig allies, he announced his support for the administration initiative. Calhoun, however, wanted to modify it by turning Treasury notes into a permanent government currency and by phasing in over four years a requirement that the Treasury Department accept only specie or

---

[17]Wilson, *The Presidency of Martin Van Buren*, offers the most complete (indeed almost the only) discussion of the alternative versions of the Independent Treasury and the differing views of its supporters. Schlesinger's *The Age of Jackson*, pp. 227–29, is still one of the best accounts of the intellectual origins of this idea, but also see Joseph Dorfman, *The Economic Mind in American Civilization, 1606–1865* (New York: Viking Press, 1946), pp. 610–14. The Jacksonian hard-money theoretician, William M. Gouge, first proposed it in *A Short History of Paper Money and Banking in the United States*, (Philadelphia: T.W. Ustick, 1833). In 1834 Philadelphia economist Condy Raguet tried to interest members of Congress in the proposal, and Congressman William Fitzhugh Gordon of Virginia, a former democrat who had followed Calhoun out of the party, aired the idea in the House. Meanwhile Jackson's acting secretary of the treasury, Roger B. Taney, hired Gouge as a clerk in the department. Thus Calhoun's claim, endorsed by his biographer, Charles M. Wiltse in *John C. Calhoun*, vol. 2, pp. 343–61, that it was the Nullifier who prompted Van Buren into pushing the Independent Treasury is ludicrous.

its own notes. Since a specie-requirement was already implicit in Van Buren's message, the administration had to accept this amendment. Although the widespread bank suspensions had tended to discredit state banks as government depositories, Calhoun's amendment now stiffened the opposition of Conservative Democrats to the divorce bill. Nor did it help when the Calhounites portrayed divorce as a sectional issue that would free the South from Northern capital, linking the question to the interminable debates over abolitionist petitions that were preoccupying Congress at the time. The amended divorce bill passed the Senate by two votes, but it was tabled in the House. In later sessions, when the administration reluctantly dropped the specie requirement in order to pick up Conservative votes, the Nullifier turned against the measure.

Yet de facto the Treasury was already independent. The Currency Resolution of 1816 forbade the government to receive bank notes not redeemable in specie, another law forbade paying them out, and the Deposit–Distribution Act of 1836 did not permit the Treasury to hold funds in any suspended bank. The president ordered federal officials to comply with these regulations as far as possible, which meant that, with the exception of the balance in deposits tied up at the time of the panic, the Treasury was only receiving, holding, and paying out either specie or Treasury notes. Once the banks resumed specie payments in May 1838, most of them still could not qualify as depositories under the Deposit Act's restrictions because during the suspension they had issued small-denomination notes. Frustrated at Congressional obstinacy, Van Buren considered emulating Old Hickory's high-handedness by establishing an Independent Treasury through executive order, but such a violation of legislative prerogatives suited neither his temperament nor his philosophy.

The depression meanwhile politically hurt the administration. Elections in the fall of 1837 turned against the Democrats in many states, particularly New York, where the Whigs gained an overwhelming majority in the state legislature's lower house by winning a stunning sixty-seven seats. The "New York tornado," as the shocked Van Buren called it, was followed a year later by the capture of the Empire State's governorship by Whig candidate William H. Seward. The combination of Whigs and Conservative Democrats in the Twenty-fifth Congress continued to block enactment of the Independent Treasury throughout much of the eighth president's term. Despite favorable votes in the Senate, the House of Representatives voted against a divorce bill during the first regular session in 1837–1838 and refused to vote on it at all during the second regular session of 1838–1839. The legislators were far more interested in a scandal that the Treasury had just uncovered in the New York City Customs House. The collector, Samuel Swartwout, had allegedly embezzled over the previous eight years the astonishing sum of $1.23 million and then fled to Europe. Even though Swartwout was an old Jackson appointee to whom Van Buren had vigorously objected, and moreover a former Calhoun favorite who was now a Whig, the Democratic administration was put on the defensive.[18]

Van Buren nonetheless scored some unheralded successes. After bank resumption in 1838, administration stalwarts in Congress defanged a new Whig–Conservative effort to revoke the Specie Circular by converting it into an act that merely made it unlawful to treat receipts from public land differently than other revenue. The secretary of the Treasury thereby gained the discretionary authority to accept only specie for all payments or also bank notes for all payments. The divorce bills furthermore had shifted the terms of the debate and forestalled any proposal for a new national bank. The Little Magician had instead maneuvered Clay and the Whigs into a political defense of the same "pet" bank system they had so vociferously denounced during Jackson's presidency. He also had achieved an uneasy reconciliation with Calhoun and a few other states'-rights Southerners, whom the autocratic Jackson had driven out of the Democratic camp. Finally, the Conservative insurgency, if not smoothed over, was at least contained. Failing to gain dominance within democratic councils, conservatives faced the alternatives of either following their prominent leaders Tallmadge and Rives into the Whig Party or of again submitting to their own party's discipline. One indication of increasing Conservative isolation was the editorial shift of the New York democracy's official newspaper, the *Albany Argus*. It went from lukewarm about the Independent Treasury to a ringing announcement in June 1838

---

[18]For a revisionist defense that asserts the amount that the New York collector owed was only $200,000, exactly as much as he admitted to, see B.R. Brunson, *The Adventures of Samuel Swartwout in the Age of Jefferson and Jackson* (Lewiston, N.Y.: Edwin Mellen Press, 1989).

that "[w]e believe the time has emphatically come for the separation of bank and state."[19]

Van Buren's refusal to abandon the goal of divorce ultimately paid off as the political tide turned in late 1839. When a second suspension of specie payments spread to half the country's banks that October, it seemed to verify the administration's suspicion of state depositories. The Democrats managed to retain control of both houses of the Twenty-sixth Congress, which met for its first session in December. The president's annual message renewed the call for an Independent Treasury, reinforced with new arguments. The latest suspension was more obviously the result of international factors than had been the panic of 1837, which had coincided with all the confusing policy changes of Jackson's Bank War. Van Buren now argued that only divorce could free the U.S. economy from "this chain of dependence" on credit flows of "the money power in Great Britain." The message also dampened the laissez-faire tone of Van Buren's earlier message to the special session and accentuated its hard-money radicalism with a willingness to consider "additional legislation, or, if that be inadequate . . . such further constitutional grants or restrictions" that might check "excessive note issues."[20]

Fortunately the legislators voted down both a bankruptcy bill, similar to the one the president had suggested in his earlier message, and Senator Buchanan's proposed constitutional

---

[19]Wilson, *The Presidency of Martin Van Buren*, p. 113.

[20]Richardson, ed., *Messages and Papers of the Presidents*, vol. 3, pp. 1762, 1766, 1769. Congress had already enacted a series of Jackson administration proposals designed to promote hard money: (1) an 1834 change in the mint ratio to encourage the circulation of gold coins; (2) an 1835 expansion of the United States Mint; (3) a renewal of the legal-tender status of foreign coins; and (4) a phased-in prohibition in the Deposit–Distribution Act of 1836 against the issue of small bank notes by government depositories, which replaced prohibitions the secretary of the Treasury had already administratively imposed. See David A. Martin, "Metallism, Small Notes, and Jackson's War With the B.U.S.," *Explorations in Economic History* 11 (Spring 1974): 227–47. The hostility to small bank notes dated back to Adam Smith, it was not confined to hard-money advocates, and it was implemented by many state statutes. It was, however, at cross purposes with the new mint ratio, which tended after the California gold discoveries to drive silver coins out of circulation. Since silver coins were more suitable for small transactions, the interaction of the mint ratio with prohibitions on small notes created a shortage of cash in small denominations.

amendment authorizing Congress to ban bank notes of less than $20. The tireless Senator Wright again introduced a divorce bill in the Senate, this version including both special subtreasuries to hold government funds and Calhoun's specie requirement for receiving payments. The bill sailed through the Senate at the end of January 1840, but the House, experiencing more than its usual disorder and delay over disputed seats and choice of speaker, did not pass the measure until June. Van Buren waited until July 4, 1840, to sign the law, symbolically confirming the words of *The Washington Globe*, the administration's mouthpiece, which nearly three years earlier had hailed the Independent Treasury as "the second declaration of independence."[21]

III

The Independent Treasury ushered in an era of financial deregulation at the national level. Although repealed in 1841, after the Whigs captured the White House, they could not agree among themselves about an alternative. President William Henry Harrison died after less than a month in office and was succeeded by Vice President John Tyler, an apostate Democrat. Tyler vetoed Henry Clay's two bank bills, leaving the government's deposit system unregulated by law. Use of state banks remained at the secretary of the treasury's discretion until President James Knox Polk, a doctrinaire Jacksonian who enthusiastically embraced the fiscal heritage of Martin Van Buren, secured reenactment of what he preferred to call a Constitutional Treasury in August 1846. The act of 1846 was identical in substance to that of 1841 and determined the country's financial regime until the outbreak of the Civil War.

Laissez-faire may not have been the intent of all those who supported the divorce of bank and government. And perhaps a more efficient way to attain that goal would have been to freely

---

Timberlake, *Monetary Policy in the United States*, chap. 9, is the only economist to seriously examine this problem. The Coinage Act of 1853 subsequently tried to rectify the deficiency by authorizing subsidiary silver coins, but the economy still relied heavily on private alternatives. Details are in Neil Carothers, *Fractional Money: A History of the Small Coins and Fractional Paper Currency of the United States* (New York: John Wiley and Sons, 1930).

[21]*Washington Globe* (September 5, 1837), as quoted in Schlesinger, *The Age of Jackson*, p. 236.

charter competitors with the Second Bank, with equal powers of interstate branching, rather than abolishing that institution altogether. Nonetheless, laissez-faire was the Independent Treasury's primary consequence. There was no nationally chartered bank, the Treasury for the most part avoided dealing with the many state-chartered banks, and the only legally recognized money was gold and silver coins. Because the economy's currency consisted solely of bank notes redeemable in specie on demand, private competition regulated the circulation of paper money.

Although traditional historians have subjected this era of relatively unregulated banking to trumped-up charges of financial instability, many economists are coming to agree that it was probably the best monetary system the United States has ever had. The alleged excesses of the fraudulent, insolvent, or highly speculative "wildcat" banks were highly exaggerated. Total losses that bank note holders suffered from 1836 to 1861 in all the states that enacted free-banking laws would not equal the losses for one year from an inflation of 2 percent, if superimposed onto the economy of 1860. Moreover, most of these losses resulted from too much regulation, not too little. Lingering at the state level were prohibitions on branch banking, mandates for minimum specie reserves, restrictions on the issue of small-denomination bank notes, and requirements that banks purchase state bonds, which at this time were among the most dubious investments. The banks were also still vulnerable to international flows of specie. No monetary system is perfect. But by any objective comparison, this one was relatively stable and crisis-free.[22]

---

[22]The standard condemnation of the free-banking era is most readily accessible in Bray Hammond, *Banks and Politics in America: From the Revolution to the Civil War* (Princeton, N.J.: Princeton University Press, 1957). Subsequent research has so thoroughly overturned everything Hammond had to say about the politics of banking, and modern economic and financial theory has so thoroughly outdated all of his theoretical analysis, that it is astonishing that scholars still take this work seriously. The revisionist research on free banking has been spread mainly through journal articles, and three summaries are Larry J. Sechrest, *Free Banking: Theory, History, and a Laissez-Faire Model* (Westport, Conn.: Quorum Books, 1993), chap. 6; Kevin Dowd, "U.S. Banking in the 'Free Banking' Period," in Dowd, ed., *The Experience of Free Banking* (London: Routledge, 1992); and Hugh Rockoff, "Lessons from the American Experience with Free Banking," in *Unregulated Banking: Chaos or Order*, Forrest Capie and Geoffrey E. Woods, eds. (New

Those historians who dismiss the Independent Treasury as constraining the government "to accept payments and to make them in an antiquated medium" more "suitable for the War of the Roses" have never adequately explained the relative quiescence of monetary debates during its operation.[23] The First and Second U.S. Banks had divided political parties since the adoption of the Constitution. The Civil War's national banking system and Greenbacks subsequently induced fresh convulsions over currency questions. If the Independent Treasury was in fact so obviously deficient, why did it provoke no similar political outcry? Moreover, its reenactment coincided with heavy expenditures for Polk's war against Mexico, yet that military effort caused the economy less financial dislocation than any previous American war. During the nation's next financial panic in 1857, the Treasury was effectively insulated from the bank suspension. There is also no evidence that the Independent Treasury hobbled the country's economic growth.[24]

York: St. Martin's Press, 1991). Most contributions to this revision are either by Hugh Rockoff—"Money, Prices and Banks in the Jacksonian Era," in *The Reinterpretation of American Economic History*, Robert W. Fogel and Stanley L. Engerman, eds. (New York: Harper and Row, 1971), pp. 448–58; "American Free Banking Before the Civil War: A Reexamination," *Journal of Economic History* 32 (March 1972): 417–20; "New Evidence on Free Banking in the United States," *American Economic Review* 75 (September 1985): 886–89; and "The Free Banking Era: A Reexamination," *Journal of Money, Credit and Banking* 6 (May 1974): 141–67—or by Arthur J. Rolnick and Warren E. Weber, "Free Banking, Wildcat Banking, and Shinplasters," *Federal Reserve Bank of Minneapolis Quarterly Review* (Fall 1982): 10–19; "New Evidence on the Free Banking Era," *American Economic Review* 73 (December 1983): 1080–91; "The Causes of Free Bank Failures: A Detailed Examination," *Journal of Monetary Economics* 14 (November 1984): 267–91; "Banking Instability and Regulation in the U.S. Free Banking Era," *Federal Reserve Bank of Minneapolis Quarterly Review* (Summer 1985): 2–9; and "Explaining the Demand for Free Bank Notes," *Journal of Monetary Economics* 21 (Winter 1986): 877–90.

[23]Bray Hammond, *Sovereignty and an Empty Purse: Banks and Politics in the Civil War* (Princeton, N.J.: Princeton University Press, 1970), pp. 23, 24.

[24]Works on the operation of the Independent Treasury include David Kinley, *The History, Organization, and Influence of the Independent Treasury of the United States* (New York: Thomas Y. Crowell, 1893); John Burton Phillips, "Methods of Keeping the Public Money of the United States," in *Publications of the Michigan Political Science Association* 4, no. 3; Ester Rogoff Taus, *Central Banking Functions of the United States Treasury, 1789–1941* (New York:

The domestic policies of the Van Buren presidency, however, did more than bequeath a superior financial regime. They also thwarted all attempts to use economic depression as an excuse for expanding government's role. Prior to the panic of 1837, state governments—in an uncanny parallel to the recent currency crises in east Asia and Russia—had borrowed more than $100 million from abroad to finance lavish and wasteful internal improvements. Most states experienced financial stringency as a result of the panic, and many became desperate. By 1844, $60 million worth of state bonds were in default. Three states—Arkansas, Michigan, and Mississippi—as well as the Florida territory repudiated their debts outright.[25] Henry Clay saw this as a heaven-sent opportunity to revive his distribution scheme under a new pretext. The Whigs of the Twenty-sixth Congress hence advocated that the national government bail out the states by assuming their debts. Clay's party also had its own proposal for a bankruptcy law—not like Van Buren's that would close banks involuntarily, but rather one that would allow individual debtors voluntarily to escape their obligations.

Democrats under the Little Magician's leadership not only blocked these initiatives but pushed government involvement in the opposite direction. Although total national expenditures suddenly spiked to $37.2 million in 1837, overall they declined through Van Buren's four years, from $30.9 million in 1836 to $24.3 million in 1840. That represents a 21 percent fall in nominal terms, no more than half as much if you adjust for price

---

Russell and Russell, 1943); and Richard H. Timberlake, Jr., "The Independent Treasury and Monetary Policy before the Civil War," *Southern Economic Journal* 27 (October 1960): 92–103. (The Timberlake article is reprinted as chap. 6 in his *Monetary Policy in the United States*.) Subtreasury vaults for holding government funds formally lingered on until 1921, when the Federal Reserve System superseded them, but none of the motivating hard-money features remained. The Civil War's national banking system and Greenbacks had eviscerated the Independent Treasury.

[25]B.U. Ratchford, *American State Debts* (Durham, N.C.: Duke University Press, 1941), pp. 77–134; Reginald Charles McGrane, *Foreign Bondholders and American State Debts* (New York: Macmillan, 1935); and William A. Scott, *The Repudiation of State Debts: A Study in the Financial History of Mississippi, Florida, Alabama, North Carolina, South Carolina, Georgia, Louisiana, Arkansas, Tennessee, Minnesota, Michigan, and Virginia* (New York: Thomas Y. Crowell, 1893).

changes, but somewhere in between if you also adjust for population growth or the economy's size.[26] Many of these spending cuts came in the realm of internal improvements, especially for rivers and harbors, where Van Buren was far more stringent than Old Hickory had been.[27] As for revenue, tariff rates were already falling as a result of programmed reductions worked out during the compromise over nullification. So the president threw his weight behind two measures that would bring the allocation of public land into closer alignment with the homestead principle: preemption, giving settlers who cultivated the land first option to buy; and graduation, reducing the price on unsold land. Graduation failed to pass, but Congress renewed earlier preemption acts twice during Van Buren's term.[28] At the end of the four years, with significant cuts in both national spending and revenue, the depression-generated debt was holding near $5 million.[29]

[26]U.S. Department of Commerce, *Historical Statistics of the United States: Colonial Times to 1970* (Washington, D.C.: U.S. Government Printing Office, 1975), pt. 2, Series Y335–38.

[27]Speech of Congressman J.A. Rockwell of Connecticut, *Congressional Globe*, 30th Cong., 1st Sess. (January 11, 1848) app. p. 106; "Appropriations and Expenditures for Public Buildings, Rivers and Harbors, Forts, Arsenals, Armories, and Other Public Works from March 4, 1789, to June 30, 1882," 47th Cong., 1st Sess (1881–82), Senate Executive Documents, no. 196, pp. 114, 286, 340, 521, 529.

[28]Daniel Feller, *The Public Lands in Jacksonian Politics* (Madison: University of Wisconsin Press, 1984), which supersedes both George M. Stephenson, *The Political History of Public Lands from 1840 to 1862: From Pre-Emption to Homestead* (Boston: Richard G. Badger, 1917), and Raynor G. Wellington, *The Political and Sectional Influence of the Public Lands, 1828–1842* (Cambridge, Mass.: Riverside Press, 1914). Congress had passed the first preemption act in 1830, but it was retrospective, applying to past squatters on government land, and so required periodic renewal.

[29]Van Buren, in December 1840 after his defeat for reelection, summarized what he felt were his administration's accomplishments. His fourth annual message to Congress listed "two-contested points in our public policy" that had dominated his term: "I allude to a national debt and a national bank. . . . Coming into office the declared enemy of both, I have earnestly endeavored to prevent a resort to either." Unwilling to raise taxes to balance the budget, Van Buren could claim: "The small amount of Treasury notes . . . still outstanding" is less "than the United States have in deposit with the States." Van Buren is here referring to the $28 million distributed to the states, technically in the form of a loan, by the Deposit–Distribution

Closer examination of the economy's fluctuations reveals the enormous benefits of this retrenchment. The two banking crises that dominated the Van Buren administration had similar causes but different outcomes. In both cases, the proximate cause was a decline in foreign inflows of specie precipitated when the Bank of England raised its discount rate. The panic of 1837, however, was a sharp and short correction that followed right on the heels of two years of price inflation at an annual rate approaching 15 percent. After wholesale prices fell back nearly 20 percent over a year, and output less than 5 percent, the economy seemed to recover. The suspension of 1839, in contrast, hit fewer banks but foreshadowed a protracted deflation. The country's total money stock—specie, banknotes, and bank deposits—declined by one-third during the next four years, and prices plummeted 42 percent.[30]

Act of 1836. Richardson, ed., *Messages and Papers of the Presidents*, vol. 3, pp. 1828 and 1824.

[30]The best overall treatment of these economic fluctuations and their causes is Peter Temin, *The Jacksonian Economy* (New York: W.W. Norton, 1969). But also consult chap. 5 of Timberlake, *Monetary Policy in the United States*. Together Timberlake and Temin have demolished the traditional view that Jackson's Specie Circular brought on the banking crisis of 1837. As Timberlake concludes (p. 61), "[T]he Specie Circular was dramatic but inconsequential." However, Temin inexplicably rejects Timberlake's persuasive case that Clay's distribution of the surplus was a major contributing factor to the earlier panic. Additional details are in Reginald Charles McGrane, *The Panic of 1837: Some Financial Problems of the Jacksonian Era* (Chicago: University of Chicago Press, 1924); Walter Buckingham Smith and Arthur Harrison Cole, *Fluctuations in American Business, 1790–1860* (Cambridge, Mass.: Harvard University Press, 1935); Samuel Rezneck, "The Social History of an American Depression, 1837–1843," *American Historical Review* 40 (July 1935): 662–87 (reprinted as chap. 4 of Rezneck, *Business Depressions and Financial Panics: Essays in American Business and Economic History* [New York: Greenwood, 1968]); George Macesich, "Sources of Monetary Disturbances in the U.S., 1834–1845," *Journal of Economic History* 20 (September 1960): 407–34; and Rockoff "Money, Prices, and Banks in the Jacksonian Era." Although there are crude consumer price indices dating back to this period, I have followed Temin and other authorities in quoting the more reliable and extensive wholesale price indices. Presumably consumer prices would show less amplitude in their fluctuations. Non-economists tend automatically to assume that because the price decline was more severe after the suspension of 1839 than after

Many economists have been struck by the comparison between this second episode, the deflation of 1839–1843, and the subsequent Great Depression of 1929–1933. Qualifying as the two most massive monetary contractions in American history, they were of identical magnitude and extended over the same length of time. But there the similarities end. During the Great Depression, as unemployment peaked at 25 percent of the labor force in 1933, U.S. production of goods and services collapsed by 30 percent. During the earlier nineteenth-century contraction, investment fell, but amazingly the economy's total output did not. Quite the opposite; it actually rose between 6 percent and 16 percent. This was nearly a full-employment deflation. Nor are economists at any loss to account for this widely disparate performance. The American economy of the 1930s was characterized by prices, especially wages, that were rigid downward, whereas in the 1840s, prices could fall fast and far enough to quickly restore market equilibrium.[31]

But why were prices and wages so much more flexible when Van Buren was at the helm? The fact that the Great Depression, America's deepest and longest economic downturn, was also the first to be met with a comprehensive program of federal intervention offers some hint. Intervention commenced, furthermore, not with the well-known New Deal of President Franklin D.

1837 that the resulting depression must also have been more severe. As we shall see, the evidence does not support this conclusion.

[31]Most of this comparison is drawn from Temin, *The Jacksonian Economy*, p. 157. His table shows the money stock falling by 27 percent during the Great Depression, but that is because he is looking at M1. If he had used M2 instead, which is more consistent with his nineteenth-century definition of the money stock, the two monetary contractions are of almost identical magnitudes. To get the 16 percent increase in output for 1839–1843, Temin relies on Robert E. Gallman's unpublished annual estimates of U.S. GDP. Thomas Senior Berry offers less satisfactory estimates in *Production and Population Since 1789: Revised GNP Series in Constant Dollars* (Richmond, Va.: Bostwick Press, 1988), which yield only a 6 percent rise in output over the four years. Others who have noted similarities between the two episodes include Milton Friedman and Anna Jacobson Schwartz, *A Monetary History of the United States, 1867–1960* (Princeton, N.J.: Princeton University Press, 1963), p. 299; Douglass C. North, *The Economic Growth of the United States, 1790–1860* (New York: Prentice Hall, 1961), p. 202; and Hammond, *Banks and Politics in America*, p. 529. Hammond as usual misinterprets the evidence and draws the wrong conclusion.

Roosevelt, who did not enter office until early 1933 when the economy was almost at rock bottom, but with his predecessor, Herbert C. Hoover. This progressive Republican's long tenure during the 1920s as secretary of commerce, promoting trade associations, product standardization, and business cartels, prepared him to meet the stock-market crash of October 1929 with a vigorous effort to stop any fall of prices. Starting with a series of White House conferences jawboning business leaders into "voluntarily" holding up wage rates, Hoover pressed with mixed results for further cartelization in agriculture, in the cotton textile industry, in commercial aviation, and in the energy industries—coal, oil, and electricity. He also signed into law in 1932 the largest peacetime tax increase in U.S. history, and practically closed the borders to foreign trade with the Smoot-Hawley Tariff of 1930, the highest in American history, in an effort to hold up prices internationally. Roosevelt's National Recovery Administration and Agricultural Adjustment Administration simply made this concerted campaign for price supports more formal.[32] Prices did indeed still drop by 31 percent from 1929 to 1933, but not nearly as much as during the deflation of the 1830s and 1840s. Although government policies may not explain fully the price rigidity of the 1930s, they explain a lot.

The Little Magician, of course, was not single-handedly responsible for preventing the earlier deflation from becoming another Great Depression. His heroic resistance to the expansion of central power received vital aid from the Democratic coalition that he had helped to forge. And given that total federal spending started at less than 2 percent of GDP in the mid 1830s, as compared with nearly twice that in the 1920s, Clay's misguided

---

[32]Hoover's contributions to price rigidity are exposed in three works by Murray Rothbard: "The Hoover Myth," in *For a New America: Essays in History and Politics from Studies on the Left, 1959–1967*, James Weinstein and David W. Eakens, eds. (New York: Vintage, 1970), pp. 162–79; "Herbert Hoover and the Myth of Laissez-Faire," in *A New History of Leviathan: Essays on the Rise of the American Corporate State*, Ronald Radosh and Murray Rothbard, eds. (New York: E.P. Dutton, 1972), pp. 111–45; and *America's Great Depression*, 5th ed. (Auburn, Ala.: Mises Institute, 2000). See also Richard K. Vedder and Lowell E. Gallaway, *Out of Work: Unemployment and Government in Twentieth-Century America*, rev. ed. (New York: New York University Press, 1997), pp. 74–111, 128–49.

recovery measures would probably not have been as economically devastating as those of Hoover and Roosevelt. Once Van
Buren's term ended, a few of Clay's measures were implemented
briefly. Congressional Whigs were able to secure President
Tyler's assent to their voluntary bankruptcy bill, to a watered-
down distribution of the proceeds from land sales to the states,
and to a tariff hike justified as a way to eliminate depression
deficits. But the distribution was abruptly ended in 1842, after
only a year, in order to secure enough legislative votes for the
tariff increase, whereas the Whigs themselves were embarrassed
into repealing the bankruptcy act in 1843 after thirty thousand
fortune-seekers had used its provisions to get out of more than
$400 million worth of debt.[33] The deflation had just about run
its course, anyway, and by 1846 the new Polk administration
had brought the tariff back down. The refusal to bail out
defaulting state governments produced a widening ripple of
salutary effects, not the least of which was making more difficult any future squandering of state money on public works
and government-owned railroads. The Red Fox of Kinderhook
thus had held the pass at the crucial time, when doing so was
politically unpopular, against powerful mercantile, financial,
and other special interests clamoring for national assistance. The
depression of 1837, more than any other factor, brought about
his overwhelming trouncing in the presidential election of 1840 at
the hands of General Harrison, hero of the battle of Tippecanoe.

IV

No politician, especially one successful enough to be elected to
the United States's highest office, can be perfect. Martin Van Buren's
most morally egregious and fiscally exorbitant compromises with
government coercion stemmed from his faithful adherence to
Andrew Jackson's ruthless program of Indian removal. Most of
the tribes of the Southwest had already gone to Oklahoma, but

---

[33]Charles Warren, *Bankruptcy in United States History* (Cambridge, Mass.:
Harvard University Press, 1935), pp. 56–85. A compromise bill, providing
for both voluntary and involuntary bankruptcy but exempting corporations (which means all state-chartered banks), passed the Senate on June 25,
1840, while Van Buren was still in office, but was rejected by the Democra-
tic-controlled House. The Whigs were only able in 1841 to pass a similar
measure with some blatant logrolling, in which Western votes for bankruptcy were bought with the promise of Eastern votes for distribution.

an assortment of Northwest tribes still awaited deportation beyond the Missouri River. More troublesome, seventeen thousand Cherokee had legally delayed eviction from their homes in North Carolina, Georgia, Tennessee, and Alabama, whereas approximately four thousand Seminoles mingled with more than one thousand blacks, many of them escaped slaves, were putting up effective military resistance in Florida. Although General Winfield Scott did his best to ensure that Cherokee removal was peaceful and humane, bad weather and inadequate appropriations turned the journey into a "Trail of Tears," in which hundreds perished before the process was completed in early 1839. The second Seminole war, having erupted in 1835 prior to Van Buren's inauguration, degenerated into a vicious and unrelenting counterinsurgency struggle that was still raging as he left office. President Tyler finally ended what had become the U.S. Army's most costly and lengthy Indian war with a proclamation in 1842 that permitted three hundred surviving Seminoles to remain in Florida on reservations, essentially the same terms that Van Buren had rejected in 1838. The war and other removals occasioned a one-half increase in the regular army's authorized size—from around eight thousand to more than twelve thousand soldiers—and a new string of forts. The most that can be said in the Little Magician's behalf is that these burdensome expenses make his success at rolling back federal expenditures all the more remarkable.[34]

Because the Seminoles harbored fugitive slaves, the Florida war was intimately intertwined with concessions that Van Buren made to slaveholders. During his first presidential bid, the Calhounite press had tried to cripple the New Yorker's candidacy

[34]Ronald N. Satz, *American Indian Policy in the Jacksonian Era* (Lincoln: University of Nebraska Press, 1975); Francis Paul Prucha, *The Sword of the Republic: The United States Army on the Frontier, 1783–1846* (New York: Macmillan, 1969), pp. 249–306; John K. Mahon, *History of the Second Seminole War, 1835–1842* (Gainesville: University of Florida Press, 1967); Grant Foreman, *Indian Removal: The Emigration of the Five Civilized Tribes of Indians* (Norman: University of Oklahoma Press, 1932). The authorized increase in the regular army took effect in July 1838, but an examination of the U.S. Department of Commerce, *Historical Statistics of the United States*, pt. 2, Series Y904-16, reveals that total army personnel had risen to 12,449 by 1837. That is because the Seminole War had already induced Congress to authorize in May 1836, while Jackson was still president, enlistment of 10,000 additional emergency troops to serve for six to twelve months.

in the South by branding him an abolitionist. Van Buren countered with an announcement that he was "the inflexible and uncompromising opponent of any attempt on the part of Congress to abolish slavery in the District of Columbia, against the wishes of the slaveholding states."[35] He also went along with various "Gag Rules" on receiving abolitionist petitions that Congress implemented between 1836 and 1844, and during the 1840 election promised to veto any antislavery restrictions Congress might place on Florida's admission to the Union. His accommodation with the peculiar institution had greatest practical impact in the case of the *Amistad*, a Spanish schooner that had fallen into the custody of a U.S. revenue cutter in 1839, after the slaves on board had successfully mutinied. The president stood ready to hand the blacks over to Spanish authorities, despite their having been illegally kidnapped from Africa. But the case became tied up in U.S. courts, and after the administration appealed, the Supreme Court in March 1841 freed the Africans.[36]

Although the Little Magician's Faustian bargain to hold together the sectional wings of a national party dedicated to frugal government was more pronounced during his presidency than either before or after, its extent should not be exaggerated. Nearly twenty years earlier Van Buren, serving in the New York legislature, had endorsed the prohibition of slavery in Missouri, as he would later support the Wilmot Proviso, barring the extension of slavery into the territories acquired from Mexico. Not only was the eighth president quite capable of disappointing slaveholder hopes for Texas annexation, but he never appeased Southerners to the lengths that a James Buchanan would endorse or a John C. Calhoun would demand. The president refused to overturn the conviction of a navy lieutenant court-martialed for excessive flogging, in spite of Southern complaints that the prosecution had relied on testimony of two

[35]As quoted by Van Buren in his first inaugural, Richardson, ed., *Messages and Papers of the Presidents*, vol. 2, p. 1535.

[36]William Lee Miller, *Arguing About Slavery: The Great Battle in the United States Congress* (New York: Alfred A. Knopf, 1996); Howard Jones, *Mutiny on the Amistad: The Saga of a Slave Revolt and Its Impact on American Abolition, Law, and Diplomacy* (New York: Oxford University Press, 1987); and Mary Cable, *Black Odyssey: The Case of the Slave Ship* Amistad (New York: Viking Press, 1971).

black seamen.[37] The New Yorker's vice-presidential running mate in both 1836 and 1840 was a Southerner, Colonel Richard M. Johnson of Kentucky, yet hardly one who made his fellow slave-holders comfortable. Johnson had violated the color line by openly living with a black mistress and acknowledging their two daughters. Such limits on Van Buren's ability to placate Southerners were reflected by the stiff presidential opposition he faced in 1836 in the South, a region that had gone solidly for Old Hickory. The Little Magician did even worse in the South in 1840 running against Harrison, an Ohioan who was Virginia-born.[38]

The Van Buren administration's readiness to return the *Amistad* mutineers was also motivated in part by diplomatic considerations. The objective of friendly relations with foreign powers was responsible for another of the president's lapses in 1837. To supplement efforts to calm tensions during the Canadian rebellions, he asked Congress for a new neutrality law. The existing act of 1818 was mainly maritime, and Van Buren wanted the power to prevent private citizens from organizing raids on foreign soil. Congress was in this instance more sensitive to civil liberties, so it declined to permit the use of military

[37]Cole, *Martin Van Buren and the American Political System*, pp. 362–63; Wilson, *The Presidency of Martin Van Buren*, p. 200.

[38]Richard H. Brown, "The Missouri Crisis, Slavery, and the Politics of Jacksonianism," *South Atlantic Quarterly* 65 (Winter 1966): 55–72, is an influential but simplistic argument that Martin Van Buren's Democracy was intentionally and unequivocally proslavery—an argument which is echoed in Leonard L. Richards, "The Jacksonians and Slavery," in *Antislavery Reconsidered: New Perspectives on the Abolitionists*, Lewis Perry and Michael Fellman, eds. (Baton Rouge: Louisiana State University Press, 1979), pp. 99–118. For more sophisticated and balanced considerations of this question, see John McFaul, "Expediency vs. Morality: Jacksonian Politics and Slavery," *Journal of American History* 62 (June 1975): 24–39; William H. Riker, *Liberalism Against Populism: A Confrontation Between the Theory of Democracy and the Theory of Social Choice* (San Francisco: W.H. Freeman, 1982), pp. 213–32; William W. Freehling, *The Road to Disunion: Secessionists at Bay, 1776–1854* (New York: Oxford University Press, 1990), pp. 287–352; J. David Greenstone, *The Lincoln Persuasion: Remaking American Liberalism* (Princeton, N.J.: Princeton University Press, 1993), pp. 154–85; and Sean Wilentz, "Slavery, Antislavery, and Jacksonian Democracy," in *The Market Revolution in America: Social, Political, and Religious Expressions, 1800–1880*, Melvyn Stokes and Stephen Conway, eds. (Charlottesville: University Press of Virginia, 1996), pp. 202–23.

force against groups merely organizing and planning such an expedition. Instead, under a new law that would expire two years after its passage in 1838, civil authorities could seize arms, ammunition, vehicles, and vessels attempting to cross the border.[39]

Two years later Van Buren carelessly passed along to Congress a report from his secretary of War, Joel R. Poinsett. Poinsett (for whom the poinsettia was named) was a staunch Unionist from South Carolina, more nationalistic than his chief executive. The administration's frequent diplomatic and military tribulations inspired the secretary to request a militia reorganization similar to what had been suggested by nearly every president since George Washington. Under the plan, the regular army each year would call out and rigorously drill from the state militia rolls an active force of one hundred thousand men, who would then be available for rapid mobilization. Once the Whigs got wind of this scheme for universal military training, they set off an uproar. Many states were already undermining the basis for such a reorganization by replacing their compulsory militias with voluntary systems. The Little Magician, who had not previously read the plan, promptly disavowed it. To the charge of favoring standing armies, he responded:

> If I had been charged with the design of establishing among you at public expense, a menagerie of two hundred thousand wild beasts, it would not have surprised me more, nor would it, in my judgment, have been one jot more preposterous.[40]

But the disavowal was not in time to avoid political damage in the ongoing presidential race. Poinsett's proposal was destined to be the last effort to nationalize the state militias until after the Civil War.[41]

---

[39]Stevens, *Border Diplomacy*, pp. 27–28.

[40]As quoted in Curtis, *The Fox at Bay*, p. 201.

[41]Marcus Cunliffe, *Soldiers and Civilians: The Martial Spirit in America, 1775–1865* (Boston: Little, Brown, 1968), pp. 197–99; Russell F. Weigley, *History of the United States Army* (New York: Macmillan, 1967), pp. 156–57; J. Fred Rippy, *Joel R. Poinsett: Versatile American* (Durham, N.C.: Duke University Press, 1935), pp. 175–77; Curtis, *The Fox at Bay*, pp. 199–201; Wilson, *The Presidency of Martin Van Buren*, pp. 188–89. For background on the evolution of the militia during this period, consult John K. Mahon, *History of the Militia and National Guard* (New York: Macmillan, 1983), pp. 63–96.

The New Yorker's years in the White House saw the first national regulation of steamboats and a nationally funded scientific expedition. President Jackson had recommended "precautionary and penal legislation" after an explosion on a Red River steamboat in 1833 had killed Senator Josiah S. Johnston of Louisiana. Not until 1838 did Congress enact a law that required federal inspection of boilers and hulls on passenger vessels. They entrusted supervision to district judges, however, and the creation of a regular inspection bureaucracy within the Treasury Department had to await the future Whig presidency of Millard Fillmore.[42] The navy's South Sea Exploring Expedition, under the command of Lieutenant Charles Wilkes, set sail in August 1838 on a four-year voyage that would claim discovery of Antarctica. But it had been the brainchild of former President John Quincy Adams, and Congress had appropriated the money nearly a year before Van Buren entered office.

To offset these relatively minor transgressions on market enterprise, the eighth president deserves credit for enthusiastically embracing reforms suggested by his postmaster general Amos Kendall of Kentucky. Kendall wanted to eliminate the heavy postal subsidy for newspapers, instituted back in 1792, which resulted in newspapers providing no more than 15 percent of postal revenue even though they accounted for more than 95 percent of deliveries by weight. The head of the Post Office also tried to rein in the congressional franking privilege. Needless to say, Congress was not interested in either of these reforms.[43] Mention should be made of Van Buren's executive order, in the midst of his campaign for reelection, mandating a ten-hour day on all federal public works.

[42]Leonard D. White, *The Jacksonians: A Study in Administrative History, 1829–1861* (New York: Free Press, 1954), pp. 442–46; Lloyd M. Short, *Steamboat-Inspection Service: Its History, Activities and Organization* (New York: D. Appleton, 1922), pp. 1–6; John H. Morrison, *History of American Steam Navigation* (New York: W.F. Sametz, 1903), pp. 591–92. Neither Curtis, *The Fox at Bay*, nor Wilson, *The Presidency of Martin Van Buren*, mentions this regulatory development. To my knowledge, there is no economic study of steamboat inspection's efficacy, but we may safely assume that it was as inefficient and counterproductive as nearly all other federal regulation.

[43]Richard R. John, *Spreading the News: The American Postal System from Franklin to Morse* (Cambridge, Mass.: Harvard University Press, 1995), p. 40, passim; Wilson, *The Presidency of Martin Van Buren*, pp. 172–75.

V

The election of 1840 turned into a political circus. Under the savvy management of such rising Whig politicos as Thaddeus Stevens of Pennsylvania and Horace Greeley, William Seward, and Thurlow Weed of New York, the apologists for mercantilism learned to throw off the historic taint of elitist privilege and appeal for the first time directly to the masses. William Henry Harrison earned the sobriquet "General Mum" for obscure positions on the issues, while his party adopted no platform and emphasized its candidate's military record during the War of 1812 and his alleged frontier, log-cabin origins. Harrison was in reality the scion of Virginia aristocracy, but that did not stop the Whigs from falsely portraying Martin Van Buren as the *effete grandee*, extravagant with public money. The popular rallies, colorful slogans, and huckster excitement surrounding the Whigs's "Log Cabin and Hard Cider" campaign caused the *Democratic Review* to cry out in despair: "We have taught them to conquer us!"[44] Still, it was the lingering trauma of hard times, coupled with disgruntled Southern and Northern expansionism and the exaggerated fears of Democratic Caesarism, that brought about the Little Magician's political defeat at the hands of "Tippecanoe and Tyler too." Voter turnout was much higher in 1840 than four years earlier—jumping from 57.8 percent of those eligible to 80.2 percent—so that Van Buren actually received 400,000 more votes, but he carried only seven out of twenty-six states.[45]

Heading back to Kinderhook in March of 1841 with his usual good cheer, Van Buren felt confident of future vindication. Instead, he would watch the Democracy abandon his peaceful

---

[44]As quoted in Glyndon G. Van Deusen, *The Jacksonian Era, 1828–1848* (New York: Harper and Brothers, 1959), p. 148.

[45]Robert Gray Gunderson, *The Log-Cabin Campaign* (Lexington: University of Kentucky Press, 1957), and Michael F. Holt, "The Election of 1840, Voter Mobilization, and the Emergence of the Second American Party System: A Reappraisal of Jacksonian Voting Behavior," in Holt, *Political Parties and American Political Development: From the Age of Jackson to the Age of Lincoln* (Baton Rouge: Louisiana State University Press, 1992), pp. 151–91. See also articles by Joel H. Silbey, "Election of 1836," and William Nisbet Chambers, "Election of 1840," both in *History of American Presidential Elections*, Arthur M. Schlesinger, Jr., Fred L. Israel, and William P. Hansen, eds. (New York: Chelsea House, 1971), vol. 1.

foreign policy and, as a result, tear itself apart along with the Union, as he had foretold; he did not live to see his economic precepts go out of fashion as well. Nevertheless, the Little Magician could feel justifiable pride in his single term. Glyndon G. Van Deusen, a historian not at all sympathetic to laissez-faire, provides one of the fairest modern assessments:

> [W]ith all his weaknesses, the fact remains that Van Buren was honest; that he knew the value of and habitually sought counsel; that he deliberated before making decisions; and that his four years in the White House demonstrated, for better or for worse, a perfectly logical development of the left-wing tendencies of Jacksonian Democracy, a development which it took courage to foster in the face of a catastrophic depression.[46]

Defying the median voter model of public-choice theory, the eighth president moved, not toward the center, but risked political injury to become more radical while in office. As a result, this admirer of both Thomas Jefferson and Andrew Jackson presided himself over an administration marred by none of their inconsistencies. Nothing like the Sage of Monticello's despotic embargo, his unconstitutional Louisiana Purchase, or his vindictive witch-hunt against Aaron Burr disfigured the New Yorker's term. Nor anything to compare with Old Hickory's executive bullying of South Carolina, France, or Congress (to name just a few). The Little Magician remained truer to Old Republican principles than either of these more renowned known champions of liberty, even though the panic of 1837 arguably proffered as weighty a temptation for compromise.

Since Van Buren is being held up to a libertarian yardstick, perhaps it would be more appropriate to compare him with other nonactivist chief executives, those that mainstream historians tend to dismiss. Grover Cleveland, a later Democratic president who similarly confronted major depression, is actually in my opinion the strongest contender for superior accolades, but his signing the Interstate Commerce Act, his use of troops during the Pullman strike, and his involvement in the Venezuelan boundary dispute demonstrate a weaker commitment to free markets, civil liberties, and nonintervention. Warren Harding and Calvin Coolidge, it is true, implemented the brilliant fiscal

---

[46]Van Deusen, *The Jacksonian Era*, p. 114.

program of Secretary of the Treasury Andrew Mellon, yet the economic meddling of their secretary of Commerce, Herbert Hoover, cancels that out. John Tyler looks good as long as you focus only on his vetoes; we have already mentioned the bills he signed and his Texas intrigue, to which you can add suppression of the Dorr Rebellion in Rhode Island. One thing alone disqualifies Millard Fillmore from consideration: the Fugitive Slave Act of 1850, among the most draconian laws Congress ever passed. As for Franklin Pierce and James Buchanan, even if we overlook their proslavery policies in Kansas, Pierce still has his imperialistic ambitions revealed in the Ostend Manifesto, whereas Buchanan stands indicted for dispatching the army to Utah in the Mormon War. And the single-term, post-Civil War Republicans—Rutherford B. Hayes, James A. Garfield–Chester A. Arthur, and Benjamin Harrison—with their high protective tariffs, pork-barrel subsidies, and profligate veterans' benefits, are not even in the running.

But the case for Van Buren's greatness goes beyond his being the least bad U.S. president. While avoiding foreign wars, he did more than maintain the domestic *status quo*. He reduced the power and reach of central authority in the face of stiff resistance and thereby helped the American economy weather one of its most severe deflations. The Little Magician also brought an ideological clarity to American politics that has seldom been equaled. Although the Democracy would stray in significant and reprehensible ways from the principled course he had charted, his imprint still left an enduring legacy. The Democratic Party remained the political alliance with the strongest affinity for laissez-faire, personal liberty, and free trade until almost the turn of the century. All will acknowledge, I believe, that Americans once enjoyed greater freedom from government intervention than any other people on the face of the earth. For that accomplishment, Martin Van Buren deserves as much credit as any other single individual—and certainly more credit than any other president of the United States.

I thank Fabbian George Dufoe III, Lynda Esko, K.R. Constantine Gutzman, Michael F. Holt, Ross Levatter, Charles J. Myers, Robert V. Remini, Larry Schweckart, Richard H. Timberlake, Jr., and Dyanne Petersen for their comments. Of course, I alone am responsible for any remaining errors.

7

ABRAHAM LINCOLN AND THE TRIUMPH OF MERCANTILISM

THOMAS J. DILORENZO

I presume you all know who I am. I am humble Abraham Lincoln. I have been solicited by many friends to become a candidate for the legislature. My politics are short and sweet, like the old woman's dance. I am in favor of a national bank . . . in favor of the internal improvements system and a high protective tariff.

—Abraham Lincoln, 1832
The Collected Works of Abraham Lincoln

This statement by Abraham Lincoln is a succinct summary of what he devoted virtually his entire political career to prior to being elected president in 1860. Lincoln was always a Whig and was almost single-mindedly devoted to the Whig agenda of protectionism, central banking, and corporate welfare for the railroad and shipping industries—euphemistically referred to as "internal improvements."

Although he will forever be remembered as the "Great Emancipator," Lincoln was not particularly concerned with the slavery issue prior to 1860. According to Roy Basler, the editor of Lincoln's collected works, as of 1857, Lincoln "had no solution to the problem of slavery except the colonization idea which he had inherited from Henry Clay . . . when he spoke . . . of respecting the Negro as a human being, his words lacked effectiveness."[1]

What *did* preoccupy Lincoln's political mind throughout his career was the Whig Party's mercantilist economic agenda, which was named "The American System" by Henry Clay, the undisputed leader of the Whigs and Lincoln's professed political idol and role model. Lincoln spent nearly three decades preceding his election as president working tirelessly in the trenches of the Whig and (after 1856) Republican parties to organize voters in

---

[1]Roy Basler, *Abraham Lincoln: His Speeches and Writings* (New York: Da Capo, 1946), p. 23.

Illinois and other states on behalf of the Whigs' mercantilist agenda. It is not surprising, therefore, that once he was elected president, he presided over the enactment of that agenda. Thus, Lincoln's election as president signified the triumph of mercantilism—a set of economic policies that would become a permanent drag on the economy and a source of pervasive political corruption for decades to come.

ALWAYS A WHIG

> Mercantilism, which reached its height in the Europe of the seventeenth and eighteenth centuries, was a system of statism which employed economic fallacy to build up a structure of imperial state power, as well as special subsidy and monopolistic privilege to individuals or groups favored by the state.
>
> — Murray N. Rothbard
> *The Logic of Action Two*

In 1859 Lincoln declared that he was "always a whig in politics."[2] And indeed he was. Both he and his wife were ardent admirers of Henry Clay, the leader of the Whigs. In his 1852 eulogy to Clay, Lincoln called him "the great parent of Whig principles" and "the fount from which my own political views flowed."[3] Indeed, "one could hardly read any paragraph" in the eulogy, writes Roy Basler, "without feeling that Lincoln was, consciously or unconsciously, inviting comparison and contrast of himself with Clay."[4] "From the moment Lincoln first entered political life as a candidate for the state legislature during the . . . 1832 presidential election," writes historian Robert Johannsen, "he had demonstrated an unswerving fidelity to the party of Henry Clay and to Clay's American System, the program of internal improvements, protective tariff, and centralized banking."[5]

---

[2]David Herbert Donald, *Lincoln* (New York: Simon and Schuster, 1996).

[3]Basler, *Abraham Lincoln*, p. 264.

[4]Ibid., p. 18.

[5]Robert Johannsen, *Lincoln, the South, and Slavery: The Political Dimension* (Baton Rouge: Louisiana State University Press, 1991), p. 14.

THE MASTER POLITICIAN

Lincoln began a very active career in Illinois politics in 1832, but the citizens of that state never elected him to any major office, such as U.S. senator or governor. He only served one term in Congress and eight years in the state legislature, along with several more menial positions, such as county surveyor.

Nevertheless, Lincoln was a skilled politician, described by historian David Donald as "the master wirepuller who operated the state political organization first of the Whig Party and, after its decay, that of the Republicans."[6] Lincoln made hundreds of "stump speeches" on behalf of the Whigs and was extraordinarily gifted in the use of rhetoric. (Of course, saying that a politician is gifted in the use of rhetoric is a polite way of saying he is a talented liar, deceiver, and manipulator.) Contrary to the impression one gets from reading popular historical accounts of Lincoln as statesman and constitutional philosopher, he spent virtually his entire political career prior to 1860 engulfed in the dirty work of party politics. For example, in the 1840 presidential election, Lincoln sent written instructions to party activists within the state informing them that "the whole state must be so well organized that every Whig can be brought to the polls."[7] He then went on in great detail:

> So divide your county into "small districts" and appoint in each a subcommittee; make a perfect list of all the voters, and ascertain with certainty for whom they will vote. Designate doubtful voters in separate lines, indicating their probable choice. Each subcommittee must keep a constant watch on the doubtful voters and have them talked to by those in whom they have the most confidence—also Whig documents must be given them . . . on election day see that every Whig is brought to the polls.[8]

By 1860, after nearly thirty years as a "party operative," Lincoln "had maneuvered himself into a position where he controlled the party machinery, platform, and candidates of one of

---

[6]Donald, *Lincoln*, p. 66.

[7]Ibid., p. 104.

[8]Ibid.

the pivotal states in the Union."[9] One biographer described him as "the smartest parliamentarian and cunningest logroller" in the Illinois legislature.[10]

Lincoln was not a guileless, naive, and unsophisticated "backwoodsman" and "rail splitter." He was a shrewd, cynical, manipulative politician who was not above playing dirty tricks, such as writing *anonymous* letters to the editor of newspapers denouncing his political opponents.[11] Perhaps his most success-ful political trick was to portray himself as an innocent babe-in-the-woods when it came to politics. One of the biggest lies he ever told was to a group of Pennsylvania politicians who had come to the White House to confer with him: "You know I never was a contriver," the consummate political contriver and manipulator said; "I don't know much about how things are done in politics."[12] Lincoln was also fond of portraying himself as a friend of the "farmer and the mechanic," although in real-ity the Whig Party championed tariffs, inflationary finance, and corporate welfare for the benefit of big business *at the expense of* farmers and mechanics.

THE CENTRAL BANK CRUSADER

Lincoln was such a blind follower of the Whig Party line that many of his economic policy speeches were embarrassingly illogical and sounded dumb and foolish. In 1840 he made numerous speeches in favor of establishing a central bank even though he had no educational background at all in economics and merely mouthed slogans that may well have been written by someone else. Like all Whigs, Lincoln was in favor of infla-tionary finance through the printing of paper money by a cen-tral bank or, if need be, by state government banks, and was an ardent opponent of a monetary system based on gold or any other precious metal.

After Andrew Jackson destroyed the Second Bank of the United States in the early 1830s, Lincoln and the Whigs turned

[9]Ibid., pp. 66–67.

[10]Paul M. Angle, ed., *The Lincoln Reader* (New York: Da Capo Press, 1947), p. 83.

[11]Edgar Lee Masters, *Lincoln, The Man* (Columbia, S.C.: Foundation for American Education, 1997), p. 77.

[12]Donald, *Lincoln*, p. 66.

(for the moment) from advocating central banking to championing fiat currency issue by state government banks, ostensibly to pay for their "internal improvements" schemes. As a member of the Illinois legislature, Lincoln repeatedly opposed proposals by Democratic legislators to investigate the Illinois State Bank.[13] In December of 1840, the Democrats, who were in the majority in the legislature, wanted to force the bank to make payments in specie instead of paper. The bank was authorized to continue its suspension of specie payment through the end of the year, after which it would have to make specie payments.

Lincoln and the Whigs wanted desperately to avoid this move toward sound money based on gold so, in an attempt to stop the adjournment of the legislature, Lincoln and his fellow Whigs bolted for the door, which unfortunately was locked and guarded. Their objective was to leave the room so that there was no quorum to vote for adjournment. Blocked from the normal entrance, Lincoln then jumped out of the first-story window and was followed by his lemming-like Whig compatriots. The Democrats began calling them "Lincoln and his flying brethren."[14]

THE LIFELONG PROTECTIONIST

In the 1844 elections, he championed the second plank of the Whig platform, protectionist tariffs, with the most absurd economic arguments. He argued that protectionist tariffs would not harm the average consumer at all because they would be collected only from "those whose pride, whose abundance of means, prompt them to spurn the manufactures of our own country, and to strut in British cloaks, and coats and pantaloons."[15] He told a newspaper reporter that "he could not tell the reason," but he was sure that protectionist tariffs would "make everything the farmers bought cheaper."[16]

Like many other Whig politicians, Lincoln familiarized himself with the protectionist writings of Henry C. Carey, who apparently earned a living by popularizing protectionist myths on behalf of the Pennsylvania steel industry. One of these myths

[13]Ibid., p. 77.
[14]Ibid.
[15]Ibid., p. 110.
[16]Ibid.

adopted and repeated by Lincoln was that free trade would supposedly increase costs and prices because so much "useless labor" would be employed transporting goods from one country to another.[17] According to this "logic," the importation of goods to Illinois from Kentucky, Ohio, Indiana, and Pennsylvania would also have been undesirable, in Lincoln's opinion, because of all the "useless labor" expended in transporting them across state lines. Mercantilism relies crucially on the spreading of economic fallacies.

Lincoln also believed in a crude version of the Marxian labor theory of value, announcing that free trade perpetuated a system whereby "some have laboured, and others have, without labour, enjoyed a large portion of the fruits. . . . To secure to each labourer the whole product of his labour, or as nearly as possible, is a most worthy object of any good government."[18]

CHAMPION OF CORPORATE WELFARE

By 1838, Lincoln had worked his way up to the position of leader of the Illinois Whig Party. In that capacity, he was influential in passing legislation with regard to the third major element of Whigism: corporate welfare, or "internal improvements." At the time, the use of federal funds for so-called internal improvements, such as subsidies to the railroad industry, were widely believed to be unconstitutional. But thanks to Lincoln's political skills, Illinois was a leader in using state tax revenues for such purposes.

The Illinois experience in government-funded "internal improvements" during the late 1830s, under Lincoln's political leadership, provided a case study of why such uses of tax dollars were viewed with great suspicion. William H. Herndon, Lincoln's law partner and one of his closest friends, described the Illinois "internal improvement" program in 1838 as

> reckless and unwise. The gigantic and stupendous operations of the scheme dazzled the eyes of nearly everybody, but in the end it rolled up a debt so enormous as to impede the otherwise marvelous progress of Illinois. The burdens imposed by this Legislature under the guise of improvements became so

[17]Ibid.
[18]Ibid.

monumental in size it is little wonder that at intervals for years afterward the monster of [debt] repudiation often showed its hideous face above the waves of popular indignation.[19]

George Nicolay and John Hay, who studied law in Lincoln's Springfield law offices and later served as his personal secretaries in the White House, described the internal improvements debacle as follows:

> The market was glutted with Illinois bonds; one banker and one broker after another, to whose hands they had been recklessly confided in New York and London, failed, or made away with the proceeds of sales. The [internal improvements] system had utterly failed; there was nothing to do but repeal it, stop work on the visionary roads, and endeavor to invent some means of paying the enormous debt. This work taxed the energies of the Legislature in 1839, and for some years after. It was a dismal and disheartening task. Blue Monday had come after these years of intoxication, and a crushing debt rested upon a people who had been deceiving themselves with the fallacy that it would somehow pay itself by acts of the legislature.[20]

The Illinois legislature allocated $12 million in 1838 for this "gigantic and stupendous" boondoggle. What Lincoln and the Whigs promised, but did not deliver upon (according to Herndon), was that

> Every river and stream . . . was to be widened, deepened, and made navigable. A canal to connect the Illinois River and Lake Michigan was to be dug . . . cities were to spring up everywhere; capital from abroad was to come pouring in; attracted by the glowing reports of marvelous progress and great internal wealth, people were to come swarming in by colonies, until in the end Illinois was to outstrip all others, and herself become the Empire State of the Union.[21]

After spending the $12 million, observed Nicolay and Hay,

> Nothing was left of the brilliant schemes of the historic Legislature of 1836 but a load of debt which crippled for many years

[19]Paul M. Angle, *The Lincoln Reader*, p. 82.
[20]Ibid., pp. 100–01.
[21]Ibid., p. 83.

the energies of the people, a few miles of embankments which the grass hastened to cover, and a few abutments which stood for years by the sides of leafy rivers, waiting for their long delaying bridges and trains.[22]

Herndon wrote that "The internal improvement system, the adoption of which Lincoln had played such a prominent part, had collapsed, with the result that Illinois was left with an enormous debt and an empty treasury."[23]

Similar financial disasters were created by Whig politicians throughout the country. As described by John Bach McMaster in his *History of the People of the United States,*

In every State which had gone recklessly into internal improvements the financial situation was alarming. No works were finished; little or no income was derived from them; interest on the bonds increased day by day and no means of paying it save by taxation remained.[24]

The Illinois scheme was nevertheless a marvelous *political* success from the Whigs' perspective, for they were able to take credit for having dispensed $12 million in patronage. This is what the Whigs really stood for: the acquisition of political power through the dispensation of patronage. They had no grand philosophy or ideology; they wanted political power and private riches and had no qualms about using the taxpayers' money as the mechanism for acquiring these things.

Discussing his involvement in the Illinois internal improvements boondoggle of the late 1830s, Lincoln explained to a friend that his career ambition was to become known as "the DeWitt Clinton of Illinois."[25] New York Governor DeWitt Clinton, explains historian Paul Johnson, "invented the 'spoils system,' whereby an incoming governor turned out all officeholders and rewarded his supporters with their jobs."[26]

---

[22]Ibid., p. 102.

[23]William H. Herndon and Jesse W. Weik, *Life of Lincoln* (New York: Da Capo, 1983), p. 161.

[24]John Bach McMaster, *A History of the People of the United States*, vol. 6, *1830–1842* (New York: D. Appleton, 1914), p. 628.

[25]Ibid.

[26]Paul Johnson, *A History of the American People* (New York: HarperCollins, 1997), p. 336.

Thus, Lincoln aspired to be a midwestern "Boss Tweed," a political string-puller and patronage-dispenser, the "Godfather" of Illinois politics. He understood that patronage was the route to political power and, potentially, to personal wealth. It is not just coincidental that while championing taxpayer-funded corporate welfare for the railroad industry as a politician, Lincoln was also one of the attorneys representing the Illinois Central Railroad and was paid as much as $5,000 for a single case in 1853.[27]

During the next several years, Lincoln honed his skills as a pork-barrel politician by guiding through the legislature a bill to move the state capitol from Vandalia to Springfield, Illinois. There was no particular reason why Springfield was necessarily a better location. As explained by Illinois Governor Thomas Ford in 1847, Lincoln and the Whigs in the state legislature simply solicited and received political and financial support from various interest groups in and around Springfield in return for their legislative efforts. As the governor explained:

> Thus it was made to cost the State about six millions of dollars to remove the seat of government from Vandalia to Springfield, half which sum would have purchased all the real estate in that town at three prices; and thus . . . by multiplying railroads . . . by distributing money to some of the counties, to be wasted by the county commissioners, and by giving the seat of government to Springfield, was the whole State bought up and bribed, to approve the most senseless and disastrous policy which ever crippled the energies of a growing country.[28]

WHO WERE THE WHIGS?

To better understand Lincoln's slavish devotion to Whig politics (which he declared to be identical to Republican Party politics as of 1856), it will be useful to present a brief overview of American Whigism.

The American Whig Party was founded in 1832 as a reaction to President Andrew Jackson's abolition of the Second Bank of the United States. The name "Whig" was chosen to imply that these men were opposed to despotism and centralized governmental tyranny, as were the American Whigs of 1776 and, earlier, the British Whigs who advocated classical liberalism.

[27]Masters, Lincoln, The Man, p. 123.
[28]Angle, The Lincoln Reader, pp. 87–88.

But the very name "Whig" was a cleverly-contrived decep-tion. The nineteenth-century American Whigs were in fact the *champions* of centralized, consolidated government, and all stu-dents of political philosophy understood at the time (much bet-ter than they do today) that centralization of political power was destructive of liberty. They claimed to be opposed to "exec-utive power" (as opposed to the power of Congress), but in real-ity they were only opposed to the kind of executive power that was exercised by President Jackson in destroying the central bank. If Jackson had been a supporter of central banking, it is doubtful that the Whigs would ever have given a second thought to the "dangers" of "executive power." Indeed, they lusted after such power for themselves.

There were Northern Whigs, like Lincoln, and there were Southern Whigs, like John C. Calhoun, who opposed Jackson but for different reasons. Calhoun battled Jackson over the 1828 Tariff of Abominations, which a South Carolina political con-vention nullified. The nullification crisis was a battle between states'-rights Southerners, like Calhoun, and Jackson. The Northern Whigs were not in favor of Calhoun's (and the Found-ing Fathers') cherished system of limited, decentralized govern-ment; they merely found it to be politically convenient to form a coalition with the Southern Whigs, among others.

The Northerners dominated the Whig coalition, which was virtually defined by Henry Clay and Daniel Webster—especially Clay. Edgar Lee Masters, the Illinois poet, playwright, and one-time law partner of Clarence Darrow, provided what I believe to be a perfect description of the nineteenth-century American Whigs:

> Clay was the champion of that political system [the Whigs] which doles favors to the strong in order to win and to keep their adherence to the government. His system offered shelter to devious schemes and corrupt enterprises. . . . He was the beloved son [figuratively speaking] of Alexander Hamilton with his corrupt funding schemes, his superstitions concern-ing the advantage of a public debt, and a people taxed to make profits for enterprises that cannot stand alone. His example and his doctrines led to the creation of a party that had no platform to announce, because its principles were plunder and nothing else. . . . These Whigs adopted the tricks of the pickpocket who

dresses himself like a farmer in order to move through a rural crowd unidentified while he gathers purses and watches.[29]

The battle with Andrew Jackson over the rechartering of the Second Bank of the United States is what ignited the creation of the Whig Party in the North. The Whig political strategy was as simple as it was corrupt: promise to plunder the taxpayers for the benefit of corporations and banks, in return for the everlasting financial support (and kickbacks) from those same entities, all the while drowning the public in the false rhetoric of opposing executive tyranny, championing the small family farm, etc.

A central bank and a high protectionist tariff were the keystones to the Whigs' plan for political plunder, for that is how their massive "internal improvements" schemes were to be funded and monopolies created. Jackson was their mortal political enemy, for he regarded the bank as "dangerous to the liberty of the American people because it represented a fantastic centralization of economic and political power under private control."[30] Jackson understood the implications of a politicized money supply as well as the Whigs did. The difference between them was that Jackson thought the results would be unequivocally bad for the country; the Whigs understood that a politicized money supply was a key to their personal political advancement and wealth accumulation. Jackson condemned the bank as "a vast electioneering engine" which had the "power to control the Government and change its character."[31] That is exactly what the Whigs wanted to do.

Roger B. Taney, who was Jackson's Treasury secretary, also complained of the bank's "corrupting influence" with "its patronage greater than that of the Government" and its ability to "influence elections" by engineering what contemporary public choice scholars call a "political business cycle."[32]

[29]Masters, *Lincoln, The Man*, p. 27.

[30]Robert V. Remini, *Andrew Jackson* (New York: Harper and Row, 1966), p. 141.

[31]Ibid., p. 142.

[32]Ibid., p. 144.

Whig politicians barely hid the fact that one of the reasons they were such fierce champions of central banking is that they could receive kickbacks in return for their support for the bank. While the Second Bank of the United States was still chartered, Henry Clay left Congress for two years in 1822, after having accumulated some $40,000 in personal debt, to become general counsel of the bank. Clay biographer Maurice Baxter explains that Clay's

> income from this business apparently amounted to what he needed: three thousand dollars a year from the bank as chief counsel; more for appearing in specific cases; and a sizable amount of real estate in Ohio and Kentucky in addition to the cash. . . . When he resigned to become Secretary of State in 1825, he was pleased with his compensation.[33]

Daniel Webster never bothered resigning; he just demanded a "retainer" from the bank while remaining in Congress. He once wrote to Nicholas Biddle, the bank's president: "I believe my retainer has not been renewed or refreshed as usual. If it be wished that my relation to the Bank should be continued, it may be well to send me the usual retainer."[34]

Most Lincoln biographers invent excuses for virtually every questionable decision or action he ever made. In the case of the disastrous $12 million internal improvements debacle of the late 1830s, the excuse given is that the spending projects were harmed by the panic of 1837. This may be true, but it is worth noting that the Second Bank of the United States had a lot to do with creating that panic. A case can be made that the panic was the result of the inevitable boom-and-bust cycle spawned by central-bank money creation. The stock of money (currency plus bank deposits) increased by 42 percent between 1834 and 1837, which must have contributed to a false sense of prosperity and the extension of credit for myriad uncreditworthy ventures, such as the ones financed by the Illinois Legislature.[35] By

---

[33]Maurice Baxter, *Henry Clay and the American System* (Lexington: University Press of Kentucky, 1995), p. 75.

[34]Remini, *Andrew Jackson*, p. 145.

[35]Richard H. Timberlake, *Monetary Policy in the United States: An Intellectual and Institutional History* (Chicago: University of Chicago Press, 1993), p. 47.

the end of Jackson's two terms (January 1837), the Second Bank of the United States was dead.

Long before the creation of the Whig Party, Henry Clay, Daniel Webster, and other like-minded politicians promoted the idea of government-funded "internal improvements," but such schemes were routinely vetoed by presidents who uniformly believed that such expenditures of tax dollars were unconstitutional. "Internal improvements" bills sponsored by Henry Clay were vetoed by President James Madison, the acknowledged "father" of the Constitution, as well as his successor, James Monroe.

But by 1840, Clay and the Whigs thought they finally had a chance to break the constitutional logjam with the election of their candidate, William Henry Harrison, to the presidency. Clay was an extraordinarily powerful force in Congress. He was such a natural politician that after just one year in the House of Representatives (1811), he was elected Speaker of the House. By 1840, he and his followers were sure they could get much of his "American System" through Congress and have it rubber-stamped by Harrison. Lincoln did his part by organizing the Illinois Whigs, as was his forte, and tirelessly campaigning for Harrison.

Unfortunately for the Whigs, however, Harrison dropped dead after only one month in the White House, placing the burden of the presidency on his vice president, the Virginian John Tyler. Tyler was a Southern Whig, and little attention was paid to the contest for the vice presidency. Tyler biographer Oliver Chitwood writes that "what little attention was paid to Tyler's role in the campaign was due mainly to the fact that 'Tyler too' rhymed with 'Tippecanoe.'"[36]

The Whigs controlled both houses of Congress, and Henry Clay immediately proposed establishing a new central bank and a sharp increase in tariffs without even consulting with Tyler.[37] These proposals were never mentioned by the national Whig Party during the campaign and for good reason—they were wildly unpopular with the citizens.

---

[36]Oliver Perry Chitwood, *John Tyler: Champion of the Old South* (New York: Russell and Russell, 1964), p. 184.

[37]Ibid., p. 213.

Clay was like a shark with the smell of blood in the water. Believing that he was "in perfect control" of the entire government he "predominated over the Whig Party in a despotic way," according to the *New York Herald*.[38]

Much to Clay's chagrin, however, Tyler was not a pushover and considered himself a philosophical heir to his Virginia predecessors in the highest office in the land—Jefferson, Madison, and Monroe. He was a strong believer in states' rights and thought that a national bank was unconstitutional. He vetoed the bank bill by saying, "The power of Congress to create a national bank to operate *per se* over the Union has been a question of dispute from the origin of the Government . . . my own opinion has been uniformly proclaimed to be against the exercise of any such power by this Government."[39] Like most other Southern statesmen, Tyler was also highly suspicious of protectionist tariffs and internal improvement boondoggles.

The Whigs went berserk. They organized a mob that appeared in front of the White House "with blunderbusses, drums, and trumpets," shouting "A Bank! A Bank!" and "Down with the veto" while burning Tyler in effigy.[40] The Whigs expelled President Tyler from their party. The central bank idea was dead for another twenty years—until Lincoln's election.

There was never much public support for the Whig economic agenda. Nevertheless, this band of unscrupulous and imperious politicians continued promoting it in national elections by nominating a succession of former military generals—General William Henry Harrison, General Zachary Taylor, and General Winfield Scott, for example—as their presidential candidates. Taylor was elected president in 1848 but died two years later. Neither he nor his vice president and successor, Millard Fillmore, succeeded in implementing the American System. By 1856, Clay, Webster, and the Whig Party were dead; its Northern element had become part of the Republican Party.

[38]Ibid., p. 217.
[39]Ibid., pp. 226–27.
[40]Ibid., pp. 228–29.

THE TRIUMPH OF MERCANTILISM

The tariff was the centerpiece of the Republican program.

—Richard Bensel
Yankee Leviathan

The Northern industrialists and bankers who, for decades, had been lobbying for a central bank, for monopolistic privileges via protectionism, and for corporate welfare in the form of federally-funded "internal improvements," were defeated at every step along the way by American presidents who believed in and enforced the Constitution. Nowhere in Article 1, Section 8, is there mention of subsidies for railroads or any other private corporation, and so presidents typically vetoed internal improvements bills on constitutional grounds.

A central bank was also opposed on constitutional grounds by Jackson, Tyler, and others, who believed it was an unconstitutional imposition on state sovereignty. These men understood, as James Madison said, that whatever authority the Constitution had was derived from the states, for it was the state conventions which adopted the Constitution in the first place.

Protectionist tariffs were also viewed by defenders of the Constitution as an unconstitutional plundering of one segment of the population for the benefit of another which violated the clause in the Constitution that mandates uniformity in taxation.

Thus by 1860, the Whigs—and their successors, the Republicans—had been waging political war on the Constitution for nearly three decades. The purpose of this "war" was to adopt mercantilism—a system of centralized state power and special-interest subsidies and monopolistic privileges for individuals and groups favored by the state at the expense of the general public. That is why Lincoln was just their man in 1860. He quickly demonstrated that he had little regard—if not outright contempt—for constitutional restrictions on governmental power.

Samuel Morison and Henry Steele Commager described Lincoln as "a dictator from the standpoint of American Constitutional law and practice."[41] The political scientist Clinton Rossiter made the "Lincoln dictatorship" a major case study in his book,

---

[41]Samuel E. Morison and Henry Steele Commager, *The Growth of the American Republic* (New York: Oxford University Press, 1942), pp. 699–700.

Constitutional Dictatorship.[42] As long ago as 1897, the historian William Archibald Dunning referred to the Lincoln administration as a "temporary dictatorship."[43] Even Lincoln's defenders and idolaters have called him a "dictator," but one who "was a benevolent dictator," writes James G. Randall.[44] James Ford Rhodes called Lincoln a "dictator" but, as is typical of the history profession, which seems to be completely incapable of objective analysis of Lincoln, he added that "never had the power of a dictator fallen into safer and nobler hands."[45]

Among the reasons these commentators all labeled Lincoln a "dictator" are his initiating and conducting a war by decree for months without the consent of Congress; suspending *habeas corpus*; conscripting the railroads and censoring telegraph lines; imprisoning without trial as many as thirty thousand Northern citizens for voicing opposition to war; deporting a member of Congress—Clement L. Vallandigham of Ohio, a fierce opponent of the Morrill Tariff and the central bank—for merely opposing Lincoln's income tax at a Democratic Party rally in Ohio; and shutting down hundreds of Northern newspapers and imprisoning some of their editors for simply disagreeing in print with his war policies.[46]

Lincoln only exercised his veto power on two occasions while president, and both of them were with regard to minor and relatively inconsequential bills. Many historians have interpreted this as evidence that Lincoln delegated virtually all domestic legislation to Congress and showed little interest in it. This is not the case. Vetoing the Whig–Republican mercantilist schemes was *exactly* the problem this political coalition had faced for nearly fifty years. With Lincoln they finally got a president who shared their disdain for the Constitution and *would*

---

[42]Clinton Rossiter, *Constitutional Dictatorship: Crisis Government in the Modern Democracies* (Princeton, N.J.: Princeton University Press, 1948).

[43]William Archibald Dunning, *Essays on the Civil War and Reconstruction* (New York: Macmillan, 1897).

[44]James G. Randall, *Constitutional Problems Under Lincoln* (Urbana: University of Illinois Press, 1951), p. 30.

[45]James Ford Rhodes, *History of the United States from the Compromise of 1850 to the Final Restoration of Home Rule at the South in 1877* (New York: Macmillan, 1900), p. 441.

[46]See Randall, *Constitutional Problems Under Lincoln*.

not veto their tariff, internal improvement, and central banking schemes.

Lincoln was not a political "outsider." He had been laboring mightily for thirty years for the same mercantilist schemes that the Republicans who controlled the Congress had been working for. He was their man, and he proved it by virtually giving up his presidential veto power.

This was all explained by Senator John Sherman, who was a powerful figure in the Republican Party (and brother of General William Tecumseh Sherman).

> [T]hose who elected Mr. Lincoln expect him . . . to secure to free labor its just right to the Territories of the United States; to protect . . . by wise revenue laws, the labor of our people; to secure the public lands to actual settlers . . . ; to develop the internal resources of the country by opening new means of communication between the Atlantic and Pacific.[47]

Pulitzer Prize-winning Lincoln biographer David Donald interprets this statement as meaning that Lincoln and the Republicans "intended to enact a high protective tariff that mothered monopoly, to pass a homestead law that invited speculators to loot the public domain, and to subsidize a transcontinental railroad that afforded infinite opportunities for jobbery."[48] This is exactly what they did.

THE TARIFF

In his classic 1931 book, *The Tariff History of the United States*, Frank Taussig observed that as of 1857

> the level of duties on the whole line of manufactured articles was brought down to the lowest point which has been reached in this country since 1815. It is not likely that we shall see, for a great many years to come, a nearer approach to the free-trade ideal.[49]

[47]Quoted in David Donald, *Lincoln Reconsidered* (New York: Vintage, 1961), pp. 105–06.

[48]Ibid., p. 106.

[49]Frank Taussig, *The Tariff History of the United States* (New York: Putnam, 1931), p. 157.

Once the Republicans were confident that Lincoln would win the 1860 election, and especially once the Southern Democrats began leaving the U.S. Congress, the Republicans did what they had been dreaming of doing for decades: They went on a protectionist frenzy that lasted for decades after the war.

The Morrill Tariff was passed by the House of Representatives in May 1860 and by the Senate in March 1861, just prior to Lincoln's inauguration. Thus, the apparatus of protectionism was initiated *before* Fort Sumter and before the war. The Morrill Tariff was not passed to finance the war; it was passed because the old Whigs, who were now Republicans, finally had the power to do it. Even though it was passed before Lincoln officially took office, it is important to note that, as the Republicans' presidential candidate, he was the leader of the party and, as such, most likely had a great deal to do with the political maneuvering on behalf of the tariff.

As Murray Rothbard noted, mercantilism always relied on the espousal of economic fallacies. To support the Morrill Tariff, Lincoln and the Republicans relied on the hoary, mercantilist notion, long since disproved by economic scholars, that "that country is most independent, and consequently most prosperous, which produces within her own borders all articles needful for the use of her citizens."[50]

Taussig further explains that "in the next regular [congressional] session, in December 1861, a still further increase of duties was made. From that time until 1865, no session, indeed, hardly a month of any session, passed in which some increase of duties on imports was not made."[51] By 1862, the average tariff rate had crept up to 47.06 percent which "established protective duties more extreme than had been ventured on in any previous tariff act in our country's history."[52]

The Republicans openly admitted that the purpose of their protectionist policy was not necessarily to raise money to finance the war but to pay off Northern manufacturers for their political support. The manufacturers were being taxed explicitly

---

[50]Heather Cox Richardson, *The Greatest Nation of the Earth: Republican Economic Policies During the Civil War* (Cambridge, Mass.: Harvard University Press, 1997), p. 108.

[51]Taussig, *The Tariff History of the United States*, p. 160.

[52]Ibid., p. 167.

(through excise taxes) to help finance the war, and the tariff was a way to offset those losses. Congress enacted and Lincoln signed into law tariff legislation "whose chief effect was to bring money into the pockets of private individuals."[53] Long after the war, Taussig concluded, "almost any increase in duties demanded by domestic producers was readily made" and "great fortunes were made by changes in legislation urged and brought about by those who were benefited by them."[54]

In his First Inaugural Address, Lincoln promised over and over again that he had no intention to disturb Southern slavery and that, even if he did, it would be unconstitutional to do so in light of the 1857 *Dred Scott* decision. But he also issued a *promise* that he would launch an invasion of any state that failed to collect its share of tariff revenues. To Lincoln, Southern slavery was perfectly tolerable; free trade was not. "The power confided in me will be used to hold, occupy, and possess the property, and places belonging to the government," Lincoln announced, "and to collect the duties and imposts; but beyond what may be necessary for these objects, there will be no invasion."[55]

If he was to succeed politically Lincoln had to start a war (by maneuvering the South into firing the first shot), for the Confederate Constitution outlawed protective tariffs altogether, as the British government did in 1850 and as France was in the process of doing as well. A high protectionist tariff in the Northern United States, coupled with free trade in the South, would have guaranteed that most international commerce would have entered Southern rather than Northern ports and would have ruined the Republican dream of a highly centralized, patronage-based superstate that could keep them in power indefinitely.

Ever since the nullification crisis of the 1820s, Southerners had been threatening nullification and secession because they viewed protectionist tariffs as a tool of political plunder whereby Southerners paid the lion's share of the tariff (because they relied so heavily on Northern and European manufacturers for their manufactured goods), but the bulk of the tariff revenues were spent in the North. Free trade would put an end to this plunder, which was simply intolerable to the Republicans.

---

[53]Ibid.

[54]Ibid., p. 166.

[55]"Lincoln's First Inaugural Address," in Basler, *Abraham Lincoln*, p. 583.

Newspapers in the 1860s were generally affiliated with one political party or another. As such, they tended to espouse a strict party line. The *Daily Chicago Times*, a Republican Party mouthpiece, explained the strategy of plundering the South with the tariff on December 10, 1860:

> The South has furnished near three-fourths of the entire exports of the country. Last year she furnished seventy-two percent of the whole . . . we have a tariff that protects our manufacturers from thirty to fifty percent, and enables us to consume large quantities of Southern cotton, and to compete in our whole home market with the skilled labor of Europe. This operates to *compel the South to pay an indirect bounty to our skilled labor, of millions annually.*[56]

"Let the South adopt the free-trade system," the paper warned, and the North's "commerce must be reduced to less than half what it now is," a "large portion of our shipping interest would pass into the hands of the South," and "these revulsions will bring in their train very general bankruptcy and ruin."[57]

The *New York Post* advocated on March 12, 1861, that the U.S. Navy "abolish all ports of entry" in the South.[58] The *Newark Daily Advertiser* warned ominously on April 2, 1861, that Southerners had apparently "taken to their bosoms the liberal and popular doctrine of free trade" and that free trade with Europe "must operate to the serious disadvantage of the North" as "commerce will be largely diverted to the Southern cities."[59] The "chief instigator" of "the present troubles"—South Carolina—has all along been "preparing the way for the adoption of free trade" and must be stopped at any cost by "the closing of the ports" by military force.[60]

The war was just what was needed to break the logjam behind which the Whigs' mercantilist agenda had languished for decades.

---

[56]Howard Perkins, *Northern Editorials on Secession* (Gloucester, Mass.: Peter Smith, 1964), p. 573 (emphasis added).

[57]Ibid.

[58]Ibid., p. 600.

[59]Ibid., p. 601.

[60]Ibid., p. 602.

CORPORATE WELFARE

The fifty-year debate over the constitutionality of spending federal tax revenues on "internal improvements" or corporate welfare was ended once and for all by force of arms. What virtually every president since Jefferson had believed to be unconstitutional was now acceptable to the unprincipled Republicans, led by Lincoln. That the Confederate Constitution outlawed the use of tax dollars for "internal improvements" and deleted the "General Welfare" clause of the U.S. Constitution was another reason why the Republicans had to go to war if they were to finally implement the Whig agenda.[61]

The military–industrial–congressional complex was invented during the War Between the States as hundreds of Northern businesses developed "partnerships" with the federal government and fleeced the taxpayers in the process. As historian Leonard Curry observed, "Throughout the remainder of the nineteenth century [and beyond], corporate interests—apparently insatiable—returned again and again to demand direct and indirect federal subsidies."[62]

Lincoln and the Whig–Republicans had been promising taxpayer-funded subsidies to the railroad industry for so long, and were under such pressure to deliver once they controlled the entire federal government, that during the dark days of 1862, when the Confederates were clearly winning the war, they passed legislation and allocated millions of dollars to begin building a subsidized transcontinental railroad from the Midwest to California—far removed from the war in the East and of no military significance.

Railroad lobbyists descended on Washington in early 1862, the result of which was the creation of the federally-funded Union Pacific (UP) and Central Pacific (CP) Railroad Companies. Each company was given sections of land for each mile of track completed and $16,000 in loans for each mile of track on flat

[61]Marshall DeRosa, *The Confederate Constitution of 1861: An Inquiry into American Constitutionalism* (Columbia: University of Missouri Press, 1992).

[62]Leonard Curry, *Blueprint for Modern America: Nonmilitary Legislation of the First Civil War Congress* (Nashville, Tenn.: Vanderbilt University Press, 1968), p. 247.

prairie land, $32,000 for hilly terrain, and $48,000 per mile in the mountains.[63]

The chief engineer of the Union Pacific was Grenville Dodge, a close friend of Lincoln's who had also been appointed as a general in the Union army despite his lack of military training. Dodge and other federal officers organized federal armies to massacre American Indians whose property was "in the way" of their grandiose plans for a socialized railroad industry. Thus, the killing of the Indians was another form of indirect corporate welfare for the railroad businesses.

The only thing that was "efficient" about the construction of the Union Pacific was the way in which Dodge and Thomas Durant, the vice president of the company, bilked the taxpayers. Since they were being paid by the mile, they built wastefully circuitous routes to collect for more mileage. They used the cheapest construction materials and stressed speed, not workmanship. Not only Indians, but also white farmers were evicted from their land, which led to violence and bloodshed as the farmers tried to protect their property with firearms.[64]

Dodge laid track on the ice and snow during the winters, and when the line had to be rebuilt in the spring, the railroad company pocketed even more federal subsidies. The officers of the two companies set up their own supply companies and used their government funds to purchase supplies from themselves on a noncompetitive-bid basis, thereby making money from both building and running the railroads. This practice was the source of the Credit Mobilier scandal which was aired during the Grant administration. (Credit Mobilier was the name of one of the construction companies).

Republican legislators accepted bribes in return for appointing railroad commissioners who were political appointees with no experience in the railroad business. By the time the line was completed in May 1869, the UP and CP were bankrupt. And the root cause of the corruption and bankruptcy was the fact that the railroads were not built on the free market but were part of a "partnership" with government. Government-subsidized industries will *inevitably* become corrupt and inefficient. Surely the Whig–Republicans understood this, in light of their

[63]Richardson, p. 178.

[64]Burton W. Folsom, Jr., *The Myth of the Robber Barons* (Herndon, Va.: Young America's Foundation, 1991), pp. 18–19.

previous experiences with government-subsidized "internal improvements" by state governments in earlier years. To these politicians, what mattered most was not the efficient operation of a railroad "in the public interest," but all the patronage opportunities such an undertaking presented to them. Their emphasis was never on efficiency and was always on politics. For example, in 1866:

> Thomas Durant wined and dined 150 "prominent citizens" (including Senators, an ambassador, and government bureaucrats) along a completed section of the railroad. He hired an orchestra, a caterer, six cooks, a magician, . . . and a photographer. For those with ecumenical palates, he served Chinese duck and Roman goose; the more adventurous were offered roast ox and antelope. All could have expensive wine and, for dessert, strawberries, peaches, and cherries. After dinner some of the men hunted buffalo from their coaches. Durant hoped that all would go back to Washington inclined to repay the UP for its hospitality.[65]

Credit Mobilier stock was given out to congressmen as a form of bribery, and General William Tecumseh Sherman who, after the war, was in charge of "clearing" the American Indians away from the areas in which the railroad lines were being built, was allowed to purchase land near Omaha at less than one-third of the going market rate ($2.50 per acre versus $8).[66]

Once the floodgates of corporate welfare were open, graft and corruption inevitably became commonplace during the Grant administrations (1869–1877). The Speaker of the House of Representatives, Schueler Colfax, who was later President Grant's vice president, was a beneficiary of the Credit Mobilier scandal, as were over a dozen prominent Republican congressmen. Grant's war secretary, W.W. Belknap, was forced to resign for having taken bribes; his private secretary, Orville Babcock, was involved with a ring of swindlers; his Treasury secretary, W.W. Richardson, was implicated in a tax swindle; and even Grant's ambassador to England, Robert Schenck, had to plead diplomatic immunity to avoid being arrested for selling Londoners worthless stock in American mining companies.[67]

[65]Ibid., pp. 20–21.

[66]Ibid., p. 21.

[67]Johnson, *A History of the American People*, p. 544.

All of these scandals were the inevitable consequence of the "partnership" between business and government that had been championed by Lincoln during his entire political career and put more fully into place by his fellow Republicans after his death. As Leonard Curry remarked, "the railway interests of the country . . . sustained and encouraged by federal funds, mushroomed into one of the most powerful and ruthless lobbies that the republic had ever known."[68] Following the cue of the railroad lobbyists, many other industries aspired to bilk the taxpayers as well. "Other interests, desirous of demonstrating that they, too, were powerful, and hence deserving of preference, hastened to the feast [of corporate welfare]."[69] Timber and mining companies essentially "captured" the 1862 Homestead Act for themselves by bribing politicians to give them a majority share of all the free land; and the U.S. Department of Agriculture was created in 1862 to dispense farm welfare, as it has done ever since.

The major economic fallacy that was employed to "justify" corporate welfare for the railroads was the assertion that private capital markets in particular, and free enterprise in general, could not be relied upon to build a transcontinental railroad. But railroad entrepreneur James J. Hill proved what a lie that was by building what was by far the most efficient transcontinental railroad—the Great Northern—without a penny of government subsidies or land grants.[70] "Our own line in the North," Hill proudly boasted, "was built without any government aid, even the right of way, through hundreds of miles of public lands, being paid for in cash."[71]

If it were not for the massive amounts of corporate welfare that were ladled out to railroad companies, there would certainly have been more companies like Hill's Great Northern that would have built transcontinental railroads faster, better, and cheaper. To make matters worse, the corruption that accompanied the federally-funded railroads led angry taxpayers to

[68]Curry, *Blueprint for Modern America*, p. 134.

[69]Ibid., p. 148.

[70]Folsom, *The Myth of the Robber Barons*, pp. 26–36; James J. Hill, *Highways of Progress* (New York: Doubleday, 1910); and Albro Martin, *James J. Hill and the Opening of the Northwest* (New York: Oxford University Press, 1976).

[71]Ibid., pp. 410–11.

demand regulation of the railroads, which made a truly free market in railroading an impossibility.

THE BANK! THE BANK!

The Whig dream of a central bank was also realized during the war. The National Currency Acts of 1863 and 1864 created a network of nationally chartered banks that issued national bank notes supplied to them by the comptroller of the Currency. The national banks were required to hold federal government bonds as backing for their note issues, thereby artificially increasing the demand for the Treasury's bonds.

State banks were driven into bankruptcy by a prohibitive 10 percent federal tax on the issuance of their bank notes. The Secret Service was created to police counterfeiting, thereby assuring that the federal government would have a monopoly in the counterfeiting business.

The nation's monetary system was finally nationalized, as the constitutional roadblocks that had previously been laid in place by Jacksonian Democrats were removed when the Southern Democrats left the Congress during the war (and for years thereafter). One lone dissenter was Representative Lazarus Powell of Kentucky, who presciently forecast that central banking "would enable the national Congress to destroy every institution of the States and cause all power to be consolidated and concentrated here [in Washington, D.C.]."[72] The Clay–Lincoln "American System" was complete.

LINCOLN'S MERCANTILIST LEGACY

Lincoln's economic legacy is the fraud, waste, abuse, economic inefficiency, and corruption of mercantilism which Lincoln's idol, Henry Clay, referred to as "The American System." The massive corruption of the notorious Grant administrations was the direct and inevitable consequence of the political triumph of Abraham Lincoln and the Whigs' mercantilist agenda.

Lincoln always maintained that his goal in life was to be "the DeWitt Clinton of Illinois"—the king of the patronage politicians. As such, he was the perfect front man for the collection of special interests that had been lobbying for protectionism,

---

[72]Cited in Richardson, *The Greatest Nation of Earth*, p. 90.

mercantilism, corporate welfare, and inflationism for the previous half century.

Like many prominent figures of his time—such as Robert E. Lee, who freed the slaves he had inherited—Lincoln was bothered by slavery and wished that it would disappear from the face of the earth. But he admittedly viewed his own emancipation policy as a means to an end, with the end being to "save the union" or, more precisely, to establish federal supremacy over the states and the citizens in order to implement the Whig economic agenda. "My paramount object in this struggle," Lincoln wrote in his famous August 22, 1862, letter to Horace Greeley, "is to save the Union, and is not either to save or destroy slavery. If I could save the Union without freeing any slave I would do it."[73]

During a debate with Stephen Douglas on September 18, 1858, Lincoln stated that he was never "in favor of bringing about in any way the social and political equality of the white and black races."[74] He was opposed to ever making voters or jurors of black people or ever allowing them to hold office or intermarry with white people.[75] He was "in favor of having the superior position assigned to the white race" and proposed sending all ex-slaves back to Africa.[76] In his December 1, 1862, message to Congress, Lincoln said, "I cannot make it better known than it already is, that I strongly favor colonization" back to Africa.[77]

Whenever Lincoln and the Republicans did propose doing something about slavery prior to 1861, it was only in the new territories, not in the South. But even then, the main reason for objecting to the extension of slavery into the new territories was not always a moral one. As William Seward explained: "The motive of those who protested against the extension of slavery had always really been concern for the welfare of the white man, and not an unnatural sympathy for the Negro."[78] That is,

---

[73]Basler, *Abraham Lincoln*, p. 652.

[74]Roy Basler, *The Collected Works of Abraham Lincoln* (New Brunswick, N.J.: Rutgers University Press, 1953), pp. 145–46.

[75]Ibid.

[76]Ibid.

[77]Ibid., p. 685.

[78]Cited in James McPherson, *The Struggle for Equality: Abolitionists and the Negro in the Civil War and Reconstruction* (Princeton, N.J.: Princeton University Press, 1966), p. 24.

the opponents of the extension of slavery into the new territories opposed it because they didn't want the slaves or ex-slaves to compete for jobs with white men. As Pennsylvania Representative David Wilmot stated when he introduced his famous proviso that forbade slavery in the new territories acquired after the Mexican War, he "had no morbid sympathy for the slave," but would "lead the cause and the rights of white freedmen."[79]

There was also a political concern. Because of the three-fifths clause of the Constitution, which counted each five slaves as three citizens for purposes of congressional representation, the extension of slavery into the new territories would artificially inflate Democratic Party representation there, and this was intolerable to the Republicans.

Even the vaunted Emancipation Proclamation failed to free a single slave. It only applied to rebel territory, and specifically exempted those parts of the South that were at the time (January 1863) occupied by federal armies. The president "has proclaimed emancipation only where he has notoriously no power to execute it," observed the *New York World*, while the *London Spectator* cynically noted that "the principle [embodied in the Emancipation Proclamation] is not that a human being cannot justly own another, but that he cannot own him unless he is loyal to the United States."[80] Indeed, federal troops who occupied Southern territory often enslaved the slaves for their own uses.[81]

The purpose of the Emancipation Proclamation may have been to attempt to make a statement to other countries—especially Britain and France—that they should not support the slave-holding South in the war. If that was its purpose, however, it was a failure. Most British opinion-makers were Southern sympathizers who believed the war was being fought against governmental tyranny by the United States, not over slavery.[82]

---

[79]Leon Litwack, *North of Slavery: The Negro in the Free States, 1790–1860* (Chicago: University of Chicago Press, 1961), p. 47.

[80]Shelby Foote, *The Civil War: A Narrative* (New York: Random House, 1986), pp. 707–08.

[81]James McPherson, *For Cause and Comrades: Why Men Fought the Civil War* (New York: Oxford University Press, 1997), p. 119.

[82]Sheldon Vanauken, *The Glittering Illusion: English Sympathy for the Southern Confederacy* (Washington, D.C.: Regnery, 1989).

After the war, many Southern whites were prohibited from voting during Reconstruction, while Republican Party activists made sure that the uneducated and propertyless ex-slaves voted for tax increase after tax increase at the state and local levels of government, ostensibly to pay for "internal improvements." All too often, however, the improvements never materialized, while the Republican Party hacks lined their personal bank accounts with confiscated tax dollars.

This, of course, spawned even greater resentment toward Northerners, with the resentment frequently vented in a violent way against the ex-slaves. Most countries in the Western Hemisphere that ended slavery during the first half of the nineteenth century (and there were dozens of them) did so peacefully through compensated emancipation, something that was never seriously attempted in the U.S.[83] The economic destruction of the South during the war and the continued looting of Southern citizens for many years thereafter, wherein the ex-slaves were used as political pawns by the Republicans, guaranteed that a tremendous amount of racial animosity would exist in the South long after the war ended.

Thus, in a way, Lincoln's mercantilist legacy is also a root cause of many of the race relations problems that plague America to this day.

[83]Thomas J. DiLorenzo, "The Great Centralizer: Abraham Lincoln and the War Between the States," *The Independent Review* (Fall 1998).

8

LINCOLN AND THE
FIRST SHOT: A STUDY
OF DECEIT AND DECEPTION

JOHN V. DENSON

In almost every poll of public opinion or assessment by professional historians which has been published since World War II, Presidents Abraham Lincoln and Franklin Roosevelt rank in the top three as two of our "greatest."[1] Arthur M. Schlesinger, Sr., who conducted the first poll of historians in 1948, concluded that the ratings as to "greatness" were heavily influenced by a particular president's connection with "some turning point in our history."[2] Undoubtedly, the American Civil War and World War II were major "turning points" in American history and therefore greatly influenced the high ratings of these two presidents. The position of "greatness," however, necessarily assumes that neither of these presidents had any guilt in bringing on these wars. Instead, it is assumed that both presidents were peace-seekers, trying to lead the nation toward a reconciliation of its problems and trying to avoid a war until the enemy fired the first shot and forced an unwanted war upon these presidents and the American people.

The Roman lawyer Cicero struggled with the question of what is a "just war," as did the Christian philosophers of the Medieval period, from Augustus to Aquinas. Later, the father of international law, the Dutchman Hugo Grotius, addressed the question also because he was concerned that wars which Christians might fight would be done with a clear conscience toward God. As a result of these developing ideas, Western political leaders have tried to convince their citizens or subjects that their wars met one of the main criteria; that is, that the wars were

---

[1]Robert Murray and Tim H. Blessing, "The Presidential Performance Study: A Progress Report," *Journal of American History* 70 (December 1983): 535.

[2]Ibid., p. 553.

"defensive." President John F. Kennedy declared in January 1961 that "Our arms will never be used to strike the first blow in any attack. . . . It is our national tradition."[3] It has always been important to American presidents to try to demonstrate that the enemy fired the first shot and started the war.

Those who support the mythology that surrounds Lincoln and Franklin Roosevelt have tried to resist the nagging question which continues to assert itself about whether these presidents actually maneuvered the enemy into firing the first shot in order to produce wars that they wanted but that the people did not. In both cases, war caused great power and prestige to flow to the presidency, and most of the imagined "greatness" of these two presidents therefore arises from their perceived conduct as war leaders and protectors of "American liberty and rights." The question concerning the Lincoln administration will be dealt with here and a subsequent chapter will examine President Franklin Roosevelt. Nonetheless, the question in regard to both is whether they provoked the enemy into firing the first shot.

Most wars are fought for economic reasons, but the general population will rarely rally around the flag for such causes; therefore, other reasons are usually given for the purpose of any war, in order to persuade mothers and fathers to send their sons off to an uncertain future which could very easily result in their return in body bags. For this reason, both the Civil War and World War II have been clothed in a mythology which states that the Civil War was fought for the purpose of "abolishing slavery" and World War II was fought to oppose "tyranny" or "Fascism."

The investigation of why the South fired the first shot at Fort Sumter raises the question of whether the firing on Fort Sumter by the South started the war or whether there were preceding, provocative, and precipitating acts on the part of President Lincoln and his administration which caused the South to fire first.

One of the essential reasons the South wanted out of the Union was to avoid economic exploitation by the North, and one of the main reasons the Northern political and economic interests refused to allow the South to secede was that they wanted to continue this economic exploitation. The long–standing

[3]Richard N. Current, *Lincoln and The First Shot* (Prospect Heights, Ill.: Waveland Press, 1963), p. 7.

dispute over slavery that existed between the North and South was not whether slavery should be abolished where it already existed but, rather, whether slavery should be expanded into the new territories and new states. The small but vociferous band of abolitionists in the North were the only ones calling for the abolition of slavery where it already existed and could be accomplished through the secession of the North. The abolitionists argued that secession would relieve the North from the obligation to enforce the fugitive slave clause in the Constitution, which required the North to return slaves. Both Horace Greely, owner of the *New York Tribune*, and the abolitionist Harry Ward Beecher said, "Let the South go."[4] The abolitionists, however, were very unpopular in the North, primarily because secession was not a popular issue there just before the Civil War, although it had been in previous times.[5] The concern of the North was that if slavery was expanded into new states, the South would have more representation in Congress in both the House and Senate, thereby allowing the South to protect itself from economic exploitation.

The story of the cause of the Civil War goes all the way back to the Constitutional Convention in which one of the major disputes was whether a simple majority vote or a two-thirds vote would be required for the passage of the Navigation Acts, which included the tariff legislation. Both at the time of the adoption of the Constitution and the Civil War, the tariff constituted the primary (more than 80 percent) of the revenue for the federal government. George Mason, one of the Virginia delegates to the Constitutional Convention, argued for a two-thirds vote as follows:

> If the Government is to be lasting, it must be founded in the confidence and affections of the people, and must be so constructed as to obtain these. The *Majority* will be governed by their interests. The Southern States are the *minority* in both

[4]W.A. Swanberg, *First Blood: The Story of Fort Sumter* (New York: Charles Scribener's Sons, 1957), p. 155.

[5]See David Gordon, ed., *Secession, State and Liberty*, (New Brunswick, N.J.: Transaction Publishers, 1998), which covers the subject of secession in America thoroughly and shows that both the North and the South had championed this "right" and both had threatened to secede on numerous occasions before the Civil War.

Houses. Is it to be expected that they will deliver themselves bound hand & foot to the Eastern States, and enable them to exclaim, in the words of Cromwell on a certain occasion—"the lord hath delivered them into our hands."[6]

Fellow Virginia delegate James Madison, who was a strong supporter of the Constitution and, in fact, is known to us today as "The Father of the Constitution," resisted Mason's request for a two-thirds vote and argued that there would be no exploitation of the South if there was a simple majority vote to enact tariff legislation.[7] The final draft of the Constitution that was approved in Philadelphia had only a simple majority requirement for tariff legislation, and Mason refused to sign the document. One writer, in analyzing this dispute over the tariff between Mason and Madison—which later became the most important cause of the American Civil War—shows that Mason continued his opposition to the Constitution in the Virginia ratification convention by continuing to demand a two-thirds vote on any tariff legislation.[8]

At the time of the adoption of the Constitution, the North had a larger population than the South, but there was an attempt to compensate for this by counting a fraction of the slave population

---

[6]Gaillard Hunt and James Brown Scott, eds., *The Debates in the Federal Convention of 1787 Which Framed the Constitution of the United States of America* (Buffalo, N.Y.: Prometheus Books, 1987), vol. 2, p. 485. Also see p. 575 for Mason's statement about the two-thirds vote and p. 582 for his refusal to sign the Constitution along with Randolph and Gerry.

[7]Ibid., p. 485.

[8]See K.R. Constantine Gutzman, "'Oh, What a Tangled Web We Weave . . .': James Madison and the Compound Republic," *Continuity: A Journal of History* 22 (1998): 24.

> In our own day, with the NAFTA and GATT controversies, we have been reminded of the potentially contentious nature of trade arguments. In Madison's day, such disputes were even more contentious, even more acrimonious. Especially after Henry Clay's "American System" speech of 1824, in which the Kentuckian frankly admitted that his program was an intersectional transfer of wealth, tariff arguments were potentially violent. Mason predicted in Philadelphia that the requirement of a bare majority for the enactment of tariff legislation would lead to Northern exploitation of the South of the kind Clay later made famous. Madison immediately issued a long declamation on the impossibility of such a turn of events.

as part of the total population for determining representation in the House of Representatives—a concept that became known as the "federal ratio." One of the reasons the Northern politicians opposed slavery was that it gave the South too much political power. Another factor was that the North quickly adapted to the Industrial Revolution which had started in England and then crossed the Atlantic, causing the North to become more industrial than agricultural by 1820. The new industrial jobs caused a rapid increase in the population of the North, which gave it much more representation in the House of Representatives, but this factor was partially balanced by the practice of admitting two new states at a time with one being a slave state and the other being a free state (so that representation in the Senate was equal). The South also sought to protect itself by sending its most prominent citizens to Congress and by a close cooperation with Northern Democrats.

In 1824, Kentuckian Henry Clay made his famous "American System" speech and frankly admitted that the tariff should be high enough to protect "American" industry from manufactured imports from Europe, primarily England. A tariff levied on an import could be made high enough that a purchaser would be better off buying the Northern-made product. As the South was almost entirely an agricultural region, it had to buy almost all of its manufactured products either from Europe, and pay the protective tariff, or from Northern industries, and pay, in most cases, an excessive price. About three-fourths of the total tariff collected in the U.S. was paid by the Southerners. Another development which began to divide the North and South was that the political power of the North also allowed it to keep a vast majority of the tariff revenue and use it for "internal improvements," such as building harbors and canals, which was, in effect, a corporate welfare program. The North claimed a right to do this under the "general welfare" clause of the Constitution, but the South objected, stating that this was an incorrect understanding of the meaning of this clause. Internal improvements were also a major part of Henry Clay's "American System," which in reality was a partnership between government and the business interests in the North.

In 1828, the North had enough political power to pass an extremely high protective tariff, which became known as the "Tariff of Abominations." This led to the nullification movement in South Carolina in 1832 under the leadership of John C. Calhoun.

South Carolina declared that the tariff was nullified or void in the state of South Carolina; however, a subsequent reduction in the tariff by Congress settled the problem temporarily. Charleston, South Carolina, was the primary focus of this entire battle because this was where most of the tariff was collected, and Fort Sumter, manned by federal troops, constituted the means for enforcement of the collection of the tariff. The tariff continued to be an extremely hot issue between the North and South up to the Civil War, with Henry Clay being both an instigator and pacificator of the conflict until his death in 1852.[9]

The new Republican Party, which had only come into existence in 1854, adopted a platform in 1860 that explicitly called for a high protective tariff and internal improvements and, therefore, was a direct threat to the South. Lincoln fully subscribed to this platform before and after his presidential nomination by the Republicans. Lincoln won his election with less than 40 percent of the popular vote, carrying only eighteen of thirty-three states, and he did not have a single electoral vote cast for him in the South. While Lincoln's position on the tariff and internal improvements was an ominous economic sign, the South still had hope that Lincoln would not oppose secession. During Lincoln's one term in Congress, he had been a vocal opponent of the U.S.–Mexican War of 1846 and had supported the right of secession as a way of protesting the war. The threat of secession had been asserted, not only by the South because of the tariff, but by the North, especially New England, on numerous occasions: in 1803 with the Louisiana Purchase, at the Hartford Convention in opposition to the War of 1812, and then

---

[9]For a full discussion of the tariff issue, see three books by Charles Adams, *For Good and Evil: The Impact of Taxes on the Course of Civilization*, 2nd ed. (New York: Madison Books, 1999), pp. 329–43, *Those Dirty Rotten Taxes: The Tax Revolts that Built America* (New York: The Free Press, 1998), pp. 81–112, and *When In The Course of Human Events: Arguing the Case for Southern Secession* (Lanham, Md.: Rowman and Littlefield, 2000). See also Kenneth M. Stampp, *And the War Came: The North and the Secession Crisis, 1860–1861* (Baton Rouge: Louisiana State University Press, 1990), pp. 2, 4, 43–44, 161–64, 231–38. Finally, see Phillip S. Foner, *Business and Slavery: The New York Merchants and The Irrepressible Conflict* (Chapel Hill, N.C.: Duke University Press. 1941), pp. 275–305.

again, at the time of the Mexican War.[10] Lincoln proclaimed his strong endorsement of the right of secession in 1847 as follows:

> Any people, anywhere, being inclined and having the power, have the right to rise up and shake off the existing government, and form a new one that suits them better. *This is a most valuable, a most sacred right, a right which we hope and believe is to liberate the world.*[11]

After the election of 1860, the new Republican Party was very much a minority in both the House and Senate, and it claimed only one Supreme Court justice. This new political party was made up of some abolitionists and former Democrats, but mostly former Whigs like Lincoln, who stood for a strong centralized government, a high protective tariff, internal improvements, a loose interpretation of the Constitution, and a partnership between big business in the North and government that would allow business to expand westward, and even to other countries, if necessary.

As soon as Lincoln was elected, attention again focused on South Carolina because of the tariff issue. There were three federal forts in the Charleston harbor, but Fort Sumter stood squarely in the middle of the channel and constituted the main weapon for enforcement of the tariff. Should South Carolina secede, it would be imperative to reclaim the fort. At the time of South Carolina's coming into the Union, it had made a gift or deed of trust of the land and Fort Sumter to the federal government. Because the fort also provided the ultimate defense from invasion of the harbor, whoever controlled Fort Sumter would control Charleston, a key Southern city.

On December 9, 1860, all the congressmen from South Carolina met with President Buchanan in Washington and got a verbal pledge from him that he would not make any move to reinforce Fort Sumter.[12] Unknown to the South, President-elect Lincoln, who would not take office until March 4, 1861,

---

[10]For a full discussion, see Donald W. Livingston, "The Secession Tradition in America," pp. 1–33, and Thomas J. DiLorenzo, "Yankee Confederates: New England Secessionists Movement Prior to the War Between the States," pp. 135–53, in *Secession, State and Liberty*, David Gordon, ed. (New Brunswick, N.J.: Transaction Publishers, 1998).

[11]John Shipley Tilley, *Lincoln Takes Command* (Nashville, Tenn.: Bill Coats, 1991), p. xv (emphasis added).

[12]Ibid., p. 121.

communicated directly on December 12, 1860, with General Winfield Scott, head of the army under the Buchanan administration, and told him to be sure to hold and retake all federal forts in the South.[13] Soon thereafter, on December 20, South Carolina became the first state to leave the Union. Six days later, Major Robert Anderson, on his own initiative, moved his federal troops into Fort Sumter from Fort Moultrie, a nearby military installation. There was an immediate uproar throughout the South, and Senator Jefferson Davis of Mississippi asserted that this was an overt act of war on the part of President Buchanan, who indicated truthfully that he had not authorized this reinforcement of Fort Sumter.[14] Governor F.W. Pickens of South Carolina complained to President Buchanan and again received assurances from him that there would not be any further reinforcement of any forts in South Carolina, and especially Fort Sumter.[15]

Major Anderson wrote a letter to his commanding officer in Washington on December 26, 1860, reporting that he had one year's supply of hospital stores as well as food provisions for about four months, which would be through April 26, 1861.[16] This food supply was that which was available in Fort Sumter, but Anderson quickly developed a good relationship with the mayor of Charleston and other local Charleston merchants, so that from that point on, he was getting daily supplies from grocers and butchers. Therefore, Anderson was in no danger of lack of food supplies from this point up until just a few days before the firing on Fort Sumter. Also, following Anderson's move to Fort Sumter, Secretary of War Floyd resigned, stating that Anderson's action was an act of bad faith on the part of the Buchanan administration which he could no longer support.[17]

Before continuing with the full story of Fort Sumter, it is important to look at the other key fort that was a focal point of dispute between the North and South at this time—that is, Fort Pickens in Pensacola Bay, Florida—because this also sheds light upon Lincoln's intentions and actions at Fort Sumter. While Fort Pickens was not a primary tariff collection port, it was an essential military installation for the Southern part of

---

[13]Ibid., pp. 105–06.
[14]Ibid., p. 110.
[15]Ibid., p. 122.
[16]Ibid.
[17]Ibid., p. 126.

the United States and for the Confederacy. The state of Florida seceded from the Union on January 10, 1861, and through its former U.S. senator, Stephen Mallory, and its governor, made an immediate demand upon President Buchanan on January 15, for the return of Fort Pickens and the immediate evacuation of all federal troops. After much discussion and threats from both sides, the state of Florida and the Buchanan administration entered into a formal truce on January 29. The agreement was that if there was no reinforcement of Fort Pickens by the North, then the South would not fire upon the fort, which would allow time for the parties to attempt to work out their other differences.

After Lincoln's inauguration on March 4, 1861, he violated this truce by issuing secret executive orders on March 11 and 12 to send reinforcements to Fort Pickens. The order was actually signed by General Winfield Scott, who kept the same position in the Lincoln administration as he had in the previous administration as head of the army. When Captain Adams of the U.S. Navy, who was in charge of Fort Pickens, received the order from General Scott in March 1861 to send out boats to pick up reinforcements on the warships that were near the harbor, Adams refused to obey the order. Adams was very familiar with the terms of the truce and thought there had been some misunderstanding by the new administration. He knew this reinforcement was an explicit violation of the agreement without any provocation on the part of the South. He fully realized that this act alone would start the war. Furthermore, as a captain in the navy, he was unwilling to take an order from General Scott, who was head of the army, so he sent word back that he wanted clarification from his naval commander.[18]

On April 1, President Lincoln issued a series of secret executive orders, some over his name and some over the name of Secretary of the Navy Gideon Welles, to send troops to reinforce Fort Pickens. Captain M.C. Meigs was present in the office of the president when he issued these orders, and Meigs wrote a letter dated April 6, in which he explained his reaction to the events he had observed on April 1.

> While the mere throwing of a few men into Fort Pickens may seem a small operation, the opening of the campaign is a great one. Unless this movement is followed up by the navy and

[18]Ibid., pp. 48–52.

supported by ample supplies . . . it will be a failure. This is the beginning of the war.[19]

Captain Meigs clearly saw that the act of reinforcement was an act of war and violated the truce that existed between the United States and Florida (and the Confederacy), and that war was being started secretly by the act of the president without any consultation with Congress. The warships came to Pensacola harbor, but because reinforcement actually did not take place until the night of April 12 under the complete cover of darkness, it was not perceived by the South until the next day.[20] Negotiations continued, however, after the South discovered the violation of the truce, and the military commanders were still exchanging communications until April 17, before any shots were fired.[21]

Later, after the war had started and Lincoln had addressed Congress on July 4, 1861, Congress made a written inquiry dated July 19, requesting documents about the armistice at Fort Pickens. President Lincoln replied by sending Navy Secretary Welles to Congress with a written message dated July 30, in which the president declined to produce any documents, claiming executive privilege, and stating "it is believed the communication of the information called for would not, at this time, comport with the public interest."[22]

Returning now to the developments at Fort Sumter, a major event occurred there on January 9, 1861. Without prior notice to or knowledge of Major Anderson at Fort Sumter, a merchant ship named *Star of the West* entered Charleston harbor and headed toward Fort Sumter. It had been learned by the South, just prior to this event, that hidden below the deck were two hundred armed soldiers with ammunition, and supplies; therefore, the South Carolina troops fired a shot across the bow as a warning to the ship, which then reversed its course and left the area. Secretary of Interior Thompson resigned his position in the Buchanan administration over this incident, saying that it indicated bad faith on the part of the administration.[23] President

[19]Ibid., p. 63.

[20]Ibid., p. 66.

[21]Ibid., p. 75.

[22]Ibid., p. 92.

[23]Ibid., p. 156.

Buchanan again claimed that the event occurred without his authority, but actually he had authorized the attempt to reinforce and then unsuccessfully tried to revoke the order.[24] On January 12, Governor Pickens of South Carolina again demanded the return of the fort, but President Buchanan stated he had no authority to do so.[25] Even though the fort had been a gift from South Carolina to the Union, South Carolina was willing to pay fair-market value for all of the land and improvements in exchange for its return and the evacuation of the federal troops. Governor Pickens at this time made it clear to President Buchanan and his administration, a position which soon became public knowledge, that any future attempt by any ship to provide reinforcements would immediately cause South Carolina to fire directly upon the ship and Fort Sumter.[26] Also in the discussions with President Buchanan, it was pointed out that simply the act of sending the ship for reinforcement was an act of war and would not be tolerated.[27]

On February 4, the Confederate government had taken over jurisdiction of all federal property still located in the South, which included both Forts Sumter and Pickens.[28] On February 6, President Buchanan also reaffirmed the armistice in regard to Fort Pickens to the effect that there would be no further reinforcements. As he had earlier indicated, this was also the case at Fort Sumter. In return, the South would not fire on either fort as long as no reinforcement was attempted.

On February 7, retired Navy Captain Gustavus Fox approached the Buchanan administration and General Winfield Scott, in particular, with his secret plan to reinforce Fort Sumter successfully. It called for a nighttime maneuver involving several tugs to go first, pulling whaling boats full of men and supplies, and then several warships with more troops to follow. General Scott presented Fox and his plan to Secretary of War Holt, who liked the plan, but on the next day Scott informed Fox

---

[24]Swanberg, *First Blood*, pp. 121, 123, 127, 145.

[25]Tilley, *Lincoln Takes Command*, pp. 149–51.

[26]Ibid., p. 152.

[27]Ibid.

[28]Ibid., p. 154.

that any plans to reinforce Fort Sumter were being abandoned by the Buchanan administration.[29]

On March 2, President Buchanan signed the Morrill Tariff into law, which was the highest protective tariff in American history, and by early 1862, it reached the average amount of 47.06 percent.[30] The Morrill Tariff remained the cornerstone policy of the Republican Party up through the twentieth century. President Buchanan was from Pennsylvania, a traditional high-tariff state, and even though he was leaving office in two days, he wanted to protect his political career by signing this act, which was popular in Pennsylvania but an ominous threat to the South. Two days later, on March 4, the nation waited with great anticipation for President Lincoln's Inaugural Address. Lincoln addressed the question of slavery directly and openly by quoting from one of his previously published speeches:

> I have no purpose, directly or indirectly, to interfere with the institution of slavery in the States where it exists. I believe I have no lawful right to do so, and I have no inclination to do so.[31]

Lincoln had also required each of his cabinet members to take a solemn pledge that they would enforce the Constitution, and particularly the fugitive slave clause, which required the North to return fugitive slaves to the South.[32] Lincoln specifically promised in his speech to enforce this clause. Furthermore, historian David Potter points out that:

> Lincoln returned, later in his speech, to the question of Constitutional protection for slavery in the states. He alluded to the proposed Thirteenth Amendment, just passed by Congress, to guarantee slavery in the states, and added that, although he wished to speak of general policy, rather than specific measures, he would say that, holding such a guarantee to be

---

[29]Ibid., p. 153.

[30]Frank Taussig, *The Tariff History of the United States* (New York: Putnam, 1931), p. 167.

[31]David M. Potter, *Lincoln and His Party in the Secession Crisis* (Baton Rouge: Louisiana State University Press, 1995), p. 321.

[32]John Nevin, *Gideon Welles, Lincoln's Secretary of Navy* (Baton Rouge: Louisiana State University Press, 1994), p. 311.

implied in the existing Constitution, "I have no objection to its being made express and irrevocable."[33]

President Lincoln thereby completely removed the slavery issue from contention between the North and South by promising to enforce the fugitive slave clause and supporting a Constitutional amendment which would explicitly protect slavery. The protection for slavery had only been implied in the original Constitution in three places; that is, the fugitive slave clause, the ban on the slave trade, and the three-fifths ratio clause.

Lincoln apologists often point to the following concluding gesture to the South in the Inaugural Address to prove that he wanted peace instead of war:

> In your hands, my dissatisfied fellow countrymen, and not in mine, is the momentous issue of civil war. The government will not assail you. You can have no conflict without being yourselves the aggressors.[34]

The mythology which has surrounded Lincoln usually cites the above quotation as showing that Lincoln was doing everything within his power to prevent a war. However, immediately after his Inaugural Address, the South considered the speech to have been a declaration of war by Lincoln, even though Lincoln said nothing that threatened the institution of slavery in the South. Therefore, there must have been other words in his address which caused the South to consider that he had declared war. We find those words in his speech:

> The power confided to me will be used to hold, occupy, and possess the property and places belonging to the government, *and to collect the duties and imposts*; but beyond what *may be necessary for these objects*, there will be no *invasion*, no *using of force* against or among the people anywhere.[35]

---

[33]Potter, *Lincoln and His Party in the Secession Crisis*, p. 321.

[34]Charles W. Ramsdell, "Lincoln and Fort Sumter," *The Journal of Southern History* 3 (Southern Historical Association, February–November, 1937): 264.

[35]Carl Van Doren, ed., "First Inaugural Address," *The Literary Works of Abraham Lincoln* (Norwalk, Conn.: Easton Press, 1970), pp. 177–78 (emphasis added).

Senator Wigfall of Texas immediately notified Governor Pickens that the address meant war sooner or later, and in all likelihood, no time should be lost in sending reinforcements to Fort Sumter.[36] Another prominent Southerner, L.Q. Washington, who was in Washington, D.C., and heard the address, forwarded to Confederate Secretary of War Leroy Walker a letter echoing Wigfall's opinion, which undoubtedly was shared with the members of the Confederate cabinet. The letter stated:

> We all put the same construction on the inaugural, which we carefully went over together. We agreed that it was *Lincoln's purpose at once to attempt the collection of the revenue*, to reenforce and hold Forts Sumter and Pickens, and to retake the other places.
>
> We believe that these plans will be put into execution immediately. I learned five or six United States ships are in New York Harbor, all ready to start. The United States steamer *Pawnee* came here the other day suddenly from Philadelphia, fully provisioned and ready to go to sea.[37]

Furthermore, President Lincoln, in his Inaugural Address, repudiated his prior stand taken during the U.S.–Mexican War that secession was a "most valuable, a most sacred right" of each state within the Union and proclaimed that "no state upon its own mere motion, can lawfully get out of the Union."[38] Later, during the war, however, Lincoln again recognized the right of forty-nine counties to secede from Virginia and to become the new state of West Virginia. The creation of the new state in this manner violated Article V, Section 3, of the Constitution, but nevertheless took place solely because of the pledge of loyalty of the residents of West Virginia. Of course, this added two new senators and additional representatives, who were all loyal to Lincoln.

In accordance with the resolution of the Confederate Congress, President Davis appointed three commissioners to negotiate with the United States all questions of disagreement between the two governments.[39] The appointments took place

---

[36]Tilley, *Lincoln Takes Command*, p. 163.

[37]Ibid., pp. 163–64, (emphasis added).

[38]Potter, *Lincoln and His Party in the Secession Crisis*, p. 322.

[39]Ramsdell, "Lincoln and Fort Sumter," p. 264.

on February 25, and reached Washington on March 5, the day after Lincoln's inauguration. The Confederate government was offering to assume its proportion of any federal debt and pay fair market value for all federal property remaining within the seceding states. It also sought recognition of its independence as a separate government by the Lincoln administration. Davis had stated that the South simply wanted to be let alone and constituted no threat to the existing government in Washington: "We seek no conquest, no aggrandizement, no concession of any kind . . . all we ask is to be let alone."[40]

President Lincoln refused to see the commissioners, refused to negotiate any peace terms, and, furthermore, refused to recognize the Confederate government. In regard to Fort Sumter, he continued to deal only with Governor Pickens of South Carolina. The commissioners were never able to speak directly with President Lincoln; and, as will be shown in more detail later, their negotiations had to go through two U.S. Supreme Court justices to Secretary of State Seward, who led them to believe that he spoke for the Lincoln administration.

Meanwhile, on March 9, President Lincoln asked his primary military adviser, General Scott, to investigate Major Anderson's condition at Fort Sumter and advise him on the feasibility of reinforcement. The diary of Attorney General Edward Bates reveals that a cabinet meeting was held on March 9 to consider the desirability of sending reinforcements to Charleston. The army and navy military representatives presented their opinions, which were recorded by Bates with the following language in his diary: "The naval men have convinced me fully that the thing can be done, *and yet as the doing of it would be almost certain to begin the war* . . . I am willing to yield to the military counsel and evacuate Fort Sumter."[41] However, on March 11, as we have already seen, President Lincoln told General Scott to issue an order to reinforce Fort Pickens, which order was refused by Captain Adams. Also, on March 11, Senator Wigfall of Texas telegraphed General Beauregard stating that the opinion in Washington was that there had been a cabinet meeting, and it had been decided that Anderson would be ordered to evacuate

[40]William C. Davis, *A Government of Our Own: The Making of the Confederacy* (New York: The Free Press, 1994), pp. 340–41.

[41]Tilley, *Lincoln Takes Command*, p. 165 (emphasis added).

Fort Sumter within five days.[42] On March 12, Postmaster General Montgomery Blair contacted his brother-in-law, retired naval officer Gustavus Fox, and took him personally to see President Lincoln in order to explain his reinforcement plan which had been rejected by the Buchanan administration.[43] After hearing Fox's plan, as well as the recommendation of the military advisers, including Generals Scott and Totten, Lincoln called another cabinet meeting for March 15 and asked for each member of his cabinet to respond in writing about what should be done regarding Fort Sumter. All the cabinet members opposed in writing any reinforcement of Fort Sumter, except Postmaster General Blair, who offered to resign from the cabinet when the Fox plan was rejected.[44] Secretary of State Seward, who was generally considered the number two man to Lincoln, consistently opposed any reinforcement of Fort Sumter because he thought it would initiate a war with the South. His written note to the president contained these words:

> Suppose the expedition successful, we have then a garrison in Fort Sumter that can defy assault for six months. What is it to do then? Is it to make war by opening its batteries and attempting to demolish the defenses of the Carolinians? . . . I may be asked whether I would in no case, and at no time advise force—whether I propose to give up everything? I reply no. *I would not initiate war to regain a useless and unnecessary position on the soil of the seceding States.*[45]

Secretary of Treasury Chase said in his note to the president:

> *If the attempt will so inflame civil war* as to involve an immediate necessity for the enlistment of armies and the expedition of millions, I cannot advise it in the existing circumstances of the country and in the present condition of the national finances.[46]

---

[42]Ibid.

[43]Ibid., p. 166.

[44]Ibid., p. 167.

[45]Edgar Lee Masters, *Lincoln, the Man* (Columbia, S.C.: The Foundation for American Education, 1997), p. 392 (emphasis added).

[46]Ibid. (emphasis added).

Secretary of War Cameron advised against reinforcement with these words:

> Whatever might have been done as late as a month ago, it is too sadly evident that it cannot now be done without the sacrifice of life and treasure not at all commensurate with the object to be attained; and as the abandonment of the fort in a few weeks, sooner or later, appears to be an inevitable necessity, it seems to me that the sooner it is done the better.[47]

Cameron also stated that:

> The proposition presented by Mr. Fox, so sincerely entertained and ably advocated, would be entitled to my favorable consideration if, with all the light before me and in the face of so many distinguished military authorities on the other side, I did not believe that *the attempt to carry it into effect would initiate a bloody and protracted conflict.*[48]

Secretary of Navy Welles opposed either sending *provisions* or reinforcing the fort with troops and stated:

> *By sending, or attempting to send provisions into Sumter, will not war be precipitated?* It may be impossible to escape it under any course of policy that may be pursued, *but I am not prepared to advise a course that would provoke hostilities.* It does not appear to me that the dignity, strength, or character of the government will be promoted by an attempt to provision Sumter in the manner proposed, even should it succeed, while a failure would be attended with untold disaster.[49]

Attorney General Bates opposed the plan with these words:

> The possession of the fort, as we now hold it, *does not enable us to collect the revenue* or enforce the laws of commercial navigation. It may indeed involve a point of honor or a point of pride, but I do not see any great national interest involved in the bare fact of holding the fort as we now hold it.[50]

---

[47]Ibid., pp. 392–93.

[48]Tilley, *Lincoln Takes Command*, p. 171 (emphasis added).

[49]Masters, *Lincoln, the Man*, p. 393 (emphasis added).

[50]Ibid., (emphasis added).

General Scott and General Totten both appeared before the cabinet meeting, and Scott submitted a written memorandum stating his military opinion. He not only opposed the Fox plan, but recommended that Forts Sumter and Pickens be evacuated immediately. He further stated that Captain Fox's plan of *simply making the attempt to approach the Fort with the ships "will inevitably involve a collision."*[51] Scott further pointed out that even if the plan was successful, they would not be able to hold the fort for any appreciable time. General Scott stated also that the evacuation of Forts Sumter and Pickens would strongly impress to the eight remaining slave states that had not seceded and this might hold them in the Union.[52] President Lincoln received the advice both from the military officers and his cabinet and, with only one member of the cabinet supporting the plan, it was determined not to implement the Fox plan since the mere attempt to initiate the plan would undoubtedly cause a war.

Charles W. Ramsdell, in his excellent study of all the official records and diaries of the people involved, also points out:

> One plan which he [Lincoln] seems to have entertained for a short while, just after the adverse cabinet vote on relieving Sumter, contemplated the collection of customs duties on revenue vessels, supported by ships of war, just outside the Confederate ports; and there were hints in the press that Anderson's force was to be withdrawn to a ship off Charleston. If it were seriously considered, the plan was soon abandoned, possibly because of legal impediments or more probably because it did not fully meet the needs of the situation.[53]

Fox was a very persistent person, however, and, subsequent to this cabinet meeting, he asked Lincoln if he could go to Fort Sumter before a final decision was made in order to see for himself the conditions that were there. Lincoln had General Scott authorize a visit by Fox to Charleston to meet with Major Anderson, which Fox did on March 22. Also on that date, President Lincoln authorized two personal delegates, S.A. Hurlbut and Ward H. Lamon, to go to South Carolina. Hurlbut was to determine if there was any Unionist sympathy within South

[51]Tilley, *Lincoln Takes Command*, p. 172 (emphasis added).

[52]Ibid.

[53]Ramsdell, "Lincoln and Fort Sumter," p. 268.

Carolina and particularly in Charleston. Lamon was a longtime trusted friend of the president, having been his law partner, and he was to visit both Governor Pickens and Major Anderson at Fort Sumter.[54]

Fox met directly with Anderson, who informed him that it would be impossible to reinforce the fort from the sea. Anderson stated that the only way to reinforce the fort successfully would be to have a massive army come from Morris Island. Anderson further warned Fox that any attempts to send reinforcements from the sea would cause the South to fire, thereby causing an unnecessary war. *It would be a provocative act merely to make the attempt.*[55] Anderson also informed Fox that there was *no need for food*, as he had an agreement with Governor Pickens and merchants in Charleston to furnish fresh groceries and meat on a daily basis. Anderson had already written his superior officers in Washington, "I do hope that no attempt will be made by our friends to throw supplies in; their doing so would do more harm than good."[56]

Hurlbut found that there was no significant amount of Unionist sympathy in Charleston, and therefore it could not be depended upon for any assistance. Lamon met with Governor Pickens and represented to him that he had come to arrange for the removal of Major Anderson and his entire garrison, and even described the type of ships that would come later to remove the troops. He informed Governor Pickens that he would be coming back soon and personally participating in the removal of the troops.[57] Lamon also learned from Governor Pickens that any attempt to send any ships to Fort Sumter, even if only bringing supplies, would cause the South to fire on the fort.[58] In fact, both Hurlbut and Lamon reported back to the president the key information he was seeking and that would be essential for his cabinet meeting on March 29—that is, *even sending supplies would cause the South to fire on the fort.*[59]

---

[54]Potter, *Lincoln and His Party in the Secession Crisis*, pp. 340–41.

[55]Tilley, *Lincoln Takes Command*, pp. 176–78.

[56]Ibid., p. 147.

[57]Potter, *Lincoln and His Party in the Secession Crisis*, p. 340.

[58]Ramsdell, "Lincoln and Fort Sumter," p. 274.

[59]Bruce Catton, *The Coming Fury* (Garden City, N.Y.: Doubleday, 1961), pp. 281–82.

Meanwhile, Congress was still in session and the U.S. Senate became interested in the negotiations and sent word to President Lincoln that they wanted to be informed about the matters regarding Fort Sumter. President Lincoln sent General Scott who testified that he had recommended abandonment of Fort Sumter and felt that this was imperative. The Senate then passed a resolution requesting that President Lincoln furnish them copies of all correspondence with Major Anderson, but Lincoln refused, claiming executive privilege in a document dated March 26, 1861.[60]

It became obvious to the public, and especially to those in Washington, D.C., that Lincoln's refusal to offer any peace proposal or to meet with the Confederate commissioners was preventing any negotiations between the North and the South. Therefore, two U.S. Supreme Court justices, Samuel Nelson from the North and John Campbell from the South, approached Secretary of State Seward, and offered themselves as intermediators to meet with the commissioners and Seward in order to communicate peace offers, etc., and attempt to resolve the difficulties without a war. Seward began meeting with the justices soon after the cabinet meeting on March 15, and at that time, Justice Campbell received specific authority from Seward to write to President Jefferson Davis informing him that Fort Sumter would be evacuated within five days.[61] Once the commissioners had received such a strong statement from Seward, they dropped the demand for recognition of the South by Lincoln. Again, on March 21, Justice Campbell passed along a second note from Seward which stated Sumter would be evacuated, and Seward promised a further statement. Finally, on March 22, there was a third note authorized by Seward to be passed from Justice Campbell to the commissioners, and this note stated, "I [Secretary of State Seward] have still unabated confidence that Fort Sumter will be evacuated."[62] On March 30, the commissioners received word from Governor Pickens that Lamon's visit with him on March 25 was a commitment from the Lincoln administration that Sumter would be evacuated soon and that Lamon had

[60]Tilley, *Lincoln Takes Command*, p. 191.

[61]Potter, *Lincoln and His Party in the Secession Crisis*, p. 345.

[62]Ibid., p. 347.

represented himself to Governor Pickens to be the personal delegate of President Lincoln.[63]

An extremely important cabinet meeting occurred, however, on March 29, which produced a completely different result than the cabinet meeting which had occurred on March 15. One day before this meeting on the 29th, President Lincoln told Fox that his plan regarding Sumter would be put into effect.[64] At the cabinet meeting on March 29, all but two of the cabinet members voted to reinforce Fort Sumter. Secretary of State Seward continued to oppose reinforcement, as did cabinet member Caleb Smith, and both called for evacuation of the troops.[65] Immediately following this cabinet meeting, Lincoln issued an order to Fox to prepare the expedition to leave for Fort Sumter no later than April 6.[66] Furthermore, Lincoln issued secret executive orders for troops to be assembled and for the warships to be made ready.[67]

A major question arises as to what happened between March 15 and March 29 to change the cabinet's position and why Lincoln would indicate to Fox on the day before the cabinet meeting of March 29 that the plan was to be put into effect. David Potter renders his opinion that at the cabinet meeting on March 29, it was decided that General Scott's recommendation to evacuate Sumter was more a political decision to keep in the border states, rather than a military opinion.[68] There is little evidence of this and overwhelming evidence that other factors caused the change. There had been speculation for some time in the Northern press that the Morrill Tariff might create a problem for the North if the South adopted a low tariff position. A good example is the *New-Haven Daily Register*, which editorialized on February 11, 1861, that:

> There never was a more ill-timed, injudicious and destructive measure proposed, (so far as northern interests are concerned) than the Morrill tariff bill, now pending before Congress. It

[63]Ibid.

[64]Tilley, *Lincoln Takes Command*, pp. 197–99.

[65]Potter, *Lincoln and His Party in the Secession Crisis*, p. 361.

[66]Ibid.

[67]Tilley, *Lincoln Takes Command*, p. 197.

[68]Potter, *Lincoln and His Party in the Secession Crisis*, p. 363.

proposes to greatly increase the duties on all imported goods, and in many articles to carry up the increase to the prohibitory point . . . so that while Congress is raising the duties for the Northern ports, the Southern Convention is doing away with all import duties for the Southern ports. . . . More than three fourths of the seafront of the Atlantic States—extending from the Chesapeake inclusive, to the furtherest boundary of Texas, would be beyond the reach of our Congress tariff. Their ports would invite the free trade of the world! And what would the high tariff be worth to us then, with only a one-fourth fragment of our former seacoast left?[69]

Tax historian Charles Adams analyzes this Northern realization of what the comparative tariffs of the North and South would do to their industries:

The war started, not because of the high Morrill Tariff, but just the opposite: it was the low southern tariff, which created a free trade zone. That tariff and its economic consequences for the North—disastrous consequences—were what aroused the anger of northern commercial interests and turned their apathy toward the seceding states into militant anger. It united the money interests in the North, and they were willing to back the president with the capital needed to carry on the war. Here is the scenario:

1. On March 11, 1861, the Confederate Constitution was adopted. It created what was essentially a free trade zone in the Confederacy, in contrast to the new high-tax, protective zone in the North.

2. Within less than two weeks, northern newspapers grasped the significance of this and switched from a moderate, conciliatory policy to a militant demand for immediate action.[70]

The New York *Evening Post*, a Republican newspaper, published an editorial on March 12 as follows:

There are some difficulties attending the collection of the revenue in the seceding states which it will be well to look at attentively.

---

[69]Howard Cecil Perkins, ed., *Northern Editorials on Secession* (Gloucester, Mass: Peter Smith, 1964), vol. 2, pp. 589–91.
[70]Charles Adams, *Those Dirty Rotten Taxes*, pp.102–03.

That either the revenue from duties must be collected in the ports of the rebel states, or the ports must be closed to importations from abroad, it is generally admitted. If neither of these things be done, our revenue laws are substantially repealed; the sources which supply our treasury will be dried up; we shall have no money to carry on the government; the nation will become bankrupt before the next crop of corn is ripe. . . . Allow railroad iron to be entered at Savannah with the low duty of ten percent, which is all that the Southern Confederacy think of laying on imported goods, and not an ounce more would be imported at New York; the railways would be supplied from the southern ports.

What, then, is left for our government? Shall we let the seceding states repeal the revenue laws for the whole Union in this manner? Or will the government choose to consider all foreign commerce destined for these ports where we have no custom-houses and no collectors, as contraband, and stop it, when offering to enter the collection districts from which our authorities have been expelled? Or will the president call a special session of Congress to do what the last unwisely failed to do—to abolish all ports of entry in the seceding states?[71]

The *Philadelphia Press*, on March 18, 1861, demanded a war by calling for a blockade of all Southern ports. The paper pointed out that the vast border from the Atlantic Ocean to West Texas would have no protective tariff and European goods would underprice Northern goods in Southern markets, and that this would ruin Northern business.[72] Previously, on January 15, 1861, the same paper had been against any military action, arguing that the South should be allowed to go peacefully, but this was before the Morrill Tariff passed with its call for a high protective tariff and the Southern Confederacy passed its Constitutional prohibition against protective tariffs.[73] The *New York Times* also changed its position over the tariff issue, and on March 22 and 23, stated, "At once shut up every Southern port, destroy its commerce, and bring utter ruin on the Confederate states. . . . A state of war would almost be preferable to the passive action the government had been following."[74]

[71]Perkins, ed., *Northern Editorials on Secession*, pp. 598–601.

[72]Adams, *Those Dirty Rotten Taxes*, p. 103.

[73]Ibid.

[74]Ibid.

The most explicit article on this issue which now faced the Lincoln administration appeared in the *Boston Transcript* for March 18, 1861:

> It does not require extraordinary sagacity to perceive that trade is perhaps the controlling motive operating to prevent the return of the seceding states to the Union which they have abandoned. Alleged grievances in regard to slavery were originally the causes for separation of the cotton states; but the mask has been thrown off and it is apparent that the people of the principal seceding states are now for commercial independence. They *dream* that the centres of traffic can be changed from Northern to Southern ports. The merchants of New Orleans, Charleston and Savannah are possessed with the idea that New York, Boston, and Philadelphia may be shorn, in the future, of their mercantile greatness, by a revenue system verging on free trade. If the Southern Confederation is allowed to carry out a policy by which only a nominal duty is laid upon imports, no doubt the business of the chief Northern cities will be seriously injured thereby.
>
> The difference is so great between the tariff of the Union and that of the Confederate States that the entire Northwest must find it to their advantage to purchase their imported goods at New Orleans rather than New York. In addition to this, the manufacturing interests of the country will suffer from the increased importation resulting from low duties. . . . The [government] would be false to its obligations if this state of things were not provided against.[75]

Lincoln was also getting pressure from the Radical Republicans, especially governors, that he needed to adopt a strong policy and go to war, if necessary, over Fort Sumter. Typical of the reaction of the Radical Republicans was a letter dated March 27, 1861, from J.H. Jordon to Secretary of Treasury Chase, which undoubtedly was discussed with the cabinet members along with many other letters and newspaper editorials on this subject. This letter read as follows:

> In the name of God! why not hold the Fort? Will reinforcing & holding it cause the rebels to attack it, and thus bring on "civil

---

[75]Ibid., pp. 104–05 (emphasis in the original).

war"? What of it? That is just what the government ought to wish to bring about, and ought to do all it can . . . to bring about. Let them attack the Fort, if they will—it will then be *them* that commence the war.[76]

It was also being widely reported in the press that the reason the Republicans were showing up poorly in elections in Ohio, Connecticut, and Rhode Island was that the administration was showing a weakness by abandoning Fort Sumter. Rutherford B. Hayes had declared, "Yes, giving up Fort Sumter is vexing. It hurts our little election, too."[77]

Charles W. Ramsdell considered the evidence and argued that Lincoln was in a terrible bind by getting military advice that the reinforcement or bringing supplies would be a failure, but that politically he could not afford to evacuate the fort. Ramsdell states: "Could the Southerners be *induced* to attack Sumter, to assume the aggressive and thus put themselves in the wrong in the eyes of the North and of the world?"[78] He continues, that if the South could be induced to start the war, then:

> The two wings of his party would unite, some at least of the Democrats would come to his support, even the border-state people might be held, if they could be convinced that the war was being forced by the secessionists. Unless he could unite them in defense of the authority of the government, the peaceable and the "stiff-backed" Republicans would split apart, the party would collapse, his administration would be a failure, and he would go down in history as a weak man who had allowed the Union to crumble in his hands. As things now stood, the only way by which the Union could be restored, his party and his administration saved, was by an unequivocal assertion of the authority of the government; that is, through war. But he must not openly assume the aggressive; that must be done by the secessionists.[79]

Lincoln, with over 60 percent of the vote against him and his party being one of many clashing ideas, knew that his minority

---

[76]Ramsdell, "Lincoln and Fort Sumter," p. 272 (emphasis in the original).

[77]Potter, *Lincoln and His Party in the Secession Crisis*, p. 342 (emphasis in the original).

[78]Ramsdell, "Lincoln and Fort Sumter," p. 272 (emphasis in the original).

[79]Ibid., pp. 272–73.

party could fall apart under the crisis. Shelby Foote has described this dilemma and Lincoln's strategy:

> Walking the midnight corridors of the White House after the day-long din of office seekers and divided counsels, Lincoln knew that his first task was to unite all these discordant elements, and he knew, too, that the most effective way to do this was to await an act of aggression by the South, exerting in the interim just enough pressure to provoke such an action, without exerting enough to justify it.[80]

On April 1, there was a flurry of activity in the Lincoln administration. As already mentioned, Lincoln issued new executive orders for Fort Pickens to be reinforced as election results came in which were unfavorable to the Republicans, who lost an important election in Ohio.[81] Secretary of State Seward on this day also recommended in writing that Lincoln start a war with either France or Spain instead of the South. Seward pointed out that there had been recent Spanish and French aggressions in Mexico and Santo Domingo, and he recommended that Lincoln demand explanations from Spain and France, and if satisfactory explanations were not received, to declare war against them.[82] Seward had already received much criticism in January of 1861, when he stated that, "If the Lord would only give the United States an excuse for a war with England, France, or Spain, that would be the best means of reestablishing internal peace."[83] Seward recognized the tremendous value to the Lincoln administration of having a war, since this would unite the Republican Party, cause great power to flow to the president, and end most dissent and opposition. Lincoln had also learned this when he tried to oppose President Polk in the Mexican War.

---

[80]Shelby Foote, *The Civil War: A Narrative, Fort Sumter to Perryville* (New York: Vintage Books, 1986), p. 44.

[81]Potter, *Lincoln and His Party in the Secession Crisis*, p. 341.

[82]Ibid., pp. 368–69; for original documents, see *Collected Works of Abraham Lincoln*, Roy P. Basler, ed. (New Brunswick, N.J.: Rutgers University Press, 1953–55), pp. 316–18, 136–37, 153–55. See also, Howard K. Beale, *Diary of Gideon Welles: Secretary of Navy Under Lincoln and Johnson* (New York: Norton, 1960), vol. 1, p. 37.

[83]Potter, *Lincoln and His Party in the Secession Crisis*, pp. 369–70.

However, Lincoln preferred a war with the South rather than England, Spain, or France. Lincoln answered Seward's note of April 1 with a note of his own on the same day, turning down the advice on foreign policy. Seward, in his note, had also criticized Lincoln for having no domestic policy, and Lincoln responded to this charge in the same note by reminding Seward that in his first Inaugural Address, he set out his policy, which was to hold the forts and collect the taxes, and he said at the time this would be done by force or invasion, if necessary.[84]

Meanwhile, the Confederate commissioners were detecting much military activity and becoming very suspicious of what Lincoln was doing secretly. On April 1, Justice Campbell went to Secretary of State Seward and demanded confirmation that Fort Sumter was to be abandoned, but at this point, he heard a different story which he considered a change in position. Seward now informed him that the president might desire to supply Fort Sumter with food and provisions but not reinforce it with troops. However, Seward stated that Lincoln "will not undertake to do so without first giving notice to Governor Pickens."[85] Now the Lincoln administration was taking a different position and making a distinction between providing food or supplies and reinforcing with troops by having the public believe that Major Anderson and his troops were "starving." However, Anderson continued to get daily supplies from Charleston until the South realized for certain that the North was sending troops and ships to precipitate an attack on Fort Sumter, and his food supplies were not cut off until April 7. Seward however, continued to guarantee to Justice Campbell that the cabinet and the president had decided to evacuate Fort Sumter eventually.[86] Seward informed Justice Campbell that the delay by the administration regarding evacuation was being forced because certain Republicans had asked the president to wait for an outcome of the elections in Connecticut and Rhode Island, and the administration had made a commitment to wait on those results.[87] Finally, on April 8, Justice Campbell pushed Seward for a response, as there was much rumor of military activity going

---

[84]Van Doren, ed., *The Literary Works of Abraham Lincoln*, pp. 183–84.

[85]Potter, *Lincoln and His Party in the Secession Crisis*, p. 347.

[86]Ibid., p. 348.

[87]Ibid.

on, and Seward sent a note to Campbell which stated, "Faith as to Sumter fully kept; wait and see."[88] On April 2, Confederate Secretary of State L.P. Walker, upon learning from the commissioners that there was much military activity and a rumor that the Lincoln administration might try to reinforce Fort Sumter, told General Beauregard in Charleston that he should consider discontinuing food supplies to Major Anderson.[89]

On April 3, Lincoln and Seward decided to send a delegate, Allen B. McGruder, to the Virginia Secession Convention to try to get a commitment from Virginia that it would not secede. On February 13, the state of Virginia had initiated a convention to consider the question of its secession and what to do about the seven states which had already seceded. There was strong sentiment against secession in Virginia, but it was obvious there was a very dangerous situation existing, especially regarding Forts Pickens and Sumter, with armed troops having guns trained on each other. The Buchanan administration was a lame duck administration, and it was unknown at that time how President Lincoln would deal with the crisis. Virginia was the key Southern state: There were seven other border states that also had not seceded, and they looked to Virginia for leadership.

McGruder was sent on April 4 to invite representatives of the convention to come to Washington and discuss these matters directly with President Lincoln. The convention chose three commissioners, but they were told that this must be a very secret mission, and since these individuals were so well-known in Washington, it was decided to send Colonel John B. Baldwin, who was well-known in Virginia but not in Washington. He was also a person known to be opposed to secession.[90] Colonel Baldwin's interview with Lincoln is related by Rev. R.L. Dabney, based on a personal interview with Baldwin in 1865, but Baldwin also testified under oath before the Joint Commission of Reconstruction in the same year with the same testimony.[91]

---

[88]Ibid.

[89]Tilley, *Lincoln Takes Command*, p. 202.

[90]Robert L. Dabney, "Memoir of a Narrative Received of Colonel John B. Baldwin of Staunton, Touching the Origin of the War," *Discussions* (Harrisonburg, Va.: Sprinkle Publications, 1994), pp. 87–110.

[91]Potter, *Lincoln and His Party in the Secession Crisis*, pp. 354–58 and see footnote 47, p. 357.

Colonel Baldwin reported that he met Secretary of State Seward on April 4, and was taken to the White House and introduced to President Lincoln. Lincoln was meeting in a room with numerous individuals, but after being told by Seward that Colonel Baldwin was present, he excused himself and went upstairs with Baldwin, locked the door, and had a private conversation.

Baldwin reported to Lincoln that Virginia wanted to stay in the Union and that this would help keep the other border states from joining the seven states which had seceded. The Virginia Convention was not worried about the issue of slavery, but it was worried about Lincoln using force to bring back the seceding states. Therefore, it wanted a written proclamation of not more than five lines to state simply that the Lincoln administration would uphold the Constitution and federal laws. The convention wanted a firm commitment that Lincoln would not use force to bring the states back. Baldwin reported further, that if Lincoln would sign such a proclamation, Virginia would not secede and would use its best efforts to get all the seceded states back into the Union. Then, Baldwin reported, Lincoln stood up and seemed very frustrated and stalked around the room and said, "I ought to have known this sooner! You are too late, sir, *too late!* Why did you not come here four days ago, and tell me all this?"[92] Baldwin protested that he came as soon as he was invited to do so and he got here as soon as possible. Lincoln again replied: "Yes, but you are too late, I tell you, *too late!*"[93]

Baldwin then related that he came to the conclusion that a policy of compulsion had already been decided upon and it was too late to stop it. Baldwin stated that Lincoln seemed to be impressed with the sincerity with which he reported that Virginia wanted to stay in the Union and that the Virginians would use their best efforts to try to bring the seceded states back; however, Lincoln asked him, "But what am I to do in the meantime with those men at Montgomery? Am I to let them go on?"[94] Baldwin replied, "Yes sir, until they can be peaceably brought back."[95] Lincoln then replied, "And open Charleston,

[92]Dabney, *Discussions*, p. 92 (emphasis in the original).
[93]Ibid. (emphasis in the original).
[94]Ibid., p. 94.
[95]Ibid.

etc., as ports of entry, with their ten-percent tariff. *What, then, would become of my tariff?"*[96]

Baldwin concluded sadly that there could be no agreement on the part of Lincoln about a commitment not to use force, so he returned to Virginia and reported his findings to the three commissioners and to the convention. The three Virginia commissioners then decided to go to Washington and meet with Lincoln. They spoke directly with Lincoln in the White House and again urged forbearance and evacuation of the forts. Lincoln objected that all goods would then be imported through Charleston and his source of revenue would be dried up. His statement was, "If I do that, what would become of my revenue? I might as well shut up housekeeping at once!"[97]

Baldwin also told Reverend Dabney that, after the war, he had talked with a personal friend and apologist of Secretary of State Seward, and Baldwin inquired as to why Seward had misled Justice Campbell of the U.S. Supreme Court about Lincoln's intentions concerning Fort Sumter, as well as misleading the Confederate commissioners. The friend of Seward stated that Lincoln was swayed from taking Seward's and General Scott's advice about Fort Sumter by "Thad. Stevens and the radical governors."[98] Colonel Baldwin continued with the statement from Seward's friend, who stated that there was "great wrath" shown by the radical governors and they spoke to Lincoln as follows:

> Seward cries perpetually that we must not do this, and that, for fear war should result. Seward is shortsighted. War is precisely the thing we should desire. Our party interests have everything to lose by a peaceable settlement of this trouble, and everything to gain by collision. For a generation we have been "the outs"; now at last we are "the ins." While in opposition, it was very well to prate of the Constitution, and of rights; but now we are the government, and mean to continue so; and our interest is to have a strong and centralized government. It is high time now that the government were revolutionized and consolidated, and these irksome "States' rights" wiped out. We need a strong government to dispense much wealth and power to its adherents; we want permanently high tariffs, to make the South tributary to the North; and now

[96]Ibid. (emphasis in the original).
[97]Ibid., p. 97.
[98]Ibid., p. 98.

these Southern fellows are giving us precisely the opportunity we want to do all this, and shall Seward sing his silly song of the necessity of avoiding war? War is the very thing we should hail! The Southern men are rash, and now profoundly irritated. Our plan should be, by some artifice, to provoke them to seem to strike the first blow. Then we shall have a pretext with which to unite the now divided North, and make them fly to arms. The Southerners are a braggart, but a cowardly and effeminate set of bullies; we shall easily whip them in three months. But this short war will be, if we are wise, our sufficient occasion. We will use it to destroy slavery, and thus permanently cripple the South. And that is the stronghold of all these ideas of "limited government" and "rights of the people." Crush the South, by abolishing slavery, and we shall have all we want—a consolidated government, an indefinite party ascendancy, and ability to lay on such tariffs and taxes as we please, and aggrandize ourselves and our section![99]

On April 4, Martin J. Crawford, who was one of the Confederate commissioners, telegraphed Governor Pickens expressing his opinion that the president intended to shift the responsibility to Major Anderson by simply taking no action and leaving Anderson to make his own decisions. Governor Pickens had also, on the same day, received word from the Confederate government that the food supplies from Charleston to Major Anderson should be cut off. Therefore, Governor Pickens sent a messenger to Major Anderson at Fort Sumter telling him that the privilege of getting food supplies from Charleston would end soon, and he also relayed the information he had received from Mr. Crawford, in order to tell Anderson what was being said in Washington. The rumor reported to Major Anderson was that: "Mr. Lincoln would not order Major Anderson to withdraw from Fort Sumter, and would leave him to act for himself."[100] The messenger reported back to Governor Pickens that Anderson became extremely upset with the report. Anderson's written reply of April 5 is part of the official records and was sent to his superiors in Washington reporting the rumor and asking if it was true that he was to be abandoned without any orders. It appears clear from this that Major Anderson did not know that any reinforcements were being sent. In his report he states that his food

[99]Ibid., pp. 98–99.
[100]Tilley, *Lincoln Takes Command*, p. 211.

supplies were soon to be cut off from Charleston.[101] As we know now, Lincoln had already issued the orders to reinforce Fort Sumter and was using the pretext that he was "sending bread to the starving garrison," when in fact, it was not until April 7 that the South cut off Anderson's food supply, and this was entirely the result of provocative acts of the president.[102] Also, Anderson had previously let it be known that even if his supplies were cut off from Charleston, he would still have enough food to last until April 26.

On April 7, the *New York Herald* published the substance of a message from Confederate President Jefferson Davis:

> Dispatches received here to-day from Montgomery render it perfectly certain that no attack will be made by the Confederate troops on either Fort Sumter or Fort Pickens. President Davis is determined that this administration shall not place him in a false position, by making it appear to the world that the South is the aggressor. This has been and still is the policy of Mr. Lincoln. It will not be successful. Unless Mr. Lincoln's administration makes the first demonstration and attack, President Davis says there will be no collision or bloodshed. *With the Lincoln administration, therefore, rests the responsibility of precipitating a collision*, and the fearful evils of protracted civil war.[103]

Furthermore, on April 7, Major Anderson received a letter composed by President Lincoln but signed by Secretary of War Cameron that was dated April 4, which informed Anderson that Lincoln was actually sending troops and ships to reinforce Fort Sumter. Anderson had warned Lincoln earlier that any successful reinforcement would have to be done by sending in thousands of troops from Fort Moultrie and that any reinforcement attempt from the sea would not be successful and would only cause the South to fire on the fort, and this would start a war.

On April 8, Anderson composed a letter to be sent back to President Lincoln; however, the South had not only cut off his

---

[101]Ibid., p. 212.

[102]Stampp, *And the War Came: The North and the Secession Crisis, 1860–1861*, p. 282.

[103]Tilley, *Lincoln Takes Command*, p. 219 (emphasis in the original).

food supply at this point but also confiscated all the mail delivery, including this letter which read, in part, as follows:

> I had the honor to receive by yesterday's mail the letter of the honorable Secretary of War, dated April 4, and confess that what he there states surprises me very greatly, following as it does in contradicting so positively the assurance Mr. Crawford telegraphed he was authorized to make. I trust that this matter will be at once put in a correct light, as a movement made now, when the South has been erroneously informed that none such will be attempted, would produce most disastrous results throughout our country.
>
> We have not oil enough to keep a light in the lantern for one night. The boats will have, therefore, to rely at night entirely upon other marks. I ought to have been informed that this expedition was to come. Colonel Lamon's remark convinced me that the idea, merely hinted at to me by Captain Fox, would not be carried out. We shall strive to do our duty, though I frankly say that *my heart is not in the war which I see is to be thus commenced*. That God will still avert it, and cause us to resort to pacific measures to maintain our rights, is my ardent prayer.[104]

By intercepting this letter, the South now knew that Lincoln was not just sending food supplies but was sending massive forces for the reinforcement of Fort Sumter in complete violation of all assurances previously made. They knew that great deception had been practiced by Lincoln in his representations to various agents of the Confederacy. President Davis now understood, not only from this letter, but also other sources, that Lincoln was sending a threatening army of reinforcements in the form of eight ships, with twenty-six cannons and fourteen hundred men, which would arrive in Charleston within a few days.[105] Also on April 8, a special messenger from President Lincoln, by the name of Robert L. Chew, a mere clerk in the State Department rather than an official, arrived in Charleston and went with Captain Theo Talbot to meet with Governor Pickens. Mr. Chew delivered a written message composed by Lincoln which stated:

---

[104]Ibid., pp. 223–24 (emphasis added).

[105]Jefferson Davis, *Rise and Fall of the Confederate Government* (Nashville, Tenn: William Mayes Coats, 1996), vol. 1, p. 284.

I am directed by the President of the United States to notify you to expect an attempt will be made to supply Fort Sumter with provisions only; and that, if such an attempt be not resisted, no effort to throw in men, arms, or ammunition will be made without further notice, or in case of an attack upon the fort.[106]

On April 10, the New York *Tribune* published an editorial which stated, "We are enabled to state, *with positive certainty*, that the principal object of the military and naval expedition which has sailed from this harbor, within the past four days, is *the relief of Fort Sumter.*"[107] As soon as the editorial appeared, the three Confederate commissioners in Washington telegraphed General Beauregard in Charleston that the "The *Tribune* of to-day declares the main object of the expedition to be the relief of Sumter, and that a force will be landed which will overcome all opposition."[108]

Meanwhile, in Montgomery, Secretary of War Leroy Walker had received word from General Beauregard in Charleston that Governor Pickens had received an official notice through Robert Chew from President Lincoln, that the reinforcements were coming, and Walker sent a telegram back to Beauregard stating,

If you have no doubt of the authorized character of the agent who communicated to you the intention of the Washington Government to supply Fort Sumter by force you will at once demand its evacuation, and if this is refused proceed, in such manner as you may determine, to reduce it.[109]

The next day General Beauregard sent two representatives to deliver a message to Major Anderson at Fort Sumter and asked if he would immediately evacuate the fort, and if he agreed to do so, they would allow him to do so with honor and without harm. Anderson sent back a reply in writing that he refused to leave, but he stated orally to the messengers "I will await the first shot, and if you do not batter us to pieces, we will be starved out in a few days."[110] General Beauregard and the

---

[106]Ramsdell, "Lincoln and Fort Sumter," p. 280.

[107]Tilley, *Lincoln Takes Command*, p. 230 (emphasis in the original).

[108]Ibid.

[109]Ibid., p. 231.

[110]Ibid., p. 233.

South's military leaders all knew that Lincoln's ships and armed forces would arrive no later than April 12, and probably sooner. Therefore, they reasoned that they were left with no alternative but to tell Major Anderson they could not wait any longer, and if he did not evacuate now, they would begin firing on April 12.

Bruce Catton, a prominent Civil War historian, explains how Lincoln maneuvered Davis into firing the first shot:

> Lincoln had been plainly warned by Lamon and by Hurlbut that a ship taking provisions to Fort Sumter would be fired on. Now he was sending the ship, with advance notice to the men who had the guns. He was sending war ships and soldiers as well, but they would remain in the background; if there was going to be a war it would begin over a boat load of salt pork and crackers—over that, and the infinite overtones which by now were involved. Not for nothing did Captain Fox remark afterward that it seemed very important to Lincoln that South Carolina "should stand before the civilized world as having fired upon bread."[111]

One biographer of Jefferson Davis, Robert McElroy, described the thinking of Davis and his cabinet in sending the order to fire on Sumter: "The order [by Lincoln] for the sending of the fleet was a declaration of war."[112] Shelby Foote describes the dilemma as follows:

> Lincoln had maneuvered them into the position of having either to back down on their threats or else to fire the first shot of the war. What was worse, in the eyes of the world, that first shot would be fired for the immediate purpose of keeping food from hungry men.
>
> Davis assembled his cabinet and laid the message before them. Their reactions were varied. Robert Toombs, the fire-eater, was disturbed and said so: "The firing on that fort will inaugurate a civil war greater than any the world has yet seen, and I do not feel competent to advise you." He paced the room, head lowered, hands clasped beneath his coattails. "Mr. President, at this time it is suicide, murder, and you will lose us every friend at the North. You will wantonly strike a hornets' nest which extends from mountains to ocean. Legions now

---

[111]Catton, *The Coming Fury*, p. 297.
[112]Tilley, *Lincoln Takes Command*, p. 263.

REASSESSING THE PRESIDENCY

quiet will swarm out and sting us to death. It is unnecessary. It puts us in the wrong. It is fatal."

Davis reasoned otherwise, and made his decision accordingly. It was not he who had forced the issue, but Lincoln, and this the world would see and know, along with the deception which had been practiced.[113]

The logic of Davis was reasonable in light of all he knew about the negotiations over Pickens and Sumter. He knew Lincoln had decided not to abandon the forts and was prepared to send in reinforcements. It would not be reasonable to wait until the forts had been resupplied and reinforced with men and ammunition before firing on them. Davis could not have a federal fort left in Charleston harbor after secession any more than the American colonists could have allowed the British to continue having a fort in the New York or Boston harbors after secession from England. It was clear that Lincoln had deceived the South in his various promises, especially through Seward, to evacuate the forts. Now he was clearly provoking a war by resupplying Fort Sumter and showing thereby that it would not be evacuated. However, the public did not have the benefit of all the information concerning negotiations over the forts and did not understand all the correspondence that had gone back and forth to indicate clearly that the sending of the ships for reinforcement, or sending them bread, was to be considered an act of war by the South. The public simply saw what appeared to be an innocent act of "sending bread to the starving garrison," and the South opened fire. If the South had won the war, Davis's viewpoint would have been in the history books along with the reasons the North would not allow the South to secede. But nothing is more certain in history than the fact that the winners write it.

When the South commenced firing, in the early morning hours of April 12, the first Lincoln ship, *The Harriet Lane*, had arrived near the Charleston harbor. The South continued to fire upon the fort for thirty-six hours and during this time the remainder of the ships arrived. However, the ships never returned any fire, indicating their mission had been accomplished simply by drawing the first shot from the South.

Many newspapers in the North reacted to the firing on Fort Sumter and Lincoln's deception in provoking the South to fire

---

[113]Foote, *The Civil War*, pp. 47–48.

the first shot. Representative of these reports in the North is an editorial in the *Buffalo Daily Courier*, dated April 16, 1861.

> The news of the fall of Fort Sumter has been received at the North more with astonishment than any other feeling. Every mind is full of questions. Has the administration been in earnest in this first strangely disastrous battle? If the fort was to be reinforced, why was not the attempt made? . . . The affair at Fort Sumter, it seems to us, has been planned as a means by which the war feeling at the North should be intensified, and the administration thus receive popular support for its policy. . . . If the armament which lay outside the harbor, while the fort was being battered to pieces, had been designed for the relief of Major Anderson, it certainly would have made a show of fulfilling its mission. But it seems plain to us that no such design was had. The administration, virtually, to use a homely illustration, stood at Sumter like a boy with a chip on his shoulder, daring his antagonist to knock it off. The Carolinians have knocked off the chip. War is inaugurated, and the design of the administration is accomplished.[114]

The New York *Evening Day–Book*, in its editorial dated April 17, stated as follows:

> We have no doubt, and all the circumstances prove, that it was a cunningly devised scheme, contrived with all due attention to scenic display and intended to arouse, and, if possible, exasperate the northern people against the South. Lincoln and Seward know very well that the right to send a vessel with provisions to Major Anderson *involved just the same issue as a reinforcement*. Hence it was made in a way that enabled them to get up a story about "humanity," "relieving a starving garrison." It would be impossible for Seward to do anything openly and above board.
>
> We venture to say a more gigantic conspiracy against the principles of human liberty and freedom has never been concocted. Who but a fiend could have thought of sacrificing the gallant Major Anderson and his little band in order to carry out a political game? Yet there he was compelled to stand for thirty-six hours amid a torrent of fire and shell, while the fleet sent to assist him, coolly looked at his flag of distress and moved not to his assistance! Why did they not? Perhaps the

---

[114]Perkins, *Northern Editorials on Secession*, p. 716.

archives at Washington will yet tell the tale of this strange proceeding.

Pause then, and consider before you endorse these mad men who are now, under pretense of preserving the Union, doing the very thing that must forever divide it.[115]

The *Providence Daily Post*, on April 13, 1861 editorialized as follows:

We are to have civil war, if at all, because Abraham Lincoln loves a [the Republican] party better than he loves his country. . . . [He] clings to his party creed, and allows the nation to drift into the whirlpool of destruction. While commerce is languishing, and all our industrial interests are threatened with ruin, he calls upon the people of the North—Democrats, Conservatives, and Republicans—to march to the South, and vindicate—what? The national honor? By no means; but the Chicago platform! . . . The cotton States, despairing of justice under such circumstances, have withdrawn from the Union, asking only to be let alone.

We are told, however, just now, that war results, if at all, from an act of humanity on the part of our government—that the garrison at Fort Sumter needs food, and the effort is to supply them. That is all. Is it all? Look at the facts. For three weeks the administration newspapers have been assuring us that Fort Sumter would be abandoned. They said it could not be provisioned or reinforced without a great sacrifice of life, and without greatly exasperating the whole South; that to abandon it would certainly disappoint and embarrass the secessionist, and kill the spirit of secession in all the border slave States. They had got the public mind all ready for the event, when—*presto!*—the tables are turned, and Fort Sumter is to be provisioned! Secession is *not* to be killed! Why?

We think the reader will perceive why. Mr. Lincoln saw an opportunity to inaugurate civil war without appearing in the character of an aggressor. There are men in Fort Sumter, he said, who are nearly out of provisions. They ought to be fed. We will attempt to feed them. Certainly nobody can blame us for that. We ought to feed our gallant soldiers by all means. *We will* attempt to feed them. The secessionists, who are both mad and foolish, will resist us. Then will commence civil war. Then I will appeal to the North to aid me in putting down rebellion, and the North must respond. How can it do otherwise?[116]

---

[115]Ibid., pp. 718–19 (emphasis in the original).
[116]Ibid., pp. 711–13 (emphasis in the original).

Finally, another representative editorial from the Northern press comes from New Jersey and the Jersey City *American Standard*. This was published on the day of the firing on Fort Sumter, April 12, 1861:

There is a madness and a ruthlessness in the course which is attributed to the government which is astounding. It would seem as if it were bent upon the destruction instead of the preservation of the Union, and as if all wisdom and patriotism had departed from it, or had been forced to succumb to the demands of its infuriated partisan leaders. . . . [T]he government seeks to mask this, its real purpose, by pretending that humanity requires them to succor the gallant Major Anderson and his troops, and that an unarmed vessel is to be sent to him with stores and that if it is not permitted peaceably to fulfill its errand it shall be done by force. The measure is a disingenuous feint. . . . This unarmed vessel, it is well understood, is a mere decoy to draw the first fire from the people of the South, which act by the pre-determination of the government is to be the pretext for letting loose the horrors of war. It dare not itself fire the first shot or draw the first blood, and is now seeking by a mean artifice to transfer the odium of doing so to the Southern Confederacy. . . . The assumption of a regard for humanity and the actions which the government base upon it are a sham the most transparent, a mockery the most unsubstantial, an hypocrisy which is only more infamous than the low cunning with which it is commingled.

No intelligent man will be deceived by the plea, and if blood be shed it will be laid where it justly ought to be laid, at the door of an Administration which had not the courage to surrender an abstraction in order to preserve the peace and unity of the country, but was brave enough to dare to close its ear against all the persuasive ties of common brotherhood, a common country, a common ancestry, a common religion and a common language, and by plunging the nation into civil war to demolish the noble fabric which our fathers founded.

If this result follows—and follow civil war it must—the memory of ABRAHAM LINCOLN and his infatuated advisors will only be preserved with that of other destroyers to be scorned and execrated. . . . And if the historian who preserves the record of his fatal administration needs any motto descriptive of the president who destroyed the institutions which he swore to protect, it will probably be some such an one as this:

Here is the record of one who feared more to have it said that he deserted his party than that he ruined his country, who had a greater solicitude for his consistency as a partisan than for his wisdom as a Statesman or his courage and virtue as a patriot, and who destroyed by his weakness the fairest experiment of man in self government that the world ever witnessed.[117]

There were no casualties on either side as a result of the bombardment of Fort Sumter, and after the firing ended, the South sent a doctor to see if Anderson needed his services. Major Anderson replied that there were no injuries or casualties and he needed no assistance, but he did request, and was then allowed, to have a ceremony to lower the flag and to leave with honor. However, during this ceremony, one of his cannons exploded and a Northern soldier was killed, which was the only casualty involved in the Fort Sumter incident.

Shelby Foote records the respect which both sides demonstrated toward each other, and especially the Southerners who admired the bravery of Major Anderson and his troops for enduring the assault. Foote states, "As the weary artillerymen passed silently out of the harbor, Confederate soldiers lining the beaches removed their caps in salute. There was no cheering."[118] The matter could have ended here with only one accidental death. The South would have seceded and preserved the ideas of a limited central government and states' rights advocated by the Founding Fathers. Slavery would have died a natural death soon, without a war, as it did everywhere else in Western civilization. Instead, President Lincoln, without consulting Congress, called for seventy-five thousand militia and unconstitutionally invaded the South as a "retaliation" for the firing on Fort Sumter. Also, on April 15, Lincoln called for Congress to meet, but not until July 4, 1861. Without any threat to the government in Washington or to the North, Lincoln began the war through illegal and unconstitutional means, claiming he was acting under the "war powers" of the president set out in the Constitution.

Since Congress never declared war, the question has arisen as to when the Civil War started. The U.S. Supreme Court was called on to decide this question in several cases which arose both

[117]Ibid., pp. 706–08 (emphasis in the original).
[118]Foote, *The Civil War*, p. 50.

during and immediately after the war. The popular opinion has been that the war officially started when the South fired on Fort Sumter; however, the Supreme Court stated that the war had two starting dates subsequent to the Fort Sumter incident, both initiated by President Lincoln in calling for a blockade of Southern ports. The first Presidential Proclamation was issued on April 19, 1861, applying to South Carolina, Georgia, Alabama, Florida, Mississippi, Louisiana, and Texas; the second, issued on April 27, 1861, applied to Virginia and North Carolina.[119]

After the Fort Sumter incident, Justice Campbell of the U.S. Supreme Court realized that he had been badly misled by Secretary of State Seward during their negotiations, and he wrote to Seward criticizing him for this deception:

> I think no candid man who will read what I have written and consider for a moment what is going on at Sumter but will agree that the equivocating conduct of the Administration, as measured and interpreted in connection with these promises, is the proximate cause of the great calamity.[120]

Secretary of State Seward never responded to this letter; however, his biographer, Thornton K. Lothrop, revealed Seward's opinion about Sumter: "The Sumter expedition failed of its ostensible object, but it brought about the Southern attack on that fort. The first gun fired there effectively cleared the air . . . and placed Lincoln at the head of the united people."[121]

Charles Ramsdell, a prominent historian, argues convincingly that Lincoln's whole purpose in using the Fox plan was to prompt the South into firing the first shot:

> Although there were no casualties during the bombardment, the mere news that the attack on the fort had begun swept the entire North into a roaring flame of anger. The "rebels" had fired the first shot; they had chosen to begin war. If there had been any doubt earlier whether the mass of the Northern people would support the administration in suppressing the secessionists, there was none now. Lincoln's strategy had been

---

[119]James G. Randall, *Constitutional Problems Under Lincoln* (Chicago: University of Chicago Press, 1951), p. 50.

[120]Tilley, *Lincoln Takes Command*, p. 288.

[121]Ibid., p. 265.

completely successful. He seized at once the psychological moment for calling out the militia and committing the North to support of the war. This action cost him four of the border slave states, but he had probably already discounted that loss.[122]

Lincoln never ceased to blame the South for causing the war, and even in his State of the Union Address on December 6, 1864, Lincoln stated, "In stating a simple condition of peace, I mean simply to say that the war will cease on the part of the Government whenever it shall have ceased on the part of *those who began it.*"[123]

After the war, Confederate President Jefferson Davis explained his reasons for giving the order to fire on Fort Sumter:

> The attempt to represent us as the *aggressors* in the conflict which ensued is as unfounded as the complaint made by the wolf against the lamb in the familiar fable. He who makes the assault is not necessarily he that strikes the first blow or fires the first gun. To have awaited further strengthening of their position by land and naval forces, with hostile purpose now declared, for the sake of having them "fire the first gun," would have been as unwise as it would be to hesitate to strike down the arm of the assailant, who levels a deadly weapon at one's breast, until he has actually fired. The disingenuous rant of demagogues about "firing on the flag" might serve to rouse the passions of insensate mobs in times of general excitement, but will be impotent in impartial history to relieve the Federal Government from the responsibility of the assault made by sending a hostile fleet against the harbor of Charleston, to cooperate with the menacing garrison of Fort Sumter. After the assault was made by the hostile descent of the fleet, the reduction of Fort Sumter was a measure of defense rendered absolutely and immediately necessary.
>
> Such clearly was the idea of the commander of the *Pawnee*, when he declined, as Captain Fox informs us, without orders from a superior, to make any effort to enter the harbor, "there to inaugurate civil war." The straightforward simplicity of the sailor had not been perverted by the shams of political sophistry.

---

[122]Ramsdell, "Lincoln and Fort Sumter," pp. 284–85.

[123]Tilley, *Lincoln Takes Command*, p. 227 (emphasis added).

But, suppose the Confederate authorities had been disposed to yield, and to consent to the introduction of supplies for the maintenance of the garrison, what assurance would they have had that nothing further would be attempted? What reliance could be placed in any assurances of the Government of the United States after the experience of the attempted *ruse* of the *Star of the West* and the deceptions practiced upon the Confederate Commissioners in Washington? He says we were "expressly notified" that nothing more "would *on that occasion* be attempted"—the words in italics themselves constituting a very significant though unobtrusive and innocent-looking limitation. But we have been just as expressly notified, long before, that the garrison would be withdrawn. It would be as easy to violate the one pledge as it had been to break the other.

Moreover, the so-called notification was a mere memorandum, without date, signature, or authentication of any kind, sent to Governor Pickens, not by an accredited agent, but by a subordinate employee of the State Department. Like the oral and written pledges of Mr. Seward, given through Judge Campbell, it seemed to be carefully and purposely divested of every attribute that could make it binding and valid, in case its authors should see fit to repudiate it.[124]

President Davis went on to say:

The bloodless bombardment and surrender of Fort Sumter occurred on April 13, 1861. The garrison was generously permitted to retire with the honors of war. The evacuation of that fort, commanding the entrance to the harbor of Charleston, which, if in hostile hands, was destructive of its commerce, had been claimed as the right of South Carolina. The voluntary withdrawal of the garrison by the United States Government had been considered, and those best qualified to judge believed it had been promised. Yet, when instead of the fulfillment of just expectations, instead of the withdrawal of the garrison, a hostile expedition was organized and sent forward, the urgency of the case required its reduction before it should be reinforced. Had there been delay, the more serious conflict between larger forces, land and naval, would scarcely have been bloodless, as the bombardment fortunately was. The event, however, was seized upon to inflame the mind of the Northern people, and the disguise which had been worn in the

[124]Davis, *The Rise and Fall of the Confederate Government*, vol. 1, pp. 292–95 (emphasis in the original).

communications with the Confederate Commissioners was now thrown off, and it was cunningly attempted to show that the South, which had been pleading for peace and still stood on the defensive, had by this bombardment inaugurated a war against the United States.[125]

Following the maneuver of getting the South to fire the first shot and "start the war," Lincoln then set out to become America's first dictator. One of his strongest supporters, historian Arthur M. Schlesinger, Jr., describes Lincoln's initial conduct of the war as follows:

> Lincoln chose nevertheless to begin by assuming power to act independently of Congress. Fort Sumter was attacked on April 12, 1861. On April 15, Lincoln summoned Congress to meet in special session—but not until July 4. He thereby gained ten weeks to bypass Congress, ruled by decree, and set the nation irrevocably on the path to war.
>
> On April 15, he called out state militia to the number of seventy-five thousand. Here he was acting on the basis of a statute. From then on he acted on his own. On April 19, he imposed a blockade on rebel ports, thereby assuming authority to take actions hitherto considered as requiring a declaration of war. On May 3, he called for volunteers and enlarged the army and navy, thereby usurping the power confided to Congress to raise armies and maintain navies. On April 20, he ordered the Secretary of Treasury to spend public money for defense without congressional appropriation, thereby violating Article I, section 9, of the Constitution. On April 27, he authorized the commanding general of the army to suspend the writ of *habeas corpus*—this despite the fact that the power of suspension, while not assigned explicitly to Congress, lay in that article of the Constitution devoted to the powers of Congress and was regarded by commentators before Lincoln as a congressional prerogative. Later he claimed the *habeas corpus* clause as a precedent for wider suspension of constitutional

[125]Ibid., pp. 297. Also, see explanation of Confederate Vice President Alexander H. Stephens, *A Constitutional View of the War Between the States* (Harrisonburg, Va.: Sprinkle Publications, 1994), vol. 2, pp. 34–36, 349. For another compact and reasonable interpretation of Lincoln's first shot maneuver, see Stampp, *And the War Came*, pp. 263–86.

rights in time of rebellion or invasion—an undoubted stretching of original intent.[126]

The question that history must eventually determine is whether Lincoln maneuvered the South into firing the first shot in order that the public would believe, and history would record, that the South started the war which Lincoln actually started and wanted? While Lincoln was a very manipulative and secretive person, there is hard evidence which clearly indicts him of this offense. Not only do the official records, revealed particularly by the study of John Shipley Tilley, indicate this, but Lincoln himself leaves the evidence.[127] First, there is his letter to Gustavus Fox dated May 1, 1865, in which he consoled Fox and told him he should not be worried about the fact that his attempt to bring supplies to Fort Sumter was unsuccessful. Lincoln assured him that he still had confidence in him and praised him for the effort. Lincoln states in his letter,

> You and I both anticipated that the cause of the country would be advanced by making the attempt to provision Fort Sumter, even if it should fail; and it is no small consolation now to feel that our anticipation is justified by the result.[128]

Lincoln also demonstrated his appreciation to Fox by elevating him to a high position of assistant secretary of the Navy in 1865.[129] Second, Lincoln's two trusted confidential secretaries, John G. Nicolay and John Hay, recorded their accounts of Lincoln's efforts to get the South to fire the first shot. One of their references states, "Abstractly it was enough that the Government was in the right. But to make the issue sure, he determined that in addition the rebellion should be put in 'the wrong.'"[130] Also, they state,

---

[126]Arthur M. Schlesinger, Jr., "War and the Constitution: Abraham Lincoln and Franklin D. Roosevelt," in *Lincoln The War President: The Gettysburg Lectures*, Gabor S. Boritt, ed. (New York: Oxford University Press, 1992), pp. 155–56; Also for other details of Lincoln's unconstitutional conduct see James G. Randall, *Constitutional Problems Under Lincoln*.

[127]Tilley, *Lincoln Takes Command*.

[128]Ramsdell, "Lincoln and Fort Sumter," p. 285.

[129]Tilley, *Lincoln Takes Command*, p. 152.

[130]Ramsdell, "Lincoln and Fort Sumter," p. 286.

President Lincoln in deciding the Sumter question had adopted a simple but effective policy. To use his own words, he determined to "send bread to Anderson"; if the rebels fired on that, they would not be able to convince the world that he had begun the civil war.[131]

Finally, these two secretaries concluded the Fort Sumter matter by stating,

When he finally gave the order that the fleet should sail, he was master of the situation . . . master if the rebels hesitated or repented, because they would thereby forfeit their prestige with the South; master if they persisted, for he would then command a united North.[132]

The best evidence, however, is contained in the diary of Lincoln's close and trusted friend, Senator Orville H. Browning. Senator Stephen A. Douglas from Illinois died after the war started, and on June 3, 1861, the Republican Governor, Richard Yates, appointed Browning to fill the vacancy. Browning had been a close personal friend of Lincoln for more than twenty years, and after becoming a senator he became a principal spokesman for the Lincoln administration. Lincoln had called Congress into session for July 4, 1861, but Senator Browning reported early and went to the White House to meet privately with his old friend on the night of July 3. Unknown to Lincoln, Browning kept a meticulous diary and he made an entry that night after returning to his hotel room about the discussion he just had with the president. The diary reports that after Lincoln read to Browning the message he was going to give Congress on July 4, he then put the document aside and Browning reports the conversation as follows:

He told me that the very first thing placed in his hands after his inauguration was a letter from Major Anderson announcing the impossibility of defending or relieving Sumter. That he called the cabinet together and consulted General Scott—that Scott concurred with Anderson, and the cabinet, with the exception of PM General Blair were for evacuating the Fort, and all the troubles and anxieties of his life had not equalled those which intervened between this time and the fall of

---

[131]Ibid.

[132]Ibid.

Sumter. He himself conceived the idea, and proposed sending supplies, without an attempt to reinforce giving notice of the fact to Governor Pickens of S.C. *The plan succeeded. They attacked Sumter—it fell, and thus, did more service than it otherwise could.*[133]

If "the plan" was "to bring food to the starving garrison" then it failed. But if "the plan" was to provoke the South into firing the first shot, then it succeeded, and this is exactly what Lincoln stated.

Charles Ramsdell states that this diary entry "completes the evidence" that Lincoln provoked the South into firing the first shot, and Ramsdell explains Lincoln's conduct with Browning as follows:

It is not difficult to understand how the usually secretive Lincoln, so long surrounded by strangers and criticized by many whom he had expected to be helpful, talking that night for the first time in many months to an old, loyal, and discreet friend, though a friend who had often been somewhat patronizing, for once forgot to be reticent. It must have been an emotional relief to him, with his pride over his consummate strategy bottled up within him for so long, to be able to impress his friend Browning with his success in meeting a perplexing and dangerous situation. He did not suspect that Browning would set it down in a diary.[134]

Rarely do historians find any better clue or "smoking gun" about a clever politician's hidden purpose than Browning's diary entry. On the next day, July 4, 1861, Lincoln gave his message to Congress and informed them that he had been trying to bring about a peaceful solution to the problem when he sent his ships merely to "deliver bread to a few brave and hungry men at Fort Sumter." He ended his message with these words, "And having thus chosen our course *without guile and with pure purpose*, let us renew our trust in God, and go forward without fear and with manly hearts."[135] Although Browning was a close friend and supporter of Lincoln, he must have blanched when he heard

---

[133]Ibid., pp. 287–88 (emphasis added).

[134]Ibid., p. 288.

[135]Masters, *Lincoln, the Man*, p. 418 (emphasis added).

these words after having heard Lincoln's true story the night before.

There are many Lincoln supporters who maintain that Lincoln could never have used a trick to start a war because this would be out of character for a man who had expressed his anti-war opinions so strongly during his one term in Congress when he opposed President Polk's Mexican war. Lincoln charged Polk with provoking that war by ordering troops into a disputed boundary which caused the Mexicans to fire the first shots. One of Lincoln's most admiring historians has commented upon Lincoln's opposition to that war with the following comment:

> Politics of course also intertwined with Lincoln's moral revulsion to the Mexican War, as opposition to it became largely a party matter. Yet it is difficult to miss the fundamental anti-war meaning of his 1848 stand. He denounced the president of the United States, James K. Polk, for provoking the conflict: "The blood of this war, like the blood of Abel, is crying to Heaven against him." Lincoln made no apologies for attacking the commander in chief, for throughout history rulers [Lincoln said] "had always been . . . impoverishing their people in wars, pretending . . . that the good of the people was the object." This, he argued, was "the most oppressive of all Kingly oppressions." "Military glory," Lincoln defined as "that attractive rainbow, that rises in showers of blood—that serpent's eye, that charms to destroy."[136]

Gabor Boritt is obviously quoting, in part, from Lincoln's letter to his law partner, William H. Herndon, who had taken the position that Lincoln should not be criticizing President Polk for starting the war with Mexico and by tricking Congress into declaring war. Lincoln thought the war was unconstitutional because, in fact, President Polk had started it rather than submitting the question to Congress for a declaration of war. Lincoln's letter to Herndon stated that:

> The provision of the Constitution giving the war-making power to Congress, was dictated, as I understand it, by the following reasons. Kings had always been involving and impoverishing

---

[136]Boritt, "War Opponent and War President," in *Lincoln, the War President: The Gettysburg Lectures*, Gabor S. Boritt, ed. (New York: Oxford University Press, 1992), pp. 190–91. Also, for a more full explanation of Lincoln's attack on President Polk, see Masters, *Lincoln, the Man*, pp. 97–98.

their people in wars, pretending generally, if not always, that the good of the people was the object. This, our Convention understood to be the most oppressive of all Kingly oppressions; and they resolved to so frame the Constitution that *no one man* should hold the power of bringing this oppression upon us. But your view destroys the whole matter, and places our President where kings have always stood.[137]

However, Lincoln learned many valuable lessons during his opposition to President Polk. He knew that Polk wanted the war in order to take property away from the Mexicans which they had refused to sell. He also knew that Polk could not afford to be perceived as the aggressor in starting the war. Lincoln learned from Polk that if you provoke the other side into firing the first shot and the American troops are thereby under fire, it is very difficult for Congress not to support the president and, therefore, to declare war, since to do otherwise would be a failure to support the troops in the field. He also learned that immense power and prestige immediately flowed to Polk as soon as the war began. Lincoln learned that once war is underway, all dissent from your opponents is stamped out, and the party in power is assisted greatly in getting its way with Congress. Lincoln also had endured much criticism for his attack on President Polk, and he had learned how unpopular it is to oppose a war in progress. The Democrats especially condemned him in 1848 for, "corruption" and "treason" of this new "Benedict Arnold."[138] Although most Whigs in Illinois agreed with Lincoln's opposition to Polk and accused the president of starting the war, one politician, who had been an opponent of the War of 1812, did not, and he explained that he would not oppose the Mexican war thusly: "No, by God, I opposed one war, and it ruined me, and henceforth, I am for *War, Pestilence,* and *Famine.*"[139]

Lincoln's Mexican war experience, far from proving that he would have been acting out of character by causing the Civil War, shows that he had an opportunity to learn many lessons which he could put into practice as president, especially for one

---

[137]Mark E. Neely, Jr., *The Fate of Liberty: Abraham Lincoln and Civil Liberties* (New York: Oxford University Press, 1991), p. 213 (emphasis in the original).

[138]Boritt, ed., "War Opponent and War President," p. 191.

[139]Ibid. (emphasis in the original).

who had less than 40 percent of the vote and minority representation in both Houses of Congress. With a war in progress, and the South not represented in Congress, the entire Republican agenda could be put into law. The South had always opposed the plan of the Federalist Party for a strong centralized government; the South had further opposed the Whigs, and now the South opposed Republicans, who stood for the same strong centralized government and also wanted a high protective tariff, internal improvements, as well as a partnership between big business and government.

Fareed Zakaria, managing editor of the influential magazine *Foreign Affairs*, is a great admirer of Lincoln's accomplishment in creating a strong centralized government, which changed America from a "backward" country to one that resembled the European powers. In his book, *From Wealth to Power*, he supports the fact that Lincoln was the first man to make America into a great war power, and he fully agrees with the change in foreign policy which finally occurred with the Spanish–American War and World War I. He concludes that a rich country like the U.S. should also be a "powerful country" through its military might, which helps it to expand its economic empire abroad. Zakaria describes the change of perception by European statesmen and especially Great Britain's Prime Minister Disraeli as a result of Lincoln's Civil War:

> European statesmen believed the Civil War represented a watershed from which there could be no turning back. Benjamin Disraeli explained in the House of Commons that the war would produce "a different America from that which was known to our fathers and even from that which this generation has had so much experience. It would be an America of armies, of diplomacy, of Rival States and maneuvering Cabinets, of frequent turbulence, and probably of frequent wars."[140]

Very different ideas are contained in the correspondence after the Civil War between two prominent men, who both loved liberty and saw that a strong centralized government was a great threat to individual freedom and the whole concept of the

---

[140]Fareed Zakaria, *From Wealth to Power: The Unusual Origins of America's World Role* (Princeton, N.J.: Princeton University Press, 1998), p. 48.

American Republic created by our Founders. The great historian of liberty, Lord Acton, had been asked to write his opinions on the American Civil War, which he had followed very closely and had written about contemporaneously with the events. At the end of the war, he wrote to General Robert E. Lee, asking for Lee's opinions about the effect of the North's victory. In a letter dated November 4, 1866, Lord Acton lamented the defeat of the South and stated:

> I saw in State Rights the only availing check upon the abso-
> lutism of the sovereign will, and secession filled me with hope,
> not as the destruction but as the redemption of Democracy. . . .
> Therefore I deemed that you were fighting the battles of our
> liberty, our progress, and our civilization; and I mourn for the
> stake which was lost at Richmond more deeply than I rejoice
> over that which was saved at Waterloo.[141]

General Lee replied to Lord Acton in a letter dated December 15, 1866, and, in part, stated:

> I can only say that while I have considered the preservation of
> the constitutional power of the General Government to be the
> foundation of our peace and safety at home and abroad, I yet
> believe that the maintenance of the rights and authority
> reserved to the states and to the people, not only essential to the
> adjustment and balance of the general system, but the safe-
> guard to the continuance of a free government. I consider it as
> the chief source of stability to our political system, *whereas the
> consolidation of the states into one vast republic, sure to be aggres-
> sive abroad and despotic at home, will be the certain precursor of
> that ruin which has overwhelmed all those that have preceded it.*[142]

General Lee continued by stating:

> The South has contended only for the supremacy of the con-
> stitution, and the just administration of the laws made in pur-
> suance to it. Virginia to the last made great efforts to save the
> union, and urged harmony and compromise. Senator Douglass,
> in his remarks upon the compromise bill recommended by the
> committee of thirteen in 1861, stated that every member from

---

[141] J. Rufus Fears, ed., *Essays in the History of Liberty, Selected Writings of Lord Acton* (Indianapolis, Ind.: Liberty Fund, 1985), vol. 1, p. 363.

[142] Ibid. (emphasis added).

the South, including Messrs. Toombs and Davis, expressed their willingness to accept the proposition of Senator Critten-den from Kentucky, as a final settlement of the controversy, if sustained by the republican party, and that the only difficulty in the way of an amicable adjustment was with the republican party. Who then is responsible for the war?[143]

Carl N. Degler, a Pulitzer Prize-winning historian, states that most historians do not like to compare Lincoln with Bismarck of Germany, but he shows that they were both men of "blood and iron" and their achievements were very similar.[144] Both Lincoln and Bismarck converted their respective governments, which were both confederations of states, into consolidated *nations*. Degler concludes that both needed wars to accomplish this feat. Although Degler doesn't mention the welfare-state compar-isons, Bismarck was very explicit in creating the first modern welfare state through the first social security system and the first workmen's compensation act, while Lincoln's creation of the welfare state in America was mainly corporate welfare, and then after the war there were pensions for the veterans. Degler points out, however, that there is a very direct parallel in their respective creations of the warfare state.

One comparison leading to the warfare state which Degler omits is that in the process of destroying confederacies to create nations, both Bismarck and Lincoln became virtual dictators essentially during the same period of time. Bismarck gained this distinction from 1862 to 1871 and Lincoln from 1861 to 1865.[145] Professor Forrest McDonald, in his excellent book sur-veying the American presidency, cites numerous sources, both by Lincoln's contemporaries and by current historians who all agree that Lincoln became a dictator:

> Many people, then and later, criticized Lincoln's conduct as excessive. The abolitionist Wendell Phillips called Lincoln an "unlimited despot," and Justice Benjamin R. Curtis wrote that he had established "a military despotism." When William Whiting, solicitor of the War Department, published a book

---

[143]Ibid., p. 366.

[144]Carl N. Degler, "The United States and National Unification," in *Lincoln, the War President: The Gettysburg Lectures*, Gabor S. Boritt, ed. (New York: Oxford University Press, 1992), p. 106.

[145]Randall, *Constitutional Problems Under Lincoln*, p. 57.

called *War Powers under the Constitution*, in which he maintained that in wartime the president's actions are subject to no constitutional restraints whatever, Sen. Charles Sumner thundered that that doctrine (and Lincoln's behavior under it) was "a pretension so irrational and unconstitutional, so absurd and tyrannical" as to deserve no respect. The doctrine when followed changed the federal authority "from a government of law to that of a military dictator." Twentieth-century historians and political scientists routinely characterized Lincoln's presidency as a "dictatorship" or as a "constitutional dictatorship"—sometimes using the word in the benign Roman sense, sometimes in a sinister modern sense."[146]

Lincoln, as America's first dictator, brought some of the horrors of the French Revolution to our shores. He signed a warrant for the arrest of the chief justice of the Supreme Court because the judge rendered an opinion that Lincoln acted unconstitutionally by suspending the writ of *habeas corpus*. Lincoln persecuted Northern objectors to the war by having more than thirteen thousand people arrested without warrants, tried, and convicted in military courts unfairly and without due process of law, even though the civil courts were fully available for the trials.[147] After the war, the U.S. Supreme Court, in the case of *Ex Parte Milligan* (1866) rendered one of its greatest decisions against presidential war power and in favor of individual rights by deciding that President Lincoln acted unconstitutionally by permitting the military trial of these civilians.

The government urged in the *Milligan* case that in the absence of restrictions imposed by Congress, the president is "sole judge of the exigencies, necessities, and duties of the occasion, their extent and duration," and that "during the war, his powers must be without limit." The Court unanimously disagreed, proclaiming,

> The Constitution of the United States is a law for rulers and people, equally in war and in peace. . . . No doctrine, involving more pernicious consequences, was ever invented by the wit of

---

[146]Forrest McDonald, *The American Presidency* (Lawrence: University Press of Kansas, 1994), p. 400.

[147]Neally, Jr., *The Fate of Liberty*, pp. 10, 23.

man than that any of its provisions can be suspended during any of the great exigencies of government.[148]

Lincoln had numerous members of the state legislature of Maryland arrested and placed in prison merely on the suspicion that they *might* vote for secession.[149] He also confiscated many railroads and more than three hundred "disloyal" newspapers. The supreme irony occurred when Lincoln had the grandson of the author of the *Star-Spangled Banner* arrested without a warrant and held in prison without any charges, merely on suspicion of disloyalty to Lincoln. This occurred at Fort McHenry, the very scene that had inspired the writing of the national anthem. Frank Key Howard wrote about this horrible experience in a book which was first published in 1881:

> When I looked out in the morning, I could not help being struck by an odd and not pleasant coincidence. On that day, forty-seven years before, my grandfather, Mr. F.S. Key, then a prisoner on a British ship, had witnessed the bombardment of Fort McHenry. When, on the following morning, the hostile fleet drew off, defeated, he wrote the song so long popular throughout the country, the "Star-spangled Banner." As I stood upon the very scene of that conflict, I could not but contrast my position with his, forty-seven years before. The flag which he had then so proudly hailed, I saw waving, at the same place, over the victims of as vulgar and brutal a despotism as modern times have witnessed.[150]

Secretary of State Seward basked in the power and the glory of the Lincoln dictatorship, even to the extent that he bragged to Lord Lyons, the British ambassador, "I can touch a bell on my right hand and order the arrest of a citizen of Ohio. I can touch the bell again and order the arrest of a citizen of New York. Can Queen Victoria do as much?"[151]

---

[148]Christopher N. May, *In the Name of War: Judicial Review and the War Powers Since 1918* (Cambridge, Mass.: Harvard University Press, 1989), p. 19.

[149]Bart Rhett Talbert, *Maryland: The South's First Casualty* (Berryville, Va.: Rockbridge, 1995), pp. 59–66 (emphasis added).

[150]John A. Marshall, *American Bastile: A History of the Illegal Arrests and Imprisonment of American Citizens in the Northern and Border States, on Account of Their Political Opinions, During the Late Civil War* (Wiggins, Miss.: Crown Rights, [1881] 1998), pp. 645–46.

[151]Masters, *Lincoln, the Man*, p. 411.

Degler points out that both Lincoln and Bismarck lived in a time when the trends were very different from today. While the approval of secession has been evident and was a very live issue during the last years of the twentieth century in Russia, Canada, Italy, France, Belgium, Britain, and even in the United States, Degler points out that between 1845 and 1870, there was much nation-building going on in the world. He gives six examples where there was either a failed secession or wars which brought about unification: (1) There was the revolt of Hungary against Austria which failed in 1848; (2) The Poles failed in a secession movement against Russia in 1863; (3) In 1847, the Swiss completed a Union under a new constitution modeled after that of America as a result of a civil war between the Catholic and Protestant cantons, which had caused a separation; (4) In 1860, Italy became united for the first time since Ancient Rome; (5) In 1870, Germany became united for the first time; and (6) Japan reorganized into a strong centralized government to replace the feudal society in the course of the Meiji Restoration.[152] Degler then analyzes the American Civil War, which he states is the best example of the unification process that was taking place at the time. He points out that under the original American Constitution there was a confederation of states, and America was not a nation in the "usual" or European sense. There had been many prior threats of disunion through the Kentucky–Virginia resolutions of nullification, the threat of New England states to secede after the Louisiana Purchase, the threat of New England states to secede after the War of 1812, and the South Carolina tariff nullification threat in 1832.[153]

Degler analyzes Bismarck's process of unification and states that he had to *provoke* two wars to create the German nation. Degler states that "all of the struggles for national unification in Europe, as in the United States, required military power to bring the nation into existence and to arm it with state power."[154] The German unification of its various states under Bismarck was not complete until the end of both wars. First, the Seven Weeks War was *provoked* by Bismarck on behalf of Prussia against Austria for the purpose of excluding Austria from Germany so that the

[152]Degler, "The United States and National Unification," pp. 92–93.
[153]Ibid., pp. 95–96.
[154]Ibid., p. 102.

militaristic state of Prussia would be the center and head of a future united Germany. By defeating Austria in 1866, he created a North German Confederation under the leadership of Prussia. Degler states: "Bismarck had provoked Austria into war to achieve his end."[155] The second step in the unification process was the Franco-Prussian War, which brought into the newly formed German nation the Catholic states of Bavaria, Württemberg, and Baden with Protestant Prussia, and the other Northern states.[156] Bismarck boasted in his memoirs that he *provoked* the war with France by deliberately editing a report from the Prussian King, who was making a response to the French government. This has become known as the "Ems dispatch," and upon receipt of the reply, which greatly angered the French government, they declared war against Germany. Bismarck accomplished his purpose by committing the first act of aggression which provoked the French into declaring war, thus uniting all the German states into one nation under the leadership of Prussia and Bismarck himself.[157] He was in tune with Lincoln regarding the appearance of a defensive war in order to make it appear to be a "just war." Bismarck stated, "Success essentially depends upon the impression which the origination of the war makes upon us and others; it is important that we should be the party attacked."[158]

The foreign policy viewpoint of Great Britain, as seen through the eyes of its prime minister, Benjamin Disraeli, regarding the effect of the American Civil War has already been stated. It is interesting to compare here Disraeli's ideas about the newly unified Germany:

> As far as Germany was concerned, Disraeli's well-known remark in February, 1871 on "the German revolution" captured some of Europe's apprehensive reaction to the newly unified Germany. That revolution, Disraeli dramatically asserted, is "a greater political event than the French Revolution of the last century." He admitted that it was not as great

---

[155]Ibid., p. 103.

[156]Ibid., pp. 107–08.

[157]Ibid., p. 108.

[158]Charles L.C. Minor, *The Real Lincoln: From the Testimony of His Contemporaries*, 4th ed. (Harrisonburg, Va.: Sprinkle Publications, 1992), p. 256.

a social event as the French upheaval, but "there is not a diplomatic tradition which has not been swept away. You have a new world. . . . The balance of power has been entirely destroyed, and the country which suffers most, and feels the effects of this great change most, is England."[159]

The editors of the book *On the Road to Total War*, from which the above quotation was taken, reached the following conclusion:

After all, in the making of nations, as Sherman advised, one must be prepared to use violence, even to the extreme of total war, if necessary. Abraham Lincoln, the lowly born democrat, and Otto von Bismarck, the aristocratic autocrat, could have agreed on that.[160]

Carl Degler, in commenting upon the American Civil War, stated that it "in short, was not a struggle to save a failed Union, but to create a nation that until then had not come into being."[161] Degler continues, "Lincoln then emerges as the true creator of American nationalism, rather than as the mere savior of the Union."[162] Degler's conclusion about the significance of the war is that:

What the war represented, in the end, was the forceful incorporation of a recalcitrant South into a newly created nation. Indeed, that was exactly what abolitionist Wendell Phillips had feared at the outset. "A Union," he remarked in a public address in New York in 1860, "is made up of willing states."[163]

Degler also addresses the question of Lincoln's maneuvering the South into firing the first shot as follows:

---

[159]Stig Forster and Gorg Nagler, eds., *On the Road to Total War: The American Civil War and the German Wars of Unification, 1861–1871* (Washington, D.C.: German Historical Institute and Cambridge University Press, 1997), p. 71.

[160]Ibid.

[161]Degler, "The United States and National Unification," p. 102.

[162]Ibid., p. 106.

[163]Ibid., p. 109.

Over the years, the dispute among United States historians whether Lincoln maneuvered the South into firing the first shot of the Civil War, has not reached the negative interpretation that clings to Bismarck's Ems dispatch. Yet Lincoln's delay in settling the issue of Sumter undoubtedly exerted great pressure upon the Confederates to fire first. To that extent his actions display some of the earmarks of Bismarck's maneuvering in 1870. For at the same time Lincoln was holding off from supplying Sumter he was firmly rejecting the advice of his chief military advisor, Winfield Scott, that surrendering the fort was better than provoking the Confederates into beginning a war. *Lincoln's nationalism needed a war, but one that the other side would begin.*[164]

In summary, Lincoln brought about the "American System" envisioned by his hero Henry Clay, which included extremely high tariffs to protect Northern industry from foreign competition, internal improvements for Northern business from tax revenues collected primarily in the South, and a centralized federal government strong enough to be "aggressive abroad and despotic at home" as stated by Lee.[165] None of this could have been achieved without destroying the American Republic created by the Founding Fathers, and this could not have been done without a war that excluded the South from Congress and then left this region prostrate from 1865 until the middle of the twentieth century—a century which saw Lincoln's *nation* involved in two world wars with the German *nation*, which Bismarck had created.

---

[164]Ibid., p. 108 (emphasis added).

[165]See the excellent book by Frank Van der Linden, *Lincoln: The Road to War* (Golden, Colo.: Fulcrum Publishing, 1998), p. 329, where the author supports this general conclusion but fails to recognize the tariff issue which caused Northern political and economic interests to demand a war to prevent Southern secession.

9

PRESIDENT ANDREW JOHNSON: TRIBUNE OF STATES' RIGHTS

H. ARTHUR SCOTT TRASK AND CAREY ROBERTS

During the first half of the twentieth century, most American historians regarded Andrew Johnson as a courageous and strong-willed politician who defended the prerogatives and independent position of the presidency from a usurping Congress. Defenders of the imperial presidency saw in Johnson a strong leader. If Johnson had not resisted the attempt of the Radical Republicans in Congress to create a congressional system of government, so the thinking ran, the presidency may never have reached the heights of power and leadership that it attained under Theodore Roosevelt, Woodrow Wilson, and Franklin Roosevelt. In addition, historians praised Johnson for resisting what was regarded, even in the North, as the shameful period of congressional Reconstruction.

Beginning as early as the 1890s, the consensus opinion in the North began to regard their attempt to "reconstruct" the Southern states as an unnecessary, vengeful, misguided, and corrupt enterprise. In the latter half of the century, the perspective changed somewhat. Race-obsessed American historians began to condemn Johnson as a narrow-minded fool who obstructed the noble experiment of congressional Reconstruction. If only Johnson had cooperated with, instead of fighting, the efforts of Republicans to reconstruct the South, then America's "unfinished revolution" would have been completed well before 1900. At the same time, presidential historians continued to respect Johnson for his courageous stand on behalf of the prerogatives of the presidency.

Our view rejects both positions. We see Johnson as an unlikely hero for liberty during his presidency. Unlikely, because he supported the Northern war to coerce the Southern states back into the Union, and he served the president who dealt a series of hammer blows to the federal constitutional order from which it has never recovered. As such, Johnson was an accomplice and abettor of the man and party who killed America's great heritage of constitutional and federative liberty. Yet in the aftermath of that war, Johnson set himself in the path of those who intended to complete and institutionalize the statist revolution inaugurated by Lincoln. Johnson was not a forerunner of the modern imperial president who views his office as the ideal ground from which to transform the polity from the top down. Rather, Johnson the president acted more like a tribune whose duty was to defend the liberties and laws of the land from the usurpations of other branches of government. He thus employed the veto power as a conservative, constraining force upon the excesses of a vindictive and revolutionary Northern majority.

Andrew Johnson was born in Raleigh, North Carolina, in 1808. As a young man, he worked as a tailor in Greenville, Tennessee. He began his political career in east Tennessee, climbing the ladder from alderman (1828–1830) to mayor (1830–1833) to state representative (1835–1837; 1839–1841), to state senator (1841–1843). In 1842, he was elected to the U.S. Congress, where he served six terms; he was elected governor of Tennessee in 1852, where he served until 1857; and he was elected to the U.S. Senate in 1856, where he served until 1862.

In politics, Johnson was a Jacksonian Democrat. As such, he opposed the Whig economic program of high tariffs, federal subsidies for internal improvements, and a national bank. Also typical of many Jacksonians, he defended the institution of slavery and consistently supported proslavery legislation (the fugitive slave law, the Kansas–Nebraska Act, etc.) in Congress. Like Andrew Jackson, he was a states'-rights nationalist, which means that while he believed in preserving the rights of the states, he denied the state remedies of nullification (state veto) and secession. As many Jeffersonians of the time pointed out, and as experience was to confirm, this was a fatal concession to federal power, for without some means of preserving states' rights, they were vulnerable to the encroachments of the federal authority.

From the perspective of state politics, Johnson was regarded as a spokesman for the yeomanry and poor whites of Tennessee. He did not represent the interests of the planters, most of whom were Whigs, nor did he associate with them socially or politically. Not surprisingly, when Tennessee withdrew from the

Union in June 1861, Johnson refused to go with his state. He was the only Southern senator not to resign his seat. His decision was influenced both by his humble background and his nationalist principles. In March 1862, Lincoln appointed Johnson military governor of Tennessee, and, in 1864, chose him to be his running mate on the "National Union," or Union–Republican, ticket. By choosing a Southerner and an ex-Democrat (Johnson switched parties during the war) as his running mate, Lincoln angered the Republican leaders. But Lincoln was already looking toward reuniting the country after the war. As the historian Otto Scott observed, Lincoln believed that a Northern victory would settle the vexing questions of secession and slavery, but nothing more. Once the war was over and those two issues were settled, "the nation should resume its normal patterns."[1]

Like other conservative Whigs and Democrats who decided to support "the war for the Union," Johnson was no radical, and he had no intention of helping to bring about a constitutional revolution or perpetuating Republican control over the national government. He honestly believed that the war could be limited to the conservative end of reuniting the states on the old federal basis. In July of 1861, Senator Johnson introduced a resolution, soon passed by the Senate, which explained Northern war aims:

> This war is not prosecuted upon our part in any spirit of oppression, nor for any purpose of conquest or subjugation, nor for the purpose of overthrowing or interfering with the rights or established institutions of those States, but to defend and maintain the supremacy of the Constitution and all laws made in pursuance thereof, and to preserve the Union, with all the dignity, equality, and rights of the several States unimpaired; that as soon as these objects are accomplished the war ought to cease.[2]

Thousands of Northerners enlisted in the army and fought bravely on the grounds that they were fighting to preserve the

---

[1] Otto Scott, "The Fourteenth Amendment," *Otto Scott's Compass* 5 (May 1995): 1.

[2] Quoted in Hans L. Trefousse, *Andrew Johnson: A Biography* (New York: W.W. Norton, 1989), p. 144.

Union, nothing more. In retrospect, Johnson's belief that the Union could be restored on the old basis after the secession of eleven states and a war of coercion to bring them back to federal allegiance appears naive at best. Like many other conservative Unionists, he failed to see that military coercion was incompatible with the federated and consensual character of the Union formed in 1788, and that to wage a war of subjugation was to wage war upon the same principles of self-determination and self-government upon which a previous generation of Americans had fought the British Crown. War always brings with it fundamental, unforeseen, and often revolutionary changes in the body politic, and the Republican leaders were not going to voluntarily relinquish their political power and their economic policies upon the cessation of hostilities. From its inception in 1854, the Republican Party had been the political expression of the will-to-power of Northern capital. What Northern bankers, manufacturers, and investors wanted was a close partnership between themselves and the federal government in which the revenue, power, and resources of the latter would be put to work to further the interests of the former. The Republican victory in 1860, in which the party captured not only the presidency but both houses of Congress, promised them a feast of long-awaited sweets—a protective tariff, a national bank, a national paper currency, and federal subsidies for railroads and other internal improvements. The unexpected secession of the seven states of the lower South threatened to deprive them of the fruits of their long-awaited political victory, for it meant both a drastic reduction in federal tariff revenue (most of which was paid by the cotton-exporting states) and the loss of the Southern market for their manufactures. When the Northern states slipped into economic depression during "the secession winter" (1860–1861), the business community threw its support behind war to restore the Union.

The War Between the States is a classic case of Clausewitz's dictum that war is the continuation of politics by other means. Johnson simply lacked the political insight or genius to recognize the deeper meaning of the war. He was not alone. Even the brilliant Northern writer Orestes Brownson supported the Northern war effort because he believed it was "a war in defense of government, of authority, and the supremacy of law. It is a war in vindication of national integrity, and in defense of American constitutionalism."[3] Only in retrospect did Brownson realize that the war had been

> a struggle of interests. The abolition fanatics were only the fly on the wheel, and the question they raised amounted to nothing in itself, and it was of importance only as it was seized upon as a pretext, and had only this significance, that the business interests of the North could subject the interests of the South to their control only by destroying the southern capital invested in labor.[4]

Despite his radicalism and contempt for constitutional limitations, Lincoln wanted to restore the Southern states to their previous status as full and equal members of the Union with only a minimum of conditions—loyalty oaths, requests for presidential pardons from high-ranking Confederate officers and officials, repudiation of the Confederate war debt, and ratification of the Thirteenth Amendment. Lincoln decided to pursue such a policy based on three considerations. First, he believed that a statesman should be magnanimous and generous in victory. (See his Second Inaugural Address.) Second, he feared the possibility of a long, drawn-out guerrilla war between ex-Confederates and Northern troops if the government were to impose harsh peace terms. Third, he hoped to rebuild the antebellum Whig coalition of Northern businessmen and Southern planters under the banner of the Republican Party.

Lincoln was as dedicated as any Radical to assuring the political ascendancy of the Republican Party and to maintaining the mercantilist national economic policies favored by the party. However, he disagreed with the Radicals on the proper strategy to follow to achieve these goals. The Radicals wanted to disenfranchise Southern whites and enfranchise Southern blacks; Lincoln wanted to enlist the Southern gentry in the Republican Party. As the war drew to a close in the spring of 1865, Lincoln showed unmistakable signs that he intended to abide by a generous policy of restoration, rather than reconstruction.

---

[3]Orestes Brownson, "Liberalism and Progress," *Brownson's Quarterly Review* (October 1864); reprinted in *Orestes Brownson: Selected Political Essays*, Russell Kirk, ed. (New Brunswick, N.J.: Transaction Publishers, 1990), p. 166.

[4]Brownson, "The Democratic Principle," *Brownson's Quarterly Review* (April 1873); reprinted in Brownson, *Selected Essays*, p. 202.

In a speech just a few days before his assassination, Lincoln explained that "the sole object of the government, civil and military, in regard to those States," is to get them back into "their proper practical relation with the Union."[5] With regard to the state government of Louisiana, which he had already recognized, "the question is not whether the Louisiana government, as it stands, is quite all that is desirable. The question is, will it be wiser to take it as it is and help to improve it, or to reject and disperse it?"[6] The day before he was shot, he told Gideon Welles, his secretary of the Navy, that "civil government [in the South] must be reestablished as soon as possible—there must be courts, and law, and order, or society would be broken up—the disbanded armies would turn into robber bands and guerrillas."[7] During a cabinet meeting the same day, he expressed his belief that it was "providential" that "the rebellion" had been subdued just as Congress had adjourned for the summer, thus giving them time to carry out a restoration policy without "the disturbing elements of that body to hinder and embarrass us."[8] He hoped to "reanimate the States and get their governments in successful operation, with order prevailing and the Union reestablished, before Congress came together in December." Referring to the Republican Radicals in Congress,

> there was too much of a desire on the part of some of our good friends to be masters, to interfere with and dictate to those States, to treat the people not as fellow citizens; there was too little respect for their rights. He did not sympathize in these feelings.[9]

Lincoln hoped to restore the Union by December 1865, with functioning state governments and full political rights for ex-Confederates, and so present the Radical leaders with a fait accompli. Lincoln for the first time in his political life was acting

---

[5]Quoted in Howard K. Beale, *The Critical Year: A Study of Andrew Johnson and Reconstruction* (New York: Frederick Ungar, [1958] 1970), p. 56.

[6]Ibid.

[7]Ibid., p. 57.

[8]Ibid. For Lincoln's millennial understanding of the war, see Allen C. Guelzo, *Abraham Lincoln: Redeemer President* (Grand Rapids, Mich.: William B. Eerdmans, 1999).

[9]Ibid., p. 57.

the part of a statesman, and the Radicals did not like it. Thaddeus Stevens wrote fellow Radical Charles Sumner to complain that "the president is precipitating things. . . . I fear before Congress meets he will have so be-deviled matters as to render them incurable." In a later letter, he cried out "Is there no way to arrest the insane course of the president? . . . If something is not done the president will be crowned king before Congress meets."[10]

Not surprisingly, Republican leaders in Congress reacted to the news of President Lincoln's assassination with a mixture of shock and elation. Many of them regarded it as an act of providence. B. Gratz Brown, a Radical leader from Missouri, wrote Johnson to express his belief that "God in His providence has called you to complete the work of rebuilding this nation that it might be stamped with radical democracy in all its parts."[11] What they meant was that now that Lincoln had fulfilled his mission of saving the union, it was up to firmer hands (Johnson's) to secure the blessings of victory (i.e., spoils). The Radicals had regarded Lincoln's policy both as too lenient and as politically suicidal. They feared that to readmit Southern representatives and senators to Congress would be to throw away the well-deserved fruits of victory at the very moment when they were to be enjoyed in peace and security. Thaddeus Stevens (R–Penn.) told Confederate General Richard Taylor a few weeks after the end of the war that "the white people of the South ought never again to be trusted with power, for they would inevitably unite with the Northern Copperheads and control the government."[12] The Republican leadership understood that their party did not yet command majority support in the country and that few Southerners were going to want to join forces with the party of abolition and military coercion. On these matters, they probably were being more realistic than the president. What is more, many Radicals hoped to make money in the South after the war. The restoration of home rule in the South would mean considerably fewer opportunities to profit from the prostration of the Southern economy, for Southerners would be less than friendly to Yankee efforts to buy up their

[10]Ibid., pp. 63–64.

[11]Ibid., pp. 60–61.

[12]Richard Taylor, *Destruction and Reconstruction: Personal Experiences of the Late War* (Nashville, Tenn.: J.S. Sanders, [1879] 1998), p. 251.

plantations and natural resources and establish an economic thralldom over them.

However, the Radicals erred in assuming that Johnson shared their desire to impose harsher terms upon "the rebels" or that at least he would not stand in their way. When Johnson took office after Lincoln's assassination, he at first appeared to be on their side. He spoke of hanging the chief "traitors" and even ordered the arrest of Robert E. Lee, the latter of which was prevented only by the timely protest and intervention of General Grant. However, after Johnson's passions had cooled, he decided to follow the basic lines of Lincoln's policy. In early May, he recognized the legitimacy of the provisional state governments set up by Lincoln in Louisiana, Tennessee, Arkansas, and Virginia. On May 29, he announced two proclamations. The first granted a general pardon to all Confederates who agreed to take an oath of allegiance to the union; only high-ranking officers and officials were excluded. The president invited the latter group to apply for special pardons from the executive branch. In the next six months, Johnson issued more than 13,500 of these pardons.

The second proclamation that Johnson issued laid down the procedures and conditions to be followed in order to obtain executive recognition of state governments in the seven remaining Southern states. A provisional governor appointed by the president was empowered to call a state convention to frame a new constitution. All ex-Confederates who had been pardoned were eligible to vote or serve as delegates. Johnson expected the conventions to abolish slavery, revoke their secession ordinances, and repudiate the Confederate war debt (both confederate and state). Johnson did not consider granting black suffrage as a condition for restoration, for that was a "power the people of the several States have rightfully exercised from the origin of the Government to the present time." Johnson's restoration policy became known as the North Carolina Plan. In the next six months, state conventions met in six of the seven unreconstructed states. (Texas's convention did not meet until March 1866.) Every state convention abolished slavery. Every one except South Carolina declared their secession ordinances to be null and void; South Carolina merely repealed its ordinance. Every convention except South Carolina and Mississippi repudiated the state debt incurred during the war. The conventions also provided for the election of state legislators, executive officials, and judges. The new state legislatures promptly ratified the Thirteenth Amendment (Mississippi excepted), chose U.S. senators, and provided for the election of federal representatives. By the time Congress convened in early December 1865, Johnson's conditions had been fulfilled in every state but two, and substantially fulfilled in those two states; and every Southern state except Texas had sent a delegation to Congress. All that was necessary to complete the process of political restoration and reunification was for Congress to seat the new members. In his first annual message on December 5, 1865, Johnson declared that the Union had been practically restored and that the revived Southern states were entitled to representation. He urged Congress to promptly admit them.

The Republican leadership, however, never considered recognizing the newly established governments or seating the Southern representatives. Even before Congress reconvened, Republican leaders met to plan strategy. They decided to form a special congressional committee to take over Reconstruction policy from the president and to refuse to seat any Southern representatives. When Congress assembled on December 6, they named a Joint Committee of Fifteen, ostensibly to determine whether the Southern states were "entitled to be represented in either House of Congress" but actually to formulate their own Southern policy. House leaders moved to excise the names of Southern representatives from the congressional rolls, and the Senate refused to hear the reading of the credentials of the Southern senators. They even refused to recognize or seat representatives and senators from Lincoln's loyalist governments set up during the war, even though they had been voting in Congress! The meaning was clear: The president's program was out, and a congressional plan was to take its place. Another deeper meaning was also clear, at least to astute Northern Democrats and Southerners: There had been a third war aim, unannounced but real. Otto Scott's induction hits the nail on the head: "To win that war, and to then refuse to allow the South to remain in the Union was not only logically perverse, but a tacit admission that the war had not been about slavery, but—as in all and every war—power."[13]

On December 18, 1865, Representative Thaddeus Stevens rose in the House to declare the intentions of the Republican leadership.

[13]Scott, "The Fourteenth Amendment," p. 3.

The president's plan was null and void. According to Stevens, the Southern states were no longer states, but were "conquered provinces," and they were no longer in the Union. Since they were out of the Union they could only be readmitted by joint action of the president and Congress. Now that the war was over, Stevens and the Republican Party were changing the rules. The Northern states had carried on the war on the theory that the Southern states had not seceded but had rebelled and hence were simply out "of their proper relations" with the federal government and the other states. Taking this theory at face value, Southerners assumed that once they accepted the verdict of the war—no secession or slavery—they could resume their place as equal states in the Union. But now that the war was over, Stevens was saying that the Southern states were out of the Union, that they had no political rights at all, and that they were going to be "reconstructed" by the Republicans.[14] Stevens declared that the Southern states should be readmitted only after they had "learn[ed] the principles of freedom, and eat[en] the fruits of foul rebellion." For Stevens and his ilk, unconditional surrender, the physical devastation of the South, and the death of one-third of Southern white males was not enough of a lesson. Stevens's speech is an example of the deep-seated moral self-righteousness of the Republicans of this period. In a postwar speech, Thaddeus Stevens exclaimed:

> What! Six millions of Rebels who had renounced the Constitution, who had murdered five hundred thousand of our citizens,

---

[14]Speech by Thaddius Stevens, *Congressional Globe*, 39th Cong., 1st Sess., pp. 72–75. General Richard Taylor, who was in command of the last Confederate forces to surrender east of the Mississippi, was asked by the governors of Alabama and Mississippi what they should do when news of the final Confederate surrender became known. After consulting with General Canby, the commander of all Northern military forces in the southwest, Taylor suggested with Canby's approval that the governors call their state legislatures back into session and repeal their ordinances of secession and abolish slavery, "thus smoothing the way to the restoration of their states to the Union." The response of the Washington government was to arrest the two governors "for abetting a new rebellion." Taylor comments:

> The North, by its Government, press, and people, had been declaring for years that the war was for the preservation of the Union, and for nothing else, and Canby and I, in the innocence of our hearts, believed it. (Taylor, p. 233)

who had loaded the nation with debt and drenched it with blood, when conquered had forfeited no right, had lost no jurisdiction or civil authority.[15]

For the Radicals, restoration of the Union on Johnson's terms was simply not enough. The South had to be made to pay for their "treason" and remade in the image of New England. Belief in the unmitigated evil of the other seems to have fulfilled some deep psychological or religious need of the Northern majority. The demonization of the South also provided a handy moral cover and rationalization for the numerous war crimes (arson, systematic theft, rape) committed by Northern troops as they rampaged through the South, as well as for what the Republicans had in store for the postwar South—namely political subordination and economic exploitation.

The Republicans realized that restoration of the Union on Lincoln's and Johnson's terms in 1865 would have meant their fall from national power sooner or later, perhaps as early as the fall elections of 1866. The loss of their congressional majority—and, in 1868, the presidency—meant not only the loss of lucrative political offices at the federal level but the dismantling of their neo-mercantilist economic program. A resurgent Democratic Party would reduce the tariff, curb federal railroad subsidies, decrease federal expenditures, begin retiring the national debt, and move the country back to a hard-money standard. Johnson's annual message only confirmed these fears with its Jacksonian overtones and themes. To them it was confirmation, if they needed any at that point, that Johnson had gone over to the Democratic enemy.

Johnson described the federal debt "as a heavy burden on the industry of the country" which should "be discharged without unnecessary delay."[16] To effect this objective, he called for the immediate adoption of a program of debt reduction designed to "discharge it fully within a definitely fixed number of years."[17] Such a policy was anathema to Republicans. Not only did federal bonds form a profitable part of the investment portfolio of many

---

[15]Quoted in Beale, pp. 372–73.

[16]James D. Richardson, ed., *A Compilation of the Messages and Papers of the Presidents, 1789–1902* (Washington: Bureau of National Literature and Arts, 1903), vol. 6, p. 366.

[17]Ibid., p. 354.

Republicans both in and out of Congress, but the Republicans had used the bonds to capitalize both the railroads and the new national banks. Rapid retirement would bring ruin to these debt-financed enterprises. Just as much an anathema were Johnson's call for diminishing the amount of federal paper money in circulation, probably through the retirement of greenbacks, and his suggestion that the tariff be "adjusted as to fall most heavily on articles of luxury, leaving the necessaries of life as free from taxation as the absolute wants of the Government economically administered will justify."[18] Johnson's adjustment policy was a subtle way of calling for reductions in the duties most favored by the textile and iron magnates who were the real power in the Republican Party.

His call for currency deflation threatened the huge profits being made by Republican national bankers and investment houses. Although the Republicans were less than candid in declaring their true motives in public, they were not so in private. General Beckwith of Massachusetts wrote Charles Sumner that they had "better let Louisiana, Arkansas, and Tennessee, all wait for years than let in a single state or man not permanently reliable for the support of the right policy."[19] Another Bostonian wrote Edwin Stanton, "We have them now under a control which we must not lose, even if we hold them as military dependencies."[20]

It is necessary to demolish a series of historical myths that have persisted to this day, which blamed the South for "the necessity" of congressional Reconstruction. According to this argument, the South refused to accept the end of slavery and so crafted a series of "black codes" designed to re-enslave the blacks in all but in name, and violent and vengeful Southerners began the wanton murder and lynchings of blacks all across the South. Under these circumstances, restoration of home-rule to the South was out of the question. Congress, led by the Republican Party, was morally obligated to intercede to protect the lives and liberty of the freedmen by assuming direct rule over the Southern states and instituting fundamental

[18]Ibid., pp. 364–65.
[19]Quoted in Beale, *Critical Year*, p. 313.
[20]Ibid.

changes. Let us examine these charges, beginning with the slavery issue. The evidence that can be gleaned from Southern diaries, letters, and published writings is overwhelming that, once the war was over, Southerners were glad to be done with slavery. Slavery had brought many benefits, but it had also entailed huge responsibilities. Richard Taylor explained the attitude of his fellow Southerners after the surrender: "extinction of slavery was expected by all and regretted by none."[21]

The second historical myth was the black codes. The first black codes were passed by the legislature of Mississippi in the late fall of 1865, and other states followed. Although the codes varied from state to state, there were common elements. Most granted, or recognized, important legal rights for the freedmen, such as the right to hold property, to marry, to make contracts, to sue, and to testify in court. Many mandated penalties for vagrancy, but the intention there was not to bind them to the land in a state of perpetual serfdom, as was charged by Northern Radicals, but to end what had become an intolerable situation—the wandering across the South of large numbers of freedmen who were without food, money, jobs, or homes. Such a situation was leading to crime, fear, and violence. Other provisions, found in some of the state codes, excluded freedmen from jury duty, mandated segregation in public facilities, and required freedmen to obtain licenses before doing certain kinds of work.

The question is not whether the passage of certain legal disabilities was just or right, but whether their passage justified the action of Congress in refusing to seat Southern delegates to Congress. There are reasons to doubt that they did constitute such a justification. First, the Constitution did not grant the federal government any authority or jurisdiction over questions of civil rights within the various states. Second, many of the legal disabilities contained in "the black codes" were already in existence in the Northern states (such as denial of jury duty). For Northerners to cite them as justification for denying Southerners their right to federal representation was gross hypocrisy. Third, the weakness of the Radicals' case can be seen in their failure to calmly explain the specific injustices of the codes. Instead of doing so, Republican newspapers and politicians systematically

---

[21]Taylor, *Destruction and Reconstruction*, p. 242.

misrepresented them, or denounced them in toto, to a gullible Northern public eager to believe the worst about the South.

Another myth was racial violence. It was simply not true that the postwar South was convulsed with white violence against blacks. After surveying the many reports made by Northern officers, businessmen, and comissioners, the historian Howard Beale concluded that "a preponderance of trustworthy opinion expressed to Johnson was sanguine about Southern conditions."[22] Most reported that Southerners had accepted the results of the war, were ready to do justice to the freedmen, and wanted to rebuild their country and resume their place in the Union. Even Generals Grant and Sherman told Johnson that the South was loyal and deserved immediate restoration.[23] The problem was that the Republicans, who had no interest in reconciliation or restoration, were citing the reports of officers and businessmen that claimed the opposite of what Johnson was hearing—that Southerners were bent on revenge and mayhem. Beale explains these negative reports as stemming from a combination of ignorance, or misunderstanding, of Southern conditions by Northerners with little experience or sympathy for the South, and distortions, and in many cases outright fabrications, of events by those who either had ideological obsessions or interests to gratify. Of course racial violence occurred in the South, but both races contributed to it; and it was unreasonable to expect that there would be no violence in the aftermath of a bitter and destructive civil war that overthrew traditional social relations and resulted in so much death and destruction. In fact, considering the circumstances, one wonders why there was so little violence.

The postwar North was hardly immune from violent conflict between labor and capital. There even is evidence that Republican leaders tried to provoke violence to create a pretext for keeping Southerners out of Congress. Secretary of War Edwin Stanton, who was secretly working with the Radical leaders, kept armed garrisons of black soldiers posted throughout the South for more than a year after the war was over. Such a policy was dictated partly by vengeance—a desire to humiliate Southerners and rub their noses in the fruit of their "rebellion"—

[22]Beale, *Critical Year*, p. 165.

[23]Ibid., pp. 165–69.

and partly by the expectation that racial violence might result which could be used for Republican political advantage.

In the Memphis race riot of May 1866, Stanton's policy of provocation bore its bitter fruit. The situation in Memphis was volatile. First, there was a garrison of four thousand black soldiers located on the outskirts of town. Many of the troops held up white citizens at gunpoint, while others made it a practice of insulting whites, jostling them on the sidewalk, or stopping them for searches. At the same time, thousands of blacks from the countryside had flocked into the city after the war, where they began competing for jobs with a large number of recently arrived Irish immigrants. In addition, as a consequence of the Northern occupation, Irish immigrants came to hold the municipal office and to constitute much of the police force. When some discharged black soldiers threw stones at police officers attempting to break up a fight, a riot broke out that soon degenerated into a systematic attack upon the black quarter by Irish police and laboring men. The riot resulted in forty-eight deaths (mostly black), three rapes, and the destruction of hundreds of buildings.[24] The important point is that Southerners were not even involved in this race riot. The obvious lesson was not that Southerners could not be trusted with self-government but that armed black garrisons were a bad idea and that Southerners, not recently arrived Irish immigrants, should be in charge of city governments in the South.

The New Orleans race riot of late July 1866 offered further proof of the role of the Republicans in provoking race violence in the South. Under Johnson's plan, Southerners were slowly resuming control of their state. By the summer, pardoned Confederates had elected a state legislature, state executive officers, and a mayor for New Orleans; it was only a matter of time before the Republicans lost control of the office of governor and hence of all political power. The Republicans in the state decided to act before it was too late. They issued a call for the reconvening of the 1864 state convention for the purpose of amending the state constitution and holding new elections. Only those who had been eligible to vote in 1864 could vote for delegates to

---

[24]For a more detailed account of the riot see Ludwell Johnson, *North Against South: The American Iliad, 1848–1877* (Columbia, S.C.: Foundation for American Education, [1978] 1993), pp. 220–21.

the new convention. The Radical delegates planned on canceling the previous state elections that had resulted in Democratic victories; disenfranchising most ex-Confederates; and enfranchising the blacks.

When President Johnson heard of these proceedings, he immediately wrote Governor Wells, asking him on what authority had the convention been called and pointing out that a convention that did not represent the qualified voters of the state, which this did not, had no legal standing. The governor ignored him. What the Radicals were doing was not simply illegal; it was revolutionary. They were actually attempting to overthrow the legally-elected state government and institute new government controlled by themselves.

Outraged, the mayor of the city and the lieutenant governor of the state asked General Baird, who was commanding Federal forces in the city, for permission to disperse the convention and arrest its key leaders. Baird refused permission or assistance and offered only to protect the convention from mob action. On the Friday night previous to the Monday convention, the Radicals held a mass meeting at which they denounced President Johnson, urged blacks to arm themselves, and warned that if the city authorities attempted to prevent or break up the convention, "the streets will run with blood." General Baird immediately telegraphed the president, asking him for instructions on what to do. Given Johnson's opinion that the convention was an illegal and revolutionary gathering, there is no doubt he would have ordered Baird to assist the city authorities in suppressing the convention. He himself admitted a few days later that he would have so acted. But Johnson did not receive the telegram until after the riot was over. Why? Secretary Stanton deliberately withheld it from him. Not surprisingly the convening of the convention was met by violence as city police and some civilians attacked the delegates and their black supporters. The violence did not last long, but close to fifty persons were killed, most of them black.[25]

As news of the riot reached the North, the Republican press, pulpit, and stump erupted in inflammatory denunciations of Southern wickedness, murder, mayhem, and continued rebelliousness. As Richard Taylor so aptly put it, "the radicals . . .

---

[25]Ibid. and Beale, *Critical Year*, pp. 344–52.

rejoiced as Torquemada might have done when the discovery of score of heretics furnished him an excuse to torment and destroy a province."[26] In a typical statement, *The Chicago Tribune* reported that "the hands of the Rebels are again red with loyal blood; rebel armies have once again begun the work of massacre."[27]

Republicans made liberal use of the Memphis and New Orleans riots in the fall election campaign to persuade Northern voters that the South was not yet deserving of self-rule or congressional representation, and that the military occupation would have to continue until Southerners were duly punished, the blacks were protected, and Southern society was transformed. Thaddeus Stevens thundered:

> Behold the awful slaughter of white men and black—of a Convention of highly respectable men, peaceably assembled in New Orleans, which General Sheridan pronounces more horrible than the massacre of Fort Pillow. Even the clergyman who opened the proceedings with prayer was cruelly murdered. All this was done under the sanction of Johnson and his office-holders. It is the legitimate consequence of his policy.[28]

In other words, if the Southerners were allowed their freedom, this was how they would behave. It is hardly just to blame the white people of New Orleans for the violent acts committed by a few dozen undisciplined policemen and some armed roughs in response to deliberate provocation and goading from Radical leaders. Taylor himself explained that most Southerners in the city disapproved of the violence employed by the police, "were indignant" at reports that some blacks had been wantonly killed, and expected that the regular civil authorities would punish those guilty of murder or of violence not committed in self-defense.[29] Yet all three agencies of Northern opinion—the press, the pulpit, and the legislative hall—blew the riots out of proportion and systematically misrepresented the facts, for they

[26]Taylor, pp. 256–57.

[27]Quoted in Beale, *Critical Year*, p. 353.

[28]Ibid., p. 354.

[29]For Taylor's account of the riot, see his *Destruction and Reconstruction*, pp. 256–57.

furnished proof for those already disposed to believe it that the South was unrepentant and in need of further chastisement.

The first major act of congressional Reconstruction was the passage of the Freedmen's Bureau Bill (February 1866). This bill authorized significant land confiscation and redistribution, social-welfare programs, and the setting up of extra-constitutional military courts for the protection of the "civil rights" of freedmen. Johnson vetoed the bill on the grounds of its gross unconstitutionality and centralizing character. The bill empowered the bureau to distribute in forty-acre plots up to three million acres of land in five Southern states to freedmen for rent with an option to buy. Johnson pointed out that this measure confiscated land "without any legal proceedings being first had."[30] The bill made the bureau a welfare agency with the power to start up and administer schools, to distribute free food and clothing to the freedmen, and to provide money by which the freedmen could pay rent for the lands they had been awarded. Johnson condemned the bill because:

> The Congress of the United States has never heretofore thought itself empowered to establish asylums beyond the limits of the District of Columbia, except for the benefit of our disabled soldiers and sailors. It has never founded schools for any class of our own people, not even for the orphans of those who have fallen in the defense of the Union, but has left the care of education to the much more competent and efficient control of the states, or communities, of private associations, and of individuals. It has never deemed itself authorized to expend the public money for the rent or purchase of homes for thousands, not to say millions, of the white race who are honestly toiling from day to day for their subsistence. A system for the support of indigent persons in the United States was never contemplated by the authors of the Constitution; nor can any good reason be advanced why, as a permanent establishment, it should be founded on one class or color of our people more than another. . . . The idea on which the slaves were assisted to freedom was that on becoming free they would be a self-sustaining population. Any legislation that shall imply that they are not expected to attain a self-sustaining condition must have a tendency injurious alike to their character and their prospects. . . . Neither is sufficient consideration given to the ability of the freedmen to protect and take

[30]Richardson, p. 402.

care of themselves. It is no more than justice to them to believe that as they have received their freedom with moderation and forbearance, so they will distinguish themselves by their industry and thrift, and soon show the world that in a condition of freedom they are self-sustaining, capable of selecting their own employment and their own places of abode, of insisting for themselves on a proper remuneration, and of establishing and maintaining their own asylums and schools. . . . It is certain that they can attain to that condition only through their own merits and exertions.[31]

While Johnson's criticism speaks for itself, three of his chief points should be emphasized. First, the adoption of such powers by the federal government was both unprecedented and unconstitutional and took it into areas that it was not competent to manage. Second, making the freedmen wards of the federal government was not only unwise, as tending to perpetuate them in a state of dependency, but was contradictory of thirty years of antislavery dogma that insisted that the slave was the equal of his master and needed only to be set free to unleash his talents and resourcefulness. Last, Johnson decried the law enforcement and judicial apparatus created by the bill which would empower bureau officials to arrest

any white person who may be charged with depriving a freedman of "any civil rights or immunities belonging to white persons" without however, defining the "civil rights and immunities" which was thus to be secured to the freedmen by military law. This military jurisdiction also extends to all questions that may arise respecting contracts.[32]

What was worse, the accused would stand trial before military tribunals

without the intervention of a jury and without any fixed rules of law or evidence. . . . The punishment will be, not what the law declares, but such as a court-martial may think proper; and from these arbitrary tribunals there lies no appeal, no writ of error to any of the courts in which the Constitution vests exclusively the judicial power of the country.[33]

[31]Ibid., pp. 401–03.
[32]Ibid., p. 399.
[33]Ibid.

One of the causes of the American Revolution had been the creation by the British of admiralty courts very similar to the ones proposed by this bill. Johnson's veto was upheld, but later, in the summer of 1866, Congress passed a modified version of this bill over his veto.

Congress next passed the Civil Rights Act of 1866 (March 16). This act granted citizenship to all persons born in the United States (except Indians) and declared that they were entitled to all civil and legal rights enjoyed by whites. Since the Southern states had already granted most of the specific rights mentioned in this bill to the freedmen, it is clear that the real intent of this act was to grant the federal government unlimited discretion to intervene in state affairs. In his veto message, Johnson pointed out that:

> hitherto every subject embraced in the enumeration of rights contained in this bill has been considered as exclusively belonging to the states. They all relate to the internal police and economy of the respective states. They are matters which in each state concern the domestic condition of its people, varying in each according to its own peculiar circumstances and the safety and well-being of its own citizens.[34]

The bill also created an even more elaborate and vigorous federal enforcement apparatus than had the Freedmen's Bureau Bill. The act granted the power of arresting anyone who violated the act or obstructed its enforcement to federal district attorneys, federal marshals, Freedmen's Bureau officials, and special federal commissioners who would be paid a fee for each arrest. All such persons were authorized to call to their aid federal troops or state militia in enforcing the act. Last, the federal courts were given exclusive jurisdiction over all cases arising under this law. Johnson pointed out that the act was revolutionary as well as unconstitutional. In the first place, it granted sweeping powers to federal officials and courts. In the second, it nationalized civil rights and thus marked a significant step away from a decentralized federal polity toward a centralized national one. Johnson stated:

[34]Ibid., p. 407.

In all our history, in all our experience as a people living under Federal and State law, no such system as that contemplated by the details of this bill has ever before been proposed or adopted. They establish for the security of the colored race safeguards which go infinitely beyond any that the General Government has ever provided for the white race. . . . They interfere with the municipal legislation of the States, with the relations existing exclusively between a State and its citizens, or between inhabitants of the same State—an absorption and assumption of power by the General Government which, if acquiesced in, must sap and destroy our federative system of limited powers and break down the barriers which preserve the rights of the States. It is another step, or rather stride, toward centralization and concentration of all legislative powers in the National Government. The tendency of the bill must be to resuscitate the spirit of rebellion and to arrest the progress of those influences which are more closely drawing around the States the bonds of union and peace.[35]

Johnson's predictions were fully vindicated. The provisions of this act, as incorporated in the Fourteenth Amendment, have been instrumental in transforming a federal constitutional order into its opposite, and they have embittered sectional relations for generations. Johnson did not believe that the protections of this bill were necessary to protect the freedmen from being re-enslaved or exploited by their former masters. And he was far from being unsympathetic to their situation, claiming:

The white race and the black race of the South have hitherto lived together under the relation of master and slave—capital owning labor. Now, suddenly, that relation is changed, and as to ownership, capital and labor are divorced. They stand now each master of itself. In this new relation, one being necessary to the other, there will be a new adjustment, which both are deeply interested in making harmonious. Each has equal power in settling the terms, and if left to the laws that regulate capital and labor it is confidently believed that they will satisfactorily work out the problem. Capital, it is true, has more intelligence, but labor is never so ignorant as not to understand its own interest, not to know its own value, and not to see that capital must pay that value. This bill frustrates

[35]Ibid., pp. 412–13.

this adjustment. It intervenes between capital and labor and attempts to settle the question of political economy through the agency of numerous officials whose interest it will be to foment discord between the two races, for as the breach widens their employment will continue, and when it is closed their occupation will terminate.[36]

Johnson did not believe that the planters had nefarious intentions. The Radical Republicans believed that they did have such intentions. But on whose judgment are we to place the most reliance: that of a Yankee Radical from Massachusetts such as Charles Sumner who was full of ideological obsessions and had no experience in the South at all, or a Southerner such as Andrew Johnson who was far from being the tool or dupe of the former Confederates? Johnson also raised the important question of whether it was just or democratic to pass such a momentous piece of legislation when ten states of the Union had no representation in Congress. He asked whether its passage in such circumstances would be consistent with the theory of self-government or of equal rights among the states on which the republic was founded.

The Republicans overrode Johnson's veto of the Civil Rights Act. It was the first time in American history that Congress had overridden a presidential veto. However, they had to resort to illegality in order to prevail. When the Republicans in the Senate fell one vote short of the necessary two-thirds majority, they decided upon the expedient of unseating, on a frivolous pretext, a Democratic senator from New Jersey, John P. Stockton, who was supporting Johnson's policy. With Stockton out of the way, they had their two-thirds majority. It was not the last time that the Republicans would trample upon democratic procedures and the law to enact their agenda. But there remained one problem: The Civil Rights Act was so blatantly unconstitutional that even many Republicans doubted its legitimacy. In addition, as a mere legislative act, it was vulnerable to being repealed by a Democratic Congress or judicially nullified by a conservative Supreme Court. To meet these dangers, the Radicals decided to incorporate the provisions of the act in a constitutional amendment, the Fourteenth.

[36]Ibid., p. 412.

The Fourteenth Amendment is best known for granting citizenship to everyone born in the United States (except Indians) and extending federal jurisdiction over many civil rights. But it was also cleverly crafted to entrench Republican political and economic hegemony. Section 2 mandated that federal representation be reduced in proportion to how many male citizens were denied the vote in a particular state. This was obviously intended to prevent Southerners from gaining representation by the repeal of the three-fifths clause while not extending the franchise to the freedmen. Section 3 debarred ex-Confederates who, previous to the war had ever taken an oath to support the federal Constitution, from ever again holding any state or federal office, political or judicial. Its effect was to proscribe almost the entire Southern leadership class from public life. Section 4 forbade any state from paying any part of the Confederate war debt or providing compensation to the former owners of slaves; it also forbade any future Congress from repudiating the federal war debt. In addition, the Republican leaders framed the amendment to protect corporations from state regulations and interference with their affairs, although for obvious reasons they did not publicly avow this intention.

The language of Section 1 refers to "persons," not citizens; of course, corporations were considered persons in the eyes of the American law. In 1882 Roscoe Conkling, who had been a member of the Committee of Fifteen, admitted that the committee crafted the language of the amendment to provide corporations with "congressional and administrative protection against invidious and discriminating state and local taxes and oppressive and ruinous rules applied under state laws." He even produced the hitherto unpublished journal of the committee to prove his point.[37]

The Republicans used methods to adopt the Fourteenth Amendment that were illegal, unconstitutional, and alien to the American political tradition as it existed at that time. In Tennessee, the Republican majority found that they lacked a quorum to pass the amendment. They actually kidnapped two Democratic members who were staying away on purpose, bound them, and carried them into the legislative hall. They ratified the amendment. But there remained a problem; no other

---

[37]Quoted in Beale, *Critical Year*, p. 218.

Southern state would ratify the amendment, even though the Republicans had made ratification a condition for representation. Their solution to this problem will be discussed below. In the meantime, during the long period between its congressional passage and its final ratification in July 1868, two Northern states, Ohio and New Jersey, rescinded their ratifications and voted against the amendment. The Republicans responded by simply ignoring this vote and considering the previous yes vote as binding.

As it became clear in the spring of 1866 that neither Johnson nor the Republican leaders in Congress were going to submit to the policies of the other, attention shifted to the fall elections. The Republican aim was to maintain, or increase, their veto-proof majority in Congress. The Republicans adopted a complex strategy of stealth and deceit. First, they concealed their more radical intentions, such as black suffrage, until after the elections. Second, they used congressional testimony and the newspapers to portray the South as a land still in rebellion and bent on murdering blacks. Third, in the Eastern states, they warned that a Democratic resurgence would mean repudiation of the federal debt and a lower tariff; in the Western states, they waved the bloody shirt.

Johnson was in the impossible position of being a leader without a party. He had the support of moderate Republicans, but they were a minority in the party. He had the support of the Northern Democrats, but this support was weakening him among his own adopted party. Some suggested that he form a third party, but as it takes time to build a third-party movement, this was unrealistic and could not in any event help in the fall. His only real option was to use his powers of patronage to purge the Radicals from the federal government, but for whatever reasons, he failed to do so before it was too late. The result was predictable. The Republicans lost a handful of seats, but they retained their commanding majority (3–1 in the House and 4–1 in the Senate). With the election behind them, the Republicans proceeded to launch the second and more radical phase of congressional reconstruction—the imposition of direct military rule over the South.

In his second annual message on December 3, 1866, a still defiant Johnson declared that by refusing to seat Southern congressional delegates the Republicans were violating "the great principle enunciated in the Declaration of Independence that no people ought to bear the burden of taxation and yet be denied the right of representation."[38] Leaving aside the fact that Johnson, by supporting the war for the Union, had denied another great principle contained in the Declaration—the right of self-determination of a people—Johnson's criticism is devastating. He also pointed out that treating the Southern states as conquered provinces was "incompatible with the nature of our republican system and with the professed objects of the war."[39] He implored the Republicans to accept Southern representation to "consummate the work of restoration and exert a most salutary influence in the reestablishment of peace, harmony, and fraternal feeling."[40] Of course, nothing could have been further from the intentions of the Republican leadership.

In March 1867, the Radical Republicans began the second phase of their revolution by passing two pieces of legislation. The first was the Tenure of Office Act, which forbade the president from removing any appointive civil or military officer without the consent of the Senate. Johnson promptly vetoed the act on the grounds of its unconstitutionality, but the Republicans just as promptly passed it over his veto. In his veto message, Johnson argued that

> the power of removal is constitutionally vested in the President of the United States, is a principle which has been not more distinctly declared by judicial authority and judicial commentators than it has been uniformly practiced upon by legislative and executive departments of the Government.[41]

In other words, the uniform precedent of seventy-five years, both judicial and political, sanctioned an exclusive executive discretion in removals, and there was nothing in the text of the Constitution or the record of the ratification debates to suggest that the original intent had been different. The Republicans were trying to deprive the president of one of his only weapons in fighting their reconstruction policy, but they also may have intended to lay a trap for him. If Johnson removed an official

---

[38]Richardson, p. 446.
[39]Ibid., p. 447.
[40]Ibid., p. 448.
[41]Ibid., p. 493.

without their consent, they could impeach him, which was exactly what happened. In February 1868, Johnson finally decided to dismiss Edwin Stanton, the secretary of war, who had been undermining the president's policy from the beginning. Stanton's Radical sympathies and activities had been known since mid-1866, but for some reason Johnson had refrained from dismissal. The House wasted no time in impeaching the president (February 24), and the case went to the Senate for trial. The Senate voted 35–19 to convict but fell one vote short of the requisite two-thirds majority due to the fact that seven moderate Republicans would not vote for conviction.

Johnson tried to persuade the public that only his plan could reunite the country: "The only safety of the nation lies in a generous and expansive plan of conciliation, and the longer this is delayed, the more difficult it will be to bring the North and South into harmony."[42] He also warned them that the Republican plan threatened the American tradition of constitutional federalism:

> We must return to constitutional limits establishing the great fact that ours is a government of limited powers with a written constitution, with boundaries both national and state, and that these limitations and boundaries must be observed and strictly enforced if free government is to exist.[43]

But while Johnson tried to reason with the public, the newspapers and the Radicals did their best to inflame them.

The second piece of Radical legislation was of far greater consequence: the Reconstruction Act, which deposed the functioning state governments in ten Southern states and placed them under martial law. It divided these states into five military districts and appointed a military governor with full and plenary powers over each. To enforce this act, Congress authorized that twenty thousand troops be stationed in the South. Almost two years after the end of the war, Congress had placed the Southern states under renewed military occupation. Congress overthrew ten state governments that had been functioning in all their political and judicial capacities for a year and a half. Moreover,

---

[42]Quoted in Beale, *Critical Year*, p. 27.
[43]Ibid., pp. 29–30.

these were governments that had accepted the results of the war and had been recognized by the president. The Republicans claimed that drastic action was necessary because the Southern states were in a state of disorder and anarchy which threatened the lives and property of all citizens, black and white. But this claim was just a pretext.

As Johnson pointed out, there was no state of anarchy or disorder. The Radicals had decided that the only way to force the Southern states to ratify the Fourteenth Amendment was to topple the existing governments and install new governments more amenable to Radical demands. In addition, they wanted to force black suffrage upon the South. It should be stressed that their motivation in doing so was purely mercenary—to gain Republican votes in the South—and had nothing to do with idealism or justice, as is evident in the gross hypocrisy of the 1868 Republican platform. The platform called for black suffrage to be imposed on the Southern states by federal military authority even while it maintained that the Northern states should be left at liberty to decide on their own for or against black suffrage. Johnson railed against the bill in his veto message:

> The military rule which it establishes is plainly to be used, not for any purpose of order or for the prevention of crime, but solely as a means of coercing the people into the adoption of principles and measures to which it is known they are opposed, and upon which they have an undeniable right to exercise their own judgment.[44]

The Reconstruction Act bears comparison with the Massachusetts Government Act (1774), one of the Coercive Acts, which annulled the Massachusetts charter and set up a new government for that province. Johnson promptly vetoed the bill on the grounds that it was,

> in its whole character, scope, and object without precedent and without authority, in palpable conflict with the plainest provisions of the Constitution, and utterly destructive to those great principles of liberty and humanity for which our ancestors on both sides of the Atlantic have shed so much blood and expended so much treasure.[45]

[44]Richardson, p. 500.
[45]Ibid.

Those great principles of liberty included the right of self-determination, the right of self-government, and no taxation without representation. What's more, the Reconstruction Act violated the clause of the Constitution guaranteeing each state a republican form of government:

> Can it be pretended that this obligation is not palpably broken if we carry out a measure like this, which wipes away every vestige of republican government in ten states and puts the life, property, liberty, and honor of all people in each of them under the domination of a single person clothed with unlimited authority.[46]

The act also required that each state hold a new constitutional convention elected by universal manhood suffrage. However, it made former Confederate leaders ineligible to serve as delegates or vote for the same. It required the conventions to grant black suffrage and exclude former Confederate leaders from voting or serving in the state government in any capacity. Johnson thundered:

> The purpose and object of this bill—the general intent which pervades it from beginning to end—is to change the entire structure and character of the State governments and to compel them by force to adoption of organic laws and regulations which they are unwilling to accept if left to themselves.[47]

Johnson went so far as to argue that the Republicans' reconstruction policy gave credence to the Southern claim that they had seceded to protect their constitutional liberties from a lawless Northern majority that had no respect for the fundamental and organic law of the republic. He added:

> Those who advocated the right of secession alleged in their own justification that we had no regard for law and that the rights of property, life, and liberty would not be safe under the Constitution as administered by us. If we now verify their assertion, we prove that they were in truth in fact fighting for their liberty, and instead of branding their leaders with the dishonoring name of traitors against a righteous and legal

---

[46]Ibid., 506.
[47]Ibid., 507.

government we elevate them in history to the rank of self-sacrificing patriots, consecrate them to the admiration of the world, and place them by the side of Washington, Hampden, and Sidney.[48]

In his third annual message, Johnson declared that the Republicans' reconstruction policy had dissolved the Union:

Candor compels me to declare that at this time there is no Union as our fathers understood the term, and as they meant it to be understood by us. The Union which they established can exist only where all the States are represented in both Houses of Congress; where one State is as free as another to regulate its internal concerns according to its own will, and where the laws of the central Government, strictly confined to matters of national jurisdiction, apply with equal force to all the people of every section.[49]

In comments designed to further antagonize the Republicans, Johnson called for a resumption of specie payments and reductions in the public debt, expenditures, and taxation. In his fourth annual message in December 1868, Johnson provided his final judgment on congressional Reconstruction. Although the Union had been on the verge of full restoration and sectional reconciliation in December 1866, Congress:

intervened, and, refusing to perfect the work so nearly consummated, declined to admit members from the unrepresented states, adopted a series of measures which arrested the progress of restoration, frustrated all that had been so successfully accomplished, and, after three years of agitation and strife, has left the country further from the attainment of union and fraternal feeling than at the inception of the Congressional plan of reconstruction. It needs no argument to show that legislation which has produced such baneful consequences should be abrogated.[50]

But the Republicans continued to exclude the Southern states from the Union and persisted in their attempts to revolutionize

---

[48]Ibid., p. 509.
[49]Ibid., p. 559.
[50]Ibid., p. 673.

Southern society for eight more years before finally, in 1877, throwing in the towel.

Perhaps the best epitaph on the Johnson presidency came from the pen of Gideon Welles, Johnson's secretary of the Navy:

> The real and true cause of assault and persecution was the fearless and unswerving fidelity of the president to the Constitution, his opposition to central Congressional usurpation, and his maintenance of the rights of the states and of the Executive Department, against legislative aggression.

The struggle was

> carried on by a fragment of Congress that arrogated to itself authority to exclude States and people from their constitutional right of representation, against an Executive striving under infinite embarrassments to preserve State, Federal and Popular Rights.[51]

---

[51]Quoted in Beale, *Critical Year*, pp. 222–23.

10

WILLIAM MCKINLEY: ARCHITECT OF THE AMERICAN EMPIRE

JOSEPH R. STROMBERG

Papa met José Martí in Key West, and admired his Cuban Revolutionary Party, but he says we should not fool ourselves about our interests. He hates the Spaniards as sincerely as the next man, but says the U.S. picked this fight in Cuba, *Maine* or no *Maine*, it's just an excuse to clean Spain out of our hemisphere once and for all, and grab the Philippines and Puerto Rico while we're at it. The War with Spain isn't one bit different than what he still calls "the War of Yankee Aggression": the Old South, says he, was the first conquest of the Yankee Empire.

—Peter Matthiessen
Killing Mr. Watson

"Our first man of destiny since Mr. Lincoln—the President, who else? The Major himself. Mr. McKinley. Don't laugh!" Adams frowned severely. "I know he is supposed to be a creature of Mark Hanna and all the other bosses, but it's plain to me that they are his creatures. They find him money—a useful art—so that he can deliver us an empire, which he has!"

—Gore Vidal
Empire

'Consent of the governed,' indeed! . . . War is the great civilizer. God commanded Moses and Joshua to exterminate the Canaanites.

—Hon. Henry Gibson of Tennessee,
Pictorial History of America's New Possessions

"Ye're a traitor," said Mr. Hennessy.
"I know it," said Mr. Dooley, complacently.
"Ye're an anti-expansionist."
"If ye say that again," cried Mr. Dooley, angrily, "I'll smash in ye'er head."

—Finley Peter Dunne
Mr. Dooley's Philosophy

The most unprofitable of all commerce is that connected with foreign dominion. To a few individuals it may be beneficial, merely because it is commerce; but to the nation it is a loss. The expense of maintaining dominion more than absorbs the profit of any trade.

—Thomas Paine
Selected Writings of Thomas Paine

William McKinley:
Architect of Overseas Empire

Wjilliam McKinley, twenty-fifth president of the United States, is, frankly, a rather boring character, although we should not consider this a bad trait in a president. Indeed, had he only been as boring as Harding or Coolidge, we would not need to worry as much as we do about the bloated office which presides over the American empire. He deployed an array of presidential powers—largely absent from the original Constitution but built up over time by "strong" presidents like Jefferson, Jackson, and Lincoln—to achieve his geopolitical and domestic goals. He left the office "enhanced," as historians like to say.[1]

McKinley's Early Career
as a Conventional Republican

William McKinley was born in Niles, Ohio, in 1843. He had some college education and taught in a country school. He served in the Twenty-third Ohio Infantry, preserving the Union, and rose to the rank of major. After the war, he studied law in Canton, Ohio; worked as an attorney; and was elected prosecuting attorney of Stark County, as a Republican in a Democratic county. In 1871 he married Ida Saxton, but their happiness was undermined by the loss of two daughters and his wife's "invalid" condition (actually, epilepsy).

McKinley was elected to Congress in 1876 and reelected in 1878, 1880, 1882, 1884, and 1888. He was a talented, highly conventional Republican noted for his dedication to sky-high

---

[1]E.S. Corwin, in *Total War and the Constitution* (New York: Alfred A. Knopf, 1947) was critical of Lincoln's "invention" of unspecified presidential "war powers," but in later writings could not get enough presidential power. Of sterner stuff is Raoul Berger, whose *Executive Privilege: A Constitutional Myth* (Cambridge, Mass.: Harvard University Press, 1974) argues persuasively that the Constitution granted no inherent executive powers.

tariffs and occasional waving of the bloody shirt.[2] He was a personal friend of Marcus Hanna, industrialist and, later, politician, and the myth arose that Hanna was his puppetmaster. Mark Hanna himself remarked to some Republican leaders that "you will find that he knows more about politics than all of us."[3]

In 1890, it was realized that the 1883 Tariff Act (largely McKinley's own work) was bringing in too much money and McKinley, now chairman of the Ways and Means Committee, undertook to subject the tariff to friendly revision.[4] The tariff cannot be discussed apart from an integrated set of political ideas and interests which emerged as a program by the 1880s. While for some of McKinley's associates the tariff may have simply been a good thing they were getting away with, for more sophisticated policymakers in the tradition of William H. Seward, tariffs were but one means of achieving a neomercantilist expansion of the American political economy. Seward's acquisition of Alaska and the Midway Islands projected U.S. power, potentially, into the Pacific toward appealing Asian markets for American goods and investment. This state-promoted expansion, at first merely desirable, soon came to be seen as absolutely essential to American prosperity and liberty.[5]

[2]Thus, in a speech at East Liverpool, Ohio, in October 1893, he said: "There is not one Southern State that is not in favor of State bank money. Do you know why? Because they still believe in State sovereignty. They don't seem to realize that State sovereignty was shot to death twenty-five years ago." (Murat Halstead, *Life and Distinguished Services of William McKinley, our Martyr President*: Memorial Association,1901), pp. 158–59.

[3]Quoted in William Appleman Williams, *The Roots of the Modern American Empire* (New York: Random House, 1969), p. 411. Henry Adams observed that McKinley, as president, "was a marvelous manager of men" who "found several manipulators, to help him, almost as remarkable as himself, one of whom was [John] Hay." *The Education of Henry Adams* (Boston, Mass.: Houghton Mifflin, [1918] 1961), p. 374.

[4]The contemporary English liberal economic historian Thorold Rogers said of the American tariff: "The American people pretend to be the freest nation in the world, and they permit themselves to be fleeced and plundered by a few interests, which dictated their own terms at a supreme crisis of the national history." *The Economic Interpretation of History* (London: T. Fisher Unwin, 1918), pp. 383–84.

[5]See Walter LaFeber, *The New Empire: An Interpretation of American Expansion, 1860-1898* (Ithaca, N.Y.: Cornell University Press, 1963). On Seward's precocious program, see pp. 24–32, and also Ernest N. Paolino,

This is the essential context—to which we shall return—of McKinley's clash with the James G. Blaine wing of the Republican Party over tariff policy. Blaine, secretary of state under Presidents Garfield and Harrison (1881 and 1889–1892), was heir to Seward's strategic vision (and perhaps Lincoln's, since Lincoln had been a disciple of the mercantilist Henry Clay). He wished to combine flexible tariffs with broad discretionary presidential power to negotiate reciprocity treaties with foreign nations to gain better access to those markets. This made tariffs a tool in a larger policy of market expansion. McKinley, still a pure protectionist, worked to achieve a traditional Republican high-tariff act which carried his name. McKinley learned from this fight and later emerged as a proponent of Blaine's strategy for expanding U.S. exports, once he took on board the widespread "overproductionist" theory of America's economic difficulties.[6]

"OVERPRODUCTION" AND THE PANACEA OF EXPORT MARKETS

William Appleman Williams argues that "farm businessmen" formulated the diagnosis of overproduction and its proposed cure—expanded export markets—even before metropolitan interests did. Southern and Western farmers sought regulation (and, ultimately, nationalization) of the railroads to ensure their equitable operation. Another agrarian goal was large-scale coinage of silver to reverse its demonetization in 1873–1874 and provide "easier" money, as well as to foster trade with countries on the sterling standard. Above all, the farm bloc wanted expanded markets for their crops.[7] The deflation of 1873–1879 gave them added reason to look abroad.

According to Williams, an "export bonanza" in 1877–1881, occasioned by natural disasters affecting European agriculture,

---

The Foundations of the American Empire: William Henry Seward and U.S. Foreign Policy (Ithaca, N.Y.: Cornell University Press, 1973).

[6]See Williams, *The Roots of the Modern American Empire*, pp. 247–48, 332–37.

[7]Ibid., pp. 132–404. For a discussion of the complex monetary issues, see Irwin Unger, *The Greenback Era* (Princeton, N.J.: Princeton University Press, 1964). Unger remarks "a rather loose connection between protectionist principles and soft money" (p. 127)—a point that probably applies to the 1870s. As yet there appears to be no real Austrian analysis of this period.

underscored the possibilities overseas markets held for U.S. prosperity. The bonanza's end, when European farmers recovered, only reinforced the growing conviction that larger export markets for U.S. farmers were both desirable and necessary. Failing at first to win government assistance to open up such markets, agrarian interests exerted substantial pressure for such expansion.[8] Many metropolitan industrial interests had also arrived at the view that foreign markets were essential to their prosperity.[9] The turning point came when metropolitan Republicans led by Governor William McKinley of Ohio presented a program attractive to industrial and agrarian interests alike.

The fundamental reason for what became informal "Open Door" empire was stated in 1899 by Francis B. Thurber, president of the United States Export Association: "We must have a place to dump our surplus, which otherwise will constantly depress prices and compel the shutting down of our mills . . . and changing our profits into losses"; or as Andrew Carnegie put it, "The condition of cheap manufacture is *running full.*" The resulting dilemma was met by selling or "dumping" the excess product abroad "at a lower price, sometimes . . . below cost."[10]

Writing not long after the Spanish–American War and the Boer War, the English anti-imperialist writer John A. Hobson, himself an overproductionist theorist, summarized matters thus:

> The economic taproot of, the chief directing motive of all the modern imperialistic expansion, is the pressure of capitalist industries for markets, primarily markets for investment, secondarily markets for surplus products of home industry. Where the concentration of capital has gone furthest, and where a rigorous protective system, prevails, this pressure is necessarily strongest. . . . This is the essential significance of the recent change in American foreign policy as illustrated by the Spanish War, the Philippine annexation, the Panama policy, and the new application of the Munroe [sic] doctrine. . . . South America is needed as preferential market for investment

---

[8]Ibid., pp. 206–31.

[9]William Appleman Williams, *Contours of American History* (New York: New Viewpoints, 1973), pp. 363–64.

[10]Quoted in Williams, *The Roots of the Modern American Empire*, p. 439, and *Contours of American History*, pp. 326–27.

of trust "profits" and surplus trust products. . . . China as a field of railway enterprise and general industrial development already begins to loom large in the eyes of foresighted American businessmen.[11]

It was the panic of 1893 and the subsequent economic crisis which set the stage for the emergence of McKinley, now governor of Ohio, as leader of an expansionist coalition:

> The majority of American interest groups, farmers as well as manufacturers, and top political leaders as well as academic theorists, changed their mind between 1892 and 1897 on the question of what had caused the panic and the ensuing depression. From explaining it as a consequence of dangerous or outmoded *monetary* theories and policies, they came to account for it in terms of overproduction and lack of markets.[12]

McKinley and his colleagues generalized the thesis of "overproduction" advanced by various interests and industries to the American economy as a whole. Their combination of protectionism and reciprocity treaties proved very attractive and contributed to Republican victory in 1896. The expansionist consensus, of which McKinley's policies were the mature expression, had long been developing. Rooted in a felt need to dominate world markets, the new policies bespoke a fundamentally *imperial* conception of America's world role. This conception was reinforced by a "frontier-expansionist" interpretation of history put forward by Frederick Jackson Turner, which regarded the frontier as the source of American republicanism, individualism, and prosperity. With the close of the continental frontier, a "new frontier" had to be found if American society was to remain free and prosperous. Brooks Adams, historian and would-be geopolitical theorist, and his associates (including Theodore Roosevelt) came to see overseas empire as the substitute West for

---

[11]John A. Hobson, *The Evolution of Modern Capitalism: A Study of Machine Production* (London: George Allen and Unwin, [1926] 1949), pp. 262–63.

[12]William Appleman Williams, "The Acquitting Judge" in *For A New America: Essays in History and Politics from Studies on the Left, 1959–1967*, James Weinstein and David W. Eakins, eds. (New York: Random House, 1970), p. 44.

industrial America.[13] To that traditional U.S. sphere of influence, Latin America, were to be added the markets of Asia—above all, China—and the world. Hence, the agitation for subsidies to shippers and a modern "blue water" navy.

Given the goal of opening up markets, U.S. policymakers sought to create political conditions favorable to trade and investment in every country regarded as a potential market. A variety of tactics, ranging from reciprocity treaties to more flexible tariffs, were employed to eliminate other countries' barriers to U.S. trade. Reform of the U.S. Consular Service, an isthmian canal in Nicaragua or Panama, Hawaiian annexation, and even meat inspection legislation to overcome European discrimination against U.S. products, were all part of a strategy of economic empire.[14] This noncolonial strategy of empire, relying on America's preponderant power to achieve "supremacy over the whole region," was remarkably like Britain's "imperialism of free trade" as analyzed by Gallagher and Robinson.[15] As free trade, it was, of course, somewhat spurious.

The panic of 1893—which probably *can* be addressed in terms of monetary factors—and the severe depression which followed enlarged the audience for "overproduction" analysis.[16]

---

[13]See LaFeber, *The New Empire*, pp. 62–101, Thomas McCormick, *China Market: America's Quest for Informal Empire, 1893–1901* (Chicago: Quadrangle Books, 1970), and Lloyd C. Gardner, *A Different Frontier: Selected Readings in the Foundations of American Economic Expansion* (Chicago: Quadrangle Books, 1966).

[14]William F. Marina points out that "[i]t is a mistake to consider anyone who believed in developing American commercial interests as an economic imperialist. . . . [T]he essence of the anti-imperialist position was an aversion to the use of force in relations between nations." See "Opponents of Empire: An Interpretation of American Anti-Imperialism, 1898–1921" (Ph.D. Dissertation, University of Denver, 1968), p. 100. Cf. Harold Baron: "The free trade concept of developing international trade had nothing in common with the neo-mercantilist governmental policy that prevailed in the United States" ("Comment on John Rollins,'The Anti-Imperialists and Twentieth Century American Foreign Policy,'" *Studies on the Left* 3, no. 1 [1962]: 26).

[15]John Gallagher and Ronald Robinson, "The Imperialism of Free Trade," *Economic History Review*, 2nd ser., 6, no. 1 (1953): 3, 1–15. For a reply which stresses the difference between "free trade" imperialism and real free trade, see Oliver MacDonagh, "The Anti-Imperialism of Free Trade," *Economic History Review*, 2nd ser., 14, no. 3 (1962): 489–501.

[16]McCormick, *China Market*, p. 34.

Implicitly rejecting Say's Law, would-be analysts across the political spectrum reasoned that U.S. industry somehow produced significantly more than could be consumed at home, at prevailing prices. The surplus had to find "vent" overseas.

One obvious reform—drastic reduction of U.S. tariffs, or outright free trade—as a means of easing entry of U.S. goods into foreign markets did not appeal to northeastern Republicans and industrialists, and their opponents—Southern and Western Democrats, Populists, and even some Republicans—seemed to think freer trade was desirable but not the entire remedy.

Many who saw foreign markets as the cure for all ills disagreed violently with one another over monetary policy. Democrats and Populists argued that in addition to easier credit, extensive coinage of silver would assist U.S. penetration of foreign markets on the silver standard. Proponents of gold monometallism were denounced as agents of London bankers and the British Empire. Eastern interests of both major parties saw the program of the silverites as dangerously inflationary (which it was) and tarred them with the brush of foreign radicalism. (The real socialists, waiting in the wings, added the obvious corollary to overproduction, namely, "underconsumption," to be solved by redistribution of wealth at home.)

In this divisive climate, accented by the depression, Governor McKinley—"the Major"—won his party's 1896 presidential nomination. He had already emerged as the chief political leader of the Republican neomercantilists, as the man who could actually implement the ideas of Captain Mahan, Senator Henry Cabot Lodge, Theodore Roosevelt, and John Hay (mentioned so often in this context that they form their own Gramscian "historical bloc" or, at least, a Gang of Four).

That McKinley was prepared for his role is clear from his address to the founding convention of the National Association of Manufacturers in January 1895 in Cincinnati, where he told the enthused delegates:

> We want our own markets for our manufactures and agricultural products; we want a tariff for our surplus products which will not surrender our markets and will not degrade our labor to hold our markets. We want a reciprocity which will give us foreign markets for our surplus products and in

turn will open our markets to foreigners for those products which they produce and which we do not.[17]

The election of 1896 pitted McKinley against Democratic nominee William Jennings Bryan, a prairie Populist, who emphasized unlimited coinage of silver and drastic tariff reduction. The Republican platform called for an isthmian canal, reciprocity, and Hawaiian annexation, and pledged loyalty to the gold standard. To give the silverites something, McKinley promised international negotiations to establish bimetallism.[18] McKinley won handily.

He came into office faced with the after-effects of the depression and the Cuban revolution against Spanish rule, which had broken out in 1895. The Cuban guerrillas' disruption of Cuban economic activity and the heavy-handed Spanish attempts at repression endangered American lives and property in the island, while Cuban propagandists headquartered in New York made the most of Spanish brutalities. Popular and congressional opinion, spurred on by the "yellow journalists" of the period, demanded American action to liberate Cuba and restore normal economic life. In its diplomatic notes, the Cleveland administration had already implied that Spain might be *allowed* to restore order within limits prescribed by the United States.[19]

---

[17]Quoted in LaFeber, *The New Empire*, pp. 192–93. (Not exactly Daniel Webster, but certainly what the N.A.M. delegates wanted to hear.) Businesses especially keen on the political finding of overseas markets included cotton, flour, and meat exporters (see Williams, *The Roots of the Modern American Empire*, p. 340). Mr. Dooley soon pictured American business representatives addressing the poor heathen Chinese as follows: "Hinceforth ye'll ate th' canned roast beef iv merry ol' stock yards or I'll have a file iv sojers fill ye full iv ondygestible lead." And: "We ar-re th' advance guard iv Westhren Civilization, an we're goin' to give ye a railroad so ye can go swiftly to places that ye don't want to see." (Peter Finley Dunne, *Mr. Dooley's Philosophy* [New York: R.H. Russell, 1900], pp. 79–80.)

[18]Reciprocity, subsidies to the merchant marine, foreign markets, and bimetallism feature prominently in McKinley's first inaugural address. See James D. Richardson, ed., *Messages and Papers of the Presidents* 10 (Washington, D.C.: Bureau of National Literature and Art, 1903), pp. 11–19.

[19]LaFeber, *The New Empire*, pp. 295–95.

THE PROSPECT OF WAR FOR EMPIRE

The Cuban revolt presented McKinley with the choice—and opportunity—of going to war to launch the imperial program. Aside from protecting investments and markets in Cuba, the administration wished to pacify the island in order to concentrate on the larger goal of penetrating Asia markets. The conjuncture of problem and opportunity led to war in 1898. The U.S. not only acquired Cuba as an informal possession but gained a foothold in Asia by taking the Philippine Islands over from Spain.

HOW MCKINLEY MANEUVERED THE SPANIARDS

It is his handling of his opportunities and his assumption of the mantle of empire that rescue McKinley from his popular image as a weak president badgered into war by the people, Congress, and the press.[20] That the cause of liberating Cuba was popular helped, but McKinley had his own schedule. More was at stake—the whole integrated extension of American commerce as a *political-economic system*. War with Spain was a positive good, given the Caribbean and Pacific insular properties that would accrue to the United States upon its conclusion. The latter, in particular, would provide coaling stations for military and commercial vessels and effectively put America's economic frontier well into Asia. In this respect, peace was hardly the first choice.

> In the end, that is to say, the United States got the war that the vast majority of its leaders and citizens wanted. Nobody thrust it upon them. They had defined their ideological and economic interests in ways that converged upon a demand for forceful action in the arena of foreign affairs. The overseas interests that they had defined may be considered mistaken by later observers (some citizens considered them such even then), but they were very real at the time.[21]

---

[20]"McKinley led by indirection . . . but he was more in charge than his colleagues realized." Michael P. Riccards, *The Ferocious Engine of Democracy: A History of the American Presidency* (New York: Madison Books, 1995), p. 364. Henry Adams wrote that "[t]he Major is an uncommonly dangerous politician" (quoted in Walter Karp, *The Politics of War* [New York: Harper Colophon Books], p. 71).

[21]Williams, "The Acquitting Judge," p. 45.

In May 1897, the president asked Congress for $50 million to assist Americans in Cuba, and in June he submitted the Hawaiian annexation treaty which his predecessor, Grover Cleveland, had buried. The administration had begun lecturing Madrid to the effect that continued disorder in Cuba severely affected American interests there. "Spain was held responsible for a prosperity to which the United States was 'entitled.'"[22]

McKinley's first annual message, in December 1897, dealt with his usual economic concerns but centered on the Cuban question. Referring to the infamous Spanish policy of *reconcentración*, the president said, "It was not civilized warfare. It was extermination."[23] The current Spanish government, in power since October, showed signs of adopting more acceptable policies.

Alarmist reports from the U.S. consul at Havana, Fitzhugh Lee, may have stimulated the administration to send the battleship *Maine* to Havana harbor. The DeLôme affair was still in the news when the battleship exploded on February 15, 1898. Both these events worsened relations with Spain and added to clamor for war. The ineffable Teddy Roosevelt, undersecretary of the Navy, cabled Commodore Dewey at Hong Kong to be ready to steam to Manila in the event of war. (Theodore Roosevelt was impetuous but not really ahead of the administration.)

On March 26, the administration insisted that Spain must negotiate with the Cuban rebels over Cuban independence. On March 31, Spain agreed to close the *reconcentración* camps, provide $600,000 "for relief," "grant an armistice to the Cuban rebels, and convene a legislative assembly at Havana in May to inaugurate autonomous government on the island." "Since the President had anticipated that Spain would reject the ultimatum and had written a war message on the basis of his expectation, the conciliatory reply from Madrid forced him into hasty revisions."[24] Nevertheless, McKinley told the cabinet on April 2 that armed U.S. intervention "would be necessary in Cuba."[25] The pattern of the negotiations raises the question of whether the administration really wanted negotiations to succeed.

---

[22]Williams, *The Roots of the Modern American Empire*, p. 417.

[23]Richardson, ed., *Messages and Papers of the Presidents*, 10, p. 31.

[24]George H. Mayer, *The Republican Party: 1854–1966* (New York: Oxford University Press, 1967), pp. 262–63.

[25]Marina, "Opponents of Empire," p. 7.

THE MAJOR GETS HIS WAR

On April 11, McKinley sent his "war message" to Congress, asking Congress "to empower the President to take measures to secure a full and final termination between the Government of Spain and the people of Cuba."[26] Congress replied with a four-part resolution on April 19, which called for Cuban independence, and Spanish withdrawal, and empowered the president to achieve these goals with military force. The fourth point, the Teller Amendment, obligated the United States to "leave the government and control of the island to its people."[27]

The war found the military unprepared for even a minor campaign, and various comic-opera episodes took place. War Secretary Russell A. Alger noted that "[t]he army had not been mobilized since the Civil War."[28] The naval campaign in the Pacific proceeded rapidly. Commodore Dewey defeated the Spanish Fleet at Manila on May 1 before the army had attempted a landing in Cuba. Spanish forces surrendered in Cuba on July 17, ending the war. General Shafter kept the Cuban rebels at arm's length, showing that Cuban "independence" was an American operation.[29] In the Pacific theater, the battle of Manila, on August 13, was largely an orchestrated affair fought for the Spanish officers' honor.

THE EMPIRE BUILDERS GO TO WORK

In the meantime, the administration had annexed Hawaii, using that old, dubiously constitutional dodge, the joint resolution, to get around the senatorial two-thirds rule. (The same dodge gave us Texan annexation and NAFTA.) As American forces

[26]Richardson, *Messages and Papers of the Presidents*, 10, p. 67.

[27]Joint Declaration in Merrill D. Peterson and Leonard W. Levy, eds., *Major Crises in American History: Documentary Problems, II: 1865–1953* (New York: Harcourt, Brace, and World, 1962), pp. 191–92.

[28]Quoted in G.J.A. O'Toole, *The Spanish War: An American Epic—1898* (New York: W.W. Norton, 1984), p. 230.

[29]Louis Pérez, Jr., says: "A Cuban war of liberation was transformed into a U.S. war of conquest" (*Cuba: Between Reform and Revolution* [New York: Oxford University Press, 1988], p. 178). In his second annual message in December 1898, McKinley stated that recognizing the Cuban rebels as belligerents would have been "logically unfounded or practically inadmissible"—whatever that might mean (Richardson, *Messages and Papers of the Presidents*, vol. 10, p. 82).

had seized Guam and were holding Manila, there was now no shortage of coaling stations and jumping-off points to Asian markets and world "responsibilities."

Before the battle of Manila, the U.S. called for Cuban independence (here the Teller Amendment tied the administration's hands) and the cession to the U.S. of Puerto Rico and Manila— the city and harbor). After Spain sued for peace on August 12— the battle on the 13th was needless—U.S. demands increased. McKinley was already thinking of keeping the island of Luzon— or, indeed, the whole archipelago. His decision to keep all the Philippines had much to do with fear of German seizure of the islands, which would interfere with the larger political-economic strategy he was following.[30]

The immediate result was a colonial war, the "Philippine Insurrection," between the Americans and Filipinos who had only recently supported the Americans against Spain. This quickly became a counter-insurgency whose conduct increasingly resembled that of the evil Spanish feudalists in Cuba, with 220,000 Filipino deaths resulting from the war. Veterans of late nineteenth-century Indian wars conducted the campaign, notable for its "marked severities."[31] No remarks were heard from McKinley about "uncivilized warfare" or "extermination" this time; only bland generalizations about the rights of conquerors under international law, good government, and uplifting the savages.

True to his interest in the practical details, the president appointed a special commission consisting of Jacob G. Schurman, Rear-Admiral Dewey, Major-General Elwell S. Otis, Charles Denby, and Dean C. Worcester to design a civil government for our new colony and, perhaps as an afterthought, to get the

---

[30]See Marina, "Opponents of Empire," pp. 150–51.

[31]See Leon Wolff, *Little Brown Brother* (Garden City, N.Y.: Doubleday, 1961); Richard Drinnon, *Facing West: The Metaphysics of Indian-Hating and Empire-Building* (New York: New American Library, 1980), pp. 307–32; and Stuart Creighton Miller, *Benevolent Assimilation: American Conquest of the Philippines, 1899–1903* (New Haven, Conn.: Yale University Press, 1982). Fierce resistance by Islamic Moro tribesmen on Mindanao, who could damage or kill an American officer with their bolos even after taking two .38 caliber bullets, led the Army to change over to the Colt .45 automatic pistol (see Geoffrey Perrett, *A Country Made by War: From the Revolution to Vietnam* [New York: Random House, 1989], p. 296).

resources of the islands into the hands of deserving U.S. corporations.[32] Something similar took place in Cuba, where the U.S. military occupation stayed in place long enough to oversee the writing of a Cuban constitution that allowed U.S. intervention at the Americans' discretion (the Platt Amendment) and presided over a virtual Enclosure Movement with respect to Cuban land and resources.[33]

In the Philippines the former anti-Spanish insurgents took up the slogan, *"No hay derecho a vender un pueblo como se vende un saco de patatas"* ("There is no right to sell a village like a sack of potatoes").[34] The Americans were up against the classic colonial problem of finding local collaborators to be their front men and man their administration once the war was won. The rebel leaders, on the other hand, coming from the native upper class—the *ilustrados*—lacked mass support, and as *hacendados*—large landowners—were hardly able to offer land reform to win a mass base.[35] The Americans, with superior resources and firepower, ultimately prevailed, although fighting continued in

---

[32]For an acid portrait of Worcester as an anthropologist whose main interest was timber, cattle, and coconuts (on which he made a lot of money), see Drinnon, *Facing West*, pp. 279–306. A Philippine nationalist newspaper in 1908 portrayed Worcester as "a bird of prey," who

> ascends the mountains of *Benguet* ostensibly to classify and measure Igorot skulls, to study and civilize the Igorots, but, at the same time, he also espies during his flight . . . where the large deposits of gold are, the real prey concealed in the lonely mountains and then he appropriates these all to himself afterward, thanks to the legal facilities he can make and unmake at will, always, however, redounding to his benefit.

(Quoted in Leonard Davis, *The Philippines: People, Poverty, and Politics* [London: Macmillan, 1987], p. 39.)

[33]See Louis Pérez, "Insurrection, Intervention, and the Transformation of Land Tenure Systems in Cuba, 1895–1902," *Hispanic American Historical Review* 65, no. 2 (May 1985): 229–54.

[34]Usha Mahajani, *Philippine Nationalism* (St. Lucia: University of Queensland Press, 1971), p. 156.

[35]See Ronald Robinson, "Non-European Foundations of European Imperialism: Sketch For a Theory of Collaboration" in *Studies in the Theory of Imperialism*, Roger Owen and Bob Sutcliffe, eds. (London: Longman Group, 1972), pp. 118–42, and Glenn A. May, "Why the United States Won the Philippine–American War, 1899–1902," *Pacific Historical Review* 52, no. 4 (November 1983): 353–77.

remote southern islands through 1910. *Ilustrados* who had col-laborated with Spain did the same with the Americans—and, in time, so did former rebels.

THE EMPIRE OF THE OPEN DOOR

McKinley invented, or at least popularized, a name for the strategy of market-expansion by political–military means. In a speech in late 1898, he said, "we seek no advantages in the Ori-ent which are not common to all. Asking only the open door for ourselves, we are ready to accord the open door to others."[36] The phrase soon became shorthand for state-driven overseas eco-nomic expansion. By asserting Americans' right to trade as equal competitors in *all* of China in the Open Door Notes of 1899 and 1900, the United States sought to prevent or reverse the division of China into exclusive spheres of trade by other, less sophisticated, imperial powers.[37] To realize the asserted right of American business to trade everywhere became the key strategy and consistent theme of U.S. foreign policy in the twentieth cen-tury. When rival powers staked out empires and when strong nationalist and national-communist movements arose in the undeveloped countries, Open Door imperialism involved Amer-ica in seemingly endless interventions and major wars.

The brutal Philippine war briefly stirred up an anti-imperi-alist movement, but the administration was able to characterize its critics as men of little vision drawing back from the glories and opportunities of empire. In the election of 1900, William Jennings Bryan, running again, made little real use of imperial-ism as a campaign issue.[38] McKinley, running with Theodore

---

[36]Quoted in Tyler Dennett, *Americans in Eastern Asia* (New York: Barnes and Noble, 1941), p. 622.

[37]On the illusory character of Open Door profits, see Charles A. Beard, *Giddy Minds and Foreign Quarrels* (New York: Macmillan, 1939), esp. pp. 36–37. That well-connected individuals, rather than whole nations or economies, gain from these exercises is made clear by David S. Landes, "The Nature of Economic Imperialism" in *Economic Imperialism*, Kenneth E. Boulding and Tapan Mukerjee, eds. (Ann Arbor: University of Michigan Press, 1972), pp. 134–41, and Robert Zevin, "An Interpretation of Ameri-can Imperialism," *Journal of Economic History* 32 (1972): 348–57.

[38]See Marina, "Opponents of Empire" generally (on Bryan's half-hearted-ness, pp. 194–203), and Robert L. Beisner, *Twelve Against Empire: The Anti-Imperialists, 1898–1900* (New York: MacGraw-Hill, 1968).

Roosevelt, was easily reelected. Finley Peter Dunne's "Mr. Dooley" summed things up well in his paraphrase of a McKinley speech:

> As f'r our newly acquired possessions, 'tis our intintion to give them a form iv government suited to their needs, which is small, an' in short to do as we blamed please with thim, makin' up our minds as we go along.[39]

WILLIAM MCKINLEY:
"AN UNCOMMONLY DANGEROUS POLITICIAN"

There might have been an American empire and a bloated presidency without William McKinley. But McKinley was indeed the man of his hour and his contribution to the destruction of republican liberty was significant. Like Tammany Hall's Mr. Plunkitt, "he seen his opportunities and he took 'em."[40]

McKinley brought factions of his own party into the new expansionist consensus and was a tireless spokesman for the Seward–Blaine tradition and the overproduction–underconsumptionist thesis that gave it new meaning.[41] He was an able

---

[39]Dunne, *Mr. Dooley's Philosophy*, p. 108.

[40]William L. Riordan, *Plunkitt of Tammany Hall* (New York: E.P. Dutton, 1963), p. ix.

[41]The cry of "overproduction" was raised to justify an aggressive foreign export policy. But the overproductionist thesis was actually (1) rationalization of entrepreneurial error (see Ludwig von Mises, *Planning for Freedom* [South Holland, Ill.: Libertarian Press, 1962], pp. 64–67); (2) an *ad hoc* argument for grants of privilege; or (3) an honest but mistaken explanation of real trends in particular sectors and markets (not "general overproduction"), trends having some relation to prior state interventions such as protectionism, subsidies, and cartelizing regulatory reform. This is the pattern of "export-dependent monopoly capitalism" (Schumpeter's term). Briefly, tariffs confer on many firms prices above world market levels, at which all their production cannot not be sold at home. To take full advantage of economies of scale, the full quantities had to be produced, leaving the manufacturers crying for foreign markets for the unsold "surplus." See esp. Joseph Schumpeter, *Imperialism and Social Classes* (New York: Meridian Books, 1955), pp. 79–80ff.; Ludwig von Mises, *Omnipotent Government* (New Haven, Conn.: Yale University Press, 1944), pp. 69–72; *Human Action: A Treatise on Economics* (Chicago: Henry Regnery, 1966), pp. 364–69; and William L. Langer, "A Critique of Imperialism" in *American Imperialism in 1898*, Theodore P. Greene, ed. (Boston: D.C. Heath, 1955),

manager and manipulator of subordinates and allies, all the more effective because he did not care that much about the final credit.[42] He shrewdly brought ex-Confederate officers into his war to make it an instrument of sectional reconciliation.

McKinley was on top of the details, political and economic, of his foreign and domestic policies. He made extensive use of the leeway given presidents in foreign affairs and the greater leeway given a president clothed in his invisible "war powers." He traveled extensively around the country expounding his ideas. He brought academics and practical men together in three presidential commissions—one to drum up support for the Open Door and two to deal with the Philippines—and thus beginning the political corruption of American higher learning. He rather quickly overcame his initial uneasiness at ruling foreign subjects by decree and went at it with a will. Although he stands, in retrospect, in the shadow of the flashy and impetuous Theodore Roosevelt, he was a very modern president—and that is the problem.[43] Diplomatic historian Tyler Dennett comments that to get his final peace treaty ratified, McKinley "created a situation . . . which had the effect of coercing the Senate."[44] By founding an overseas empire—which outlasted its colonial phase, being reborn as the permanent, global, "informal" American empire—he gave

---

pp. 15–16. Murray Greene writes that "American capitalism, which developed unimpeded by monarchical power, and German capitalism, where the monarchical element was a factor, were both characterized by strong tendencies toward protectionism and monopolism" ("Schumpeter's Imperialism—a Critical Note" in Harrison M. Wright, ed., *The New Imperialism* [Boston: D.C. Heath, 1961], p. 64). Cf. F.A. Hayek's remarks on Imperial Germany and the United States in *The Road to Serfdom* (Chicago: University of Chicago Press, 1944), p. 46.

[42]Secretary of War Elihu Root remarked that McKinley "was absolutely indifferent to credit . . . but McKinley always had his way" (quoted in Walter Karp, *The Politics of War* [New York: Harper Colophon Books, 1980], p. 70).

[43]See generally Lewis L. Gould, *The Presidency of William McKinley* (Lawrence: The Regents Press of Kansas, 1980), but esp. pp. 97, 136–37, 144–47, and chap. 10, "The First Modern President," pp. 231–53. As a presidential historian, Gould finds McKinley's activities good and writes that McKinley's policy in the Philippines "was not dictatorial, purposely oppressive, or genocidal" (p. 188), being merely, one supposes, criminal, and callous.

[44]Dennett quoted in Marina, pp. 153–54.

future presidents a vast arena within which to claim novel powers for themselves and the colossal bureaucracy they oversee. James Oliver Robertson writes:

> McKinley conjured up the image of the humble, popular Lincoln, revived Lincoln's uses of war powers, and established the image of presidential control and presidential decision-making for the United States as a world power. . . . By the use of his authority as Commander-in-Chief, McKinley acquired for the United States a territorial empire in the Caribbean and the Pacific. At the same time, the mass media spread stories of his humility, his popular origins, his prayers for guidance, and his ignorance of world geography. By his diplomatic and military direction, he "emancipated" the people of Cuba, Puerto Rico, and the Philippines from Spanish bondage, and made the United States their protector, defender and educator, and the prime user of their land, their resources, and their markets. McKinley's presidency is symbol—and reality as well—of the beginnings of the modern American focus on the presidency, and of the mythology of presidential power.[45]

McKinley was untiring. On September 5, 1901, the day of his assassination in Buffalo, New York, he had given a speech praising Blaine, reciprocity, and flexible tariffs. He stated: "The period of exclusiveness is past. The expansion of our trade and commerce is the pressing problem."[46]

By taking the step into overseas—or "salt-water"—imperialism, McKinley broke the continuity of Republican landed expansion, itself not entirely unproblematic,[47] and set the stage

---

[45] James Oliver Robertson, *American Myth, American Reality* (New York: Hill and Wang, 1980), p. 311.

[46]*Messages and Papers of the Presidents*, vol. 10, pp. 393–97. The speech resembles the old Byrds' song with the line "and you can believe the future's ahead."

[47]Some writers maintain that expansion was such an ingrained American habit that 1898 scarcely represents any change at all. See Richard Drinnon, *Facing West*; Walter A. McDougall, *Promised Land, Crusader State: The American Encounter with the World Since 1776* (New York: Houghton Mifflin, 1997); and (a classic) Richard Van Alstyne, *The Rising American Empire* (New York: W.W. Norton, [1960] 1974). William Appleman Williams's emphasis on the frontier-expansionist theory of history as a key to American thinking goes in this direction as well. And see Albert K. Weinberg, *Manifest Destiny: A Study of Nationalist Expansionism in American History* (Chicago:

for the expansion, not so much of markets, as of the American presidency and state apparatus into near-infinity. A modern president is responsible only to himself, executive traditions, and the *officium* (with a wink and a nod at his party, cronies, favored business interests, and—very distantly—the abstract "people," whose tribune and lord he is). So much meddling and control have become possible on a global scale that the question of "economic" causation seems a bit misplaced. Felix Morley—surveying the changes that took place between 1865 and 1900—comments:

> The deeper result [of 1898] was to make Washington for the first time classifiable as a world capital, governing millions of people overseas as subjects rather than as citizens. The private enslavement of negroes was ended. The public control of alien populations had begun.[48]

In the last analysis, empire is a political phenomenon not reducible to some economic "base." The empire is the extension of the area of state control. While imperialists may have *economic motives*, empire is not an "economy"; the imperialists may be seeking power, prestige, adventure, or other things. Overseas,

---

Quadrangle Books, [1935] 1963). The Anti-Imperialists of 1900, who were laissez-faire liberals with ties to the old antislavery movement, found comfort, oddly enough, in *Dred Scott v. Sandford* (1857), in which Chief Justice Taney wrote: "There is certainly no power given by the constitution to the Federal Government to establish or maintain colonies . . . to be ruled and governed at its own pleasure, nor to enlarge its territorial limits in any way except by the admission of new states" (quoted in Dennett, *Americans in Eastern Asia*, p. 625). (Taney was denying the right of Congress to exclude slavery from the territories, but from the standpoint of republican theory his larger point was well taken.)

[48]Felix Morley, *Freedom and Federalism* (Indianapolis, Ind.: Liberty Press, [1959] 1981), p. 118. Not too surprisingly, given the inner unity of statism at home and abroad, many corporate liberals (Progressives) were expansionists, and *vice versa*. As J.W. Burgess wrote in 1915, "the Jingoes and the Social Reformers have gotten together" (quoted in F.A. Hayek, *The Constitution of Liberty* [Chicago: Henry Regnery Company, 1960], p. 406). The combination of paternalistic welfarism and gunboat diplomacy symbolized by Teddy Roosevelt provides a revealing parallel to British "social imperialism." Cf. Bernard Semmel, *Imperialism and Social Reform* (Garden City, N.Y.: Anchor Books, 1968). Robert Zevin argues that the Jingoes and Social Reformers had always been together ("American Imperialism," pp. 358–60).

the empire creates a "double layer" of statism, superimposing its own power over that of local elites (*compradores*, etc.).[49]

The state organizes the political means to wealth—the "means of coercion," to quote Sir Ernest Gellner—and, in Murray Rothbard's words, "constitutes, and is the source of, the 'ruling class' . . . and is in permanent opposition to *genuinely* private capital."[50] Empire is the state *in extenso*. Different motives can drive the process. It appears that the engrossing of overseas markets has been the chief aim of American empire-builders since 1898, but we cannot overlook the possibility that some of them believe their own rhetoric about global democratic perpetual war for perpetual philanthropy and moral uplift.[51]

William McKinley was a worthy contributor in this field, just as he was in the more practical aspects of empire.[52] His quiet style of leadership, combined with mastery of the political and economic details (if there was a tariff on pig iron, he knew exactly how much revenue it brought in), made him the ideal founder of a modern nonaristocratic empire grounded in state

[49]On "two-layered" statism, see Vincent Ninelli, "On the Importance of Knowing Your Enemy: U.S. Imperialism and Movement Strategy," *The Abolitionist* 2, no. 1 (April 1971): 1.

[50]Ernest Gellner, "Soviets Against Wittfogel: Or, the Anthropological Preconditions of Mature Marxism," *Theory and Society* 14 (1985): 351, and Murray N. Rothbard, "Anatomy of the State," *Rampart Journal of Individualist Thought* 1, no. 2 (Summer 1965): 18. (Gellner's full phrase is "the means of coercion and persuasion"—suggesting that there is something for the intellectuals to do.)

[51]On the Open Door and informal empire, see William Appleman Williams, *The Tragedy of American Diplomacy* (New York: Delta, 1962), pp. 16–50.

[52]Thus one of McKinley's explanations of his Philippine policy: "Our concern was not for territory or trade or empire, but for the people whose interests and destiny, without our willing it, had been put in our hands" (quoted in Murat Halstead, ed., *Pictorial History of America's New Possessions* [Chicago: Dominion, 1899], p. 512). (This is about as convincing as Lyndon Johnson's rationales for the Vietnam War, but Johnson had five or six of them.) On American Protestant missionaries as a great force for empire, see Julius W. Pratt, *Expansionists of 1898: The Acquisition of Hawaii and the Spanish Islands* (Gloucester, Mass.: Peter Smith, 1959), chap. 8, "'The Imperialism of Righteousness,'" pp. 279–316; on post-millennial Protestants— some of them secularized (like the monstrous John Dewey)—as a force for aggravated statism generally, see Murray N. Rothbard, "Origins of the Welfare State in America," *Journal of Libertarian Studies* 12, no. 2 (Fall 1996): 193–229.

power but oriented toward commercial gain for well-connected friends and associates. It could be said that British imperial leaders employed a certain style of hypocritical legalistic and Christian rhetoric to justify what they wished to do anyway. McKinley helped establish the American variation on the theme, which is marked by an eternal innocence (accidents! collateral damage! greatness thrust upon us! totally unforeseen attacks by wily foreigners!) and a self-righteousness surpassing that of the British.

11

THEODORE ROOSEVELT
AND THE MODERN PRESIDENCY

THOMAS E. WOODS, JR.

In 1896, Brooks Adams wrote a book called *The Law of Civilization and Decay*. Like most late-nineteenth-century commentators, he believed that his country was nearing a watershed in its history. But unless America rallied around a strong leader, the center of world power, which he thought might be about to shift from England to the United States, would shift instead to Russia. In many ways, Theodore Roosevelt—who read Adams's book with interest—would prove to be this leader, invigorating the executive branch in both the domestic and the foreign arenas. In so doing, he became the first modern president.

Roosevelt was well suited for this role. Philosophically he was the consummate Progressive, determined to bring efficiency and coordinated intelligence to bear against the trusts, against despoilers of the natural environment, against international disorder. He was, as one historian put it, "the first great president–reformer of the modern industrial era."[1] He therefore had little patience with federalism and indeed with most of the constitutional impediments that stood between him and the construction of a new American state. Politically he was a committed nationalist. He thus could barely bring himself to speak of Thomas Jefferson, whom he loathed; and as late as the 1880s he was still condemning Jefferson Davis as a traitor. The Confederate cause, since it denied that a large consolidated nation was its own justification, enraged him. Roosevelt brought to the presidential office a thorough and consistent philosophy of the presidency. What a previous president may have done hesitatingly or without fanfare, Theodore Roosevelt made a matter of principle. He deserves credit for innovation even, paradoxically

---

[1]William Henry Harbaugh, *Power and Responsibility: The Life and Times of Theodore Roosevelt* (New York: Farrar, Straus and Cudahy, 1961), p. 522.

enough, in cases in which he was exercising an executive prerogative that one of his recent predecessors had in fact pioneered.

Presidential scholar Edward Corwin has spoken of the "personalization of the presidency," by which he means that the accident of personality has played a considerable role in shaping the office. And indeed it is hard to think of a man with a stronger personality than that of Theodore Roosevelt who ever served as president. One presidential scholar observed that Roosevelt gave the office "the absorbing drama of a Western movie."[2] And no wonder. Mark Twain, who met with the president twice, declared him "clearly insane." In a way, Roosevelt set the tone for his public life to come at age twenty, when, after an argument with his girlfriend, he went home and shot and killed his neighbor's dog.[3] He told a friend in 1884 that when he donned his special cowboy suit, which featured revolver and rifle, "I feel able to face anything."[4] When he killed his first buffalo, he "abandoned himself to complete hysteria," as historian Edmund Morris put it, "whooping and shrieking while his guide watched in stolid amazement." His reaction was similar in 1898 when he killed his first Spaniard.[5]

He loathed inactivity. At one point during the 1880s, he wrote to a friend that he had been working so hard lately that for the next month he was going to do nothing but relax—and write a life of Oliver Cromwell. Henry Adams said that

> all Roosevelt's friends know that his restless and combative energy was more than abnormal. Roosevelt, more than any other man living within the range of notoriety, showed the singular primitive quality that belongs to ultimate matter— the quality that medieval theology assigned to God—he was pure act.[6]

[2]Clinton Rossiter, *The American Presidency* (New York: New American Library, 1960), p. 97.

[3]Walter LaFeber, "The Making of a Bully Boy," *Inquiry*, June 11 and 25, 1979, p. 15.

[4]Emmet John Hughes, *The Living Presidency: The Resources and Dilemmas of the American Presidential Office* (New York: Coward, McCann, and Geoghegan), p. 91.

[5]Edmund Morris, *The Rise of Theodore Roosevelt* (New York: Coward, McCann, and Geoghegan, 1979).

[6]Henry Adams, *The Education of Henry Adams* (New York: Random House Modern Library, 1931), p. 417.

One of his sons is said to have remarked, "Father always wanted to be the bride at every wedding and the corpse at every funeral."[7]

Bringing such a personality to the presidency, Roosevelt increased very significantly the visibility of the office and the popular fascination with the person of the president. One presidential historian explained it this way:

> As no president in memory and probably none up to that time, Theodore Roosevelt became a "personality"—a politician whose every action seemed newsworthy and exciting. His family, his friends, his guests, his large teeth, his thick glasses, his big game hunting, and his horseback riding—all were sources of media attention and delight. In a way that Washington and Lincoln had not done, and even Jackson avoided, Theodore Roosevelt became a very visible tribune of the people, a popular advocate whose personality seemed immediate, direct, and committed to their personal service.[8]

The modern tendency to micromanage even those affairs that clearly belong to the care of civil society, and to refer even the most trivial issues to the discretion of the executive under the implicit presumption that individuals and intermediate bodies are unable to manage their affairs, also finds substantial precedent in the Roosevelt administration. The classic example occurred in 1905 when Theodore Roosevelt assembled athletic personnel from Harvard, Princeton, and Yale at the White House to reform the rules of college football to make the game safer. The 1903 season had witnessed several dozen deaths from excessively rough play. Roosevelt's small convocation was a minor incident, to be sure, but it was the first step in a long series by which the presidency would assume an aggressive and visible presence in the life of the nation, and by which the American people would grow accustomed to entrusting to the person of the executive even the most trivial aspects of everyday affairs.

This was the kind of energy and vigor that Theodore Roosevelt brought to his office and that he used to promote his

---

[7]John Milton Cooper, Jr., *The Warrior and the Priest: Woodrow Wilson and Theodore Roosevelt* (Cambridge, Mass.: Harvard University Press, 1983), p. 69.

[8]Michael P. Riccards, *The Ferocious Engine of Democracy: A History of the American Presidency*, vol. 2, *Theodore Roosevelt through George Bush* (Lanham, Md.: Madison Books, 1995), pp. 5–6.

distinct philosophy of the presidency. "There inheres in the presidency more power than in any other office in any great republic or constitutional monarchy of modern times," Roosevelt once remarked. But far from deploring this state of affairs, he went on to say, "I believe in a strong executive; I believe in power."[9] "I don't think that any harm comes from the concentration of power in one man's hands," and, arguing elsewhere, he said, "provided the holder does not keep it for more than a certain, definite time, and then returns it to the people from whom he sprang."[10]

He agreed with Andrew Jackson, who had argued that the president, by virtue of his election by the nation as a whole, possessed a unique claim to be the representative of all American people. Each member of the executive branch, but especially the president, "was a steward of the people bound actively and affirmatively to do all he could for the people," he maintained. He could, therefore, "do anything that the needs of the nation demanded" unless expressly prohibited in the Constitution. "Under this interpretation of executive power, I did and caused to be done many things not previously done. . . . I did not usurp power, but I did greatly broaden the use of executive power."[11]

The cry of "executive usurpation" had hounded Andrew Jackson during the 1830s when he attempted to put a similar theory of the presidency into practice. "What effrontery!" John C. Calhoun had exclaimed in response to the suggestion that the president was "the immediate representative of the American people." "[T]he American people are not represented in a single department of the Government," Calhoun insisted; "the people of these States [are] united in a constitutional compact . . . forming distinct and sovereign communities," and therefore, "no such community or people, as the American people, taken in the aggregate [exists]."[12] Calhoun was characteristically perceptive when he pondered why Jackson would put forth such a theory.

---

[9]Forrest McDonald, *A Constitutional History of the United States* (Malabar, Fla.: Robert E. Krieger, 1982), p. 166.

[10]John Morton Blum, *The Republican Roosevelt* (New York: Athaneum, [1954] 1962), p. 122.

[11]Ibid., pp. 107–08.

[12]Calhoun's remarks are taken from *Register of Debates in Congress, 23rd Cong., 1st sess., May 6, 1834* (Washington, D.C.: Gales and Seaton, 1834), pp. 1645–46.

But why all this solicitude on the part of the president to place himself near to the people, and to push us off to the greatest distance? Why this solicitude to make himself their sole representative, their only guardian and protector, their only friend and supporter? The object cannot be mistaken. It is preparatory to farther hostilities—to an appeal to the people; and is intended to to [sic] prepare the way in order to transmit to them his declaration of war against the Senate, with a view to enlist them as his allies in the war which he contemplates waging against this branch of the Government.[13]

Calhoun's remark applies equally well to Theodore Roosevelt. Roosevelt, as we shall see, convinced he was doing the will of the people and what was best for the country, did not hesitate to disregard the Senate or the Congress as a whole. He honestly believed himself to be doing the people's will, and his solemn responsibility to see that will vindicated overrode concerns regarding the separation of powers. He remarked privately that in the United States,

as in any nation which amounts to anything, those in the end must govern who are willing actually to do the work of governing; and insofar as the Senate becomes a merely obstructionist body it will run the risk of seeing its power pass into other hands.[14]

Roosevelt's innovations in the area of domestic policy were more subtle than those he introduced in foreign affairs. Previous presidents, following both American tradition and the spirit of the Constitution, had not entered office with an extensive legislative program whose passage they vigorously prosecuted. They deferred instead to Congress, the branch which, it was generally understood, was to retain the initiative in such matters. But Roosevelt found a certain virility in bold leadership, and in situations in which decisive action seemed called for, he considered deference to Congress or to other legal restraints on executive

---

[13]Ibid., p. 1646; see also Gary L. Gregg II, *The Presidential Republic: Executive Representation and Deliberative Democracy* (Lanham, Md.: Rowman and Littlefield, 1997), pp. 80–89.

[14]Theodore Roosevelt to John St. Loe Strachey, February 12, 1906, in Elting E. Morison, ed., *The Letters of Theodore Roosevelt*, vol. 5, *The Big Stick, 1905–1907* (Cambridge, Mass.: Harvard University Press, 1952), p. 151.

power as a sign of pusillanimity and decadence. He wrote in his *Autobiography*:

> In theory the Executive has nothing to do with legislation. In practice as things now are, the Executive is or ought to be peculiarly representative of the people as a whole. As often as not the action of the Executive offers the only means by which the people can get the legislation they demand and ought to have. Therefore a good executive under the present conditions of American political life must take a very active interest in getting the right kind of legislation, in addition to performing his executive duties with an eye single to the public welfare.[15]

Although the political parties of Roosevelt's day, as in our own, shared a great deal in common, political discourse in the United States was still fluid enough that matters of real import were still discussed within the halls of Congress. Thus Senator Isidor Rayner, aghast at Roosevelt's approach, remarked in 1906:

> Here we were day after day struggling with questions of constitutional law, as if we really had anything to do with their settlement, laboring under the vain delusion that we had the right to legislate; that we were an independent branch of the Government; that we were one department, and the Executive another, each with its separate and well-defined distinctions, imagining these things, and following a vision and a mirage, while the president was at work dominating the legislative will, interposing his offices into the law-making power, assuming legislative rights to a greater extent than if he were sitting here as a member of this body; dismembering the Constitution, and exercising precisely and identically the same power and control as if the Constitution had declared that the Congress shall pass no law without the consent of the president; adopting a system that practically blends and unites legislative and executive functions, a system that prevailed in many of the ancient governments that have forever gone to ruin, and which today still obtains in other governments, the rebellious protests of whose subjects are echoing over the earth, and whose tottering fabrics I hope are on the rapid road to dissolution.[16]

[15]Theodore Roosevelt, *The Autobiography of Theodore Roosevelt*, Wayne Andrews, ed. (New York: Octagon, 1975), p. 282.

[16]*Congressional Record*, April 5 and June 19, 1906.

The annual presidential message read to Congress in December 1905—the "State of the Union," having fallen into disuse since Jefferson's tenure, would be revived by Woodrow Wilson—contained a lengthy plea from Roosevelt for a series of regulatory legislation. The significance of Roosevelt's program was not lost on his political opponents. The *New York World*, a Democratic newspaper, called it "the most amazing program of centralization that any president of the United States has ever recommended."[17] One disgruntled commentator remarked after the legislation was passed that Roosevelt's policies betrayed "a marked tendency toward the centralization of power in the United States and a corresponding decrease in the old-time sovereignty of the states, or of the individual."[18]

Roosevelt's top legislative achievements, such as the Meat Inspection Act, the Pure Food and Drug Act, and the Hepburn Act, reflect the president's confidence in expert commissions and, more broadly, his stewardship theory of the executive branch. As one scholar put it, these acts, taken together, "might well be considered as marking the birth of the modern regulatory state."[19] Not everyone was especially sanguine at this prospect. One conservative Republican observed that the president was "consciously, or unconsciously . . . trying to concentrate all power in Washington, to practically wipe out state lines, and to govern the people by commissions and bureaus."[20]

It is fashionable in historical circles to describe Roosevelt as a conservative because he advocated domestic reform in large part simply to keep at bay more radical initiatives.[21] So, for example, he called for legislation to regulate the railroads in order to counter calls for outright nationalization. Historians of the New Left have gone even further, arguing that since big business itself frequently played a role in agitating for and even shaping the emerging regulatory apparatus, the ostensible effort

---

[17]Quoted in Lewis L. Gould, *The Presidency of Theodore Roosevelt* (Lawrence: University Press of Kansas, 1991), p. 158.

[18]Quoted in ibid., p. 169.

[19]William C. Widenor, "Theodore Roosevelt," in Frank N. Magill, ed., *The American Presidents: The Office and the Men*, vol. 2, *Lincoln to Hoover*, rev. ed. (Danbury, Conn.: Grolier Educational Corporation, 1989), p. 185.

[20]Gould, *Presidency of Theodore Roosevelt*, p. 198.

[21]See, for example, Richard Hofstadter, *The American Political Tradition and the Men Who Made It* (New York: Vintage Books, [1948] 1974), pp. 298–99.

by Roosevelt and his successors to rein in business interests was a sham. New Left scholars have indeed added a necessary corrective to the previously existing literature, and their claims certainly hold water in such obvious cases as the Federal Reserve System. The Fed, which, while perhaps still not as centralized as some bankers may have wanted, clearly served bankers' interests by socializing risk and by helping to coordinate the inflationary policies of member banks, thereby reducing the risk of runs.[22]

But it is too hasty to conclude from this that all regulation, even when corporate interests themselves may have played a role in its passage, ultimately works to the benefit of big business. That a government–business alliance characterized the emerging American regime at the turn of the century is beyond dispute; but New Left historians fail to acknowledge that the state always maintained the upper hand in this partnership. The New Left critique stems partially from the fact that its partisans would have been satisfied with nothing short of nationalizing or dismantling large interests. From such a perspective, Roosevelt can indeed seem the reactionary.

The battle over railroad regulation and the Interstate Commerce Commission provides a good example of the shortcomings of this thesis. Roosevelt supported further railroad regulation in addition to that already on the books, and had ultimately signed the Hepburn Act of 1906—which, while not as radical as what he had sought, he considered satisfactory. The act increased the number of members of the Interstate Commerce Commission and gave it the authority to set "just and reasonable" rail rates. Whatever rates the commission decided upon were to take effect immediately. Although the railroads had a right to appeal to the courts, the burden of proof rested on them and not on the commission.

The results were devastating. In a book that earned the Columbia University Prize in American Economic History in 1971, Albro Martin described the situation in detail. His thesis, stated simply, is that Roosevelt's Hepburn Act, combined with subsequent regulatory enactments—in particular William Howard Taft's Mann–Elkins Act of 1910—deprived the railroads

---

[22]See Murray N. Rothbard, *The Case Against the Fed* (Auburn, Ala.: Ludwig von Mises Institute, 1994).

of the rate increases they needed, an especially debilitating handicap in an inflationary atmosphere. The railroads needed investment capital following the reorganizations of the 1890s if they were to preserve their capital stock, rebuild, and modernize. In other words, they needed to be left alone. Instead they got policies that both increased labor costs and refused the rate increases they needed. The result was that by 1911, profits had vanished, and the collapse of the system of private management of the railroads followed soon afterward.[23]

One historian who concedes that railroad regulation ultimately proved destructive attempts to exonerate Roosevelt by claiming that the president had wanted a commission that would be fair rather than punitive; but Roosevelt can hardly be held blameless for having adopted, uncritically, the standard Progressive faith in the disinterested rationality and overall benevolence of expert commissions.[24] Indeed, Roosevelt never bothered to explain how the granting of rate-setting power to a board of supposed experts who were completely divorced from the actual operation and ownership of the railroads and for whom rational economic calculation was therefore impossible, could have yielded anything but arbitrary decrees.

This arbitrariness, this apparent belief that seeing vindication of his iron will was an adequate substitute for a sober assessment of a situation, was a central feature of Roosevelt's personality, and it appears time and again in his dealings with big business. Unlike some Progressives, whom he dubbed "the lunatic fringe," Roosevelt did not consider business concentration a trend to be avoided or reversed. He saw it as an inevitable and even beneficial development of industrial society, albeit one that had to be regulated in the public interest. It is also true that Roosevelt's reputation as a trustbuster has been exaggerated; historians rightly point out that the Taft administration initiated twice as many antitrust suits in its one term than Roosevelt did in his two. But at issue here is not so much whether Roosevelt was especially severe in this or that area or whether he was an outright radical. The question is whether he dealt justly with the private sector, what kind of precedents he set for the future, and

---

[23]Albro Martin, *Enterprise Denied: Origins of the Decline of American Railroads, 1897–1917* (New York: Columbia University Press, 1971).

[24]Gould, *Presidency of Theodore Roosevelt*, p. 165.

how he helped to strengthen the executive beyond what the framers had envisioned.

In early 1902, Roosevelt ordered Attorney General Philander Knox to file an antitrust suit against the Northern Securities Company, a holding company that had taken over two railroads—the Northern Pacific and the Great Northern—that stretched from Seattle to St. Paul.[25] This is the case that almost single-handedly earned Theodore Roosevelt his trust-busting reputation; but again, in a desperate effort to portray Roosevelt as judicious and moderate, most historians have belittled its significance. Roosevelt himself pinpointed its importance:

> From the standpoint of giving complete control to the National Government over big corporations engaged in interstate business, it would be impossible to overestimate the importance of the Northern Securities decision and of the decisions afterward rendered in line with it in connection with the other trusts whose dissolution was ordered. The success of the Northern Securities case definitely established the power of the government to deal with all great corporations.[26]

The decision at last overthrew what he called the "vicious doctrine" of the *E.C. Knight* case of 1895, which had severely limited the scope of the Sherman Act. In that case, the Supreme Court had ruled that, although the American Sugar Refining Company held about 95 percent of the American sugar market after buying the E.C. Knight Company, they had committed no actionable offense since they had done nothing, strictly speaking, to restrain trade. "This decision," Roosevelt said with some satisfaction, "I caused to be annulled by the court that had rendered it."[27] The argument that Northern Securities was neither restraining trade nor preventing other lines from providing transportation along the same route—an argument its architects had been led to believe, on the basis of the precedent in *Knight*, the federal government would consider unimpeachable—suddenly no longer held water.

---

[25]On the Northern Securities case, see Dominick T. Armentano, *Antitrust and Monopoly: Anatomy of a Policy Failure* (New York: John Wiley and Sons, 1982), pp. 53–55; Henry F. Pringle, *Theodore Roosevelt: A Biography* (New York: Harcourt, Brace, 1931), pp. 252ff.

[26]Roosevelt, *Autobiography*, pp. 228–29.

[27]Pringle, *Theodore Roosevelt*, p. 253.

Before advising Philander Knox to initiate the case, Roosevelt neglected to ask himself some fairly obvious questions. For one thing, did the new holding company in fact substitute a monopolistic arrangement for a previously existing state of competition? In fact, it did not. The Great Northern and the Northern Pacific may have appeared to be two alternative lines between St. Paul and Seattle, but in fact, as Balthasar Henry Meyer points out, price wars between the two lines were a thing of the past, and for twenty years the railroads had lived in "comparative peace." "It was assumed that competition had been stifled without first asking the question whether competition had actually existed; and whether, if competition could be perpetuated, the public would profit by it."[28] According to Dominick Armentano,

> Both railways had maintained joint rates, and the consequent backloading and even flow of freight realized from such arrangements had increased the efficiency and economy of each line, and allowed a generally low level of rates that would have bankrupted other roads.

The idea for the holding company originated partly from a desire to put the arrangement on a more stable footing and partly from concerns surrounding the designs of E.H. Harriman, who in early 1901 had tried to get a controlling interest in the Northern Pacific. In a mere four days, its common stock rose from $144 to over $1,000 per share. The holding company would put both rails beyond the reach of Harriman, and, thus, prevent him from undermining the economic advantages that obtained from the close relationship that existed between the two lines. Naturally, these advantages paid dividends to the consumer: Rail rates declined on the Hill–Morgan lines between November 1901, when the Northern Securities Company was incorporated, and 1903. There had been a chance, following *Knight*, that the arbitrariness of the antitrust laws might to some degree be mitigated; Roosevelt helped ensure that they would continue to be leveled against corporations that simplistic, static models deemed monopolistic but which nearly always brought benefits to the consumer.

In domestic affairs, then, Roosevelt greatly accelerated the process by which the executive became the de facto originator of

---

[28]Armentano, *Antitrust and Monopoly*, p. 54.

legislation, and in other ways, such as his increasing use of executive commissions, set in motion a trend toward presidential supremacy. As Forrest McDonald explains in his own study of the presidency, "Roosevelt's showmanship in pretending to be the fountain of reform legislation transformed the expectations Americans had for their presidents and thus opened the door for the emergence of the legislative presidency."[29] That his legislative record was not more impressive was not from lack of trying. But he paved the way for his successors, who would build upon Roosevelt's foundation.

Theodore Roosevelt made even more significant contributions to the modern presidency in the area of foreign affairs. In domestic affairs, Roosevelt explained, Congress could generally be trusted to come around to the correct position. But in the conduct of foreign policy, senators, who were, as he put it, "wholly indifferent to national honor or national welfare" and "primarily concerned in getting a little cheap reputation among ignorant people," could interfere with the conduct of an honorable course abroad.[30] "More and more," Roosevelt declared to Congress in 1902, "the increasing interdependence and complexity of international political and economic relations render it incumbent on all civilized and orderly powers to insist on the proper policing of the world."[31] The contention that Congress was the more popular branch of government and, therefore, even prescinding from the constitutional question, deserved special deference in matters of peace and war, would not have dissuaded him. He had privately called public opinion "the voice of the devil, or what is still worse, the voice of a fool," and in a calmer moment, speaking in particular of foreign affairs, he observed that "[o]ur prime necessity is that public opinion should be properly educated."[32] Hence, while he favored executive

---

[29]Forrest McDonald, *The American Presidency: An Intellectual History* (Lawrence: University Press of Kansas, 1994), p. 358.

[30]W. Stull Holt, *Treaties Defeated by the Senate: A Study of the Struggle Between President and Senate over the Conduct of Foreign Relations* (Baltimore, Md.: The Johns Hopkins Press, 1933; Gloucester, Mass.: Peter Smith, 1964), p. 221.

[31]Blum, *The Republican Roosevelt*, p. 127.

[32]LaFeber, "The Making of a Bully Boy," pp. 15-16; Theodore Roosevelt to William Bayard Hale, December 3, 1908, in Morison, ed., *Letters of Theodore Roosevelt*, vol. 6, *The Big Stick, 1907–1909* (Cambridge, Mass.: Harvard University Press, 1952), p. 1408.

supremacy in all areas of governance, the need for it in foreign policy was correspondingly greater.

Roosevelt's fascination with war is corroborated both by his own testimony and by that of those who knew him. A college friend wrote in 1885, "He would like above all things to go to war with some one. . . . He wants to be killing something all the time."[33] Roosevelt told another friend a few years later:

> Frankly I don't know that I should be sorry to see a bit of a spar with Germany. The burning of New York and a few other sea coast cities would be a good object lesson in the need of an adequate system of coast defenses, and I think it would have a good effect on our large German population to force them to an ostentatiously patriotic display of anger against Germany.[34]

Over and over again Roosevelt insisted that the country "needed" a war. "He gushes over war," wrote the philosopher William James,

> as the ideal condition of human society, for the manly strenuousness which it involves, and treats peace as a condition of blubberlike and swollen ignobility, fit only for huckstering weaklings, dwelling in gray twilight and heedless of the higher life. . . . One foe is as good as another, for aught he tells us.[35]

One of the top scholars of Theodore Roosevelt's foreign policy has explained that the Rough Rider "sought a big navy because it would prevent war, but also because it was such fun to have a big navy."[36]

So attached was Roosevelt to the issues of national readiness and the martial virtues that after leaving office, Roosevelt suggested adapting some of the wartime model to the needs of peacetime. He became an advocate of "universal obligatory military training" and, in a comment that unwittingly reveals the rarely acknowledged link between universal suffrage and universal conscription, Roosevelt declared: "Let us demand service

---

[33]On all this, see Howard K. Beale, *Theodore Roosevelt and the Rise of America to World Power* (Baltimore, Md.: The Johns Hopkins Press, 1956), pp. 36–38.

[34]Ibid.

[35]Ibid.

[36]Ibid., p. 36.

from women as we do from men, and in return give the suffrage to all men and women who in peace and war perform the
service." When it came to men's training, Roosevelt pointed to
the U.S. Army camps as the standard to be imitated.

> I believe that for every young man . . . to have six months in
> such a camp . . . [with] some field service, would be of incalcu-
> lable benefit to him, and . . . to the nation. . . . [M]aking these
> camps permanent would be the greatest boon this nation could
> receive.[37]

This attachment to war, combined with the various manifestations of imperialism during his presidency, earned Theodore
Roosevelt the scorn of New Left historians, after having enjoyed
a period of tremendous popularity during the 1950s. The pendulum has since swung back in Roosevelt's favor. Nearly every
historian of Roosevelt since the late 1970s, with the smug self-
satisfaction that comes from seeming to overturn the conventional wisdom, has argued that notwithstanding his reputation
and his personal bellicosity, Theodore Roosevelt was actually
much more restrained in foreign policy matters while in office
than might have been expected. The only way to make this
interpretation of Roosevelt's conduct in foreign affairs persuasive is to downplay or to eliminate altogether any mention of
the discomfiting fact that both as vice president and as president, Theodore Roosevelt presided over a vicious and brutal war
of suppression in the Philippines. It is simply not possible to pretend to assess Roosevelt's tenure as president without examining
this ugly episode in American history. This is in fact what most
of these historians, to their everlasting shame, have done.

The United States obtained the Philippines during the Spanish–American War in 1898, when Commodore George Dewey,
under instructions from Theodore Roosevelt himself (then assistant
secretary of the Navy), attacked the islands a few days after the
opening of hostilities in Cuba. Shortly after the war's conclusion,
when it became apparent that the United States had no intention
of granting independence to the islands, guerrilla warfare broke

---

[37]Matthew J. Glover, "What Might Have Been: Theodore Roosevelt's Platform for 1920," in *Theodore Roosevelt: Many-Sided American*, Natalie A. Taylor, Douglas Brinkley, and John Allen Gable, eds. (Interlaken, N.Y.: Heart of
the Lakes, 1992), pp. 488–89.

out, spearheaded by Emilio Aguinaldo, the head of the rebels. The size of the American effort to suppress the Filipino nationalists has rarely been fully appreciated: Some 126,000 American troops saw action in suppression campaigns, and an incredible 200,000 Filipinos lost their lives.[38]

While the fighting was going on, the *Philadelphia Ledger* featured a front-page story by a correspondent covering General J. Franklin Bell's campaign that read:

> The present war is no bloodless, fake, opera bouffé engagement. Our men have been relentless; have killed to exterminate men, women, children, prisoners and captives, active insurgents and suspected people, from lads of ten and up, an idea prevailing that the Filipino, as such, was little better than a dog, a noisome reptile in some instances, whose best disposition was the rubbish heap. Our soldiers have pumped salt water into men to "make them talk," have taken prisoner people who held up their hands and peacefully surrendered, and an hour later, without an atom of evidence to show that they were even insurrectos, stood them on a bridge and shot them down one by one, to drop into the water below and float down as an example to those who found their bullet-riddled corpses.

This correspondent might seem to be a critic of American policy. In fact, he joined Roosevelt's generals in pointing to the primitive and uncivilized Filipinos as an excuse for disregarding the norms of civilized warfare. "It is not civilized warfare," he

---

[38]Precise casualty figures are difficult to establish, in large part because deaths resulting from a cholera epidemic at the end of the war have often been conflated with those of the war itself. It is also unclear to what extent war conditions and American policy led to or exacerbated the spread of cholera. See Glenn A. May, "150,000 Missing Filipinos: A Demographic Crisis in Batangas, 1887–1903," *Annales de Demographie Historique* [France] 1985: 215–43; Mary C. Gillett, "U.S. Army Medical Officers and Public Health in the Philippines in the Wake of the Spanish–American War, 1898–1905," *Bulletin of the History of Medicine* 64 (1990): 567–87; Ken De Bevoise, *Agents of Apocalypse: Epidemic Disease in the Colonial Philippines* (Princeton, N.J.: Princeton University Press, 1995); Matthew Smallman-Raynor and Andrew D. Cliff, "The Philippine Insurrection and the 1902–04 Cholera Epidemic: Part I—Epidemiological Diffusion Processes in War," *Journal of Historical Geography* 24 (January 1998): 69–89; Warwick Anderson, "Immunities of Empire: Race, Disease, and the New Tropical Medicine, 1900–1920," *Bulletin of the History of Medicine* 70 (1996): 94–118. The figure of 200,000 deaths appears in McDonald, *The American Presidency*, p. 394.

admitted, "but we are not dealing with a civilized people. The only thing they know and fear is force, violence, and brutality, and we give it to them."[39] Roosevelt's own views on race, which would take an entire chapter to describe in detail, only encouraged this kind of barbarism; and more than once he insisted that he had no intention of dealing with peoples he called backward with the same treatment he afforded civilized countries. He told Rudyard Kipling how irritated he became with those who dared suggest that a country like Colombia "is entitled to just the treatment that I would give, say, to Denmark or Switzerland." The very suggestion was a "mere absurdity," he told another correspondent.[40]

Only after American conduct in the Philippines was given embarrassing publicity at home in 1902 did Roosevelt take any action at all, ordering the court-martial of General Smith and Major Glenn, and, even then, he seemed clearly displeased that the subject had been broached at all. At the same time, he denounced lynchings in the South—acts which he claimed were "worse to the victim, and far more brutalizing to those guilty of it," than any atrocities that may have been committed in the Philippines.[41] Charles Francis Adams, who suspected that the brutality of the American side of the fighting enjoyed at least the president's benign acquiescence, had predicted earlier that year that Roosevelt would "be very severe in words—on outrages; but no one will be punished." He was right: Glenn ended up being fined $50, and Smith was "admonished." Theodore Roosevelt's utter lack of interest was made especially manifest when, immediately following his court-martial of General Smith, he wrote General J. Franklin Bell to congratulate him on his conduct of the war in Batangas. Bell was a man whose methods Henry Cabot Lodge himself had described as "cruel," and it was well-known that Bell had ordered 100,000 Filipinos into

---

[39]Stuart Creighton Miller, "Benevolent Assimilation" in The American Conquest of the Philippines, 1899–1903 (New Haven, Conn.: Yale University Press, 1982), p. 211.

[40]Howard C. Hill, Roosevelt and the Caribbean (New York: Russell and Russell, 1965), p. 208.

[41]Gould, Presidency of Theodore Roosevelt, pp. 56–57.

concentration camps.[42] In 1906 Roosevelt went even further and appointed General Bell as his chief of staff.[43]

Roosevelt's approach in the Philippines was only the most spectacular indication that the content of his foreign policy left much to be desired, and it inaugurated a century of humanitarian violence that would be couched in the saccharine language of idealism and justice. Even more important from the point of view of Theodore Roosevelt's contributions to the presidency as an institution, however, is the more procedural question of how he actually carried out his policy. It is here that he demonstrated his most brazen contempt for the legislative branch.

An excellent example concerns Roosevelt's decision to take over the customs houses in the Dominican Republic. In what has become known as the Roosevelt Corollary to the Monroe Doctrine, Theodore Roosevelt had declared in 1904 that although the United States had no territorial ambitions in its own hemisphere, cases of "chronic wrongdoing" on the part of a Latin American country that might invite occupation by a European power could force America's hand. To forestall European occupation, the United States would intervene to restore order and to see that all just claims were satisfied. When it looked in early 1905 as though one or more European countries might intervene in the Dominican Republic to recover outstanding debt, Roosevelt put the corollary into effect for the first time by declaring that the United States would administer the Dominican Republic's customs collections to forestall any such foreign intervention.

From the beginning, Theodore Roosevelt seemed to have hoped to be able to avoid consulting the Senate at all. The agreement reached with the Dominican Republic was set to take effect February 1, 1905, a mere eleven days after it was signed—obviously too short an interval to allow for Senate discussion or approval. The administration had a change of heart after it found itself the subject of severe denunciations in the Senate, even among supporters of the president. Senator Augustus Bacon, not unreasonably, objected:

---

[42]Daniel B. Schirmer, *Republic or Empire: American Resistance to the Philippine War* (Cambridge, Mass.: Schenkman, 1972), pp. 238–39.

[43]Miller, "Benevolent Assimilation," p. 260.

I do not think there can be any more important question than that which involves the consideration of the powers of the president to make a treaty which shall virtually take over the affairs of another government and seek to administer them by this Government, without submitting that question to the consideration and judgment of the Senate.[44]

For his part, Senator Henry Teller added:

I deny the right of the executive department of the Government to make any contract, any treaty, any protocol, or anything of that character which will bind the United States. . . . The president has no more right and no more authority to bind the people of the United States by such an agreement than I have as a member of this body.[45]

After the treaty was finally submitted to the Senate, a special session closed without taking a vote on it. An exasperated Roosevelt simply defied the Senate, drawing up what today we would call an executive agreement—by which, he later noted in his autobiography, "I went ahead and administered the proposed treaty anyhow, considering it as a simple agreement on the part of the Executive which could be converted into a treaty whenever the Senate acted." The Senate finally did approve a modified version of the treaty two years later, but Roosevelt later wrote, "I would have continued it until the end of my term, if necessary, without any action by Congress."[46]

Forrest McDonald observes that before Theodore Roosevelt's accession to power, the last time a matter of real significance had been carried out by means of an executive agreement was the Rush–Bagot Agreement of 1817 between Britain and the United States that limited naval armaments on the Great Lakes. But even here, President Monroe eventually sought the opinion of the Senate as to whether it required ratification; and while that body gave no answer, it did approve the agreement by a two-thirds vote. It fell to Theodore Roosevelt to convert the executive agreement into a major instrument of American foreign policy, and he did so without hesitation or apology. These included

---

[44]Holt, *Treaties Defeated by the Senate*, p. 216.

[45]On all this, see ibid.; quotation on pp. 215–16.

[46]McDonald, *The American Presidency*, p. 390.

"agreements to approve Japan's military protectorate in Korea, to restrict Japanese immigration into the United States, to uphold the Open Door policy in China, and to recognize Japan's 'special interests' in China."[47]

One of the classic combinations of Roosevelt's belligerence and his contempt for Congress was the Rough Rider's decision to send the entire battle fleet on a worldwide tour, the aim of which was to impress all nations, but in particular to intimidate Japan. As presidential scholars have noted, the manner in which Roosevelt carried out this exhibition was perhaps as significant as the act itself. Congress objected immediately, threatening to withhold funds for the tour. Roosevelt saw their bluff and warned Congress that since he had the money to send the ships to the Pacific, their refusal to fund the return trip—and therefore to strip the East of its defenses—was a political decision he would leave to them.[48]

Indeed, Congress (and even Roosevelt's own cabinet) looked on impotently as much of Theodore Roosevelt's foreign policy was conducted. "I took Panama without consulting the Cabinet," Roosevelt later recalled. "A council of war never fights, and in a crisis the duty of a leader is to lead." Upon sending his Secretary of War, William Howard Taft, to restore some kind of order in Cuba, he told the future president, "I should not dream of asking the permission of Congress. . . . It is for the enormous interest of this government to strengthen and give independence to the Executive in dealing with foreign powers."[49] When the Senate insisted on modifying the language of a series of arbitration treaties between the United States and nine European countries and Mexico so that the right of the president to reach a "special agreement" with a country with whom the United States was entering arbitration would instead become the right to enter a "special *treaty*"—thereby requiring the president to secure the Senate's consent—Roosevelt rejected the treaties altogether on such a basis.[50] Senate Foreign Relations Committee Chairman Shelby M. Cullom, meanwhile, later explained that

[47]Ibid., pp. 389–90.

[48]Riccards, *Theodore Roosevelt Through George Bush*, p. 19.

[49]Hughes, *The Living Presidency*, pp. 92–93.

[50]Gould, *Presidency of Theodore Roosevelt*, p. 149.

the Senate had had no choice but to "assert and uphold its rights as part of the treaty-making power."[51]

Many of Roosevelt's contemporaries favored a strong executive and an expansionist foreign policy because they had become convinced that American business needed to seize foreign markets for their unsold surpluses. Roosevelt seems to have shared this view, but his primary concern in expansion was a geopolitical one: to elevate the United States to the great-power status to which it had an increasing claim. In fact, as Emily Rosenberg has pointed out, Roosevelt only became interested in the economic issues involved in foreign affairs when he perceived matters of national honor at stake, when a foreign power was not showing the United States the respect he thought it deserved. Thus in 1905, Roosevelt was prepared for a direct confrontation with China when that country cancelled a railroad concession it had granted to J.P. Morgan. It was not without reason that the Chinese ordered the cancellation: In five years Morgan had completed a mere twenty-eight miles of what was ultimately supposed to be an 840-mile track, and they also claimed certain violations of contract on his part. Morgan himself, perhaps recognizing the flimsiness of his case, accepted the settlement, which included a handsome compensation package for profits foregone. Roosevelt, on the other hand, was furious. He later remarked privately that if Morgan had decided to fight, "I would have put the power of the government behind them, so far as the executive was concerned, in every shape and way."[52] No wonder that a half-century later, when the proposed Bricker Amendment, which among other things would have limited the executive's free hand in foreign affairs, came up for discussion, big business was one of its most vocal opponents.[53]

Looking back on his years in office, Roosevelt told his son in 1909: "I have been a full president right up to the end."[54] And

---

[51]Shelby M. Cullom, *Fifty Years of Public Service*, 2nd ed. (Chicago: A.C. McClurg, 1911), p. 399.

[52]Emily S. Rosenberg, *Spreading the American Dream: American Economic and Cultural Expansion, 1890-1945* (New York: Hill and Wang, 1982), p. 58.

[53]See "Bricker's Battle I," *Human Events* (January 13, 1954): 1; see also Duane Tananbaum, *The Bricker Amendment Controversy: A Test of Eisenhower's Political Leadership* (Ithaca, N.Y.: Cornell University Press, 1988), pp. 58, 127.

[54]Emmet John Hughes, *The Living Presidency*, p. 93.

just as he promised, Roosevelt had seized all the power that inhered in the presidency, and through his actions in office permanently strengthened the executive for his successors.

> [W]henever I could establish a precedent for strength in the executive, as I did for instance as regards external affairs in the case of sending the fleet around the world, taking Panama, settling affairs of Santo Domingo and Cuba; or as I did in internal affairs in settling the anthracite coal strike, in keeping order in Nevada this year when the Federation of Miners threatened anarchy, or as I have done in bringing the big corporations to book—why, in all these cases I have felt not merely that my action was right in itself, but that in showing the strength of, or in giving strength to, the executive, I was establishing a precedent of value.[55]

In both domestic and foreign affairs, that meant seizing the initiative, constitutionally or not, from Congress, and in international relations it meant that the United States would force its way onto the world stage to take its rightful place among the great powers. Long gone was the view of Charles Pinckney, who had said that

> [w]e mistake the object of our Government if we hope or wish that it is to make us respectable abroad. Conquest or superiority among other Powers is not, or ought never to be, the object of republican systems. If they are sufficiently active and energetic to rescue us from contempt, and preserve our domestic happiness and security, it is all we can expect from them—it is more than almost any other government ensures to its citizens.[56]

Instead of this classical vision of the American republic, Roosevelt solidified trends toward centralization that had been at work since the 1860s and institutionalized what amounted to a revolution in the American form of government. His legacy is cherished by neoconservatives and other nationalists but deplored by Americans who still possess a lingering attachment to the republic the framers established.

---

[55]Theodore Roosevelt to George Otto Trevelyan, June 19, 1908, in Morison, ed., *The Big Stick, 1907–1909*, p. 1087.

[56]Quoted in Felix Morley, "American Republic or American Empire," *Modern Age* 1 (Summer 1957): 26.

12

THE USE AND ABUSE
OF ANTITRUST FROM
CLEVELAND TO CLINTON:
CAUSES AND CONSEQUENCES

GEORGE BITTLINGMAYER

THE STRUGGLE BETWEEN PRESIDENTS AND BIG BUSINESS:
WINNERS, LOSERS, AND BUSINESS CONFIDENCE

D ramatic conflict between the president and business is a recurring theme in U.S. history. Nineteenth-century disputes over banking, such as the struggle between Nicholas Biddle and Andrew Jackson, provide early examples. The rise of the modern corporation toward the end of the nineteenth century resulted in an intensification of this conflict. In response to the emerging "trusts" and their successors, the modern industrial corporations, individual states, and the federal government passed "antitrust" laws in the 1880s and 1890s. However, the new laws by themselves proved ineffective in curbing the growth of big business, partly because the federal judiciary resisted interpreting early antitrust laws aggressively and partly because New Jersey and Delaware offered a safe legal haven. Ironically, the new laws drove the trusts underground or stimulated the formation of corporations that were beyond the reach of the law as the courts were then interpreting it. The Supreme Court justices, steeped in the common law tradition on which the Sherman Act was allegedly based, were not ready to condemn big business.

The turning point came when Theodore Roosevelt initiated a series of antitrust suits against big business. His targets included a major railroad merger, the Chicago meat packers Armour and Swift, and Rockefeller's Standard Oil. However, the lawsuits by themselves likely would not have been enough to sway the high court. It was Roosevelt's simultaneous use of the bully pulpit that persuaded the Supreme Court to reverse itself and rescue the

Sherman Act from irrelevance. Roosevelt turned a legal and economic question into a highly charged political issue and showed that government could indeed make life tough for the trusts. The Supreme Court bowed to this political reality—though by the narrowest of margins, perhaps for fear that it would lose influence on the trust issue if it did not.

Other presidents picked up where Roosevelt left off, and the list of trustbusters turns out to be surprisingly long and bipartisan. Roosevelt's successor, William Howard Taft, though serving only one term, actually filed more cases than did Roosevelt. Taft's attorney general sued to break up U.S. Steel and promised to break up the country's one hundred largest corporations. Woodrow Wilson enacted several major pieces of antitrust legislation and conducted a vigorous campaign of enforcement. The trust-busting tradition surfaced again under Herbert Hoover, Franklin Roosevelt, Harry Truman, Dwight Eisenhower, and John Kennedy. In fact, Kennedy's famous May 1962 confrontation with Big Steel was accompanied by a major antitrust initiative.

Though the history of these struggles is well-known, their treatment by historians, even by economic historians, is unsatisfying. Historians have told us what happened: presidents and big business frequently clashed. However, the historians have not offered compelling reasons for the struggles between government and business. They also haven't offered insight into the consequences.

This neglect of the "why" and the "so what" of antitrust is unfortunate. The neglected "why" can help us illuminate the nature of economic policy and, in particular, the motivations of the chief executive. For a number of policies—and antitrust is a leading example—economists have not reached a consensus about why government does what it does. The history of presidential use of antitrust offers some clues. Presidents undertook major antitrust initiatives either (1) after a period of sustained economic change as a reaction to that change, or (2) as a way of covering up policy failures. Antitrust originated in the far-reaching economic changes that took place a century ago and received a new endorsement after the far-reaching changes that occurred in the 1920s. A similar, though muted, reaction occurred after the 1980s merger wave, which led to stepped-up antitakeover legislation and court opinions less friendly toward takeovers.

The neglect of the "so what" of antitrust is also unfortunate because antitrust mattered. In the first instance, and perhaps surprisingly, it mattered for the stock market and the economy. Antitrust was bad for the economy because politically charged and volatile attacks on business undermined business confidence. Why would corporations make investments when the future of the corporate form was uncertain? A decline in business confidence is a plausible consequence of volatile, politically charged trustbusting.

The assertion that trust-busting affected the economy is perhaps surprising today. However, it was not surprising to eminent economists writing when the trusts were under attack. Ninety years ago, the charge that Theodore Roosevelt had caused the panic of 1907 was commonplace. But the panic of 1907, though extreme, was not unique. The evidence supports the view that sporadic attacks on business hurt the stock market and the economy in 1919–1920, 1929–1930, 1937–1938, and at several other crucial points.

If beating up on big business hurts stock prices—if it lowers the traded value of big business—does a friendly attitude increase the value of business? The answer turns out to be "yes." A number of presidencies—including those of McKinley, Coolidge, Reagan, and, perhaps surprisingly, Clinton—have been marked by a friendly attitude toward business and a buoyant stock market and robust economic performance. The strong stock market returns of the last fifteen years of the twentieth century were the consequence of two happy circumstances— low inflation and policies that, more so than during any other fifteen-year period of our history, have accepted the modern corporation and the merger of large firms.

Given its woeful economic effects, antitrust also mattered for the fortunes of the two major parties and individual presidents. For example, the conflict over antitrust policy resulted in Theodore Roosevelt's Bull Moose candidacy in 1912 and contributed to the Democratic victory. Indeed the role and power of the large corporation was the single defining issue of the election of 1912. In addition, much contemporary commentary and the relevant evidence support the notion that Wilson's policies hampered economic recovery. Big business and Wall Street were afraid, and rightly so. America's antitrust struggles also explain some aspects of U.S. policies during World War I, in particular the suspension of antitrust under the War Industries Board, which gave business a safe harbor at the expense of government control.

Another example further illustrates the possible influence of antitrust on the course of presidential history. Coolidge became president by accident in 1923. He deliberately pursued antitrust liberalization over the next five years. Hoover reversed this policy in the fall of 1929, and this shift put into doubt the legal validity of the very large number of mergers that had occurred under Coolidge. This uncertainty arguably laid the basis for the 1930 recession, and hence can be viewed as a precipitating factor in the Great Depression and in Hoover's defeat in 1932.

One point deserves emphasis: The shift in antitrust policy probably created an ordinary recession; it did not cause the Great Depression. The cause of the Depression has to be found in whatever turned an ordinary downturn into a world-class, one-third decline of output. Most plausibly, the one-third decline in the price level, aggravated by U.S. adherence to the gold standard, explains the depth of the Great Depression itself. Uncertainty about the future course of government policies engendered by Hoover's New Deal-like initiatives may very well have contributed to a decline in investment by business, a decline in durable goods expenditures by the public, and increased hoarding of money. The latter no doubt contributed to the decline of the price level.

A final example concerns the very close election of 1960. With a more robust economy, Richard Nixon would likely have beaten John Kennedy. One possible cause of the low economic growth of the late 1950s may very well have been the revival of antitrust in the late Eisenhower administration. This revival was consistent with Eisenhower's concern about the "military–industrial complex." Ironically, it may have cost Nixon his first chance to move into the White House.

The view advanced here, that (1) the Sherman Act had its origins in the gains and losses of a dynamic economy and (2) the Sherman Act caused economic damage when applied in a highly charged political environment, solves some riddles. This theory of the origins and effects of antitrust explains the very large amount of attention paid to the trust problem. New business forms created winners and losers on a grand scale. The political struggle and ensuing uncertainty created recessions and stock price volatility.

However, this new view of the Sherman Act also raises a provocative question. If slowing down the redistribution of wealth that occurs with dynamic markets also hurts economic growth and financial markets, was this a price that presidents and others involved in trust-busting willingly paid? The evidence suggests that most presidents were unaware of the full extent of the trade-off.

THE MODERN CORPORATION:
ITS ECONOMIC AND POLITICAL CONSEQUENCES

From the vantage point of the early twenty-first century, we've lost sight of a fact that was once obvious. In the words of historian Martin Sklar:

> The trust question was the corporation question. The great antitrust debates were . . . in essence, debates about the role and power of the large corporations in the market and in society at large, and debates about the corresponding role and power of government in relation to the emergent corporate order.[1]

A hundred years ago, the debate revolved around a single "trust and corporation problem." Remnants of this view were evident as recently as two decades ago, when some legal scholars and economists took the view that the defense of small business and worthy men beset by larger, more efficient competitors was still a valid goal of antitrust. That debate seems quaint today. Most observers have accepted the modern corporation and the goal of economic efficiency. Today's debate over antitrust revolves around how best to protect consumers rather than how best to protect inefficient competitors.

Why was the "trust and corporation problem" important?

(1) The modern corporation constitutes the single most important innovation in the organization of business. The modern corporate form is responsible in large part for the phenomenal increase in the standard of living of the last century. By means of limited liability, the corporation can raise large amounts of capital. By means of the holding company and merger, it solves problems of coordination and control and allows valuable assets in the form of a going concern to be transferred to more valuable uses. We tend naturally to view our improved conditions as the result of a long list of specific

---

[1]Martin Sklar, *The Corporate Reconstruction of American Capitalism: 1890–1916* (Cambridge: Cambridge University Press, 1988), p. 179.

technical advances—the automobile, the airplane, electrical appliances, or the computer. But we owe our well-being to organizational as well as physical innovation. The application of new technology on a wide scale requires large amounts of capital. Indeed, even the prospective rewards for would-be innovators depend on the institutions available to implement their innovations. The integrated circuit finds wider application and has generated higher social returns because corporations produce the final products—everything from microwave ovens to handheld games to supercomputers. Any complete explanation of our material progress over the last century would also have to emphasize the role of new forms of business organization and, in particular, the modern corporation.[2]

(2) The rise of the modern corporation and new technologies generated winners and losers, and the losers turned to the political process. A hundred years ago, ever cheaper railroad transportation helped efficient large-scale producers and hurt their existing smaller competitors. Cheap kerosene was a boon to the average household but harmed candle and whale oil producers. The refrigerated railcar made centralized slaughter of hogs and cattle possible but hurt regional slaughterhouses, in particular those along the eastern seaboard. In the 1920s, the rapidly growing use of the automobile, electricity, and other innovations created higher standards of living for many and "profitless prosperity" for others. Today, information technology generates winners and losers—firms and workers whose value is increased in the marketplace by the computer and telecommunications technology, and those whose value is decreased. Even within high-tech industries, new developments create winners and losers.[3]

(3) In the U.S., the political reaction to these gains and losses often took the form of antitrust. If large firms threatened small firms, then the political policies designed to protect small firms

---

[2]Alfred D. Chandler, Jr., *The Visible Hand: The Managerial Revolution in American Business* (Cambridge, Mass.: Harvard University Press, 1977); Lester G. Telser, *A Theory of Efficient Cooperation and Competition* (Cambridge, Mass.: Cambridge University Press), chap. 8.

[3]Thomas J. DiLorenzo, "Origins of the Sherman Act: An Interest-Group Perspective" *International Review of Law and Economics* 13 (Fall 1985): 73–90; Telser, *A Theory of Efficient Cooperation and Competition*, chap. 2; Gary D. Libecap, "The Rise of the Chicago Packers and the Origins of Meat Inspection and Antitrust," *Economic Inquiry* 30, no. 2 (April 1992): 242–62.

would focus on firms grown large through merger or through colorably unfair business practices. At several points, the legal struggle threatened to involve nearly every major corporation or subject major sectors of the economy to state control on prices or profits. This happened formally with railroads, utilities, and phone companies, and informally with steel.

(4) Antitrust attacks were often linked with other antibusiness initiatives. At the turn of the century, for example, antitrust initiatives were linked in time with efforts to enact personal and corporate income taxes, with agitation against the "money trust," and with the creation of federal bureaucracies with power over business. During the late 1930s, antitrust chief Thurman Arnold's attack on business practices was accompanied by an attack on America's "hundred wealthy families" and the Temporary National Economic Committee hearings.[4]

(5) Attacks on business, though sometimes largely rhetorical, often posed a substantial threat to the continued vitality of the corporation. This is true even if the country never actually "went socialist." There were points at which there was an appreciable likelihood—perhaps small but still not negligible—that the country would go 'round the bend. A new antitrust initiative might have been successful in reaching its rhetorical aims, or it might have signaled the first step in a broader panoply of antibusiness policies. At such points, it makes sense for business to put its investment on hold, with predictable consequences.[5]

---

[4]Sam Peltzman, "Toward a More General Theory of Regulation," *Journal of Law and Economics* 19 (October): 211–40; Fred S. McChesney, "Be True to Your School: Chicago's Contradictory Views of Antitrust and Regulation," *Cato Journal* (Winter 1991): 775–98; Mark J. Roe, *Strong Managers, Weak Owners: The Political Roots of American Corporate Finance* (Princeton, N.J.: Princeton University Press, 1994); Ellis Hawley, *The New Deal and the Problem of Monopoly: A Study in Economic Ambivalence* (Princeton, N.J.: Princeton University Press).

[5]The idea that uncertainty on the trust question might affect business confidence was first proposed by Wesley Clair Mitchell, the founder of American business cycle research (Wesley Clair Mitchell, *Business Cycles* [New York: National Bureau of Economic Research, 1927]). John Bates Clark and John Maurice Clark suggested the possibility as well. Irving Fisher was undoubtedly thinking about the same debate when he wrote a scant two decades later: "During the Roosevelt and Wilson regimes, there was an organized effort at 'trust busting'; it was the popular sport of politicians" (Irving Fisher, *The Stock Market Crash—And After* [New York: Macmillan, 1930], p. 106).

FIXED COSTS:
AN ECONOMIC AND POLITICAL PERENNIAL

The trust and corporation problem had its origins in the rise of the modern corporation a century ago. One important complication arose from the problem of fixed costs. Many of the early corporations involved in transportation and manufacturing produced under conditions of high fixed costs. However, high fixed costs implied that an industry might not be able to conform to the textbook model of competition. Some sort of "noncompetitive" conduct often emerged, generating situations that were ripe for political exploitation. Even with a good-government view, the fixed-cost problem generates a policy challenge, namely that of separating good, "efficient" restrictions from "bad" inefficient restrictions.

The fixed-cost problem arose from new technologies. Substantial fixed costs came to characterize manufacturing, transportation, and telecommunications. Paradoxically, the decline in transportation costs that accompanied the rise of the railroad and steamship meant that a small, local monopoly was often displaced by regional, national, or even worldwide oligopoly of large firms.

In an older literature, the existence of several firms with high fixed costs implied "cutthroat competition," competition that drove prices below the costs of production. The idea has had fluctuating fortunes. It initially received the endorsement of leading economists but then came in for a good deal of derision. Today, the problems posed by fixed costs and the possibility of cutthroat competition have experienced a revival among economic theorists. Modern economic theory has shown that, excepting special circumstances, fixed costs are incompatible with a competitive equilibrium.[6] This opens the door to something else: prices too low to cover socially-justified costs, cartels or merger, for example.

The emergence of fixed costs generated reaction and counter-reaction on the part of business and the government. The original reaction took the form of pools in railroading and of trusts and cartels in manufacturing. Some companies also adopted merger or the holding company, a form made possible by New Jersey in the late 1880s. With the increased pressure of antitrust at both the

---

[6]Telser, *A Theory of Efficient Cooperation and Competition*, chap. 3.

state and federal levels during the 1890s, many more corporations sought refuge in merger and the holding company. The fixed-cost problem and the public's and government's reaction to the original cooperative forms—trusts, pools, cartels, and merger—are an important part of the story.

Though some firms took refuge in merger, many others continued as separate entities linked through cooperative agreements. It was a simple question of relative costs. Though cartels suffered occasional breakdowns, independent firms under the control of owner–managers were more efficient.

The question of what to do about these cooperative forms of organization surfaced repeatedly in the trust debate. The vague prohibitions of the Sherman Act against restraints of trade can be interpreted as a plea to the courts to find a solution. During Theodore Roosevelt's administration, the fixed-cost problem was reflected in the Hepburn bill—proposed legislation that would have allowed "reasonable restraints of trade." With the failure of this initiative, attention turned to Arthur Jerome Eddy's "open-price" or "association movement" and Judge Gary's steel industry dinners. The fixed-cost problem also surfaced in Supreme Court decisions that allowed for reasonable restraints of trade and in the debate leading up to the creation of the Federal Trade Commission (FTC) in 1914. Indeed, the hope was that the trade commission would be able to offer guidance on the nettlesome issues raised by restraints of trade. However, when it was finally allowed to do so in 1920s, the Supreme Court rebuffed its efforts.

In the meantime, the idea of a safe haven for cartels was implemented during World War I in the form of Webb–Pomerene exemptions for shipping and export cartels, and the War Industries Board. After the war, efforts to establish a peacetime industries board foundered, but antitrust chief "Colonel" Donovan at the Justice Department along with William Humphrey at the FTC continued with sub-rosa efforts to promote cooperative forms of organization during the 1920s. Beginning in the early 1920s, Commerce Secretary Herbert Hoover promoted similar aims, with policies designed to encourage the exchange and dissemination of information at the industry level.

The fixed-cost problem surfaced again in the infamous 1933 Appalachian Coals decision. Paying close attention to developments in the political world, the Supreme Court briefly returned to a "rule of reason" approach to cartels and approved a joint sales agency covering roughly 10 percent of U.S. production.

Possibly the most famous attempt to deal with the consequences of the fixed-cost problem was the National Industrial Recovery Act, enacted in 1933 close on the heels of the Appalachian Coals decision. The NIRA was the centerpiece of Franklin Roosevelt's First Hundred Days. It created the National Recovery Administration (NRA). Historian Robert Himmelberg convincingly argues that the NRA had its origins in the War Industries Board and the pro-association-movement policies of the antitrust agencies during the 1920s. In fact, Roosevelt had been a trade association lawyer.

The NRA was the culmination of antitrust reform efforts that began with the panic of 1907 and the ill-fated Hepburn Bill. One continuous thread connects the Sherman Act, the early cartel cases such as Trans-Missouri and Addyston, Theodore Roosevelt's proposed Sherman Act amendments to allow "reasonable restraints of trade," Eddy's "open-price associations," Judge Gary's dinners, the Federal Trade Commission Act, antitrust exemptions to export associations and ocean shipping, Bernard Baruch's War Industries Board, the activities of Hoover as Commerce secretary and Colonel Donovan as antitrust chief, the discussion over antitrust reform during Hoover's term as president, and the short-lived reforms under the NRA.

The Supreme Court declared the National Recovery Act unconstitutional in 1935, and no further attempts were made to provide a statutory haven for cartels. Over the next few decades, manufacturing industries that operated under substantial fixed costs—steel and cement, for example—adopted a variety of forms to deal with the problem: illegal cartels, vertical integration, basing point pricing, merger, and foreign ownership. A number of other industries characterized by high fixed costs—notably railroads, telephony, trucking, and airlines—either were already subject to federal or state regulation of price and entry or became subject to such a regime. In all of these cases, whether steel, cement, or airlines, the industries arguably operated with less efficiency than they would have under a system of self-regulation disciplined by common law courts, free entry, and the emergence of new products.

PRESIDENTS AND TURNING POINTS

President Benjamin Harrison signed the Sherman Antitrust Act into law in July 1890. Early enforcement was sporadic.

Indeed, early legal commentary held that the new law either merely codified the common law—and hence implied no large changes for the legality of trusts—or was bound to have limited reach because of constitutional limitations. *E.C. Knight*, the case against the infamous Sugar Trust, proved these doubters right. The case, decided in 1895, put merger out of reach of the Sherman Act, because it held that the trade in shares that effectuated a merger was not interstate commerce. Grover Cleveland's attorney general, Richard Olney, had already been skeptical of the Sherman Act's reach. This decision only confirmed his suspicion.

It would be difficult to exaggerate the importance of *Knight*. The case created a well-defined safe haven for the trusts—namely merger. At the same time, *Trans-Missouri* and *Joint Traffic*, both cases against railroads, and the *Addyston Pipe*, filed against an industrial cartel, established the *per se* rule against cartels. The resulting legal scissors created a clear incentive for the trusts to merge—and merge they did ,on a scale that has not been equaled, adjusting for the size of the economy. The ensuing Great Merger Wave of 1898–1902 involved roughly half of U.S. industrial capacity and created or greatly augmented many large firms that were household words through much of the twentieth century, including General Electric, DuPont, U.S. Steel, and Standard Oil.

The trusts played a secondary role in the election of 1896. The main issue was the currency question. However, it was clearly understood that the victory by William Jennings Bryan would imply changes for the trusts as well. Many commentators have stressed the possible link between the election of 1896 and the recession that occurred the same year. The fear of limitless money creation under Bryan's proposed free silver program may have generated part of the slump, but the prospect of stepped-up and politicized attacks on corporations may have played a role as well.

With the election of 1896 decided and William McKinley in office, the economy grew at a remarkable pace over the next four years. From a monetarist's view, one factor may have been the discovery of gold in Alaska. Arguably, the safe haven for trusts and widespread mergers of the same years also played a role. Though a renewed candidacy by Bryan in 1900 appears to have cast a momentary shadow over the economy, the economy turned robust again after the election.

The assassination of McKinley in September 1901 proved to be a crucial event. It propelled "that cowboy," Theodore Roosevelt, into the presidency. In fact, the attack on McKinley and his death a few days later unsettled the stock market. Note that Kennedy's assassination did not have similar effects. The mere fact of a lone madman attacking the president would not and should not rattle markets. Rather, commentary at the time and circumstantial evidence implicates the trust-busting inclinations that Roosevelt had already revealed as governor of New York.

Wall Street's suspicions proved well-founded. The most important case of Roosevelt's first term stemmed from the Northern Securities merger. On the basis of the facts and the law, the merger was beyond the reach of the law, by virtue of *E.C. Knight*. However, the merger generated strong emotions, and Roosevelt communicated his determination to overthrow legal precedent. Arguably, the fear that Roosevelt would be successful and attack other larger mergers contributed to the rich man's panic of 1903. In a 5–4 decision in 1904, a divided Supreme Court, in fact, overturned the Sugar Trust decision and held the Northern Securities merger in violation of the Sherman Act. This case marked the beginning of twentieth-century trust-busting.

However, 1904 was also an election year. Roosevelt's attorney general showed sensitivity to business fears when he said immediately after the decision there would be "no running amok" on antitrust. Roosevelt and Congress undertook administrative measures, forming both the Bureau of Corporations and the Antitrust Division of the Justice Department. But they did not initiate any more aggressive, high-profile cases.

This changed in 1906. Standard Oil had been one of the pioneering trusts, and independent oil producers had attacked it for two decades. Two circumstances may explain the escalating attacks of 1900–1906. First, the discovery of crude in Texas depressed crude oil prices, squeezing the margins of Pennsylvania producers. Second, Ida Tarbell had written a series of highly popular muckraking pieces about Standard Oil. The stage was set for a number of investigations and the November 1906 antitrust filing.

The Standard Oil case generated interest for a number of reasons. It represented the first attempt to use the Northern Securities precedent—which involved a railroad merger—against a large industrial trust. Moreover, when the case dragged on in 1907, Roosevelt's attorney general threatened to institute criminal proceedings—raising the prospect of substantial jail time for Rockefeller and for other leading industrialists. Third, a successful prosecution of Standard Oil would put in jeopardy nearly every major industrial consolidation. The legal posture at the time was that a violation of the Sherman Act—"bad behavior" under the antitrust laws—carried the punishment of dismemberment. This satisfied the political craving to undo the Great Merger Wave that *E.C. Knight* had permitted, but it would have implied a costly and drawn-out legal battle between government and the trusts. Finally, the *Standard Oil* case generated uncertainty because Roosevelt backed up the legal assault with a wildly popular political assault on the trusts. Two further major cases, against the Tobacco Trust (*American Tobacco*) and the "Gunpowder Trust" (*DuPont*), added to the sense that large changes were afoot.

The assault on the trusts was accompanied by what came to be called the panic of 1907, which was marked by a 50-percent decline in stock prices and a one-third decline in output over the twelve months ending December 1907. Roosevelt's critics blamed the panic on his trust-busting, and many of his friends even urged him to suspend his attacks or reverse course. In a phrase that reverberated through ensuing decades, Roosevelt responded that he had not caused the panic, but rather that "malefactors of great wealth" had provoked it in order to discredit his policies.

In fact, Roosevelt began pulling his antitrust punches in late 1907 and started to urge antitrust reform to allow "reasonable restraints of trade." The proposed legislation, which provided for an agency that would have passed judgment on proposed cooperative arrangements, eventually died, in large part because it would have strengthened the hand of the executive.

Roosevelt's successor was William Howard Taft. Taft was the author of the 1898 circuit court opinion in *Addyston Pipe*, which had established the *per se* rule against price fixing. Indeed, Taft's circuit opinion became more famous than the Supreme Court opinion that affirmed it in 1899. He argued that a *per se* prohibition of cartels under the Sherman Act merely codified the common law, though recent scholarship disputes this claim.[7]

---

[7]Mark F. Grady, "Toward a Positive Economic Theory of Antitrust," *Economic Inquiry* 30, no. 2 (April 1992): 225–41.

Ironically, his Addyston opinion had accelerated the merger wave in which many large corporations were formed.

Taft, besides having shaped early antitrust doctrine, was also a very stubborn man. Against this background, it is not surprising that he pursued an even more aggressive antitrust policy than did Roosevelt. At one point, his attorney general threatened to break up the nation's hundred largest corporations and send corporate officials to jail. Taft saw himself restoring an idealized nineteenth-century competition. "We must go back to competition: If that is impossible, then let us go to socialism, for there is no way between."[8] His most famous case involved U.S. Steel, which, with Roosevelt's approval, had acquired Tennessee Coal and Iron in the depths of the 1907 panic.

Taft's trust-busting was also accompanied by troubled financial markets and charges that his policies undermined business confidence. Unlike Roosevelt, Taft freely admitted that his policies "may make business halt." In a letter to his brother, he wrote: "We are going to enforce that law or die in the attempt." The words were prophetic.

Roosevelt, piqued because he was named as the handmaiden of the trusts and sensing that Taft was vulnerable, staged his celebrated Bull Moose candidacy. Taft and Democratic challenger Wilson adopted a strong antitrust position, while Roosevelt viewed trusts as engines of progress in part and sought to distinguish good and bad trusts. The debate over the trusts was the single defining issue of the election of 1912. A sullen Taft did little campaigning, in fact. His only goal was to deny Roosevelt the White House. With the benefit of hindsight, it is possible to argue that had Taft shown more discretion and less valor, he would not have provoked Roosevelt into running, the economy would have done better, and Taft would have been reelected.

After Wilson's victory, the trust issue continued as one of the major policy topics. In the 1911 *Standard Oil* and *American Tobacco* opinions, the Supreme Court had upheld the divestiture of these two trusts, but also had included language friendly to the "good trusts" view. Congressional attempts to take back the initiative resulted in the Clayton and Federal Trade Commission Acts. At the same time, concern about the "money trust" resulted in two major reforms. The Federal Reserve Act of 1913 gave the U.S. a central bank. At one level, this was a response to

[8]*Wall Street Journal*, October 7, 1911, p. 1, col. 4.

the perceived lack of "elasticity" in the banking system during the panic of 1907. At another level, it established a counter-weight to influential bankers, like J.P. Morgan, who had served as lenders of last resort. The second related reform emerged from Pujo Investigation. This investigation, which concerned the alleged influence of the "money trust" over industry, did not result in new law, but prominent investment bankers removed themselves from the boards of major industrial firms to avoid trouble.[9]

Wilson's first administration was not marked by a robust economy. Critics charged that unfriendly business policies hurt business confidence. Indeed the Wilson administration admitted as much. In January 1914, Wilson told Congress, "The antago-nism between business and government is over."[10] But it was not over, and his administration seemed divided between faith-fulness to the slogans of 1912 and the desire to create a favor-able business climate. World War I provided a new dimension. U.S. opportunities for ocean transport and export provided rhetorical cover for antitrust exemptions to shipping and export associations. The need to secure industrial cooperation in the war effort once the U.S. entered the war formally in 1917 caused the Wilson administration to grant a long-standing request for antitrust exemptions along the lines proposed in Roosevelt's ill-fated Hepburn bill of 1908. The War Industries Board administered the resulting industry associations. Arguably, the strong performance of the U.S. economy during the war was due in part to the restoration of business confi-dence—the knowledge that the Wilson administration was a good deal less likely to attack business on antitrust grounds. In fact, the newly created FTC, which many viewed as a potential rogue elephant from the very beginning, did not receive sub-stantial funding for several years after its creation.

After the November 1919 Armistice, U.S. policies changed rapidly. Industry hopes of a peacetime industries board were not fulfilled. In fact, public opinion turned hostile. The inflation gen-erated by wartime finance created a "cost of living" controversy, complicated by a "war profiteer" controversy. Together with

---

[9]Roe, *Strong Managers, Weak Owners*.

[10]Thomas K. McCraw, *Prophets of Regulation* (Cambridge, Mass.: Belknap Press, [1984] 1986).

high-profile antitrust cases, sharpened antibusiness rhetoric at the state and federal level in 1919–20, and sharp deflation, the business climate worsened, increasing the chances of Republican victory in 1920.

The Republicans did win, and Harding's administration continued a moderately aggressive antitrust policy, though Commerce Secretary Hoover waged bureaucratic resistance to the campaign against "open price associations" by championing the cause of information exchange at his agency. Harding's death in 1923 set the stage for more radical reform. Under Calvin Coolidge, antitrust policy was scaled back so far that prominent antitrust attorney Gilbert Montague called the Sherman Act a dead letter. The FTC saw its major function in promoting industry trade association agreements, and Department of Justice (DOJ) antitrust chief "Colonel" William Donovan attempted to establish accomplished facts administratively that the courts would have to recognize. In particular, he was providing pre-merger clearance, though he lacked statutory authority. During the three years 1926 through 1928, the two agencies filed only one merger case against a publicly traded firm. At the same time, America experienced its second large merger wave, which resulted in consolidation of electric utilities (the go-go industry of the 1920s), automobile manufacture, food processing, and the fast-growing radio and movie industries.

The rapid growth of some sectors, like automobiles and electric utilities, caused wrenching changes in others. The rise of the department store and grocery chains created problems for old-line retailers. Indeed, complaints surfaced about "profitless prosperity" and the lax enforcement of the antitrust laws.

The time was ripe for a swing of the pendulum, but Hoover might have seemed an unlikely agent. As commerce secretary under Harding, he had pursued policies sympathetic to the association movement, then under attack by the Justice Department and the courts. As commerce secretary under Coolidge, he might have been expected to have been sympathetic to the favorable attitude toward business and big business in particular. In retrospect, one early warning sign appeared when Hoover declined to make Donovan his attorney general.

During the summer of 1929, merger activity continued at a rapid pace. Hoover became uneasy and asked Attorney General William Mitchell to look into the matter. Hoover and Mitchell were appalled to discover the actual practice under Coolidge.

Major antitrust initiatives under Coolidge were quietly reversed in the fall of 1929, and on Friday, October 25, 1929, in his address at the annual meeting of the American Bar Association, Mitchell announced a new regime. He promised to enforce the laws as they were written; he characterized "the machinery of some trade associations [as] dangerously near price fixing"; he revealed that the Department of Justice had not approved a single merger since the administration took office in March; and he reserved the right to file suit against any merger not explicitly approved. This policy put at risk a large volume of mergers, and it put at risk the multitude of industry trade association agreements brokered by the two agencies. Mitchell's October 25 speech and the related policy initiatives offer a compelling explanation for the stock market crash that began the preceding Wednesday and ended with a one-third decline of the Dow Industrial Average at the close of trading on the following Tuesday. The switch in regime generated a debate over antitrust reform that lasted through the remainder of Hoover's administration. In line with experience during earlier periods in which policy took a turn for the worse from the point of view of business, economic activity declined in 1930. Clearly, a good deal of the subsequent economic decline was caused or greatly aggravated by the collapsing price level. Still, the switch to a less favorable business climate offers an explanation for the beginning of that decline in 1930, when prices were still stable.

The presidencies of Coolidge and Hoover offer compelling evidence against economic determinism. Accident thrust Coolidge into the White House, and a misunderstanding caused the public and Wall Street to think that Herbert Hoover would continue Coolidge's policies, when in fact he did not.

Historians and modern commentators focus on the rhetoric of the early New Deal, but not the substantive policies. The "First Hundred Days" are powerful legend, about which little is known today. This ignorance may be deliberate. Both writers sympathetic to Roosevelt and writers sympathetic to business are embarrassed by the cozy relationship between government and business inherent in the New Deal's first major piece of economic legislation—the National Industrial Recovery Act (NIRA) of 1933.

From an economic standpoint, the NIRA had its advantages and disadvantages. Its main advantage was that it implemented the status quo ante under Coolidge. Its main disadvantage was that it represented an adorned power grab by the executive and a politicization of issues that should have been handled by industry. Given business's worst fears in 1933, which may have included the country "going socialist" (recall that socialists of one stripe or another had prevailed in much of Europe), the good news may have outweighed the bad. Some evidence at least points to that conclusion. The passage and early implementation of the NIRA were marked by a very strong economic recovery. This may have partly reflected the net benefits of the act itself. Passage of the NIRA may have had an even greater symbolic effect by conveying the message that Franklin Roosevelt's administration was prepared to give business what it wanted, albeit at a price.

The Supreme Court declared the NIRA unconstitutional in 1935, and the monopoly issue languished until the fall of 1937. With the 1938 elections looming and no end of the Depression in sight, the administration faced a problem. The solution was to blame the alleged monopolistic practices of business and the "hundred wealthy families." This proved to be effective politically, but it had the effect of delivering a sharp blow to the already slow and faltering recovery. The 1938 recession was arguably a result of this assault. Thurman Arnold began his legendary antitrust campaign. The Temporary National Economic Committee hearings on monopoly and business practices were another reflection of this initiative.

America's entry into World War II brought an end to antibusiness actions. After the armed services complained that antitrust investigations of major defense industries were harming the war effort, Franklin Roosevelt kicked Arnold upstairs to a judgeship, and the Department of Justice largely suspended its campaign against business. Repeating a pattern seen in World War I, cooperation between government and business flourished once again. The strong performance of U.S. industry during the war was plausibly the result of lucrative cost-plus contracts (paid for by a generally lower standard of living of the general population) and relative freedom from the sorts of virulent antibusiness initiatives that had marked the late 1930s and early 1940s.

After the war, some of the old fears and politics surfaced. A largely unfounded concern about a "rising tide of concentration" led to the 1950 Celler–Kefauver Amendment to the Clayton Act. This closed the "assets loophole," which had allowed firms to merge by purchasing assets rather than actual stock shares. Like earlier wars, the Korean War generated a truce between government and business that was soon lifted. The Antitrust Division took the first steps, but the Federal Trade Commission soon followed. The Supreme Court also endorsed a more strident antitrust policy. A good deal of this initiative came from Eisenhower. Among other measures, he directed that government purchases of vehicles be carried out so as not to increase concentration among the automobile producers. These attacks coincided with the 1958–1959 recession and likely contributed to Kennedy's slim victory in the 1960 election.

Though different in other respects, Kennedy nurtured the strident antibusiness policies he inherited from Eisenhower. In fact, his celebrated 1962 confrontation with the steel companies only intensified the conflict between government and business. Already during the Eisenhower years, steel had become a regulated utility for all intents and purposes. The steel companies could not raise prices without presidential approval. However, in 1962, the industry thought it had the go-ahead to finally raise prices as well. When it did, Kennedy claimed that no agreement had been reached and forced the steel companies to roll back their prices in May. A flurry of antitrust cases against steel firms and other companies followed in mid-1962. This incident left the Kennedy administration with the reputation of being "antibusiness" and resulted in the Investment Tax Credit.

Antitrust under Lyndon Johnson came under two influences: Johnson's natural inclination to make a deal where one could be made and the Vietnam War. Antitrust enforcement was in fact scaled back. The war had several consequences. First, it distracted the chief executive. Its growing unpopularity also diminished Jackson's influence over domestic economic policy. Second, in conjunction with Johnson's Great Society programs, the war created inflation and the familiar though erroneous claims that big business was causing inflation. The departing Johnson administration filed some of the worst cases on record, though largely without Johnson's encouragement. The notorious case against IBM was filed in January 1969, just before Nixon's inauguration.

Antitrust in the 1970s under Nixon, Ford, and Carter went through its Dark Ages. The agencies engaged in new, entirely speculative antitrust crusades. Symbolic was the FTC's case against the ready-to-eat cereal companies, which alleged that the major cereal companies had jointly monopolized the market by offering too many product varieties. The FTC also filed a monopolization suit against DuPont for building a titanium dioxide plant that was too large and too efficient. Also symbolic was the fact that none of these administrations killed the *IBM* case. The revival of the large-firm deconcentration case with the filing of the AT&T divestiture case in November 1974 raised the possibility of a new, broader assault on American business.

The Reagan administration brought about two permanent shifts in economic policy. First, it brought inflation down from double-digit levels. Second, it scaled back antitrust adventure. Together, these two changes explain a good deal of the improved performance of the U.S. economy and the unprecedented performance of the U.S. stock market. The experience of the 1920s was repeated, though in much muted fashion. Again, restrained antitrust enforcement and good times went together. And again, the far-reaching restructuring that these policies permitted generated a political reaction. In the 1980s, this occurred both at the federal and state levels. At the federal level, the most noteworthy initiatives involved the proposed antitakeover legislation that researchers have implicated as a precipitating factor in the 1987 stock market crash and actual measures taken to undermine the junk-bond market, which had fueled a large fraction of the takeover activity. At the state level, the U.S. Supreme Court had declared earlier antitakeover statutes unconstitutional. However, a new generation of statutes offered takeover targets some protection. To some extent, the state-level actions were a political substitute for the federal actions that did not go very far.

Antitrust under George Bush slid back into some of the old bad habits. Bush's antitrust authorities conducted investigations of Microsoft and Intel; they brought new life to antimerger policy; they undertook quixotic attacks on Japanese business practices in Japan; they filed cases against the Ivy League colleges for alleged conspiracy in offering financial aid; and they revived the vertical restriction policy after a period of benign neglect. Indeed, these actions, together with Bush's endorsement of policies such as the Americans with Disabilities Act and the 1990 Clean Air Act, led to the charge that the 1991–1992 downturn was a "regulatory recession."

The genius of the Clinton record was its ability to implement the Reagan changes while at the same time offering some public-relations dressing. In antitrust history, the Clinton administration will forever be linked with the case against

Microsoft. Arguably, the case had its origins as much in Microsoft's failure to pay tribute in Washington as in competitor complaints. The shift in policy is apparent from the many large mergers that took place during the Clinton administration—mergers that would have been unimaginable two decades earlier.

CONCLUSION

The past has significance for our future. Consider the case of a rational, perhaps too-rational, twenty-five-year-old planning for the future, and in particular planning for retirement. She might well ask, how will the economy and the stock market do over the next forty years? The simplest predictions of the economy and the stock market merely refer to past averages—2 percent real growth and 12 percent per annual returns in the stock market. Slightly more sophisticated answers attempt to make predictions based on guesses about future technical and demographic developments. In view of our experience over the last hundred years, the best prediction of the future will be the one that correctly guesses how government deals with business and the inevitable political pressures to regulate business that economic progress and economics generate.

13

From Opponent of Empire to Career Opportunist: William Howard Taft as Conservative Bureaucrat in the Evolution of the American Imperial System

William Marina

The Evolution of the Imperial Presidency

Any reassessment of the presidency in general, or of any president in particular, must begin with some understanding of the concept of the presidency itself in American history and its evolution over the last two centuries. From the writing of the Constitution and the election of George Washington as the first president, to the election of William Jefferson Clinton in 1992, it would not be unfair to suggest that the office of the president has been viewed as something in the nature of an American "tribunate"—despite the electoral college mechanism, an individual elected by the whole people.

From its beginnings in the Renaissance with Machiavelli, modern classical-Republican political thought was permeated with a fascination for Greece and Rome—their histories and institutional structures. Thus, the protests of *Cato's Letters* against the corrupt politics of eighteenth-century Great Britain were enormously popular reading in the formation of the ideology of the generation of Americans who led the American Revolution and created the republic.[1] The terminology of Roman ideals and

---

[1]For some of the classical reading of the Americans of that generation, see H. Trevor Coulburn, *The Lamp of Experience: Whig History and the Intellectual Origins of the American Revolution* (Indianapolis, Ind.: Liberty Press, reprint, 1998).

institutions was apparent in such organizational concepts as the Senate, "virtue," and even the ill-fated Society of the Cincinnati.

But American leaders were also aware that the Roman Republic and its institutions over several centuries of warfare and conquest had evolved into the Roman Empire and the *Pax Romana*, the latter not universally acclaimed by those inhabitants who suffered under its yoke. The difference was nicely summed up in 1775 by John Adams, when, in the midst of citing Aristotle, Livy, and James Harrington, he wrote:

> [T]he British Constitution is more like a republic than an empire. They define a republic to be a government of laws, and not of men. . . . An empire is a despotism, and an emperor is a despot, bound by no law or limitation of his own will; it is a stretch of tyranny beyond absolute monarchy. For, although the will of an absolute monarch is law, yet his edicts must be registered by parliaments. Even this formality is not necessary in an empire.[2]

One of the significant aspects of the worldview of many of the Founding Fathers such as John Adams, but certainly evident in writings of intellectuals such as Baron de Montesquieu or Edward Gibbon, was a belief in a cyclical view of history. The fear was that the American republic would evolve in much the same cycle as had the Roman: into empire.[3]

As we survey the American presidency from the perspective of over two hundred years, it is difficult to disagree with the liberal historian, Arthur Schlesinger, Jr., that there has been an evolution toward an imperial presidency.[4] The difficulty with any evolutionary continuum or spectrum, of course, is to determine

---

[2]John Adams, *Novanglus Letters, 1775*, cited in William Marina, *Egalitarianism and Empire* (Menlo Park, Calif.: Institute for Humane Studies, 1975), p. 7.

[3]See, for example, Amaury de Riencourt, *The Coming Caesars* (New York: Coward-McCann, 1957).

[4]Arthur M. Schlesinger, Jr., *The Imperial Presidency* (Boston: Houghton Mifflin, 1973). It is simply foolishness to suggest that only the presidency has become, somehow, imperial. The whole American system has become imperial, including the Congress, the judiciary, and larger society itself. At the core has been a shift toward statist, positive law, by a large part of the society and away from either supernatural or natural law.

at what point a substantive transition has been made from one entity toward another—in this case, from republic to empire.[5]

In the case of classical Rome's leadership, that transitional spectrum might be said to have evolved from tribune to consul to caesar to emperor over several centuries. In the case of the United States, it took only a couple of generations before some politicians were calling popular leaders such as President Andrew Jackson "caesarian," although the Whigs backed off from that assessment when the party also began to select generals for presidential candidates in the 1840s.[6]

One of the first American political thinkers to discern this drift toward centralization and empire was Alexander Stephens, Abraham Lincoln's old friend from their service together in the House of Representatives in the 1840s. Stephens, later the vice president of the Confederacy, devoted his last years to a perceptive analysis of the evolving American political system, and argued, very much like Oswald Spengler several decades later, against "empire," and that there was "no difference between centralism and imperialism."[7]

Whether or not one agrees with the view of a drift toward empire, several definitional matters need to be explored with respect to the phenomenon of empire. From the great imperialist surge of the Western powers into both Africa and Asia during the late nineteenth century, and given even greater emphasis by the Leninist and other neo–Marxist attempts to explain those policies, empire and imperialism have come to be almost synonymous with foreign policy. But it needs to be remembered that the other definitions of empire—centralization and the erosion of the rule of law—are in no way abrogated by the attention drawn to the former. Indeed, the two aspects of empire most often function together.

The key link between the two is the emergence of bureaucracy. Empire, whether due to an acquisition of territory abroad or an expansion and centralization of the role of government at home, is never a result of some fit of "absentmindedness"; it requires an expanding bureaucracy to administer the increasing governmental role. This inevitably leads to a massive explosion

[5]Carroll Quigley, *The Evolution of Civilizations: An Introduction to Historical Analysis* (Indianapolis, Ind.: Liberty Press, 1979).

[6]Edwin A. Miles, "The Whig Party and the Menace of Caesar," *Tennessee Historical Quarterly* XXVII, no. 4 (1968): 361–79.

[7]Marina, *Egalitarianism and Empire*, p. 9.

of rules and bureaucratic law, often unclear, vague, and even perhaps contradictory—what in ancient China was called legalism.[8]

In the United States, these two impulses came together at
the end of the nineteenth century with the acquisition of an
overseas empire and a simultaneous demand for domestic
reform that numerous intellectuals and politicians came to
believe could only be achieved by an increase in the role and
function of government. If those who have argued that the
major change of the last century or so has been the emergence of
empire are correct—and this writer agrees with that view—then
any reassessment of the presidency, or of a particular president
must be undertaken in the context of that development. It is thus
fair to ask: How does the presidency of William Howard Taft
relate to that overall movement toward an imperial presidency?

At first glance, one might dismiss the Taft presidency as a
four-year interlude between the dynamic almost eight-year
Republican progressivism of the ultra-activist Theodore Roosevelt, and the eight-year Democratic progressivism of the intellectual Woodrow Wilson. To do so would be to severely under-
estimate Taft's role in the development of events between 1900
and 1912.

No president, no emperor, can rule alone. Whether there is
anyone among the people to suggest he might be without
clothes, as did the small boy in the Hans Christian Anderson
story, the executive needs a burgeoning bureaucracy to administer an expanding empire. This expansion of the role of government presents an extraordinary opportunity for those businessmen providing goods and services to the empire and those with
credentials, scholarly or otherwise, for administrative service in
the empire. Such bureaucrats are unlikely to tell the executive
any more than they believe he needs to know, and they
inevitably filter the information that he receives.

Given that reality, Taft's career in government during these
years assumes at least as great an importance as the four years
of his presidency, for his twelve years at the very cockpit of
bureaucratic decision-making at the turn of the century was
greater than any of his immediate predecessors or successors.
One would have to go back, perhaps, to John Quincy Adams, or

---

[8]Amaury de Riencourt, *The Soul of China* (New York: HarperCollins, 1958),
pp. 33–34.

forward to Franklin Delano Roosevelt to find a president or soon-to-be-president, so long near the helm of the policymaking apparat as Taft. Taft served as head of the Philippine Commission, governor–general of the Philippines (or, as he later described it, pro-consul), secretary of war, and, finally, president. William McKinley might have been directed by God to acquire the Philippines, but it was Taft who went to the islands to work out the parameters of colonial policy. Teddy Roosevelt may have "taken" Panama, but it was Taft who administered the building of the canal. The same can be said with respect to a number of other countries—such as Cuba, Haiti, Nicaragua, Mexico, and China, to name several—where in those years the United States felt it necessary to intervene. Even if Taft was not always the actual architect of a given policy, he was entrusted with the task of executing it.

THE EMERGENCE OF "BIG BILL" TAFT

The Taft family was well connected to the Ohio Republican political organization that dominated late-nineteenth-century American politics. Taft was an amiable giant of a man, weighing over three hundred pounds. After graduation from Yale University in 1878 and the University of Cincinnati Law School two years later, Taft gravitated toward the law. He later remarked that, "[I]n my early married life, I told my wife that I was so fond of judicial work that if I could be made a Common Pleas Judge in Hamilton County in Cincinnati, I would be content to remain there all my life."[9] During the next twenty years, Taft was appointed to several judgeships—once even elected to the Superior Court—as he moved with distinction up the ladder of the judiciary. By the turn of the century, it was evident he had set his sights on the U.S. Supreme Court.

Jacob Gould Schurman, president of Cornell University, and head of the first Philippine Commission to the islands in 1899, characterized himself as a "reluctant imperialist."[10] The same might also be said of Taft. When Schurman announced that he

[9]Address before the National Geographic Society, Washington, D.C., November 14, 1913, cited in Donald F. Anderson, *William Howard Taft: A Conservative's Conception of the Presidency* (Ithaca, N.Y.: Cornell University Press, 1973), p. 7.

[10]Kenneth S. Hendrickson,"Reluctant Expansionist–Jacob Gould Schurman and the Philippine Question," *Pacific Historical Review* 36 (November 1967):

could no longer continue with the work, McKinley persuaded Taft to drop his anti-imperialist feelings and help in the work of administering the islands.[11] Elihu Root, at least, understood that Taft might appreciate a good career opportunity, and Taft used his leverage to secure the chairmanship of the second commission in February 1900, as the price of participation in what we now call "nation-building." Root stressed duty and obligations to the Republican Party and the nation as reasons for Taft accepting membership on the commission:

> You have always had your platter up. You have caught the offices that have fallen; you have had an easy time; you have done good work enough but now you have an opportunity to serve your country. You are at the parting of the way and the question is whether you are going to take the easy or the heavy task.[12]

In other words, the party was now calling in its dues. Taft's feelings about the wisdom of the Spanish–American War and his opposition to the annexation of the Philippine Islands cannot, however, have been very deeply felt. If so, they were overridden by his sense that this was an opportunity to move upward politically, perhaps even toward the Supreme Court.

SWEATING IT OUT IN THE PHILIPPINES

The tropical climate of the Philippines was always a major occupational hazard for Taft. He sweated a great deal, probably not much helped by wearing a Western-style business suit. With the severe discomfort of prickly heat and its accompanying itching, the budding pro-consul by 1903 had discovered the relative comfort, during the summer, of removing the seat of civil

---

408–10; Jacob Gould Schurman, *Philippine Affairs*, 2nd ed. (New York: Scribner's, 1902).

[11]In Taft's own mind, he may still have considered himself an anti-imperialist, simply carrying out American rule in the most "benevolent" way possible. Mrs. Taft apparently considered her husband, "the *most active* anti-imperialist of them all." Quoted in Morrell Heald and Lawrence S. Kaplan, *Culture and Diplomacy: The American Experience* (Westport, Conn.: Greenwood Press, 1977), p. 151 (emphasis added). Chap. 6, "Conscience and Consciousness in the Philippines: The Imperial Impulse, 1898–1903," pp. 124–58, discusses these events in detail.

[12]Quoted in Anderson, *William Howard Taft*, pp. 6–7.

government to Baguio City, about twelve hours' travel time into the mountains outside Manila. To justify the cost of that move, Taft spoke of "a place with a climate not unlike that of the Adirondacks, or Wyoming in the summer" that would make it possible to more easily function for ten months in Manila, curtail the need for vacations in America, "reduce the number who go invalided home," and serve as a place where "Filipinos of the wealthier class" might also vacation rather than taking the now-frequent visits to China and Japan.[13] Later Taft would also be hospitalized for the various problems associated with amoebic dysentery. No doubt these health problems were all part of what Rudyard Kipling had referred to as "the White Man's Burden"!

Some of Taft's adventures in the deepest tropics were downright comical. At one point he was touring some of the outer islands with a delegation including Congressman Henry A. Cooper of Wisconsin, chairman of the influential House Insular Affairs Committee, which was charged with writing important legislation for the Philippines. Cooper described an attempt to get "Big Bill" off the boat in a situation where there was no loading platform and the level of the boat deck was not the same as that of the dock. A number of Filipino dock workers attempted to hold a ladder as the not-so-agile Taft made his way down it, the ladder teetering over the water. It was comparable to a scene from a "Keystone Cops" film and not at all what might be called pro-consul splendor.[14]

By the time Taft arrived in the islands in 1900, the Philippine Insurgency was in full swing. As one might expect with two strong personalities, there were soon problems between Taft and General Arthur MacArthur, the army's commander in the Philippines. Students of Southern history can appreciate something of their differences. The army, like Abraham Lincoln and Andrew Johnson at the conclusion of the War for Southern Independence, was willing to accept those insurgents who had laid down their arms and taken an oath back into participation within the system. Taft and the civilian authorities, however, were

[13]Quoted in Charles Burke Elliott, *The Philippines: To the End of the Commission Government; A Study in Tropical Democracy* (Indianapolis, Ind.: Bobbs-Merrill, 1917), p. 295.

[14]See the Diaries of Henry A. Cooper (1899–1908) (Madison: Wisconsin Historical Society).

more like the Radical Republicans in wanting to create a Filipino participation that would readily accept an American definition of the colonial relationship because it understood that its legitimacy rested upon American power.[15]

Lesson one about empire might be that you have to be very careful about blundering into colonial rebellions that are also internal civil wars or revolutionary social situations. The situation in the Philippines, of which America's "benevolent imperialists" were essentially in "blissful ignorance," was not unlike the American Revolution, which, as Carl Becker put it long ago, was not only about home rule, but who would rule at home. The British found themselves in a colonial rebellion that also involved an internal struggle within the colonies.

After the Civil War, the South manifested many of the same tendencies. While Northern forces finally withdrew from occupying the South after 1877—twelve years after the war's end— the United States did not promise eventual independence to the Philippines until 1917; then, in 1934, make it a definite ten years hence; and, because of the intervention of World War II, not fulfill that promise until July 4, 1946. From Taft's perspective, our "Little Brown Brothers" could never have been ready for independence in such a relatively short period of time.

In view of our continued efforts in the twentieth century to help others with respect to self-determination—as long as their understanding of that term reflects an acceptance of doing things our way (something of a contradiction in concepts, of course)—it might be useful to reflect on these rival philosophies

---

[15]To my knowledge, the parallels between the Filipino Revolution and the aftermath of the American Civil War have not been much commented upon, but see Renato Constantino, *A History of the Philippines* (New York: Monthly Review Press, 1975) and Renato Constantino, *The Philippines: A Past Revisited* (Manila, 1975). The latter was the Introduction to Captain John R.M. Taylor's *Philippine Insurrection Against the United States*, 5 vols. (Manila: University of the Philippines 1975). Constantino notes that the Filipino Katipunan Society, which marked the emergence of the revolutionary movement toward independence, was very aware of the insurrectionary efforts of the Ku Klux Klan in the American South during and after Reconstruction, and stressed the "K" common in both names in talking and writing about the Klan. While late-twentieth-century "politically correct" writers in the United States might find this difficult to grasp, Filipino revolutionaries understood that, at its most fundamental level, the Klan was part of a Southern insurrectionary movement against Northern colonialism.

of encouraging and inducing social change in other societies, what today many rather statist-oriented sociologists call "state building capacity," that is, the ability of a bureaucracy to change a society.

In Western civilization, perhaps the first discussion of this issue came when the Jesuits and the Franciscan–Dominicans faced the question of relating to social change in another society, as the West began its extensive intercourse with China in the centuries after Marco Polo. The Jesuit approach was to work with the mandarin elite and to relate in terms of what was seen as somewhat similar concepts, such as Tien–Heaven. The Dominican idea was to take the hard-core, undiluted word to the masses. Unfortunately, the squabbles between the Christians and complaints back to Rome caused the emperors, in essence, to throw out Western religious ideas altogether.

The American approach in the Philippines was a rather eclectic mix of these philosophies. We offered widespread education to what we saw as the "inferior" masses, but we coupled this early on with working with a conservative native elite that had worked as comprador–scalawags with the Spanish, rather than attempting to assimilate more of the nationalists–revolutionists.[16]

---

[16]The author was reminded of these enormous ethnic and class divisions when he lectured in the Philippines under the auspices of the U.S. Information Service in 1981. After a talk before 1,500 businessmen at the Mikati Business Club, a group rather like the New York Chamber of Commerce, because of my Spanish last name, a former economics minister and Harvard Ph.D. in economics invited me to lunch at his club, an incredibly opulent and elegant building out of late-nineteenth-century Europe, where all the wives seemed to have just returned from shopping sprees in Madrid and Paris. He assured me the Spanish had endured the Americans, the "brown" Filipinos, the "yellow" Japanese, and then the Filipinos again, but would continue to prosper and endure in the islands. Their club reminded one of the Big Five Club in Miami, a consolidation of the clubs in Havana, which excluded a mulatto such as Fulgencio Batista, who never challenged those rules even when he governed Cuba.

Later this writer learned that the whole junket away from his position with the Joint Economic Committee in Washington had been concocted as an opportunity for American diplomats to liaison with the Aquino leadership. As he lectured on about Reaganomics, and other such arcane subjects, our state department personnel used the occasion to assure the Filipino dissidents that Vice President George Bush's "under the influence" recent rash embrace of Philippine President Ferdinand Marcos was a violation of their advice, and that our policy really was in the process of changing! So much for the notion that Vice President Dan Quayle was the only "loose cannon" in the later Bush administration.

By 1901, the Philippine Insurrection had been dampened by the capture of its leader, Emilio Aguinaldo, and Taft had been installed as the civil governor of the islands, a position in which he served, despite several severe illnesses, until his recall to Washington in 1904 to become secretary of war. By that time, he had established himself as one of the prime architects of American "state-building."

A second lesson of empire is that such systems of power require a large bureaucracy to carry out imperial policies and that, once in place, it is difficult to dismantle them. Thus, by early 1902, there were already 2,777 American civilian bureaucrats in the Islands, a majority over the 2,697 Filipinos, but this did not include the numerous American teachers in the Philippines or the large contingent of soldiers in the army of occupation needed to maintain "order."[17] The key bureaucratic institution with respect to American colonialism was the Bureau of Insular Affairs, or B.I.A., not to be confused with the Bureau of Indian Affairs.

Created early in December 1898 as the Division of Customs and Insular Affairs, the organization by 1902 had evolved into the B.I.A., functioning as a part of the War Department in a number of other areas of intervention such as Santo Domingo, Haiti, Nicaragua, even Liberia and elsewhere. As Secretary Root put it, the B.I.A. was performing "with admirable and constantly-increasing efficiency the great variety of duties which in other countries would be described as belonging to a colonial office."[18]

[17]Onofre D. Corpuz, *The Bureaucracy in the Philippines* (Manila: University of the Philippines, 1957), p. 178. There is a vast literature discussing various aspects of the U.S. effort at "state-building" in the Philippines. In addition to the two-volume study of W. Cameron Forbes, cited in the next note, see for example, Joseph Ralston Hayden, *The Philippines: A Study in National Development* (New York: Macmillan, 1935); Charles B. Elliott, *The Philippines: To the End of the Military Regime, with a Prefatory Note by Elihu Root* (Indianapolis, Ind.: Bobbs-Merrill, 1917), idem, *The Philippines: To the End of the Commission Government* (Indianapolis, Ind.: Bobbs-Merrill, 1917); Peter W. Stanley, *A Nation in the Making: The Philippines and the United States, 1899–1921* (Cambridge, Mass.: Harvard University Press, 1974); Bonifacio S. Salamanca, *The Filipino Reaction to American Rule, 1901–1913* (The Shoe String Press, 1968); and Garel A. Grunder and William E. Livezey, *The Philippines and the United States* (Norman: University of Oklahoma Press, 1951).

[18]W. Cameron Forbes, *The Philippine Islands* (Boston, Mass.: Houghton Mifflin, 1928), vol. 1, p. 136. It is interesting that, for a nation that prides

Except, of course, Root didn't mention that the American equivalent was under the control of the military.

As one might expect, as with any bureaucracy, there was never any shortage of new tasks in which to prepare the natives for self-government at some point in the distant future. The importance of the bureau is indicated by the fact that its chief was raised first to brigadier and then to major general by 1912. As we shall observe later, the B.I.A. was deeply involved in the whole currency exchange question, which later became the linchpin of the American empire.

All of these colonial ventures, of course, offered career opportunities not only for the military but also for budding American progressive-oriented public administrators, newly schooled in American universities in the science of politics and thus ready to explain the virtues of democracy to those less fortunate souls in Asia. In one report, Taft even suggested that the civil service in the Philippines was less corrupt than back in America, and he may well have been right! When these administrators returned from the Philippines and other of our colonial possessions, they could then turn their attention to making American government less corrupt and to expanding its size and power—noble endeavors, indeed!

Among the social problems in Filipino society under Spanish rule—apart from the numerous languages, religions, tribes, and ethnic groups inhabiting the islands—was the lack of opportunity for the native elite. Given the church's role in administering Spanish colonialism, the Philippine revolution in the 1890s was directly related to the closing-off of increased entry into, and mobility upward within, the church hierarchy for able Filipinos. This occurred as several orders were curtailed in Europe and Spanish priests were sent to sinecures in the islands.[19] The so-called

---

itself on a separation of civil government and the military, the military was from the beginning so involved in administering all of the territories that the United States had acquired, directly or indirectly, as a result of the Spanish–American War. Not only the Philippines, but also Puerto Rico, Guam, Panama, and even Hawaii and Cuba, along with military interventions in areas ranging from China to Haiti, came under the province of the War Department. As Anderson remarked, Taft "was a *de facto* colonial secretary," *Taft*, p. 13.

[19]For a discussion of the role of elites in the revolutionary process, see, William Marina, "The American Revolution and the Minority Myth,"

Friar Lands, the extensive holdings of the church in the Islands, was one of the major areas of contention in the Philippine situation. Taft visited the Vatican in an effort to help settle this question, and, although unsuccessful in the short run, this did later lead to the church's disposing of the greater portion of these lands. That meant the Filipinos would have access to these vast land holdings.

There is not space here to detail all of Taft's actions during his four years of "empire-building" in the Philippines. Then, and later as secretary of war and finally as president, he never seemed to understand that you have to allow your comprador–scalawag to have legitimacy and credibility before his own people. Taft's papers and the files of the B.I.A. are filled with letters in which he seemed never to comprehend his conservative Filipino friends' explanations that some of their public words should not be taken literally as "anti-American," but as necessary to retain their credibility in the face of attacks by nationalists such as Manuel Quezon. Or as Franklin Roosevelt put it so succinctly from an "empire man's" perspective, speaking of Trujillo, although applicable to any number of American comprador–Scalawags, "He may be an SOB, but he's our SOB!"

We perhaps shouldn't judge Taft too harshly, however, in his inability to understand that one could be pro-American and a Filipino nationalist as well. In the 1940s and after, John Foster Dulles and numerous other American policymakers couldn't fathom the notion that Mao Tse-tung and Ho Chi Minh, among others, could be both nationalists and communists at the same time and could conceive of Chinese or Vietnamese national interests outside of the Soviet Union's own rather nationalistic version of "international communism."

We ought to welcome that failure on Taft's part, because it allowed the anti-imperialists, the Democrats (many were both, such as Cordell Hull), and the Filipino nationalists to advance the agenda toward a more rapid promise of eventual Philippine independence than men like Taft could ever have accepted. The British, in India and elsewhere in Asia, were infuriated that nationalists like Gandhi immediately asked, if the Americans could move the Philippines so rapidly toward independence, why could not the British do likewise?

Modern Age (1976); and idem, "Revolution and Social Change," *The Literature of Liberty* II (1978), pp. 1–39.

From a longer historical perspective, one of Taft's greatest policy failures with respect to the Philippines was in 1908 and after, when he refused to allow the publication of Captain John R.M. Taylor's five-volume *History of the Philippine Insurrection*, which still can be found in galley proofs in the National Archives, although it was published some years ago in a limited edition in the Philippines. He blocked the publication to keep from embarrassing some former Filipino leaders, such as Emilio Aguinaldo, who were now cooperating with the United States.[20]

TAFT AND THE PANAMA CANAL

By the time Taft returned to Washington to assume his duties as secretary of war, the United States had acquired another possession, the Panama Canal Zone. Most Americans are familiar with Teddy Roosevelt's observation that while Congress debated, he "took" Panama. While some opponents of Empire—such as Moorfield Storey, president of the Anti-Imperialist League—protested against Roosevelt's blatant action, it ultimately fell to bureaucratic administrators like Taft to actually oversee the building of the canal.[21]

Roosevelt's outlook on law, or the lack thereof which characterizes the movement toward empire, was revealed in a cabinet meeting shortly after the acquisition of the Canal Zone. The president preached on at length, justifying his reasons for taking Panama and offering the usual moral arguments about saving Western civilization—always a sure warning that one is about to be presented with a justification for yet another

---

[20]In the 1930s, after Taft's death, Captain Taylor was still trying to get the work published in case the U.S. Army should ever find itself engaged in another guerrilla insurgency in Asia. The irony is, of course, that the United States did get involved in the suppression of another anticolonial insurgency in Asia, in Vietnam from 1945 until 1975. The ultimate American victory in the Philippines was aided enormously by the facts that the Filipino elite was divided within itself and that Filipino nationalism had not developed into the kind of movement that would sustain a "people's war." Conditions were quite different in Vietnam.

[21]Storey's anti-imperialist critique of Theodore Roosevelt's actions was contained in a small pamphlet entitled, *The Recognition of Panama* (Boston: Geo. H. Ellis, 1903). For a more extended discussion of the Panama question at that time, see William Marina, "Opponents of Empire: An Interpretation of American Anti-Imperialism, 1898–1921" (doctoral dissertation, University of Denver, 1968).

government intervention! In any event, Roosevelt turned to then-secretary of war Root and asked, "Well, Elihu, have I justi-fied myself?" to which Root, a conservative and realist in foreign policy, replied, "Yes, Teddy, you certainly have! You were accused of seduction; you have proved conclusively, you were guilty of rape."[22]

Conceding Taft's role in the building of the canal, as one his-torian has put it perhaps a bit too strongly, Roosevelt could brag that he "took" the Canal Zone, but Taft could have responded, "But I built the Canal."[23] Here again, what needs to be recog-nized is the bureaucratic dimension of "empire-building." Roo-sevelt fully understood the importance of Taft and Root in mak-ing policies and in administering the growing imperial edifice that McKinley had begun and that he had also carried forward. He was profuse in his praise of both men. "If only there were three of you!" he exclaimed to Taft, "Then I would have put one of you on the Supreme Court . . . one of you in Root's place as Secretary of War . . . [and] one of you permanently as Governor General of the Philippines."[24]

The building of the canal has legitimately been described as one of the great engineering triumphs of the world, made pos-sible by the subsequent virtual elimination of yellow fever.[25] But moral and legal considerations, such as Moorfield Storey's,

[22]Recounted in Philip C. Jessup, *Elihu Root* II (Hamden, Conn.: Archon Books, [1938] 1964). Much of the material in this section is taken from William Marina, "From Rape to Seduction: Panama and the Shifting Strat-egy of the American Empire," *Reason* (January 1978): 33, 35, 38, 50. What could not be anticipated, however, in 1978, was that in 1989 President George Bush would again turn to interventionist "rape" in Panama on a scale that made Theodore Roosevelt appear as a rather "modest imperialist." The Pentagon has yet to formally acknowledge that perhaps 4,000 Pana-manians were killed in the effort to abduct President Manuel Noreiga and try him for drug trafficking. Critics have suggested that the manner in which this was done, as well as the nature of his trial, were intended to cover up American involvement in such activities.

[23]Anderson, *William Howard Taft*, p. 18.

[24]Ibid., p. 12.

[25]On the building of the Canal, see David McCullough. *Path Between the Seas: The Creation of the Panama Canal, 1870–1914* (New York: Simon and Schuster, 1977); and William Friar, *Portrait of the Panama Canal: From Con-struction to the Twenty-First Century* (New York: Graphic Arts, 1999).

aside, Americans have seldom questioned whether building the canal really made good economic sense.

Those arguing for more government intervention have always had a "gut" understanding that Americans are "suckers" for anything that has a technologically challenging dimension to it. The French couldn't build a canal, but we could! If somebody else was able to build the "bomb," they must have stolen the "secret" from us! If "they" have unmanned space vehicles, then we can and should build manned ones, or perhaps a space shield which, after the expenditure of $60 billion dollars and counting, is still far from reality.

Recall that at the time of the canal debate in 1978, that great patriotic presidential candidate, Ronald Reagan was almost accusing President Jimmy Carter of treason for daring to negotiate a treaty that would take down the American flag in the sacred Canal Zone before the end of this century. Reagan claimed to be for capitalism, along with motherhood and apple pie, but fundamentally he was just a late-twentieth-century "jingoist" and socialist. The building of the canal was one of the greatest socialist endeavors in American history, and its operation shows how an imperial bureaucracy's interests, with the passage of time, can become institutionalized.

In 1855, the Vanderbilt interests constructed a railroad across the Isthmus of Panama that operated until the canal opened in 1914, paying a nice dividend to its investors through all the years of its existence. Today, of course, in an age of shipping and railroad containerization, we have more than a dozen such railroad "bridges" from Canada southward, linking trade between the Atlantic and Pacific oceans.

Most Americans are unaware that, due to cave-ins, etc., we have dug out more dirt between 1914 and today than we excavated in originally building the canal. The dig-out of 1975, when one of the hills collapsed into the canal, cost American taxpayers $175 million. The canal has always been an American taxpayer subsidy to the shipping industry, especially the American one, and has never paid for itself.

One could say, as Theodore Roosevelt did, that it was all for the benefit of Western civilization, but in the late 1970s, when this writer last checked, the major canal users were Japanese ships hauling iron ore from Brazil to Osaka to build Toyotas and other such items needing steel. But on February 8, 1904, when the Japanese sprang their brilliant surprise attack on the czarist Russians, Theodore Roosevelt was among those Americans applauding the Asians' clever use of "pre-owned" battleships, as if they had somehow joined Western civilization! Obviously, we didn't see things the same way on December 8, 1941, and it was rather ironic that the U.S. was still indirectly subsidizing Japan through the canal in the 1970s and after.

Indeed, the only major entity that made a true market analysis of the canal in 1978 was not Ronald Reagan but *Forbes* magazine, that "tool" of the capitalists, pointing out how much cheaper in most cases railroad bridging was than paying a unionized crew to sail down south, wait to move through the lock system where there was a growing shortage of water from Lake Gaitan, and then sail back north with the cargo.

One suspects that had we never built the Canal, another railroad or two would have sprung up to compete with the Vanderbilt business before the Antitrust Division of the Justice Department would have gotten around to accusing the Vanderbilt interests of maintaining a monopoly, but one can never be certain about such things!

The only viable argument for America's twentieth-century "canal socialism" was a military one, which captured Theodore Roosevelt's public relations fancy after the battleship *Oregon* was forced to sail "around the Horn" as clipper ships had done sixty years before. That viability, however, began to erode after 1945, as aircraft carriers replaced battleships, and our largest warships thus could not navigate the canal, even though their support ships could do so.

Unlike our relatively quick departure from the Philippines, we have associations in this country consisting of hundreds of retirees from the canal bureaucracy, many of them generations of "Army brats" born and raised there. It is understandable, more so than with Reagan in 1978, that as time to relinquish the canal approached, they had emotional difficulties in dealing with the reality of this particular example of bureaucratic socialism. Environmental problems aside, if there is no hidden American financial subsidy into the twenty-first century, it will be interesting to see how long the canal can "compete" with railroad bridging.

TAFT AND CUBA

Taft's policies toward Cuba, both as secretary of war and as president, also reflect his role in the emergence of the American empire. It is, of course, impossible to assess how his experience as governor general in the Philippines, virtually an "oriental potentate" in the view of some anti-imperialists, affected his administrative style both in the cabinet and in the presidency. But recall that the major reason for what became a campaign for empire at the turn of the century was the American crusade to "free" Cuba from the cruel yoke of the Spanish Empire, a crusade that ultimately included the Philippines and Puerto Rico as well.[26]

From the standpoint of many Cuban revolutionaries then, and certainly a number of Cuban historians since, the United States had moved toward war with Spain precisely because it perceived that the revolutionists were on the verge of victory. From the American perspective, a radical revolution with strong black participation and support, not only might pose a challenge to the United States's hegemony in the Caribbean, but it was certainly not a good example for a society bent on establishing a post-Civil War segregationist policy at home.

By the time McKinley led the nation toward a declaration of war against Spain, the Congress had passed the Teller resolution, disclaiming "any disposition or intention to exercise sovereignty, jurisdiction or control" over Cuba except for its pacification.[27] The motives for the resolution were varied, ranging from Southerners who did not wish to see more "inferior" peoples incorporated into the American union; to agriculture interests, such as the sugar producers in Colorado represented by Senator Henry Teller; to idealistic Americans who genuinely believed that the United States should support movements for self-determination around the world.

In the aftermath of the war itself, as Taft was making his decision to head the Philippine Commission, events were also

---

[26]Under Spain, Puerto Rico had representatives in the Cortes. In bringing the island "the blessing of liberty," the U.S. has allowed observers to the Congress.

[27]The American promise of independence to Cuba in 1898 had influenced the Filipinos to believe they could obtain a similar promise, but for American policymakers, "independence" always included intervention, whenever that was deemed necessary.

moving forward in Cuba. As with the Philippines, a decision had been made to retain a "standing army" there as a means of insuring stability, law and order, on the assumption that the Cuban revolutionaries were incapable of doing so.[28] The inevitable social clashes between Cubans and members of this "Gringo" occupying force, were not unlike those between southerners and the northern occupation forces some three decades earlier in the United States. It greatly enhanced feelings of Cuban nationalism and self-determination much as had British occupation of Boston after 1774. Before the Spanish–American War, there had for years been a segment of American planters and conservative Cubans that favored annexation by the United States to keep the more radical elements of the island under control. The occupation had the effect of rather quickly muting expressions of that view.

American policy ultimately took form in the Platt Amendment, authored by Senator Orville Platt of New York, a member of the imperialist group. The Platt Amendment clearly reflected the outlook of another New Yorker, Secretary of War Elihu Root, who had written the guidelines for American rule in the Philippines. Its provisions effectively made Cuba a protectorate of the United States, providing for United States intervention if deemed necessary.

It took the election, and reelection, of several constituent assemblies before a vote accepting "la Emienda Platt" was secured. The ensuing problems with those arrangements carried over into Taft's years as secretary of war and as president, and as a major factor in the ongoing tensions that have characterized Cuban–American relations for decades. American troops left after the acceptance of the amendment but would return in the years ahead as support to colonial administrators. It is impossible to explain the continued, if declining, appeal of socialist dictator Fidel Castro to the Cuban people outside of this massive American military, political, and economic intervention in Cuba through the twentieth century. That nationalistic, anti-imperialist, social cement, which this country continues to reinforce, is about the only appeal Castro has left.

---

[28]Most Cuban historians long ago concluded that the U.S. intervened in 1898 to prevent a victory of the revolutionaries over Spain.

Since some Filipino leaders also advocated a protectorate as preferable to annexation, the Cuban experience suggests there would also have been problems with the Philippines, although of a different kind, from the resulting insurgency and ensuing American colonial rule. It was not long before the United States was presented with complaints from American business interests that the Cuban government was discriminating against them. American officials had to make it clear they would not intervene in that instance, but this revealed the difficulties inherent in any protectorate relationship.

In 1906, the United States had to intervene again in Cuba. By that time, Taft was serving as secretary of war and Root had moved on to secretary of state. Since the latter was on an extended goodwill tour of Latin America, Taft was dispatched to Cuba to deal with a situation in which President Estrada Palma threatened to resign unless the United States intervened to help him maintain law and order in the face of growing discontent.

Roosevelt and Taft were extremely interactive during these formative years of the empire, but they held very different views about law and governmental powers, as revealed with respect to the crisis in Cuba. A letter to Taft is indicative of Roosevelt's views about the presidency and illustrates what has become the norm for the modern presidency:

> If it becomes necessary to intervene I intend to establish a precedent for good by refusing to wait for a long wrangle in Congress. You know as well as I do that it is for . . . the enormous interest of this Government to strengthen and give independence to the Executive in dealing with foreign powers, for a legislative body, because of its very good qualities in domestic matters, is not well fitted for shaping foreign policy on occasions when instant action is demanded. Therefore, the important thing to do is for a president who is willing to accept responsibility to establish precedents which successors may follow even if they are unwilling to take the initiative themselves.[29]

Taft was a good subordinate and usually went along with the president's expansion of the executive powers, but his decision to preserve the constitutional continuity of the Palma

---

[29]Roosevelt to Taft, September 17, 1906, in *Theodore Roosevelt Papers* (Washington, D.C.: Library of Congress).

government again demonstrated the differences between the two Americans that would become increasingly evident once Taft assumed the presidency. As Roosevelt wrote:

> Upon my word, I do not see that with Cuba in the position it is we need bother our heads much about the exact way in which the Cubans observe or do not observe so much of their own Constitution as it does not concern us. . . . Neither do I understand why the fact that [the] government is not within the Constitution as you state, would alter your control of the situation for pacification.[30]

The politically astute Roosevelt understood that Americans had grown tired of the burden of neo-colonial interventionism. Having been awarded a Nobel Peace Prize, the president was already looking for more heroic areas of challenge. It was the legalistic Taft who was left to deal with the problems of empire. Actually, he was more sympathetic to the liberals in Cuba, describing the conservative Palma in a letter to Mrs. Taft as "a good deal of an old ass," but he ended up supporting the Cuban president.[31]

TAFT AND ANTITRUST

Although the major focus here is on Taft's involvement in the bureaucratic expansion of government into the empire abroad, it would be remiss not to mention one of the areas in which he continued that same approach at home: antitrust policies. It was Taft who bureaucratized the whole area of antitrust, adding considerably to the government's staff of trustbusters. Where Roosevelt had precipitated a few confrontations to gain publicity and had negotiated with businessmen at a personal level, Taft initiated far more cases and sought to legally rationalize what was essentially an irrational procedure.[32]

---

[30]Ibid.

[31]To Helen H. Taft, September 17, 1906, in ibid.

[32]A good summary of the bureaucratic expansion of antitrust under Taft is chap. 8, "A 'Nonreform': The Antitrust Crusade," in *The Presidency of William Howard Taft*, Paolo E. Coletta (Lawrence: University Press of Kansas, 1973).

TAFT'S FOREIGN POLICY—
NOT DOLLAR DIPLOMACY, BUT CURRENCY EXCHANGE

While Taft's early career, and even into his presidency, was associated with the development and administration of the emerging American colonial empire, during his years in the Oval Office he also initiated what was known as "dollar diplomacy," supposedly the substitution of "dollars for bullets." At first glance, this would appear to be an improvement over the water torture and other such methods used in the subjugation and acquisition of outright colonial possessions.

While a number of studies have explored dollar diplomacy with respect to China, Mexico, Nicaragua, and several other nations, in the view of this writer, they seemed to have missed the mark in understanding the larger dimensions of Taft's policies—which were, in fact, precursors of what would become the main thrust of American foreign policy for the rest of the century.[33]

The only historian to fully grasp the link between the American empire's evolving domestic policies and its emerging foreign policies, known under Taft as dollar diplomacy, was the great Austrian economic theorist and economic historian, Murray N. Rothbard. At the time of his death, Rothbard had begun not only to develop a reinterpretation of the origins of imperialism but to fit its development into the whole banking and currency question in the late-nineteenth and early-twentieth centuries.[34] His analysis suggests that what has been termed dollar diplomacy cannot be understood outside of the framework of elite bankers, lawyers, and policymakers who were pressing for a central banking system that was ultimately known as the Federal Reserve and that was virtually in place by the time that Taft left office early in 1913. As Rothbard observed:

---

[33]See, for example, Walter and Maria V. Scholes, *The Foreign Policies of the Taft Administration* (Columbia: University of Missouri Press, 1970); Coletta, *The Presidency of William Howard Taft*; and Anderson, *William Howard Taft*. Unfortunately, the great revisionist historian, William Appleman Williams, in his well-known, *The Tragedy of American Diplomacy* (New York: Delta Books, 1962), p. 68, mentions Taft rather briefly in moving from Theodore Roosevelt to Woodrow Wilson.

[34]Murray N. Rothbard, "The Origins of the Federal Reserve," *The Quarterly Journal of Austrian Economics* 2, no.3 (Fall 1999): 3–51. The discussion of imperialism and currency exchange covers pp. 19–35.

The years shortly before and after 1900 proved to be the beginnings of the drive toward the establishment of a Federal Reserve System. It was also the origin of the gold-exchange standard, the fateful system imposed upon the world by the British in the 1920s and by the United States after World War II at Bretton Woods. Even more than the case of a gold standard with a central bank, the gold-exchange standard establishes a system, in the name of gold, which in reality manages to install coordinated international inflationary paper money.[35]

Even before the turn of the century, a number of American intellectuals, including Brooks Adams, Henry Adams, Admiral Alfred Thayer Mahan, and Senator Henry Cabot Lodge, were involved in justifying some kind of expansionism, economic imperialism, and even colonialism, if necessary, to sustain the nation's prosperity. Thus, as Rothbard pointed out, "what would later be called the 'Leninist' theory of capitalist imperialism . . . was originated not by Lenin but by advocates of [American] imperialism.[36]

It would be difficult to improve upon Rothbard's summation of the thesis developed by these Americans, later popularized by the English economist John A. Hobson and subsequently modified by Lenin:

> The idea was that capitalism in the developed countries was "overproducing," not simply in the sense that more purchasing power was needed in recessions, but more deeply in that the rate of profit was therefore inevitably falling. The ever-lower rate of profit from the "surplus capital" was in danger of crippling capitalism, except that salvation loomed in the form of foreign markets and especially foreign investments. New and expanded foreign markets would increase profits, at least temporarily, while investments in undeveloped countries would be bound to bring a high rate of profit.[37]

Thus, a program of imperialism was necessary to open up these countries to both American products and investments. The writer who first put forward this view, based upon the erroneous assumption of David Ricardo and others "that the rate of

[35]Ibid., p. 19.
[36]Ibid.
[37]Ibid., p. 20.

profit is determined by the stock of capital investment" rather than "by the time preferences of everyone in society," was the economic writer Charles Conant.[38]

Conant saw the Philippines as the opening wedge to American access to the markets of Asia. Along with other statist advocates of empire, he argued that internally the nation would have to be transformed to make its operation as "efficient" as possible. This, of course, meant a vast centralized concentration of power along the lines of Czarist Russia, including an amending of the Constitution to greatly expand the powers of the executive in the formulation of foreign policy.[39] Given such a program, if Theodore Roosevelt had not existed, it would have been necessary to invent him.

Perhaps equally important, as Rothbard describes in detail, these ideas were embraced by a number of economists in the newly emerging economics profession, such as John Bates Clark and Edwin R.A. Seligman of Columbia University and Arthur Twining Hadley of Yale. The outright colonialism and war in the Philippines posed a problem for some of these academics like Hadley, but none disagreed with the way in which such an agenda would increase the role of the economist in policymaking.

At the same time that Taft was going out to head up the administration of the Philippines, the American Economic Association (A.E.A.) was busy carrying out its own colonial "burden," publishing a volume of *Essays in Colonial Finance*, almost half of which was underwritten by five corporate sponsors who all had a stake in the emerging empire. Thus, as Rothbard comments, not only was the A.E.A. "wholeheartedly in favor of the new American empire," but economists "were willing and eager to play a strong role in advising and administering the empire, a role which they happily filled."[40]

In less than a decade after the splendid little adventures of 1898—what with a bloody and costly insurrection in the Philippines and the anti-imperialist critics—the politicians and the public had come to see the "burden" of colonialism as not a very good bargain. Even protectorates and continued interventionism,

---

[38]Ibid.

[39]Ibid., p. 21, citing David Healy, *U.S. Expansionism: The Imperialist Urge of the 1890s* (Madison: University of Wisconsin Press, 1970), pp. 202–03.

[40]Ibid., p. 25.

such as in Cuba, were costly, and politicians like Roosevelt had found them less appealing.

The groups that really benefitted from imperialism were the burgeoning bureaucracies that included such seemingly-diverse groups as the military and its associated contractors; the B.I.A. within the military; all the administrators and business interests associated with such undertakings as the Panama Canal; the banking interests; especially those pushing for a central banking system; the newly emerging public administrative class seeking jobs both here and abroad; and their academic mentors building such programs in the universities, the economics profession which saw a leadership role for itself in the empire, and the various religious groups that early on had pushed for an imperial involvement. This emerging situation meshes rather nicely with the interpretation of imperialism developed by Ludwig von Mises and will be discussed in greater detail below.

What Rothbard cogently demonstrated was that, even with the problems inherent in colonialism and neo-colonialism, the imperialist theorists, especially Conant, understood that control of money, of the currency, was essential. With respect to Asia, this had been evident before the Industrial Revolution in the West and had made the latter's manufactured goods cheaper than those of India or China. But Asia also had many luxury items, ranging from silk to jade, and a number of raw materials and spices such as tea to trade to the West. For centuries, the East had drained specie from the West, and the latter was always searching for new products or techniques to redress the balance. What the British had discovered a century before was that Indian opium was a wonderful means to change the terms of the trade with China.

At the dawn of the twentieth century, despite its political humiliations, the economies of nations such as China were far from dead, and the monetary system was still soundly based upon silver. The acquisition of colonial possessions gave the imperialists an excellent opportunity to advance their currency exchange schemes. Rothbard offers an excellent description of how this was carried out in the newly acquired Puerto Rico, where the Spanish had already begun to debase the currency in 1895.[41]

[41]Ibid., p. 26.

The Philippines presented a greater problem because that country, like much of the Far East, was "happily using a perfectly sound silver currency, the Mexican silver dollar."[42] With Taft already in the Philippines, Secretary of War Elihu Root, who sometimes functioned as J.P. Morgan's personal attorney, got the B.I.A., America's military colonial service, to hire none other than Charles Conant, the theorist of empire, to devise a currency scheme for the islands.

At the heart of his plan was a debased new silver coin. The seigniorage profit that the U.S. Treasury obtained from this debasement was deposited in a New York bank, where it then functioned as a "reserve fund" for the debased silver currency being minted in the Philippines. As Rothbard concludes: "Thus, the New York funds would be used for payment outside of the Philippines instead of as a coin or specie. Moreover, the U.S. government could issue paper dollars based on its new silver reserve fund."[43] It took several years for this plan to be approved by Congress, but by 1903 these inflationary blessings of imperialism were being passed on to our "little brown brothers" in the islands. Naturally, a whole host of economists and social scientists was necessary to carry out this policy, including Carl C. Piehn, Bernard Moses, and David P. Barrows of the University of California, as well as Edwin W. Kemmerer of Cornell. Most of these ideologues of Empire went on to write scholarly treatises on America's role in bringing Western ideas of civilization and liberty to the Filipinos.[44]

Rothbard also describes how the effort to carry out this kind of currency scheme was developed, with varying degrees of success, in a number of countries within the American imperial sphere, including Mexico, China, Cuba, and Panama.[45]

---

[42]Ibid., p. 27.

[43]Ibid.

[44]Ibid., pp. 27–29.

[45]Ibid., pp. 29–35. Rothbard remarks about the possible role of the currency struggle as a factor on the Mexican Revolution and the need for further research on this question. The same is true with respect to China. The Revolution broke out there, also in 1911, over the issue of railroad funding. The Western powers pushed for foreign funding through the central government which could more easily be controlled. Many Chinese favored decentralization and their own funding through the provincial governments. Sun Yat-sen was at the Brown Palace Hotel in Denver raising funds

From the perspective of this exploration of the role of Taft, it is important to note that he was in a central position within the bureaucratic policymaking apparat during these years to move things along to fruition, from the Philippines to the War Department, and then, as president. As Rothbard describes these developments, it was during Taft's presidency that the work on moving from these currency plans abroad to the Federal Reserve at home was virtually put in place, with the final phase beginning in 1911.[46]

TOWARD AN AUSTRIAN INTERPRETATION OF EMPIRE

Taft's career, both before and during his presidency, illuminates the role of bureaucrats and bureaucracy in the development of that kind of centralized statism known as imperialism and empire. Ideologues and various economic, religious, or other interests may initiate the process, but as the state becomes involved, the structure and process become heavily bureaucratized with groups whose agendas are quite different. Unlike the businessman's need to make a bottom-line profit, even if often with the help of government, a bureaucrat's prime goal is to extend his own power and influence within the system.

Taft's opportunism manifested itself in his moving from an opponent of empire to one of those bureaucrats who carried out and expanded the system. Hannah Arendt was correct. There is a certain banality to that kind of evil! Bureaucrats only carry out rules and orders, but often with a vicious kind of efficiency.

In a number of his works, Ludwig von Mises touched upon imperialism, often in a critique of Marxist interpretations of that phenomenon. His work that most closely parallels the description

---

when the revolt broke out, and he had to hurry home to put himself at the head of the revolutionary surge.

One is reminded of railroad funding in the United States and the coming of the Civil War. Modern supplysiders such as Jude Wanniski are still fighting this battle with respect to the World Bank and International Monetary Fund. See Jude Wanniski, *The Way the World Works* (Washington, D.C.: Regnery, 1998), especially the chapters dealing with "The Building of Empires," "The Breakdown of Bretton Woods," "The Third World on the Laffer Curve," and "Experiment in Puerto Rico."

[46]Ibid., pp. 35–51.

of bureaucracy and imperialism as discussed here is *Omnipotent Government: The Rise of the Total State and Total War*.[47] As cited above, Murray N. Rothbard has added greatly to our understanding of these developments.

These early twentieth-century efforts at empire through currency manipulation find their lineal descendants today in the World Bank and the International Monetary Fund. As the battle over empire continues into the twenty-first century, the task of Austrian economists and historians will be to continue to show the continuity of the policies to those of the past. The evolution of the imperial presidency has been a part of that story, but it is only one part of a whole civilization's evolution toward statism and empire.

[47](Spring Mills, Penn.: Libertarian Press, 1985). Rothbard's discussion of the Bureau of Insular Affairs in the development of American empire is suggestive of the need for a thorough study of the way in which the military planners and bureaucrats in that organization helped to administer the empire. In working in the Military Section of the National Archives many years ago and helping to construct an index to the ninety-six reels of microfilm of the Philippine Insurgent Records, which is still in use there, this author had a chance to read through huge amounts of the records of the B.I.A. As one might suspect in such a bureaucracy, there is no "smoking gun" revealing the extent to which this organization shaped policy, but there was no doubt that the staff was aware that presidents might come and go—Wilson might replace Taft, for example—but the continuity of American imperial policy would carry on, safely in their hands.

14

WOODROW WILSON'S
REVOLUTION WITHIN THE FORM

RICHARD M. GAMBLE

Declaring that "Woodrow Wilson was not a revolution-ary," University of Virginia President E.A. Alderman defended the Wilsonian legacy before a joint session of Congress convened specially on December 15, 1924, to hear the late president eulogized. Seeing himself somewhat in the role of Pericles praising the Athenian war dead, Alderman elevated his friend and fellow academic into the Progressives' eclectic Pantheon to join Washington, Jefferson, and Lincoln. He marveled, he said, at the "revolutionary transformation" that in so few years had taken Wilson from schoolteacher to president—a feat matched only by Lincoln's own meteoric and seemingly inexplicable rise to power. Typical of the Progressive spirit that persisted into the 1920s, Alderman praised Wilson for having redefined America as a "servant, a minister, a friend . . . among the nations" and for establishing his foreign policy on the principle of "service to humanity" rather than on selfish national interests. Indeed, Wilson had summoned America "to a crusade, not to a war."[1]

There was nothing startling or original in Alderman's claims; they merely echoed the definition of the war and of American destiny that Wilson himself had labored to infuse into the American soul. Wilson had never tired of referring to America as the servant-nation, chosen to bring light and liberty and peace to all the world. Consistent with the habit of mind of the nineteenth-century Romantic nationalists he so admired, Wilson deified the American state and its historical mission, applying to the United States the attributes of Christ and his atoning work—the promise and hope of the Incarnation secularized and

---

[1]Edwin Anderson Alderman, *Woodrow Wilson: Memorial Address* (Garden City, N.Y.: Doubleday, Page, 1925), pp. 39 and 41.

fulfilled.[2] Alderman's tribute recognized Wilson as the one who promised to make all things new. His Fourteen Points, for example, were intended to found "a new order and a new life" and held out the promise of "a new earth arising out of horror but ennobled by the sacrifice of millions."[3]

Despite this promise of a world transformed, however, Alderman pleaded that Wilson could not properly be classified as a revolutionary because, after all, he had devoted so much of his energy and imagination to building up institutions, such as the League of Nations, instead of "breaking up" institutions as a true revolutionary would do.[4] Nevertheless, Alderman closed his eulogy by likening Wilson to Martin Luther, to the English Puritan John Milton, and to the Romantic nationalist Giuseppe Mazzini—each of them either a religious or political revolutionary.[5]

To be sure, not all contemporary Americans joined in this panegyric to Wilson. In contrast to Alderman's Periclean praise of Wilson, essayist H.L. Mencken and the Old-Right poet Robinson Jeffers offered a scathing assessment of the fallen war president. With characteristic deadpan, Mencken referred to the president as the "late Messiah" and the "deceased Moses." Rather than praise Wilson's rhetorical skill, he lamented Wilson's remarkable finesse at "reducing all the difficulties of the hour to a few sonorous and unintelligible phrases, often with theological overtones." And what troubled Mencken most was that the American people had taken this man and his words so seriously.[6] The anti-imperialist Jeffers, in a poem dated the month of Wilson's death, wrote of the president's "huge delusion" that "the God of the stars needed [his] help."[7]

After a distinguished career as a college professor, president of Princeton, and one-term reform governor of New Jersey,

[2]See, for example, Wilson's praise of Giuseppe Mazzini in remarks he made in Genoa, Italy, on January 5, 1919. Arthur S. Link, et al., eds., *The Papers of Woodrow Wilson* (Princeton, N.J.: Princeton University Press, 1986), vol. 53, pp. 614–15.

[3]Alderman, *Woodrow Wilson*, p. 44.

[4]Ibid., p. 53.

[5]Ibid., p. 79.

[6]H.L. Mencken, "The Archangel Woodrow," in *A Mencken Chrestomathy* (New York: Alfred A. Knopf, 1949), pp. 248–51.

[7]Robinson Jeffers, "Woodrow Wilson," in *Robinson Jeffers: Selected Poems* (New York: Vintage Books, 1965), pp. 35–36.

Wilson was elected president in 1912, the first Democrat to occupy the White House since Grover Cleveland nearly two decades before. But Wilson's vision of the role and scope of government differed markedly from that of the minimal-state, anti-imperialist Cleveland. "There has been a change of government," Wilson announced in 1913 in the opening sentence of his First Inaugural. Government, he promised, would now "be put at the service of humanity."[8] Having preached the "New Freedom" in his campaign, his slate of successful reform legislation in his first term alone included the Underwood Tariff (1913), the Federal Reserve System (1913), the Federal Trade Commission (1914), the Clayton Antitrust Act (1914), and the Federal Farm Loan Act (1916). In the war emergency of his second term, moreover, he nationalized the railroads and the merchant marine and expanded the use of the new income tax beyond what even the most pessimistic Cassandra had predicted possible in the hands of an imperial president.

As Murray Rothbard observed in his essay "War as Fulfillment," World War I provided the opportunity that Progressives like Wilson needed to remold the American economy and mind, taking the nation decisively toward a command economy—what the Germans were then referring to in their mobilization effort as war socialism. The editors of the *New Republic*, close associates of Wilson's, boasted during the war that "We revolutionized our society."[9] Indeed, Wilson and the Democratic Congress dramatically expanded the government's powers in wartime, including military conscription (under the euphemism of "selective service"), and silenced their critics on the Left and the Right with selective enforcement of the Espionage and Sedition acts. The irony of this war to "make the world safe for democracy" in light of these violations of American freedoms and at the expense of the Constitution did not escape courageous critics.

Rothbard traced the Progressives' wartime agenda to the postmillennial pietist impulse "to make America and eventually the world holy, and thereby to bring about the Kingdom of God on

[8]*Papers of Woodrow Wilson*, vol. 27, pp. 148, 150.

[9]Quoted in Murray N. Rothbard, "War As Fulfillment," in *The Costs of War: America's Pyrrhic Victories*, John V. Denson, ed. (New Brunswick, N.J.: Transaction Publishers, 1997), p. 229.

Earth."[10] Rothbard was correct to see this link to the theological presuppositions then guiding the Social Gospel clergy and their political and academic allies as they built the modern interventionist state. But in Wilson's case the effort to create heaven on earth fits into the larger theological problem of political gnosticism identified by Eric Voegelin.[11] Wilson typifies the profile of the gnostic prophet. Gnosticism, in Voegelin's use of the word, is the modern attempt to infuse mundane, secular human history with the transcendent mission of the kingdom of God. The gnostic prophet is a leader, a saint, convinced of his own divine commissioning, who claims to know with utter certainty the direction and resolution of history, the inexorable movement of human affairs toward apocalyptic fulfillment. The gnostic prophet promises emancipation from the constraints of the past, the abolition of war and oppression, and the coming of universal and everlasting peace, justice, and righteousness.[12] The gnostics, Voegelin wrote, "will not leave the transfiguration of the world to the grace of God beyond history but will do the work of God himself, right here and now, in history."[13] They take into their own hands the remaking of the world. Moreover, they tend to divide the world into two camps—light and dark—and to interpret all political disagreements and wars as absolute struggles between the kingdom of God and the forces of Satan. Ordinary war becomes the Last Judgment, every battle becomes Armageddon.

Wilson was not the first of America's gnostic prophets. Abraham Lincoln's gnosticism, for example, is evident throughout his speeches. Citing the Gettysburg Address in particular, M.E. Bradford called Lincoln's rhetorical strategy a "rhetoric for continuing revolution."[14] This phrase applies equally well to Wilson, the heir of Lincoln's secularized revolutionary Puritanism. Wilson betrayed the same destructive tendency to use language to wage

[10]Ibid., p. 203.

[11]See esp. Eric Voegelin's *The New Science of Politics: An Introduction* (Chicago: University of Chicago Press, 1987).

[12]Ibid., p. 121.

[13]Ibid., p. 147.

[14]M.E. Bradford, "Lincoln, the Declaration, and Secular Puritanism: A Rhetoric for Continuing Revolution," in *A Better Guide Than Reason: Federalists and Anti-Federalists* (New Brunswick, N.J.: Transaction Publishers, 1994), pp. 185–203.

an ideological war of revolutionary implications. Wilson was a gnostic revolutionary at the most elemental level in that he wished to repeal the past by waging war against the institutions of the past, especially monarchy, multinational empires, and balance-of-power diplomacy.

Wilson's gnostic temperament was evident before the U.S. entered the war in 1917 and even before the outbreak of the European war itself in 1914. In the 1912 presidential campaign, for example, Wilson explained his internationalist creed: "I believe that God planted in us the visions of liberty . . . that we are chosen and prominently chosen to show the way to the nations of the world how they shall walk in the paths of liberty."[15] And in his first term, Wilson showed his faith by his works, intervening militarily in Mexico (1914), Haiti (1915), and the Dominican Republic (1916). His wartime speeches, such as his extravagantly praised "Peace Without Victory" address (January 22, 1917), the War Message (April 2, 1917), and the Fourteen Points (January 8, 1918), ache with millennial expectancy of the "final war" and the last crusade and burn with hyper-spiritualized, gnostic longings to escape from history, materiality, and contingency. Wilson distorted a rather conventional war, fought for conventional territorial and dynastic objectives, into something unrecognizable, into an apocalyptic transformation of human nature and reality.

One speech in particular reveals Wilson's temperament. On Independence Day 1918, just over a year after America's entry into the war and four months before the guns fell silent with the Armistice, Wilson addressed a gathering of the diplomatic corps at George Washington's tomb at Mount Vernon.[16] In the shadow of the architect of America's tradition of nonintervention and neutrality, Wilson performed the alchemy of his "rhetoric for continuing revolution." Clothed, like Lincoln, with the authority of the Fathers, Wilson's words, whether consciously or not, echoed the very language of the Gettysburg Address. Like Lincoln, he sought to interpret for his hearers the real meaning of the Declaration of Independence and the true intention of the Fathers within the context of the present war—namely, to interpret intervention not as a betrayal of America's traditions but as

[15]May 26, 1912, *The Papers of Woodrow Wilson*, vol. 24, p. 443.
[16]Ibid., vol. 48, pp. 514–17.

the inevitable fulfillment and universalization of those inherited principles. Washington and the other Founders, according to Wilson, had turned their back on the past and had looked ahead to the whole wide world: "A great promise that was meant for all mankind," Wilson explained, "was here given plan and reality." It was the duty of those present at Mount Vernon

> to conceive anew the purposes that must set men free. . . . It has been left for us to see to it that it shall be understood that they [the Founders] spoke and acted, not for a single people only, but for all mankind. We are in this war to fulfill the promise of their vision; having achieved our own liberty we are to strive for the liberties of every other people as well.[17]

Throughout this July fourth oration, Wilson's totalist mind was at work, expressing the unconstrained modern worldview that leads so easily to total war. "The past and the present are in deadly grapple," he continued. America was fighting for the "final" settlement; "There can be no compromise." As a minimal condition of peace, he promised, there must be "the destruction of every arbitrary power anywhere that can separately, secretly, and of its single choice disturb the peace of the world." Furthermore, a league of nations was required to "check every invasion of right." And, remarkably, he claimed that the Founders themselves would have approved of these universal principles. Moreover, in the past century the British themselves had witnessed the very revolutionary democratic principles that they had once opposed liberate their own peoples. But the work was not over, Wilson continued; "I stand here now to speak . . . of the spread of this revolt, this liberation, to the great stage of the world itself!" These were Wilson's revolutionary principles; "deathless," he called them, "and of the very stuff of triumph!"[18]

Unfortunately, Wilson did not confine his revolutionary principles to rhetoric. What the noted historian Christopher Dawson concluded about Cromwell's revolutionary army during the English civil wars was also true of Wilson. He worked for nothing less than the "translation of the conception of the Holy Community from an ecclesiastical ideal to a principle of revolutionary political action"—or, in Wilson's case, the translation

[17]Ibid., p. 515.
[18]Ibid., pp. 516, 517.

of the ideal of the Holy Community also into a principle of revolutionary *foreign policy*.[19] Wilson's redemptive impulse to save the Old World is the high-water mark of Progressive imperialism, even though he claimed to be the sworn enemy of empire. The American mission was defined no longer simply in terms of offering an example to Europe of liberty and successful self-government, but now as a divine calling to liberate Europe itself from its past, its institutions, its imperialism, and its system of alliances. As the "trustees of liberty," Americans had to wage war on behalf of others.[20] Wilson transformed the worthy principle of liberty for *us* into the limitless and bloody promise of liberty for *all*. And he aimed this policy at Central Europe with devastating and lasting consequences.

By his own admission, Wilson waged war from 1917 to 1918 not primarily out of fear for American security or to defend U.S. interests or honor, but rather out of a sense of mission and service to humanity in obedience to a divine appointment to destroy German autocracy in the name of democracy and peace, to end multinational empires in the name of self-determination for all peoples, and to transcend balance-of-power politics in the name of benevolence and brotherhood. With the advice of his closest unofficial adviser, Colonel Edward M. House, Wilson consistently differentiated between the German people and their government in order to undermine the legitimacy of the German monarchy. As historian Lloyd Ambrosius noted, in 1917 Colonel House "recommended an appeal to the German people against their government, for 'Imperial Germany should be broken down within as well as from without.'"[21] But Wilson needed little inspiration or encouragement from House. In his War Message of April 2, 1917, and then in a Flag Day speech the following June, Wilson had already claimed that the American people entered the war as "the sincere friends of the German people."[22]

---

[19]Christopher Dawson, *The Judgment of the Nations* (New York: Sheed and Ward, 1942), p. 49.

[20]Address to the officers of the Atlantic Fleet, August 11, 1917, *The Papers of Woodrow Wilson*, vol. 43, p. 429.

[21]Lloyd E. Ambrosius, *Wilsonian Statecraft: Theory and Practice of Liberal Internationalism during World War I* (Wilmington, Del.: Scholarly Resources, 1991), p. 101.

[22]*The Papers of Woodrow Wilson*, vol. 41, p. 526. In his Flag Day speech in 1917, Wilson said that "we are not the enemies of the German people. . . .

With this sort of sophistry, he was able to claim that he was waging war not against the people of Germany but only against their system of autocratic government. He delegitimized the German government as alien to its people, as a despotic master that had enslaved its own people. On August 11, 1917, Wilson spoke of being "anxious to see that [the German people] have their glad emancipation" from the German imperial ideology "imposed upon them." "We are fighting a thing, not a people," he reasoned. And the war against this "thing" knew no limits: "we intend," he said, "to see to it that *no other people* suffers a like limitation and subordination."[23]

The key point here, and a point directly relevant to our own troubled times, is that Wilson waged ideological warfare against a form of government and not just against its behavior. Wilson tried to defeat Germany from the inside out. As the antistatist essayist Randolph Bourne (who coined the phrase, "War is the health of the State") wrote concerning one of Wilson's speeches against the German government, it "implies that America is ready to pour out endless blood and treasure, not to the end of a negotiated peace, but to the utter crushing of the Central Powers, to their dismemberment and political annihilation."[24] This strategy was crucial to Wilson's revolutionary democratism and has become a defining feature of the ongoing Wilsonianism of the White House. The peace and freedom of the world, he had said in his war message, was threatened by "the existence of the autocratic governments," unaccountable as they were to "the will of their people."[25] Wilson clearly was at war with a system of government and at war to export another system of government in its place.

Wilson implemented this policy toward Germany in two key ways. First, by refusing to accept a mediated settlement once the U.S. entered the war, and, second, by working to dismember the Central Powers' multinational empires. When Pope

---

They are themselves in the grip of the same sinister power that has now at last stretched its ugly talons out and drawn blood from us." *The Papers of Woodrow Wilson*, vol. 42, p. 500.

[23]Address to the officers of the Atlantic Fleet, ibid., vol. 43, p. 429, (emphasis added).

[24]Quoted in Ambrosius, *Wilsonian Statecraft*, p. 103.

[25]April 2, 1917, *The Papers of Woodrow Wilson*, vol. 41, p. 523.

Benedict XV proposed a negotiated end to the war in the summer of 1917, Wilson declined his offer, noting that compromise was unimaginable when the free peoples were fighting against a vast, secret conspiracy to take over the world. Wilson refused to negotiate with the German imperial government, claiming that their word could not be trusted and that no covenant could be entered into with them.[26] As Germany faced imminent defeat in the autumn of 1918, Wilson forced a political revolution as a precondition of negotiations and peace.

In hindsight, it seems clear that a constitutional monarchy in Germany would have been a more responsible alternative to the forced creation of a republic. As historian John Lukacs concluded: "That this kind of ideological democratism was disastrous should be obvious in retrospect. Had the Kaiser abdicated in favor of his son and of a constitutional monarchy, Adolf Hitler may have remained unknown to the world."[27] Unfortunately, clear thinking about the consequences of America's entry into the Great War seems impossible. It has become unassailable orthodoxy, especially among neo-Conservatives, that it was the U.S. *withdrawal* from Europe after 1918—invariably demonized as a "retreat" or "lapse" into isolationism—and the U.S. refusal to join the League of Nations that opened the way for Hitler and precipitated World War II. But it is more historically demonstrable that America's entry into Europe in 1917 and Wilson's revolutionary "People's War," as he once called it, are the main culprits. Wilson sowed the seeds of World War II by guaranteeing political instability and creating a power vacuum in the heart of Europe.

Under Wilson's leadership, furthermore, the United States entered the European war not only to defeat the abstraction of "autocracy," but also to end multinational empires. Originally disclaiming any such intention, Wilson worked systematically to dismantle the empires of Germany, Austria–Hungary, and the Ottoman Turks, while simultaneously defending the virtues of the progressive, "enlightened" imperialism of Britain and the U.S. Despite his reputation then and since as an anti-imperialist, Wilson was not opposed to empire in principle; he was not

[26]August 27, 1917, ibid., vol. 44, pp. 57–59.

[27]John Lukacs, *Outgrowing Democracy: A History of the United States in the Twentieth Century* (Garden City, N.Y.: Doubleday, 1984), p. 226.

opposed to what could be called the "redemptive imperialism" of world service, but only to the retrograde, predatory variety practiced by Germany.[28] Wilson outlined his vision of the new world order in his well-received Fourteen Points Speech.[29] As prejudicial as these points were to the Central Powers of Germany, Austria–Hungary, and the Ottoman Empire, they did form the basis for an armistice in 1918, but they were accepted in desperation by defeated empires unwilling to trust their fate to vengeful European victors and not because they saw any wisdom in Wilson's ideological crusade.

The revolutionary implications of the Fourteen Points were well understood at the time—even by the American press. The New York *Tribune*, for example, responding the day after the speech, called Wilson's Fourteen Points "a second Emancipation Proclamation." "As Lincoln freed the slaves of the South half a century ago," the editors wrote, drawing the Progressives' inevitable analogy, "Mr. Wilson now pledges his country to fight for the liberation of the Belgian and the Pole, the Serb and the Rumanian."[30] The Fourteen Points were a direct effort to rearrange Europe, marking an unprecedented entry of the U.S. into European affairs and a further departure from America's traditional foreign policy of nonentanglement and nonintervention. For Wilson to claim repeatedly that he was *fulfilling* the intentions of the Founders was tragically absurd.

Among the Fourteen Points was Wilson's guarantee of government by the consent of the governed, or self-determination for all peoples—to his mind a universalization of the Declaration of Independence. Wilson used recognition of the nationalist aspirations of Czechoslovakia and Yugoslavia as means to defeat the Austro–Hungarian Empire from within. He recognized a de facto Czech–Slovak government in 1918—before the Armistice—as a

---

[28]A prime example of Wilson's defense of benevolent, humane imperialism is included near the end of his speech to a plenary session of the Paris Peace Conference on February 14, 1919, the speech he used to present the League Covenant. *The Papers of Woodrow Wilson*, vol. 55, p. 177. See also Wilson's vision of an empire of "service" in his speech to the U.S. Senate on July 10, 1919, ibid., vol. 51, pp. 435–36.

[29]Address to a joint session of Congress, January 8, 1918, ibid., vol. 45, pp. 534–39.

[30]Reprinted in John Randolph Bolling, ed., *The Chronology of Woodrow Wilson* (New York: Frederick A. Stokes, 1927), pp. 9–11.

cobelligerent against Germany and Austria–Hungary and insisted on Yugoslavia's "destiny" and rightful place among the "family of nations."[31] Near the war's end, he refused the Austrian monarchy's offer of "autonomy" for these two regions "and instead demanded their full independence."[32] The process of carving up eastern Europe did not begin with the postwar negotiations and settlements at Versailles. Wilson first used self-determination as a weapon of war, not as an instrument of peace. For these reasons, H.L. Mencken called the Fourteen Points' ideal of self-determination "hypocritical" and "a deliberate and successful device to divide and conquer" the German people.[33]

Historians who excuse Wilson's rhetorical excess and the impracticality of his millennial schemes tend to appeal to his idealism. But Wilson was dangerous precisely because of his idealism. In this regard, University of Virginia President Alderman said more than he realized in his eulogy when he observed that Wilson was "a master and in some sense a slave of ideas and ideals."[34] The tragedy for America's subsequent history is that Wilson enslaved his country to those same ideas and ideals. Such delusions led inevitably to the "perpetual war for perpetual peace" that Charles Beard prophetically warned about. Wilson provoked revolution in Europe, but, more important, he completed a revolution in America—a revolution in how we understand ourselves and our responsibility to the rest of the world.

The problem of Wilsonianism persists, and its dangers are not abstract. There are those who intend to see Wilsonian democratism revitalized in the post-cold war world. Neoconservative pundits in particular continue to dream under the spell of Wilson's gnostic theology of empire, conjuring with the magic words "democracy," "destiny," and "mission." Joshua Muravchik, in *Exporting Democracy: Fulfilling America's Destiny*, calls upon the United States to continue its crusade for global democracy now that the cold war is over.[35] His proposal is

[31]Wilson's reply to a note from Austria–Hungary, October 7, 1918. Excerpted in Bolling, et al., eds. *Chronology of Woodrow Wilson*, pp. 117–18.

[32]Holger H. Herwig, *The First World War: Germany and Austria–Hungary, 1914–1918* (London: Arnold, 1997), p. 436.

[33]*Prejudices: Fourth Series* (New York: Alfred A. Knopf, 1924), p. 202.

[34]Alderman, *Woodrow Wilson*, p. 48.

[35]Paperback, rev. ed. (Washington, D.C.: AEI Press, 1992).

frightening enough, but his reasoning is more alarming. He explains that America was founded on an "idea," that she has to be true to that idea, and that such fidelity means democratizing the world. If Americans don't crusade for global democracy then they are "selfish"—the worst epithet from the Progressive lexicon. Tony Smith's *America's Mission*, while a much more substantial and sophisticated work than Muravchik's, also advocates a renewal of America's global democratic mission primarily on the basis of national security and American interests, in the vain hope that a democratic world will be a world at peace and therefore a world safer for America.[36]

While loudly trumpeting the supposed blessings of America's mission, the proponents of Wilsonianism offer no serious consideration of what this crusade for global democracy has done and will do domestically to America's own free institutions. What are the costs of "exporting democracy"? What are the costs to America, or any nation for that matter, of pursuing a divine mission and serving as the Christ among nations? As critics of empire have been asking for the past century, what does this ideological imperialism do to the size of our government, to the burden of taxation, to the power of the presidency, to our own tradition of self-government, to our free-market economy, and to the moral character of our people? These are the questions William Graham Sumner and other anti-imperialists had the courage to ask in 1898 when it still seemed possible to prevent America's plunge into empire. These are the questions we must have the courage to ask again. We must reevaluate Wilson's place in the American Pantheon and recognize, in John Lukacs' words, that Wilson, not Lenin, "turned out to be the real revolutionary."[37]

[36]Tony Smith, *America's Mission: The United States and the Worldwide Struggle for Democracy in the Twentieth Century* (Princeton, N.J.: Princeton University Press, 1994).

[37]Lukacs, *Outgrowing Democracy*, p. 223.

15

FRANKLIN DELANO ROOSEVELT'S NEW DEAL: FROM ECONOMIC FASCISM TO PORK-BARREL POLITICS

THOMAS J. DILORENZO

Before the massive government intervention of the 1930s, all recessions were short-lived. The severe depression of 1921 was over so rapidly, for example, that Secretary of Commerce Herbert Hoover, despite his interventionist inclinations, was not able to convince President Harding to intervene rapidly enough; by the time Harding was persuaded to intervene, the depression was almost over. . . . When the stock market crash arrived in October 1929, Herbert Hoover, now the president, intervened so rapidly and so massively that the market adjustment process was paralyzed, and the Hoover–Roosevelt New Deal policies managed to bring about a permanent and massive depression.

—Murray N. Rothbard
America's Great Depression

The biggest economic myth of the twentieth century is the notion that President Franklin D. Roosevelt's unprecedented peacetime economic interventions "got us out of the Great Depression" and thereby "saved capitalism" from itself.[1] This tale was repeated frequently during the 1990s by the former Speaker of the U.S. House of Representatives, Newt Gingrich (R–Ga.), who said that FDR "did bring us out of the Depression" and was therefore "the greatest figure of the twentieth century."[2] Virtually every U.S. history book repeats this falsehood, despite readily-available evidence to the contrary.

In reality, FDR's economic policies made the Great Depression much worse; caused it to last much longer than it otherwise would

---

[1] I consider myself somewhat of an expert on the subject of government lies. See James T. Bennett and Thomas J. DiLorenzo, *Official Lies: How Washington Misleads Us* (Alexandria, Va.: Groom Books, 1992).

[2] Cited in Robert Higgs, "How FDR Made the Depression Worse," *The Free Market* (February 1995).

have; and established interventionist precedents that have been a drag on economic prosperity and a threat to liberty to this day.

WHAT RECOVERY?

Despite a doubling of federal government expenditures from 1933 (Roosevelt's first year in office) to 1940, the creation of dozens of new federal programs, and the direct employment of some ten million Americans in government "relief" jobs, the economy was basically no better off in 1938 than it was in 1933. Indeed, as will be discussed below, it was precisely *because* of all these programs and expenditures that the Great Depression dragged on until after World War II.

Table 1 shows the official U.S. unemployment rate from 1929—the year of the stock market crash—until 1940. As seen here, unemployment remained extraordinarily high for the first three years of FDR's first term.

Table 1
U.S. Unemployment Rate
(Percent of Civilian Labor Force), 1929–1940

Year	Unemployment Rate
1929	3.2%
1930	8.7
1931	15.9
1932	23.6
1933	24.9
1934	21.7
1935	20.1
1936	16.9
1937	14.3
1938	19.0
1939	17.2
1940	14.6

Source: U.S. Department of Commerce, *Historical Statistics of the United States* (Washington, D.C.: U.S. Government Printing Office, 1961), p. 73.

A short and shallow recovery was followed by the "Roosevelt recession" of 1938, where the unemployment rate shot back up from 14.3 percent to 19.0 percent in a single year as a result of what economist Benjamin Anderson called a "sudden, extraordinarily severe and precipitous break both in the volume of business and in stock market prices running through autumn 1937 and into spring 1938."[3] There were more than ten million unemployed Americans in 1938, compared to eight million in 1931, the year before Roosevelt's election.

The average rate of unemployment during the 1933–1940 period was 17.7 percent—more than five times the 1929 level. In terms of unemployment, FDR never did "end" the Great Depression. (Conscripting millions of men and sending them to an overseas war subjected them to a fate much worse than temporary unemployment.)

Table 2
Per Capita GNP, 1929–1940

Year	Per-Capita GNP
1929	$857
1930	772
1931	721
1932	611
1933	590
1934	639
1935	718
1936	787
1937	846
1938	794
1939	847
1940	916

Source: U.S. Department of Commerce, *Historical Statistics of the United States* (Washington, D.C.: U.S. Government Printing Office, 1961), p. 139.

The government's own per-capita GNP statistics also reveal that, in terms of aggregate production, there was no recovery until after World War II was ended and a massive reduction in government expenditures and employment occurred. As seen in Table 2, per-capita GNP did not recover to its 1929 level until

[3]Benjamin M. Anderson, *Economics and the Public Welfare: A Financial and Economic History of the United States, 1914–1946* (Indianapolis, Ind.: Liberty Press, 1979), p. 474.

1940, and even then, just barely so. Moreover, by 1940 government statistics on GDP were virtually useless as a basis of determining the extent, if any, of economic recovery; much of the
U.S. economy was being redirected toward wartime production,
and the economic data were distorted by price controls.

Data on personal consumption expenditures tell the same
story: There was no economic recovery. Table 3 shows that personal consumption expenditures were approximately 8 percent
less in 1940 than they were in 1929.

Table 3
Personal Consumption Expenditures, 1929–1940 ($billions)

Year	Total Consumption Expenditures
1929	$78.9
1930	70.9
1931	61.3
1932	49.3
1933	46.4
1934	51.9
1935	56.3
1936	62.6
1937	67.3
1938	64.6
1939	67.6
1940	71.9

Source: U.S. Department of Commerce, *Historical Statistics
of the United States* (Washington, D.C.: U.S. Government
Printing Office, 1961), p. 179.

There was also a massive reduction in private capital investment. From 1930 to 1940, net private investment was *minus* $3.1
billion, as Americans failed to add anything to their capital stock.[4]
No economy can grow without capital accumulation. American
manufacturing equipment had grown so obsolete that by 1940,

[4]Robert Higgs, "Regime Uncertainty: Why the Great Depression Lasted So
Long and Why Prosperity Resumed After the War," *Independent Review*
(Spring 1997): 561–90.

70 percent of all metalworking equipment was over ten years old, a 50 percent increase over the 1930 level of obsolescence.[5]

The American recovery from the Great Depression was also more sluggish and slower to emerge than in most European nations. By 1937, Great Britain's unemployment rate had declined to 10.3 percent (4 percentage points below the U.S. rate), for example.[6]

It is foolish to argue that World War II ended the Great Depression, as most economists and historians have done. Sure, unemployment was virtually ended when more than twelve million men were conscripted into the armed services, but this cannot be interpreted as a return to prosperity. Consumer goods production was replaced by the production of military goods; price controls were pervasive; and rationing was imposed for consumer goods. Consequently, economic data on GNP and inflation during the war years are useless as barometers of economic health. As of 1940, the economy had not recovered from the Great Depression, and for the next six years economic data were essentially useless. Consumer welfare continued to *decline* during the war years.

It was not until 1947, when the wartime economic controls ended and government spending and employment levels fell dramatically, that prosperity was restored.[7] Federal government expenditures fell from $98.4 billion in 1945 to $33 billion by 1948, the first full year of genuine recovery.[8] Keynesian economists expected a two-thirds reduction in government spending to lead to another depression, and they were dead wrong. With the price controls and rationing schemes of the war years out of the way and with the dramatic reduction in government spending, the private economy quickly blossomed. Private-sector production increased by almost one-third in 1946 alone, as private

[5]Ibid.

[6]Richard K. Vedder and Lowell E. Gallaway, *Out of Work: Unemployment and Government in Twentieth-Century America* (New York: Holmes and Meier, 1993), p. 129.

[7]Robert Higgs, "Wartime Prosperity? A Reassessment of the U.S. Economy in the 1940s," *Journal of Economic History* (March 1992): 41–60.

[8]*Historical Statistics of the United States* (Washington, D.C.: U.S. Government Printing Office, 1961), p. 711.

investment boomed for the first time in eighteen years and corporate share prices soared.[9]

WHAT DID FDR DO?: THE "FIRST NEW DEAL"

Historians distinguish between FDR's First New Deal (1933–1934) and his Second New Deal (1935–1938). Dozens of new federal laws and programs were initiated during the First New Deal, including the creation of the Civilian Conservation Corps, Federal Emergency Relief Administration, and Tennessee Valley Authority. But the crowning "achievements" of FDR's first two years in office were the National Industrial Relations Act (June 16, 1933) and the Agricultural Adjustment Act (May 12, 1933).

In *The Roosevelt Myth*, John T. Flynn devotes his sixth chapter to "The Dance of the Crackpots," which describes many of the quite literally crackpot ideas that were widely discussed in Washington during the early 1930s.[10] Unfortunately, FDR adopted one of these crackpot ideas as the primary basis of his economic policy. The central idea was based on an interpretation of the Depression that had cause and effect exactly backward. The main cause of the Depression, FDR and his advisers believed, was low prices. The Depression did not cause low prices and wages, then contended; low prices and wages caused the Depression. Therefore, the "obvious solution" to the Depression was government-mandated price and wage increases (to ostensibly increase "purchasing power"), which is what the National Industrial Recovery Act (NIRA) and the Agricultural Adjustment Act attempted to do. The former act sought to cartelize virtually every industry in America under the auspices of the federal government (while suspending the antitrust laws); the latter act sought to do the same for agriculture.

The First New Deal was essentially a scheme to turn the U.S. economy into one massive, government-run system of industrial and agricultural cartels. At a time when underemployment or unemployment of resources, including labor resources, was of tragic proportions, the focus of the government was to *restrict* output and employment even further with supply-reducing cartel schemes and limitations on hours worked.

---

[9]Higgs, "Regime Uncertainty," p. 586.

[10]John T. Flynn, *The Roosevelt Myth* (New York: Devin-Adair, 1948).

The scheme was always destined to fail, of course, because of several major confusions. First, if wages are forced up by government fiat, the effect is to reduce the demand for labor, which creates *more* unemployment.

It is well-known that the minimum wage law causes unemployment, especially among lower-skilled workers. But at least the minimum wage law primarily applies only to entry-level employees and is therefore limited in the amount of harm it can do. The NIRA was an *economy-wide* minimum wage (and maximum hour) program that rendered the job-destroying effect of the minimum wage law universal.

Second, higher prices caused by a government-run cartel scheme may increase the incomes of some sellers, but only by reducing the incomes of buyers by an equivalent amount. On net, the economy is not "stimulated." The NIRA was the public policy equivalent of a Rube Goldberg machine.

The NIRA created the National Recovery Administration (NRA), which was a bureaucratic monstrosity. The NRA organized each industry into a federally-supervised trade association called a "Code Authority" which had the authority to regulate production, prices, and distribution methods. Every businessperson was required to sign a pledge to observe the government's minimum wage, maximum hours, prohibitions on "child labor," and myriad other regulations. Signers of the pledge were given a Blue Eagle badge that they were to wear to show their compliance.

The NRA was administered by a former Army general, Hugh Johnson, who adopted more than seven hundred industry codes and employed thousands of code-enforcement police. It was empowered to enforce *minimum* prices, but not maximum prices. Prices were not legally permitted to fall below "costs of production," even if weak consumer demand would necessitate such pricing (temporarily) on the free market. Moreover, what counted as allowable "costs of production" for pricing purposes was determined arbitrarily by government bureaucrats in an unholy collaboration with industry executives. In the lumber industry, for example, prices were prohibited from falling below a "weighted average cost of production," which included thirteen different cost categories. "When all of these items are thrown in," Henry Hazlitt wrote, "the lumber industry should be able to present a very impressive figure for cost of production. In other words, it can fix a very substantial minimum price."[11] Once again the corporate world confirmed Adam Smith's dictum that businessmen seldom meet, even for "merriment," when the discussion doesn't turn to some conspiracy against the public. (As always, effective price-fixing conspiracies must utilize the coercive powers of the state to enforce compliance by the conspirators.)

> In the New York garment industry the code-enforcement police roamed through the garment district like storm troopers. They could enter a man's factory, send him out, line up his employees, subject them to minute interrogation, take over his books on the instant. Night work was forbidden. Flying squadrons of these private coat-and-suit police went through the district at night, battering down doors with axes looking for men who were committing the crime of sewing together a pair of pants at night.[12]

A New Jersey tailor named Jack Magid was arrested, convicted, fined, and imprisoned for the "crime" of pressing a suit of clothes for 35¢ when the Tailors' Code fixed the price at 40¢.[13] Every town in America, wrote John T. Flynn, could offer a similar example.

More than six thousand patronage jobs were ladled out to "statisticians" who prepared reports regarding the "appropriate" prices that ought to be charged in each and every industry, a sort of Soviet-style central planning bureaucracy. Henry Hazlitt explained the work of some of these statistical wizards in a December 1933 article in *The American Mercury*:

> [T]he corset and brassiere industry, while permitting manufacturers or wholesalers to contribute up to 50 percent of the net cost of a retailer's advertising space, prohibits them from paying any of the cost of advertising on "corsets, combinations, girdle-corsets, or step-in corsets which are advertised for retail sale at less than $2, or on brassieres which are advertised for retail sales at less than $1."[14]

---

[11]Ibid., p. 422.

[12]Ibid., p. 45.

[13]Ibid., p. 44.

[14]Henry Hazlitt, "The Fallacies of the N.R.A.," *The American Mercury* (December 1933): 421.

Of course, the codes were in reality nothing but a blatant monopoly scheme. Government-enforced high prices were said to constitute "fair competition," much to the delight of the industries who believed that they would benefit from the scheme—and who would likely make hefty campaign contributions to FDR in return. In short, the NRA—and the New Deal in general—was a giant shakedown operation.

The oil industry was also cartelized by a provision in the NIRA that created state "control boards" that could restrict the amount of oil sold in interstate and international commerce.[15]

A massive government-funded propaganda campaign complete with a mammoth New York City parade, was launched to promote acceptance of the NRA by the public. The campaign championed the NRA Codes while smearing and denigrating capitalists and capitalist institutions. Competition was called "economic cannibalism"; rugged individualists were "industrial pirates"; competitive price-cutting was denounced by the government as "cutthroat and monopolistic price-slashing"; price cutters were branded as "chiselers"; and government-enforced cartels were praised as "cooperative arrangements."[16] It is important to recognize that whenever government itself enters into a policy debate, it has the ability to drown out all other voices, and it did so in this case.

Henry Hazlitt perfectly summarized the essence of the NRA in 1933 as a government program under which

> the American consumer is to become the victim of a series of trades and industries which, in the name of "fair competition," will be in effect monopolies, consisting of units that agree not to make too serious an effort to undersell each other; restricting production, fixing prices—doing everything, in fact, that monopolies are formed to do. . . . Instead of a relatively flexible system with some power of adjustment to fluid world economic conditions we shall have an inadjustable structure constantly attempting—at the cost of stagnant business and employment—to resist these conditions.[17]

---

[15]Robert Higgs, *Crisis and Leviathan: Critical Episodes in the Growth of American Government* (New York: Oxford University Press, 1987), p. 178.

[16]Ibid., p. 179.

[17]Hazlitt, *The Fallacies of the N.R.A.*, p. 422.

The Agricultural Adjustment Act created the Agricultural Adjustment Administration (AAA) within the Department of Agriculture, which was similar to the NRA; the only real difference was that the former sought to cartelize agricultural markets. Even as many Americans were going hungry, FDR adopted a program to pay farmers millions of dollars annually to literally burn their crops and slaughter their livestock. One corporation alone that was in the business of refining sugar was paid $1 million for not producing sugar.[18] This created a public relations disaster for Roosevelt, who then wised-up and began paying farmers and ranchers for not raising livestock and planting crops in the first place. The AAA initiated acreage allotments, restrictive marketing agreements, the licensing of food processors and dealers to "eliminate unfair pricing," and numerous other agricultural cartel schemes. The agency was an awful burden on poor sharecroppers, thousands of whom were evicted so that the landowners could collect their governmental bounties for not producing.[19] Who needs sharecroppers when one is being paid not to grow crops?

Perhaps the worst of FDR's price-fixing schemes had to do with his handling of gold prices. Roosevelt abandoned the gold standard, the only certain restraint on federal government growth and inflation. He nationalized the gold stock by making the private ownership of gold illegal (except for jewelry, scientific or industrial uses, and foreign payments) and by nullifying all contractual promises to pay for anything in gold.

This was an act of outright theft, and it didn't even inflate prices, as FDR hoped it would. Due to the severity of the Depression, the price level remained fairly steady for the entire decade of the 1930s. Roosevelt failed in his harebrained scheme to make everyone "rich" through inflation.

FDR's "bank holiday," in which he invoked the 1917 "Trading with the Enemy Act" to order the closing of banks, served only to heighten the state of panic in the minds of the public and did nothing to improve the banking system or alleviate the Depression. This crisis mentality allowed Roosevelt to further

[18]Flynn, *The Roosevelt Myth*, p. 49.

[19]David E. Conrad, *The Forgotten Farmers* (Urbana: University of Illinois Press, 1965).

ignore constitutional constraints on governmental power and to act, more or less, like a dictator. One of FDR's advisers, Raymond Moley, absurdly proclaimed that because of his boss' bank closings, "Capitalism was saved in eight days."[20]

ECONOMIC FASCISM

The NRA and AAA were essentially modeled after the Italian fascist system that had been put in place by Benito Mussolini in the 1920s. Under Mussolini's system, Italian businesses were grouped into "legally recognized syndicates," which were essentially regional trade associations with names like "National Fascist Confederation of Commerce," and the "National Fascist Confederation of Credit and Insurance."[21] The ostensible purpose of these groupings was to enable government to secure "collaboration . . . between the various categories of producers" to assure that "the principle of private initiative" would not serve the purposes of private citizens, such as consumers,but would be "useful in the service of the national interest."[22] The "national interest" as defined by Mussolini, of course.

Each regional trade association, or syndicate, was overseen and regulated by a central government "planning agency" or "corporation." There was one such corporation for each industry. The supposed purpose of this arrangement was to counter—if not eliminate—free-market competition and replace it with "a spirit of collaboration that would not be possible under any other system," according to the fascist economist Luigi Villari, an adviser to Mussolini.[23]

Like FDR and his NRA appointees, the Italian fascists waged a fierce propaganda campaign against the principles of free markets and individual liberty. In numerous speeches Mussolini bemoaned the "selfish pursuit of material prosperity," explained that fascism was "a reaction against the flaccid materialistic positivism of the nineteenth century," and urged Italians to abandon

[20]William E. Leuchtenberg, *Franklin D. Roosevelt and the New Deal* (New York: Harper and Row, 1963), p. 45.

[21]Fausto Pitigliani, *The Italian Corporative State* (New York: Macmillan, 1934).

[22]Ibid., p. 93.

[23]Luigi Villari, *Bolshevism, Fascism, and Capitalism* (New Haven, Conn.: Yale University Press, 1932), p. 107.

the ideas of Adam Smith and "the economistic literature of the eighteenth century."[24] "If the nineteenth century was the century of the individual (liberalism implies individualism)," Mussolini wrote, then "this [the twentieth century] is the 'collective' century, and therefore the century of the State. . . . Fascism spells government."[25]

That the First New Deal was strikingly similar to Italian fascism was noted by John T. Flynn, who observed that many American intellectuals, politicians, and businessmen greatly admired Mussolini.

> What they liked particularly was his corporative system. He organized each trade or industrial group or professional group into a state-supervised trade association. He called it a cooperative. These cooperatives operated under state supervision and could plan production, quality, prices, distribution, labor standards, etc. The NRA provided that in American industry each industry should be organized into a federally supervised trade association. It was not called a cooperative. It was called a Code Authority. But it was essentially the same thing. . . . This was fascism.[26]

American businessmen were the primary promoters of economic fascism, although many of FDR's advisers endorsed the idea as well. In 1932, Henry I. Harriman, president of the U.S. Chamber of Commerce, was impressed at how businessmen had been "conspicuously zealous in promoting the effort to carry into practical effect the philosophy of the planned economy."[27]

In the 1920s, Gerard Swope, chief executive officer of General Electric, offered a "plan" that was very popular among business executives. His system would "operate through compulsory trade associations, made up of all major firms and empowered by law to regulate production, prices, and trade practices."[28]

---

[24]Benito Mussolini, *Fascism: Doctrine and Institutions* (Rome: Adrita Press, 1935), p. 8.

[25]Ibid., p. 29.

[26]Flynn, *The Roosevelt Myth*, p. 43.

[27]Cited in Charles and Mary Beard, *America in Midpassage* (New York: Macmillan, 1932), p. 100.

[28]Martin Fausold and George T. Mazuzan, *The Hoover Presidency: A Reappraisal* (Albany: State University of New York Press, 1974), p. 107.

In the June 1931 issue of *Harper's* magazine, economist Stuart Chase offered a "Ten Year Plan for America" that was extremely popular among businessmen. Chase sneered at the Soviets for believing that they, and not Americans, had invented central planning. "These Slavs seem to think that they discovered national planning," Chase stated, but in reality the "credit" for it should go to Woodrow Wilson and his "War Industries Board" during World War I, described by Chase as "fifteen hundred businessmen, economists, engineers, statisticians, map makers, running the country."[29]

So enamored with Mussolini were America's political and business elite that in the foreword to Mussolini's 1928 autobiography, former American ambassador to Italy Richard Washburn Child wrote that "In our time it may be shrewdly forecast that no man will exhibit dimensions of permanent greatness equal to those of Mussolini . . . the Duce is now the greatest figure of this sphere and time."[30] Similar sentiments were expressed by many other business and political leaders during the 1920s and '30s.

The idea that war planning can be a model for peacetime planning of the economy permeated the Roosevelt administration, as did admiration for something even more totalitarian than Italian fascism: Soviet central planning. FDR's most influential economic adviser was Rexford G. Tugwell of Columbia University. In his 1930 book, *American Economic Life*, Tugwell praised Soviet communism, which he believed would be more prosperous and more egalitarian than capitalism.

> Her [the Soviet Union's] worst enemies are being forced to admit that the system appears to be able to produce goods in greater quantities than the old one and to spread such prosperity as there is over wider areas of the population.[31]

Soviet central planning enabled the Soviets to plan and to "carry out their industrial operations in accordance with a completely thought-out program," Rexford Tugwell admiringly

---

[29]Stuart Chase, "A Ten Year Plan for America," *Harpers* (June 1931): 2.

[30]Benito Mussolini, *My Autobiography* (New York: Charles Scribener's Sons, 1928), pp. xi, xix.

[31]Rexford Tugwell, Thomas Munro, and Roy E. Stryker, *American Economic Life* (New York: Harcourt Brace, 1930), p. 707.

commented.[32] "The available evidence as to the success of the scheme seems to indicate clearly enough that it works."[33] There were admittedly "those who suffer under it," but according to Tugwell, "the major advantages . . . outweigh the disadvantages of the supposed loss of incentive, red tape, unimaginative centralized authority."[34] As Stalin reportedly said, one must break a few eggs to make an omelet.

Yes, there might have been "a ruthlessness, a disregard for liberties and rights" in the Soviet Union, and there was an awful lot of "repression, spying, and violence," but it was not caused by socialism, Tugwell contends.[35] Anyone who was interested "in peace, prosperity, and progress must, in the coming years, devote much study and thought to Russia and the Russians."[36]

Writing in the *American Economic Review* in 1932, the year of Franklin Roosevelt's election, Tugwell denounced capitalistic profits as being responsible for producing "insecurity" by creating "overcapacity" and "inflation, essentially echoing Karl Marx's theory of surplus value.[37] Profits were said to "create unemployment and hardship" and to "persuade us to speculate" in "dangerous endeavors" and, most harmfully, to "hinder measurably the advance of [centralized] planning."[38] To Tugwell, the NRA, as onerous and as unconstitutional as it was, did not nearly go far enough in regulating and regimenting the U.S. economy.

The First New Deal was such a debacle that both the NRA and AAA were ruled unconstitutional by the U.S. Supreme Court in early 1935. The NRA created such a protest with its storm-trooper tactics that the U.S. Senate forced FDR to appoint a commission to evaluate the agency in 1934. The commission was headed by renowned attorney Clarence Darrow, who described the NRA as "harmful, monopolistic, oppressive,

[32]Ibid., p. 709.
[33]Ibid., p. 711.
[34]Ibid., p. 712.
[35]Ibid.
[36]Ibid., p. 716.
[37]Rexford G. Tugwell, "The Principle of Planning and the Institution of Laissez Faire," *American Economic Review* (May 1932): 79.
[38]Ibid., p. 82.

grotesque, invasive, fictitious, ghastly, anomalous, preposterous, irresponsible, savage, wolfish."[39]

General Hugh Johnson resigned on October 1, 1934 as the head of the NRA because of a dispute with FDR. The man whom FDR chose to head his most important effort to "revive" the economy gave a farewell speech to NRA employees in which he compared himself to "Christ and Madame Butterfly, quoting in Italian the words on the latter's Samurai dagger, 'To die with honor when you can no longer live with honor.'"[40] The Italian language was an especially appropriate touch. Mussolini would have liked it.

But many of these programs were resurrected by the wiley and irrepressible Roosevelt. The AAA programs were continued under the subterfuge of a "soil conservation program" and, thanks to Roosevelt's court-packing scheme, many other programs that the U.S. Supreme Court had ruled unconstitutional were continued—many of them to this day. As economist Charlotte Twight observed in her book, *America's Emerging Fascist Economy*, many (perhaps most) of the governmental institutions that Americans take for granted today and that were introduced during the New Deal were explicitly modeled after the fascist economies of Italy and Germany of the 1930s. Economic fascism sought to "empower an elite to determine the specific purposes that other individuals in the society are compelled to serve"; it "is the antithesis of limited government and individualism," as it "uncompromisingly seeks to obliterate individual rights"; its view of capitalism is "regulated capitalism" and "government intervention in the economy on a massive scale"; it "supplants . . . market considerations with political considerations" with only "perfunctory regard for economic costs or consumers' wishes"; it uses the language of "the national interest" to justify myriad government interventions; and it "attempts to fuse management and labor, molding them into a monolithic instrument for achieving whatever government officials decree to be the national interest."[41]

[39]Report of the National Recovery Review Board," *New York Times*, May 21, 1934.

[40]Jordan A. Schwartz, *The New Dealers* (New York: Alfred A. Knopf, 1993), p. 104.

[41]Charlotte Twight, *America's Emerging Fascist Economy* (New Rochelle, N.Y.: Arlington House, 1975), pp. 13–29.

Economic fascism is perhaps Roosevelt's most enduring legacy to America. So was the art of lying through one's teeth and political viciousness. After modeling his First New Deal almost exclusively along the lines of Italian fascism sprinkled with outright socialism and filling the top levels of his administration with wide-eyed idolaters of Stalinist central planning, FDR had the gall to warn the country in an ominous voice that "Tory Republicanism" may lead to fascism. Just before the 1938 election he stated:

> As of today, Fascism and communism and old-line Tory Republicanism are not threats to the continuation of our form of government, but I venture the challenging statement that if American democracy ceases to move forward as a living force . . . then Fascism and Communism, aided, unconsciously perhaps, by old-line Tory Republicanism, will grow in strength in our land.[42]

THE SECOND NEW DEAL

We shall tax and tax, spend and spend, and elect and elect.

—Harry Hopkins
Adviser to President Roosevelt

On January 4, 1935—only a few months before most of his "First New Deal" was ruled unconstitutional by the U.S. Supreme Court—Franklin Roosevelt announced his Second New Deal. The principal additions were the Social Security Act, the National Labor Relations Act, the Fair Labor Standards Act (the minimum wage law), the Works Progress Administration, and punitive taxes imposed ostensibly to punish "economic royalists" and other entrepreneurs whom Roosevelt wanted to blame for the country's troubles. Every one of these programs was a drain on the private sector of the economy and an impediment to the employment of labor. As such, they all made the Great Depression even worse.

The Social Security payroll tax and the two labor laws increased the cost to employers of hiring workers, which led to higher unemployment. The payroll tax was a straightforward increase in the cost of labor, as was the minimum wage law. The

---

[42]James MacGregor Burns, *Roosevelt: The Lion and the Fox* (New York: Macmillan, 1956).

National Labor Relations Act, or Wagner Act, created a system of government-sanctioned legal privileges for labor unions that greatly enhanced their bargaining powers and, in many ways, enabled them to become more or less outlaw organizations. The Norris–LaGuardia Act, signed by President Hoover in 1932 and vigorously enforced during the Roosevelt administration, made it extremely costly and difficult to obtain an injunction against union violence. Laws against extortion exempted unions as long as the extortion involved "the payment of wages by a *bona fide* employer to a *bona fide* employee."[43]

Thanks primarily to FDR's Depression-era labor legislation, labor unions have been able to compel even nonmembers to pay dues, which are often used for political purposes unrelated to collective bargaining. Unions are immune from most injunctions by federal courts; can compel workers to pay dues as a condition of keeping their jobs; are legally empowered to "represent" all workers in a bargaining unit, regardless of whether they are union members; can compel employers to make their private property available to union officials; are all but immune from paying damages for personal and property injury that they inflict; and can force employers to open up their books to them.[44] As Friedrich Hayek wrote in *The Constitution of Liberty*:

> We have now reached a state where they [unions] have become uniquely privileged institutions to which the general rules of law do not apply. They have become the only important instance in which governments fail in their prime function— the prevention of coercion and violence.[45]

These new laws that granted special privileges to unions—and at the same time, expanded state control over labor relations—were virtually identical to the kind of arrangements that had been adopted in Germany and Italy in the 1920s and '30s. In each instance, the objective was to put the state in control of regulating labor relations in such a way as to achieve *the state's* objectives— higher wages to "enhance purchasing power," in Roosevelt's case.

[43]*Congressional Record* 78, 402–03 (1934).

[44]Morgan O. Reynolds, *Power and Privilege: Labor Unions in America* (New York: Universe Books, 1984), p. 265.

[45]Friedrich A. Hayek, *The Constitution of Liberty* (Chicago: University of Chicago Press, 1960), p. 267.

In each instance *individual* bargaining with employers was all but outlawed and was replaced by state-supervised and controlled *collective* bargaining, with unions as the state-sponsored bargaining agents for all workers within a unionized workplace. According to labor historian Howard Dickman, New Deal labor legislation was "the beginning of a fascistic regulation of our quasi-syndicalist system of industrial democracy."[46]

The virtual exemption from the rule of law allowed unions to force wages up during the Great Depression at a much faster pace than labor productivity was increasing, thereby causing higher unemployment. Wages rose by a phenomenal 13.7 percent during the first three quarters of 1937 alone.[47] Due largely to the legislated powers granted to unions, the union–non-union wage differential increased from 5 percent in 1933 to 23 percent by 1940.[48] On top of this, the Social Security payroll and unemployment insurance taxes contributed to a rapid rise in government-mandated fringe benefits, from 2.4 percent of payrolls in 1936 to 5.1 percent just two years later.

Richard Vedder and Lowell Gallaway have estimated a statistical model of unemployment that leads them to conclude that, by 1940, the unemployment rate was more than 8 percentage points higher than it otherwise would have been due to the legislation-induced growth in unionism and government-mandated fringe benefit costs imposed on employers.[49] They conclude that "the Great Depression was very significantly prolonged in both its duration and its magnitude by the impact of New Deal programs."[50] Most of the abnormal unemployment of the 1930s would have been avoided had it not been for the New Deal.

In addition to fascistic labor policies and government-mandated wage and fringe benefit increases that destroyed millions of jobs, the Second New Deal was responsible for economy-destroying tax increases and massive government spending on myriad government make-work programs. "I've got four million at

---

[46]Howard Dickman, *Industrial Democracy in America: Ideological Origins of National Labor Relations Policy* (LaSalle, Ill.: Open Court, 1987), p. 287.

[47]Vedder and Gallaway, *Out of Work*, p. 134.

[48]Ibid., p. 139.

[49]Ibid., p. 141.

[50]Ibid.

work [in federal jobs]," Harry Hopkins told the president in 1935, "but for God's sake, don't ask me what they are doing."[51] Even before the military mobilization for World War II was under way, federal spending nearly doubled, from $4.6 billion in 1932 to $9.1 billion in 1940, while approximately $24 billion in deficits were accumulated. Annual deficits during this time averaged 42 percent of the federal budget.[52] Prior to Roosevelt's terms in office budget deficits were universally denounced, even by Roosevelt himself during the election campaign of 1932.

Franklin Roosevelt proposed to have government spend the country out of the Great Depression, but of course, neither he nor any other politician could possibly have done so. There is no free lunch. Every dollar spent by government on whatever kind of make-work programs that can be dreamed up must necessarily depress genuine, market-driven economic growth by diverting resources from the private to the governmental sector. Every dollar spent by the state must be taken from private citizens one way or another—either through taxation, through government borrowing that crowds out private borrowers, or by inflating the currency, which reduces the value of all privately-held wealth. That is why, despite a more than doubling of the federal budget in eight years, the Depression did not end. Indeed, unemployment was higher in 1938 than it was in 1931.

Roosevelt's vaunted "jobs" programs unequivocally destroyed jobs. Government "jobs" programs, such as the Works Progress Administration and the Civilian Conservation Corps, can only destroy private-sector jobs in order to "create" government make-work jobs. And since government bureaucrats spend the taxpayers' money much more inefficiently than the taxpayers themselves do, government jobs that are "created" usually come at the expense of destroying *several* private-sector jobs. For example, the federal government's own General Accounting Office has estimated that some federal jobs programs have provided $14,000-per-year jobs at a total cost of more than $100,000 per job, once one accounts for all the administrative expenses. Thus, in this case, about seven $14,000-per-year entry-level jobs must be destroyed in order to create one government job.

[51]Flynn, *The Roosevelt Myth*, p. 132.
[52]*Historical Statistics of the United States*, p. 711.

THE NEW DEAL PORK BARREL

Most historians have perpetuated the myth that Roosevelt spent the U.S. out of the Great Depression. There are two fundamental flaws in these assertions. First, as mentioned above, it is impossible for government spending to create prosperity out of thin air. Only production can create prosperity. Second, the assumption behind the claims that government spending somehow ended the Depression is that Roosevelt made spending decisions based on economic "need." That is, government spending programs are said to have targeted the neediest areas of the country.

There is little evidence of this. In fact, there is much evidence that New Deal spending was designed with one overriding objective: to use the money to buy votes in order to assure Roosevelt's reelection, regardless of regional disparities in the degree of economic hardship. The South was the most devastated region of the country during the Great Depression, for example, yet it received a disproportionately small amount of federal subsidies. John T. Flynn discussed how thoroughly politicized New Deal spending was by reporting the conclusions of a 1938 Official Report of the U.S. Senate Committee on Campaign Expenditures. Among the findings of the report were:[53]

- In one Works Progress Administration (WPA) "district" in Kentucky, 349 WPA employees were put to work preparing forms listing the electoral preferences of every employee on work relief. Many of those who stated that they did not intend to vote for Roosevelt were laid off.

- In another Kentucky WPA district, government workers were required, as a condition of employment, to pledge to vote for the senior senator from Kentucky, who was a Roosevelt supporter. If they refused, they were thrown off the relief rolls.

- Republicans in Kentucky were told that they would have to change party affiliations if they wanted to keep their WPA jobs.

- Letters were sent out to WPA employees in Kentucky, instructing them to donate 2 percent of their salaries to the Roosevelt campaign if they wanted to keep their jobs.

[53]Cited in Flynn, *The Roosevelt Myth*, pp. 133–37.

- In Pennsylvania, businessmen who leased trucks to the WPA were solicited for $100 campaign contributions.

- As in Kentucky, Pennsylvania WPA workers were told to change their party affiliation if they wanted to keep their jobs. Many people refused and were fired.

- Government employment was increased dramatically right before elections. In Pennsylvania, "employment cards" were distributed, entitling holders of the cards to "two to four weeks of employment around election time."

- A Pennsylvania man who was given a $60.50-per-month white-collar job was transferred to a pick-axe job in a limestone quarry after refusing to change his voter registration from Republican to Democrat.

- Tennessee WPA workers were also instructed to contribute 2 percent of their salaries to the Democratic Party as a condition of employment.

- In Cook County, Illinois, 450 men were employed in one congressional election district by the WPA and were instructed to canvass for (Democratic) votes around election time. They were all laid off the day after the 1938 election.

The U.S. Senate report only surveyed four states, but there is every reason to believe that similar practices occurred in all states. Economist Gavin Wright conducted a more systematic examination of WPA spending patterns and concluded that, in general, "WPA employment reached peaks in the fall of election years, and the pattern is most pronounced when employment is measured relative to indices of need."[54] In a 1939 magazine article entitled "The WPA: Politicians' Playground," historian Stanley High observed that "In states like Florida and Kentucky— where the New Deal's big fight was in the primary elections—the rise of WPA employment was hurried along in order to synchronize with the primaries."[55]

---

[54]Gavin Wright, "The Political Economy of New Deal Spending: An Econometric Analysis," *Review of Economics and Statistics* (February 1974): 35.

[55]Stanley High, "The WPA: Politicians' Playground," *Current History* (May 1939): 23–25.

More recently, in 1969, economic researchers uncovered governmental data sets depicting the distribution of New Deal spending, and that has enabled them to examine more fully the extent to which programs such as the WPA were motivated by politics, i.e., the reelection of Franklin D. Roosevelt. In general, the relatively well-off Western states tended to receive the lion's share of New Deal subsidies, whereas the Southern states, where the Depression was most severe, received the least. The average resident of a Western state received 60 percent more in federal subsidies than did the average Southerner.[56] This is sharply at odds with the New Deal rhetoric of compassion and "relief" for the most "downtrodden." As soon as these data were discovered, statist apologists in academe began constructing excuses and rationales for the pattern of New Deal spending. The cost of living was much lower in the South, they said, so naturally there would have been less spending there. Cost-of-living differences existed but were rather small, whereas there were very large differences in the distribution of spending on a regional basis. For example, the annual cost-of-living estimate for Jacksonville, Florida, in 1938 was $1,260.44; the corresponding estimate for Buffalo, New York, was $1,283.81.[57]

A second rationale offered by New Deal apologists is that, since standards of living were so low in the South, it didn't take much to satisfy Southerners. But this rationale is clearly at odds with all the "compassionate" rhetoric of the New Deal.

A third excuse for the New Deal's odd spending patterns has to do with matching requirements. The argument is that since some New Deal programs had matching requirements that required state and local governments to match federal subsidies, it should be expected that more affluent states—that is, states in the West and Northeast—would receive more in subsidies, since they could afford greater matching amounts. But the key question is this: If the New Deal programs were truly motivated by a desire to help those who most needed economic assistance, why were such matching requirements implemented in the first place? Surely Roosevelt's vaunted "Brains Trust" knew that the

---

[56]Jim F. Couch and William F. Shughart, II, *The Political Economy of the New Deal* (Northampton, Mass.: Edward Elgar, 1998), p. 130.

[57]Ibid., p. 139.

requirements would skew the distribution of subsidies in this way.[58]

In contrast to these questionable excuses, a number of economists have begun to examine the notion that politics may have been a more reliable and consistent explanation for the pattern of New Deal spending than "compassion" or "need." Couch and Shughart explain why so much federal money was showered on the Western states:

> The support of these states was instrumental in securing Franklin Roosevelt's nomination as the Democratic Party's standard-bearer in 1932. History might have played out very differently had "favorite son" candidates William Gibs McAdoo of California and Speaker of the House (and soon-to-be vice presidential nominee) John Nance Garner of Texas not released the delegates pledged to them and thrown their support behind FDR on the convention's fourth ballot. Two years later, the West was again of the highest political importance to the New Dealers "because of crucial senatorial races involving Democratic incumbents in Utah, Arizona, Montana, and in other states where they hoped to gain a seat: Nebraska, Wyoming, New Mexico, Washington, and California.[59]

Since the War Between the States, the South had been solidly Democratic. Few self-respecting Southerners could bring themselves to vote for the "party of Lincoln." Thus, Franklin Roosevelt knew that he had little need to buy the electoral votes of the Southern states with federal funds. He only needed to throw them enough crumbs to avoid a political revolt. His main priority was to use tax dollars to buy votes in those states where his electoral margins were slim.

Gavin Wright was the first economist to publish in 1974 a statistical analysis of New Deal spending that explored the hypothesis that the spending was driven by politics more than economic "need."[60] He found that in those states (mostly Western) where the percentage of the electoral vote going to the Democratic Party in 1932 and 1936 was lower, New Deal spending tended to be highest. In other words, FDR directed New Deal spending to where it was most "needed" by him, not by Americans suffering

---

[58]Ibid., p. 143.

[59]Ibid., p. 145.

[60]Gavin Wright, "The Political Economy of New Deal Spending."

from the effects of the Depression. Wright also found little statistical support for the hypothesis that New Deal spending patterns were determined by economic need across regions.

More recently, Gary Anderson and Robert Tollison also found that electoral votes per capita were an important determinant of the allocation of New Deal spending. They found that congressional districts whose representatives were members of House or Senate appropriations committees received disproportionate New Deal subsidies.[61]

Couch and Shughart found the "perverse" result that "states with healthier economies [during the Great Depression] received proportionately more federal aid in the form of [New Deal] grants they were not expected to repay while repayable loans were directed in slightly greater amounts to their harder-hit sisters."[62] They also found that "New Dealers allocated significantly more funds to states where the nation's most valuable . . . farms were located. . . . Little flowed to sharecroppers and other tenants or to farm laborers."[63]

Couch and Shughart also concluded that

> the states that gave Franklin Roosevelt larger percentages of the popular vote in 1932 were rewarded with significantly more federal aid than less-supportive constituencies . . . a one percentage point increase in support of FDR in the 1932 presidential election translated into nearly $300 in additional per-capita federal aid over the 1933–1939 period.[64]

The New Dealers'—and their contemporary descendants'— claims of special sensitivity to the hardships of blacks during the Great Depression is also challenged by Couch and Shughart's research: "[S]tates where blacks accounted for larger percentages of the farm population received fewer New Deal dollars."[65] In light of all these findings these authors conclude that:

---

[61]Gary Anderson and Robert Tollison, "Congressional Influence and Patterns of New Deal Spending," *Journal of Law and Economics* (April 1991): 161–75.

[62]Couch and Shughart, *The Political Economy of the New Deal*, p. 187.

[64]Ibid.

[64]Ibid., p. 188.

[65]Ibid., p. 192.

[T]he distribution of the billions of dollars appropriated by Congress to prime the economic pump was guided less by considerations of economic need than by the forces of ordinary politics. Perhaps the New Deal failed as a matter of economic policy because it was so successful in building a winning political coalition: FDR was reelected overwhelmingly in 1936 and again in 1940 in part due to the support of the big-city machines, organized labor, and other constituencies which benefited disproportionately from New Deal largesse. Insofar as the region was "safe" for the Democrats, the administration's comparative neglect of the nation's number one economic problem—the South—can likewise be explained by politics.[66]

As David Gordon has written, Franklin Roosevelt was a most ordinary and familiar kind of politician. That is, he "was a vain, intellectually shallow person whose principal interest was to retain at all costs his personal power," and whose priorities were the "total subordination of his country's welfare to his personal ambition."[67] All politicians are power-hungry egomaniacs, but Roosevelt was hungrier and more egomaniacal than most.

CONCLUSION

A "comprehensive" treatment of Franklin Delano Roosevelt and the New Deal would require a very long book, many of which have been written. The purpose here has been to highlight two overriding features of the New Deal: the adoption of economic fascism, modeled directly after Mussolini's system in Italy (and Hitler's in Nazi Germany), and the unrestrained orgy of vote-buying and pork-barrel politics. This latter policy was famously described by Roosevelt confidant Harry Hopkins as the strategy of "tax and tax, spend and spend, and elect and elect."

Roosevelt virtually destroyed what was left, by the 1930s, of the old Constitutional order that was established by the American Founding Fathers. Legal scholar Richard Epstein was right when he wrote in his treatise on governmental "takings"

---

[66]Ibid., p. 228.

[67]David Gordon, "Power Mad," *The Mises Review* (Spring 1999): 7–12.

that the New Deal was unconstitutional, as is most of what the federal government does today.[68]

Roosevelt's critics, such as John T. Flynn, Albert J. Nock, and H.L. Mencken, were labeled "Roosevelt Haters" and their criticisms were dismissed by most of the American journalistic and political elite. Whatever one may wish to call them, the "Roosevelt Haters" have been proven right by history. Roosevelt was a disaster for American liberty and prosperity.

Now that we know that John T. Flynn was prescient in his analyses of Roosevelt and the New Deal, it is perhaps worth reconsidering his assessment of Roosevelt's role in getting the United States involved in World War II. Having failed miserably for eight years to end the Depression (actually making it worse, as we have seen), Roosevelt must have been thrilled when, in 1940, Germany, France, England, Italy, China, and Japan were all "clamoring for steel, scrap iron, planes, plane parts. The time was here when thousands of Americans who, seeking immediate riches, fool's gold, would attempt to break down or evade our neutrality."[69] What would Roosevelt do? According to Flynn:

> Here he was with a depression on his hands—eleven million men out of work, the whole fabric of his policy in tatters, his promise only a few months old to balance the budget still fresh in the minds of the people and yet the pressing necessity, as he put it himself, of spending two or three billion a year of deficit money and, most seriously of all, as he told Jim Farley, *no way to spend it.*
>
> Here now was a gift from the gods—and from the gods of war at that. Here was the chance to spend. Here now was something the federal government could really spend money on—military and naval operations. . . . He promptly set off on an immense program of military and naval expenditures, . . . all with borrowed money and more government debt.[70]

To assure that he could engage in the Mother of All Spending Binges, Roosevelt abandoned the Neutrality Act, which he

---

[68]Richard A. Epstein, *Takings: Private Property and the Power of Eminent Domain* (Cambridge, Mass.: Harvard University Press, 1985).

[69]Flynn, *The Roosevelt Myth*, p. 171.

[70]Ibid.

had previously invoked in 1936 when Mussolini invaded Ethiopia and in 1937 when Japan invaded China.

Every American has viewed film footage of the weeping crowds mourning the sudden and unexpected death of Roosevelt in 1945, which made him a political icon for the ages. But Americans also need to confront the fact that, for the last years of his life, he was a terribly sick man whose doctors advised him not to work more than four hours a day and who was heavily medicated. Always putting his own personal political fortunes above all else, Roosevelt apparently never even seriously considered not running for reelection in 1944 or stepping down when he was deathly ill and expected to negotiate the postwar "peace" with Joseph Stalin and Winston Churchill. The disastrous result was that the smiling, jocular Roosevelt, with his ever-present cigarette holder protruding from his mouth, sat next to Stalin at Yalta and agreed to condemn the people of Eastern Europe and much of Asia to forty-five years of communist hell. To Roosevelt, this was apparently a necessity. After all, the political fortunes of Franklin D. Roosevelt were at stake.

16

FRANKLIN DELANO ROOSEVELT AND THE FIRST SHOT: A STUDY OF DECEIT AND DECEPTION

JOHN V. DENSON

The question was how we should maneuver them into the position of firing the first shot without allowing too much danger to ourselves.[1]

W orld War II is the favorite war of modern liberals and neoconservatives who worship both a large, activist central government and an interventionist foreign policy. Part of the mythology that surrounds this war is that it was the "last good war." It was a "just" war because it was defensive. Despite President Roosevelt's supreme efforts to keep America neutral regarding controversies in Europe and Asia, the Japanese launched an *unprovoked surprise attack* at Pearl Harbor, thereby "forcing" America into the fray. It was also a "noble" war because America fought evil tyrannies known as Nazism in Germany and fascism in Italy and Japan. The fact that Stalin and Soviet Russia were our allies and that we aided them with their oppression of millions of people during the war and thereafter is ignored.[2] Finally, the advocates of the "last good war"

---

[1]Quotation is from the diary of Secretary of War Henry Stimson concerning the meeting with President Roosevelt and his cabinet on November 25, 1941, just prior to the "surprise" attack at Pearl Harbor. See George Morgenstern, *Pearl Harbor: The Story of the Secret War* (Old Greenwich, Conn.: Devin-Adair, 1947), p. 292.

[2]For the tyranny of Stalin and the Soviet Union generally, see R.J. Rummel, *Death by Government* (New Brunswick, N.J.: Transaction Publishers, 1995) and his more recent book, *Power Kills: Democracy as a Method of Nonviolence* (New Brunswick, N.J.: Transaction Publishers, 1997). For American help to the Soviet Union during and after the war, see Werner Keller, *Are the Russians Ten Feet Tall?* Constantine FitzGibbon, trans. (London: Thames and Hudson, 1961) and also Major George R. Jordan (USAF), *From Major Jordan's Diaries*

---

say the Americans were generally united in their patriotic efforts to support the war. This helped to make us a great *nation* with a strong centralized government in Washington, D.C., which propelled America into an international leadership position as the world's policeman, thereby bringing "stability" to the world. World War II and the United States' participation have become patriotic myths to the American public, and all questioning of the official version of these events is discouraged, even viciously condemned, by the political, intellectual, and media establishment.[3]

This author will argue, however, that President Roosevelt desperately wanted and sought a war. He not only provoked the Japanese into firing the first shot at Pearl Harbor, but he was ultimately responsible for withholding vital information from the Pearl Harbor military commanders which, if conveyed to them, probably would have prevented the surprise attack altogether.

Unlike the story in the previous chapter, "Lincoln and the First Shot," where there was no official investigation of the Fort Sumter "incident," there were ten official investigations into the debacle at Pearl Harbor to see how such a tragedy could occur, killing nearly three thousand American servicemen, wounding thousands more, and causing massive damage to our Pacific Fleet. Many scholars, writers, and politicians who have studied the evidence gathered by these investigations have found, in fact, that President Roosevelt provoked the Japanese; that he withheld critical information from the commanders at Pearl Harbor; and that he misled the American people and Congress. Nevertheless, these Roosevelt admirers continue to defend and even praise him for his deceitful conduct. Typical of such apologists is Professor Thomas Bailey, a Stanford University historian of diplomatic relations, who declares:

(New York: Harcourt, Brace, 1952). For British and American assistance to the tyranny of Stalin after the war, see Nicholas Bethell, *The Last Secret: The Delivery to Stalin of Over Two Million Russians by Britain and the United States* (New York: Basic Books, 1974).

[3]A classic example is the vicious smear tactics used against Pat Buchanan concerning his book, *A Republic, Not an Empire: Reclaiming America's Destiny* (Washington, D.C.: Regnery, 1999). See for example the articles about Buchanan and his book by Tucker Carlson, Robert G. Kaufman, and William Kristol in *The Weekly Standard* 5, no. 2 (September 27, 1999).

Franklin Roosevelt repeatedly deceived the American people during the period before Pearl Harbor. . . . If he was going to induce the people to move at all, he would have to trick them into acting for their best interests, or what he conceived to be their best interests. He was like the physician who must tell the patient lies for the patient's own good. . . . The country was overwhelmingly noninterventionist to the very day of Pearl Harbor, and an overt attempt to lead the people into war would have resulted in certain failure and an almost certain ousting of Roosevelt in 1940, with a consequent defeat for his ultimate aims.[4]

The same Professor Bailey quotes Congresswoman Claire Booth Luce, who was also the wife of media mogul Henry Luce, as saying Roosevelt "lied us into war because he did not have the political courage to lead us into it."[5]

To address the defense of Roosevelt made by Professor Bailey requires a thorough discussion on allowing the president of the United States to become a virtual dictator, and that is not the focus of this chapter. Bailey's defense of Roosevelt sacrifices all the safeguards provided by the Constitution and the democratic process, which try to prevent the executive branch from having control over starting American wars. The Founding Fathers intended that only Congress should have the right to declare war and explicitly deprived the president of any war-making power in the Constitution. History, and especially English history, which was well-known by our Founders, clearly demonstrates that the king, or a few people in the executive branch, cannot be trusted with war-making powers.[6]

To study an event in history, such as the "surprise attack" at Pearl Harbor, it is necessary to study the ideas and events which preceded it, because history is like a seamless piece of cloth. The

---

[4]Thomas A. Bailey, *The Man in the Street: The Impact of American Public Opinion on Foreign Policy* (New York: Macmillan, 1948), pp. 11–12; see also Bruce R. Bartlett, *Cover-Up: The Politics of Pearl Harbor, 1941–1946* (New Rochelle, N.Y.: Arlington House, 1978), p. 64.

[5]Thomas A. Bailey, *Presidential Greatness: The Image and the Man from George Washington to the Present* (New York: Appleman Century-Crofts, 1966), p. 155.

[6]See John V. Denson, "War and American Freedom" in *The Costs of War: America's Pyrrhic Victories*, John V. Denson, ed., 2nd ed. (New Brunswick, N.J.: Transaction Publishers, 1999), pp. 1–11.

Pearl Harbor story is tied directly to British influence going back to World War I, and the British accomplishment of bringing America into that war. There are numerous books on the subject of this "surprise attack," but they differ in their conclusions on whether Roosevelt provoked the attack, whether he withheld information from the Pearl Harbor commanders, and whether Churchill and Roosevelt conspired to get America into the European war through the "back door" of a war first between America and Japan. However, all the books with which this author is familiar on the subject of Pearl Harbor primarily examine the period of time from early 1939 through December 7, 1941. One cannot truly understand and appreciate the story of Pearl Harbor without seeing it as a part of the period starting in 1914 with America's entry into World War I and coming up through 1946 to the Pearl Harbor congressional investigations. World War II was actually a continuation of World War I and therefore, needs to be studied as one war which had a recess of twenty years, from 1919 to 1939.

Many people simply refuse to believe that President Roosevelt would conspire secretly with Winston Churchill to bring America into World War II by putting the Pacific Fleet at risk in Pearl Harbor to carry out this plan. If you only look at the period from 1939 to 1941, you do not get the complete picture. The picture becomes clear only when you recognize the tremendously powerful political and economic forces at work in both the British Empire and America that caused Great Britain to enter World War I and then later got America into that war. Key British members of this same group, which has now become known as the Anglo-American Establishment, also practically wrote the Treaty of Versailles, which ended World War I. This unfair treaty led directly to the resumption of war in 1939 between Germany, France, and Great Britain, and that evolved into World War II. There are many events which Presidents Wilson and Roosevelt could not have brought about acting on their own to bring America into these two wars; but with both the public and secret participation of the powerful Anglo-American Establishment, America was dragged into these European wars against the wishes of the vast majority of American citizens. There is a well-established pattern by this Anglo-American group from World War I to Pearl Harbor, and the Pearl Harbor story fits into this pattern like a hand into a glove. In order to tell the Pearl Harbor story one must begin with World War I.

Another point needs to be made here. The "court historians"—or establishment journalists and historians whose main roles are to serve as both the progenitors and guardians of the political and patriotic myths of the nation, as well as protectors of the political leaders and special interest groups involved—accomplish their purpose by denigration and dismissal of any adverse explanation or exposure of these myths.[7] In most cases the court historians dismiss a refutation of the myth by simply stating that it is just another "conspiracy theory." They tend to explain most controversial historical events with their "lone nut" theory. While the court historians can't explain Pearl Harbor with the "lone nut" theory, they do dismiss the version related herein as merely another "conspiracy theory." They also attempt to explain the Pearl Harbor story by stating that the very nature of the Japanese people is that they are treacherous and vicious and have a long history of "surprise attacks," which is really only a reference to their surprise attack on Port Arthur in their victory over Russia in 1905.

First, to tell the Pearl Harbor story, we need to recall the original ideas of our Founders regarding America's foreign policy—ideas which we have completely repudiated in the twentieth century. The original American foreign policy, which began with President George Washington and continued for one hundred years thereafter, is well stated in Washington's *Farewell Address* in 1797, which contained this prescient advice:

> Against the insidious wiles of foreign influence, (I conjure you to believe me fellow citizens) the jealousy of a free people ought to be *constantly* awake; since history and experience prove that foreign influence is one of the most baneful foes of Republican Government. . . .
>
> The Great rule of conduct for us, in regard to foreign Nations is in extending our commercial relations to have with them as little *political* connection as possible. . . .

---

[7] See Harry Elmer Barnes, "Revisionism and the Historical Blackout," in *Perpetual War for Perpetual Peace: A Critical Examination of the Foreign Policy of Franklin Delano Roosevelt and its Aftermath*, Harry Elmer Barnes, ed. (New York: Greenwood Press, 1969), pp. 1–78.

Europe has a set of primary interests, which to us have none, or a very remote relation. Hence she must be engaged in frequent controversies, the causes of which are essentially foreign to our concerns. Hence therefore it must be unwise in us to implicate ourselves, by artificial ties, in the ordinary vicissitudes of her politics, or the ordinary combinations and collisions of her friendships, or enmities. . . .

Why, by interweaving our destiny with that of any part of Europe, entangle our peace and prosperity in the toils of European Ambition, Rivalship, Interest, Humor or Caprice?

'Tis our true policy to steer clear of permanent Alliances, with any portion of the foreign world.[8]

Murray Rothbard wrote a brilliant essay about American foreign policy and its change to interventionism at the end of the nineteenth century, expressly repudiating Washington's advice. This first put America at odds with the worldwide British Empire and its economic interests in our hemisphere in Venezuela over a boundary dispute:

The great turning point of American foreign policy came in the early 1890s, during the second Cleveland administration. It was then that the U.S. turned sharply and permanently from a policy of peace and non-intervention to an aggressive program of economic and political expansion abroad. At the heart of the new policy were America's leading bankers, eager to use the country's growing economic strength to subsidize and force-feed export markets and investment outlets that they would finance, as well as to guarantee Third World government bonds. The major focus of aggressive expansion in the 1890s was Latin America, and the principal Enemy to be dislodged was Great Britain, which had dominated foreign investments in that vast region.[9]

The leading investment bank in America at that time was the House of J.P. Morgan, which had tremendous influence over

---

[8]George Washington, *George Washington: A Collection*, W.B. Allen, ed. (Indianapolis, Ind.: Liberty Classics, 1988), pp. 524–25 (emphasis in the original).

[9]Murray N. Rothbard, *Wall Street, Banks, and American Foreign Policy* (Burlingame, Calif.: Center for Libertarian Studies, 1995), p. 4.

some members of the Cleveland administration, if not Cleveland himself. Rothbard continues:

> Long-time Morgan associate Richard Olney heeded the call, as Secretary of State from 1895 to 1897, setting the U.S. on the road to Empire. After leaving the State Department, he publicly summarized the policy he had pursued. The old isolationism heralded by George Washington's Farewell Address is over, he thundered. The time has now arrived, Olney declared, when "it behooves us to accept the commanding position . . . among the Power[s] of the earth." And, "the present crying need of our commercial interests," he added, "is more markets and larger markets" for American products, especially in Latin America.[10]

This new foreign policy, which was announced, if not implemented, during the Cleveland administration, led directly to McKinley's Spanish–American War in 1898 and to America's acquisition of a foreign empire in Asia, thereby repudiating the traditional American foreign policy.

At the turn of the twentieth century, as America started its new interventionist foreign policy, the British Empire was the largest the world had ever known. The Industrial Revolution began in England, and, therefore, the British became the first nation to acquire all of the advantages of industrialization, including the creation of massive amounts of new wealth. A.J.P. Taylor, a prominent British historian, comments on how Britain became and remained a great world power for more than three centuries:

> Though the object of being a Great Power is to be able to fight a great war, the only way of remaining a Great Power is not to fight one, or to fight it on a limited scale. This was the secret of Great Britain's greatness so long as she stuck to naval warfare and did not try to become a military power on the continental pattern.[11]

Through limited wars and military actions, the British had acquired numerous colonies throughout the world. It was perceived that these possessions were necessary for industrial development, to secure these colonies' natural resources and to

---

[10]Ibid., p. 5.

[11]A.J.P. Taylor, *The Origins of the Second World War*, 2nd ed. (Greenwich, Conn.: Fawcett Publications, 1961), p. 284.

provide markets for the manufactured products of the British economy. These basic factors of British and American political and economic development set the stage for World War I and America's entry into that war.

Neither World War I nor World War II was inevitable or necessary, especially from an American perspective; they were caused primarily by bad political choices that were greatly influenced by very large economic interests of a small number of politically powerful people. In fact, the entire twentieth century, in regard to the issues of war and peace, has been greatly influenced, if not controlled, by this Anglo-American group, which represents some of the world's most important economic interests. This group has supported the idea in America of a bipartisan foreign policy that causes little debate or discussion of the issues relating to foreign policy or to war and peace, and it has supported the concept of the "imperial presidency," which has given the president almost unlimited power over foreign policy. Arthur M. Schlesinger, Jr., in his book *The Imperial Presidency*, discusses the origins of the American bipartisan foreign policy, pointing out that it started when President Roosevelt put Republicans in his cabinet but that it became a dominant policy under President Truman. He points out that Senator Robert A. Taft strongly opposed both Roosevelt and Truman in this regard:

> "There are some who say that politics should stop at the water's edge," Senator Robert A. Taft had said in 1939. ". . . I do not at all agree. . . . There is no principle of subjection to the Executive in foreign policy. Only Hitler or Stalin would assert that." Taft retained that belief after the war. In January 1951 he called the bipartisan foreign policy "a very dangerous fallacy threatening the very existence of the Nation."[12]

This Anglo-American group is not a dark, illegal conspiracy, although it does try to withhold its ultimate aims from public scrutiny. These people, or their minions, are openly active in American and British politics by holding elective offices and holding cabinet positions in their respective governments. Their

---

[12]Arthur M. Schlesinger, Jr., *The Imperial Presidency* (Boston: Houghton Mifflin, 1973), p. 129; see also the condemnation of the bipartisan foreign policy by Felix Morley in his excellent book, *The Foreign Policy of the United States* (New York: Alfred A. Knopf, 1951), pp. vi–vii.

financial contributions and political propaganda are immensely effective. They fully support the *private*-enterprise system, or *private* ownership of property and the means of production, but they strongly oppose the *free*-enterprise system advocated by Ludwig von Mises and the Austrian School of economics. The *free*-enterprise system proposes the complete separation of the economy from the government, whereas the *private*-enterprise system advocates a partnership between government and the economic interests involved, thus providing many economic and military benefits to businesses. This Anglo-American group has little difficulty with a controlled economy. That is part of the price they pay for this partnership, because they have such immense political influence that they actually use this governmental power to deter their less politically-positioned competitors.

WORLD WAR I AND THE TREATY OF VERSAILLES AS CAUSES OF WORLD WAR II

The Pearl Harbor "incident" brought America into World War II, in 1941, two years after it had begun in Europe. In order to understand why World War II *started* in Europe, it is necessary to understand how World War I, in 1918–1919, *ended*. As stated earlier, World War II was actually a continuation of World War I in Europe, primarily because of the vindictive and fraudulent Versailles treaty that ended World War I. Prior to World War II, Germany attempted to revise the treaty peacefully and, after being rebuffed by the Allies, decided to revise it forcibly. A.J.P. Taylor has written the definitive work on the true origins of World War II in Europe by cutting through the myths and false propaganda presented by the Allies. He comments that:

> The second World war was, in large part, a repeat performance of the first. . . . Germany fought specifically in the second war to reverse the verdict of the first and to destroy the settlement which followed it. Her opponents fought, though less consciously, to defend that settlement. . . . If one asks the rather crude question, "what was the war about?" the answer for the first is: "to decide how Europe should be remade," but for the second merely: "to decide whether this remade Europe should continue." The first war explains the second and, in fact, caused it, in so far as one event causes another.[13]

---

[13]Taylor, *The Origins of the Second World War*, pp. 22–23.

Taylor goes on to explain how the peace treaty that ended World War I was a major cause of World War II and concludes that, "The peace of Versailles lacked moral validity from the start."[14] Therefore, in order to understand the causes of World War II in Europe, we need to take a brief look at World War I and why it was fought, as well as how it was concluded by this treaty.

The entry of Great Britain into World War I was greatly influenced by the same British political and economic interests who later joined with J.P. Morgan to bring America into World War I and World War II. The story of this Anglo-American group is told by Professor Carroll Quigley from Georgetown University, who has studied its organization and its tremendous influence on British and American foreign policy throughout the twentieth century. Quigley held positions at Harvard and Princeton prior to going to Georgetown University—where, incidentally, he had a student by the name of Bill Clinton. (President Clinton has stated that Professor Quigley was one of his favorite teachers at Georgetown.) Quigley wrote a book published in 1965 that discussed the Anglo-American group and its beginnings in England in the late nineteenth century:

> There does exist, and has existed for a generation, an international Anglophile network. . . . I know of the operations of this network because I have studied it for twenty years and was permitted for two years, in the early 1960s, to examine its papers and secret records. I have no aversion to it or most of its aims and have, for much of my life, been close to it and to many of its instruments. I have objected, both in the past and recently, to a few of its policies (notably to its belief that England was an Atlantic rather than a European Power and must be allied, or even federated, with the United States and must remain isolated from Europe), but in general my chief difference of opinion is that it wishes to remain unknown, and I believe its role in history is significant enough to be known.[15]

Quigley explained that the group started in England under the leadership of Professor John Ruskin at Oxford University

---

[14]Ibid., pp. 32, 277.

[15]Carroll Quigley, *Tragedy and Hope: A History of the World in Our Time* (New York: Macmillan, 1974), p. 950.

and received most of its money from the imperialist Cecil Rhodes. The American contingent was consolidated initially around the House of J.P. Morgan, which helps explain Morgan's key role in getting America into World War I to help the British. He goes on to explain that,

> The original purpose of these groups was to seek to federate the English-speaking world along lines laid down by Cecil Rhodes (1853–1902) and William T. Stead (1849–1912), and the money for the organizational work came originally from the Rhodes Trust.[16]

Soon after Quigley published his book *Tragedy and Hope*, the publisher took the book out of print and destroyed the plates without consulting Quigley.[17] That is probably why his next book, *The Anglo American Establishment*, was much more critical of the group.[18] An accurate understanding of how and why the United States got into two world wars in the twentieth century to help the British Empire cannot be obtained without reading these two books by Quigley and Rothbard's *Wall Street, Banks, and American Foreign Policy*.

Quigley concludes his analysis of this Anglo-American group and its influence on world events with this sobering thought: "In foreign policy their actions almost destroyed Western civilization, or at least the European center of it."[19] Quigley also comments on the long-term significance of this group, especially the British portion thereof:

> [O]ne of the chief methods by which this Group works has been through propaganda. It plotted the Jameson Raid of 1895; it caused the Boer War of 1899–1902; it set up and controls the Rhodes Trust; it created the Union of South Africa in 1906–1910 . . . it was the chief influence in Lloyd George's

---

[16]Ibid.

[17]Popular American columnist Charley Reese from Orlando, Florida, confirmed this fact in a personal interview with Quigley's widow. Reese reported, "I verified this myself in a telephone interview with his widow. She said he had been extremely upset when he learned of it. He died not long afterward." (Charley Reese, *The Orlando Sentinel*, January 26, 1999).

[18]Carroll Quigley, *The Anglo-American Establishment: From Rhodes to Cliveden* (New York: Books in Focus, 1981).

[19]Ibid., p. 309.

war administration in 1917–1919 and dominated the British delegation to the Peace Conference of 1919; it had a great deal to do with the formation and management of the League of Nations and of the system of mandates; it founded the Royal Institute of International Affairs in 1919 and still controls it; it was one of the chief influences on British policy toward Ireland, Palestine, and India in the period 1917–1945; it was a very important influence on the policy of appeasement of Germany during the years 1920–1940; and it controlled and still controls, to a very considerable extent, the sources and the writing of the history of British Imperial and foreign policy since the Boer War.[20]

The British were the first modern nation to make imperialism into an "art of government," and they created their empire over several centuries by following three main aims: control of the sea, control of international banking, and control of the world's natural resources.[21] The foreign policy of the British Empire since the latter part of the sixteenth century has been to prevent the rise of any strong power on the continent, something they accomplished by forming various alliances to prevent any one power from achieving supremacy. However, with the consolidation of the German states under the leadership of Bismarck in the Franco-Prussian War of 1870–1871, an aggressive and economically powerful German *nation* burst forth. Thereafter, the British political and economic leadership perceived this new German nation as an extreme threat to their balance of power policy in Europe and to their dominance in the world, both economically and militarily.

Karl Helfferich, a prominent German banker and the finance minister during the war, commented in 1918 upon the economic rivalry of Germany and the British Empire, as well as the reason the British declared war in August 1914:

> England's policy was always constructed against the politically and economically strongest Continental power. . . . Ever since Germany became the politically and economically strongest Continental power, did England feel threatened from Germany more than from any other land in its global economic position

---

[20]Ibid., p. 5.

[21]F. William Engdahl, *A Century of War: Anglo-American Oil Politics and the New World Order* (Concord, Mass.: Paul and Company, 1993), pp. 8–19.

and its naval supremacy. Since that point, the English–German differences were unbridgeable, and susceptible to no agreement in any one single question.[22]

Helfferich sadly noted the accuracy of the declaration by Bismarck in 1897: "The only condition which could lead to improvement of German–English relations would be if we bridled our economic development, and this is not possible."[23]

American diplomat Henry White was instructed by his government in 1907 to meet with the appropriate British representatives in order to determine their views regarding the rising power of Germany. He met with Arthur James Balfour, who would later serve as the British foreign secretary during World War I and would become famous for the Balfour Declaration that led to the creation of the State of Israel in 1948. As reported by historian Allan Nevins, White's daughter overheard the following conversation at this meeting:

> Balfour (*somewhat lightly*): "We are probably fools not to find a reason for declaring war on Germany before she builds too many ships and takes away our trade."
>
> White: "You are a very high-minded man in private life. How can you possibly contemplate anything so politically immoral as provoking a war against a harmless nation which has as good a right to a navy as you have? If you wish to compete with German trade, work harder."
>
> Balfour: "That would mean lowering our standard of living. Perhaps it would be simpler for us to have a war."
>
> White: "I am shocked that you of all men should enunciate such principles."
>
> Balfour (*again lightly*): "Is it a question of right or wrong? Maybe it is just a question of keeping our supremacy."[24]

Also, by 1910, two of the new industrial powers, Germany and the United States, both had acquired strong centralized governments through their respective wars from 1861 through 1871, and this began to upset the "balance of power" in the world. Furthermore, Japan, with one of the world's oldest

[22]Ibid., p. 38.

[23]Ibid.

[24]Allan Nevins, *Henry White: Thirty Years of American Diplomacy* (New York: Harper and Brothers, 1930), pp. 257–58.

monarchies and a strong centralized government, became the only country in Asia that decided to industrialize, and it shocked the world by defeating Russia in 1905. Therefore, the British political leadership perceived that their world supremacy was threatened on the continent and in both the Atlantic and the Pacific regions. From an economic standpoint, America in 1910 moved into first place in the world of manufacturing output while Germany was second and Great Britain was third.[25] In addition, the rapid industrial progress that was taking place in America, Germany, Japan, and the British Empire had shown the extreme importance of oil. By 1912, the United States produced more than 63 percent of the world's petroleum, while England commanded no more than 12 percent of the oil production.[26] Germany and Japan, on the other hand, had no independent, secure supply of oil.[27]

Great Britain's balance-of-power policy, as applied by the British political leadership, viewed all these economic rivalries as a threat to its empire but saw Germany, which was the new strong man of Europe and which was only a short distance across the channel, as a far greater threat than either America, which was all the way across the Atlantic Ocean, or Japan, in the Pacific. The author of *A Century of War* concludes in his analysis of World War I that:

> The British establishment had determined well before 1914 that war was the only course suitable to bring the European situation "under control." British interests dictated, according to their balance-of-power logic, a shift from her traditional "pro-Ottoman and anti-Russian" alliance strategy of the nineteenth century, to a "pro-Russian and anti-German" alliance strategy as early as the late 1890s."[28]

The British political and economic establishment did not expect the war to be as difficult or to last as long as it did and certainly did not think their "victory," with American help, would be as debilitating and costly as it turned out to be. A.J.P. Taylor explains that, "The first World war would obviously

---

[25]Fareed Zakaria, *From Wealth to Power: The Unusual Origins of America's World Role* (Princeton, N.J.: Princeton University Press, 1998), p. 190.

[26]Engdahl, *A Century of War*, pp. 37 and 75.

[27]Ibid., p. 36.

[28]Ibid., p. 38.

have had a different end if it had not been for American inter-vention: the Allies, to put it bluntly, would not have won."[29] He states further that, "The German army had been beaten in the field. It was in retreat. But it had not been routed or destroyed. The British and French armies, although victorious, were also near exhaustion."[30] Germany had not been invaded; in fact, its army still occupied foreign territory, and although it was in retreat, it could still fight. It was, obvious, however, that with American intervention, the eventual outcome of the war was certain to cause their defeat.

In the recently published book, *The Pity of War*, British histo-rian Niall Ferguson asserts that Great Britain should not have entered the European war (helping to make it a world war) and that the German government, under the kaiser, was not truly a military or economic threat to the British Empire.[31] Ferguson concludes that if Britain had not entered the war, then America would not have entered, it would not have lasted so long, and it would have ended with a victory for the kaiser's Germany. He points out that there were no binding legal ties with either Bel-gium or France to cause Great Britain to enter the war:

> Britain's decision to intervene was the result of secret planning by her generals and diplomats, which dated back to late 1905. . . . When the moment of decision came on 2 August 1914, it was by no means a foregone conclusion that Britain would intervene against Germany; the majority of ministers were hesitant, and in the end agreed to support [Foreign Secretary Sir Edward] Grey partly for fear of being turned out of office and letting in the Tories. It was a historic disaster.[32]

He further argues that, "[I]f a war had been fought, but without Britain and America, the victorious Germans might have created a version of the European Union, eight decades ahead of schedule," and the British would have remained strong, especially financially.[33] Ferguson then states that a short war won by the kaiser's Germany would have produced

[29]Taylor, *The Origins of the Second World War*, p. viii.

[30]Ibid., p. 26.

[31]Niall Ferguson, *The Pity of War* (London: Allen Lane, Penguin Press, 1998).

[32]Ibid., p. 443.

[33]Ibid., pp. 458 and 460.

a far different world for the remainder of the twentieth century, without Nazism in Germany or Communism in Russia:

> With the Kaiser triumphant, Adolph Hitler could have eked out his life as a mediocre postcard painter and a fulfilled old soldier in a German-dominated Central Europe about which he could have found little to complain. And Lenin could have carried on his splenetic scribbling in Zurich, forever waiting for capitalism to collapse—and forever disappointed. . . . It was ultimately because of the war that both men were able to rise to establish barbaric despotisms which perpetrated still more mass murder.[34]

Ferguson closes his book by recognizing that World War I was horrible not only because of its destructiveness, but, more importantly, because it was avoidable, not inevitable. British leaders made a great error in judgment by taking Britain into the war, changing the whole course of the twentieth century:

> World War I was at once piteous, in the poet's sense, and "a pity." It was something worse than a tragedy, which is something we are taught by the theater to regard as ultimately unavoidable. It was nothing less than the greatest *error* of modern history.[35]

Murray Rothbard agrees with Ferguson's assessment of World War I and the great error made by Britain in entering that war, but he laments even more the great *error* that President Wilson made:

> American entry into World War I in April 1917 prevented [a] negotiated peace between warring powers, and drove the Allies forward into a peace of unconditional surrender and dismemberment, a peace which, as we have seen, set the stage for World War II. American entry thus cost countless lives on both sides, chaos and disruption throughout central and eastern Europe at war's end, and the consequent rise of Bolshevism, fascism, and Nazism to power in Europe. In this way, Woodrow Wilson's decision to enter the war may have been the single, most fateful action of the twentieth century, causing

---

[34]Ibid., p. 460.

[35]Ibid., p. 462 (emphasis in the original).

untold and unending misery and destruction. But Morgan profits were expanded and assured.[36]

Rothbard comments further about Morgan's direct financial interest in getting America into the war, which Morgan claimed was only to help the British:

> At the moment of great financial danger for the Morgans, the advent of World War I came as a godsend. Long connected to British, including Rothschild, financial interests, the Morgans leaped into the fray, quickly securing the appointment, for J.P. Morgan and Company, of fiscal agent for the warring British and French governments, and monopoly underwriter for their war bonds in the Unites States. J.P. Morgan also became the fiscal agent for the Bank of England, the powerful English central bank. Not only that: the Morgans were heavily involved in financing American munitions and other firms exporting war material to Britain and France. J.P. Morgan and Company, moreover, became the central authority organizing and channelling war purchases for the two Allied nations.[37]

As we all know, hindsight is easier than foresight, but lessons should be learned from history; these lessons come by studying the political choices that were available and then by following the consequences of the choices that were made, as well as the probable consequences of the choices that were not made.[38] The British decided to enter the war for very poor reasons, mainly economic, and thought that, with the French and Russians, they could defeat the Germans quickly and conclusively. This did not turn out to be the case; therefore, the British desperately sought American intervention in order to crush the German economic and military "threat" completely. Even if the British had entered the war, but without American intervention, and regardless of who the victors were, a peace treaty would have been entered into much earlier and would have been concluded on much more equal terms, with the original German government—and probably the original Russian government—still in place. In this case also, the twentieth century

---

[36]Rothbard, *Wall Street, Banks, and American Foreign Policy*, pp. 20–21.

[37]Ibid., pp. 15–16.

[38]See Niall Ferguson, ed., *Virtual History: Alternatives and Counterfactuals* (London: Papermac, [1977] 1997).

would have been far different without Nazism ruling Germany and probably without Communism ruling Russia.

Colonel Edward Mandell House, President Woodrow Wilson's primary adviser, frequently visited England in 1914 and 1915 in order to discuss America's possible entry into the war. Finally, on October 17, 1915, and in spite of his political speeches calling for neutrality, President Wilson wrote a secret letter to the leaders of the British government, offering to bring America into the war on the side of the Allies in order to cause them to win decisively. That would then allow Wilson to be the major player in dictating a *permanent peace* for the world.[39] House appealed to Wilson's insatiable ego by telling the president that he would be the "Savior of the World" and the new "Prince of Peace."[40] House praised Wilson's humanitarian motives for bringing America into the war, stating that he would play the "the noblest part that has ever come to a son of man."[41]

President Wilson was naive enough to believe that the only war aims of the Allies (England, France, and Russia) were those stated publicly, "which included the restoration of Belgium, the return of Alsace–Lorraine to France, and the annexation of Constantinople by Russia."[42] However, one of the American delegates to the Paris Peace Conference that followed World War I was a knowledgeable diplomat by the name of William C. Bullitt. He later resigned his position as a delegate in protest of Wilson's actions at the peace conference, saying that Wilson did not understand the secret war aims of the Allies, and particularly those of the British, until the peace negotiations were all under way in regard to the Treaty of Versailles. Bullitt states the secret aims the British hoped to achieve at the peace conference:

[T]he destruction of the German Navy, the confiscation of the German merchant marine, the elimination of Germany as an economic rival, the extraction of all possible indemnities from Germany, the annexation of German East Africa and the

---

[39]William C. Bullitt and Sigmund Freud, *Woodrow Wilson: A Psychological Study* (New Brunswick, N.J.: Transaction Publishers, [1967] 1999), pp. 170–71.

[40]Ibid., p. 170.

[41]Ibid.

[42]Ibid., p. 174.

Cameroons, the annexation of all German colonies in the Pacific south of the Equator . . . Palestine and as much of Syria as they might be able to get away from the French, the extension of their sphere of influence in Persia, the recognition of their protectorates of Cyprus and Egypt.[43]

Bullitt then concludes that "All of these secret war aims of the British were actually achieved in one form or another by the Treaty of Versailles."[44]

The great *classical* liberal American writer, Albert Jay Nock, commented on World War I and the Treaty of Versailles:

The war immensely fortified a universal faith in violence; it set in motion endless adventures in imperialism, endless nationalistic ambition. Every war does this to a degree roughly corresponding to its magnitude. *The final settlement at Versailles, therefore, was a mere scramble for loot.*[45]

It was also during World War I that the British clearly recognized how important, even critical, the abundant supply of oil was, not only for industrial purposes but also for military purposes. Therefore, one of their main economic and military aims was to help free the Arabs from the rule of the Turks (the Ottoman Empire) and then to take over the Arab oil interests after the war. The British used their agent "Lawrence of Arabia" to lead the Arab revolt against the Turks. Then, during the negotiations that led to the Treaty of Versailles, the British doublecrossed the Arabs by grabbing their oil for themselves. By 1925 the British controlled a major part of the world's future supplies of petroleum.[46] It was not until World War II that America, through the trickery of President Roosevelt, was able to grab "its share" of the Arabs' oil that the British had taken in World War I. William Engdahl states:

They [the Rockefeller companies of the Standard Oil Group, together with the Pittsburgh Mellon family's Gulf Oil] had

---

[43]Ibid., p. 173.

[44]Ibid.

[45]Albert Jay Nock, *The State of the Union: Essays in Social Criticism* (Indianapolis, Ind.: Liberty Press, 1991), p. 89 (emphasis added).

[46]Engdahl, *A Century of War*, p. 75.

secured a major stake in concessions for oil in the Middle East, above all in Saudi Arabia. Partly through the clever diplomacy of President Roosevelt and the bungling of Britain's Winston Churchill, Saudi Arabia slipped from the British grip during the war. Saudi King Abdul Aziz gained an unprecedented Lend-Lease agreement in 1943 from Roosevelt, a gesture to ensure Saudi goodwill to American oil interests after the war.[47]

Engdahl also comments on the Versailles peace treaty and the League of Nations:

> Britain's creation of the League of Nations through the Versailles Peace Conference in 1919, became a vehicle to give a facade of international legitimacy to a naked imperial territory seizure. For the financial establishment of the City of London, the expenditure of hundreds of thousands of British lives in order to dominate future world economic development through raw materials control, especially of the new resource, oil, was a seemingly small price to pay.[48]

Engdahl further states that by 1919, after the signing of the Treaty of Versailles, the Persian Gulf became an "English lake."[49]

Murray Rothbard points out that the first formal joining of the Anglo-American group occurred at the Versailles peace conference in Paris when:

> [T]he British and U.S. historical staffs at Versailles took the occasion to found a permanent organization to agitate for an informally, if not formally, reconstituted Anglo-American Empire.
>
> The new group, the Institute of International Affairs, was formed at a meeting at the Majestic Hotel in Paris on May 30, 1919.[50]

Rothbard continues by revealing the heavy representation of the House of Morgan in this Anglo-American group. He also points out that the intense economic and political warfare between the Morgan and the Rockefeller interests, which began in the early

---

[47]Ibid., p. 102.

[48]Ibid., p. 50.

[49]Ibid., p. 51.

[50]Rothbard, *Wall Street, Banks, and American Foreign Policy*, pp. 25–26.

years of the twentieth century, eventually ceased and that they joined forces to become the main leaders of the American portion of this group just before World War II.[51]

It is important to recall that, after World War I, a better informed and more realistic President Wilson admitted to the American people that World War I had not been an idealistic and humanitarian war to "make the world safe for democracy," nor had it been the "war to end all the wars." He toured the U.S. to try to influence public opinion to pressure the U.S. Senate to approve the Treaty of Versailles and to have the United States join the League of Nations, which the Senate wisely failed to do. Near the end of the tour, the discouraged president made a speech in St. Louis, Missouri, on September 5, 1919, wherein he abandoned his lofty statements and confessed to the American people what the real purpose of the war had been:

> Why, my fellow-citizens, is there any man here, or any woman—let me say, is there any child here, who does not know that the seed of war in the modern world is industrial and commercial rivalry? . . . This war, in its inception, was a commercial and industrial war. It was not a political war.[52]

The complete injustice of the Treaty of Versailles is a story that most British and American historians refuse to tell and one that very few of the American and British public know. In fact, the modern liberal line today, which is completely fallacious, is that World War II resulted mainly from the failure of the U.S. Senate to ratify the treaty and the failure of America to join the League of Nations. However, the true story of the Versailles

---

[51]Ibid., pp. 27–37.

[52]Arthur S. Link, ed., *The Papers of Woodrow Wilson* (Princeton, N.J.: Princeton University Press, 1990), vol. 63, pp. 45–46. The Wilson administration discovered a silver lining in the cloud caused by the failure of the U.S. Senate to ratify the Versailles treaty, thereby leaving America technically at war until November 1921 when new treaties were signed proclaiming the end of the war. During this interim period, the Wilson administration pushed through legislation which still claimed to be part of the war effort. The Supreme Court, which traditionally had avoided judicial review of wartime measures, saw the danger, broke their long-standing rule, and began to judicially review these power-seeking measures. See Christopher N. May, *In the Name of War: Judicial Review and the War Power Since 1918* (Cambridge, Mass.: Harvard University Press, 1989).

treaty is very different and teaches an important lesson of history, as we shall see.

President Wilson, after injecting America into World War I, promised the Germans that a peace treaty would be effected with America as the leader of the conference and that the terms would be equitable and would not demand punitive war payments from Germany. The treaty, he promised, would allow self-determination for people throughout Europe so they could select their own governments. America, France, and the British entered into a pre-armistice agreement with Germany on November 5, 1918, with America and its Allies agreeing to make peace on the basis of President Wilson's famous Fourteen Points.[53] This promise proved to be fraudulent, and instead, a vindictive treaty was *forced* on Germany. A.J.P. Taylor describes the coercive measures, applied primarily by the British:

> There were other measures of coercion than the renewal of the war and occupation of German territory. These measures were economic—some form of the blockade which was believed to have contributed decisively to Germany's defeat. The blockade helped push the German government into accepting the peace treaty in June, 1919. . . . The negotiations between Germany and the Allies became a competition in blackmail, sensational episodes in a gangster film. The Allies, or some of them, threatened to choke Germany to death.[54]

After the signing of the formal armistice on November 11, 1918, the fighting stopped, but the British blockade of Germany continued, thereby causing the death by starvation of eight hundred thousand Germans, and resulting in a much-justified hatred of the Allies.[55] It was mainly the continuation of this naval blockade for six months after the war ended that forced the Germans into signing the unfair treaty.

The Treaty of Versailles divested Germany of its colonial possessions, allowing the British to expand their control in

---

[53]Quigley, *The Anglo-American Establishment*, p. 237.

[54]Taylor, *The Origins of the Second World War*, p. 33.

[55]Charles Callan Tansill, "The United States and the Road to War in Europe" in *Perpetual War for Perpetual Peace: A Critical Examination of the Foreign Policy of Franklin Delano Roosevelt and its Aftermath*, Harry Elmer Barnes, ed. (New York: Greenwood Press, 1969), p. 96.

Africa to fulfill Cecil Rhodes's dream of an all-British route from Cairo to the Cape by taking the German colonies under the "mandate" in 1919. Most important, from a future political standpoint, it deprived Germany of any military defense by reducing the maximum number of its armed forces to only one hundred thousand men, which could hardly defend Germany from its traditionally hostile neighbors, especially the French and now *Soviet* Russia. The treaty prohibited Germany from having any airplanes, submarines, heavy artillery, or tanks. Germany had scuttled its own high-seas fleet under the waters of Scapa Flow to prevent its capture while the British retained the world's largest navy. The French, through the treaty, required the demilitarization of the Rhineland west of the bank of the Rhine which bordered on France, thereby keeping an open, undefended access to Germany's industrial heart in the Ruhr. France also maintained on Germany's border a great army, which was considered one of the world's finest.[56] In complete violation of Wilson's Fourteen Points, which called for self-determination, more than three million Germans were forcibly included in the country of Czechoslovakia and six million in Austria.[57] Furthermore, the treaty saddled Germany with the complete war guilt by branding her as the country that started the war, a conclusion which she did not agree with or accept.[58] Another great injustice done to Germany in the treaty is the one that became the immediate cause of World War II. The treaty carved a wide path, or "corridor," through Germany from Poland to the German seaport city of Danzig, the strip of land that was taken from Germany in order to give Poland an outlet to the sea. The corridor completely separated East Prussia from the remainder of Germany, and the League of Nations took over the government of Danzig, declaring it a "Free City." Half a million German citizens within Danzig and the corridor suddenly became subject to the government of Poland, in complete violation of Wilson's promise of self-determination.[59] Finally, another great injustice

---

[56]J. Kenneth Brody, *The Avoidable War: Lord Cecil and the Policy of Principle— 1933–1935* (New Brunswick, N.J.: Transaction Publishers, 1999), vol. 1, pp. 1–6, 99–123.

[57]Taylor, *The Origins of the Second World War*, pp. 146–81, 278.

[58]Ibid., p. 50; see also M.H. Cochran, *Germany Not Guilty in 1914* (Colorado Springs, Colo.: Ralph Myles, 1972).

[59]Taylor, *The Origins of the Second World War*, p. 189.

was the creation of the huge debt for reparation payments or damages caused to the Allies, which was imposed on Germany in complete violation of Wilson's promises and the pre–armistice agreement. William Engdahl states:

> In May 1921, the Allied Reparations Committee met and drew up what was called the London Ultimatum, the "final" payments plan demanded of Germany. It fixed Germany's Reparations Debt to the victorious Allies at the astronomical sum of 132 billion gold Marks, an amount which even British reparations expert, John Maynard Keynes, said was more than 3 times the maximum which Germany could possibly pay.[60]

Taylor comments about the reparation payments, which lasted for thirteen years, from 1919 to 1932: "At the end the French felt swindled; and the Germans felt robbed. Reparations had kept the passions of war alive."[61] He comments further: "Reparations counted as a symbol. They created resentment, suspicion, and international hostility. More than anything else, they cleared the way for the second World war."[62]

Germany had been totally betrayed by America and the Allies in the peace negotiations. Delegate Bullitt commented upon the German reaction to the treaty:

> The Treaty of Versailles was delivered to the Germans on May 7, [1919]. The President of the National Assembly at Weimar, upon reading it, remarked, "it is incomprehensible that a man who had promised the world a peace of justice, upon which a society of nations would be founded has been able to assist in framing this project dictated by hate." The first German official comment on the treaty was made on May 10, 1919. It stated that a first perusal of the treaty revealed that "on essential points the basis of the Peace of Right, agreed upon between the belligerents, has been abandoned," that some of the demands were such as "no nation could endure" and that "many of them could not possibly be carried out."[63]

---

[60]Engdahl, *A Century of War*, p. 81.

[61]Taylor, *The Origins of the Second World War*, p. 47.

[62]Ibid., p. 48.

[63]Bullitt and Freud, *Woodrow Wilson*, pp. 268–69.

Many of Wilson's advisers told him not to participate any further in the treaty negotiations and advised him to use his financial leverage over France and England to cause them not to enforce such a vindictive treaty against Germany. Wilson refused and continued to state publicly that he thought the treaty would be revised later by the League of Nations in order to make it fair.[64] Bullitt recounts that Wilson stated to Professor William E. Dodd later, "I ought not to have signed; but what could I do?" Bullitt then concludes, "He [Wilson] seems to have realized at times that the treaty was in truth a sentence of death for European civilization."[65]

William Bullitt resigned from the Paris Peace Conference and wrote a letter of resignation to President Wilson dated May 17, 1919, which contained the following statement:

> But our government has consented now to deliver the suffering peoples of the world to new oppressions, subjections, and dismemberments—*a new century of war*. And I can convince myself no longer that effective labor for "a new world order" is possible as a servant of this Government.[66]

Delegate Bullitt went on to state that this treaty would:

> [M]*ake new international conflicts certain*. It is my conviction that the present League of Nations will be powerless to prevent these wars, and that the United States would be involved in them by obligations undertaken in the covenant of the league and in the special understanding with France. Therefore the duty of the Government of the United States to its own people and to mankind is to refuse to sign or ratify this unjust treaty, to refuse to guarantee its settlements by entering the League of Nations, to refuse to entangle the United States further by the understanding with France.[67]

---

[64]Ibid., pp. 261–63.

[65]Ibid., p. 294.

[66]Ibid., p. 271 (emphasis added).

[67]Ibid., pp. 271–72 (emphasis added). The "special understanding with France" was a proposed collective security agreement to be entered into jointly by the British and the Americans to protect France from a future invasion by Germany. When the U.S. Senate failed to approve this agreement, the British refused to guarantee this security alone and the agreement failed altogether.

The Treaty of Versailles destroyed Germany's form of government, again violating Wilson's promise of self-determination, and created instead the puppet-like democratic Weimar Republic, which virtually assured continued political convulsions within Germany itself. This unpopular government, which was enforcing the treaty against Germany's interests, was finally overthrown by Hitler's murderous Nazi movement, which won its power through the democratic and constitutional process with two main commitments: to fight communism and to end the unfair and vindictive treaty. Although the payments stopped in 1932, just before Hitler took office in 1933, the injustice of the payments had been a major part of his campaign. He continued to campaign against the remainder of the treaty after taking office and stated: "My programme was to abolish the Treaty of Versailles. . . . No human being has declared or recorded what he wanted more often than I. Again and again I wrote these words—the Abolition of the Treaty of Versailles."[68] After gaining power, Hitler repeatedly petitioned the Allies to revise the treaty either to allow Germany to restore at least the equality of defense in military personnel and equipment with the other nations or to call for total disarmament by everyone. The Allies refused both offers.[69] Hitler then acted unilaterally to keep his promise to the German people by disregarding the treaty's limitations on Germany's defense and he rearmed Germany, first only to an adequate defensive position.

Hitler made one peace offer in 1936 that would have provided European security for the British and the French. He offered to agree that there would be no territorial claims in Europe, thereby accepting the German losses of territory in the treaty. He even proposed a twenty-five-year pact of nonaggression with all Western powers except Russia. Hitler had always maintained that the only war he wanted was with communism and Soviet Russia. In response to this peace offer, the British asked a few questions for further definitions but then refused to reply, and the French never replied at all.[70] A.J.P. Taylor comments on Hitler's foreign policy as follows:

[68]Alan Bullock, *Hitler, A Study in Tyranny* (New York: Harper and Row, 1962), p. 315; also see Brody, *The Avoidable War*, p. 99.

[69]Ibid., pp. 99–123.

[70]Taylor, *The Origins of the Second World War*, p. 100.

There was one element of system in Hitler's foreign policy, though it was not new. His outlook was "continental," as Stresemann's had been before him. Hitler did not attempt to revive the "World Policy" which Germany had pursued before 1914; he made no plans for a great battle-fleet; he did not parade a grievance over the lost colonies, except as a device for embarrassing the British; he was not even interested in the Middle East—hence his blindness to the great opportunity in 1940 after the defeat of France. . . . He did not wish to destroy the British Empire, nor even to deprive the French of Alsace and Lorraine. In return, he wanted the Allies to accept the verdict of January 1918; to abandon the artificial undoing of this verdict after November 1918; and to acknowledge that Germany had been victorious in the East. This was not a preposterous program. Many Englishmen, to say nothing of Milner and Smuts,[71] agreed with it even in 1918; many more did so later; and most Frenchmen were coming round to the same outlook.[72]

There has been much criticism of the Munich Pact as appeasement, but Taylor comments:

Only those who wanted Soviet Russia to take the place of Germany are entitled to condemn the "appeasers"; and I cannot understand how most of those who condemn them are now equally indignant at the inevitable result of their failure.[73]

Britain's reason for appeasement was primarily caused by the sense of guilt on the part of the political and economic interests identified by Rothbard and Quigley as the British portion of the Anglo-American Establishment, because they were the principal authors and beneficiaries of the unfair Versailles treaty. This British group, usually called the Milner Group, negotiated the treaty and virtually controlled British foreign policy during World War I and thereafter. They were willing for Hitler to set

---

[71]Sir Alfred Milner was the key leader of the British portion of the Anglo-American Establishment, and Jan C. Smuts was an important member who was located in South Africa. Lord Robert Cecil was the leader of another bloc within the British portion of the Anglo-American group. However, Milner became the dominant member, and the group is often referred to as "The Milner Group." See Quigley, *The Anglo-American Establishment*, pp. 15–32, 51–100.

[72]Taylor, *The Origins of the Second World War*, p. 71.

[73]Ibid., p. 292.

aside much of the treaty on a piecemeal basis, which would allow Germany to reclaim certain territory in Europe. However, the Milner Group would not give up *its* economic gains received through the treaty. These British leaders especially wanted Hitler to rearm to a sufficient extent so that he could prevent Russian Communism from taking over Europe, but they wanted it done unilaterally by Hitler without their specific agreement, because that might reflect badly on their "wisdom" in negotiating the original treaty.

The real irony of the beginning of World War II is that it started over Danzig and the Polish Corridor question, which both the British and French political leaders found to be the most indefensible part of the treaty and one which most needed to be revised peacefully. Hitler made numerous offers to the Allies and to Poland for settlement of the corridor question, one being to take Danzig back and letting the people inside the corridor remain subjects of the Polish government. Another offer was to let the people within the corridor vote on which government they wanted. The British and the French, who were formal allies of Poland, pushed the Poles to accept these offers from Hitler.[74] Britain and France also requested that President Roosevelt push the Poles to accept Hitler's offers, but Roosevelt refused even to discuss the matter with Poland's representatives.[75] The Polish government arrogantly refused even to reply to these offers, and Hitler finally attacked Poland on September 1, 1939. Because of their treaty obligations, France and England then declared war against Germany on September 3 but refused to assist Poland in any way. Hitler had not expected the British and French to go to war over a treaty provision that they knew and declared to him to be completely unfair to Germany and to her people located in Danzig and the corridor. Taylor comments on this irony:

> In this curious way the French who had preached resistance to Germany for twenty years appeared to be dragged into war by the British who for twenty years preached conciliation. Both countries went to war for that part of the peace settlement which they had long regarded as least defensible. . . .

---

[74]Ibid., pp. 239–68.
[75]Ibid., p. 262.

> Such were the origins of the second World war, or rather the war between the three Western Powers over the settlement of Versailles; a war which had been implicit since the moment when the first war ended. . . . Great Britain and France did nothing to help the Poles, and little to help themselves. The European struggle which began in 1918 when the German armistice delegates presented themselves before Foch in the railway–carriage at Rethondes, ended in 1940 when the French armistice delegates presented themselves before Hitler in the same carriage. There was a "new order" in Europe; it was dominated by Germany.[76]

It is both ironic and noteworthy that Germany and Soviet Russia attacked Poland in September 1939 but that France and England only declared war against Germany while the Soviets became the allies of Britain and America thereafter. The final irony at the end of World War II was that Poland was not saved from tyranny at all but was simply transferred from German domination to that of Soviet Russia.

The French and British war on Germany was called "the phony war" because there was little activity on either side. However, in April and May of 1940, the Germans shocked the world by defeating the French in about thirty-five days of combat and drove an Allied army of 335,000 men, who were mostly British, to the beach at Dunkirk where they were hopelessly trapped.[77] Hitler gave orders to allow the helpless British army to escape in order to demonstrate dramatically that he had no quarrel with the British and desperately wanted to negotiate a treaty with them. He thought that a massacre at Dunkirk would inflame British public opinion and preclude a settlement with them. However, Winston Churchill became prime minister on May 10, 1940, and not only did he refuse to negotiate, but he immediately initiated bombing raids on German cities and civilians. War propaganda by the Allies, including America, has always stated that Hitler started the bombing of cities with his attack on the British city of Coventry, but the records now clearly indicate that Churchill initiated this.[78] Taylor, the British historian,

---

[76]Ibid., p. 267.

[77]See generally, Nicholas Harman, *Dunkirk: The Patriotic Myth* (New York: Simon and Schuster, 1980).

[78]James E. Spaight, *Bombing Vindicated* (London: G. Bles, 1944); Air Marshall Sir Arthur Harris, *Bomber Offensive* (London: Kimber, 1963).

comments on this propaganda by stating that there was "almost universal belief that Hitler started the indiscriminate bombing of civilians, whereas it was started by the directors of British strategy, as some of the more honest among them have boasted."[79] During the summer of 1940, after the bombing of civilians in German cities by the British, Hitler again tried desperately to reach a settlement with Churchill, but Churchill flatly refused to negotiate. It was not until November 1940 that Hitler retaliated by bombing British civilians and cities that were not military targets, such as Coventry.[80]

Therefore, we see that one of the main causes of World War II in Europe was the vindictive Versailles treaty and the failure of the Allies to revise it peacefully in the interim period between the wars. However, the Allies continued their parade of injustice at the Nuremberg war trials after World War II. One of the charges contained in count two was "crimes against peace," which was interpreted to mean that Germany had violated the Versailles peace treaty. The initial unfairness of the treaty was considered irrelevant and inadmissible testimony; this effectively prevented Germany from explaining any of her actions from 1919 to 1939, and prohibited her from showing the attempts to revise the treaty peacefully. At the trials, the Allies made it appear that Germany was simply an unprovoked aggressor against the peaceful powers of Europe, just as the war guilt clause of the Versailles treaty branded the Germans with sole responsibility for the outbreak of World War I.

None of this explanation for the cause of World War II should absolve Hitler for his murderous domestic policy. As Taylor points out, it was *not* Hitler's foreign policy that was evil; in fact, it was understandable and just, up to a point. Instead, it was Hitler's evil domestic policy, which resulted in the deaths of twenty-one million innocent, unarmed men, women, and children killed during the war after Hitler had taken total control of the German government. Although Hitler achieved his office in a democratic and constitutional manner by promising to revise the Versailles treaty and oppose communism, after he obtained office, he went beyond Bismarck's consolidation of the states into a nation by *abolishing* all the states and creating a

---

[79]Taylor, *The Origins of the Second World War*, p. 284.
[80]Ibid., pp. 284–87.

strong, totalitarian government. He finally declared himself dictator. As Taylor states:

> He changed most things in Germany. He destroyed political freedom and the rule of law; he transformed German economics and finance; he quarrelled with the Churches; he abolished the separate states and made Germany for the first time a united country. In one sphere alone he changed nothing. His foreign policy was that of his predecessors, of the professional diplomats at the foreign ministry, and indeed of virtually of all Germans. Hitler, too, wanted to free Germany from the restrictions of the peace treaty; to restore a great German army; and then make Germany the greatest power in Europe from her natural weight.[81]

Hitler's domestic policy, however, was again proof of Lord Acton's famous phrase, "All power tends to corrupt; absolute power corrupts absolutely." There is no question that Hitler ranks as one of the most evil murderers in all history, but he still ranks third behind Soviet Russia's Stalin and Mao of Communist China. Stalin was personally responsible for more than forty-two million murders of innocent men, women, and children from 1929 to 1953, and the Soviet Empire itself ranks as the greatest political tyranny the world has ever known, with a total of sixty-two million murders of its own citizens from 1917 until 1987.[82] Mao ranks number two behind Stalin because as the Chinese dictator from 1923 to 1976, he murdered more than thirty-seven million of his own people.[83] One of the bizarre results of World War II was that it enhanced the two great Communist powers of Russia and China and destroyed the three most anticommunist governments: Germany, Japan, and Italy. World War II made the world much safer for communism and, thereby, more at risk to tyranny.

Finally, in regard to World War I and America's intervention, it is important to note that two of the key players in that war were also important figures in World War II. Franklin Roosevelt served in the Wilson administration as assistant secretary of Navy, and Winston Churchill played a much more significant role in the British government as the first lord of the Admiralty.

[81]Ibid., p. 70.

[82]R.J. Rummel, *Death by Government*, pp. 4, 8, 79–89.

[83]Ibid., pp. 8, 91.

Churchill's role in the *Lusitania* incident is remarkable, and this event became one of the major "reasons" Wilson used to bring America into World War I.

Just prior to World War I, the Cunard steamship company in England had received a government subsidy in order to build the *Lusitania*, which was the world's fastest ocean liner. This subsidy allowed the government to participate in the design of the ship, which included a secret compartment where weapons and ammunition could be stored aboard ship. This subsidy further allowed the British government to take over full control of this ship during wartime. Colin Simpson, in his explosive 1972 best-seller, *The Lusitania*, gives the details of how the British, primarily through the actions of Churchill, used the sinking of the *Lusitania* to bring America into World War I to help defeat Germany.[84] When the *Lusitania* sank, more than one hundred Americans lost their lives.[85] On this fateful voyage, the British Admiralty, under Churchill's leadership, changed captains, substituting Captain William Turner for the usual captain. As the *Lusitania* drew near to its final destination, orders came from the British Admiralty to the military escort ship, the *Juno*, to abandon its usual mission, thereby leaving the ocean liner without protection from submarines. The *Lusitania* was not told that it was now alone, nor was it told that a German submarine was directly in its path—a fact known by the Admiralty. Finally, the Admiralty ordered Captain Turner to reduce his speed, thereby making the *Lusitania* an easy target for torpedoes.

At the hearing held in England following this disaster, Captain Turner was made the scapegoat and found guilty of negligence, just as the American commanders at Pearl Harbor would later be made scapegoats for that disaster in World War II.

WORLD WAR II AND BRITISH INFLUENCE ON AMERICAN FOREIGN POLICY PRIOR TO PEARL HARBOR

Britain learned the hard way in World War I that it could not preserve and protect its empire without having the United States, with its economic and military strength, to help fight its

---

[84]Colin Simpson, *The Lusitania* (New York: Ballantine Books, 1974).

[85]William Stevenson, *A Man Called Intrepid: The Secret War* (New York: Ballantine Books, 1976), pp. 267–68.

wars to ultimate victory. The British openly sought American aid in advance of the European war that started in September 1939. On June 10, 1939, King George VI and his wife, Queen Mary, came to America and visited the Roosevelts at Hyde Park. According to King George's biographer, Roosevelt, in private conversations with the king, secretly promised the king full American support for the British Empire. Roosevelt agreed to set up a zone in the Atlantic to be patrolled by the U.S. Navy, and the king's notes show that Roosevelt intended to sink German U-boats and await the consequences. The biographer of King George VI, John W. Wheeler-Bennett, concludes that these agreements served as the basis for the destroyer deal as well as for the Lend-Lease Agreement made much later.[86]

Another very important matter, related directly to secret conversations between Roosevelt and Churchill before America entered the war, is known as the "Tyler Kent Affair." Tyler Kent, a code clerk in the American Embassy in London, intercepted coded communications between Roosevelt and Churchill, who at that time was merely the first lord of the Admiralty. The code was supposed to be used only by the American Embassy in communications with the president and diplomats back in Washington. In other words, in violation of proper protocol, the president of the United States was not communicating with the head of the British government but was secretly negotiating with Churchill, who would not become prime minister for several months. Tyler Kent became concerned about the fact that these conversations revealed secret plans by which America was to be brought into the war in violation of the U.S. Constitution without a declaration of war by Congress. Scotland Yard learned that Kent had discussed these decoded messages with, and possibly showed them to, Captain Archibald Ramsay, who was a member of the British Parliament and known to be unsympathetic to the jingoistic Churchill.

Churchill became prime minister in May 1940 and immediately ordered the arrest of both Kent and Ramsay. The American government (Roosevelt) could have asserted diplomatic immunity

---

[86]See John W. Wheeler-Bennett, *King George VI: His Life and Reign* (New York: St. Martin's, 1958), pp. 390–92; also, see Ralph Raico "Re-Thinking Churchill" in *The Costs of War: America's Pyrrhic Victories*, John V. Denson, ed., 2nd ed. (New Brunswick, N.J.: Transaction Publishers, 1999), p. 337.

for Kent and thereby prevented his trial but instead conspired with the British government (Churchill) to waive that immunity, and allow Kent to be tried secretly in a British court. Kent was found guilty of violating the British Official Secrets Act of 1911 and was placed in a British prison, where he remained for seven years and was not allowed to return to America until after World War II ended. Tyler Kent's information concerning the secret plans of Roosevelt and Churchill to bring America into the war, if revealed to the American people through a public trial in Britain, would have proved at least embarrassing to Roosevelt's administration and may even have led to his impeachment. Churchill also wanted the matter kept from the British people, therefore Ramsay, even though he was a member of Parliament, was held at Brixton Prison without any charges or a trial and was not released until September 1944. On the morning following his release from prison, he resumed his seat in the House of Commons and remained there until the end of that parliament.[87]

Another important matter to consider for the background of the Pearl Harbor story relates to a close personal friend of Winston Churchill, a Canadian citizen by the name of William Stephenson, who later became known by his code name, Intrepid. The full story of how Intrepid helped Churchill and Roosevelt drag America into World War II can be seen in three books: *A Man Called Intrepid*, *The Quiet Canadian*, and the very recent *Desperate Deception*.[88] One of Intrepid's agents was Ian Fleming, the author who popularized this secret British agency in novels and movies about James Bond.

Stephenson had made millions through the military-industrial complex of Great Britain during World War I, and it was at this time he became a close personal friend of Churchill. When Churchill became prime minister in May 1940, a year and a half

---

[87]See John Holland Snow, *The Case of Tyler Kent* (New Canaan, Conn.: The Long House, 1982); also, see David Irving, *Churchill's War: The Struggle for Power* (Western Australia: Veritas, 1987), vol. 1, pp. 193–96, 287–88.

[88]Stevenson, *A Man Called Intrepid: The Secret War* (New York: Ballantine, 1976); H. Montgomery Hyde, *The Quiet Canadian: The Secret Service Story of Sir William Stephenson* (London: Hamish Hamilton, 1963); Thomas E. Mahl, *Desperate Deception: British Covert Operations in the United States, 1939–44* (Washington: Brassey's, 1998).

before Pearl Harbor, he immediately arranged for financing from the royal family and, without any knowledge of Parliament, established a secret organization headed by Stephenson to be located rent-free in Rockefeller Center in New York.[89] Roosevelt had full knowledge of and was in agreement with this, but the U.S. Congress knew nothing of this deceitful action. The primary purpose of this organization was to help Roosevelt and Churchill bring America into the war through false propaganda, the creation of false documents, and whatever other means were necessary, apparently even including the murder of an American citizen who had established a supply of oil for Germany—a completely legal business relationship at the time.[90] Roosevelt stayed in constant contact with Intrepid primarily through an American lawyer by the name of Ernest Cuneo, whose code name was Crusader.[91]

Two false documents used by Intrepid were important in bringing America and Germany into the war against each other. First, Intrepid provided a false map that knowingly was used by Roosevelt in a national radio speech to the American people on October 27, 1941.[92] This document allegedly was obtained from a German spy and purported to show Hitler's secret plans for an invasion of South America, thereby demonstrating an imminent danger to America. Intrepid also created a false document that was put into Hitler's hands as an allegedly stolen secret plan of the American government.[93] It was received by Hitler on December 3, 1941, and purported to show Roosevelt's secret plans to make a preemptive strike against Germany without a declaration of war by the U.S. Congress. This document played a role in Hitler's decision to declare war against America on December 11, 1941, which surprised almost everyone except Roosevelt, Intrepid, and Churchill.

Intrepid also provided ammunition to attack Roosevelt's political enemies, such as Charles Lindbergh and Henry Ford, by

[89]Stevenson, *A Man Called Intrepid*, pp. 30, 47.

[90]Ibid., pp. 317–26.

[91]Mahl, *Desperate Deception*, pp. 47, 120, 193.

[92]Stevenson, *A Man Called Intrepid*, pp. 326–28; Mahl, *Desperate Deception*, pp. 55–56.

[93]Stevenson, *A Man Called Intrepid*, pp. 326–34.

creating false information that made it appear they were Nazi sympathizers.[94] Also, he launched a concerted effort that eventually destroyed the political career of a very distinguished Congressman, Hamilton Fish, who represented Roosevelt's district and who had opposed almost all of Roosevelt's foreign policy ideas on interventionism.[95] Intrepid exercised heavy influence over popular political writers like Dorothy Thompson, Walter Winchell, and Walter Lippman.[96]

It is important here to interrupt the story about Intrepid to discuss Lippman's views and the British group he worked with to influence America's entry into the war. The immense value of Walter Lippman to the British as a propagandist is clearly shown in David Gordon's excellent study of false war propaganda in general, and his case study of Lippman in particular.[97] Lippman argued that America should intervene in World War II because Germany was clearly a "menace" to the British Empire, and he concluded that since America's interests were "equated" with the British, Germany was equally a threat to America. Gordon points out that Lippman was the most influential American political commentator from 1930 through 1950 but that he did not manifest his real intentions until after World War II ended. In a short volume entitled *Isolation and Alliances*, which appeared in 1952, Lippman wrote about the American and British alliance:

> We were on the right course, as I see it, during the war— specifically, between 1942 and 1945. . . . During those years we had a close partnership, one might call it an organic alliance, which managed the business of war and peace in the Western world—managed it for what we have come to call the Atlantic Community.[98]

[94]Mahl, *Desperate Deception*, pp. 23, 34–35.

[95]Ibid., pp. 107–35.

[96]Ibid., pp. 47–68.

[97]David Gordon, "A Common Design: Propaganda and World War" in *The Costs of War: America's Pyrrhic Victories*, John V. Denson, ed., 2nd ed. (New Brunswick, N.J.: Transaction Publishers, 1999), pp. 301–19; see also Rothbard's account of Lippman's important role in *Wall Street, Banks, and American Foreign Policy*, pp. 19–20.

[98]Quoted by Gordon in "A Common Design," pp. 318–19.

Lippman wanted a partial repeal or reversal of the American Revolution and the establishment of at least a permanent alliance with the British Empire. Gordon concludes that:

> Lippman, like Woodrow Wilson, had a hidden agenda. For this foremost columnist, the aim was not world government based on universal principles. Rather, it was a permanent union of the United States and Britain.[99]

Professor Carroll Quigley tells us that the British portion of the Anglo-American Establishment was very much in control of the intelligence and propaganda activities of the British government in America, with two of the British members of the Milner Group—Lord Lothian and Lord Halifax—serving as ambassadors to America. Quigley points out how significant this group was just prior to World War II:

> Of even greater significance was the gathering of Milner Group members and their recruits in Washington. The Group had based most of their foreign policy since 1920 on the hope of "closer union" with the United States, and they realized that American intervention in the war was absolutely essential to insure a British victory. Accordingly, more than a dozen members of the Group were in Washington during the war, seeking to carry on this policy.[100]

Intrepid, who was obviously working for the Milner Group as a propaganda specialist, influenced Roosevelt even to the point that most of Roosevelt's important speeches on foreign policy were first cleared with Intrepid before they were actually given, so that the British agent could edit and revise them.[101] Also, Intrepid's agency became intimately involved in changing the results reached by Gallup polls.[102] Furthermore, Intrepid and his organization helped rig the Republican Party nomination for

---

[99]Ibid., p. 319; for a current statement on the idea of Great Britain merging with America as a full voting entity, see the article by popular British historian Paul Johnson, "Why Britain Should Join America," *Forbes*, April 5, 1999, pp. 82–87.

[100]Quigley, *The Anglo-American Establishment*, p. 303.

[101]Mahl, *Desperate Deception*, p. 58.

[102]Ibid., pp. 69–86.

Wendell Willkie, whose foreign policy stance was almost identical to that of Roosevelt, thereby removing foreign policy as an issue in Roosevelt's bid for an unprecedented third term.[103] Intrepid's agency created false passes for a large number of Willkie supporters to come into the convention hall and chant for him throughout the convention, and they cut off the microphone for Herbert Hoover's speech.[104]

Intrepid's agency neutralized the opposition from Michigan Senator Arthur H. Vandenberg, who was a Republican and a staunch opponent of an interventionist foreign policy, thereby removing a strong potential threat to Roosevelt's reelection. The British provided three mistresses to Vandenberg, and then the senator's opposition to Roosevelt was compromised by the threat of disclosure.[105] Vandenberg later became a staunch interventionist and even helped President Harry Truman launch America into the cold war after World War II.

Intrepid followed the example first set by Sir William Wiseman, head of the British Secret Service in America during World War I, who had played a major role in getting the U.S. into that war. Wilson's adviser, Colonel House, "habitually permitted Sir William Wiseman . . . to sit in his private office in New York and read the most secret documents of the American Government. House's father and mother had both been English."[106]

PEARL HARBOR

Now we turn to how America got into World War II at Pearl Harbor, events that propelled Franklin D. Roosevelt to "greatness." Roosevelt has always been ranked by "court historians" next to Lincoln as either the second or third greatest president in American history, and this is due primarily to his involvement in World War II. Roosevelt struggled mightily to get America into the war by provoking "incidents" with both Germany and

---

[103]Ibid., pp. 155–76.

[104]Ibid., pp. 160–61.

[105]Ibid., pp. 137–54.

[106]Bullitt and Freud, *Woodrow Wilson*, p. 160; see also Rothbard's account of the important role played by Wiseman in *Wall Street, Banks, and American Foreign Policy*, pp. 19–20.

Japan, but it was the "surprise" attack at Pearl Harbor that finally did the trick. As will be shown, this attack was no surprise to Roosevelt and his key advisers in Washington. In fact, was it provoked by Roosevelt and his policies.

Background Specific to Pearl Harbor

In 1932, as a part of the annual maneuvers, it was documented by American naval planners that if there ever was a war with Japan, the Japanese would strike the Pacific Fleet wherever it was located. It was realized then that Pearl Harbor created a very vulnerable target for a surprise attack by aircraft carriers.[107] The studies revealed that, in order to prevent such an attack, a large contingent of American aircraft would be needed for a 360-degree surveillance, which would stretch out for long distances in order to provide sufficient warning to prevent disaster. The Japanese were very familiar with the findings of this naval maneuver in 1932; in fact, the Japanese patterned their attack of December 7, 1941, on the various studies done by the Americans concerning their own weaknesses.

In January 1940, Roosevelt ordered the Pacific Fleet transferred from its home base at San Diego to Pearl Harbor, with very little air cover or support.[108] On May 7, 1940, it was announced that the entire fleet would remain in Pearl Harbor indefinitely, which was a radical departure from American naval policy. Roosevelt further weakened the fleet by transferring many of its ships to the Atlantic to assist in delivering supplies and ammunition to the British and to try to provoke the Germans into firing the first shot against America.[109] Admiral James O. Richardson, commander of the Pacific Fleet, was so strongly opposed to these ridiculous orders that he made a personal visit to the White House to protest to Roosevelt, telling him that key naval officers were losing confidence in the president. As a result of this meeting, Roosevelt removed Richardson from command and placed Admiral Husband E. Kimmel in control.[110]

---

[107]Morgenstern, *Pearl Harbor*, pp. 68–84; see also Bartlett, *Cover-Up*, pp. 52–53.

[108]Morgenstern, *Pearl Harbor*, pp. 51–67.

[109]Ibid., p. 53; Bartlett, *Cover-Up*, pp. 29, 30.

[110]Morgenstern, *Pearl Harbor*, p. 63; Edward L. Beach, Captain, USN Ret., *Scapegoats: A Defense of Kimmel and Short at Pearl Harbor* (Annapolis, Md.:

The American people had become very disillusioned over being misled into World War I by President Wilson and were decidedly against entering another European war. Therefore, as Roosevelt sought to be elected to an unprecedented third term, he had to campaign for reelection as a peace candidate, as Wilson had before World War I. On September 11, 1940, Roosevelt stated, "We will not participate in foreign wars and we will not send our army, naval or air forces to fight in foreign lands outside of the Americas, *except in case of attack.*"[111] Later, on October 30 in Boston, he told American mothers and fathers, "Your boys are not going to be sent into any foreign wars. I have said this before but I shall say it again."[112] Two months after this promise, in early January 1941, he sent Harry Hopkins, his alter ego, to London to deliver a much different message. This secret message was just like the one President Wilson's alter ego, Colonel House, delivered to the British government on January 16, 1916, to promise American entry into World War I. Roosevelt made the same promise to the British. We now know through Churchill that on this visit, Hopkins reported to the prime minister the following:

> The president is determined that we shall win the war together. Make no mistake about it. He has sent me here to tell you that at all costs and by all means he will carry you through . . . *there is nothing that he will not do so far as he has the human power.*[113]

Later, Roosevelt and Churchill held a meeting, which became known as the Atlantic Conference, and released a statement in August 1941 called the Atlantic Charter. The British archives

---

Naval Institute Press, 1995) p. 13; James O. Richardson, *On the Treadmill to Pearl Harbor: The Memoirs of Admiral James O. Richardson USN (Ret.) as told to Vice Admiral George C. Dyer, USN (Ret.)* (Washington, D.C.: Naval History Division, Department of Navy, 1973).

[111]Benjamin Colby, *'Twas a Famous Victory: Deception and Propaganda in the War Against Germany* (New Rochelle, N.Y.: Arlington House, 1974), p. 21 (emphasis added).

[112]Ibid.

[113]Winston Churchill, *The Second World War,* vol. 3, *The Grand Alliance* (Boston: Houghton Mifflin, 1950), p. 23 (emphasis added); Colby, *'Twas a Famous Victory,* p. 22.

were opened on this subject in 1971, and soon thereafter, in January 1972, *The New York Times* reported that Churchill had told his war cabinet, upon his return from the Atlantic Conference with Roosevelt, the following statement which was recorded in the cabinet minutes:

> If he [Roosevelt] were to put the issue of peace and war to Congress, they would debate it for months. . . . The president had said he would wage war but not declare it, and that he would become more and more provocative. If the Germans did not like it, they could attack American forces.[114]

Churchill also reported that a decision had been made that the U.S. Navy would escort the British ships across the Atlantic, and the minutes of the British cabinet meeting contained these words from Churchill,

> The president's orders to these [United States Navy] escorts were to attack any [German] U-boat which showed itself, even if it was 200 or 300 miles away from the convoy. . . . *The president made it clear that he would look for an incident which would justify him in opening hostilities.*[115]

After America had actually entered the war, Churchill made a speech to the House of Commons on January 27, 1942, reflecting on the secret plans that he and Roosevelt had for America to come into the war, which is what they had discussed at the Atlantic Conference in August of 1941: "It has been the policy of the cabinet at almost all cost to avoid embroilment with Japan until we were sure that the United States would also be engaged."[116] Soon thereafter, on February 15, 1942, Churchill told the House of Commons:

> When I survey and compute the power of the United States and its vast resources and feel that they are now in it with us, with the British commonwealth of nations all together, however long it lasts, till death or victory, I cannot believe that there is any other fact in the whole world which can compare

---

[114]*New York Times*, January 2, 1972; Colby, *'Twas a Famous Victory*, p. 35.

[115]Colby, *'Twas a Famous Victory*, p. 36 (emphasis added).

[116]Morgenstern, *Pearl Harbor*, p. 115.

with that. This is what I dreamed of, aimed at, and worked for, and now it has come to pass.[117]

We now have the recollections of Churchill's son, Randolph, who relates that he had a conversation with his famous father before America entered the war, and he asked his father how he was going to win the war. Churchill told his son, "I shall drag the United States in."[118]

One member of Churchill's war cabinet, Captain Oliver Lylleton, who was the British production minister, was well aware of the secret maneuverings of Churchill and Roosevelt to get America into the war, and he stated in a speech in London on June 20, 1944: "America provoked Japan to such an extent that the Japanese were forced to attack Pearl Harbor. It is a travesty on history ever to say that America was forced into war."[119] A member of the Roosevelt cabinet, Harold L. Ickes, stated, "For a long time I've believed our best entrance into the war would be [via] Japan . . . [which] will inevitability lead to war against Germany."[120]

In his excellent book on Pearl Harbor, George Morgenstern devotes an entire chapter to an analysis of the secret agreements made primarily between Churchill and Roosevelt before America entered the war. He also points out that the Dutch were included, mainly because of their oil resources in the Pacific. Roosevelt had secretly committed America to a war in the event the British and Dutch oil interests were put at risk by the Japanese, who desperately needed oil.[121] The military plan drawn up to carry this out, called "Rainbow Five," and this amounted to a commitment by Roosevelt to protect British, Dutch, and Chinese economic interests.[122] This secret agreement actually became public on December 6, 1941, but its significance was lost in the Pearl Harbor news the next day.[123] This secret agreement had been in place for eight months before Pearl Harbor, but it was

[117]Ibid., p. 116.

[118]Mahl, *Desperate Deception*, p. 1.

[119]Morgenstern, *Pearl Harbor*, p. 116.

[120]Beach, *Scapegoats*, p. 26.

[121]Morgenstern, *Pearl Harbor: The Story of the Secret War*, pp. 104–16.

[122]Ibid., p. 115.

[123]Ibid., p. 104.

never put into a formal treaty or even an executive agreement. It was simply an oral commitment by Roosevelt which had been committed into a definite written war plan for the Army and Navy. The plan had actually been approved in Washington by Secretary of Navy Frank Knox on May 28, 1941, and by Secretary of War Henry Stimson on June 2, 1941.[124]

Another close associate of Roosevelt and a frequent administration spokesman, Senator Claude Pepper of Florida (whose nickname was "Red" Pepper because of his leftist leanings), stated in an interview in Boston on November 24, 1941, that the United States was not far from a shooting war with Japan and that "we are only waiting for Japan to cross a line before we start shooting. I don't know exactly where that line is . . . and I am not sure the president knows exactly where it is, but when they cross it we'll start shooting." Pepper added that "actual declaration of war is a legal technicality, and such technicalities are being held in abeyance as long as those brigands [the Japanese] continue in force."[125] Pepper was obviously aware to some extent of the "Rainbow Five" plan.

It was Secretary of War Stimson, however, who revealed after the war Roosevelt's secret wish of getting the Japanese to fire the first shot. In a statement to the congressional committee investigating the attack at Pearl Harbor, Stimson said, in looking back:

> If war did come, it was important, both from the point of view of unified support of our own people, as well as for the record of history, that we should not be placed in the position of firing the first shot, if this could be done without sacrificing our safety, but that Japan should appear in her true role as the real aggressor. . . . If there was to be war, moreover, we wanted the Japanese to commit the first overt act.[126]

Stimson's diary entry of November 25, 1941, thirteen days before Pearl Harbor, describes a meeting of the cabinet at the White House:

---

[124]Ibid., p. 109.

[125]Ibid., p. 290.

[126]Ibid., p. 292.

There the president . . . brought up entirely the relations with the Japanese. He brought up the event that we were likely to be attacked, perhaps [as soon as] next Monday, for the Japanese are notorious for making an attack without warning and the question was what we should do. *The question was how we should maneuver them into the position of firing the first shot without allowing too much danger to ourselves.*[127]

Provocations by Roosevelt

After the war had started in Europe in September 1939, but before America entered the war, Roosevelt committed numerous provocative acts in an attempt to create an incident that would involve America in the war to help the British.[128] One of the most provocative acts addressed to Germany was the Lend–Lease Act of March 1941, which was a virtual declaration of war. Roosevelt's action of sending fifty destroyers to England was clearly intended to provoke the Germans, and to aid the British.[129] In regard to provoking the Germans, one critic has stated:

Many have found Roosevelt's behavior on the eve of America's intervention in World War II especially reprehensible. Edward S. Corwin and Louis W. Koenig protested that, in the destroyer deal, "what President Roosevelt did was to take over for the nonce Congress's power to dispose of property of the United States . . . and to repeal at least two statutes," while Senator

---

[127]Ibid. (emphasis in original).

[128]While Roosevelt claimed that the primary aim of America entering World War II was to defend the British from German "aggression," toward the end of the war, and during the wartime conferences—Yalta in particular—he seemed to have little concern for the British or for western Europe. At the wartime conferences, he was more concerned with his place in history and in achieving what his favorite president and idol Woodrow Wilson could not achieve; that is, creating a world organization with America playing a major role in it. Roosevelt repeatedly made concessions to Stalin in order to get Stalin's cooperation and agreement to form the United Nations wherein America and the Soviet Union would control the two largest spheres of influence. See also generally Amos Perlmutter, *FDR and Stalin: A Not So Grand Alliance, 1943–1944* (Columbia: University of Missouri Press, 1993), and Townsend Hoopes and Douglas Brinkley, *FDR and the Creation of the U.N.* (New Haven, Conn.: Yale University Press, 1997).

[129]Colby, *'Twas a Famous Victory*, p. 17.

William Fulbright accused Roosevelt of having "usurped the treaty power of the Senate" and of having "circumvented the war powers of the Congress." His detractors point out that six months before Pearl Harbor, on shaky statutory authority, the president used federal power to end strikes, most notably in sending troops to occupy the strike-bound North American Aviation plant in California; and that in the same period he dispatched American forces to occupy Iceland and Greenland, provided convoys of vessels carrying arms to Britain, and ordered U.S. destroyers to shoot Nazi U-boats on sight, all acts that infringed Congress's warmaking authority."[130]

Also unknown to the American people was the fact that Roosevelt put an American airplane with an American commander at the service of the British Admiralty to assist in tracking down the German warship *Bismarck*. Roosevelt commented to his speech writer, Robert Sherwood, that if it was found out he had done this, he would be impeached.[131] Roosevelt tried to use conflicts that he intentionally provoked between U.S. Navy ships and German submarines in the Atlantic as causes for America's entry into the war. On September 4, 1941, the USS *Greer*, was attacked by a German submarine off the coast of Iceland. The *Greer* had provoked the attack, but the president lied to the American people, stating that the ship was only carrying American mail to Iceland and was attacked without warning in international waters. The truth came out shortly thereafter when Admiral Harold Stark, chief of naval operations, disclosed that the *Greer* had actually been giving chase to the German submarine for more than three hours; the sub finally turned and fired two torpedoes at the *Greer*, which responded with depth charges.[132] Another incident is described as follows:

> A few weeks later another American warship, the USS *Kearny*, was attacked and damaged by a German submarine. On October 27 the president told the country: "We have wished to avoid shooting. But the shooting has started. And history has recorded who fired the first shot. In the long run, however, all

[130]Fred I. Greenstein, ed., *Leadership in the Modern Presidency* (Cambridge, Mass.: Harvard University Press, 1988), p. 35.

[131]Bartlett, *Cover-Up*, p. 9.

[132]Ibid., p. 29.

that will matter is who fired the last shot. America has been attacked."

When the truth of the *Kearny* incident finally came out, it became clear that Germany had not fired the first shot at all. Like the *Greer*, the *Kearny* had sighted the German sub and fired first. The result was that the American people refused to become inflamed by the incident. Thus when the first American ship, the USS *Reuben James*, was actually sunk on October 30, the president did not make much of it.[133]

These efforts to provoke the Germans into firing the first shot were unsuccessful because, more than anything else, Hitler wanted to avoid a war with America.

Roosevelt also tried to provoke the Japanese into firing the first shot, and eventually he was successful. An absolutely sensational book, and maybe the most important ever written on Roosevelt's role in the Pearl Harbor attack, was published in 2000.[134] The author, Robert Stinnett, a veteran of the Pacific war during World War II, devoted seventeen years to researching this subject. The book shows beyond any reasonable doubt that Roosevelt was directly involved in provoking the Japanese into firing the first shot at Pearl Harbor, that he was responsible for almost all of the critical military information being withheld from the Pearl Harbor commanders, and that he immediately launched a cover-up to make them the scapegoats while he pretended to be surprised and blameless. Stinnett states:

> By provoking the attack, Roosevelt accepted the terrible truth that America's military forces—including the Pacific Fleet and the civilian population in the Pacific—would sit squarely in harm's way, exposed to enormous risks. The commanders in Hawaii, Admiral Husband Kimmel and Lieutenant General Walter Short, were deprived of intelligence that might have made them more alert to the risk entailed in Roosevelt's policy, but they obeyed his direct order: "The United States desires that Japan commit the first overt act." More than 200,000 documents and interviews have led me to these conclusions. I am indebted to the Freedom of Information Act and its author,

[133]Ibid., pp. 29–30.

[134]Robert B. Stinnett, *Day of Deceit: The Truth about FDR and Pearl Harbor* (New York: The Free Press, 2000).

the late Congressman John Moss (D–Cal.) for making it possible for me to tell this story.[135]

Stinnett discovered the crucial document concerning Roosevelt's provocation in the personal files of Lieutenant Commander Arthur H. McCollum in 1995. The document reveals the eight-step plan Roosevelt used to cause the Japanese to fire the first shot. At Roosevelt's request, McCollum prepared the document, which is dated October 7, 1940, and McCollum and Roosevelt met at the White House immediately thereafter to discuss the same.[136] Stinnett relates how Roosevelt adopted the plan step by step. The plan set out the eight steps as follows:

A. Make an arrangement with Britain for the use of British bases in the Pacific, particularly Singapore;

B. Make an arrangement with Holland for the use of base facilities and acquisition of supplies in the Dutch East Indies;

C. Give all possible aid to the Chinese Government of Chiang-Kai-shek;

D. Send a division of long-range heavy cruisers to the Orient, Philippines, or Singapore;

E. Send two divisions of submarines to the Orient;

F. Keep the main strength of the U.S. Fleet, now in the Pacific, in the vicinity of the Hawaiian Islands;

G. Insist that the Dutch refuse to grant Japanese demands for undue economic concessions, particularly oil; and

H. Completely embargo all U.S. trade with Japan, in collaboration with a similar embargo imposed by the British Empire.[137]

Lieutenant Commander McCollum commented at the end of the plan, "If by these means Japan could be led to commit an overt act of war, so much the better."[138]

The recurring theme in American history is that certain ships are offered by presidents as bait to get the enemy to fire the first shot.[139] Stinnett comments on this as follows:

[135]Ibid., p. xiv.

[136]Ibid., pp. 6-10, 13–17, 28–29; see also Appendix A at the end of this volume, which sets out this secret document in full, pp. 261–68.

[137]Ibid., p. 8.

[138]Ibid., p. 265.

[139]Lincoln, McKinley, Wilson, and Lyndon Johnson are good examples.

Roosevelt's "fingerprints" can be found on each of McCollum's proposals. One of the most shocking was Action D, the deliberate deployment of American warships within or adjacent to the territorial waters of Japan. During secret White House meetings, Roosevelt personally took charge of Action D. He called the provocations "pop-up" cruises: "I just want them to keep popping up here and there and keep the Japs guessing. I don't mind losing one or two cruisers, but do not take a chance on losing five or six." Admiral Husband Kimmel, the Pacific Fleet commander, objected to the pop-up cruises, saying: "It is ill-advised and will result in war if we make this move."[140]

Admiral Kimmel was notified by the chief of naval operations on July 25, 1941, to be prepared to send a carrier-load of fighter planes to Russia which had been attacked by Germany in June 1941. Kimmel objected very strongly because he thought this would provoke the Japanese to fire the first shot and start a war and also because it would sacrifice a carrier and its airplanes. The idea finally was dropped.[141] Roosevelt also ordered separate suicide missions for three small ships based in the Philippines. With American captains and Filipino crews, these vessels, each of which carried at least one gun, were to sail at different times toward Japan in an effort to draw Japanese fire, but the Japanese refused the bait.[142]

Roosevelt continued to follow the McCollum plan in all respects and, on July 25, 1941, he ordered all Japanese assets in the United States frozen, thus effectively ending all trade between the countries. This freezing order, in conjunction with an identical one from the British and Dutch, effectively cut off all oil from Japan that left them with approximately one year's supply in reserve at the time of Pearl Harbor and with no prospects for new supplies.[143]

The Japanese were aware that Roosevelt and Churchill were trying to provoke a war between America and Japan as a

---

[140]Stinnett, *Day of Deceit:*, p. 9.

[141]Morgenstern, *Pearl Harbor*, p. 303.

[142]Bartlett, *Cover-Up*, pp. 56–59; see also Kemp Tolley, *Cruise of the Lanikai: Incitement to War* (Annapolis, Md.: Naval Institute Press, 1973), p. 77f.

[143]Bartlett, *Cover-Up*, pp. 32, 38–39; and see Beach, *Scapegoats*, p. 28.

"back-door" entry into the European war. Japanese Ambassador Nomura in Washington sent a coded message to Tokyo on August 16, 1941, two days after the announcement of the Roosevelt–Churchill Atlantic Charter Conference, which was decoded by the U.S. as follows: "I understand that the British believe that if they could only have a Japanese–American war started at the back door, there would be a good prospect of getting the United States to participate in the European war."[144] The Japanese, in an unprecedented diplomatic move following the Atlantic Conference between Roosevelt and Churchill, offered to send Prince Fumimaro Konoye, the prime minister, and a member of the royal family to America to negotiate personally with Roosevelt in a desperate effort to preserve peace. Roosevelt flatly refused such a meeting, thereby causing the downfall of the moderate, peace-seeking Konoye government, which was then replaced by Tojo's militant jingoistic government.[145] Furthermore, Roosevelt and Secretary of State Cordell Hull, in their negotiations with Japanese diplomats, presented ultimatums requiring Japan to get out of China completely, knowing that the Japanese would not accept those terms.[146] Japan was finally placed in the position of choosing either to lose the war without even fighting—basically because all of its oil supplies and essential war materials had been cut off—or gamble that a surprise attack at Pearl Harbor would cripple the American naval forces and cause America either to negotiate a peace treaty or to be so weakened that she would be unable to win a war in the Pacific.

[144]Morgenstern, *Pearl Harbor*, p. 173.

[145]Bartlett, *Cover-Up*, pp. 39–41; also, see Morgenstern, *Pearl Harbor*, pp. 127–43. This refusal of Roosevelt to meet with the Japanese prime minister is very much like Lincoln's refusal to meet and discuss peace terms with the Confederate commissioners, with very similar results in regard to preserving the peace.

[146]Beach, *Scapegoats*, p. 32. A.J.P. Taylor states that Manchuria received "mythical importance" and was "treated as a milestone on the road to war," when, in fact, the commission designated by the League of Nations investigated the Manchurian incident at the initiative of the Japanese and found that the Japanese grievances were justified and Japan was not condemned as an aggressor, although Japan was condemned for resorting to force before all peaceful means had been exhausted. Taylor states, "The Chinese reconciled themselves to the loss of a province which they had not controlled for some years; and in 1933 peace was restored between China and Japan." See Taylor, *The Origins of the Second World War*, p. 65.

Information Withheld by Roosevelt and Marshall

The extreme deceit of the Pearl Harbor attack is revealed further by the fact that Roosevelt and his key advisers in Washington had a tremendous amount of information that clearly pointed to Japan's intentions of launching a surprise attack at Pearl Harbor many days in advance and with plenty of time to either prevent the same or prepare for the event, but they withheld most of it from the Pearl Harbor commanders. Both Admiral Husband E. Kimmel and Lieutenant General Walter C. Short, the military commanders at Pearl Harbor, had been promised in writing by their respective chiefs of service that all information pertaining to their posts, regardless of the source of the information, would be delivered immediately from Washington to them directly. In fact, Admiral Kimmel made a special trip to Washington in June 1941 to meet with Admiral Harold R. Stark, chief of naval operations, requesting this pledge to get the information. Stark, in turn, gave his absolute assurance that all information would be passed along.[147]

On January 27, 1941, the American ambassador to Japan, Joseph Grew, sent the following dispatch to Washington:

> My Peruvian colleague told a member of my staff that he had heard from many sources including a Japanese source that the Japanese military forces planned, in the event of trouble with the United States, to attempt a surprise mass attack on Pearl Harbor using all of their military facilities. He added that although the project seemed fantastic the fact that he had heard it from many sources prompted him to pass on the information.[148]

Admiral Stark relayed this information to Admiral Kimmel but reported that it was only a rumor and that he should put no stock in it.[149] The fact that "a rumor" was reported clearly led Admiral Kimmel to believe he was receiving all the information available to his superiors in Washington.

---

[147]Beach, *Scapegoats*, p. 11.

[148]Bartlett, *Cover-Up*, p. 53.

[149]Beach, *Scapegoats*, p. 48.

Prior to Stinnett's book, it was known that certain Japanese spies were sending messages to Japan stating the location and activity of the ships in Pearl Harbor. Also, it was known that American cryptographers had solved the purple, or diplomatic, code of the Japanese. However, the critical information about the attack was in the naval or military code of the Japanese, and Stinnett discovered these secret messages that were known to Roosevelt and withheld from the Pearl Harbor commanders and the American public for more than fifty years. Stinnett states "The truth of Pearl Harbor is found in the Naval Codes, not in the diplomatic codes."[150] The American cryptographers broke the naval or military code of the Japanese in October 1940.[151]

Some of the most startling revelations made by Stinnett show that, contrary to prior assertions made in sworn testimony at congressional hearings, the Japanese fleet that set out for Pearl Harbor on November 25, 1941, did *not* maintain radio silence up through December 7, 1941. In fact, American cryptographers were decoding the military communications and sending them directly to Roosevelt; through directional radio finders, they were able to determine the exact location of the fleet all the way through their fateful journey. Roosevelt ordered all ships out of the North Pacific Ocean when he learned that the Japanese forces were in that area, and he did this to prevent any discovery of the Japanese presence there. Stinnett reports:

> Navy officials declared the North Pacific Ocean a "Vacant Sea" and ordered all U.S. and allied shipping out of the waters. An alternate trans-Pacific route was authorized through the Torres Strait, in the South Pacific between Australia and New Guinea. Rear Admiral Richmond K. Turner, War Plans officer for the United States Navy in 1941, explained the reasoning with a startling admission: "We were prepared to divert traffic when we believed that war was imminent. We sent the traffic down via Torres Strait, so that the track of the Japanese task force would be clear of any traffic." On November 25, the day that the Japanese carrier force sailed for Pearl Harbor, Navy headquarters sent this message to Kimmel and San Francisco's Twelfth Naval District:

---

[150]Stinnett, *Day of Deceit*, p. 21.

[151]Ibid., p. 22.

ROUTE ALL TRANSPACIFIC SHIPPING THRU TORRES STRAITS. CINCPAC AND CINCAF PROVIDE NECESSARY ESCORT. REFER YOUR DISPATCH 230258.

The order was dispatched about an hour after Admiral Nagumo's carrier force departed Hitokappu Bay and entered the North Pacific.

The "vacant sea" order dramatizes Admiral Kimmel's helplessness in the face of Roosevelt's desires. The admiral tried on a number of occasions to do something to defend Pearl Harbor, based on Rochefort's troubling intercepts. Exactly two weeks prior to the attack, Kimmel ordered a search for a Japanese carrier force north of Hawaii. Without White House approval, he moved the Pacific Fleet into the North Pacific Ocean in the precise area where Japan planned to launch her carrier attack on Pearl Harbor. But his laudable efforts came to naught. When White House military officials learned Kimmel's warships were in the area of what turned out to be the intended Japanese launch site, they issued directives that caused Kimmel to quickly order the Pacific Fleet out of the North Pacific and back to its anchorages in Pearl Harbor.[152]

Stinnett reports further that:

At the time, of course, Kimmel did not know of Washington's eight-action policy. If McCollum's action policy was to succeed in uniting America, Japan must be seen as the aggressor and must commit the first overt act of war on an unsuspecting Pacific Fleet, not the other way around. FDR and his highest-level commanders gambled on Japan committing the first overt act of war, and knew from intercepted messages that it was near. An open sea engagement between Japan's carrier force and the Pacific Fleet would have been far less effective at establishing American outrage. Japan could claim that its right to sail the open seas had been deliberately challenged by American warships if Kimmel attacked first.[153]

Stinnett further shows how Roosevelt ordered Kimmel's ships around like they were on strings:

On orders from Washington, Kimmel left his oldest vessels inside Pearl Harbor and sent twenty-one modern warships,

---

[152]Ibid., pp. 144–45.
[153]Ibid., p. 151.

including his two aircraft carriers, west toward Wake and Midway. Those were strange orders, for they dispatched American forces directly into the path of the oncoming Japanese fleet of thirty submarines. The last-minute circumstances that moved the warships out of Pearl Harbor were discussed during the 1945–46 Congressional inquiry. Members wondered whether the sorties were genuine efforts to reinforce Wake Island and Midway or merely ploys to move all the modern warships from the Pearl Harbor anchorages prior to the attack so they would not be hit by the First Air Fleet. . . . With the departure of the Lexington and Enterprise groups, the warships remaining in Pearl Harbor were mostly twenty-seven-year-old relics of World War I.[154]

Prior to Stinnett's book, a British code-breaker published a book entitled *Betrayal at Pearl Harbor*.[155] This sensational book states that on or about November 25, 1941, the British were able to overhear the Japanese military commands relating to a large military operation, including aircraft carriers, battleships, and other vessels that were leaving Japanese waters headed to Hawaii. The book's co-author, Captain Eric Nave, personally passed this information—which clearly indicated the Japanese were headed for a surprise attack at Pearl Harbor—directly to Churchill. The book is inconclusive, however, as to whether Churchill actually relayed this message to Roosevelt.[156] Prior to

---

[154]Ibid., p. 152 and 154.

[155]James Rusbridger and Eric Nave, *Betrayal at Pearl Harbor: How Churchill Lured Roosevelt into World War II* (New York: Summit Books, 1991).

[156]Another sensational book published recently describes and quotes verbatim the alleged intercepted radio communications between Churchill and Roosevelt concerning the essential message that the Japanese were headed to Pearl Harbor for a surprise attack. There is a series of books relating to alleged interviews by an American CIA agent with Heinrich Müller, who was the Gestapo chief under Hitler. These interviews with Müller allegedly took place at the end of the war, and Müller states that the Germans were able to intercept the radio communications between Roosevelt and Churchill because the Germans had the identical communications system. The German interception of these comments between Churchill and Roosevelt shows that Churchill gave explicit information to Roosevelt that the Japanese were headed to Pearl Harbor for a surprise attack. See Gregory Douglas, *Gestapo Chief: The 1948 Interrogation of Heinrich Müller* (San Jose, Calif.: R. James Bender, 1998), vol. 3, pp. 48–99.

the Stinnett book, a book by former CIA director William Casey, entitled *The Secret War Against Hitler*, states:

> As the Japanese storm began to gather force in the Pacific, the most private communications between the Japanese government and its ambassadors . . . were being read in Washington. Army and Navy cryptographers having broken the Japanese diplomatic cipher, were reading messages that foretold the attack. *The British had sent word that a Japanese fleet was steaming east toward Hawaii.*[157]

Some of the most important information that was *never* passed along to Kimmel and Short and was never even available to them to use in their own defense were the "bomb plot" messages of September 24, 1941, and thereafter.[158] Japanese spies in Hawaii regularly were reporting the positions of all ships in Pearl Harbor and this information drastically increased the week before the attack, even including information that ships were not moved. A grid system was set up so that they could tell the position of the ships within that system—a clear indication that an air attack was a strong probability.[159]

Admiral Kimmel, in his own book that was published before it was known that the Japanese military orders had been intercepted, stated that key information was withheld from him and that he thought the bomb plot messages were probably the most essential pieces of military information that should have been communicated to him:

> The deficiencies of Pearl Harbor as a fleet base were well known in the Navy Department. In an interview with Mr. Roosevelt in June 1941, in Washington, I outlined the weaknesses and concluded with the remark that the only answer was to have the fleet at sea if the Japs ever attacked.
>
> I accepted the decision to base the fleet at Pearl Harbor in the firm belief that the Navy Department would supply me promptly with all pertinent information available and in

---

[157]William Casey, *The Secret War Against Hitler* (Washington, D.C.: Regnery Gateway, 1988), p. 7 (emphasis added).

[158]Beach, *Scapegoats*, p. 34.

[159]Ibid., pp. 35–36, 92.

particular with all information that indicated an attack on the fleet at Pearl Harbor. . . .

The care taken to keep the commander-in-chief of our Asiatic Fleet and the British in London informed of Japanese intentions while withholding this vital information from our commanders at Pearl Harbor has never been explained. . . .

The Navy Department thus engaged in a course of conduct which definitely gave me the impression that intelligence from important intercepted Japanese messages was being furnished to me. Under these circumstances a failure to send me important information of this character was not merely withholding of intelligence. *It amounted to an affirmative misrepresentation.* I had asked for all vital information. I had been assured that I would have it. I appeared to be receiving it. . . . Yet, in fact, the most vital information from the intercepted Japanese messages was withheld from me. This failure not only deprived me of essential facts. It misled me.

I was not supplied with any information of the intercepted messages showing that the Japanese government had divided Pearl Harbor into five areas and was seeking minute information as to the berthing of ships of the fleet in those areas, which was vitally significant.[160]

Admiral Kimmel testified under oath that "Had we been furnished this information as little as two or three hours before the attack, which was easily feasible and possible, much could have been done."[161]

At the time of the Pearl Harbor congressional hearings in 1945–1946, the only code the investigators knew that the Navy had broken was the diplomatic code. Much testimony was taken regarding what information was known in Washington by Roosevelt and Marshall concerning the diplomatic code and what was not passed along to Admiral Kimmel and General Short.[162] One of these important messages was that the Japanese indicated that if they were not able to secure a peace agreement with the Americans by November 26, 1941, things would automatically go into operation, indicating that an attack would occur

---

[160]Kimmel as quoted in Beach, *Scapegoats*, pp. 57–59.

[161]Morgenstern, *Pearl Harbor*, p. 253.

[162]The bomb-plot messages were not part of the diplomatic intercepts, but were messages from spies in Hawaii.

after that point. This was not delivered to the military commanders at Pearl Harbor.[163]

Another critical diplomatic code interception received in Washington and not delivered to Pearl ·Harbor was called the "winds execute" message, which was received during the night of December 3, 1941. Captain Laurence F. Safford received and translated the message to mean "War with America, War with England, and Peace with Russia."[164] The written evidence of the "winds execute" message mysteriously disappeared from Navy files before the first congressional investigation, but Captain Safford was absolutely certain of the receipt and content of the message and was certain that it was delivered to President Roosevelt immediately.[165]

Finally, the code interceptors received and translated a fourteen-part message from the Japanese government to its diplomats in Washington, D.C.; the first thirteen parts were received on December 6, 1941.[166] The first part of this message was delivered about 9:15 P.M. to Lieutenant Lester R. Schulz at the White House, and he immediately took the locked pouch containing the message to Roosevelt. Harry Hopkins, of course, was also present, and Schulz heard Roosevelt state to Hopkins, "This means war!" Hopkins then replied, "It's too bad we can't strike the first blow and prevent a surprise." Roosevelt replied, "No, we can't do that. We are a democracy and a peaceful people. But we have a good record!"[167]

There is a great deal of controversy about what transpired between this point and the actual bombing the next morning. However, Captain Edward L. Beach's recent book, *Scapegoats*, addresses the issue of why the fourteen-part message was not delivered to the Pearl Harbor commanders. He references the new evidence concerning a meeting at midnight at the White House on December 6, which lasted until approximately 4:00 A.M. on December 7. According to Beach's

---

[163]Ibid., p. 184.

[164]Bartlett, *Cover-Up*, p. 100; see also Morgenstern, *Pearl Harbor*, pp. 198–211.

[165]Ibid.

[166]Beach, *Scapegoats*, pp. 87–109.

[167]Ibid., p. 89.

book, James G. Stahlman, a close friend of Secretary of Navy Frank Knox, said that Knox told him he attended this meeting, along with Secretary of War Henry Stimson, General Marshall, Admiral Stark, Harry Hopkins, and Roosevelt. The purpose was to discuss the message already received and to review the fourteenth part of the message, which was expected to be delivered at any moment but did not come while the meeting was taking place. Stahlman did not report that Secretary Knox informed him about the actual content of the discussions, but one is led to surmise what occurred by the actions of the parties after their meeting during the early morning hours of December 7.[168] This particular decoded message has been called the "delivery message" which informed the Japanese diplomats that the fourteenth part of the message must be delivered to Secretary of State Hull on December 7 no later than 1:00 P.M. Washington time—which was dawn, Pearl Harbor time. The intent of the Japanese was to give notice to the American government that an attack was going to be made on Pearl Harbor just before the attack actually occurred, so that they could never be accused of launching a surprise attack. The fourteenth part was late in being delivered to Hull, but of course, the key people in Washington—especially Roosevelt and Marshall—had full knowledge of all the decoded messages before this, so the attack was clearly no "surprise" to them.

When Admiral Stark arrived at his office at 8:00 A.M. on December 7, he was met by Rear Admiral Theodore S. Wilkinson and Commander Arthur McCollum. These two officers had with them the first thirteen parts of the message and stated that they were waiting to receive the "delivery message," which arrived while they were meeting with Stark. Wilkinson indicated that it was absolutely imperative that Admiral Stark get on his scrambler telephone and issue a warning first to Admiral Kimmel in Pearl Harbor and then to Admiral Thomas C. Hart in Manila.[169] The scrambler telephone was an instrument that allowed direct and immediate contact between the parties, but the message was scrambled so it could not be intercepted and understood; however, at each end, it was

---

[168]Ibid. (specifically for the letter of Stahlman, see pp. 203–05).
[169]Ibid., p. 95.

unscrambled and immediately understood. Kimmel would have received this warning at 3:00 P.M. Pearl Harbor time, and that would have given him sufficient time to either prepare for or prevent the surprise attack. According to these witnesses, Stark picked up his scrambler telephone and hesitated for a long period of time, then put the phone down and instead tried to call President Roosevelt. The White House operator stated that the president was unavailable! The witnesses then stated that Stark tried to reach General Marshall, who was not in his office, and all witnesses agreed that Stark did nothing at all after that for the next few hours, until Marshall finally returned his call.[170]

The transcript of the Joint Congressional Committee hearings in 1945–1946 shows that General Marshall testified he had been riding his horse during the early morning hours of December 7, and that he did not arrive at his office until about 11:00 A.M. at which time he was given the complete, fourteen–part message by two of his most senior intelligence officers, Brigadier General Sherman Miles and Colonel Rufus Bratton. Marshall also had a scrambler telephone on his desk that would have allowed him to make a direct call to General Short, but instead of making the call he slowly and deliberately read through the message while both Miles and Bratton frantically tried to tell him about the crucial delivery message and the time limitation of 1:00 P.M. Washington time. Finally, with the office clock showing nearly noon, Marshall wrote out a warning message in pencil in nearly illegible handwriting and then told Miles and Bratton that the message was to be sent to Admiral Kimmel on a nonpriority basis. The message, therefore, went by normal Western Union telegram and arrived at Kimmel's office after the attack had occurred.[171] General Marshall then returned the call to Admiral Stark, who had been waiting for about two hours to talk with him.

Admiral J.O. Richardson, the original commander at Pearl Harbor who was relieved by Roosevelt, wrote his memoirs in 1956 but delayed publication until 1973, a year after his friend Admiral Stark died and a year before Richardson's own death.[172]

[170]Ibid.

[171]Ibid., pp. 96–97.

[172]Richardson, *On the Treadmill to Pearl Harbor*.

He gave his opinion that Stark and Marshall were under orders from President Roosevelt not to warn Kimmel and Short. Elsewhere Richardson has written:

> I am impelled to believe that sometime prior to December 7, the president had directed that only Marshall could send any warning message to the Hawaiian area. I do not know this to be a fact and I cannot prove it. I believe this because of my knowledge of Stark and the fact that his means of communications with Kimmel were equal to, if not superior to those available to Marshall for communication with Short. He made no effort to warn Kimmel on the morning of December 7, but referred the matter to Marshall.[173]

Captain Beach has also written:

> Richardson stated that he was positive that there had been "some directive from higher authority" that only Marshall was to make any such call, but he believed Stark should have done it anyway, and he never forgave him. Richardson was clearly outraged, and the entire Navy would have been also, had it known.[174]

The obvious question is, why would President Roosevelt not want Marshall and Stark to communicate the warnings to General Short and Admiral Kimmel at Pearl Harbor? During the Joint Commission hearings, Senator Homer Ferguson of Michigan questioned General Short about what he thought would have happened had the commander at Pearl Harbor been notified of the impending attack. General Short testified:

> There would have been a very excellent chance that they would have turned back. . . . That would have been the tendency, because they would have felt, or they would be sure, that they would take heavy losses. Surprise was the only opportunity they had to succeed.[175]

The conclusion seems obvious: Roosevelt did not want to take a chance on the Japanese backing off from firing the first shot, and therefore he gambled that the losses would not be too heavy

---

[173]Quoted by Beach, *Scapegoats*, p. 201.

[174]Ibid., p. 96.

[175]Morgenstern, *Pearl Harbor*, p. 259.

if the Japanese achieved total surprise. Unlike Lincoln at Fort Sumter, where no injuries or deaths occurred as a result of the South firing the first shot, Roosevelt suffered immense damages with his gamble.

Secretary of War Henry Stimson recorded in his diary the relief from the anxiety over the question of how to get into the war by the fact that the Japanese had now bombed Pearl Harbor. He wrote that at 2:00 P.M. on Sunday, December 7, he received a telephone call from the president informing him that the Japanese were bombing Pearl Harbor. He confided in his diary, "We three [Hull, Knox, and Stimson] all thought that we must fight if the British fought. *But now the Japs have solved the whole thing by attacking us directly in Hawaii.*"[176] Stimson also wrote in his diary:

> When the news first came that Japan had attacked us my first feeling was of relief that the indecision was over and that a crisis had come in a way which would unite all our people. This continued to be my dominant feeling in spite of the news of catastrophes which quickly developed. For I feel that this country united has practically nothing to fear; while the apathy and divisions stirred up by unpatriotic men had been hitherto very discouraging.[177]

Morgenstern's editorial comment at this point about Stimson's diary entry is, "In other words, Stimson's view was that it was patriotic to go to war for the British and Dutch empires, and unpatriotic to try to stay at peace."[178] Stimson was clearly stating the viewpoint of the American portion of the Anglo-American Establishment, which now was the combined Morgan and Rockefeller interests.[179] Murray Rothbard comments on the merger of the Morgan and Rockefeller efforts for the purpose of getting America into World War II:

[176]Ibid., p. 308 (emphasis in original).

[177]Ibid., p. 309.

[178]Ibid.

[179]Stimson was a close associate of the Morgan interests, a Wall Street lawyer and a protégé of Morgan's personal attorney, Elihu Root. He served as secretary of war for Presidents Taft and Franklin Roosevelt and as secretary of state under Herbert Hoover. See Rothbard, *Wall Street, Banks, and American Foreign Policy*, p. 18.

During the 1930s, the Rockefellers pushed hard for war against Japan, which they saw as competing with them vigorously for oil and rubber resources in Southeast Asia and as endangering the Rockefellers' cherished dreams of a mass "China market" for petroleum products. On the other hand, the Rockefellers took a non-interventionist position in Europe, where they had close financial ties with German firms such as I.G. Farben and Company, and very few close relations with Britain and France. The Morgans, in contrast, as usual deeply committed to their financial ties with Britain and France, once again plumped early for war with Germany, while their interest in the Far East had become minimal. Indeed, U.S. Ambassador to Japan, Joseph C. Grew, former Morgan partner, was one of the few officials in the Roosevelt Administration genuinely interested in peace with Japan.

World War II might therefore be considered, from one point of view, as a coalition war: the Morgans got *their* war in Europe, the Rockefellers *theirs* in Asia.[180]

Roosevelt knew that if Japan entered the war, Germany would soon follow. One of the diplomatic messages intercepted by the Americans on November 29, 1941, was a conversation between the Japanese ambassador and Von Ribbentrop, the German foreign minister, in which Ribbentrop stated, "Should Japan become engaged in a war against the United States, Germany, of course, would join the war immediately."[181] On the night of December 7, 1941, after the bombing, Roosevelt summoned his cabinet members and congressional leaders to the White House to discuss the Pearl Harbor attack. He said to the assembled group that, "We have reason to believe that the Germans have told the Japanese that if Japan declares war, they will too. In other words, a declaration of war by Japan automatically brings."[182] The president was interrupted at this point and did not finish his sentence, but this comment indicates clearly that he was familiar with the Japanese code intercepts and knew that an attack by Japan would open the back door to a war with Germany, and that was Roosevelt's real intention.

Roosevelt's defenders have maintained that adequate warnings were sent to the Pearl Harbor commanders by his administration

---

[180]Ibid., pp. 27–28 (emphasis in original).

[181]Morgenstern, *Pearl Harbor*, p. 189.

[182]Ibid., p. 298.

in Washington. The following warnings were sent and are summarized by Morgenstern as follows[183]:

1. On October 16, 1941, Kimmel received a message that a new cabinet had been formed in Japan and that war between Japan and Russia was a strong possibility. It was also stated that a possible war by Japan could occur with the U.S. and Britain.

2. On November 24, 1941, Admiral Kimmel received word that successful negotiations were doubtful and to look for a possible attack by Japan on the Philippines or Guam.

3. On November 25, 1941, there was a message which hardly constituted a warning at all.

4. On November 27, 1941, the message stated "consider this dispatch a war warning."[184] It speculated that the likely targets for Japan would be the Philippines, the Kar Peninsula or Borneo. The message specifically stated to take precautions against sabotage, which caused the airplanes to be moved to the middle portion of the airfield to guard against sabotage, but this made them an easy target to be bombed on December 7.

5. Finally, a second warning on November 27, 1941, stated that the negotiations with Japan had ended. This message included a specific statement that, "the United States desires that Japan commit first overt act." It also instructed Kimmel that they should not make any movements or demonstrate actions which might "alarm the civil population."[185]

It is obvious in comparing these warnings with all of the information that was known in Washington, but was not communicated to the Pearl Harbor commanders that Roosevelt did not want to destroy the surprise element and thereby take the chance that the Japanese would call off the attack and not fire the first shot. He needed to comply with his campaign promise that he would not go into a foreign war unless attacked first. He needed

[183]Ibid., pp. 223–42.
[184]Ibid., p. 225.
[185]Ibid., p. 226.

to comply with his commitment to Churchill and the British that he would get into the war against Germany by some means, even if it required going through the "back door" by having a war with Japan.

Cover-up

One of the first actions Roosevelt took after asking Congress for a declaration of war was to form a commission that was limited in its scope to the investigation of what happened at Pearl Harbor to allow the surprise attack to succeed with such disastrous results. The directions to the committee specifically excluded any investigation of what went on in Washington, D.C.[186] This commission held secret hearings in Pearl Harbor; neither Commander Kimmel nor Short was allowed to submit any evidence or confront any witnesses, and they were completely denied due process. The commission concluded that these two commanding officers, Kimmel and Short, were solely at fault for the lack of preparation that caused the debacle. President Roosevelt had both of them reduced in rank and forced them to resign in disgrace.[187]

Stinnett reports the following reaction by the admiral who preceded Kimmel at Pearl Harbor: "Admiral James Richardson condemned the findings. 'It is the most unfair, unjust and deceptively dishonest document ever printed by the government printing office. I cannot conceive of honorable men serving on the commission without greatest regret and deepest feelings of shame.'"[188]

It was not until Stinnett's book was published that it was learned that the official cover-up began before the commission even began its work. Stinnett reports:

---

[186]Ibid., p. 41; Roosevelt appointed Supreme Court Justice Owen J. Roberts as chairman of this commission. Justice Roberts had made a speech at Madison Square Garden on August 19, 1941, advocating America's entrance into the war as a means of achieving world government which he strongly supported.

[187]Ibid., pp. 38–50; and see Beach, *Scapegoats*, pp. 113–17. This is almost the same scenario that occurred with Captain Turner of the *Lusitania* in World War I, who was blamed for the disaster and made the scapegoat, thereby diverting the attention away from Churchill and the British government.

[188]Stinnett, *Day of Deceit*, p. 255.

The key evidence of what really happened began to be concealed as early as December 11, 1941, only four days after the
attack. The first step in the clean-up came from Rear Admiral
Leigh Noyes, the Navy's Director of Communications. He
instituted the fifty-four-year censorship policy that consigned
the pre-Pearl Harbor Japanese military and diplomatic intercepts and the relevant directives to Navy vaults. "Destroy all
notes or anything in writing," Noyes told a group of his subordinates on December 11.[189]

Stinnett shows how the cover-up continued even after the
war:

> Two weeks after Japan surrendered in August 1945, the Navy
> blocked public access to the pre-Pearl Harbor intercepts by clas-
> sifying the documents TOP SECRET. Even Congress was cut
> out of the intercept loop. The Navy's order was sweeping; it
> gagged the cryptographers and radio intercept operators who
> had obtained the Japanese fleet's radio messages during the fall
> of 1941. Fleet Admiral Ernest King oversaw the censorship. He
> threatened imprisonment and loss of Navy and veteran's ben-
> efits to any naval personnel who disclosed the success of the
> code-breaking. . . .
>
> When the congressional investigation into the Pearl Harbor
> attack began on November 15, 1945, Americans believed they
> would be given full details on breaking the Japanese code prior
> to the attack. Witnesses introduced intercepts into evidence and
> read decrypted messages to the senators and representatives of
> the Joint Committee. It was a total sham. None of the details
> involving the interception, decoding, or dissemination of the
> pre-Pearl Harbor Japanese naval messages saw the light of
> day. Only diplomatic messages were released. Republicans sus-
> pected a stranglehold but could not pierce King's gag order.[190]

It was not until May 1999, almost fifty-eight years later,
that the U.S. Senate held another hearing and tried to rectify this
grave injustice inflicted by President Roosevelt upon these capable
career officers by making them the scapegoats for the "surprise

---

[189]Ibid.
[190]Ibid., pp. 256–57.

attack" on Pearl Harbor. A Senate resolution posthumously restored their full rank and declared that both men had performed their duties "completely and professionally" and that the Japanese attack was "not a result of dereliction of the performance" of their duties.[191] The U.S. Senate further made an extremely important finding:

> Numerous investigations following the attack on Pearl Harbor have documented that then Admiral Kimmel and then Lieutenant General Short were not provided necessary and critical intelligence that was available, that foretold of war with Japan, that warned of imminent attack, and that would have alerted them to prepare for the attack, including such essential communiques as the Japanese Pearl Harbor Bomb Plot message of September 24, 1941, and the message sent from the Imperial Japanese Foreign Ministry to the Japanese Ambassador in the United States from December 6-7, 1941, known as the Fourteen-Part Message.[192]

The Senate did not know about the sensational revelations in Robert Stinnett's book, which was published after the hearings. Perhaps someday the American people will finally understand that the real reason the day of December 7, 1941, will "live in infamy" will be because their president had become an "imperial president" who betrayed the American servicemen at Pearl Harbor and badly misled the U.S. Congress and the American people into an unnecessary war.

Stinnett's book reveals the ugly truth of the crimes, if not treason, of President Roosevelt and leaves no doubt about how Roosevelt provoked the Japanese into firing the first shot and how he withheld essential information from his Pearl Harbor commanders that would have allowed them either to prevent the attack or protect themselves. The book further shows the massive cover-up instigated by President Roosevelt. It further shows the sinister conspiracy instigated by the president and carried out by his military and civilian subordinates to make Admiral Kimmel and General Short the scapegoats by diverting

---

[191]See Roth Amendment No. 388 to the Defense Authorization Act passed by the United States Senate for the 106th Congress, First Session May 25, 1999, and the Senate Congressional Record for May 24, 1999, Sec. 582, p. S 5879.

[192]Ibid., Senate Congressional Record, p. 5878.

the attention away from the political intrigue in Washington. The book confirms that the power of the presidency and the executive branch has led to deceit and corruption the depths of the worst caesars of Rome. The Roosevelt supporters are now reduced to the erroneous, ridiculous, and evil Machiavellian defense that the end—(war with Germany—justified the means—provoking the Japanese to fire the first shot by sacrificing the men and ships at Pearl Harbor.[193]

[193]A new revelation of the treachery of Roosevelt has been disclosed in *The Washington Times* section entitled "Inside the Beltway" for the April 22, 1999 issue. This newspaper report refers to an article by Daryl S. Borgquist, a Justice Department media affairs officer. The article, "Advance Warning: The Red Cross Connection," appears in the May–June 1999 issue of *Naval History* magazine, published by the U.S. Naval Institute at Annapolis, Maryland. Borgquist points out that a Mrs. Helen E. Hamman wrote a letter to President Clinton, dated September 5, 1995, when she heard that the families of Admiral Kimmel and General Short were trying to clear their names in the Pearl Harbor matter. She reported that she was the daughter of Mr. Don C. Smith who died in 1990 at the age of 98. Mr. Smith directed the War Service for the Red Cross before World War II, and he informed his daughter during the 1970s that he had worried for years about the fact that he had been called to the White House shortly before the Pearl Harbor attack in 1941 and had a personal meeting with President Roosevelt. The letter of Mrs. Hamman states the following account of the meeting:

> Shortly before the attack in 1941, President Roosevelt called him [Smith] to the White House for a meeting concerning a Top Secret matter. At this meeting the president advised my father that his intelligence staff had informed him of a pending attack on Pearl Harbor, by the Japanese. He [FDR] anticipated many casualties and much loss; he instructed my father to send workers and supplies to a holding area . . . on the West Coast. When he protested to the president, President Roosevelt told him that the American people would never agree to enter the war in Europe unless they were attack[ed] within their own borders. . . . He followed the orders of the president and spent many years contemplating this action which he considered ethically and morally wrong.

Borgquist reports that the Red Cross records indicate a substantial supply of personnel and medical equipment was sent by the Red Cross to Hawaii shortly before the Pearl Harbor attack.

A huge monument has been erected in Washington, D.C., to celebrate the "greatness" of President Franklin D. Roosevelt. On the monument is a quotation from Roosevelt—"I hate war"—indicating falsely to the public that he was a president who sought peace rather than war. It is the ultimate

Conclusion:

Comparison of Lincoln and Roosevelt

At this point, it is interesting to compare Lincoln and his activity in causing the "enemy" to fire the first shot, as was shown in my earlier essay, with Roosevelt's similar activity. Arthur M. Schlesinger, Jr., a well-known American "court historian," has written the definitive defenses for both Abraham Lincoln and Franklin D. Roosevelt regarding their reprehensible behavior in causing their respective unnecessary American wars. He clearly documents the unconstitutional behavior of both and offers great praise for the same. He attempts to justify the actions of both presidents on grounds that they were acting during a "crisis" pertaining to the "survival of the American government," and that their unconstitutional actions were thereby made "necessary." Schlesinger has stated that "Next to the Civil War, World War II was the greatest crisis in American history."[194] His defense of these two "great" presidents is as follows:

> Roosevelt in 1941, like Lincoln in 1861, did what he did under what appeared to be a *popular demand* and a *public necessity.* Both presidents took their actions in light of day and to the accompaniment of *uninhibited political debate*. They did what they thought they had to do to *save the republic*. They threw themselves in the end on the justice of the country and the rectitude of their motives. Whatever Lincoln and Roosevelt felt compelled to do under the pressure of crisis did not corrupt their essential commitment to constitutional ways and democratic processes.[195]

---

example of false propaganda that is being perpetrated upon the American people. We learn from the investigation of the Pearl Harbor matter that after the attack ended, some of the crew of the battleship *Oklahoma* were still alive and trapped inside the hull of the partially sunken ship. The survivors outside could hear the trapped men knocking against the hull with metal objects desperately seeking rescue, but no rescue was possible (Beach, *Scapegoats*, p. 111). A recording should be made to duplicate their desperate sounds and have it played every hour at the Roosevelt Memorial to remind Americans of the treachery of their commander-in-chief.

[194]Schlesinger, *The Imperial Presidency*, p. 116.

[195]Arthur M. Schlesinger, Jr., "War and the Constitution: Abraham Lincoln and Franklin D. Roosevelt" in *Lincoln, the War President: The Gettysburg*

Schlesinger, however, recognizes the terrible precedents that were created by these presidents' violations of the clear Constitutional restrictions on their office:

> Yet the danger persists that power asserted during *authentic emergencies* may create precedents for transcendent executive power during emergencies that exist only in the hallucinations of the Oval Office and that remain invisible to most of the nation. The perennial question is: How to distinguish real crises threatening the life of the republic from bad dreams conjured up by paranoid presidents spurred on by paranoid advisers? Necessity, as Milton said, is always "the tyrant's plea."[196]

Let us add to John Milton's statement a more specific warning by William Pitt in his speech to the House of Commons on November 18, 1783: "Necessity is the plea for every infringement of human freedom. It is the argument of tyrants."[197]

Finally, it is instructive to compare the circumstances for Lincoln at Fort Sumter with those for Roosevelt at Pearl Harbor. In neither case was there an actual "surprise" attack by the enemy. In fact, there was an extended period of time, many months prior to the "first shot," in which both Lincoln and Roosevelt had ample opportunity to attempt to negotiate with the alleged "enemy," who was desperately trying to reach a peaceful settlement. In both cases, the presidents refused to negotiate in good faith. Lincoln sent completely false and conflicting statements to the Confederates and to Congress; even refused to talk with the Confederate commissioners. Roosevelt also refused to talk with Japanese Prime Minister Konoye, a refusal that brought down the moderate, peace-seeking Konoye government and caused the rise of the militant Tojo regime. Both Lincoln and Roosevelt repeatedly lied to the American people and to Congress about what they were doing while they were secretly provoking the "enemy" to fire the first shot in their respective wars. Both

---

Lectures, Gabor S. Boritt, ed. (New York: Oxford University Press, 1992), p. 174 (emphasis added).

[196]Ibid., p. 176 (emphasis added).

[197]John Bartlett, *Familiar Quotations*, Emily Morrison Beck, ed., 14th ed. (Boston: Little, Brown, 1968), p. 496.

intentionally subjected their respective armed forces to being bait to get the enemy to fire the first shot.

Also, a comparison of circumstances clearly shows that both Lincoln and Roosevelt had ample opportunity to present their arguments and the question of war to Congress as the Constitution clearly required them to do. In fact, Congress in both cases was desperately trying to find out what the presidents were doing, and in both cases the presidents were hiding evidence from them. In Lincoln's case, Congress probably would not have declared war for either the real reasons Lincoln went to war or for those he used only for propaganda. Similarly, Roosevelt could have presented the question of war to Congress and attempted to persuade Congress and the American people that we needed to join Soviet Russia and Great Britain to fight tyranny in Germany. This might have been embarrassing to the Roosevelt administration in light of the fact that Congress may not have wanted to declare war and join with Soviet Russia, which was already one of the greatest tyrannies the world had ever known, while Germany was Russia's main enemy. A majority in Congress surely were aware of the dangers of Communism, while Roosevelt never seemed to grasp the total evil of Stalin or Communism. Roosevelt gave Stalin everything he wanted throughout the war and referred to this mass murderer as "Uncle Joe." The wartime conferences at Teheran and Yalta clearly demonstrated Roosevelt's complete and secret capitulation to Communism in Russia and China.[198]

Before World War II started in Europe in 1939, it was widely known that Stalin had already murdered more than ten million innocent, unarmed people, three million of whom were Russian peasants he killed between 1928 and 1935. Communism believed that private property was the main source of evil in the world, and therefore he took the privately owned land from these self-sufficient people.[199] Also, in the period from 1936 through

[198]George N. Crocker, *Roosevelt's Road to Russia* (Chicago: Henry Regnery, 1959); and for an explanation of Roosevelt's delivery of China to the communists, see Anthony Kubek, *How the Far East Was Lost: American Policy and the Creation of Communist China, 1941–1949* (Chicago: Henry Regnery, 1963); see also Perlmutter, *FDR and Stalin*.

[199]Rummel, *Death by Government*, p. 10; see also Robert Conquest, *The Harvest of Sorrow: Soviet Collectivization and the Terror-Famine* (New York: Oxford University Press, 1986).

1938, Stalin murdered millions more during his reign of terror after the "show trials," purging from the Communist Party those he thought were disloyal.[200] Hitler, on the other hand, before 1939, and primarily from June to July 1934, had murdered fewer than one hundred in his purge of the Storm Troopers.[201] This is not to defend Hitler, or to deny that he was evil, but comparison of these two murderers and tyrants (as Stalin and Hitler were known in the period from 1939 to 1941), shows that Roosevelt could hardly have asked Congress to declare war and to join with Stalin and Communism, yet still argue that he was fighting a noble war against tyranny.

Private Enterprise Compared with Free Enterprise

Another interesting comparison of the situations affecting the decisions of Lincoln and Roosevelt is that economic interests of an elite few played a major role in the decisions of both presidents to instigate a war. It is doubtful that either Lincoln or Roosevelt would have wanted to disclose the influence of these economic interests to the public in a congressional hearing where the question of war was to be decided upon. The study of the history of wars indicates that economic factors have always played a major role in starting wars, but rarely are these economic factors disclosed to the public as the reasons.

Many businessmen and bankers believe in *private* enterprise but do not believe in *free* enterprise. In Lincoln's case, the private-enterprise capitalists wanted Lincoln to have a war in order to prevent the South from establishing a free-trade zone with a low tariff. They wanted Lincoln to protect their special interests by keeping the tariff high, while still forcing the South to remain in the Union to pay the tax. These types of people want a partnership between private enterprise and the government, which is the essence of fascism and the cause of many wars. In the case of Roosevelt, he was greatly influenced, even controlled at times, by the Anglo-American Establishment that was composed of prominent businessmen and bankers who owned or represented large economic interests, both domestically and globally. They also wanted a partnership with government to protect their private businesses and economic interests, especially from formidable

---

[200]Rummel, *Death by Government*, p. 10; see generally Robert Conquest, *The Great Terror: Stalin's Purge of the Thirties* (New York: Macmillan, 1968).

[201]Rummel, *Death by Government*, pp. 111–22.

industrial and commercial competitors like Germany and Japan. Today the economic establishment in America is much larger than just the Morgan and Rockefeller interests but is just as active in trying to influence government, especially the foreign policy, primarily through the president to further their economic interests.

Ludwig von Mises made a clear distinction between private enterprise and free enterprise. Mises wanted a complete separation of the economy from the government, just like separation of church and state, which meant no regulation or control by the government but also no partnership with or help from the government, either economically or militarily. In the free-enterprise system, if any business or any bank wants to transact business globally, it must do so at its own risk and without the help of the government. There would be no foreign aid, especially no aid to prop up dictators in order for them to do business with any particular economic interests. There would be no war in order to create a devastated area like Bosnia or Yugoslavia that needs to be rebuilt by American businesses who have the political influence to get these foreign contracts. Mises thought that separation of the economy from the government was necessary in order to produce peace rather than war.

A major contribution of Mises and the Austrian School of economics is to show that government intervention and regulation of the economy is the actual cause of the boom and bust cycles, while a free market is very stable and self-correcting in a short period of time. Furthermore, Mises showed that coercive monopolies are created by government and not by the free market. Therefore, the economy does not need government regulation or control to stabilize it and will function better by being completely separated.

Mises's other recommendation, seen in the following statement, is to reduce the size and power of the central government in general in order to protect individual liberty:

> Durable peace is only possible under *perfect capitalism*, hitherto never and nowhere completely tried or achieved. In such a Jeffersonian world of unhampered market economy the scope of government activities is limited to the protection of the lives, health and property of individuals against violence or fraudulent aggression.[202]

---

[202]Ludwig von Mises, *Omnipotent Government: The Rise of the Total State and Total War* (New Rochelle, N.Y.: Arlington House, 1969), p. 284 (emphasis added).

Mises goes on to state that:

> All the oratory of the advocates of government omnipotence
> cannot annul the fact that there is but one system that makes
> for durable peace: a free market economy. Government control
> leads to economic nationalism and thus results in conflict.[203]

This complete separation of the economy and the government is
what Mises meant by "perfect capitalism," which promotes
peace and prosperity rather than war and welfare.

Foreign Influence—The Anglo-American Establishment

In Roosevelt's case, a foreign government clearly influenced
and literally worked secretly and directly with him to cause the
U.S. to enter World War II in complete violation of President
Washington's warning in his *Farewell Address* against allowing
the influence of foreign governments to control American policy. This is still a major problem today with America's foreign
policy. American political leaders have not only ignored President Washington's warning about the dangerous influence of
foreign powers, but they have also ignored his excellent advice
that we should avoid permanent entangling alliances, such as
the United Nations and NATO. Washington advised us to have
as little *political* connection with other governments as possible,
while having *trade* relationships with *all* and without preferen-
tial status. Mises and President Washington are not advocating
isolationism; they are advocating global trade with all nations.

President Washington warned emphatically against getting
involved in the quarrels of Europe. Under President Clinton,
the U.S. readopted the Wilsonian foreign policy of crusading
throughout the world as its policeman by disguising imperialism with the term "humanitarianism," a policy that involves
American armed forces in matters which have no relationship
to real American interests or the defense of the American people and their homeland. Many members of Congress are now
calling for the draft again in order to have enough soldiers to be
the world's policeman. Charles Beard, the famous historian,
warned that we would lose our freedom if we adopted a policy

---

[203]Ibid., p. 286.

524

of "perpetual war for perpetual peace,"[204] and it was one of our Founders, James Madison, who warned that, "No nation could preserve its freedom in the midst of continual warfare."[205] War necessarily concentrates political power into the hands of a few—especially the president—and diminishes the liberty of all.

Reclaiming the Dream of Our Founders

If Americans are to reclaim the dream of our Founders and have peace and prosperity instead of war and welfare, we must understand the ideas and institutions that promote those conditions. Americans must appreciate and adopt the free-enterprise system and reject the private-enterprise system. Since the beginning of the twentieth century, we have been on a collision course with disaster by following political leaders who got elected and maintained their power through the war and welfare system of politics. Americans will never reclaim the dream of their Founders if presidents like Lincoln and Roosevelt are held up as examples of "great" presidents. We must impeach those presidents who ignore that the Constitution grants the warmaking power exclusively to Congress, and certainly impeach those who mislead Congress into a declaration of war with false information.

Americans need to oppose and destroy the "imperial presidency" because of what it has already done and will do to our country and to our individual freedom. The first step toward that goal is to recognize Presidents Lincoln and Roosevelt for what they really were: American Caesars.

---

[204]Harry Elmer Barnes, ed., *Perpetual War for Perpetual Peace*, p. viii.

[205]James Madison, "Political Observations," *Letters and Other Writings of James Madison (1795)* (Philadelphia: J.B. Lippincott, 1865), 4, pp. 491–92; also see further quotations from Madison in John V. Denson, "War and American Freedom" in *The Costs of War: America's Pyrrhic Victories*, John V. Denson, ed., 2nd ed. (New Brunswick, N.J.: Transaction Publishers, 1999), pp. 6–11.

17

DESPOTISM LOVES COMPANY: THE STORY OF FRANKLIN D. ROOSEVELT AND JOSEF STALIN

YURI N. MALTSEV AND BARRY DEAN SIMPSON

Many people consider Franklin D. Roosevelt one of the greatest presidents of the United States. Republican Party leaders solemnly invoke him as a protector and not a destroyer of liberty.[1] Historians such as Arthur M. Schlesinger, Jr., look to him as a model and hero.[2] Public opinion seems to agree with prominent magazines that Roosevelt's legacy is unmatched by any other American president.[3] But for all his tributes, the damage Roosevelt inflicted on the U.S. through his affinity for and mishandling of the Soviet leader Josef Stalin, set the stage for the cold war and communist expansion.

---

[1]See J. Jennings Moss, "Reverence for FDR Crosses Spectrum," *Insight on the News* 11, no. 19, May 15, 1995; "Newt and Franklin," *National Journal* 27, no. 1 (January 1995); "The Roosevelt Legacy," *The Economist* 340, no. 7985 (September 28, 1996): 38; and *Polio Survivor's Page* "President Franklin Delano Roosevelt: A Disability Hero," http://www.eskimo.com/%7Edempt/fdr.htm. April 4, 1995.

[2]See Arthur M. Schlesinger, Jr., "Franklin Delano Roosevelt," *Time* 151, no. 14, April 13, 1998, p. 98, "The Real Roosevelt Legacy," *Newsweek* 128, no. 16, October 1996, p. 43; and "A Conversation with Historian Arthur Schlesinger," *All Things Considered*, National Public Radio Broadcast, December 18, 1994.

[3]In a 1997 CNN/*USA Today*/Gallup Poll, 32 percent of Americans rated FDR an outstanding president, and 36 percent rated him an above average president. See also Milton Cooper, Jr., "Great Expectations and Shadowlands," *The Virginia Quarterly Review* 72, no. 3 (Summer 1996): 377. For magazine support, see "The Roosevelt Centennial," *America* 146, February 13, 1982, p. 104; Toast to a Hero," *Time* 119, February 8, 1982, p. 30; "Roosevelt's Long Shadow," *Newsweek* 99, February 1, 1982, p. 30; and "The Unforgotten Man," *Newsweek* 99, January 11, 1982, p. 26.

Thus, the concern here is with Roosevelt's general approach to foreign policy, his goals in the field, and possible reasons for his pursuit of Marshal Stalin. Roosevelt's urge to meet Stalin manifested itself at Yalta and the Atlantic Charter Conference through various concessions made to the Soviets in the hopes of attaining foreign policy goals after the war. Roosevelt had a flair for the dramatic, so many of his pronouncements and decisions resulted from these conferences. The relationship between Roosevelt and Stalin leads to our conclusion that history will not be as kind to Franklin Roosevelt as Schlesinger and current public opinion.

Roosevelt's approach to foreign policy was decidedly progressive. He introduced internationalism and globalism to foreign policy.[4] According to Amos Perlmutter:

> Projecting Wilsonian idealism, Roosevelt was the offspring of the old expansionists. The Calvinist origins of Wilsonian idealism were congenial with Roosevelt's own protestantism; but his instincts governed his foreign policy, and those instincts were patrician and expansionist. Roosevelt was not a disappointed Wilsonian, but rather a combination of both Wilson and Theodore Roosevelt. FDR, not Henry Luce, authored the American century.[5]

The president viewed himself as fulfilling the mission that Woodrow Wilson began in World War I: to take upon himself the moral leadership of making the world safe for democracy.[6] After implementing the New Deal at home, Roosevelt wanted to give the entire world a New Deal.[7] Globalization of his welfare state required the support of the competing socialist model of the Soviet Union. Sir John Wheeler-Bennett summarizes:

[4]See "From Isolationism to Global Leadership," U.S. Department of State Dispatch, no. 21, U.S. Government Printing Office, May 2, 1991, p. 391.

[5]Amos Perlmutter, FDR and Stalin (Columbia: University of Missouri Press, 1993), p. 28.

[6]John T. Flynn, The Roosevelt Myth (San Francisco: Fox and Wilkes, 1998), p. 293. See also John Charmley, Churchill (London: Hodder and Stoughton, 1993), pp. 460, 486.

[7]Perlmutter, FDR and Stalin, p. 31. See also Ted Morgan, FDR (New York: Simon and Schuster, 1985), pp. 633f.

President Roosevelt's ambition was to establish the United Nations but to superimpose upon it an American–Soviet alliance, which should dominate world affairs to the detriment of Britain and France, and to this end he made copious concessions to Marshal Stalin.[8]

ADULATION

Two factors led to Roosevelt's desire to secure the confidence of Stalin. The first followed from his quest for a global new deal. In this manner, he could obtain his goals of universal democracy and an end to colonialism.[9] Roosevelt was suspicious and resentful of what he saw as English imperialism and colonialism.[10] Elliott, his son, even managed to blame the British for the failure of the finer points of the Atlantic Charter.

The second factor was Roosevelt's admiration of the power of Stalin. Roosevelt's own love of power is self-evident in his court-packing and economic schemes. He saw Stalin as using his power on behalf of the Russian people, and he saw this somehow as a bond with Stalin.[11] In fact, the entire Roosevelt family seemed to harbor a fascination with the Soviet Union.[12] Tansill's description of the Roosevelt administration's position on Russia is certain: "Russia was to be courted, not criticized."[13]

Of course, this does not mean that Stalin did nothing worthy of criticism. Scholars knew of Stalin's reputation for ruthlessness before 1940. Marshal Stalin had already killed millions of Ukrainians, and innumerable Spanish socialists, and he had purged his own Communist Party during the Moscow Trials of the 1930s. In 1939 Stalin, along with Hitler, was busy dividing

[8]Sir John Wheeler-Bennett, et al., *The Semblance of Peace* (New York: St. Martin's, 1972), p. 8. See also Charmley, *Churchill*, pp. 538f, 550f.

[9]Willard Range, *Franklin D. Roosevelt's World Order* (Athens: University of Georgia Press, 1959), p. 137.

[10]Ibid., pp. 102ff. See also Elliott Roosevelt, *As He Saw It* (New York: Duell, Sloane, and Pearce, 1945), pp. 71–75, 115–16, 121–22, and Charmley, *Churchill*, p. 555.

[11]Robert A. Nisbet, *Roosevelt and Stalin* (Washington, D.C.: Regnery, 1988), p. 108. See also James M. Burns, *Roosevelt, the Lion and the Fox, 1912–1940* (New York: Harcourt, Brace, and World, 1956), p. 373.

[12]George N. Crocker, *Roosevelt's Road to Russia* (Chicago: Regnery, 1959), p. 60.

[13]Charles Tansill, "Japanese-American Relations," in *Perpetual War for Perpetual Peace*, Harry Elmer Barnes, ed. (Caldwell, Idaho.: Caxton Printers), p. 282.

the spoils from Poland and the Baltic States.[14] Moreover, Russia's invasion of Finland led to an eviction from the League of Nations in the same year.[15] FBI Director J. Edgar Hoover told of Stalin's desire for imperial expansion, and a report from Virgil Pinkley of the *United Press* noted the build-up of a huge military machine for the purpose of taking countries by force. Pinkley described the political structure in the Soviet Union as moving toward a dictatorship, with Stalin gaining more power than Hitler.[16]

If President Roosevelt up to this point denied knowledge of these events, there is one event in particular of which he could not deny knowledge—the Katyn Forest Massacre. The Russians in 1939 had taken fifteen thousand Polish officers captive and promptly murdered them in the Katyn Forest. Germans discovered the corpses in 1943, and the Red Cross was ready to investigate the matter. Roosevelt reacted with anger toward the messengers when presented with factual evidence of the atrocity. Quickly and quietly, the president swept the incident under the rug and suppressed the potential investigation.[17]

Roosevelt's pursuit of Stalin materialized in the form of aid and propaganda from the United States. The president had already informed British Prime Minister Churchill that he could "personally handle Stalin."[18] According to William Bullitt, Roosevelt's method of handling the dictator consisted of giving him everything he wanted and asking nothing in return.[19] This acquiescence to Soviet command began with the Lend-Lease Act.

---

[14]Nisbet, *Roosevelt and Stalin*, p. 3. See also Burns, *Roosevelt*, pp. 393f. Michael Parrish, *The Lesser Terror* (Westport, Conn.: Praeger, 1996), p. 53, estimates one million people had been murdered under Stalin's rule by 1940. See also Robert Conquest, *The Great Terror: A Reassessment* (New York: Oxford University Press, 1990); Robert Thurston, *Life and Terror in Stalin's Russia* (New Haven, Conn.: Yale University Press, 1996); J. Arch Getty and Roberta T. Manning, *Stalinist Terror* (New York: Cambridge University Press, 1993).

[15]Wheeler-Bennett, et al., *The Semblance of Peace*, p. 234. See also Nikolai Tolstoy, *Stalin's Secret War* (New York: Holt, Rinehart, 1981).

[16]Don Whitehead, *The FBI Story* (New York: Random House, 1956), p. 267.

[17]Crocker, *Roosevelt's Road to Russia*, pp. 28f., 221, 247f. See also Robert Conquest, *Stalin: Breaker of Nations* (New York: Penguin, 1991), pp. 258, 261.

[18]Nisbet, *Roosevelt and Stalin*, p. 15.

[19]Ibid., p. 6.

Roosevelt developed the Lend–Lease proposal in early 1941, shortly after the 1940 election. The president had promised to keep America out of the war when he signed the Neutrality Act in 1937, hence he could not afford the appearance of belligerence. Once passed, Lend–Lease allowed him to circumvent the Neutrality Act by sending arms and supplies to England and the Soviet Union in return for repayment at war's end.[20] The bill breached the concepts of neutrality in international law; in fact, Senator Burton K. Wheeler argued that Lend–Lease entitled Roosevelt to wage an undeclared war on Germany. No conditions or warnings accompanied the billions of dollars worth of aid that flowed to the totalitarian Communist state.[21]

The fact that Russia became an ally of Great Britain immediately changed the status of Stalin in the eyes of Roosevelt's administration. Overnight, the official propaganda shifted its slant on the Russian dictator and his American Communists and fellow-travelers. The official Communist line turned squarely from urging the country to stay out of the European war at all costs to strong pleas that America must now enter this great fight to save democracy.[22]

Pro-Soviet propaganda blanketed the country from Washington to Hollywood. Joseph E. Davies's 1941 book *Mission to Moscow* was released as a movie in 1943. According to George N. Crocker, "Stalin was pictured as a sort of combination of Pavel Milyukov, Harry Emerson Fosdick, Bernard Baruch, and Jane Addams."[23] Harry Hopkins, Roosevelt's intimate friend and confidante, published an article in *American* magazine after his first meeting with Stalin and portrayed the dictator as "an austere, rugged, determined figure in boots that shone like mirrors." Robert Nisbet describes the Hopkins article as "rapturous."[24]

Perhaps the most incredulous of Roosevelt's actions was his attempt to appease Christians against Soviet atheism. At a press conference in November 1941, Roosevelt invoked Article 124 of

---

[20]Flynn, *The Roosevelt Myth*, p. 295. See also Lloyd C. Gardner, *Economic Aspects* (Boston: Beacon Press, 1964), pp. 168f.; and Burns, *Roosevelt*, p. 457.

[21]Nisbet, *Roosevelt and Stalin*, pp. 19–20.

[22]Perlmutter, *FDR and Stalin*, p. 102.

[23]Crocker, *Roosevelt's Road to Russia*, p. 12.

[24]Nisbet, *Roosevelt and Stalin*, p. 22.

the Russian constitution which, according to the president, affords freedom of religion to the Soviet people. Roosevelt held that the rule in Russia was "essentially what is the rule in this country; only we don't put it quite the same way."[25] As Robert Dallek points out, Roosevelt knew that freedom of religion was nonexistent in Russia, but he needed it to make the war acceptable to his constituency.[26]

THE ATLANTIC CHARTER

The propaganda and preludes to war continued with the meetings between Roosevelt and Churchill. The two leaders met in a bay off the coast of Newfoundland. Roosevelt considered a meeting aboard a ship as a great show that would play well in the press. His first candidate for such a meeting was Adolf Hitler, but he could hardly meet with the German leader once the war began. Roosevelt retained the stage and the props; only the cast changed.[27]

The White House cloaked the August 1941 meeting in secrecy, conveying the semblance of a fishing vacation for the president.[28] Roosevelt carefully and skillfully pacified Americans before his departure by assuring them he would do everything within his power to avoid getting into a "shooting war."[29] His true intentions, however, were anything but an attempt to avoid war. On the first day of the conference, Roosevelt and Hopkins attended an intimate lunch with the British prime minister. Churchill expressed his desire that the United States enter the war immediately. Rather than showing antiwar disgust at such a plan, Roosevelt was much more concerned with "public opinion, American politics, all the intangibles that lead to action and at once betray it."[30]

Roosevelt made two military commitments to Churchill during this clandestine affair. Churchill expected the Nazis to overtake Spain within the month. England would have to evacuate

---

[25]Ibid., p. 25.

[26]Robert Dallek, *Franklin D. Roosevelt and American Foreign Policy* (New York: Oxford University Press, 1979), p. 298.

[27]Flynn, *The Roosevelt Myth*, p. 300.

[28]Crocker, *Roosevelt's Road to Russia*, p. 97.

[29]Ibid., p. 96.

[30]Roosevelt, *As He Saw It*, p. 27.

Gibraltar and would no longer be able to honor its commitment to Portugal to protect the Azore Islands. Roosevelt agreed to assume this role. The second commitment involved the Japanese seizure of Indochina. With this capture, the position of Singapore became a precarious one. Roosevelt issued a warning to the Japanese ambassador in Washington that amounted to an ultimatum. The warning conveyed the simple message that if Japan continued in her conquest of the Pacific, the United States would take the necessary means, in the name of national security, to stop Japanese expansion.[31]

The concessions to Russia at this meeting embodied more than semantics to convince United States citizens that Stalin was one of the leaders of the free world. The first piece of propaganda included the loss of two of Roosevelt's four freedoms. The Atlantic Charter consisted of eight points. Churchill had crafted a point stating that the signers would defend freedom of speech and religion throughout the world. Roosevelt could not allow the word "defend" and still keep up the appearance of avoiding war. More important, however, he could not pursue his courtship of Stalin through such a statement when it was well known that freedom of speech and religion did not exist in Soviet Russia. The solution was a simple one: Roosevelt allowed no mention of freedom of speech and religion in the charter.[32]

Such a result did not restrain Roosevelt in his effort to convince Americans that entry into the war would exist for the purpose of bringing freedom to the world. The following February, Roosevelt delivered a speech in honor of George Washington's birthday. In his speech, Roosevelt claimed that

> [t]he Atlantic Charter applies not only to the parts of the world that border the Atlantic but to the whole world; disarmament of aggressors, self-determination of nations and peoples, and the four freedoms—freedom of speech, freedom of religion, freedom from want, and freedom from fear.[33]

This speech was made with the knowledge that the prime minister had announced to the House of Commons in September

---

[31]Flynn, *The Roosevelt Myth*, pp. 300–01.

[32]"Declaration of the Atlantic," *Saturday Evening Post*, September 27, 1941, p. 26.

[33]Samuel I. Rosenman, *Public Papers* (New York: Random House, 1938).

that the Atlantic Charter referred only to the states that had lost their rule to the Nazis.[34]

Although he excluded freedom of speech and religion from the Atlantic Charter, Roosevelt in public implied that the Soviets exercised such freedoms. In February, he gave a radio address commemorating the 150th anniversary of the Bill of Rights. In that address, he pronounced that the principles enunciated in the Bill of Rights were accepted around the globe, with the exception of the three Axis countries: Germany, Italy, and Japan.[35]

CASABLANCA

After American entry into the war, Russian aid, or "requisitions" as they were known, became the top priority of the Washington bureaucracy. As Roosevelt and Hopkins left for Casablanca in January 1943, however, they had a much different type of Russian aid in mind. Churchill had made his military intentions clear to the president: Once the Allies conquered Africa, naval and air installations should facilitate an expeditionary force in Turkey through which an invasion of the Balkans could occur. Germany had experienced defeat in Africa and at Stalingrad. It seemed only a matter of time before the Axis powers were crushed. Churchill's long-range goal was clear: He wished to protect eastern Europe from the threat of communist expansion after the war.[36]

Stalin and Molotov had a different plan of attack in mind. The Russians had wished for an assault on France for an entire year. At Casablanca, it seemed that such an effort would be postponed for another year. Although Roosevelt could not yet bring the assault on French shores to a head, he did manage to quell British hopes for a Balkan invasion once and for all.[37] Moreover, the Red Army was beginning to push the German army back after the German surrender at Stalingrad. As the Soviet military gained strength, the Allies would lose political leverage. Roosevelt, however, had already failed to take advantage of Russia's weak position. According to Flynn, "[t]wo full years had been

[34]Chester Wilmot, *The Struggle for Europe* (New York: Harper, 1952), p. 633.

[35]Rosenman, *Public Papers*.

[36]Roosevelt, *As He Saw It*, pp. 93, 96.

[37]Ibid., pp. 94, 108–09.

wasted, instead of applying to Stalin the only pressure he could understand. All he could hope for in arms and material aid he got as fast as we could get them to him without laying down a single condition."[38]

Perhaps the most regrettable episode at Casablanca was Roosevelt's pronouncement that the only condition that would end the war was the *unconditional* surrender of Germany and Japan. According to Roosevelt, that phrase was not preconceived. As the press conference began, the president considered bringing two French generals together as difficult as arranging a meeting between Grant and Lee would have been. Suddenly, he remembered that Grant had been nicknamed "Old Unconditional Surrender." At this point, in the president's own words, "the next thing I knew, I had said it."[39]

Sherwood's comment on this Roosevelt quote is a testament to the precocious nature of the American president:

> Roosevelt, for some reason, often liked to picture himself as a rather frivolous fellow who did not give sufficient attention to the consequences of chance remarks. In this explanation, indicating a spur-of-the-moment slip of the tongue, he certainly did considerably less than justice to himself. For this announcement of unconditional surrender was very deeply deliberated. Whether it was wise or foolish, whether it prolonged the war or shortened it—or even if it had no effect whatsoever on the duration (which seems possible)—it was a true statement of Roosevelt's considered policy and he refused all suggestions that he retract the statement or soften it and continued refusal to the day of his death.[40]

Elliott Roosevelt attributes this quote to his father concerning this "frivolous" phrase:

> Of course, it's just the thing for the Russians. They couldn't want anything better. "Unconditional surrender," he repeated, thoughtfully sucking a tooth. "Uncle Joe might have made it up himself."[41]

---

[38]Flynn, *The Roosevelt Myth*, p. 314.

[39]Robert E. Sherwood, *Roosevelt and Hopkins, An Intimate History* (New York: Harper, 1950), p. 696.

[40]Ibid., p. 696.

[41]Roosevelt, *As He Saw It*, p. 117.

Sherwood's implication of a benign effect from the statement is wrong. Shortly before Casablanca, two anti-Nazi Germans had inquired of Bishop Chichester in Stockholm whether the Allies would negotiate with a democratic German government if Hitler was overthrown. Mutiny had already crossed the minds of several of Hitler's senior officers.[42] The bishop tried to obtain a reply from the Allies, but his entreaties would not invoke a response. According to Crocker, "[a]ll moves toward peace were peremptorily brushed aside."[43]

Roosevelt's turn of phrase unquestionably prolonged the war. The Germans equated unconditional surrender with slavery and, as such, were prompted to fight on for over two more years. Moreover, Hirohito perceived defeat during 1943 and would have accepted any terms but unconditional surrender. Roosevelt, however, had no time for the diplomacy of peace. After Casablanca, he had to press on to Marrakech for a short vacation replete with wine, Scotch, picnic lunches, and the singing of songs—at an exorbitant price to American taxpayers.[44]

CAIRO

Roosevelt had satisfied all of Stalin's requests except one: an all-out attack on France. An allied invasion of France to solidify the Soviet position after the war was slow but soon to come. So far, Stalin had coyly eluded the American president. In light of such conditions, it is plausible that the marshal was using himself as a bargaining chip to be dangled like a carrot in front of Roosevelt.[45] The Cairo conference in November 1943 presented an opportunity for Roosevelt to show his magnanimity toward the Russian cause in an attempt to gain an audience with the Soviet leader.

The ostensible pretense of the Cairo conference was to help China out of her current situation. Chiang Kai-shek had battled

---

[42]See B.S. Liddell Hart, *The German Generals Talk* (London: Cassell, 1951); William D. Leahy, *I Was There* (New York: Whittlesey House, 1950); Hans Rothfells, *The German Opposition to Hitler* (New York: Regnery, 1948); and Wilmot, *The Struggle for Europe*.

[43]Crocker, *Roosevelt's Road to Russia*, p. 169.

[44]Ibid., pp. 182–83.

[45]Ibid., p. 196.

an internal Communist rebellion during the 1930s. War with Japan caused Chiang to reach an agreement with the Communists in 1937. The Communists would fight Japan alongside the national army in return for a discontinuance of Communist suppression by Chiang. But the Communists would renege on the deal as soon as Chiang was driven to Chungking. Communists seized this opportunity to drop out of the war with Japan and occupy the rural areas between the Japanese occupied cities in the north. The Japanese only wanted Manchuria—the northern, resource-rich section of China. Japan's goal was to install a puppet government to funnel resources to the motherland. Whoever controlled the north controlled China, so the Communists were content to bide their time until Japan fell.[46]

Roosevelt's solution for China was to make her more democratic. Engaged in pro-Soviet propaganda at home, his method for accomplishing such a task consisted of talking Chiang into recognizing and forming a unity government with the Communists.[47] Chiang's reward for this coalition was a deal to send Allied troops into Burma. Churchill was opposed to sending troops to Burma. He still felt that a Balkan invasion represented the best course of action. But Chiang felt that the opening of the Burma Road would enhance his position with his countrymen. So Roosevelt did what any seasoned politician would do—he lied to everyone. First, he neglected to inform the prime minister of the Burma mission. Second, after Chiang left Cairo with Roosevelt's assurance that the Burma Road would soon be opened, Roosevelt threw the plan away ten days later, once he received a guarantee that Russia soon would join in the war against Japan.[48]

Presumably, Stalin expected the exact results. Chiang went south to Burma, leaving the important north open for the Communists. So Stalin would be the puppet master, as he was in Yugoslavia and Poland later. According to Crocker, "Chiang

[46]Hollingsworth K. Tong, *Chiang Kai-shek* (China Publishing, 1953), pp. 323ff. See also Flynn, *The Roosevelt Myth*, pp. 321f.

[47]John T. Flynn, *The Lattimore Story* (New York: Devin-Adair, 1953), p. 53. See also idem, *The Roosevelt Myth*, p. 328.

[48]Sherwood, *Roosevelt and Hopkins*, p. 800. See also Leahy, *I Was There*, p. 202.

was never able to recover the military advantage over Mao Tse-tung and the Red Army.[49]

TEHERAN

Egypt was merely a diversion for Roosevelt. The real challenge was Stalin himself, and this challenge the president undertook at Teheran in November 1943. Notable Stalin biographer Adam Ulam calls Teheran Stalin's greatest victory.[50] Roosevelt's failure to factor the nature of a dictator into his calculus predicated such a victory. As Robert Nisbet notes, Stalin had made a career "based upon exploitation of those who came bearing gifts and seeking friendship."[51] At Teheran, Stalin was to extract the most precious of gifts from Franklin Roosevelt.

Roosevelt's first present to Stalin was the Balkans. In defiance of the acts of Congress in 1940 supporting the independence of the Baltic states, Roosevelt suggested that Estonia, Latvia, and Lithuania, as well as the eastern portion of Poland which Stalin seized as part of his 1939–1941 pact with Hitler, remain under Soviet tyranny. The only string attached was that the deal not be made public. Stalin must remain quiet in order for Roosevelt to get the Polish vote in the 1944 election. Roosevelt accepted the idea of postwar eastern European governments friendly to the Soviet Union, and promised Stalin vast territorial gains in the Far East if he agreed to join in the war against Japan once Hitler was defeated. No prolonged arguments or sleepless nights occurred, nor was this a business deal with an aforementioned quid pro quo. All Roosevelt asked in return was Stalin's participation in the president's dream of a peacekeeping United Nations in the postwar era.[52]

Czechoslovakia and Yugoslavia became casualties of war at Teheran. The gains of Stalin's Red Army were not questioned. Teheran also marked the realization of Stalin's anticipated second front. Plans to launch an attack in May 1944 were agreed upon and finalized.[53]

---

[49]Crocker, *Roosevelt's Road to Russia*, p. 207.

[50]Adam Ulam, *Stalin: The Man and His Era* (Boston: Beacon Press, 1973), p. 587.

[51]Nisbet, *Roosevelt and Stalin*, p. 27.

[52]Crocker, *Roosevelt's Road to Russia*, pp. 209–10.

[53]Flynn, *The Roosevelt Myth*, pp. 328f., 361.

Contrary to popular opinion, the decision on the partition-
ing of Poland took place at Teheran rather than Yalta. Roosevelt
did not heed the "self-determination of nations" rhetoric found
in the Atlantic Charter. Not one single Pole was invited to attend
the conference at which more than half of their country was
given to the Soviet Union. It was Germany's invasion of Poland,
moreover, that evoked the British declaration of war against
Germany. Roosevelt's decision was an affront to every allied soldier who gave his life for the hope of a freer world.[54]

George Crocker holds that Teheran was the turning point
that led to postwar horrors. The contention is that Roosevelt
could have sided with Churchill, making it harder for Stalin to
negotiate. The German army was still on Russian soil, and the
American and British armies and navies were not committed,
hence could strike anywhere. But negotiation was not part of
Roosevelt's plan. He wanted to be liked.[55]

Evidence of this puerile need of the president is found in the
small talk that took place at the Russian-sponsored banquet
after the second plenary session. In the midst of many toasts
and jokes, Stalin proposed a toast to killing the fifty thousand
German officers and technicians as soon as they were captured.
Churchill was aghast; he announced that the British would not
sanction such butchery. Next, the great diplomat Franklin D.
Roosevelt chimed in with a compromise: "We should settle on a
smaller number. Shall we say 49,500?"[56] When the president's
son, Elliott, rose in agreement with Stalin's plan, Prime Minister
Churchill left the table, surrounded by the laughter of Russians
and Americans.[57]

Historian Keith Sainsbury also argues that Teheran constituted a turning point. Militarily, Teheran marked the end of
British plans and the ascendance of American plans for the duration of the war. It was also clear that the Soviet Union would be
the dominant power in eastern and possibly central Europe at
war's end. Politically, Roosevelt and Stalin drafted plans for a
Soviet–American concord on Europe and the Far East. According
to Sainsbury:

---

[54]Crocker, *Roosevelt's Road to Russia*, pp. 210, 221–22.

[55]Ibid., pp. 218.

[56]Ibid., p. 219.

[57]Wheeler-Bennett, et al., *The Semblance of Peace*, p. 153.

The breaking up of Germany and control of its major industrial areas, the maintenance of a large number of small States in central and eastern Europe, the annexation of part of prewar Poland by Russia, and of German territory by Russia and Poland, the permanent reduction of France to a minor power, and easy Soviet access to the Baltic and Mediterranean were indicated as part of the future pattern for Europe.[58]

QUEBEC II: THE MORGENTHAU PLAN

Germany had reasons to suspect Western democracy. The Germans believed that the president of the United States had stuck a knife in their back at Versailles. In their view, the Morgenthau Plan represented the twisting of the blade.

The first Quebec conference was fairly innocuous compared with the atmosphere the Morgenthau Plan brought to Quebec II in September 1944. The plan was to render Germany a pasture. All industries would be stripped from the area in such a manner as to prevent their return. The program even listed some German citizens for death at war's end. Those lucky enough to live would be relegated to subsistence level. Such a bare existence would continue over several generations.[59]

Roosevelt approved the Morgenthau Plan. According to Sir John Wheeler-Bennett, "the president was guilty of none of the humanitarian impulses which had motivated Woodrow Wilson. Roosevelt had his own large-scale plan for the breakup of Germany and he was happy to fall in with the rigorous demands of Stalin."[60] Fortunately, the version of the plan determined at Potsdam was watered down compared with the original version.[61] But its existence at the time allowed Goebbels to rally German troops for seven more months. As Secretary of State Cordell Hull feared, the leaking of the plan led to the loss of thousands more American lives. The coinciding result instilled a

---

[58]Keith Sainsbury, *The Turning Point* (Oxford: Oxford University Press, 1985), pp. 1–2.

[59]Crocker, *Roosevelt's Road to Russia*, p. 231. See also Charmley, *Churchill*, p. 585.

[60]Wheeler-Bennett, et al., *The Semblance of Peace*, p. 174.

[61]Flynn, *The Roosevelt Myth*, p. 363.

hatred of Western democracy within the minds and hearts of the peoples of eastern Europe.[62]

YALTA

The most celebrated meeting of the allied powers came at Yalta in February 1945. Most of the groundwork had been set by the time of the conference, but the secret agreements had not been made public. At Yalta, the world saw for the first time the gravity of the postwar situation. Even today, Yalta cannot be seen in its true light, for the historians who compiled the various papers from the meeting have confessed to tampering.[63]

Yalta provided a more profound function than a simple meeting place for deals and diplomacy. Nisbet describes the importance of Yalta in this manner:

> Yalta performed a service to the Soviets that was almost as important to Stalin as the occupied areas themselves. This was the invaluable service of giving moral legitimization to what Stalin had acquired by sheer force. The Declaration on Liberated Europe alone accomplished that.[64]

At the Yalta Conference, Roosevelt felt morally bound to legitimize Stalin's claims. Harry Hopkins wrote to Roosevelt at the conference, "[t]he Russians have given us so much at this conference that I don't think we should let them down."[65] What had Stalin given? He had agreed that in the new United Nations, the Soviet Union would have only three votes—one for the USSR, one for the Soviet Ukraine, and one for Soviet White Russia—instead of sixteen votes, or one for each of the Soviet Republics.[66]

Of course, Stalin's promises to the West did not bind him. His promise to work for a new Rooseveltian world order and to guarantee free elections in the eastern European nations that the Red Army conquered on its way to Berlin lasted less than two months. In early April 1945, a Yugoslav Communist delegation

---

[62]Crocker, *Roosevelt's Road to Russia*, p. 238. See also Gardner, *Economic Aspects*, pp. 267f.

[63]Cordell Hull, *The Memoirs of Cordell Hull* (New York: Macmillan, 1948), p. 1606.

[64]Nisbet, *Roosevelt and Stalin*, pp. 70–71.

[65]Ibid., p. 77.

[66]Flynn, *The Roosevelt Myth*, p. 390.

led by Marshal Tito visited Moscow. At a late-night banquet in their honor, Stalin ruminated on the postwar era. During the feasting and toasting, Stalin explained to his guests, "[t]his war is not as in the past; whoever occupies a territory also imposes on it his own social system."[67] As for the future, Stalin assured his guests that "[t]he war shall soon be over. We shall recover in fifteen or twenty years, and then we'll have another go at it."[68] Here was the true Stalin, the real "Uncle Joe," as Roosevelt and Churchill affectionately referred to the dictator.

After Franklin Roosevelt's death, President Truman took over at the Potsdam Conference outside of Berlin in July 1945. Germany had surrendered, thus her fate hung in the balance. While Truman allowed a milder Morgenthau Plan to be selected, "[a]ll the major decisions which make up the incredible record of surrender, blunder and savagery had already been made long before President Truman . . . went to Potsdam."[69] And although Truman should not be excused for dropping the bomb to end the war with Japan, Roosevelt's insistence on unconditional surrender prolonged the war and left President Truman few alternatives.

Traveling in free Lithuania a couple of years ago, this co-writer was struck by a huge poster displayed near Vilnius Airport. It was a famous "troika" picture with something different in it: Instead of FDR, Stalin, and Churchill, the picture depicted Roosevelt, Stalin, and Hitler. Lithuanians, like all other east Europeans, believe that the West "betrayed" them twice—to Hitler in Munich in 1938 and to Josef Stalin at Yalta in 1945. In truth, Yalta was only the final betrayal of eastern Europe, and both FDR and Churchill bear a large measure of responsibility for a half-century of communist rape and enslavement of its people.

CONCLUSIONS

Franklin Roosevelt's mark on the political landscape of the twentieth century cannot be overlooked or whitewashed. His naivete and propitiation to Stalin turned half of the population of this planet over to communism. Roosevelt, representing a

---

[67]Milovan Djilas, *Conversations with Stalin* (New York: Harvest, 1962), p. 114.

[68]Ibid., pp. 114–15.

[69]Flynn, *The Roosevelt Myth*, p. 362.

resourceful country that Russia needed in order to defeat Germany, never asked for any postwar concessions from Stalin. Roosevelt was in a position to dictate terms to a dictator, but he never did.

While mainstream politicians praise Roosevelt as a genius, the critical analysis of Roosevelt's legacy is based on the premise that he was a well-meaning but naive politician. Amos Perlmutter was the first Western scholar granted access to recently declassified key Soviet foreign ministry documents. Perlmutter provides a provocative portrait of a popular leader whose failure to comprehend Stalin's long-range goals had devastating results for the postwar world.[70] Keith Sainsbury adds that, "[Roosevelt] knew little of Stalin, or indeed of Russia and the Soviet system, but he had confidence in his ability to establish a good personal relationship."[71]

John Flynn claims that Churchill and Stalin considered postwar goals, while Roosevelt's two concerns were winning the war and establishing the United Nations. Roosevelt thought Stalin would cease annexing territory with a world policeman to quell Soviet fears against invasion. But Stalin's "policy was to commit himself to nothing, to admit nothing and to demand and demand and demand."[72] In Flynn's opinion, only an infatuated man could not see Stalin's plan to hold the territories gained by the Red Army. Roosevelt's foreign policy was not goal-directed but was obscure and whimsical—a direct result of his pet project of wooing Stalin into the Rooseveltian dream of a world government.[73] Flynn concludes, "[i]t is all the more incredible when we remember that the things he was laying in Stalin's lap were the existence of little nations and the rights of little peoples we had sworn to defend."[74]

Perhaps the most eminent of the "well-meaning naivete" theses comes from historian Robert Nisbet. For Roosevelt, Hitler and Mussolini were merely gangsters, and the law-abiding nations of the world were using their police to take them off the streets of the world. The same naivete, insists Nisbet, hovered

---

[70]See Perlmutter, *FDR and Stalin*.

[71]Sainsbury, *The Turning Point*, p. 149.

[72]Flynn, *The Roosevelt Myth*, p. 325.

[73]Ibid., pp. 323f.

[74]Ibid., p 363.

over Roosevelt's relationship with Josef Stalin. World politics seemed to be nothing more to Roosevelt than local ward politics writ large—a matter of horse-trading, personalities, and power. Personal loyalties and relationships were the heart of politics for the president. Roosevelt believed that the same methods that got things done in Albany, New York, or Washington, D.C., would work with Stalin at Teheran and Yalta.[75]

Nisbet claims that the Rooseveltian legacy is twofold. First is the legacy of New Deal domestic policy.[76] Franklin Delano Roosevelt's hand could be found in Lyndon Johnson's Great Society, which was proudly modeled after the New Deal. Roosevelt's corporate bureaucratic state is praised by Democrats and Republicans alike; his and Eleanor's ideas of social and economic engineering found their way into subsequent legislation, platforms of the two parties, and political philosophies of today's leaders. Within the Clinton administration, the first and second families themselves could be called Roosevelt's offspring. Numerous social engineers and tinkers like Al Gore, Hillary Rodham Clinton, Donna Shalala, or Ira Magaziner proudly used the name, legacy, and ideologies of Franklin and Eleanor Roosevelt to legitimize further destruction of the constitutional freedoms and cultural norms of America.

The second legacy of Roosevelt concerns his foreign policy shaped by his alliance with Stalin. Roosevelt's affair with Stalin left thirty-seven European and Asian nations betrayed.[77] The Soviet Empire, with a antebellum population of 170 million, grew to a size of 800 million after the war.[78] Roosevelt's foreign policy not only set the stage for the cold war but resulted in the death and forced enslavement of millions of people. As a global power, the Soviet Union was able to apply leverage in the United Nations and impose communism both directly and indirectly by funding revolutions around the world.

[75]See Nisbet, *Roosevelt and Stalin.*

[76]Ibid., p. 109.

[77]William Henry Chamberlin, "The Bankruptcy of a Policy," in *Perpetual War for Perpetual Peace*, Harry Elmer Barnes, ed. (Caldwell, Idaho: Caxton Printers, 1953), pp. 502f. See also Alan Bullock, *Hitler and Stalin* (New York: Alfred A. Knopf, 1992), p. 973; and Flynn, *The Roosevelt Myth*, p. 364.

[78]Crocker, *Roosevelt's Road to Russia*, p. 7.

Ironically, World War II is still seen as a war for freedom, and Roosevelt is hailed as a great president. While historians label him "well-meaning" or "naive" to make their stories more palatable, such adjectives are certainly not synonymous with the word "great." The word "great" when applied to a political leader should imply an amount of vision. But Roosevelt had no long-range goals; in the words of Topitsch, "Roosevelt was not at all conscious of what had really happened."[79] Hence, the Roosevelt legacy is not one of greatness, but one of ineptness, blindness, stubbornness, and ignorance. By the time historians complete their account, the role of the most celebrated American president in solidifying the power and influence of history's greatest mass murderer doubtless will be a cursed memory.

[79]Ernst Topitsch, *Stalin's War* (London: Fourth Estate, 1987), p. 139.

18
HARRY S. TRUMAN:
ADVANCING THE
REVOLUTION

RALPH RAICO

A "NEAR-GREAT"?

When Harry Truman left office in January 1953, he was intensely unpopular, even widely despised. Many of his most cherished schemes, from national health insurance (socialized medicine) to universal military training (UMT) had been soundly rejected by Congress and the public. Worst of all, the war in Korea, which he persisted in calling a "police action," was dragging on with no end in sight.

Yet today, Republican no less than Democratic politicians vie in glorifying Truman. When historians are asked to rank American presidents, he is listed as a "near-great." Naturally, historians, like everyone else, have their own personal views and values. Like other academics, they tend to be overwhelmingly left of center. As Robert Higgs writes: "Left-liberal historians worship political power, and idolize those who wield it most lavishly in the service of left-liberal causes."[1] So it is scarcely surprising that they should venerate men like Woodrow Wilson, Franklin Roosevelt, and Harry Truman, and agitate to get a credulous public to do the same.

But for anyone friendlier to limited government than the ordinary run of history professors, the presidency of Harry Truman will appear in a very different light. Truman's predecessor had vastly expanded federal power, especially the power of the president, in what amounted to a revolution in American government. Under Truman, that revolution was consolidated and advanced beyond what even Franklin Roosevelt had ever dared hope for.

---

[1]Robert Higgs, "No More 'Great Presidents,'" *The Free Market* (February 1997): 2.

THE ONSET OF THE COLD WAR—
SCARING HELL OUT OF THE AMERICAN PEOPLE

Most pernicious of all, Truman's presidency saw the genesis of a world-spanning American political and military empire.[2] This was not simply the unintended consequence of some alleged Soviet threat, however. Even before the end of World War II, high officials in Washington were drawing up plans to project American military might across the globe. To start with, the United States would dominate the Atlantic and Pacific Oceans and the Western Hemisphere through a network of air and naval bases. Complementing this would be a system of air transit rights and landing facilities from North Africa to Saigon and Manila. This planning continued through the early years of the Truman administration.[3]

But the planners had no guarantee that such a radical reversal of our traditional policy could be sold to Congress and the people. It was the confrontation with the Soviet Union and "international communism," begun and defined by Truman and then prolonged for four decades, that furnished the opportunity and the rationale for realizing the globalist dreams.

That after World War II the Soviet Union would be predominant in Europe was inevitable, given the goals pursued by Roosevelt and Churchill: Germany's unconditional surrender and its total annihilation as a factor in the balance of power.[4] At Yalta, the two Western leaders acquiesced in the control over eastern Europe that had been won by Stalin's armies, while affecting to

---

[2]Even such a defender of U.S. policy as John Lewis Gaddis, in "The Emerging Post-Revisionist Synthesis on the Origins of the Cold War," *Diplomatic History* 7, no. 3 (Summer 1983): 171–93, states that part of the "post-revisionist" consensus among diplomatic historians is that an American empire did indeed come into being. But this American empire, according to Gaddis, is a "defensive" one. Why this should be a particularly telling point is unclear, considering that for American leaders "defense" has entailed effectively controlling the world.

[3]Melvyn P. Leffler, "The American Conception of National Security and the Beginnings of the Cold War, 1945–1948," *American Historical Review* 89, no. 2 (April 1984): 346–81. See also the comments by John Lewis Gaddis and Bruce Kuniholm, and Leffler's reply, pp. 382–400.

[4]See Ralph Raico, "Rethinking Churchill," in *The Costs of War: America's Pyrrhic Victories*, John V. Denson, ed., 2nd ed. (New Brunswick, N.J.: Transaction Publishers, 1999).

believe that the Red dictator would cheerfully assent to the establishment of democratic governments in that area. The trouble was that genuinely free elections east of the Elbe (except in Czechoslovakia) would inescapably produce bitterly anti-Communist regimes. Such a result was unacceptable to Stalin, whose position was well-known and much more realistic than the illusions of his erstwhile allies. As he stated in the spring of 1945: "Whoever occupies a territory also imposes on it his own social system [as far] as his army can reach."[5]

When Truman became president in April 1945, he was at first prepared to continue the "Grand Alliance," and in fact harbored sympathetic feelings toward Stalin.[6] But differences soon arose. The raping and murdering rampage of Red Army troops as they rolled over eastern Europe came as a disagreeable surprise to Americans who had swallowed the wartime propaganda, from Hollywood and elsewhere, on the Soviet "purity of arms." Stalin's apparent intention to communize Poland and include the other conquered territories within his sphere of influence was deeply resented by leaders in Washington, who at the same time had no qualms about maintaining their own sphere of influence throughout all of Latin America.[7]

Stalin's predictable moves to extend his sway around the periphery of the USSR further alarmed Washington. Exploiting the presence of Soviet forces in northern Iran (a result of the wartime agreement of the Big Three to divide up control of that country), he pressed for oil concessions similar to those gained by the United States and Britain. After the Soviets withdrew in return for a promise of concessions by the Iranian parliament,

[5]Walter LaFeber, *America, Russia, and the Cold War, 1945–1990*, 6th rev. ed. (New York: McGraw-Hill, 1991), p. 13. Cf. Stalin's comment at Yalta: "A freely elected government in any of these countries would be anti-Soviet, and that we cannot allow." Hans J. Morgenthau, "The Origins of the Cold War," in Lloyd C. Gardner, Arthur Schlesinger, Jr., and Hans J. Morgenthau, *The Origins of the Cold War* (Waltham, Mass.: Ginn, 1970), pp. 87–88.

[6]Melvyn R. Leffler, "Inside Enemy Archives: The Cold War Reopened," *Foreign Affairs* (July/August 1996): 134–35.

[7]At the State Department, Henry Stimson and John J. McCloy agreed in May 1945 that (in McCloy's words) "we ought to have our cake and eat it too," that is, control South America and "at the same time intervene promptly in Europe; we oughtn't to give away either asset [sic]." Stephen E. Ambrose, *Rise to Globalism: American Foreign Policy Since 1938*, 3rd rev. ed. (New York: Penguin, 1983), p. 103.

Iran, supported by the United States, reneged on the deal. Turning to Turkey, Stalin revived traditional Russian claims dating from Czarist days, pressuring Ankara to permit unimpeded transit for Soviet warships through the straits.

Most ominous, in Washington's view, was the civil war in Greece, where royalist forces faced Red insurgents. Britain, bankrupted by the war, was compelled to abandon its support of the royalist cause. Would the United States take up the torch from the faltering hand of the great imperial power? Here, Truman told his cabinet, he "faced a decision more serious than ever confronted any president."[8] The hyperbole is inane, but one can appreciate Truman's problem. The United States had never had the slightest interest in the eastern Mediterranean, nor was it possible to discern any threat to American security in whatever outcome the Greek civil war might yield. Moreover, Stalin had conceded Greece to Britain, in his famous deal with Churchill in October 1944, whereby Russia was given control of most of the rest of the Balkans (a deal approved by Roosevelt). Accordingly, the Greek Communists did not enjoy Soviet backing: they were not permitted to join the Cominform, for instance, and their provisional government was not recognized by the Soviet Union or any other communist state.[9]

Given all this, how would Truman be able to justify U.S. involvement? Urged on by hardliners like Navy Secretary James Forrestal, who were emboldened by the (temporary) American monopoly of the atom bomb, he decided to frame the Communist uprising in Greece, as well as Soviet moves in Iran and Turkey, in apocalyptic terms. In countering them, he mused: "We might as well find out whether the Russians are as bent on world conquest now as in five or ten years."[10] World conquest. Now, it seems, it was a Red Hitler who was on the march.[11]

---

[8]Alonzo L. Hamby, *Man of the People: A Life of Harry S. Truman* (New York: Oxford University Press, 1995), p. 391.

[9]Frank Kofsky, *Harry S. Truman and the War Scare of 1948: A Successful Campaign to Deceive the Nation* (New York: St. Martin's Press, 1993), pp. 244–45.

[10]Ambrose, *Rise to Globalism*, p. 117.

[11]In their attacks on Patrick Buchanan's *A Republic, Not an Empire: Reclaiming America's Destiny* (Washington, D.C.: Regnery, 1999) for his insistence that Nazi Germany posed no threat to the United States after 1940, Buchanan's critics have generally resorted to fatuous smears. This is

Still, after the landslide Republican victory in the congressional elections of 1946, Truman had to deal with a potentially recalcitrant opposition. The Republicans had promised to return the country to some degree of normalcy after the statist binge of the war years. Sharp cuts in taxes, abolition of wartime controls, and a balanced budget were high priorities.

But Truman could count on allies in the internationalist wing of the Republican Party, most prominently Arthur Vandenberg, a former "isolationist" turned rabid globalist, now chairman of the Senate Foreign Relations Committee. When Truman revealed his new "doctrine" to Vandenberg, the Republican leader advised him that, in order to get such a program through, the president would have to "scare hell out of the American people."[12] That Truman proceeded to do.

On March 12, 1947, in a speech before a joint session of Congress, Truman proclaimed a revolution in American foreign policy. More important than the proposed $300 million in aid for Greece and $100 million for Turkey was the vision he presented. Declaring that henceforth "it must be the policy of the United States to support free peoples who are resisting attempted subjugation by armed minorities or by outside pressure," Truman situated aid to Greece and Turkey within a world-encompassing, life-or-death struggle "between alternative ways of life."[13] As one historian has written, he

> escalated the long, historic struggle between the Left and Right in Greece for political power, and the equally historic Russian urge for control of the Dardanelles [sic], into a universal conflict between freedom and slavery. It was a very broad jump indeed.[14]

---

understandable, since they are wedded to a fantasy of Hitlerian power that, ironically, is itself a reflection of Hitlerian propaganda. The fact is that Nazi Germany never conquered any militarily important nation but France. The danger of 80 million Germans "conquering the world" is a scarecrow that has, obviously, served the globalists well.

[12]Ambrose, *Rise to Globalism*, pp. 132–33.

[13]Ronald E. Powaski, *The Cold War: The United States and the Soviet Union, 1917–1991* (New York: Oxford University Press, 1998), p. 72.

[14]Ambrose, *Rise to Globalism*, p. 133. That self-interest played a role in the exaggeration of the "crisis" is the conclusion of Ronald Steel, "The End of the Beginning," *Diplomatic History* 16, no. 2 (Spring 1992): 297, who writes that universalizing the struggle would "enable the United States greatly to expand its military and political reach," which "enhanced its

At first, Truman's radical initiative provoked uneasiness, even within his administration. George Kennan, often credited with fathering the cold war "containment" idea, strongly opposed military aid to Turkey, a nation which was under no military threat and which bordered the Soviet Union. Kennan also scoffed at the "grandiose" and "sweeping" character of the Truman Doctrine.[15] In Congress, the response of Senator Robert Taft was to accuse the president of dividing the world into Communist and anti-Communist zones. He asked for evidence that our national security was involved in Greece, adding that he did not "want war with Russia."[16] But Taft turned out to be the last, often vacillating, leader of the Old Right, whose ranks were visibly weakening.[17] Although he was called "Mr. Republican," it was the internationalists who were now in charge of that party. In the Senate, Taft's doubts were answered with calm, well-reasoned rebuttals. Vandenberg intoned: "If we desert the President of the United States at [this] moment we cease to have any influence in the world forever." Henry Cabot Lodge averred that repudiating Truman would be like throwing the American flag on the ground and stomping on it.[18] In May, Congress appropriated the funds the president requested.

Meanwhile, the organs of the national-security state were being put into place.[19] The War and Navy Departments and the Army Air Corps were combined into what was named, in

---

appeal to American foreign policy elites eager to embrace the nation's new opportunities."

[15]LaFeber, *America, Russia, and the Cold War*, pp. 53–54.

[16]Ronald Radosh, *Prophets on the Right: Profiles of Conservative Critics of American Globalism* (New York: Simon and Schuster, 1975), pp. 155–56.

[17]See Ted Galen Carpenter's informative *The Dissenters: American Isolationists and Foreign Policy, 1945–1954* (Ph.D. dissertation, University of Texas, 1980). On the same topic, but concentrating on the intellectual leaders of the Old Right, see Joseph R. Stromberg's perceptive analysis, *The Cold War and the Transformation of the American Right: The Decline of Right-Wing Liberalism* (M.A. thesis, Florida Atlantic University, 1971).

[18]Melvyn P. Leffler, *A Preponderance of Power: National Security, the Truman Administration, and the Cold War* (Stanford, Calif.: Stanford University Press, 1992), p. 146.

[19]See Michael J. Hogan, *A Cross of Iron: Harry S. Truman and the Origins of the National Security State, 1945–1954* (Cambridge: Cambridge University Press, 1998).

Orwellian fashion, the Defense Department. Other legislation established the National Security Council and upgraded intelligence operations into the Central Intelligence Agency.

In the following decades, the CIA was to play a sinister, extremely expensive, and often comically inept role—especially in its continually absurd overestimations of Soviet strength.[20] In establishing the CIA, Congress had no intention of authorizing it to conduct secret military operations, but under Truman this is what it quickly began to do, including waging a secret war on the Chinese mainland even before the outbreak of the Korean War (with no appreciable results).[21] In 1999, after it targeted the Chinese embassy in Belgrade for bombing—supposedly a mistake, even though American diplomats had dined at the embassy and its location was known to everyone in the city—CIA has come to stand, in the words of one British writer, for "Can't Identify Anything."[22]

In June 1947, Secretary of State George Marshall announced a wide-ranging scheme for economic aid to Europe. In December, the Marshall Plan was presented as an appropriations bill calling for grants of $17 billion over four years. The plan, it was claimed, would reconstruct Europe to the point where the Europeans could defend themselves. Congress at first was cold to the

[20]Cf. Daniel Patrick Moynihan, *Secrecy: The American Experience* (New Haven, Conn.: Yale University Press, 1997), pp. 195–99 and passim. In 1997, former President Gerald Ford recalled his days as a member of the House Defense Appropriations Committee, when spokesmen for the CIA would warn over and over again of the imminent danger of the Soviet Union's surpassing the United States "in military capability, in economic growth, in the strength of our economies. It was a scary presentation."

[21]Truman later maintained that he never intended the CIA to involve itself in "peacetime cloak-and-dagger operations." This, however, was a lie. See John Prados, *Presidents' Secret Wars: CIA and Pentagon Covert Operations from World War II through the Persian Gulf War*, rev. ed. (Chicago: Ivan R. Dee, 1996), pp. 20–21, 28–29, 65–67; also Peter Grose, *Operation Rollback: America's Secret War Behind the Iron Curtain* (Boston: Houghton Mifflin, 2000), which discusses George Kennan's 1948 plan, approved by the Truman administration, to carry out paramilitary actions behind the Iron Curtain, including guerrilla attacks and sabotage.

[22]Geoffrey Wheatcroft, in the *Times Literary Supplement* (July 16, 1999): 9. For an excellent analysis of the United States' and NATO's successive lies on the bombing of the Chinese embassy, and the American media's endorsement and propagation of the lies, see Jared Israel, "The Arrogance of Rome," www.emperors-clothes.com, April 18, 2000.

idea. Taft grumbled that American taxpayers should not have to support an "international WPA," arguing that the funds would subsidize the socialization programs under way in many of the recipient countries.[23] The Marshall Plan led to intensified tensions with the Russians, who saw it as further proof that Washington aimed to undermine their rule over eastern Europe. Stalin instructed his satellite states to refuse to take part.[24]

"WORLD-CONQUEST" RED ALERT

Nineteen forty-eight was a decisive year in the cold war. There was great reluctance in the conservative Eightieth Congress to comply with Truman's program, which included funding for the European Recovery Act (Marshall Plan), resumption of the draft, and Universal Military Training (UMT). To deal with this resistance, the administration concocted the war scare of 1948.

The first pretext came in February, with the so-called Communist coup in Czechoslovakia. But Czechoslovakia, for all

---

[23]Radosh, *Prophets on the Right*, pp. 159–61. The Marshall Plan and its supposed successes are now enveloped by what Walter A. McDougall, in *Promised Land, Crusader State: The American Encounter with the World Since 1776* (Boston: Houghton Mifflin, 1997), p. 180, rightly calls a "mythology." The basic cause of Europe's recovery was the relatively free-market principles put into practice (in West Germany, for instance), and, more than anything else, the character of the European peoples, sometimes called "human capital." What the Marshall Plan and the billions in U.S. military aid largely accomplished was to allow the European regimes to construct their welfare states, and, in the case of France, for one, to continue trying to suppress colonial uprisings, as in Vietnam. Cf. George C. Herring, *America's Longest War: the United States and Vietnam, 1950–1976* (New York: Knopf, 1979), p. 8: "substantial American funds under the Marshall Plan enabled France to use its own resources to prosecute the war in Indochina." See also Tyler Cowen, "The Marshall Plan: Myths and Realities," in *U.S. Aid to the Developing World: A Free Market Agenda*, Doug Bandow, ed. (Washington, D.C.: Heritage, 1985), pp. 61–74; and Alan S. Milward, "Was the Marshall Plan Necessary?" *Diplomatic History* 13 (Spring 1989): 231–53, who emphasizes the pressures placed on European governments by the Plan's administrators to adopt Keynesian policies.

[24]Vladislav Zubok, "Stalin's Plans and Russian Archives," *Diplomatic History* 21, no. 2 (Spring 1997): 299. The Soviet documents show that Stalin and Molotov were "convinced that the U.S. aid was designed to lure the Kremlin's East European neighbors out of its orbit and to rebuild German strength." See also Leffler, "Inside Enemy Archives," p. 133.

intents and purposes, already a Soviet satellite. Having led the Czechs in the "ethnic cleansing" of 3.5 million Sudeten Germans, the Communists enjoyed great popularity. In the general elections, they won 38 percent of the vote, constituting by far the largest single party. The American ambassador reported to Washington that Communist consolidation of power in early 1948 was the logical outgrowth of the Czech–Soviet military alliance dating back to 1943. George Marshall himself, in private, stated that "as far as international affairs are concerned," the formal Communist assumption of power made no difference: it would merely "crystallize and confirm for the future previous Czech policy."[25] Still, the Communist "coup" was painted as a great leap forward in Stalin's plan for "world conquest."

Then, on March 5, came the shocking letter from General Lucius Clay, U.S. military governor in Germany, to General Stephen J. Chamberlin, head of Army Intelligence, in which Clay revealed his foreboding that war "may come with dramatic suddenness." Years later, when Clay's biographer asked him why, if he sensed an impending war, this was the only reference he ever made to it, he replied:

> General Chamberlin . . . told me that the Army was having trouble getting the draft reinstituted and they needed a strong message from me that they could use in congressional testimony. So I wrote this cable.[26]

On March 11, Marshall solemnly warned in a public address that: "The world is in the midst of a great crisis." Averell Harriman asserted:

> There are aggressive forces in the world coming from the Soviet Union which are just as destructive as Hitler was, and I think are a greater menace than Hitler was.[27]

And so Harriman laid down the Hitler card, which was to become the master trump in the globalist propaganda hand for the next half-century and most likely for centuries to come.

---

[25]Kofsky, *Truman*, p. 99.

[26]Ibid., p. 106.

[27]Ronald E. Powaski, *Toward an Entangling Alliance: American Isolationism, Internationalism, and Europe, 1901–1950* (Westport, Conn.: Greenwood, 1991), pp. 201–02.

Taft, campaigning for the Republican presidential nomination, was angered by the war hysteria drummed up by the administration:

> I know of no indication of Russian intention to undertake military aggression beyond the sphere of influence that was originally assigned to them [at Yalta]. The situation in Czechoslovakia was indeed a tragic one, but Russian influence has predominated there since the end of the war.

Taft tried to introduce a note of sanity: "If President Truman and General Marshall have any private intelligence" regarding imminent war, "they ought to tell the American people about it." Otherwise, we should proceed on "the basis of peace."[28]

In reality, the administration had no such "private intelligence," hence the need to stage-manage Clay's letter. On the contrary, Colonel Robert B. Landry, Truman's air aide, reported that in their zone in eastern Germany, the Russians had dismantled hundreds of miles of railroad track and shipped it home—in other words, they had torn up the very railroads required for any Soviet attack on western Europe.[29] Field Marshal Montgomery, after a trip to Russia in 1947, wrote to General Eisenhower: "The Soviet Union is very, very tired. Devastation in Russia is appalling, and the country is in no fit state to go to war."[30] Today it would be very difficult to find any scholar willing to subscribe to Truman's frenzied vision of a Soviet Union about to set off to conquer the world. As John Lewis Gaddis wrote:

> Stalin is now seen as a cagey but insecure opportunist, taking advantage of such tactical opportunities as arose to expand Soviet influence, but without any long-term strategy for or even very much interest in promoting the spread of communism beyond the Soviet sphere.[31]

---

[28]Harry W. Berger, "Senator Robert A. Taft Dissents from Military Escalation," in *Cold War Critics: Alternatives to American Foreign Policy in the Truman Years*, Thomas G. Paterson, ed. (Chicago: Quadrangle Books, 1971), pp. 181–82; and Kofsky, *Truman*, p. 130.

[29]Ibid., pp. 294–95.

[30]Michael Parenti, *The Sword and the Dollar: Imperialism, Revolution, and the Arms Race* (New York: St. Martin's, 1989), p. 147.

[31]Gaddis, "The Emerging Post-Revisionist Synthesis," p. 181. Morgenthau, "The Origins of the Cold War," p. 95, anticipated this conclusion: "The

The nonexistence of Soviet plans to launch an attack on Europe holds for the entire cold war period. One scholar in the field concludes:

> despite the fact that the Russian archives have yielded ample evidence of Soviet perfidy and egregious behavior in many other spheres, nothing has turned up to support the idea that the Soviet leadership at any time actually planned to start World War III and send the "Russian hordes" westward.[32]

---

limits of Stalin's territorial ambition were the traditional limits of Russian expansionism." Even Vladislav Zubok, who believes that the now available Soviet documents show the U.S. leaders in a much better light than many had thought, nonetheless concedes, "Stalin's Plans," p. 305:

> there was an element of overreaction, arrogance, and selfish pragmatism in the American response to Stalin's plans. . . . The Soviet military machine was not a military juggernaut, western Europe was not under threat of a direct Soviet military assault, and the Sino–Soviet bloc lacked true cohesion. . . . American containment of Stalin's Soviet Union may indeed have helped the dictatorship to mobilize people to the task of building a superpower from the ashes and ruins of the impoverished and devastated country. It may even have helped Stalin to trample on the seeds of liberalism and freedom in Soviet society.

Cf. Leffler, "Inside Enemy Archives," pp. 132, 134: "The new research clearly shows that American initiatives intensified Soviet distrust and reinforced Soviet insecurities . . . [recent research indicates] that American policies made it difficult for potential reformers inside the Kremlin to gain the high ground."

[32]Matthew Evangelista, "The 'Soviet Threat': Intentions, Capabilities, and Context," *Diplomatic History* 22, no. 3 (Summer 1998): 445–46. On how information from recently opened Soviet archives has undermined the old cold war account, see also the account by Leffler, "Inside Enemy Archives," pp. 120–35. Leffler, hardly a "New Left" (or libertarian) historian, concludes: "Americans should reexamine their complacent belief in the wisdom of their country's cold war policies."

The fact that Stalin was the worst tyrant and greatest mass-murderer in twentieth-century European history has by now been established beyond a doubt. However, here one should heed Murray Rothbard's admonition against doing "*a priori* history," that is, assuming that in a given international conflict it is always the relatively liberal state that is in the right as against the relatively illiberal state, which must always be the aggressor. Murray N. Rothbard, *For a New Liberty: The Libertarian Manifesto*, rev. ed. (New York: Collier-Macmillan, 1978), pp. 289–91.

So why the war scare in 1948? In a 1976 interview, look-ing back on this period, Air Force Brigadier General Robert C. Richardson, who served at NATO headquarters in the early 1950s, candidly admitted:

> there was no question about it, that [Soviet] threat that we were planning against was way overrated and intentionally overrated, because there was the problem of reorienting the [U.S.] demobilization . . . [Washington] made this nine-foot-tall threat out there. And for years and years it stuck. I mean, it was almost immovable.[33]

Yet, anyone who doubted the wisdom of the administra-tion's militaristic policy was targeted for venomous smears. According to Truman, Republicans who opposed his universal crusade were "Kremlin assets," the sort of traitors who would shoot "our soldiers in the back in a hot war," a good example of Truman's acclaimed "plain speaking."[34,35] Averell Harriman

---

[33]Evangelista, "The Soviet 'Threat,'" p. 447. See also Steel, "The End of the Beginning," "Unquestionably, the Soviet Union was far weaker ideologi-cally, politically, structurally, and, of course, economically, than was gen-erally assumed." An astonishing admission that the whole cold war was fueled, on the American side, by wild overestimations of Soviet strength was made in 1990 by Strobe Talbott, deputy secretary of state:

> for more than four decades, Western policy has been based on a grotesque exaggeration of what the USSR could do if it wanted, therefore what it might do, therefore what the West must be pre-pared to do in response. . . . Worst-case assumptions about Soviet intentions have fed, and fed upon, worst-case assumptions about Soviet capabilities.

John A. Thompson, "The Exaggeration of American Vulnerability: The Anatomy of a Tradition," *Diplomatic History* 16, no. 1 (Winter 1992): 23. Thompson's article is highly instructive on how hysteria regarding impend-ing attacks on the United States during the twentieth century—a time when America grew ever stronger—has contributed to entanglement in foreign conflicts.

[34]Justus D. Doenecke, *Not to the Swift: The Old Isolationists in the Cold War Era* (Lewisburg, Penn.: Bucknell University Press, 1979), p. 216. Truman's slanders were particularly vile, since his own motivation in generating the war-scare was at least in part self-aggrandizement. As his trusted political adviser Clark Clifford noted in a memo to the president:

> There is considerable political advantage to the administration in its battle with the Kremlin. The worse matters get up to a fairly certain point—real danger of imminent war—the more is there

charged that Taft was simply helping Stalin carry out his aims. *The New York Times* and the rest of the establishment press echoed the slanders. Amusingly, Republican critics of the war hysteria were labeled pro-Soviet even by journals like *The New Republic* and *The Nation*, which had functioned as apologists for Stalin's terror-regime for years.[36]

Truman's campaign could not have succeeded without the enthusiastic cooperation of the American media. Led by the *Times*, the *Herald Tribune*, and Henry Luce's magazines, the press acted as volunteer propagandists for the interventionist agenda, with all its calculated deceptions. (The principal exceptions were the *Chicago Tribune* and the *Washington Times-Herald*, in the days of Colonel McCormick and Cissy Paterson.)[37] In time, such subservience in foreign affairs became routine for the "fourth estate," culminating during and after the 1999 Yugoslav war in reporting by the press corps that was as biased as the Serbian Ministry of Information.

Overwhelmed by the propaganda blitz from the administration and the press, a Republican majority in Congress heeded the secretary of state's high-minded call to keep foreign policy "above politics" and voted full funding for the Marshall Plan.[38]

---

a sense of crisis. In times of crisis, the American citizen tends to back up his president. (Kofsky, *Truman*, p. 92)

[35]Cf. George Will's judgment, in *The Leveling Wind: Politics, the Culture, and Other News, 1990–1994* (New York: Viking, 1994), p. 380: "Truman's greatness was a product of his goodness, his straight-ahead respect for the public, respect expressed in decisions briskly made and plainly explained." In truth, despite Will's blather, Truman was all of his life a demagogue, a political "garbage-mouth" whose first instinct was to besmirch his opponents. In his tribute to Truman, Will employs his usual ploy whenever he is moved to extol some villainous politico or other: his subject's greatness could only be denied by pitiful post-modernist creatures who reject all human excellence, nobility of soul, etc. This maneuver is nowhere sillier than in the case of Harry Truman.

[36]Doenecke, *Not to the Swift*, pp. 200, 216.

[37]Ted Galen Carpenter, *The Captive Press: Foreign Policy Crises and the First Amendment* (Washington, D.C.: Cato Institute, 1995), pp. 45–52. Carpenter's excellent study covers the whole period of the cold war.

[38]The commotion over Soviet plans to "conquer the world" intensified in June 1948 with the blockade of West Berlin. The United States and its allies had unilaterally decided to jettison four-power control of Germany, and instead to integrate their occupation zones and proceed to create a west

The next major step was the creation of the North Atlantic Treaty Organization. The true significance of the NATO treaty was hidden, as new Secretary of State Dean Acheson assured Congress that it would not be followed by other regional pacts, that no "substantial" numbers of American troops would be stationed in Europe, and that the Germans would under no circumstances be rearmed. Congress was likewise promised that the United States was under no obligation to extend military aid to its new allies, nor would an arms race with the Soviet Union ensue.[39] Events came to the aid of the globalists. In September 1949, the Soviets exploded an atomic bomb. Congress approved the military appropriation for NATO that Truman had requested, which, in the nature of things, was followed by a further Soviet buildup. This escalating back and forth became the pattern for the cold war arms race for the next fifty years, much to the delight of U.S. armaments contractors and the generals and admirals on both sides.

The Korean War

In June 1950, the National Security Council adopted a major strategic document, NSC-68, which declared, implausibly enough, that "a defeat of free institutions anywhere is a defeat everywhere." The United States should no longer attempt to "distinguish between national and global security." Instead, it must stand at the "political and material center with other free nations in variable orbits around it." NSC-68, which was not declassified until 1975, called for an immediate three- or four-fold increase in military spending, which would serve also to prime the pump of economic prosperity—thus formalizing military Keynesianism as a permanent fixture of American life. Moreover, public opinion was to be conditioned to accept the "large

---

German state. Stalin's clumsy response was to exploit the absence of any formal agreement permitting the western powers access to Berlin, and institute the blockade.

[39]LaFeber, *America, Russia, and the Cold War*, pp. 83–84. Some award for Orwellian Newspeak is due the Democratic foreign affairs leader in the Senate, Tom Connally, who stated that NATO "is but the logical extension of the principle of the Monroe Doctrine."

measure of sacrifice and discipline" needed to meet the protean Communist challenge for the indefinite future.[40]

Even Truman was dubious on the prospects for such a quantum leap in globalism in a time of peace. But again, events—and Truman's shrewd exploitation of them—came to the aid of the internationalist planners. As one of Truman's advisers later expressed it: In June 1950, "we were sweating over it," and then, "thank God Korea came along."[41]

For years, skirmishes and even major engagements had occurred across the 38th parallel, which divided North Korea from South Korea. On January 12, 1950, Secretary of State Acheson described the American defensive perimeter as extending from the Aleutians to Japan to the Philippines. South Korea (as well as Taiwan) was conspicuously placed outside this perimeter. One reason was that it was not considered to be of any military value. Another was that Washington did not trust South Korean strong man Syngman Rhee, who repeatedly threatened to reunite the country by force. Rhee was advocating a march north to American officials as late as mid-June 1950.[42]

On June 25, it was North Korea that attacked.[43] The next day, Truman instructed U.S. air and naval forces to destroy Communist supply lines. When bombing failed to prevent the headlong retreat of the South Korean army, Truman sent American troops stationed in Japan to join the battle. General Douglas MacArthur was able to hold the redoubt around Pusan, then, in an amphibious invasion at Inchon, to begin the destruction of the North Korean position.

---

[40]See especially Jerry W. Sanders, *Peddlers of Crisis: The Committee on the Present Danger and the Politics of Containment* (Boston: South End Press, 1983); also Gabriel Kolko, *Century of War: Politics, Conflict, and Society Since 1914* (New York: New Press, 1994), pp. 397–98; and Powaski, *Cold War*, pp. 85–86.

[41]Michael Schaller, *The United States and China in the Twentieth Century* (New York: Oxford University Press, 1979), pp. 131–32.

[42]Bruce Cumings, *Korea's Place in the Sun: A Modern History* (New York: Norton, 1997), pp. 257–58. Japan was unable to act as a counterweight to Communist regimes in east Asia because, like Germany, it had been annulled as a power. In addition, the constitution imposed on Japan by the American occupiers forced it to renounce warmaking as a sovereign right.

[43]The attack was authorized by Stalin, "in expectation that the United States might eventually turn [South Korea] into a beachhead for a return to the Asian mainland in alliance with a resurgent Japan" (Zubok, "Stalin's Plans," p. 301).

After the North Koreans retreated behind the 38th parallel, Truman decided against ending the war on the basis of the status quo ante. Instead, he ordered MacArthur to move north. Pyongyang was to be the first Communist capital liberated and the whole peninsula to be unified under the rule of Syngman Rhee. As U.N. forces (mainly U.S. and South Korean) swept north, the Chinese issued warnings against approaching their border at the Yalu River. These were ignored by an administration somehow unable to comprehend why China might fear massive U.S. forces stationed on its frontier. Chinese troops entered the war, prolonging it by another three years, during which most of the American casualties were sustained.[44] MacArthur, who proposed bombing China itself, was dismissed by Truman, who at least spared the nation an even wider war possibly involving Russia as well.

Korea afforded unprecedented opportunities for advancing the globalist program. Truman assigned the U.S. Seventh Fleet to patrol the strait between Taiwan and the mainland. Four more U.S. divisions were sent to Europe, to add to the two already there, and another $4 billion was allocated for the rearmament of our European allies. Some months before the start of the Korean War, Truman had already initiated America's fateful involvement in Indochina, supporting the French and their puppet ruler Bao Dai against the nationalist and Communist revolutionary Ho Chi Minh. Korea furnished welcome cover for stepping up aid to the French, which soon amounted to a half-billion dollars a year. The United States was thus providing the great bulk of the material resources for France's colonialist war. The State Department defended this commitment, rather ridiculously, by citing Indochina's production of "much-needed rice, rubber, and tin." More to the point was the fear expressed that the "loss" of Indochina, including Vietnam, would represent a defeat in the struggle against what was portrayed as a unified and coordinated Communist push to take over the world.[45]

---

[44]Eric A. Nordlinger, *Isolationism Reconfigured: American Foreign Policy for a New Century* (Princeton, N.J.: Princeton University Press, 1995), pp. 168–69.

[45]Walter LaFeber, *America, Russia, and the Cold War*, pp. 107–08; see also Herring, *America's Longest War*, pp. 6–23. France's war against the Viet Minh began in 1946 with a typical colonialist atrocity, when a French cruiser bombarded Haiphong, killing 6,000 civilians; ibid., p. 5. Acts of brutality such as this were on the minds of the "isolationist" Republicans

At the same time, the degradation of political language went into high gear, where it remained for the rest of the cold war and probably permanently. To the authoritarian regimes in Greece and Turkey were now added, as components of the "free world" which Americans were obligated to defend, Rhee's autocratic Republic of Korea, Chiang's dictatorship on Taiwan, and even colonialist French Indochina.

With the outbreak of the Korean War, the Republicans' capitulation to globalism was practically complete.[46] As is standard procedure in American politics, foreign policy was a nonissue in the 1948 presidential campaign. Thomas E. Dewey, a creature of the Eastern establishment centered in Wall Street, was as much of an overseas meddler as Truman. Now, in the struggle against "international Communism," even erstwhile "isolationists" showed themselves to be arch-interventionists when it came to Asia, going so far as to make a hero of MacArthur for demanding an expansion of the war and the "unleashing" of Chiang's army on the mainland. Taft supported sending troops to fight in Korea, while entering one major objection. Characteristically, it was on the constitutional question.

THE PRESIDENT AS WAR-MAKER AT WILL

When North Korea invaded the South, Truman and Acheson claimed unlimited presidential authority to engage the United States in the war, which they kept referring to as a "police action." Truman stated: "The president, as Commander-in-Chief of the Armed Forces of the United States, has full control over the use thereof."[47] This flies in the face of Article 1, section 8 of the U.S. Constitution, where the power to declare war is vested in Congress. The deliberations at the Constitutional Convention and other statements of the Founding Fathers are unequivocal in

---

like Taft, George Bender, and Howard Buffet when they inveighed against American support of Western imperialism in terms which would be considered "leftist" today.

[46]On the shift of conservatives from "isolationism" to internationalism, see Murray N. Rothbard, "The Transformation of the American Right," *Continuum* (Summer 1964): 220–31.

[47]John Hart Ely, *War and Responsibility: Constitutional Lessons of Vietnam and Its Aftermath* (Princeton, N.J.: Princeton University Press, 1993), pp. 10–11.

this respect. While the president, as commander-in-chief, is given authority to deploy American forces in wartime, it is Congress that decides on war or peace. Wouldn't it be surpassing strange if the Founders, so concerned to limit, divide, and balance power, had left the decision to engage the country in war to the will of a single individual?[48]

So well-established was this principle that even Woodrow Wilson and Franklin Roosevelt, no minimizers of executive prerogatives, bowed to it and went to Congress for their declarations of war. It was Truman who dared what even his predecessor had not. As two constitutional scholars, Francis D. Wormuth and Edwin B. Firmage, have written:

> The Constitution is not ambiguous. . . . The early presidents, and indeed everyone in the country until the year 1950, denied that the president possessed [the power to initiate war]. There is no sustained body of usage to support such a claim.[49]

At the time, college history professors rushed to blazon the allegedly countless occasions when presidents sent U.S. forces into war or warlike situations without congressional approval. Lists of such occasions were afterward compiled by other apologists for executive power in foreign affairs—in 1971, for instance, by the revered conservative Barry Goldwater. These incidents have been carefully examined by Wormuth and Firmage, who conclude:

> One cannot be sure, but the number of cases in which presidents have personally made the decision [in contrast, for instance, to overzealous military and naval officers], unconstitutionally, to engage in war or in acts of war probably lies

---

[48]See, for example, James Wilson's statement: "This system will not hurry us into war; it is calculated to guard against it. It will not be in the power of a single man, or a single body of men, to involve us in such distress; for the important power of declaring war is vested in the legislature at large." Ibid., p. 3. Illustrative of the present-day decay of constitutional thinking is the statement of the noted conservative advocate of the doctrine of "original intent," Robert Bork (ibid., p. 5): "The need for presidents to have that power [to use military force abroad without Congressional approval], particularly in the modern age, should be obvious to almost anyone."

[49]Francis D. Wormuth and Edwin B. Firmage, *To Chain the Dog of War: The War Power of Congress in History and Law*, 2nd ed. (Urbana: University of Illinois Press, 1989), p. 151.

between one and two dozen. And in all those cases the presidents have made false claims of authorization, either by statute or by treaty or by international law. They have not relied on their powers as commander in chief or as chief executive.[50]

At all events, as Chief Justice Earl Warren held in 1969, articulating a well-known constitutional principle on behalf of seven other justices: "That an unconstitutional action has been taken before surely does not render that action any less unconstitutional at a later date."[51]

The administration sometimes alluded to the vote of the U.N. Security Council approving military action in Korea as furnishing the necessary authority. This was nothing but a smokescreen. First, because according to the U.N. Charter, any Security Council commitment of members' troops must be consistent with the members' "respective constitutional processes." The United Nations Participation Act of 1945 also required congressional ratification for the use of American forces. In any case, Truman stated that he would send troops to Korea whether or not authorized by the Security Council. His position really was that a president may plunge the country into war simply on his own say-so.[52]

Today presidents assert the right to bomb at will countries which, like North Korea in 1950, never attacked us and with which we are not at war—Sudan, Afghanistan, Iraq, and, massively, Yugoslavia. They are eagerly seconded in this by "conservative" politicians and publicists, nor does the American public demur. Back in 1948, Charles Beard already noted the dismal

---

[50]Wormuth and Firmage, *To Chain the Dog of War*, p. 151.

[51]Ibid., p. 135.

[52]Ely, *War and Responsibility*, pp. 151–52, n. 60. A year earlier the North Atlantic Treaty had been submitted to the Senate for approval. Article 5 specifically ensured that "U.S. response to aggression in the area covered by the alliance would be governed by 'constitutional processes,' thereby requiring congressional approval." Ponawski, *Toward Entangling Alliance*, pp. 208–09. On the origins of unlimited presidential warmaking powers, see Robert Shogan, *Hard Bargain: How FDR Twisted Churchill's Arm, Evaded the Law, and Changed the Role of the American Presidency*, paperback edition (Boulder, Colo.: Westview, 1999), preface to the paperback edition, "Paving the Way to Kosovo."

ignorance among our people of the principles of our republican government:

> American education from the universities down to the grade schools is permeated with, if not dominated by, the theory of presidential supremacy in foreign affairs. Coupled with the flagrant neglect of instruction in constitutional government, this propaganda . . . has deeply implanted in the minds of rising generations the doctrine that the power of the president over international relations is, for all practical purposes, illimitable.[53]

Needless to say, the situation has in no way improved, as the public schools grind out tens of millions of future voters to whom the notion, say, that James Madison had something to do with the Constitution of the United States would come as an uninteresting revelation.

The Korean War lasted three years and cost 36,916 American deaths and more than 100,000 other casualties. Additionally, there were millions of Korean dead and devastation of the peninsula, especially in the north, where the U.S. Air Force pulverized the civilian infrastructure—with much "collateral damage"—in what has since become its emblematic method of waging war.[54]

---

[53]Charles A. Beard, *President Roosevelt and the Coming of the War, 1941: A Study in Appearances and Realities* (New Haven, Conn.: Yale University Press, 1948), p. 590. Beard listed as among the major purveyors of this doctrine "powerful private agencies engaged nominally in propaganda for 'peace,'" which look to the president to advance their ideas for "ordering and reordering the world."

[54]Kolko, *Century of War*, pp. 403–08. General Curtis LeMay boasted of the devastation wreaked by the Air Force: "We burned down just about every city in North and South Korea both . . . we killed off over a million civilian Koreans and drove several million more from their homes." Callum A. MacDonald, *Korea: The War Before Vietnam* (New York: Free Press, 1986), p. 235. I am grateful to Joseph R. Stromberg for drawing my attention to this quotation. It gives one pause to realize that the savagery of the U.S. air war was such as to lead even Winston Churchill to condemn it. Ibid., pp. 234–35. In Fall 1999, it was finally disclosed that "early in the Korean War, American soldiers machine-gunned hundreds of helpless civilians under a railroad bridge in the South Korean countryside," allegedly in order to thwart the infiltration of North Korean troops. Former U.S. soldiers "described other refugee killings as well in the war's first weeks, when U.S. commanders ordered their troops to shoot civilians of an allied nation, as a

Today, nearly a half-century after the end of the conflict, the United States continues to station troops as a "tripwire" in yet another of its imperial outposts.[55]

The indirect consequences of Truman's "police action" have been equally grim. Hans Morgenthau wrote:

> The misinterpretation of the North Korean aggression as part of a grand design at world conquest originating in and controlled by Moscow resulted in a drastic militarization of the cold war in the form of a conventional and nuclear armaments race, the frantic search for alliances, and the establishment of military bases.[56]

Truman is glorified for his conduct of foreign affairs more than anything else. Whether one concurs in this judgment depends mainly on the kind of country one wishes America to be. Stephen Ambrose has summed up the results of the foreign policy of Harry Truman:

> When Truman became president he led a nation anxious to return to traditional civil–military relations and the historic American foreign policy of noninvolvement. When he left the White House his legacy was an American presence on every continent of the world and an enormously expanded armament industry. Yet so successfully had he scared hell out of the American people, the only critics to receive any attention in the mass media were those who thought Truman had not gone far

---

defense against disguised enemy soldiers, according to once-classified documents found in U.S. military archives" (*Washington Post*, September 30, 1999). A few months later, other declassified U.S. military documents revealed that the South Korean government executed without trial more than 2,000 leftists as its forces retreated in the first stages of the war; the occurrence of such executions was known to the American military authorities at the time (*New York Times*, April 21, 2000). In addition, there is evidence that the United States may, in fact, have experimented with bacteriological warfare in Korea, as charged by China and North Korea. See Stephen Endicott and Edward Hagerman, *The United States and Biological Warfare: Secrets from the Early Cold War and Korea* (Bloomington: Indiana University Press, 1998).

[55]Doug Bandow, *Tripwire: Korea and U.S. Foreign Policy in a Changed World* (Washington, D.C.: Cato Institute, 1996).

[56]Morgenthau, "Origins of the Cold War," p. 98.

enough in standing up to the communists. For all his troubles, Truman had triumphed.[57]

THE FÜHRERPRINZIP IN THE ECONOMIC ARENA

Harry Truman's conception of presidential power as in principle unlimited was as manifest in his domestic as in his foreign policy. Some key episodes illustrate this.

In May 1946, Truman decided that the proper response to the strike of railroad workers was to draft the strikers into the Army. Even his attorney general, Tom Clark, doubted that the Draft Act permitted "the induction of occupational groups" or that the move was at all constitutional. But, as Truman's Pulitzer Prize-winning biographer David McCullough wrote, in his typical stupefied admiration: "Truman was not interested in philosophy. The strike must stop. 'We'll draft them and think about the law later,' he reportedly remarked."[58] McCullough neglects to note that bold "action" in defiance of law is considered a characteristic of fascist regimes.

On May 25, Truman addressed Congress, requesting the authority "to draft into the Armed Forces of the United States all workers who are on strike against their government." His proposal was greeted with tumultuous applause, and the House quickly approved the bill by 306 to 13. In the Senate, though, the bill was stopped in its tracks by Senator Taft. He was joined by left-liberals like Claude Pepper of Florida. Eventually, the Senate rejected the bill by 70 to 13.

Later that year, another "crisis" led Truman to contemplate further exercise of dictatorial power. While most of the wartime price controls had been lifted by this time, controls remained on a number of items, most prominently meat. Strangely enough, it was precisely in that commodity that a shortage and a black market developed. The meat shortage was eroding support for the Democrats, who began to look with trepidation on the upcoming congressional elections. Party workers were told by

---

[57]Ambrose, *Rise to Globalism*, p. 185. On the ultimate price paid by the nation for Truman's "triumph," see the important article by Robert Higgs, "The Cold War Economy: Opportunity Costs, Ideology, and the Politics of Crisis," *Explorations in Economic History* 31 (1994): 283–312.

[58]David McCullough, *Truman* (New York: Simon and Schuster, 1992), pp. 501–06.

usually loyal voters, "No meat, no votes." Truman was forced to act. He would address the nation again, announcing and explaining the decision he had made.

In his draft for the speech, Truman was bitter. He indicted the American people for their greed and selfishness, so different from the selfless patriotism of the heroes who had won the Medal of Honor. The draft continued:

> You've deserted your president for a mess of pottage, a piece of beef—a side of bacon. . . . If you the people insist on following Mammon instead of Almighty God, your president can't stop you all by himself. I can no longer enforce a law you won't support. . . . You've gone over to the powers of selfishness and greed.[59]

This crazy tirade was omitted from the speech Truman made on October 14.[60] But ever the cheap demagogue, he pilloried the meat industry as responsible for the shortage, "those who, in order further to fatten their profits, are endangering the health of our people by holding back vital foods which are now ready for market and for which the American people are clamoring." The failed haberdasher, it appears, had little understanding of the role that *prices* might play in a market economy. In his speech, Truman confided that he had carefully weighed and discussed with his cabinet and economic experts a number of possible solutions. One was "to have the Government seize the packing houses." But this would not have helped, since the packing houses were empty. Then came a notion that "would indeed be a drastic remedy": "that the government go out onto the farms and ranges and seize the cattle for slaughter." Truman gave the idea "long and serious consideration." Here is why, in the end, he declined to go the route of the Bolsheviks in the Ukraine:

> We decided against the use of this extreme wartime emergency power of Government. It would be wholly impracticable because the cattle are spread throughout all parts of the country.[61]

---

[59]Hamby, *Man of the People*, pp. 382–83.

[60]*Public Papers of Harry S. Truman*, 1946 (Washington, D.C.: U.S. Government Printing Office, 1962), pp. 451–55.

[61]Ibid., p. 453.

This statement from the feisty, "near-great" Man of the People deserves to be read more than once.[62]

So, sadly and reluctantly, Truman announced the end of price controls on meat, although he advised the country that "some items, like rent, will have to be controlled for a long time to come."

On April 8, 1952, as a nationwide strike loomed in the steel industry, Truman issued Executive Order 10340, directing his Secretary of Commerce Charles Sawyer to seize the steel mills.

He acted, he claimed, "by virtue of the authority vested in me by the Constitution and the laws of the United States, and as President of the United States and Commander-in-Chief of the armed forces of the United States."[63] He could not, however, point to any such law, despite his reference to "the laws of the United States." Nor did any provision of the Constitution give the president the right to seize private property by proclamation. But, as McCullough tells us, Truman was convinced "from his reading of history" that "his action fell within his powers as President and Commander-in-Chief." After all, hadn't Lincoln suspended the writ of habeas corpus during a national emergency?[64] On April 9, the Star-Spangled Banner was raised over the nation's steel mills, and the steel companies immediately took the case to court.

At a news conference on April 17, Truman was asked: "Mr. President, if you can seize the steel mills under your inherent powers, can you, in your opinion, also seize the newspapers and/or the radio stations?" Truman replied: "Under similar circumstances the President of the United States has to act for whatever is for the best of the country. That's the answer to your question."[65]

---

[62]Murray N. Rothbard dealt with this grab for power in a brilliant piece of economic journalism, "Price Controls Are Back!" in his *Making Economic Sense* (Auburn, Ala.: Ludwig von Mises Institute, 1995), pp. 123–27.

[63]Wormuth and Firmage, *To Chain the Dog of War*, p. 174.

[64]McCullough, *Truman*, pp. 896–97. McCullough's implied apology for Truman here is a good indication of the tenor and caliber of his gargantuan puff-piece. For a debunking of McCullough by two scholars, see the review by Gar Alperovitz and Kai Bird, "Giving Harry Hell," *The Nation* (May 10, 1993): 640–41.

[65]*The Public Papers of Harry S. Truman, 1952–53* (Washington, D.C.: U.S. Government Printing Office, 1966), pp. 272–73.

The next day, the *New York Times* reported:

> The president refused to elaborate. But White House sources said
> the president's point was that he had power in an emergency, to
> take over "any portion of the business community acting to
> jeopardize all the people."

The case of *Youngstown Sheet & Tube Co. v. Sawyer* quickly
reached the Supreme Court, where Truman's argument was
rejected by a vote of 6 to 3. Speaking for the three was Truman's
crony, Chief Justice Fred Vinson, who argued that the president
had the authority to enact all laws necessary for carrying out
laws previously passed by Congress. Any man worthy of the
office of president, Vinson wrote, should be "free to take at least
interim action necessary to execute legislative programs essential to the survival of the nation." The majority, including Hugo
Black, William O. Douglas, Felix Frankfurter, and even Truman's
former attorney general, Tom Clark, decided otherwise.[66]

At that April 17 news conference, no reporter thought to ask
a follow-up question to Truman's stunning reply. His claim of
the unlimited right to dispose at his discretion of the property of
any and all citizens—a viewpoint for which a king of England
was beheaded—made as little impression on the press then as it
has on his admirers ever since. One wonders what it would take
to spark their outrage or even their interest.[67]

In economic policy, the years of Truman's "Fair Deal" were a
time of consolidation and expansion of government power. In
February 1946, the Employment Act was passed. Inspired by the

---

[66]McCullough, *Truman*, pp. 900–01.

[67]One Congressman was led by Truman's remarks and his seizure of the
steel mills to demand his impeachment (*New York Times*, April 19, 1952).
George Bender, Republican of Ohio, stated:

> I do not believe that our people can tolerate the formation of a pres-
> idential precedent which would permit any occupant of the White
> House to exercise his untrammeled discretion to take over the
> industry, communications system or other forms of private enter-
> prise in the name of "emergency."

But Bender was one of the last, and best, of the Old Right leaders (much more
consistent and outspoken than Taft) and thus out of tune with the times. Of
course the American people could and did tolerate such a precedent. What is
still uncertain is whether there is any limit whatever to their tolerance of acts
of oppression by their government.

newly dominant Keynesian economics, it declared that henceforth the economic health of the nation was primarily the responsibility of the federal government. With the coming of the Korean War, economic controls were again the order of the day. (Bernard Baruch was once more, for the third time since 1917, a prime agitator for their introduction.) Truman declared a "national emergency." New boards and agencies oversaw prices and wages, established priorities in materials allocation, and instituted controls over credit and other sectors of the economy.[68] As in the world wars, the aftermath of Truman's Korean War exhibited the "ratchet-effect," whereby federal government spending, though diminished, never returned to the previous peacetime level.[69]

A HERITAGE OF SINKHOLES

Truman's legacy includes programs and policies that continue to inflict damage to this day. Three cases are especially noteworthy.

In his message to Congress on January 20, 1949, Truman launched the concept of aid from Western governments to the poorer nations that were soon to be called, collectively, the Third World. Point Four of his speech sketched a new program to provide technical assistance to the "more than half the people of the world [who] are living in conditions approaching misery," and whose "economic life is primitive and stagnant." This was to be "a cooperative enterprise in which all nations work together through the United Nations and its specialized agencies"—in other words, a state-funded and state-directed effort to end world poverty.[70]

[68]Robert Higgs, *Crisis and Leviathan: Critical Episodes in the Growth of American Government* (New York: Oxford University Press, 1987), pp. 227, 244–45.

[69]Jonathan R.T. Hughes, *The Governmental Habit: Economic Controls from Colonial Times to the Present* (New York: Basic Books, 1977), pp. 208–09. Federal expenditures in the early Eisenhower years were, on average, twice as high as in the period 1947–1950.

[70]*The Public Papers of Harry S. Truman, 1949* (Washington, D.C.: U.S. Government Printing Office, 1964), pp. 114–15.

According to Peter Bauer, Point Four "inaugurated a far-reaching policy and a supporting terminology."[71] In the decades that followed, foreign aid was promoted by a proliferating international bureaucracy, as well as by religious and secular zealots ignorantly confident of the purity of their antisocial cause. Western guilt feelings, fostered by the leftist intelligentsia and self-seeking Third World politicians, facilitated the channeling of hundreds of billions of dollars to governments in Asia, Africa, and Latin America. Today, even "conservative" politicians and publicists are devotees. "Development aid" has become institutionalized and is intended to continue indefinitely, with all its attendant harm: reinforced statism, inferior economic performance, and corruption on the greatest scale the world has ever known.[72]

Truman began the "special relationship" between the United States and Zionism. Franklin Roosevelt, while not blind to Jewish interests, favored an evenhanded approach in the Middle East as between Arabs and Jews. Truman, on the other hand, was an all-out champion of the Zionist cause.[73]

There were two major reasons for Truman's support. One was a sentimental attachment that was strongly reinforced by many who had influence with him, including his old business partner, Eddie Jacobson as well as David K. Niles, and Eleanor Roosevelt.[74] Visiting the president, the Chief Rabbi of Israel told him: "God put you in your mother's womb so that you could be the instrument to bring about the rebirth of Israel after two thousand years." Instead of taking offense at such chutzpah, the

---

[71]Peter Bauer, *Equality, the Third World, and Economic Delusion* (Cambridge, Mass.: Harvard University Press, 1981), pp. 139, 275, n. 1. See also Peter Bauer and Cranley Onslow, "Fifty Years of Failure," *The Spectator* (September 5, 1998): 13–14.

[72]Graham Hancock, *Lords of Poverty: The Power, Prestige, and Corruption of the International Aid Business* (New York: Atlantic Monthly Press, 1989).

[73]Alfred M. Lilienthal, *The Zionist Connection: What Price Peace?* (New York: Dodd, Mead, 1978), pp. 45–100.

[74]The depth of Eleanor's understanding of the Middle East situation is illustrated by her statement: "I'm confident that when a Jewish state is set up, the Arabs will see the light: they will quiet down; and Palestine will no longer be a problem." Evan M. Wilson, *Decision on Palestine: How the U.S. Came to Recognize Israel* (Stanford, Calif.: Hoover Institution Press, 1979), p. 116.

president was deeply moved. One of his biographers reports: "At that, great tears started rolling down Harry Truman's cheeks."[75]

The second reason for Truman's support was political opportunism. With congressional elections coming up in 1946 and then a very difficult presidential campaign in 1948, the votes of Zionist Jews in New York, Illinois, California, and other states could be critical. White House Counsel Clark Clifford was particularly persistent in arguing this angle, to the point that Secretary of State Marshall, who was skeptical of the pro-Zionist bias, angrily objected. Clifford, said Marshall, was trying to have the president base a crucial foreign policy position on "domestic political considerations."[76]

American backing was indispensable in the birth of the state of Israel. In November 1947, the United Nations, led by the United States, voted to partition Palestine. The mandate had to be gerrymandered in order to create a bare majority in the territory allotted the Jews, who, while comprising one-third of the population, were given 56 percent of the land. On America's role, veteran State Department official Sumner Welles wrote:

> By direct order of the White House every form of pressure, direct and indirect, was brought to bear upon countries outside the Moslem world that were known to be either uncertain or opposed to partition.[77]

In her biography of her father, Margaret Truman spoke, in terms that today would be viewed as verging on anti-Semitism, of "the intense pressure which numerous Jews put on Dad from the moment he entered the White House and his increasing resentment of this pressure." She quotes from a letter Truman sent to Eleanor Roosevelt:

> I fear very much that the Jews are like all underdogs. When they get on top, they are just as intolerant and as cruel as the people were to them when they were underneath. I regret this

---

[75]Merle Miller, *Plain Speaking: An Oral Biography of Harry S. Truman* (New York: G.P. Putnam, 1973), p. 218.

[76]Wilson, *Decision on Palestine*, pp. 134, 142; Lilienthal, *The Zionist Connection*, pp. 82–83.

[77]Wilson, *Decision on Palestine*, p. 126.

situation very much, because my sympathy has always been on their side.[78]

But Truman's sporadic resentment did not prevent him from promoting Zionist plans for Palestine at the important points. He stubbornly ignored the advice not only of his own State Department, but also of his British ally, who kept reminding him of the commitment made by Roosevelt and by Truman himself, that the Arab states would be consulted on any settlement of the Palestine question.[79] When Israel declared its independence, on May 15, 1948, the United States extended de facto recognition ten minutes later. Since then, with the exception of the Eisenhower years, the bonds linking the United States to Israel have grown ever tighter, with American leaders seemingly indifferent to the costs to their own country.[80]

In the end, the part of Truman's legacy with the greatest potential for harm is NATO. Allegedly created in response to a (nonexistent) Soviet threat to overrun Europe, it has already outlived the Soviet Union and European communism by a decade. At the beginning of the new century, there is no possibility that this entrenched military and civilian bureaucratic apparatus will simply fade away. When did such a huge collection of

---

[78]Margaret Truman, *Harry S. Truman* (New York: William Morrow, 1973), pp. 381, 384–85.

[79]Clement Attlee, British prime minister during the decisive years, was a strong critic of Truman's policy:

> The president went completely against the advice of his own State Department and his own military people. . . . The State Department's view was very close to ours, they had to think internationally, but most of the politicians were influenced by voting considerations. There were crucial elections coming up at the time, and several big Jewish firms had contributed to Democratic Party funds. (p. 181)

Attlee reminded Truman of the American promises to Arab leaders that they, as well as the Zionists, would be fully consulted on Palestine: "It would be very unwise to break these solemn pledges and so set aflame the whole Middle East." Clement Attlee, *Twilight of Empire: Memoirs of Prime Minister Clement Attlee*, Francis Williams, ed. (New York: A.S. Barnes, 1963), pp. 181, 190.

[80]See Lilienthal, *The Zionist Connection*, and Sheldon L. Richman, *"Ancient History": U.S. Conduct in the Middle East Since World War II and the Folly of Intervention* (Washington, D.C.: Cato Institute, 1991).

functionaries ever surrender their lucrative, tax-funded positions without a revolution?

In the course of NATO's aggression against Yugoslavia—illegal, according to the U.S. Constitution, the Charter of the United Nations, and NATO's own charter—its mission has been "redefined." No longer merely a defensive alliance (against whom?), it will now roam the world, a law unto itself, perpetually "in search of monsters to destroy." In 1951, General Eisenhower, then supreme Allied commander in Europe, stated: "If in ten years time, all American troops stationed in Europe for national defense purposes have not been returned to the United States, then this whole project [NATO] will have failed."[81] A growing threat to the independence, the well-being, and the very lives of the peoples of the world, NATO may turn out in the end to have been Truman's greatest failure.

There are also episodes in Truman's presidency that have been forgotten in the rush to certify him as a "near-great" but that should not go unmentioned. Among the more notable ones:

Truman endorsed the Nuremberg trials of the top German leaders, appointing Robert H. Jackson, a justice of the Supreme Court, as chief American prosecutor.[82] The trials were exposed as a vindictive violation of the canons of Anglo-American law by Senator Taft, who was labeled a pro-Nazi by Democratic and labor union leaders for his pains.[83] At Nuremberg, when the question came up of responsibility for the murder of thousands of Polish POWs at Katyn, Truman followed the cowardly policy laid down by FDR: the proof already in the possession of the U.S. government—that it was the Soviets who had murdered the Poles—was suppressed.[84]

In the early months of Truman's presidency, the United States and Britain directed the forced repatriation of tens of

---

[81]Eugene J. Carroll, Jr., "NATO Enlargement: To What End?" in *NATO Enlargement: Illusions and Reality*, Ted Galen Carpenter and Barbara Conry, eds. (Washington, D.C.: Cato Institute, 1998), p. 199.

[82]See, for example, *The Public Papers of Harry S. Truman*, 1946, pp. 455, 480–81.

[83]James A. Patterson, *Mr. Republican: A Biography of Robert A. Taft* (Boston: Houghton Mifflin, 1972), pp. 327–29.

[84]Werner Maser, *Nuremberg: A Nation on Trial*, Richard Barry, trans. (New York: Scribener's, 1979), pp. 112–13.

thousands of Soviet subjects—and many who had never been Soviet subjects—to the Soviet Union, where tens of thousands were executed by the NKVD or cast into the gulag. Their crime had been to fight against Stalinist domination on the side of the Germans. Terrible scenes occurred in the course of this repatriation (sometimes called "Operation Keelhaul"), as the condemned men, and in some cases women with their children, were forced or duped into returning to Stalin's Russia. American soldiers had orders to "shoot to kill" those refusing to go. Some of the victims committed suicide rather than fall into the hands of the Soviet secret police.[85]

At home, the Truman administration brought the corrupt practices of the president's mentor to the White House. Truman had entered politics as the protégé of Tom Pendergast, the boss of the Kansas City Democratic machine. One of Truman's first acts as president was to fire the U.S. attorney general for western Missouri, who had won 259 convictions for vote fraud against the machine and had sent Boss Pendergast to federal prison, where he died. Over the years, the Truman administration was notorious for influence-peddling, cover-ups, and outright theft.[86] It ranks with the administration of Bill Clinton for the dishonest practices of its personnel, although Truman and his wife Bess were never themselves guilty of malfeasance.

HIROSHIMA AND NAGASAKI

The most spectacular episode of Truman's presidency will never be forgotten, but will be forever linked to his name: the atomic bombings of Hiroshima on August 8, 1945 and of Nagasaki three days later. Probably around two hundred thousand persons were killed in the attacks and through radiation poisoning; the vast majority were civilians, including several thousand

---

[85] Julius Epstein, *Operation Keelhaul: The Story of Forced Repatriation from 1944 to the Present* (Old Greenwich, Conn.: Devin-Adair, 1973), esp. pp. 99–104. See also Nicholas Bethell, *The Last Secret: Forcible Repatriation to Russia, 1944–47* (London: Andre Deutsch, 1974); and Jason Kendall Moore, "Between Expediency and Principle: U.S. Repatriation Policy Toward Russian Nationals, 1944–1949," *Diplomatic History* 24, no. 3 (Summer 2000).

[86] Jules Abels, *The Truman Scandals.* (Chicago: Regnery, 1956); Henry Regnery, *Memoirs of a Dissident Publisher* (New York: Harcourt, Brace, Jovanovich, 1979), pp. 132–38.

Korean workers. Twelve U.S. Navy fliers incarcerated in a Hiroshima jail were also among the dead.[87]

Great controversy has always surrounded the bombings. One thing Truman insisted on from the start: The decision to use the bombs, and the responsibility it entailed, was his. Over the years, he gave different, and contradictory, grounds for his decision. Sometimes he implied that he had acted simply out of revenge. To a clergyman who criticized him, Truman responded, testily:

> Nobody is more disturbed over the use of Atomic bombs than I am but I was greatly disturbed over the unwarranted attack by the Japanese on Pearl Harbor and their murder of our prisoners of war. The only language they seem to understand is the one we have been using to bombard them.[88]

Such reasoning will not impress anyone who fails to see how the brutality of the Japanese military could justify deadly retaliation against innocent men, women, and children. Truman doubtless was aware of this, so from time to time he advanced other pretexts. On August 9, 1945, he stated: "The world will note that the first atomic bomb was dropped on Hiroshima, a military base. That was because we wished in this first attack to avoid, insofar as possible, the killing of civilians."[89]

This, however, is absurd. *Pearl Harbor* was a military base. Hiroshima was a *city*, inhabited by some three hundred thousand people, which contained military elements. In any case, since the harbor was mined and the U.S. Navy and Air Force were

---

[87]On the atomic bombings, see Gar Alperovitz, *The Decision to Use the Atomic Bomb and the Architecture of an American Myth* (New York: Knopf, 1995); and idem, "Was Harry Truman a Revisionist on Hiroshima?" *Society for Historians of American Foreign Relations Newsletter* 29, no. 2 (June 1998); also Martin J. Sherwin, *A World Destroyed: The Atomic Bomb and the Grand Alliance* (New York: Vintage, 1977); and Dennis D. Wainstock, *The Decision to Drop the Atomic Bomb* (Westport, Conn.: Praeger, 1996).

[88]Alperovitz, *Decision*, p. 563. Truman added: "When you deal with a beast you have to treat him as a beast. It is most regrettable but nevertheless true." For similar statements by Truman, see ibid., p. 564. Alperovitz's monumental work is the end-product of four decades of study of the atomic bombings and is indispensable for comprehending the often complex argumentation on the issue.

[89]Ibid., p. 521.

in control of the waters around Japan, whatever troops were stationed in Hiroshima had been effectively neutralized.

On other occasions, Truman claimed that Hiroshima was bombed because it was an industrial center. But, as noted in the U.S. Strategic Bombing Survey, "all major factories in Hiroshima were on the periphery of the city—and escaped serious damage."[90] The target was the center of the city. That Truman realized the kind of victims the bombs consumed is evident from his comment to his cabinet on August 10, explaining his reluctance to drop a third bomb: "The thought of wiping out another 100,000 people was too horrible," he said; he didn't like the idea of killing "all those kids."[91] *Wiping out another one hundred thousand people . . . all those kids.*

Moreover, the notion that Hiroshima was a major military or industrial center is implausible on the face of it. The city had remained untouched through years of devastating air attacks on the Japanese home islands, and never figured in Bomber Command's list of the 33 primary targets.[92]

Thus, the rationale for the atomic bombings has come to rest on a single colossal fabrication, which has gained surprising currency: that they were necessary in order to save a half-million or more American lives. These, supposedly, are the lives that would have been lost in the planned invasion of Kyushu in December, then in the all-out invasion of Honshu the next year, if that was needed. But the worst-case scenario for a full-scale invasion of the Japanese home islands was forty-six thousand American lives lost.[93] The ridiculously inflated figure of a half-million

---

[90]Ibid., p. 523.

[91]Barton J. Bernstein, "Understanding the Atomic Bomb and the Japanese Surrender: Missed Opportunities, Little-Known Near Disasters, and Modern Memory," *Diplomatic History* 19, no. 2 (Spring 1995): 257. General Carl Spaatz, commander of U.S. strategic bombing operations in the Pacific, was so shaken by the destruction at Hiroshima that he telephoned his superiors in Washington, proposing that the next bomb be dropped on a less populated area, so that it "would not be as devastating to the city and the people." His suggestion was rejected. Ronald Schaffer, *Wings of Judgment: American Bombing in World War II* (New York: Oxford University Press, 1985), pp. 147–48.

[92]This is true also of Nagasaki.

[93]See Barton J. Bernstein, "A Post-War Myth: 500,000 U.S. Lives Saved," *Bulletin of the Atomic Scientists* 42, no. 6 (June–July 1986): 38–40; and idem, "Wrong Numbers," *The Independent Monthly* (July 1995): 41–44.

for the potential death toll—nearly twice the total of U.S. dead in all theaters in the Second World War—is now routinely repeated in high-school and college textbooks and bandied about by ignorant commentators. Unsurprisingly, the prize for sheer fatuousness on this score goes to President George W. Bush, who claimed in 1991 that dropping the bomb "spared millions of American lives."[94]

Still, Truman's multiple deceptions and self-deceptions are understandable, considering the horror he unleashed. It is equally understandable that the U.S. occupation authorities censored reports from the shattered cities and did not permit films and photographs of the thousands of corpses and the frightfully mutilated survivors to reach the public.[95] Otherwise, Americans—and the rest of the world—might have drawn disturbing comparisons to scenes then coming to light from the Nazi concentration camps.

The bombings were condemned as barbaric and unnecessary by high American military officers, including Eisenhower and MacArthur.[96] The view of Admiral William D. Leahy, Truman's own chief of staff, was typical:

> the use of this barbarous weapon at Hiroshima and Nagasaki was of no material assistance in our war against Japan. . . . My own feeling was that in being the first to use it, we had adopted an ethical standard common to the barbarians of the Dark Ages. I was not taught to make wars in that fashion, and wars cannot be won by destroying women and children.[97]

---

[94]J. Samuel Walker, "History, Collective Memory, and the Decision to Use the Bomb," *Diplomatic History* 19, no. 2 (Spring 1995): 320, 323–25. Walker details the frantic evasions of Truman's biographer, David McCullough, when confronted with the unambiguous record.

[95]Paul Boyer, "Exotic Resonances: Hiroshima in American Memory," *Diplomatic History* 19, no. 2 (Spring 1995): 299. On the fate of the bombings' victims and the public's restricted knowledge of them, see John W. Dower, "The Bombed: Hiroshimas and Nagasakis in Japanese Memory," in ibid., pp. 275–95.

[96]Alperovitz, *Decision*, pp. 320–65. On MacArthur and Eisenhower, see ibid., pp. 352 and 355–56.

[97]William D. Leahy, *I Was There* (New York: McGraw-Hill, 1950), p. 441. Leahy compared the use of the atomic bomb to the treatment of civilians by Genghis Khan, and termed it "not worthy of Christian man." Ibid., p. 442. Curiously, Truman himself supplied the foreword to Leahy's book. In a private letter written just before he left the White House, Truman referred to

The political elite implicated in the atomic bombings feared a backlash that would aid and abet the rebirth of horrid prewar "isolationism." Apologias were rushed into print, lest public disgust at the sickening war crime result in erosion of enthusiasm for the globalist project.[98] No need to worry. A sea-change had taken place in the attitudes of the American people. Then and ever after, all surveys have shown that the great majority supported Truman, believing that the bombs were required to end the war and save hundreds of thousands of American lives, or more likely, not really caring one way or the other.

Those who may still be troubled by such a grisly exercise in cost-benefit analysis—innocent Japanese lives balanced against the lives of Allied servicemen—might reflect on the judgment of the Catholic philosopher G.E.M. Anscombe, who insisted on the supremacy of moral rules.[99] When, in June 1956, Truman was awarded an honorary degree by her university, Oxford, Anscombe protested.[100] Truman was a war criminal, she contended, for what is the difference between the U.S. government massacring civilians from the air, as at Hiroshima and Nagasaki, and the Nazis wiping out the inhabitants of some Czech or Polish village?

---

the use of the atomic bomb as "murder," stating that the bomb "is far worse than gas and biological warfare because it affects the civilian population and murders them wholesale." Barton J. Bernstein, "Origins of the U.S. Biological Warfare Program," *Preventing a Biological Arms Race*, Susan Wright, ed. (Cambridge, Mass.: MIT Press, 1990), p. 9.

[98]Barton J. Bernstein, "Seizing the Contested Terrain of Early Nuclear History: Stimson, Conant, and Their Allies Explain the Decision to Use the Bomb," *Diplomatic History* 17, no. 1 (Winter 1993): 35–72.

[99]One writer in no way troubled by the sacrifice of innocent Japanese to save Allied servicemen—indeed, just to save him—is Paul Fussell; see his *Thank God for the Atom Bomb and Other Essays* (New York: Summit, 1988). The reason for Fussell's little *Te Deum* is, as he states, that he was among those scheduled to take part in the invasion of Japan, and might very well have been killed. It is a mystery why Fussell takes out his easily understandable terror, rather unchivalrously, on Japanese women and children instead of on the men in Washington who conscripted him to fight in the Pacific in the first place.

[100]G.E.M. Anscombe, "Mr. Truman's Degree," in idem, *Collected Philosophical Papers*, vol. 3, *Ethics, Religion and Politics* (Minneapolis: University of Minnesota Press, 1981), pp. 62–71.

Anscombe's point is worth following up. Suppose that, when we invaded Germany in early 1945, our leaders had believed that executing all the inhabitants of Aachen, or Trier, or some other Rhineland city would finally break the will of the Germans and lead them to surrender. In this way, the war might have ended quickly, saving the lives of many Allied soldiers. Would that then have justified shooting tens of thousands of German civilians, including women and children? Yet how is that different from the atomic bombings?

By early summer 1945, the Japanese fully realized that they were beaten. Why did they nonetheless fight on? As Anscombe wrote: "It was the insistence on unconditional surrender that was the root of all evil."[101]

That mad formula was coined by Roosevelt at the Casablanca conference, and, with Churchill's enthusiastic concurrence, it became the Allied shibboleth. After prolonging the war in Europe, it did its work in the Pacific. At the Potsdam conference, in July 1945, Truman issued a proclamation to the Japanese, threatening them with the "utter devastation" of their homeland unless they surrendered unconditionally. Among the Allied terms, to which "there are no alternatives," was that there be "eliminated for all time the authority and influence of those who have deceived and misled the people of Japan into embarking on world conquest [sic]." "Stern justice," the proclamation warned, "would be meted out to all war criminals."[102]

To the Japanese, this meant that the emperor—regarded by them to be divine, the direct descendent of the goddess of the sun—would certainly be dethroned and probably put on trial as a war criminal and hanged, perhaps in front of his palace.[103] It was not, in fact, the U.S. intention to dethrone or punish the emperor. But this implicit modification of unconditional surrender was never communicated to the Japanese. In the end, after

---

[101]Anscombe, "Mr. Truman's Degree," p. 62.

[102]Hans Adolf Jacobsen and Arthur S. Smith, Jr., eds., *World War II: Policy and Strategy. Selected Documents with Commentary* (Santa Barbara, Calif.: ABC-Clio, 1979), pp. 345–46.

[103]For some Japanese leaders, another reason for keeping the emperor was as a bulwark against a possible postwar communist takeover. See also Sherwin, *A World Destroyed*, p. 236: "the [Potsdam] proclamation offered the military die-hards in the Japanese government more ammunition to continue the war than it offered their opponents to end it."

Nagasaki, Washington acceded to the Japanese desire to keep the dynasty and even to retain Hirohito as emperor.

For months before, Truman had been pressed to clarify the U.S. position by many high officials within the administration, and outside of it, as well. In May 1945, at the president's request, Herbert Hoover prepared a memorandum stressing the urgent need to end the war as soon as possible. The Japanese should be informed that we would in no way interfere with the emperor or their chosen form of government. He even raised the possibility that, as part of the terms, Japan might be allowed to hold on to Formosa (Taiwan) and Korea. After meeting with Truman, Hoover dined with Taft and other Republican leaders, and outlined his proposals.[104]

Establishment writers on World War II often like to deal in lurid speculations. For instance: if the United States had not entered the war, then Hitler would have "conquered the world" (a sad undervaluation of the Red Army, it would appear; moreover, wasn't it Japan that was trying to "conquer the world"?) and killed untold millions. Now, applying conjectural history in this case: assume that the Pacific war had ended in the way wars customarily do—through negotiation of the terms of surrender. And assume the worst—that the Japanese had adamantly insisted on preserving part of their empire, say, Korea and Formosa, even Manchuria. In that event, it is quite possible that Japan would have been in a position to prevent the Communists from coming to power in China. And that could have meant that the thirty or forty million deaths now attributed to the Maoist regime would not have occurred.

But even remaining within the limits of feasible diplomacy in 1945, it is clear that Truman in no way exhausted the possibilities of ending the war without recourse to the atomic bomb. The Japanese were not informed that they would be the victims of by far the most lethal weapon ever invented (one with "more than two thousand times the blast power of the British 'Grand Slam,' which is the largest bomb ever yet used in the history of warfare," as Truman boasted in his announcement of the Hiroshima attack). Nor were they told that the Soviet Union was set to declare war on Japan, an event that shocked some in

---

[104]Alperovitz, *Decision*, pp. 44–45.

Tokyo more than the bombings.[105] Pleas by some of the scientists involved in the project to demonstrate the power of the bomb in some uninhabited or evacuated area were rebuffed. All that mattered was to formally preserve the unconditional surrender formula and save the servicemen's lives that might have been lost in the effort to enforce it. Yet, as Major General J.F.C. Fuller, one of the century's great military historians, wrote in connection with the atomic bombings:

> Though to save life is laudable, it in no way justifies the employment of means which run counter to every precept of humanity and the customs of war. Should it do so, then, on the pretext of shortening a war and of saving lives, every imaginable atrocity can be justified.[106]

Isn't this obviously true? And isn't this the reason that rational and humane men, over generations, developed rules of warfare in the first place?

While the mass media parroted the government line in praising the atomic incinerations, prominent conservatives denounced them as unspeakable war crimes. Felix Morley, constitutional scholar and one of the founders of *Human Events*, drew attention to the horror of Hiroshima, including the "thousands of children trapped in the thirty-three schools that were destroyed." He called on his compatriots to atone for what had been done in their name, and proposed that groups of Americans be sent to

---

[105]Cf. Bernstein, "Understanding the Atomic Bomb," p. 254: "it does seem very likely, though certainly not definite, that a synergistic combination of guaranteeing the emperor, awaiting Soviet entry, and continuing the siege strategy would have ended the war in time to avoid the November invasion." Bernstein, an excellent and scrupulously objective scholar, nonetheless disagrees with Alperovitz and the revisionist school on several key points.

[106]J.F.C. Fuller, *The Second World War, 1939–45: A Strategical and Tactical History* (London: Eyre and Spottiswoode, 1948), p. 392. Fuller, who was similarly scathing on the terror-bombing of the German cities, characterized the attacks on Hiroshima and Nagasaki as "a type of war that would have disgraced Tamerlane." Cf. Barton J. Bernstein, who concludes, in "Understanding the Atomic Bomb," p. 235:

> In 1945, American leaders were not seeking to avoid the use of the A-bomb. Its use did not create ethical or political problems for them. Thus, they easily rejected or never considered most of the so-called alternatives to the bomb.

Hiroshima, as Germans were sent to witness what had been done in the Nazi camps. The Paulist priest, Father James Gillis, editor of *The Catholic World* and another stalwart of the Old Right, castigated the bombings as "the most powerful blow ever delivered against Christian civilization and the moral law." David Lawrence, conservative owner of *U.S. News and World Report*, continued to denounce them for years.[107] The distinguished conservative philosopher Richard Weaver was revolted by

> the spectacle of young boys fresh out of Kansas and Texas turning nonmilitary Dresden into a holocaust . . . pulverizing ancient shrines like Monte Cassino and Nuremberg, and bringing atomic annihilation to Hiroshima and Nagasaki.

Weaver considered such atrocities as deeply "inimical to the foundations on which civilization is built."[108]

Today, self-styled conservatives slander as "anti-American" anyone who is in the least troubled by Truman's massacre of so many tens of thousands of Japanese innocents from the air. This shows as well as anything the difference between today's "conservatives" and those who once deserved the name.

Leo Szilard was the world-renowned physicist who drafted the original letter to Roosevelt that Einstein signed, instigating the Manhattan Project. In 1960, shortly before his death, Szilard stated another obvious truth:

> If the Germans had dropped atomic bombs on cities instead of us, we would have defined the dropping of atomic bombs on cities as a war crime, and we would have sentenced the Germans who were guilty of this crime to death at Nuremberg and hanged them.[109]

---

[107]Felix Morley, "The Return to Nothingness," *Human Events* (August 29, 1945) reprinted in *Hiroshima's Shadow*, Kai Bird and Lawrence Lifschultz, eds. (Stony Creek, Conn.: Pamphleteer's Press, 1998), pp. 272–74; James Martin Gillis, "Nothing But Nihilism," *The Catholic World*, September 1945, reprinted in ibid., pp. 278–80; Alperovitz, *Decision*, pp. 438–40.

[108]Richard M. Weaver, "A Dialectic on Total War," in idem, *Visions of Order: The Cultural Crisis of Our Time* (Baton Rouge: Louisiana State University Press, 1964), pp. 98–99.

[109]Wainstock, *Decision*, p. 122.

The destruction of Hiroshima and Nagasaki was a war crime worse than any that Japanese generals were executed for in Tokyo and Manila. If Harry Truman was not a war criminal, then no one ever was.

19

FROM KENNEDY'S "NEW ECONOMICS" TO NIXON'S "NEW ECONOMIC POLICY": MONETARY INFLATION AND THE MARCH OF ECONOMIC FASCISM

JOSEPH T. SALERNO

On August 15, 1971, President Richard Nixon in a nation-wide radio and television address informed the American public that he was ordering the implementation of "the most comprehensive New Economic Policy to be undertaken by this nation in four decades."[1] The centerpiece of his New Economic Policy was a wage–price freeze, which he introduced in the following words:

> The time has come for decisive action—action that will break the vicious circle of spiraling wages and costs. I am today ordering a freeze on all prices and wages throughout the United States for a period of 90 days. . . . I have today appointed a Cost of Living Council within the Government. I have directed this Council to work with leaders of labor and business to set up the proper mechanism for achieving contin-ued price and wage stability after the 90-day freeze is over.[2]

Nixon proceeded to deny that the freeze would involve "the mandatory wage and price controls that crush personal and

---

[1]Richard M. Nixon, "Remarks of the President on Nationwide Radio and Tele-vision, August 15, 1971," reprinted in Roger Leroy Miller and Raburn M. Williams, *The New Economics of Richard M. Nixon: Freezes, Floats, and Fiscal Policy* (San Francisco: Canfield Press, 1972), p. 75.

[2]Ibid., pp. 72–73.

economic freedom."[3] Nixon's denial was a bald-faced and absurd prevarication, given his caveat that the wage–price freeze "will be backed by Government sanctions, if necessary." The initial ninety-day wage–price freeze soon gave way to three subsequent phases of mandatory price controls that lasted until April 1974 and revealed the Nixonian New Economic Policy as the usual coercive and heavy-handed attempt at political price fixing involving gross abrogation of economic freedoms and private property rights.[4]

What was more surprising than the imposing of wage and price controls by a Republican president during peacetime, however, was the sparseness and mildness of the critical reaction among market-oriented economists and business leaders to Nixon's announcement of a policy that would, in one fell swoop, effectively suspend the operation of the market economy. Indeed, for some time leading up to the imposition of controls, an important segment of the business community had been clamoring for "direct action" on inflation, particularly on its manifestation in rising wage rates.[5] Thus, *The Washington Post* was probably not exaggerating when, on the day after Nixon unveiled his wage–price freeze, it described the mood of business and banking as "almost euphoric."[6] Also, in late 1970, the conservative economist Arthur Burns, a former chairman of the Council of Economic Advisers (CEA) during the Eisenhower administration and Nixon's new appointee as the chairman of the Federal Reserve System, suddenly joined such longtime left-wing advocates of wage and price controls as John Kenneth Galbraith in the chorus of voices calling for an "incomes policy" to

[3]Ibid., p. 73.

[4]For an insider's account of his experience administering Phase II (November 1971 to January 1973) of Nixonian price controls, see C. Jackson Grayson, Jr., with Louis Neeb, *Confessions of a Price Controller* (Homewood, Ill.: Dow Jones-Irwin, 1974).

[5]Herbert Stein, *Presidential Economics: The Making of Economic Policy From Roosevelt to Clinton*, 3rd ed. (Washington, D.C.: American Enterprise Institute for Public Policy Research, 1994), p. 175; and Arnold R. Weber, *In Pursuit of Price Stability: The Wage-Price Freeze of 1971* (Washington, D.C.: The Brookings Institution, 1973), pp. 6–7.

[6]Quoted in Murray N. Rothbard, "The End of Economic Freedom," *The Libertarian Forum* 3 (September 1971): 1.

moderate inflation.[7] Moreover, a number of prominent conservative economists long associated with the Republican Party—including Burns himself, Paul McCracken, Herbert Stein, and George P. Schultz—were directly involved in crafting the Nixonian program of wage and price controls.

While there were a few free-market economists who did criticize the wage–price freeze, including Milton Friedman and a group of Chicago School economists headed by Allen Meltzer, their criticisms were relatively mild and did not reflect recognition that the New Economic Policy marked the abolition of the market economy and its replacement by a regime of national economic planning.[8] Perhaps the only economist to fully identify and clearly express the origins, nature, and momentous implications of the New Economic Policy was Murray Rothbard, a student of Ludwig von Mises and the leader of the Austrian School in the United States. Rothbard wrote:

> It is now clear that price and wage controls of some sort will succeed the 90-day freeze—in short that we now have entered a political economy of permanent direct controls. There is only one word for this New Economic Policy, a word that is at first glance harsh and exaggerated, but in fact is precisely appropriate. That word is "fascism." A system of permanent price and wage controls, administered by a central government bureaucracy, probably headed by some form of tripartite board including Big Business, Big Labor, and Big Government—this is precisely what fascism is, precisely the economic system of Mussolini's Italy and Hitler's Germany. This is the economy of the "corporate state," administered by dictation from the top, controlled and monopolized by Big Business and Big Union interests, with the individual, and the consumer, the person who suffers. In short, the mass of the American public

---

[7] Weber, *In Pursuit of Price Stability*, pp. 5–6.

[8] See for example, Milton Friedman, "Why the Freeze is a Mistake," *Newsweek* (August 30, 1971), reprinted in idem, *An Economist's Protest: Columns in Political Economy* (Glen Ridge, N.J.: Thomas Horton, 1972), pp. 15–16, where Friedman emphasizes the unworkability and inefficiency of the freeze and its ineffectiveness in curing inflation. A few months later, Friedman published a far more vigorous denunciation of Nixonite price controls on political and moral grounds, but still failed to recognize the radical transformation of the U.S. political–economic system that it portended. See Milton Friedman, "Morality and Controls," *The New York Times* (October 28–29, 1971), reprinted in ibid., pp. 31–34.

will suffer from this system of corporate statism, from the death of the free price system, from the invasion of individual rights, from the hampering of growth, efficiency, and productivity, that the system will entail.[9]

In January 1971, eight months before the imposition of the wage–price freeze, Rothbard had foretold the coming of wage and price controls, which he characterized as the natural culmination of fascistic trends in the U.S. economy that had been developing since the beginning of the 1960s and that had gathered significant momentum during the Nixon administration. He also foresaw the surprising complicity of conservative "free-market" economists in bringing about these controls and the favorable reaction of the leaders of big business to their implementation. Rothbard's prescient and perceptive analysis of the emerging fascist political economy is worth quoting at length:

> Well, we have had two years of Nixonism and what we are undergoing is a super-Great Society—in fact, what we are seeing is the greatest single thrust toward socialism since the days of Franklin Roosevelt. It is not Marxian socialism, to be sure, but neither was FDR's; it is . . . a big-business socialism, or state corporatism, but that is cold comfort indeed. There are only two major differences in content between Nixon and Kennedy–Johnson . . . (1) that the march into socialism is faster because the teeth of conservative Republican opposition have been drawn; and (2) that the erstwhile "free-market" conservatives, basking in the seats of Power, have betrayed whatever principles they may have had for the service of the State. Thus, we have Paul McCracken and Arthur F. Burns, dedicated opponents of wage–price "guideline" dictation and wage–price controls when out of power, now moving rapidly in the very direction they had previously deplored. . . .
>
> But now the administration has swung around to the Liberal thesis of monetary fiscal expansion to cure the recession, while yelling and griping at labor and employers not to raise wages and prices—a "guidelines" or "incomes" policy that is only one step away from wage and price controls. . . .
>
> Not only is it impossible for direct controls to work; their imposition adds the final link in the forging of a totalitarian economy, of an American fascism. What is it but totalitarian

[9]Rothbard, "The End of Economic Freedom," p. 7.

to outlaw any sort of voluntary exchange, any voluntary sale of a product, or hiring of a laborer? But once again Richard Nixon is responsive to his credo of big business liberalism, for direct controls satisfy the ideological creed of liberals while at the same time they are urged by big business in order to try to hold down the pressure of wages on selling prices which always appear in the late stages of a boom.[10]

Early in this passage, Rothbard hints at the substantial continuity between the economic policies of the Kennedy and Johnson administrations on the one hand, and the Nixon administration on the other. This chapter elaborates this hint into the thesis that much of the ideological and institutional groundwork for the economic fascism of Nixon's New Economic Policy was laid by the proponents and policies of Kennedy's "new economics" in the early 1960s. It argues, in particular, that monetary inflation was a neglected but key element propelling the march toward the corporate statism that emerged during the Nixon administration. Furthermore, it seeks to demonstrate that the unleashing of the long-running monetary inflation that was initiated during the Kennedy years and culminated in the inflationary recession of 1973–1975 was a direct result of the radical reshaping of the opinions of the political establishment and the general public toward monetary policy, which was accomplished in a remarkably short time by Kennedy's new economist-advisers.

The chapter is structured in the following way. Section 2 presents a rigorous definition of economic fascism adopted in emended form from the American journalist and political commentator John T. Flynn. Section 3 is devoted to a discussion of the origins of the new economics, which was developed in the latter half of the 1950s by American followers of John Maynard Keynes, most of whom served in some administrative capacity in the U.S. planned economy during World War II. Section 4 critically analyzes the main tenets of the new economics and argues that the doctrine served as a blueprint for the macroeconomic national planning regime that began to take shape under Kennedy and that progressively evolved through the Johnson

---

[10]Murray N. Rothbard, "Nixonite Socialism," *The Libertarian Forum* 3 (January 1971): 1.

and Nixon administrations. The influence of the new economics on Kennedy and the implementation of its fiscal policy during his administration are detailed in Section 5. Section 6 discusses the radically inflationary shift in monetary policy that was inspired by the new economics and argues that it was this change and not the much-ballyhooed revolution in fiscal policy that constituted the core of Kennedy's economic policy revolution. Finally, Section 7 examines Kennedy's attempt in 1962 to compel leading steel corporations to rescind an announced price increase, an event that foreshadowed and facilitated the economic fascism of Nixon's New Economic Policy.

WHAT IS ECONOMIC FASCISM?

Fascism is an emotion-laden term that is burdened with many negative connotations, so it must be carefully defined to be useful in analyzing politico-economic doctrines, policies and institutions.[11] One of the most rigorous attempts to define fascism was undertaken by John T. Flynn, the great American journalist and essayist of the Old Right, a diverse movement of libertarians, conservatives, and anti-FDR liberals and Old Progressives that coalesced in the 1930s.[12] In his classic work, *As We Go Marching*, published in 1944, Flynn enumerated what he called "the essential ingredients of fascism."[13] According to Flynn, the first ingredient is a large centralized government that spends large sums on "planned consumption"—or what today is euphemistically called welfare—financed by means of huge budget deficits. The second ingredient is what Flynn called "the planned economy," which involves systematic government interference with prices, wages, rents, and interest rates within the formal structure of a capitalist economy. Militarism as a deliberate and permanent economic institution and imperialism

---

[11]In Charlotte Twight's words, "The term 'fascism' is an emotionally charged, vituperative label more often mindlessly affixed to one's opposition than dispassionately analyzed." *America's Emerging Fascist Economy* (New Rochelle, N.Y.: Arlington House, 1975), p. 13.

[12]For a description of this movement, see Justin Raimondo, *Reclaiming the American Right: The Lost Legacy of the Conservative Movement* (Burlingame, Calif.: Center for Libertarian Studies, 1993).

[13]John T. Flynn, *As We Go Marching* (Garden City, N.Y.: Doubleday, Doran, 1944), p. 67.

as its handmaiden represent the third and fourth ingredients, respectively. The combination of these four ingredients Flynn labeled the "prologue to fascism."[14] Here, we will refer to it either as "economic fascism" or, more descriptively, "the welfare–warfare state."[15]

For Flynn, full fascism comes into being when to the ingredients constituting economic fascism is added a totalitarian state with a "leader" or dictator at its head. Although Flynn derived this definition from Fascist Italy, he argued compellingly that it fully described National Socialist Germany as well. Moreover, he demonstrated that by the 1930s, the U.S. had arrived at economic fascism and was precariously poised on the precipice of a headlong plunge into full fascism in the 1940s.[16] Flynn graphically described the evolving American style of fascism in the following passage:

> The test of fascism is not one's rage against the Italian and German war lords. The test is—how many of the essential principles of fascism do you accept and to what extent are you prepared to apply those fascist ideas to American social and economic life? When you can put your finger on the men or the groups that urge for America the tax-supported state, the autarchical corporative state, the state bent on the socialization of investment and the bureaucratic government of industry and society, the establishment of the institution of militarism as the great glamorous public works project of the nation and the institution of imperialism under which it proposes to regulate and rule the world and, along with this, proposes to alter the forms of our government to approach as closely as possible the unrestrained, absolute government—then you will know you have located the authentic fascist. . . . Fascism will come at the hands of perfectly authentic Americans, as violently against Hitler and Mussolini as the next one, but who are convinced that the present economic system is washed up and that the present political system in America has outlived its usefulness and who wish to commit this country to the rule of the bureaucratic state; interfering in the affairs of the states and cities; taking part in the management of industry and finance and agriculture; assuming the role of great

---

[14]Ibid., pp. 67, 226–27.

[15]This felicitous term was coined by Murray Rothbard.

[16]Flynn, *As We Go Marching*, pp. 226–58.

national banker and investor, borrowing billions every year and spending them on all sorts of projects through which such a government can paralyze opposition and command public support; marshaling great armies and navies at crushing costs to support the industry of war and preparation for war which will become our greatest industry; and adding to all this the most romantic adventures in global planning, regeneration, and domination all to be done under the authority of a powerfully centralized government in which the executive will hold in effect all the powers with Congress reduced to the role of a debating society. There is your fascist.[17]

Despite the rigor and historical applicability characterizing Flynn's definition of fascism, however, it lacked a crucial ingredient. This lack was manifest in Flynn's prediction, which since has been falsified on numerous occasions, that economic fascism could not last very long without being ruthlessly imposed by a totalitarian dictatorship á la National Socialist Germany or Fascist Italy. In other words, for Flynn, economic fascism was inconsistent with a liberal-democratic political order so that the only choice in both the short run and the long run was between full fascism and the free-market economy. He reasoned that as soon as the citizenry was hit with the immense tax bill required to finance the interest payments on the accumulating debt generated by the welfare–warfare state, it would spontaneously rise up in a glorious tax revolt and either abolish it in short order or be crushed by a totalitarian dictator who comes to the fore. In Flynn's words:

> The spending of borrowed money as a permanent policy with a continuous rise in the public debt can have only one effect. As the debt rises, the yearly interest charge increases. In time the interest charge gets to be more than all the other costs of government. Funds for interest can be obtained only by taxes. A rising public debt means a continuously rising interest charge and persistently rising taxes to service the debt. . . . Of course businessmen and individuals will resist such taxes. The free society knows such a device as the "tax strike". . . . Only in a totalitarian state can these oppressive levies be imposed and enforced. And even in such a state there is a limit. But the

[17]Ibid., pp. 252–53.

limit in the free society is swiftly reached. . . . It is for this reason—and there are other reasons as well—that I make the
statement that this managed public-debt-supported autarchy
must turn to the totalitarian government or abandon its
plans.[18]

Unfortunately, here's where Flynn was misled by his own
inadequate definition of the fascist political economy, for he left
out its most important component: monetary inflation, the
unrestrained creation of fiat money by the government or its
central bank. Thus, if a democratic government is able to finance
its spending on domestic welfare programs and imperialist military adventures by money creation, it can effectively hide the
true costs of these programs from its citizens for years or
decades, during which economic fascism could come to thrive
under mass democracy. This has been the experience of the U.S.
since the early 1960s.

There is a second problem with Flynn's definition, however,
in that it does not provide the causal mechanism by which huge
government deficits and spending programs transform a market
economy with an unhampered price system into a centrally
planned economy with all-around controls of prices, wage rates,
profits, and interest rates. Once again, monetary inflation provides the key. When the consequences of monetary expansion
become visible in the form of rapidly rising prices, the government may at first react to suppress these symptoms by employ-
ing "jawboning" or "moral suasion" to convince big business
and labor unions to abide by "voluntary" wage and price guidelines or incomes policy. Of course, this policy is completely ineffective in preventing the depreciation of the monetary unit in the
face of the relentless and ongoing expansion of the supply of
money. Nonetheless, it does serve to obscure the responsibility of
the State for accelerating price inflation and to direct the attention and ire of the public onto "grasping" corporations and "pig-
gish" labor unions. In fact, it is precisely the inevitable failure of
such moderate incomes policy that smooths the way for the
later imposition of mandatory wage and price controls, which
are then touted as a necessary final resort for curing a mani-
festly intractable problem. However, coercive wage and price
controls, if they are not to result in a systemic breakdown of the

[18]Ibid., p. 228.

entire economy, must be supplemented by a comprehensive and detailed system of government directives to private resource owners and firms regarding the allocation of land, labor, and capital goods in the production process and the rationing of the final products to consumers. This policy is, of course, tantamount to abolishing the market economy and instituting central planning.

Thus, contrary to Flynn, the unrestrained spending on welfare and warfare programs and the bloated budget deficits that are essential characteristics of economic fascism do not necessarily give rise in the short run to a war to the knife between a dictatorial regime and a mass tax-resistance movement. It is more likely that economic fascism will evolve slowly under the guise of mass democracy as the monetary inflation undertaken as a surreptitious method of confiscatory taxation eventually, yet inevitably, begins to engender the highly unpopular consequence of accelerating price inflation. This outcome will compel the incumbent administration to devise and implement progressively more thoroughgoing interventions into the price system that end up in comprehensive economic planning within the nominal property rights structure of a market economy.

THE ORIGINS OF THE NEW ECONOMICS

Economics has come of age in the 1960s. Two presidents have recognized and drawn on modern economics as a source of national strength and presidential power. . . . The paralyzing grip of economic myth and false fears on policy has been loosened, perhaps even broken. We at last accept in fact what was accepted in law twenty years ago (in the Employment Act of 1946), namely that the Federal government has an overarching responsibility for the nation's economic stability and growth. . . . These are profound changes. What they have wrought is not the creation of a "new economics," but the completion of the Keynesian Revolution—thirty years after John Maynard Keynes fired the opening salvo. And they have put the political economist at the president's elbow.[19]

[19]Walter W. Heller, *New Dimensions of Political Economy* (New York: W.W. Norton, 1967), pp. 1–2.

Thus wrote Walter Heller, the primary architect of the new economics.[20] In a similar vein, another prominent new economist, Arthur Okun, described the role of the economist in advising government as assisting in the effective exercise of presidential leadership, which "consists of selecting priorities, making commitments, identifying the aims of the nation, and then working to fulfill them."[21] In frankly characterizing the new economics as a "source" of the growing strength of the central state and of its embodiment in presidential power, the new economists ironically confirmed Murray Rothbard's later evaluation of Keynesian economics as ultimately "the pure economics of power."[22] For as Heller also recognized, such an expansion of the power of the federal government and its centralization in the executive branch is necessary for "unleash[ing] fiscal and monetary policy for the aggressive pursuit" of both short-run stabilization and long-run growth objectives.[23]

The crucial link between Keynesian macroeconomics on the one hand and centralized and unrestrained political power on the other was revealed much earlier by Keynes himself. Writing in the foreword to the German edition of the *General Theory*, which was published almost contemporaneously with the English edition, Keynes declared:

> The theory of aggregate production, which is the point of the following book, nevertheless can be much easier adapted to the conditions of a totalitarian state than the theory of production and distribution of a given production put forth under conditions of free competition and a large degree of laissez-faire.[24]

[20]For a description of the central role played by Heller in the development of the "new economics," see E. Ray Canterbery, *Economics on a New Frontier* (Belmont, Calif.: Wadsworth Publishing, 1969), pp. 139–52, and Susan Lee, *Hands Off: Why the Government Is a Menace to Economic Health* (New York: Simon and Schuster, 1996), pp. 80–99.

[21]Arthur M. Okun, *The Political Economy of Prosperity* (Washington, D.C.: The Brookings Institution, 1970), p. 23.

[22]Murray N. Rothbard, *Making Economic Sense* (Auburn, Ala.: Ludwig von Mises Institute, 1995), p. 55.

[23]Heller, *New Dimensions of Political Economy*, p. 2.

[24]John Maynard Keynes, Foreword to the 1936 German Edition of the *General Theory* translated and reprinted in James J. Martin, *Revisionist Viewpoints:*

The stronghold of the new economists during the Kennedy and Johnson administrations was centered in the membership, staff, and outside consultants of the Council of Economic Advisers.[25] The most prominent among them were, almost to the man, academicians from Eastern establishment universities. Besides Heller and Okun who were from the University of Minnesota and Yale respectively, there were Robert Solow and Paul Samuelson from MIT, James Tobin from Yale, Otto Eckstein and Kenneth Arrow from Harvard, and Gardner Ackley from the University of Michigan. Two Harvard professors, John Kenneth Galbraith, who served on the White House staff during the early months of the Kennedy administration, and Seymour Harris, who headed up a standing committee of academic consultants to the Treasury Department under Kennedy and Johnson, were, along with Samuelson, also personal economic consultants to Kennedy during and after his campaign for the presidency.

These liberal economists were part of the coterie of left-leaning academicians who surrounded President Kennedy. As described by John H. Makin and Norman J. Ornstein, these liberal intellectuals

> were impatient with the fundamentally conservative Truman and Eisenhower administrations. They viewed the decade and

---

Essays in a Dissident Historical Tradition (Colorado Springs, Colo.: Ralph Myles, 1971), pp. 203–05. As Martin has pointed out,

> One can read whole reams of economic literature written by both fervent followers of John Maynard Keynes and his attackers as well and never know that there was a German language edition of his profoundly influential *General Theory* late in 1936, for which Keynes wrote a special foreword addressed solely to German readers. (p. 197)

[25]As Susan Lee vividly puts it, "The Keynesian shock troops were bunkered in Kennedy's Council of Economic Advisers" (*Hands Off: Why the Government Is a Menace to Economic Health* [New York: Simon and Schuster, 1996], p. 81). A complete list of the professional staff and outside consultants of the CEA for the years 1961–1964 can be found in Canterbery, *Economics on a New Frontier* (pp. 317–18). Capsule biographies of some of the more important economists associated with the Kennedy administration are provided by B. Hughel Wilkins and Charles B. Friday, eds., *The Economists of the New Frontier: An Anthology* (New York: Random House, 1963), pp. 14–17.

a half after 1945 as an interruption of what they saw as the thrust of the New Deal away from laissez-faire capitalism.[26]

From the left side of the political spectrum, economic historian Anthony S. Campagna has expressed a similar view, writing that:

> The liberals, so weary of the dullness of the Eisenhower administrations, cheered as Kennedy raided the universities for advisers and searched for talent from previous public servants, so long on the sidelines. The eggheads from Cambridge, Massachusetts, together with the "Irish Mafia" from anywhere, gave the administration and Washington an intellectual excitement not felt since the New Dealers.[27]

Campagna's choice of the term "eggheads" to describe the new economists is indeed an apt one, though probably unwittingly so. The new economists fit to a T John Flynn's much earlier definition of an egghead, as

> a character who pretends to the title of philosopher—a sort of professional intellectual—dedicated to the theory that the eggheads are the appointees of Destiny who will bring about something known in the trade as "security" to a creature known as the "common man" in return for which all they ask is that he deliver his soul to the management of a government operated by the eggheads.

For Flynn, the term described "the intellectual lacking in common sense, a doctrinaire contemptuous of experience, a fuzzy-minded, starry-eyed dreamer." Flynn perceptively summed up the egghead's philosophy "in the two words which describe it—the Planned Society or Economic Planning."[28]

---

[26]John H. Makin and Norman J. Ornstein, *Debt and Taxes* (New York: Times Books, 1994), p. 119.

[27]Anthony S. Campagna, *U.S. National Economic Policy: 1917–1985* (New York: Praeger, 1987), p. 277.

[28]John T. Flynn, "Eggheads through History," *The Freeman* (March 1954), reprinted in *Forgotten Lessons: Selected Essays of John T. Flynn*, Gregory P. Pavlik, ed. (Irvington-on-Hudson, N.Y.: Foundation for Economic Education, 1996), pp. 144–45. Flynn also says here that he adopted this definition of "egghead" from Louis Bromfield.

Thus, it is no surprise that a number of the new economist-eggheads had served in economic planning capacities during and immediately after World War II. Heller was attached to the occupational military government of Germany, while Tobin and Ackley served with the Office of Price Administration (OPA). The OPA was headed for a time by Galbraith, before he was unceremoniously ejected. Harris was a senior member of the OPA staff and served as its liaison with the Board of Economic Warfare and with the State Department.[29] The heady experience of the economist's brush with the exercise of political power during the New Deal, and the psychological consequences of suddenly being stripped of such power, has been well described by Galbraith. In his memoirs, Galbraith comments on being ousted from his position as the first director of the OPA in 1943:

> The sudden loss of power leaves you suddenly, unimaginably empty, facing decompression and a psychic case of the bends. You are assailed, however unnaturally, by self-doubt. And by continuous thought of the decisions that now lack your guiding hand. Worst of all, and least expected, you are now naked to your enemies.[30]

Thus when Galbraith was asked by Arthur Schlesinger on behalf of Kennedy if he wished to serve as chairman of the CEA, a post eventually given to Walter Heller, he refused. "I was little enchanted by the thought of doing with slight authority, what I had done with vast power twenty years earlier," he said.[31] Galbraith, in other words, as an unrepentantly old-fashioned New Deal socialist, saw the job of the new economist policymaker fundamentally as planning the national economy. So did his fellow new economists, although their rhetoric, as we shall see, was couched in more contemporary macroeconomic terms of

---

[29]For a biographical sketch of Harris, see John Kenneth Galbraith, "Seymour Edwin Harris," in idem, *A View from the Stands: Of People, Politics, Military Power and the Arts* (Boston: Houghton Mifflin, 1986), pp. 397–99.

[30]John Kenneth Galbraith, *A Life in Our Times: Memoirs* (New York: Ballantine Books, 1982), p. 190.

[31]Ibid., p. 389.

"stabilizing" the economy and ensuring that its "actual" rate of growth coincided with its "potential" rate of growth.[32]

The New Economics as a Blueprint for Economic Fascism

The new economics provided an elaboration of the theoretical framework of Keynesian economics into the rhetoric of comprehensive economic planning adapted to American political conditions. As Makin and Ornstein astutely note, "the young liberal economists around Kennedy were interested not just in avoiding depression and unemployment. They began to see Keynes's ideas as the basis for a magic formula that could be used to create growth and prosperity by government fiat."[33] Actually, it was not Keynes himself but extreme postwar Keynesians such as Alvin Hansen and Abba Lerner who were the direct forebears of the new economists.[34] It was these economists who developed the doctrine of "functional finance" (Lerner's term), according to which the overriding purpose of the federal budget was to regulate the rate of total spending in the economy in the interest of economic stabilization.

The doctrinal development of the new economics began in earnest in the waning years of the second Eisenhower administration, when younger American Keynesians associated with the left wing of the Democratic Party produced a stream of academic and popular articles that delineated the political–economic principles they were to help implement as government advisers and policymakers in the 1960s. These writings were in part a response to what the new economists saw as the policy inaction of the Eisenhower administration in the face of the recessions of 1958 and 1960, the mediocre growth performance of the United

---

[32]Despite their rhetorical differences, however, Galbraith was considered by the new economists as one of their own. See, for example, James Tobin's description of the differences between himself, Heller, and Galbraith on fiscal policy during the Kennedy administration in James Tobin, *Policies for Prosperity: Essays in a Keynesian Mode*, Peter M. Jackson, ed. (Cambridge, Mass.: MIT Press, 1989), pp. 426–27. Also see Stein, *Presidential Economics*, p. 103.

[33]Makin and Ornstein, *Debt and Taxes*, p. 122.

[34]See for example, Abba Lerner, *Economics of Employment* (New York: McGraw-Hill, 1951) and Alvin H. Hansen, *Monetary Theory and Fiscal Policy* (New York: McGraw-Hill, 1949).

States relative to the Soviet Union during the 1950s, and the bogus missile and technology gaps that were alleged to yawn between the two mega-states at the end of that decade.[35] A few of these articles also attempted to grapple with the intellectual problem presented by the failure of prices to fall during the recession of 1958, a phenomenon that was fundamentally inconsistent with Keynesian theory.[36] Finally, to some degree, the development of this new political economy reflected the partisan sympathies of its Democratic liberal architects, since it served to undermine the widespread perception among the lay public that economic performance under Eisenhower was satisfactory.[37] Thus it was that when the new economists attained positions of influence within the Kennedy administration, they came fully armed with a set of ready-made doctrines that could be put at the service of presidential power to revolutionize the American economy and drive it toward economic planning. The programmatic statement of the new economics appeared in 1962 in the first economic report of the Kennedy administration.[38]

Unlike Keynesian theory, the fundamental concepts and principles of which were esoteric and inaccessible to noneconomists as well as economists trained in pre-Keynesian traditions, the basic doctrine of the new economics was—and was intended to be—straightforward. The new economists saw the molding of public opinion as an important part of the role of economic adviser. In Heller's words, the main task of the economist as presidential adviser is "economic education of, by and for

[35]Wilkins and Friday, eds., *The Economists of the New Frontier* includes programmatic articles by Heller, Tobin, Galbraith, and Ackley, among other new economists.

[36]See, for example, Gardner Ackley, "Administered Prices and the Inflationary Process," in ibid., pp. 114–30; Galbraith, "Market Structure and Stabilization Policy," in ibid., pp. 131–54.

[37]Herbert Stein notes.

[38]The Annual Report of the Council of Economic Advisers, written by Heller, Tobin, and Kermit Gordon, is excerpted in Council of Economic Advisers, "Toward Full Recovery," in *American Fiscal Policy: Experiment for Prosperity*, Lester C. Thurow, ed. (Englewood Cliffs, N.J.: Prentice-Hall, [1962] 1967), pp. 29–50.

presidents."[39] In other words, the new economics was to be taught to the president and then, through both the properly instructed president and his economic advisers directly, to the public.

The key concept of the new economics is "potential output," which refers to the total quantity of goods and services or "real GNP" that would be produced by the economy when labor and other resources are fully employed. During the 1950s and early 1960s, the U.S. economy was considered by the new economists to be operating at full employment and, therefore, performing up to its full potential when the unemployment rate among labor was equal to 4 percent. At this rate of unemployment, the only workers without jobs were either those who were voluntarily unemployed because they were in the process of searching for better jobs that existed or those whose skills currently did not match the requirements of existing jobs. In either case, Keynesian macroeconomic demand management policies could not improve the situation. However, if the unemployment rate rose above 4 percent, then the dread "GNP gap" would emerge, as the economy's actual output declined below its potential output. This gap measuring the excess of potential over actual output at the same time measures the real social costs of unemployment in terms of lost output and also indicates the extent to which "aggregate demand" or total spending must be increased by expansionary government policies to reestablish full employment.[40]

According to the new economists, the cumulative real GNP gap for the decade of the 1950s totaled $175 billion (in 1961 dollars). Even more troubling to them was their perception that the GNP gap had endured without interruption from the end of 1955 to the accession of the Kennedy administration to power in 1961. The gap persisted throughout the entire recovery from the 1958 recession and reached a high of 8 percent of GNP on an annualized basis in the recessionary first quarter of 1961. In light of this, the 1962 annual report of Kennedy's CEA concluded: "We

[39]Heller, *New Dimensions of Political Economy*, p. 26.

[40]For a discussion of the concepts of potential output and the GNP gap, see Arthur Okun, "The Gap between Actual and Potential Output," in Paul A. Samuelson and Robert A. Solow, *The Battle against Unemployment*, Arthur M. Okun, ed. (New York: W.W. Norton and Company, 1965), pp. 13–22; and Council of Economic Advisers, "Toward Full Recovery," in Thurow, *American Fiscal Policy*, pp. 29–41.

face a stubborn problem of chronic slack, and the road to full recovery is a long one."[41]

Thus, the new economists forecast an era of chronic and extravagantly wasteful unemployment of resources for the American economy, unless the federal government under their tutelage intervened with demand management policies on a massive scale. The prescription of the new economists for the elimination of the pesky GNP gap and the "full recovery" of the U.S. economy was for the government to run deficits, deficits and more deficits. As Samuelson put it in 1961:

> In principle, though, there is only one correct rule about budget balance—Smith's Law (not from Adam Smith but Professor Warren Smith from the University of Michigan). It goes as follows:
>
> Smith's Law: There is only one rule about budget balancing, and it is that the budget should never be balanced.
>
> Never? Well, hardly ever. Economic conditions will generally call for either a surplus or a deficit. Only in the transition as the budget is passing from the black to the red (or from the red to the black) should the budget be fleetingly in balance.[42]

Despite Samuelson's purely formal admission that a surplus might be required under certain conditions, Smith's Law in conjunction with the new economists' diagnosis of "chronic slack," implied a sea of red ink on the long road to "full recovery." But Samuelson and his fellow new economists recognized the formidable political obstacle to the implementation of their remedy: the American public's deep-seated ideological commitment to balanced budgets.[43] In an effort to camouflage and

---

[41]Quoted in Arthur F. Burns, "The New Stagnation Theory and Our Current Economic Policies," in Thurow, *American Fiscal Policy*, p. 58.

[42]Paul A. Samuelson, "Functional Fiscal Policy of the 1960s," in Okun, *The Battle against Unemployment*, p. 104.

[43]As Samuelson lamented,

> The real barrier to optimal fiscal policy is not procedural or administrative. It is ideological. . . . The American public simply cannot stomach budget deficits of the size sometimes needed for stability, high employment and growth. Or what is really an indistinguishable variant, the American public cannot be persuaded or persuade itself that such sizable deficits are truly needed and feasible. (Ibid., p. 103)

divert attention from their emphasis on deficit spending, the new economists devised the concept of the "full-employment surplus." As Herbert Stein, a right-wing Keynesian and a critic of the new economics has pointed out, in the early postwar period the orthodox Keynesians rejected the concept of a full-employment budget.[44] This concept had been developed by the more conservative economists associated with the Committee on Economic Development as a benchmark for the "automatic stabilization" policies they favored, but the left-wing Keynesian economists of the early postwar years summarily rejected it on the grounds that there was no compelling reason for the budget to be balanced or in surplus at full employment. However, according to Stein, "The Kennedy team recognized that there might be some people out there who cared about balancing the budget, and for them they offered the comfort that the budget would be balanced at full employment."[45]

According to the new economists, a full-employment budget surplus may exist even when the actual budget is in deficit, if the current situation involves unemployment. The reason is that, as aggregate demand increases and the economy begins to recover, the increased employment and production will generate additional income. Thus, without any change in the tax structure, the rising economic activity and prosperity will cause the federal government to realize a progressive increase in its tax revenues, while enabling it to also restrict its expenditures on unemployment benefits and welfare programs. Once the recovering economy has attained the level of income consistent with full employment and potential output, revenues may very well exceed expenditures so that the budget is now in surplus. This analysis allowed the new economists to disguise their persistent advocacy of pumping up aggregate demand by expanding the actual budget deficit as merely a call for trimming back a

---

[44]Stein himself prefers the term "conservative macroeconomists" to designate those economists who, like himself, accepted Keynes's basic thesis that the market economy left to its own devices was prone to destabilizing fluctuations in aggregate demand but also regarded inflation as potentially as much of a problem as unemployment and believed monetary policy was also an important policy tool in maintaining an optimal level of aggregate demand (*Presidential Economics*, p. 73).

[45]Ibid., p. 107.

full-employment budget surplus that proved too large to sustain full employment. This also allowed the new economists to argue that an actual budget deficit of a given size may, under certain circumstances, prove restrictive rather than stimulative of economic activity, and this certainly suited their purposes in the recession year of 1961.

The rhetorical value of the concept of the full-employment surplus is emphasized in the sympathetic retrospective assessment of the new economics by Keynesian macroeconomists Rudiger Dornbusch and Stanley Fischer:

> The New Economists planned to use fiscal policy as the instrument with which to close the GNP gap. It was important to get across to Congress and the public the idea of the full-employment surplus because the unemployment rate was high in 1961, and the federal budget was in an actual deficit. Any proposals to increase spending or cut taxes would certainly imply a larger deficit if GNP were to remain unchanged. Members of Congress could be relied upon to look with great suspicion on any policy that might increase the budget deficit. By focusing attention on the full-employment budget, the New Economists appropriately succeeded in shifting attention away from the state of the actual budget to concern with how the budget would look at full employment—which had the side benefit of focusing attention on the full employment issue itself.[46]

Unfortunately for the new economists, Congress didn't fully absorb the lesson on deficits they sought to teach. This fact is evinced in a hilarious exchange during a Joint Economic Committee meeting in 1965 between a bewildered and increasingly frustrated Senator William Proxmire and an embarrassed and equivocating Gardner Ackley, by then a member of the Johnson administration's CEA:

> Senator Proxmire. I notice that the national accounts budget has been in deficit . . . until the first quarter of this year. Therefore it is stimulating at this level of unemployment; is that correct?
>
> Mr. Ackley. That is correct in the sense that efforts to reduce this deficit by raising taxes or reducing expenditures would have created even more unemployment. . . .

[46]Rudiger Dornbusch and Stanley Fischer, *Macroeconomics* (New York: McGraw-Hill, 1978), p. 300.

Senator Proxmire. I take it that this means that during this entire period the contribution of the Federal Government has been stimulative.

Mr. Ackley. I think the best measure of the impact of the budget is not the actual figure, which reflects a lot of things, but rather the full-employment budget, and that is why we focus on it.

Senator Proxmire. You can take 3 percent [unemployment], 2 percent, 1 percent, but why not take what is going on right now? . . . Right now it is 4.7 percent. If the national accounts budget is in deficit, is it not clear that the contribution of the Federal Government at this level tends to be stimulative?

Mr. Ackley. It tends to be more stimulative than if the deficit were smaller, or if there were a surplus.[47]

If the full-employment surplus doctrine was concocted to make budget deficits an acceptable tool of stabilization policy, the twin concepts of "fiscal drag" and "fiscal dividend" were invented to justify perennial deficits and continually increasing government expenditures as a permanent feature of a growing economy. Fiscal drag was the term the new economists used to denote the deflationary effect of the automatic increase in tax revenues that resulted when an economy's potential output was growing at a normal rate. With a given tax structure and a constant level of government expenditure, growing incomes would engender additional tax payments, producing an unwarranted and contractionary rise in the full-employment budget surplus, and thereby dragging output and employment below their potential levels. The remedy for this phenomenon, according to the new economists, was for the government to declare a "fiscal dividend" and use the growth-induced increases in tax revenues to increase its expenditures or to reduce tax rates or to combine both policies.

---

[47]Quoted in George Terborgh, *The New Economics* (Washington, D.C.: Machinery and Allied Products Institute, 1968), p. 39. Terborgh characterizes the implications drawn by the new economists from the full-employment surplus doctrine as "a Nietzschean 'transvaluation of values' with a vengeance: deficits may be more restrictive than surpluses, surpluses more stimulative than deficits" (ibid., p. 40).

Thus, the new economists raised the specter of the progressive growth in the full-employment budget surplus—which was as inexorable as the march of time itself—as a rationale to justify a perpetual stream of budget deficits stretching out into the indefinite future. Wrote Heller:

> Bitter experience shows that there is nothing easier than letting the full employment surplus grow. Time, bringing with it ever increasing productivity and rapid additions of young new workers to the labor force . . . will rapidly raise the full-employment surplus unless deliberate and repeated steps are taken to prevent it. . . . Present programs [implemented from 1961 to 1965] have eliminated the full-employment surplus. But in the future it will again and again rear its ugly head in the form of a growing fiscal drag, or its lovely head in the form of recurring fiscal dividends.[48]

For Heller, the prospective "huge growth" in the "lovely" fiscal dividend would mainly be used to expand the size, scope, and power of the federal government via "support for vital new or expanded federal programs; well-timed tax cuts; more generous transfers of funds to hard-pressed state and local governments; perhaps even a helping hand to the social security system."[49]

Heller and the new economists' "new look in fiscal policy" also required an enormous augmentation in presidential power, especially over the tax system. This was necessary to render fiscal policy as flexible as possible in quickly responding to the rapid and unforeseen fluctuations in aggregate demand that are the putative cause of recession and inflation. Consequently, the new economists advocated policies designed "to shorten the period between fiscal decision and fiscal action, either by carefully hedged standby powers for the president or by streamlined congressional procedures, or by some combination of the two."[50] An example of the first was embodied in the request by President Kennedy to Congress in 1962 for authority to make cuts of up to 5 percentage points in individual income tax rates as a means of fighting recession.[51]

[48]Walter Heller, "The Future of Our Fiscal System," in Thurow, *American Fiscal Policy*, p. 169.

[49]Ibid., p. 140.

[50]Heller, *New Dimensions of Political Economy*, p. 102.

[51]Ibid., p. 101.

A second effect of the rhetoric about the full-employment budget surplus was to obfuscate and suppress the all-important question of how the anticipated deficits in the real-world budget were to be financed. In other words, to be effective in closing the GNP gap and counteracting fiscal drag, must it be the case that such budget deficits are "monetized" by the Federal Reserve System? Answering this question openly in the affirmative would naturally open up the new economists to charges of hawking old wine in new bottles, advocating monetary inflation as a panacea for all economic ailments.[52] The new economists of the CEA gingerly addressed this issue in the *Economic Report of the President* of 1963:

> How can the Federal Government raise the money to finance a budget deficit? At one logical extreme—which of course no one seriously contemplates—the Federal Reserve could buy Treasury securities and increase the quantity of bank reserves in an amount equal to the deficit. In this way the reserve base of the banking system would be increased by virtually the entire amount of the deficit, paving the way for a multiple expansion of bank deposits and bank credit. This is the most liquid and most expansionary way of increasing the debt of the Federal Government.
>
> At the other extreme, the Government might finance a deficit while the Federal Reserve permitted no increase in bank reserves. This means that the Treasury would not be able to sell any of its securities, directly or indirectly, to the Federal Reserve Banks. The Treasury would have to sell them either to the public or to the commercial banks; and the banks would be able to buy them only to the extent that they in turn sold other securities to the public or denied loan accommodation to private borrowers.[53]

---

[52]In response to the question posed by Buchanan and Wagner, I believe that this was the reason that the new economists chose to emphasize the "second-best" alternative of the issuance of public debt rather than the creation of money as the source of financing for budget deficits (James M. Buchanan and Richard E. Wagner, *Democracy in Deficit: The Political Legacy of Lord Keynes* [New York: Academic Press, 1977], pp. 32–33).

[53]Quoted in Terborgh, *The New Economics*, p. 53.

Note that the option of financing a budget deficit wholly through the issuance of public debt—that is, without recourse to monetary inflation—is here characterized as an "extreme" position. The unspoken implication, of course, is that the prerequisite for an effectively expansionary fiscal policy is continuing additions to the quantity of money. Indeed, when pressed on this point before the Joint Economic Committee in 1963 by a bemused Senator Paul Douglas, a former economics professor at the University of Chicago, Heller reluctantly and somewhat evasively conceded that an effective policy of deficit financing necessitated monetary inflation. Douglas posed the following question: "[I]f the Federal Reserve Board insisted that the deficit must be met out of the savings of individuals, would not this divert capital from industry and result in no net increase in monetary purchasing power, and, consequently, no net increase in demand?" Heller's response to this query was, "If the policy were . . . to raise interest rates to a point where private spending, capital spending in particular, were depressed by as much as the tax cut expanded spending, surely it would be a self-defeating proposition."[54] In effect, Heller was admitting that expansionary fiscal policy was impotent unless it was supplemented by monetary inflation.

The emphasis of the new economics, however, was not merely on the "short-run" concern of closing the gap between actual and potential GNP and ensuring full employment. It also stressed the importance of achieving and maintaining a high rate of growth of potential output. In Heller's words, "The new economics has made a major shift in economic targetry. . . . Now, the policy focus is centered on the ever-rising potential of the economy, on gap-closing and growth."[55] Makin and Ornstein perceptively characterize the underlying theoretical impetus, which first emerged in the 1950s, for this momentous policy innovation:

> At the time, growth theory was an esoteric, highly mathematical branch of economics, but it was beginning to be seen as a dynamic extension of Keynesian principles. The idea was not just to dampen business cycles but perhaps to alter the

---

[54]Quoted in ibid., p. 55.
[55]Ibid., p. 19.

trajectory—the growth path—of the economy. That involved discovering ways to accelerate capital formation and thereby to increase growth, real wages, and income per capita. To many young economists of the era, it appears that Keynes had discovered the philosopher's stone that could turn base metals into gold.[56]

Since Solow and Tobin were in the vanguard of these Keynesian growth theorists, naturally the goal of high growth strongly conditioned the program of monetary and fiscal policy advocated by the new economists as they assumed positions of influence and power in the Kennedy administration. The "optimal" combination of policies for promoting a stable economy and economic growth, according to the new economists, was one of loose money and tight budgets. Writing in 1961, Samuelson said that he had been preaching such "a two-step program for growth" for half a dozen years.[57] The first step of Samuelson's program consisted of "militant monetary expansion" to drive down interest rates and cheapen credit to business borrowers in order to induce an increase in private investment. The second step involved "austere fiscal policies" in the form of an increase in tax rates relative to "needed government expenditure on current and capital goods and on welfare transfers."[58] According to Samuelson, this fiscal program of chronic overtaxation, to use his term, was necessary to effect "the reduction in consumption needed to release the scarce resources in our postulated full-employment economy that are needed for the induced investment programs."[59] In other words, Samuelsonian "austerity" applied only to the productive American families and businesses who would be forced to bear the burden of the increased taxes to pay for a federal budget surplus that would supposedly succeed in "supplementing private thrift by public thrift." The bloated federal political establishment, in sharp contrast, would be free to continue and even expand the needed"spending programs that benefitted its subsidized military-industrial, agricultural, welfare, and foreign-aid clientele.

---

[56]Makin and Ornstein, *Debt and Taxes*, p. 122.

[57]Samuelson, "Functional Fiscal Policy," pp. 108, 109.

[58]Ibid., p. 109.

[59]Ibid., pp. 109, 110.

The tax-and-spend policies so beloved by politicians of both political parties were thus given a scientific justification in cutting-edge economic theory. But even more momentously, the new economists elaborated Keynesian growth theory into a blueprint for the comprehensive macroeconomic planning of the American economy. In his article entitled "Growth through Taxation," originally published in the *New Republic* in July 1960, Tobin called for monetary and fiscal policies to be employed as instruments for centrally directing the allocation of resources to broad categories of use. Thus, he began his article with the declaration, "The overriding issue of political economy in the 1960s is how to allocate the national output."[60] He went on to frankly suggest, "The question of accelerating economic growth brings the question of allocation to the fore." Tobin posed the general case for a planning solution to this question in the form of two rhetorical questions:

> Can we as a nation, by political decision and governmental action, increase our rate of growth? Or must the rate of growth be regarded fatalistically, the result of uncoordinated decisions and habits of millions of consumers, businessmen and governments, uncontrollable in our kind of society except by exhortation and prayer?[61]

Without any more argumentation than this, Tobin took the intellectual case for macroeconomic central planning as established and went on to present his proposal for its implementation.

Tobin introduced his proposal with the dictum, "To stimulate growth we must somehow engineer two shifts in the composition of actual and potential national output."[62] The first shift was "from private consumption to the public sector." In addition to the stimulus it would provide growth via public investment in education and basic research, this shift was also mandated by the "possibly equally urgent reasons" of "increased defense, increased foreign aid, increased public consumption." The second shift involved a diversion of resources "from private consumption to private investment."

---

[60]James Tobin, "Growth through Taxation," in *Economists of the New Frontier*, Wilkins and Friday, eds., p. 263.

[61]Ibid.

[62]Ibid., p. 265.

To accomplish these two shifts, Tobin prescribed the following "program for growth" designed to "stimulate the desired government and private expenditures" and "discourage consumption."[63] First, federal, state, and local governments would increase expenditures on "education, basic and applied research, urban redevelopment, resource conservation and development, transportation and other public facilities." Second, in order to stimulate private investment, the Federal Reserve and Treasury would cooperate in an "easy money" policy that would make credit cheap and plentiful, especially on long-term capital markets. Also, tax credits for new investment by business and more generous provisions for business income averaging and loss offsets would be incorporated into the corporate income tax code. These last two measures would obviate a reduction in the corporate income tax rate. Third, the requisite restriction of consumption to finance these increased expenditures by government and business would be accomplished by a number of additional tax measures. These included an across-the-board increase in personal income tax rates, increases in state and local taxes, and a limitation on "the privilege of deducting advertising and promotional expenses from corporate income subject to tax." In attempting to reply in advance to the inevitable controversy that this last measure would elicit, Tobin completely ignored the issues of the free-speech rights of business owners and even of microeconomic efficiency. Instead, he sought to justify the restriction on advertising in terms of its efficiency in promoting his macroeconomic central plan, arguing, "From the economic point of view, it absorbs too large a share of the nation's resources; at the same time it generates synthetic pressures for higher consumption."

Tobin concluded his proposal with the emphatic declaration: "Increased taxation is the price of growth." The macroeconomic policy techniques devised by the new economists will thus ensure growth by bringing "under public decision the broad allocation of national output." Moreover, according to Tobin, this macroeconomic foray into central planning of economic activity could be accomplished without recourse to the heavy-handed direct controls of wartime. He gravely warned, however, that the absence of such direct controls put us at a disadvantage vis-à-vis "our communist competitors" in attempting to prevent the allocation of

[63]See ibid., pp. 268–70 for the general outline of this growth program.

increases in per capita income to wasteful spending on personal consumption rather than to such socially beneficial uses as forced saving–investment and government spending on the military establishment. "Since they do not pay out such increases in output as personal incomes in the first place, they do not have the problem of recapturing them in taxes or saving," he wrote.[64]

Routine budget deficits, chronic monetary inflation, confiscatory taxation, and centralized macroeconomic direction of resource allocation were not the only components of economic fascism that the new economists were eager to foist upon the American public. They also urged a vast and permanent increase in the level of spending on the military establishment and on civilian defense projects as a means of closing the alleged "missile gap" with the Soviet Union and both the domestic GNP gap.[65] In an article published in 1958,[66] Tobin criticized the cuts in the defense budget then being undertaken by the Eisenhower administration, arguing that "[t]he unfilled needs of defense are great and they are urgent."[67] From Tobin's Olympian vantage point as a macroeconomic planner, the likely alternative uses of these resources in the civilian sector were frivolous and wasteful. Queried Tobin:

> For what more pressing purposes were these resources released? For research and development of new consumer luxuries, for new plants in which to produce more consumers' goods, old and new, all to be marketed by the most advanced techniques of mass persuasion to a people who already enjoy the highest and most frivolous standard of living in history.[68]

---

[64]Ibid., p. 272.

[65]The charge of a "missile gap" leveled by Democrats against the Eisenhower administration indeed turned out to be bogus, although Kennedy continued to campaign on this issue even after he had been given classified briefings by the Eisenhower administration demonstrating its falsity. See Seymour M. Hersh, *The Dark Side of Camelot* (New York: Little, Brown, 1997), pp. 155–56; Richard Reeves, *President Kennedy: Profile of Power* (New York: Simon and Schuster, 1994), pp. 33, 37, 58–59; and Kenneth Weiher, *America's Search for Economic Stability: Monetary and Fiscal Policy Since 1913* (New York: Twayne Publishers, 1992), p. 120.

[66]James Tobin "Defense, Dollars, and Doctrines," in *The Economists of the New Frontier*, Wilkins and Friday, eds., pp. 42–57.

[67]Ibid., p. 48.

[68]Ibid., p. 46.

These and many additional resources to be extracted from the private sector would be used to much greater advantage not only in repairing the missile gap and equipping U.S. forces to wage conventional wars against local communist aggression but also in constructing shelters against nuclear attack and undertaking a thoroughgoing deconcentration of U.S. industry and subterranean installation of vital industrial plants.

Tobin went on in his article to argue on the basis of Keynesian doctrine that there was nothing to fear from the economic consequences of the institutionalized regime of militarism that he prescribed. We should not shrink from the build-up in the national debt entailed by this program because, in Tobin's words, "Since the debt is, so to speak, within the family, its size can and should be the servant of public policy, not the master."[69] The adverse effect of high government budgets and taxes on American productivity was also nothing to be afraid of because, according to Tobin, from the point of view of national security, "most of our vast production is just thrown away," i.e., on frivolous consumer goods. Furthermore, "the growth of our productive power requires expansion of government activities," such as education, libraries, police protection, highways, etc., and the spending decisions of politicians and bureaucrats are no less rational and efficient than those in the private sector.[70] Finally, the inflationary consequences of inflation "should be avoided by resolute taxation."

But the goal of the new economists to construct a massive welfare–warfare state strictly on the basis of macroeconomic policy hit a snag in the late 1950s. In the three consecutive years from 1958 to 1960, the U.S. price level, as measured by the CPI, rose at annual rates of 1.8 percent, 1.7 percent, and 1.4 percent, respectively. This occurred despite the fact that the corresponding unemployment rates for those years were stuck at recessionary levels of 6.8 percent, 5.5 percent, and 5.5 percent.[71] According to orthodox Keynesian theory, of course, the simultaneous coexistence of inflation and recession, of deficient and excess aggregate demand, was not possible. On the one hand, if aggregate demand were insufficient to maintain actual GNP at its

[69]Ibid., p. 49.

[70]Ibid., pp. 51–52.

[71]Kenneth Weiher, *America's Search for Economic Stability: Monetary and Fiscal Policy Since 1913* (New York: Twayne Publishers, 1992), p. 120.

potential level, the unemployment rate would rise to recessionary levels, and excess capacity would emerge, neutralizing any upward pull on the price level. If, on the other hand, aggregate demand exceeded potential GNP at the existing price level, prices would be pulled up to choke off the excess demand.

Recognizing that recent experience was patently inconsistent with the Keynesian "demand-pull" story of inflation, the new economists in the late 1950s formulated a "cost-push" theory of inflation that seemed to offer a more comfortable fit with the facts. According to this theory, the inflationary process might be initiated by a nonmonetary event, such as an increase in the price of an important input to the production process, like the price of steel or the wage rates of unionized labor. Since important industries in the economy were dominated, according to the new economists, by a few big oligopolistic firms that had the power to "administer" or set their prices irrespective of supply and demand conditions, these cost increases could be passed on to consumers despite the existence of economic slack. As the cost of living began to rise, however, workers, especially unionized workers, would respond by demands for higher wages to compensate for their loss of purchasing power, which would be granted by those firms possessing the power to administer their prices. But of course this would set off another round of increases in the cost of living and so on, resulting in a cost-push spiral of inflation throughout the price structure.

The new economists also incorporated the purely empirical relation depicted by the "Phillips curve" into their explanation of why inflation and underutilization of resources seemed to simultaneously afflict the U.S. economy. The Phillips curve, which the Australian economist A.W. Phillips originally fitted to data for the United Kingdom, postulates a rigid tradeoff between unemployment and inflation based purely on historical observation.[72] Thus a reduction of the rate of unemployment through Keynesian fiscal policy can only come at the cost of an increase in the inflation rate. The new economists Samuelson and Solow adapted the Phillips curve to American data and portrayed it as a menu of given policy choices for macroeconomic

---

[72]A.W. Phillips, "The Relation Between Unemployment and the Rate of Change of Money Wages in the United Kingdom, 1861–1957," in *Macroeconomic Readings*, John Lindauer, ed., pp. 107–19.

planners.[73] Thus the planners could choose, say, a 4-percent unemployment rate and a 2-percent annual rate of inflation for the American economy, or by utilizing a more expansionary fiscal policy, they could obtain a 3-percent unemployment rate combined with a 4.5-percent inflation rate.

These theoretical and empirical considerations allowed the new economists to assign blame to the unruly private sector of the economy for the inflationary consequences of their high-employment, high-growth macroeconomic policy. It was the decisions and actions of business executives and laborers that produced the intractable tradeoff between inflation and unemployment and that threatened at any time to precipitate a devastating inflationary wage–price spiral. As a means of taming and shaping up the recalcitrant and uncooperative private sector and rendering it amenable to macroeconomic planning, Kennedy's CEA devised wage–price guideposts, which were unveiled in the 1962 *Economic Report of the President*.[74] According to the guideposts, compliance with which was supposed to be strictly voluntary, the annual increase in wage rates was to be restricted to no more than the yearly increase in the average rate of labor productivity for the economy, then estimated at about 3 percent per year. If the rate of growth in productivity in a particular industry equaled the average rate for the overall economy, then that industry was to keep its prices stable because its per unit labor costs would remain constant. Those industries whose productivity growth rate exceeded the economy's average were instructed to cut their prices to reflect their declining labor costs, while those whose productivity growth rate fell short of the economy's average were permitted to raise their prices in step with the rise in their labor costs. The CEA believed that widespread compliance with the guideposts would improve the Phillips curve tradeoff while neutralizing the threat of a cost-push inflation. This would permit the Kennedy administration to

---

[73]Samuelson and Solow, "Analytical Aspects of Anti-inflation Policy," in ibid., pp. 233–43.

[74]A discussion of these guideposts can be found in Canterbery, *Economics on a New Frontier*, pp. 239–41. For a debate between a new economist and a conservative critic on the efficacy of the guideposts, see Arthur F. Burns and Paul A. Samuelson, *Full Employment: Guideposts and Economic Stability* (Washington, D.C.: American Enterprise Institute for Public Policy Research, 1967).

aggressively undertake expansionary policies that rapidly pushed actual GNP to its potential with very little increase in inflation. As we shall see below, this led to Kennedy's confrontation with the steel industry, in which, in the words of a supporter of the new economics, "Kennedy deployed every weapon conceivable at that time." These weapons went far beyond "moral suasion" to induce voluntary cooperation and included unleashing the awesome police powers of the federal government on a handful of private steel firms.

KENNEDY'S NEW ECONOMICS IN ACTION

Although Kennedy had not completely digested the lessons of the new economics until at least a year after his inauguration, he began to profess its basic principles almost immediately upon assuming the presidency.[75] In his State of the Union address of January 1961, he was already referring to the new economic doctrines on GNP gap and fiscal drag, when he declared in a famous statement: "The present state of our economy is disturbing. We take office in the wake of seven months of recession, three and one-half years of slack, seven years of diminished economic growth, and nine years of falling farm income."[76] In the same month, he urged Heller, his appointee as chairman of the CEA, "to use the White House as a pulpit for public education in economics, especially on the desirable effects of a federal deficit in a recession."[77] Heller and the other new economists heeded this exhortation with great enthusiasm, constantly touting to one and all the benefits of deliberate budget deficits.

In July 1961, during the Berlin crisis, Kennedy's adherence to the new economics, specifically its doctrine of military Keynesianism, was tested. Responding to the Soviet threat to deny the western Allies access to West Berlin, Kennedy sought to increase military expenditures by $3.25 billion, which he initially

---

[75]For details of Kennedy's education in the new economics, see Seymour E. Harris, *Economics of the Kennedy Years and a Look Ahead* (New York: Harper and Row, 1964), pp. 3–5; and Canterbery, *Economics on a New Frontier*, pp. 8–16.

[76]As quoted in Makin and Ornstein, *Debt and Taxes*, pp. 123–24.

[77]Heller notes, however, that at this stage Kennedy's "economic thinking was still in its formative stage" (*New Dimensions of Political Economy*, pp. 26–27).

planned to finance by an increase in taxes.[78] His "Berlin surcharge," which would have raised taxes by $3 billion, was reflexively and vigorously opposed by the new economists. Arguing that the tax increase would abort the incipient recovery from the 1960–61 recession, Heller, Samuelson, and Seymour Harris prevailed upon Kennedy to drop the idea and to accept the resulting deficit as a contribution toward strengthening the fragile recovery.[79] Early in 1962, Samuelson hailed the stabilization results of military Keynesianism, declaring that,

> as a result of two or three upward revisions of our defense budget, and not as a result of a cool decision on the part of the New Team to disregard ideology [of balanced budgets] and prescribe for the nation what its sound economic health required, fiscal 1962 looks to end up with the sizable deficit designed to promote a healthy rate of recovery and expansion.[80]

The Keynesian view of military spending as an engine of economic recovery was recognized and embraced by Kennedy himself in the letter that he wrote for inclusion in the *Economic Report of the President* for 1962. Wrote Kennedy:

> The Federal Budget played its proper role as a powerful instrument for promoting economic recovery . . . major increases in expenditures for national security and space programs became necessary. In a fully employed economy, these increases would have required new tax revenues to match. But I did not recommend tax increases at this point because they would have cut into private purchasing power and retarded the recovery.[81]

The hand of the new economists could also be seen in the revenue-neutral tax bill aimed at stimulating business investment in new capital equipment proposed by the Kennedy administration in the spring of 1961.[82] This bill was an attempt to induce a

---

[78]Anthony S. Campagna, *U.S. National Economic Policy: 1917–1985* (New York: Praeger Publishers, 1987), p. 283, and Canterbery, *Economics on a New Frontier*, pp. 104–05.

[79]Ibid., p. 105–06; and Reeves, *President Kennedy*, pp. 197–98.

[80]Quoted in Canterbery, *Economics on a New Frontier*, p. 106.

[81]Quoted in Lee, *Hands Off*, p. 85.

[82]For details of the bill and the controversy it engendered, see Makin and Ornstein, *Debt and Taxes*, pp. 124–28; and Stein, *Presidential Economics*, pp. 105–06.

more rapid rate of economic growth via macroeconomic planning that would be "costless" in terms of lost revenue to the Treasury. The gist of the bill was that business firms would be given a tax credit for investment in excess of their depreciation allowances, while the tax loopholes on expense account deductions would be closed and the partial tax exemptions on dividends would be repealed. It was also proposed that dividends and interest be subject to withholding and that a limit be imposed on the credit for foreign taxes. Business opposed this attempt at macroeconomic planning because it offered no tax relief and also "seemed capricious and likely to favor limited segments of industry."[83] Needless to say, investors and retirees also vociferously objected to the withholding provisions of the bill, which was only passed in 1962 after thoroughgoing congressional modifications had gutted its "revenue enhancing" provisions and its restriction of the investment tax credit to new investment only. Nevertheless, the bill as initially proposed served to demonstrate the extent of influence of the new economics in the Kennedy administration. Thus, as Makin and Ornstein point out, "The proposal to accelerate economic growth by inducing the increased purchase of specific forms of capital represented a remarkably rapid adoption by government policymakers of ideas that had appeared only five years earlier in esoteric economic journals."[84]

By the beginning of 1962, the economic recovery was still intact, and, according to the CEA, the GNP gap had narrowed from $51 billion in the first quarter of 1961 to $28 billion in the fourth quarter of the year. This was partly due to the fact that the full-employment surplus had fallen from $12.5 billion to $8.25 billion from the latter half of 1960 to the latter half of 1961 as a result of the $4 billion budget deficit in 1961.[85] However, the recovery began to lag early in 1962, and toward the summer the perception among the new economists was that a new recession threatened. They began to actively plump for a substantial cut in taxes that would further reduce the full employment surplus.[86] On June 11, 1962, in a commencement

[83]Makin and Ornstein, *Debt and Taxes*, p. 130.

[84]Ibid., p. 124.

[85]Campagna, *U.S. National Economic Policy*, p. 286; and Heller, *New Dimensions of Political Economy*, p. 72.

[86]Harris, *Economics of the Kennedy Years*, pp. 60–62.

address at Yale University, Kennedy announced his public conversion to the new economics. His speech also marked the initiation of a concerted effort to proselytize the American public into accepting this doctrine.[87]

The theme of the speech was the pernicious influence of entrenched myths on the formulation of public policy, particularly national economic policy. What Kennedy meant by myths was a coherent ideology, and specifically the classical-liberal or limited-government ideology that called for tight constraints on government action in the economic realm. He referred to the tenets and rules of application of this ideology as "the clichés of our forebears" and "a prefabricated set of interpretations."[88] In attacking the myth that "government is big, and bad—and steadily getting bigger and worse," Kennedy argued that "generalities in regard to federal expenditures . . . can be misleading."[89] Hence, federal expenditures may be appropriate in any sector and for any given purpose, and each expenditure must be evaluated on its own merits. Turning to fiscal policy, Kennedy opined that "myths are legion and the truth hard to find."[90] He challenged the "persistent" myth that "federal deficits create inflation and budget surpluses prevent it." He conceded that deficits were sometimes "dangerous" but warned that the same was true for surpluses, and concluded that "honest assessment plainly requires a more sophisticated view than the old and automatic cliché that deficits automatically bring inflation."[91] Last, Kennedy discussed the "problem of confidence," mainly the lack of confidence manifested in the stock market in response to the economic policies of his administration. But according to Kennedy, these "speculative turns of the speculative wheel" are a "false issue."[92] In proclaiming what he perceived as the "simple reality," Kennedy also revealed the fascist vision of a partnership of the various economic sectors under government tutelage

---

[87]John F. Kennedy, "Commencement Address at Yale University, June 11, 1962," in Canterbery, *Economics on a New Frontier*, pp. 331–39.

[88]Ibid., p. 332.

[89]Ibid., p. 334.

[90]Ibid.

[91]Ibid., p. 335.

[92]Ibid.

underlying his new economics of government-led growth: "The solid ground of mutual confidence is the necessary partnership of government with all of the sectors of our society in the steady quest for economic progress."[93] Kennedy concluded that economic decisions should no longer be based on ideological considerations but on the requirements for "the practical management of a modern economy."[94]

Kennedy's speech thus went beyond the standard Keynesian appeal for use of the budget for anti-cyclical purposes to a call for functional finance to promote comprehensive macroeconomic planning of the economy.[95] Thus the speech that Heller hailed as "[Kennedy's] own call for economic independence" was precisely that: a call for the independence of politicians, and particularly those manning the executive branch, from the Constitutional restraints that prevented them from using their coercive power to override the economic plans and choices of individual American citizens that were expressed and coordinated in the outcomes of the market economy. Indeed, Kennedy was intensely interested in applying western European indicative planning techniques to the American economy. In his speech, he noted that western European governments, which are "prepared to face technical problems without ideological preconceptions, can coordinate the elements of a national economy and bring about growth and prosperity." Kennedy went on to urge "the start of a serious dialog [in the U.S.] of the kind which has led in Europe to such fruitful collaboration among all the elements of economic society and to a decade of unrivaled economic progress."[96] And so

[93]Ibid.

[94]Ibid., p. 336.

[95]Perhaps that is why it has been hailed in such glowing terms by left-wing economists and planning advocates. Thus Seymour Harris characterized the speech as "perhaps the most brilliant address on economic issues ever delivered by a President of the United States" (*Economics of the Kennedy Years*, p. 61). Heller gushed, "President Kennedy's landmark speech . . . stands as the most literate and sophisticated dissertation on economics ever delivered by a President" (*New Dimensions of Political Economy*, p. 37). Arthur Okun referred to it as "a memorable commencement address" (*The Political Economy of Prosperity*, p. 45); and the prominent historian of American planning, Otis Graham, acclaimed it as "his remarkable speech on the economy" (*Toward a Planned Society: From Roosevelt to Nixon* [New York: Oxford University Press, 1976]), p. 136.

[96]Canterbery, *Economics on a New Frontier*, pp. 338–39.

we are informed by one of his court historians, Arthur M. Schlesinger, Jr., that this observation on Europe in Kennedy's speech

> reflected his marked interest in the performance of the western European economies. Early in his administration he had charged Heller on his transatlantic trips to report on European planning methods, and he used to cross-examine European visitors to learn the secret of their success. He soon discovered that western Europe was happily free of the American budgetary obsession. . . . The president learned too about European planning of the indirect or "indicative" sort—not centralized physical direction of the economy but the technique of laying down projections for major industries and then persuading everybody to do what was necessary to make the projections come true.

Lacking a principled belief in the sanctity of balanced budgets or of unregulated markets, Kennedy found all this a perfectly rational way to run a modern economy.[97]

The new economists continued to ratchet up the pressure on their protégé for implementation of their expansionary fiscal program. At the end of June 1962, a few weeks after Kennedy's clarion call for corporate statist planning of the economy, Samuelson, reacting to the slowdown of the recovery, "raised the odds on a 1962 recession from 20 percent to even." By mid-July, Samuelson and Solow were calling for temporary emergency tax cuts on top of the existing budget deficit to counteract "the developing recession," and Heller warned of a downturn "before the snow melts."[98] Kennedy, having now fully digested the teachings of the new economics, began to enthusiastically parrot its dogmas in private and in public. In August, Kennedy confided to an old crony, *Chattanooga Times* Washington Correspondent Charles Bartlett: "Everybody talks about our deficit. Everyone wants us to cut spending. They don't seem to understand that it's the deficit, the spending that's keeping the economy pumped up. I love that deficit."[99]

---

[97]Arthur M. Schlesinger, Jr., *A Thousand Days: John F. Kennedy in the White House* (Greenwich, Conn.: Fawcett Publications, 1965), p. 594.

[98]The quotations in the last two sentences are taken from Theodore C. Sorenson, *Kennedy* (New York: Harper and Row, 1965), p. 424.

[99]Quoted in Reeves, *President Kennedy*, pp. 332–33.

At the end of 1962, Kennedy gave a speech to six hundred assembled businessmen and Wall Street financiers at the Economic Club of New York. There, he unveiled his plan for a tax cut despite the existence of a budget deficit. But Kennedy did not try to justify his planned expansion of the budget deficit as a standard anti-recession device because, by December 1962, he realized the pace of the recovery had picked up again and recession no longer loomed.[100] Instead, he defended this plan by invoking the "topsy-turvy" principles of the new economics[101]:

> Surely, the lesson of the last decade is that budget deficits are not caused by wild-eyed spenders but by slow economic growth and periodic recessions. . . . In short, it is a paradoxical truth that tax rates are too high today and tax revenues are too low and the soundest way to raise the revenues in the long run is to lower the rates now.[102]

Afterward, Kennedy reveled in the success of his selling effort on behalf of the new economics: "I gave them straight Heller and Keynes and they loved it. If I can sell it to those guys, I can sell it to anyone."[103] In mid-January 1963, during his State of the Union Address, Kennedy informed Congress of his intention to propose a tax-cut bill. This proposal called for "a revenue cut equal to almost 15 percent of the federal budget" without compensating spending cuts and while the budget was already in deficit.[104] Ted Sorensen, Kennedy's special assistant and another of his court historians, revealed insight into the profound politico-economic implications of the tax cut plan when he chortled that it was

---

[100]Sorenson, *Kennedy*, p. 430.

[101]Abba Lerner, one of the forebears of the new economics, which he labeled "Functional Finance," coined the term "topsy-turvy economics" in the early 1950s. According to Lerner,

> In truth it cannot be denied that the economics of Functional Finance, in its application to a condition of unemployment, is topsy-turvy. . . . Topsy-turvy economics is just what is appropriate for an economy that is suffering from unemployment. (*Economics of Employment*, pp. 142–43)

[102]Quoted in Reeves, *President Kennedy*, p. 453.

[103]Quoted in ibid.

[104]Ibid., p. 452.

one of the boldest and most far-reaching domestic economic measures ever proposed—the $10 billion tax cut bill of 1963, [was] offered without experiencing or even predicting for the immediate future any of the three traditional occasions for a tax cut: a budget surplus, a reduction in spending or a recession.[105]

In the words of Richard Reeves, "The thoughts of Heller and Samuelson were now proposed as the law of the land."[106]

This tax-cut bill, introduced in January 1963, was passed by the House in October but was not enacted as law until it was passed by the Senate in February 1964, after Kennedy had been assassinated. In stumping for its passage, Kennedy hammered home the point that the new-economic revolution he was seeking to orchestrate in economic policy was closely related to the enhancement of U.S. military might and its successful projection abroad.[107] Indeed, Kennedy was now publicly espousing the military Keynesianism propounded by Tobin and the new economists according to which an unbalanced budget would be used to siphon resources out of civilian uses for the aggrandizement of a permanent military establishment. Thus Kennedy's proposed fiscal 1964 budget totaled $98.9 billion, $5 billion more than the fiscal 1963 budget, and this proposed spending increase was coming on the heels of the previous year's budget deficit. Of the $98.9 billion, $55.4 billion would go to the military and another $5.7 billion to the space race and to the funding of covert CIA operations.[108] During his first year in office, Kennedy had exhorted the American people to sacrifice to implement his expanded military agenda, including the militarization of many aspects of social and economic life and of foreign relations: to "pay the price for these programs . . . accept a long struggle . . . share their resources with less fortunate people . . . exercise self-restraint rather than push up wages and prices . . . strive for excellence in their schools, in their cities, in their physical fitness."[109] Wielding the new tool of macroeconomic planning via

[105]Sorensen, *Kennedy*, p. 427.

[106]Reeves, *President Kennedy*, p. 452

[107]Ibid., pp. 452–53.

[108]Ibid., p. 458.

[109]Ibid., p. 136.

budget deficits, Kennedy was now able to impose these sacrifices upon them without their informed consent.

Kennedy had finally and fully grasped that the new economics was indeed the economics of power: the power to vastly increase the resources, scope, and stature of the federal government. This was exemplified by Kennedy's attitude toward an American moon landing, a pet project he intended to complete at all costs as a manifestation to the entire world of the unchallenged technological and military predominance of the American mega-state. Thus when questioned by his Treasury Secretary in 1963 concerning the projected date of the landing, Kennedy replied, "1967. I'd rather unbalance my budget and all the rest."[110]

KENNEDY'S UNHERALDED "MONETARY REVOLUTION" AND THE TRIUMPH OF THE NEW ECONOMICS

Contrary to the fiscal doctrines of the left-wing new economists and of the politico-economic analysis of the Old Right critic of the New Deal, John Flynn, however, it was not ultimately budget deficits that allowed Kennedy to initiate the corporatist planning and militarization of the U.S. economy that bore first fruit in the emergence of the American welfare–warfare state during Johnson's Great Society and culminated in Nixon's fascist New Economic Policy. The policy that facilitated Johnson's simultaneous financing of extravagant expenditures on welfare programs and the military adventure in Vietnam and made conditions ripe for Nixon's imposition of wage and price controls was not newfangled functional finance but old-fashioned monetary inflation. As the historian of macroeconomic policy, Kenneth Weiher, has pointed out, it was not the much-vaunted "fiscal revolution" but the overlooked "monetary revolution" that took place during the Kennedy administration which turned out to be the predominant influence on the economic events of the 1960s and 1970s.[111] As Weiher stated: "There was a revolution all right, but the most important change occurred at the Federal Reserve; however, 10 years passed before more than a handful of people caught on to what was happening."[112]

---

[110]Ibid., p. 457.

[111]Weiher, *America's Search for Economic Stability*, p. 139.

[112]Ibid., p. 138.

In the three years of the Kennedy administration the growth of the money supply as measured by M2 averaged about 8 percent per year. If we take the eleven prior years going back to 1950, the rate of growth of M2 averaged 3.6 percent per year; if we go back four more years, to the first postwar year of 1946, the average annual rate of M2 growth over the fifteen-year period drops to 3.3 percent.[113]

There were basically two reasons why the role of monetary policy tended to be so grossly underplayed in the economic histories of this period. The first was that the new economists themselves, as unreconstructed Keynesians, uniformly denigrated the potency of monetary policy while touting the effectiveness of fiscal policy. Thus the Kennedy tax-cut bill, which did not even take effect until 1964, receives the lion's share of the credit for stimulating the recovery from the 1960–1961 recession. Second, because most economists since the 1930s, including and especially those of Keynesian orientation, identified inflation with increases in the price level, they interpreted the 1.2- percent average annual rate of increase of the CPI during the period 1961–1963 as evidence of the absence of inflation. But in fact, the effect on the price level of the monetary expansion during the Kennedy years was blunted by two factors. The first was the rapid rate of growth in real output that began in 1962 and continued through 1966 and that was partially induced by the monetary inflation itself. The second factor was the substantial increase in the demand for money, or the decline in the "velocity of circulation of money" that occurred from 1960 to 1965. Thus the ratio of nominal GNP—that is, total current dollars spent on final goods and services in the economy per year—to the total money stock as measured by M2 fell from 1.72 in 1960 to 1.57 at the end of 1965, indicating that the public increased the average amount of dollars they held in currency and in checking and savings accounts in relation to their money incomes. These two factors taken together meant that some of the new dollars that were being injected into the economy by the Fed were being diverted from increasing the demands for goods and services in the economy at the same time that the supplies of many of these goods and services were being rapidly augmented.

[113]These monetary growth rates were computed from the data in ibid., pp. 97, 120, 137.

This explains why general prices rose at a much lower rate than the supply of money.[114]

Despite the negligible increase in the CPI, however, the effects of the rapid, and initially unanticipated, monetary inflation were visible in credit markets as real interest rates trended steadily downward throughout the decade.[115] Unfortunately, both Keynesian and central bank orthodoxies of the 1960s focused on the nominal interest rate as an important indicator of the degree of ease or restraint of monetary policy, making no allowance for the effect of inflationary expectations on the nominal interest rate. Consequently, neither the new economists nor the monetary authorities believed that monetary policy was "unduly" expansionary because short-term nominal interest rates rose from 1961 to 1963.[116] Indeed, the new economists were quite pleased with monetary policy during this period, an attitude typified in Seymour Harris's observation that "the [Federal Reserve] board provided the country with a reasonably easy money policy."[117] Harris's judgment was echoed by another Keynesian, George Bach, who chaired a committee of academic monetary economists that began advising the Fed in 1963 and Bach wrote, "Throughout [the Kennedy years], monetary policy was permissive if not aggressively expansionary."[118]

Given that monetary policy was indeed grossly inflationary during the Kennedy years, what accounts for the sudden and radical shift in Federal Reserve policy from the moderate inflationism under the Eisenhower administration? The answer is Kennedy and his new economists, who conducted a relentless and incessant campaign for easy money from the very beginning of his administration. This campaign took the form of repeated public utterances on the part of the president and his economic advisers, as well as direct presidential pressure on William McChesney Martin, who was chairman of the Fed under Eisenhower and continued in that position until 1970.

---

[114]Ibid., pp. 138–43.

[115]Ibid., pp. 145–46.

[116]Sidney Homer, *A History of Interest Rates*, 2nd ed. (New Brunswick, N.J.: Rutgers University Press, 1977), pp. 372–78.

[117]Harris, *Economics of the Kennedy Years*, p. 110.

[118]G.L. Bach, *Making Monetary and Fiscal Policy* (Washington, D.C.: The Brookings Institution, 1971), p. 119.

Even before Kennedy was elected, he began beating the drums for a cheap-money policy. In a press conference in October 1960, then-Senator Kennedy alleged that high interest rates had induced a recession without arresting the inflation.[119] Shortly after his inauguration, in February 1961, Kennedy affirmed the need for low long-term interest rates, while allowing that short-term interest rates could not be reduced due to the balance-of-payments problems the dollar was then mired in. In a July 1963 press conference, Kennedy, while defending his platform pledge of cheap money in the face of rising short-term interest rates, boasted that "mortgage rates and other rates which affect business have dropped since this administration took office." In an address the following day, Kennedy pointed to the contemporary economic recovery as evidence that "a determined effort can succeed in keeping long-term investments and mortgage money plentiful and cheap while boosting short-term interest rates."[120]

Under the influence of the new economists, Kennedy also sought to obscure the link between cheap money and price inflation and to portray inflation as a consequence of the irresponsible behavior of private sectors of the economy. Thus in his January 1962 State of the Union message, Kennedy argued, "Our first line of defense against inflation is the good sense and public spirit of business and labor—keeping their total increases in wages and profits in line with productivity." Similarly, in an April 1963 meeting with newspaper editors, Kennedy contended that the economy was then threatened by deflation, not inflation. He argued that "a wage–price push inflation" could not be sustained given the prevailing levels of unused capacity and high unemployment. Even when Kennedy finally began to express fears about impending inflation, as he did in the following month, he did so in terms of "some concerns over the possibilities of a wage inflation."[121]

Kennedy and key members of his administration also doggedly prodded the Fed, both publicly and privately, to ease monetary policy, even threatening to terminate its independent status if it did not acquiesce. As early as his campaign for the

---

[119]Ibid., p. 114.
[120]Ibid., pp. 112–13.
[121]Ibid., p. 112.

presidency, Kennedy expressed his disappointment with the Fed's tendency to resort to restrictive monetary policy to rein in inflation and his intention to break with such a policy.[122] In April 1962, Kennedy petitioned Congress for a revision of the terms of the Fed chairmanship that would enable each president to nominate a new chairman at the beginning of his term.[123] Heller, Treasury Secretary Dillon, and Treasury Undersecretary Roosa also weighed in with calls for the Fed to ease monetary policy.[124]

Despite some initial foot-dragging and repeated caveats that the Fed would only finance real economic growth and not budget deficits, Fed Chairman Martin ultimately capitulated to the insistent demands of Kennedy and the new economists for a cheap-money policy. In fact, in February 1961, the Fed abandoned its long-standing "bills-only doctrine," which dictated that open market operations be conducted exclusively in the market for short-term securities. In doing so, the Fed was accommodating the administration's request to reduce long-term interest rates by buying long-term securities while simultaneously selling short-term securities in order to nudge up short-term interest rates. This attempt to artificially twist the interest-rate structure—nicknamed Operation Twist—was devised by the new economists to accomplish two goals: to stimulate domestic business investment and new housing purchases and to discourage the outflow of domestic and encourage the inflow of foreign short-term capital as a means of mitigating the U.S. balance-of-payments deficit.[125] Needless to say, this attempt to have one's cake and eat it too—to pursue a domestic cheap-money policy and to avoid its adverse consequences for the balance of payments—was a failure. As Weiher concludes:

> All involved were probably foolish to think the Fed could partition the markets so well as to accomplish this artificial "Operation Twist." . . . In the end, investors were not tricked,

---

[122]Ibid., p. 114.

[123]Ibid.

[124]Ibid., p. 115.

[125]For accounts of Operation Twist, see Campagna, *U.S. National Economic Policy*, pp. 284–85; Canterbery, *Economics on a New Frontier*, pp. 99, 163–65; and Dornbusch and Fischer, *Macroeconomics*, p. 303, n. 9.

and all the Fed accomplished was a significantly higher money supply growth rate.[126]

Our conclusion then is that Kennedy and the new economists succeeded in wringing from the Fed precisely the inflationary monetary policy they desired and that this policy represented a radical break with the monetary policy pursued in the 1950s. This conclusion, which is certainly reflected in the money-supply growth rates cited above, also accords with the perceptions of the new economists themselves. Seymour Harris, long-time Kennedy economic adviser and chief academic consultant to the Kennedy Treasury, made this pellucidly clear in his book on the economic policies of the Kennedy years. Harris concluded that:

> In short, monetary policy under Kennedy was much more expansionist than under Eisenhower. . . .
>
> Federal Reserve policy in 1961–1963 was not like that of 1952–1960. At the early stages of recovery in the 1950s, the Federal Reserve, overly sensitive to inflationary dangers, aborted recoveries. Whether the explanation was the growing conviction that inflation was no longer a threat, or whether it was an awareness that the Kennedy administration would not tolerate stifling monetary policies, the Federal Reserve made no serious attempts to deflate the economy after 1960. In fact, in 1963 Mr. Martin boasted of the large contributions made to expansion.
>
> An examination of rate movements; of purchases of securities by the Federal Reserve; of reductions in reserve requirements; and of inclusion of vault cash as reserves as a means of offsetting gold losses; of financing increased currency in circulation and providing a base for more money creation; and also the high volume of free reserves of commercial banks—all of these point to a degree of cooperation of the Federal Reserve which was lacking in the 1950s.[127]

---

[126]Weiher, *America's Search for Economic Stability*, p. 144. Even the leftist Keynesian economic historian Anthony Campagna admits, "On balance, Operation Twist could be considered only a very modest success at best" (*U.S. National Economic Policy*, p. 285). The monetarist Phillip Cagan, however, "suggests that the Fed merely paid lip service to Operation Twist" (Dornbusch and Fischer, *Macroeconomics*, p. 303, n. 9).

[127]Harris, *Economics of the Kennedy Years*, pp. 120–21.

Thus, inflationary monetary policy was the sine qua non for the regime of permanent budget deficits that was initiated in the early 1960s and continued uninterrupted almost to the end of the twentieth century. That private investment was able to continually expand concurrently with sharply increasing government spending on military and other programs was attributable in large measure to the fact that, during the Kennedy years, the Fed was induced to "cooperate" by routinely monetizing the cumulating budget deficits necessary to finance these programs.

A FORETASTE OF ECONOMIC FASCISM:
KENNEDY'S ASSAULT ON THE STEEL INDUSTRY

The monetary revolution inspired by the doctrines of the new economics had another momentous influence on the thrust of U.S. political economy toward economic fascism. It was during the Kennedy administration that presidential power was brought to bear—for the first time during peacetime—in an attempt to obscure the effects of monetary inflation by politically dictating the prices that private citizens could charge for their wares. During the so-called Steel Crisis of 1962, Kennedy and other members of his administration harassed and threatened the executives of U.S. Steel and a few other steel companies into rescinding an announced price increase that Kennedy's economic advisers considered to be inflationary.

In truth, the roots of the steel crisis lay not in any actions of the steel companies but in the doctrines of the new economics. For as Susan Lee points out:

> Keynesians were always hectoring the Fed to be a little looser in providing money to the economy and hectoring business and workers to hold down prices and wages. In other words, at the same time they were encouraging inflation with a loose monetary policy, they were trying to limit its impact by forbidding management and labor to cope.[128]

The new economists institutionalized such hectoring and scapegoating of business and labor by devising a set of ostensibly voluntary wage and price guideposts that the Kennedy administration would apply in assessing the inflationary impact of private wage agreements and pricing decisions.

---

[128]Lee, *Hands Off*, p. 106.

The steel crisis began in August 1961 when Walter Heller sent Kennedy an absurd memo "warning him that a steel strike or a sharp rise in the price of steel or steelworkers wages, or both, was *the greatest single threat to economic stability during his presidency.*"[129] Heller told Kennedy, "Steel bulks so large in the manufacturing sector of the economy that it can upset the applecart all by itself."[130]

Agitated by Heller's memo, Kennedy wrote an open letter to the major steel companies in September urging them to eschew any price increases after October 1, the date when wage increases negotiated earlier were scheduled to go into effect.[131] It seems the CEA, whose understanding of the technical aspects of steel production was derived from *Popular Mechanics* magazine, had calculated that the steel companies could absorb these wage increases without recourse to a price increase. Steel prices had not increased since the recession year of 1958, although cost pressures had been building and the industry's average rate of return on equity had been substantially below the average for all U.S. manufacturing since that year.[132]

As if presidential interference weren't bad enough, however, the steel companies were treated to economics lectures by the new economists. As Barbara Bergmann, a CEA staff member at the time, recollected, "We lectured them on whether they had made the correct investment decisions and told them they would lose market share [if they raised prices]." The enormity of this intrusion of the federal government into the pricing decisions of a particular industry was later remarked on by Roger Blough, chairman of U.S. Steel, the leader among the twelve major steel producers: "The president's attempt to predetermine the prices of

---

[129]Reeves, *President Kennedy*, p. 294 (emphasis added).

[130]Walter Heller, quoted in ibid.

[131]The ensuing account of the steel crisis is based on the following sources: Campagna, *U.S. National Economic Policy*, pp. 294–96; Reeves, *President Kennedy*, pp. 294–304; Canterbery, *Economics on a New Frontier*, pp. 247–59; Lee, *Hands Off*, pp. 106–08; Schlesinger, *A Thousand Days*, pp. 583–88; Sorensen, *Kennedy*, pp. 443–59; and Harris, *Economics of the Kennedy Years*, pp. 141–43.

[132]Robert W. Crandall, *The U.S. Steel Industry in Recurrent Crisis: Policy Options in a Competitive World* (Washington, D.C.: The Brookings Institution, 1981), pp. 28–29; Canterbery, *Economics on a New Frontier*, pp. 243–44; Lee, *Hands Off*, p. 107.

the steel industry was, to my knowledge, an unprecedented move in the history of our country at peacetime."[133]

In late 1961, Kennedy also began to converse regularly with Blough and David McDonald, president of the United Steelworkers union. Kennedy's objective in these conversations was to persuade them that their restraint in the upcoming contract negotiations was "the key to checking inflation." In February Kennedy began to lobby both sides to initiate early negotiations for a new industry-wide contract that was to go into effect in June. He believed that an early start to negotiations decreased the probability of a strike and that an early contract settlement was less likely to be inflationary. Negotiations between the industry and the union began in February, broke down for a while in March, and came to a successful close on March 31. The contracts between the individual steel companies and the union were signed during the following week. Kennedy was elated because the agreement provided for no increase in wage rates and a rise in fringe benefits of ten cents per hour—overall a 2.5 percent increase in hourly compensation, well within the CEA's productivity guidelines of 3 percent.

Kennedy's elation over his perceived triumph was to be short-lived, however. In the late afternoon of April 10, Blough personally delivered to Kennedy in his White House office a mimeographed copy of a statement released earlier to the press announcing U.S. Steel's intention of raising steel prices by about $6 per ton, or 3.5 percent, effective the following day. Despite the fact that Blough had made no promise to refrain from raising prices, Kennedy was furious and felt that Blough had double-crossed him, undermining his inflation policy, humiliating him personally, and damaging his relations with labor. But it was clear even to Kennedy-insider Arthur Schlesinger that Blough was not attempting to deliberately deceive Kennedy by withholding information about the impending price increase during labor negotiations. Indeed, as Schlesinger incredulously noted, "Blough's whole demeanor suggested a genuine belief that an increase in steel prices was no more the business of government than an increase in the price of the lemonade a child might sell in front of his house."[134] The behavior that

---

[133]Roger Blough, quoted in Lee, Hands Off, p. 107.

[134]Schlesinger, A Thousand Days, p. 584.

Schlesinger interpreted as stemming from political naiveté, however, may have been attributable to Blough's grasp of the fundamental economic principle that the height of prices, whether of steel or of lemonade, were not arbitrarily determined by sellers but crucially dependent on factors influencing market supply and demand, including the quantity of money created by the central bank. Be that as it may, Schlesinger tells us that Kennedy now "was coldly determined to mobilize all the resources of public pressure and private suasion to force steel to rescind the increase."[135] Other commentators on the episode noted that Kennedy "took personal charge of a campaign against U.S. Steel" and "deployed every weapon conceivable at that time."[136]

The next day, Kennedy learned that five more steel companies had matched U.S. Steel's price increase. One of the first weapons Kennedy deployed was an all-out rhetorical assault designed to inflame public opinion against the steel industry. At a previously scheduled press conference that afternoon, Kennedy excoriated "a tiny handful of steel executives whose pursuit of private power and profit exceeds their sense of public responsibility" and "a few gigantic corporations [that] have decided to increase prices in ruthless disregard of their public responsibilities." He proceeded to attribute all manner of evil consequences to their actions, including higher prices for items purchased by every American family and every American business; an exacerbation of U.S. balance-of-payments woes and worsening of the gold outflow, and the threat of an inflationary spiral capable of "eating up the pensions of our older citizens." He also contended that the rise in steel prices jeopardized national security by adding $1 billion to the defense bill, and he darkly and shamelessly insinuated that such an action was unpatriotic, if not treasonous, "when we are confronted by grave crises in Berlin and Southeast Asia . . . when we are asking reservists to leave their homes and families for months on end and servicemen to risk their lives—and four were killed in the last two days in Vietnam." Kennedy concluded his remarks by using his famous inaugural exhortation calling for the sacrifice of the individual citizen's resources and welfare to the purposes of the central

---

[135]Ibid.

[136]Reeves, *President Kennedy*, p. 298; Canterbery, *Economics on the New Frontier*, p. 251.

government as a rhetorical bludgeon against the steel companies: "Some time ago I asked each American to consider what he would do for his country, and I asked the steel companies. In the last twenty-four hours we had their answer."[137] During the question-and-answer period following his remarks, Kennedy continued to cynically play the patriotism card and "even answers to unrelated questions on service wives and Vietnam were related by the president to the actions of the steel companies."[138]

Kennedy's campaign of public vilification of the steel industry extended to arming journalists friendly to the administration with loaded questions for use at Blough's press conference the following day. In addition, cabinet members were assigned statements to make regarding the effects of the steel price rise on their various constituencies. That same evening, Kennedy complained that the *NBC Nightly News with Chet Huntley* was being much too kind to the steel industry, and he reacted by immediately telephoning Newton Minnow, chairman of the Federal Communications Commission. After expressing his dismay at the report in the strongest terms, Kennedy ordered Minnow: "I thought they were supposed to be our friends. I want you to do something about that. You do something about that."[139] In the midst of all this, the Bureau of the Budget prepared an analysis of the steel price increase on gross national product, tax revenues, and the overall budget, concluding that it "would *increase* GNP by (roughly) $2.8 billion to $2.85 billion. Very roughly, then, in fiscal 1963, Budget receipts would *rise* $900 million. Budget expenditures would *rise* $600 million. The Budget surplus would *gain* $300 million."[140] Needless to say, the administration did not release these estimates to the public.

Kennedy, at the behest of his new economic advisers, also sought to exert economic pressure on the industry. Administration officials, including Kennedy himself, contacted their friends and acquaintances at steel companies that had refrained from raising

[137]Kennedy's press conference remarks are reprinted in Canterbery, *Economics on the New Frontier*, pp. 339–41.

[138]Sorensen, *Kennedy*, p. 451.

[139]Reeves, *President Kennedy*, p. 300.

[140]Quoted in ibid. (emphasis added).

prices, particularly Inland Steel Company and Kaiser Steel Corporation, and pressed them to continue to resist following the industry leaders. Defense Secretary McNamara ordered defense contractors to shift their purchases to companies that had not raised their prices and personally ordered that a $5.5 million order for a specialty steel product originally developed by U.S. Steel for the *Polaris* submarine program be given entirely to a small steel company that had not raised its prices. Walter Heller estimated that "the government used so much steel that it could shift as much as 9 percent of the industry's total business away from the six companies that had announced price rises to six that were still holding back."[141]

Not satisfied that the pressure of adverse public opinion and economic sanctions would achieve the goal of an immediate and unconditional price rescission and determined to completely crush their resistance to save face, Kennedy also unleashed on the defiant steel companies the awesome police powers of the federal government. Thus, at Kennedy's behest, his brother, Attorney General Robert Kennedy convened a federal grand jury to investigate charges of price fixing against the steel companies and subpoenaed their records. The pretext of the investigation was a statement attributed by an AP report to the president of Bethlehem Steel at the annual stockholders meeting held just prior to the steel price increase that called into question the wisdom of raising steel prices in the near future. A day later, Edwin Martin, the company's president, denied the report and announced that Bethlehem Steel was matching U.S. Steel's price increases. The Kennedys alleged that Bethlehem Steel's sudden about-face was evidence of illegal collusion. Robert Kennedy ordered FBI agents in Philadelphia and Wilmington to search for evidence of the alleged collusion. According to Robert Kennedy's personal recollections, he told the agents:

> We're going for broke. Their expense accounts and where they'd been and what they were doing . . . I told the FBI to interview them all—march into their offices . . . subpoenaed for their personal records . . . subpoenaed for their company records. . . . We can't lose this.[142]

---

[141]Ibid., p. 298.

[142]Robert Kennedy quoted in ibid., 299.

The FBI agents responded by telephoning steel executives in the middle of the night. They also showed up at the doors of several reporters beginning at 3:00 A.M. on April 12 requesting that they turn over the notes they took while covering Bethlehem Steel's stockholder meeting. The Federal Trade Commission suddenly decided to reexamine the industry's compliance with a 1951 consent decree precluding price collusion, while Democratic Senator Estes Kefauver announced that his Antitrust and Monopoly Subcommittee would probe the pricing policies of the steel industry. President Kennedy himself implied later that the executives of the targeted steel companies were also blackmailed with threats of IRS audits of their expense accounts.[143]

The evening of April 12, Kennedy received word that Blough and U.S. Steel were considering surrender. Ironically, Kennedy was hosting a state dinner for the shah and empress of Iran when he learned of his impending victory over a handful of business firms that had the temerity to violate his futile price guideposts by peacefully exercising their rights to engage in exchange with buyers at a mutually agreeable price. The shah was the head of a U.S. puppet government that had come to power in 1953 as the result of a coup orchestrated and financed by the CIA. From 1954 to 1966, the U.S. government poured $1.3 billion of taxpayers' funds into Iran to help sustain the shah's government in power, a power that was based largely on the terror and torture tactics of SAVAK, his CIA-trained security police.[144] The next morning, April 13, Inland Steel and Kaiser Steel announced that they would hold the line on prices. One hour after Kaiser Steel's announcement, Bethlehem Steel announced that it was rescinding its price increases. Finally, at 5:30 that evening, U.S. Steel issued a press release revoking its price increases.

Unlike Nixon's much more thoroughgoing attempt to control prices through political dictation a decade later, Kennedy's assault on the steel industry elicited politically discerning commentary from across American society. For example, George

---

[143]Ibid., pp. 301–02, 304.

[144]On the deep involvement of the U.S. government in Iranian affairs after World War II, see Richard Barnet, *Intervention and Revolution: The United States in the Third World* (New York: World Publishing, 1971), pp. 225–29; and Jonathan Kwitny, *Endless Enemies: The Making of an Unfriendly World* (New York: Congdon and Weed, 1984), pp. 179–204.

McDougal, the vice president of a construction company in Greenville, South Carolina, remarked, "I just figured that this is the way Hitler took over."[145] Milton Friedman wrote, "It brings home dramatically how much power for a police state resides in Washington," while David Lawrence, the editor of *U.S. News and World Report* courageously referred to the "'quasi-Fascism' . . . [that] had led the public into believing that price increases are sinful or unpatriotic."[146] A cartoon published in the now-defunct *New York Herald Tribune* showed Kennedy Press Secretary Pierre Salinger reporting back to his boss after his recent trip to Moscow: "Khrushchev says he liked your style in the steel crisis."[147] Finally, the president of Pittsburgh Steel, Allison R. Maxwell, Jr., incisively commented during a speech: "This administration is heading toward a form of socialism in which the pretense of private property is retained while, in fact, prices, wages, production and distribution are dictated by bureaucrats."[148]

As one sympathetic commentator presciently concluded in 1969,

> By the end of a momentous week in 1962, Kennedy had seemingly unleashed all the potential power of the presidency on the steel industry, and the reverberations of his attack may last for another decade. . . . [T]he political action itself established a precedent for direct intervention by the executive branch against highly concentrated economic power when that power is believed to threaten the public interest. In the months to follow, President Lyndon B. Johnson was to use this power repeatedly, it became part of the Kennedy legacy.[149]

Two years after these words were written, Nixon used presidential power on a grand scale to implement thoroughgoing wage-and-price controls that foisted a regime of economic fascism on U.S. society. Sadly, by this time, the experience with the new economics and the accelerating monetary inflation it had

---

[145]Quoted in Reeves, *President Kennedy*, p. 298.

[146]Quoted in ibid., p. 303.

[147]Cited in ibid.

[148]Quoted in ibid., p. 316.

[149]Canterbery, *Economics on a New Frontier*, pp. 247, 259.

loosed on American society had so changed the ideological climate that almost no one, with the exception of Murray Rothbard, protested or even recognized the radical change that was being perpetrated in the economic system.

20

THE MANAGERIAL
PRESIDENT

PAUL GOTTFRIED

L egend has it that the U.S. was founded incipiently, if not explicitly as a presidential government. Whether this tendency was already present in the minds of the Founders or whether it emerged as a historical destiny to be ecstatically embraced, an executive regime is what we supposedly were meant to be. An entire school of American historical writing, which has dominated public education since mid-century, elevates presidential power to the skies. Identified with academic celebrities Arthur Schlesinger, Clinton Rossiter, William Leuchtenburg, James M. Burns, and John Morton Blum, this American historiography treats what was best in our past as the work of activist presidents.[1] Individually and collectively, these presidents led our country toward what intellectuals wanted it to be: a social democratic experiment bringing the benefits of our reformed society to a still unredeemed world. This mission is essential to presidential government as conceived by mainstream historians, and all the major conflicts into which our leaders thrust us from the Civil War on, with the possible exception of the

---

[1]Among works that best represent this presidential hagiography are James MacGregor Burns, *Roosevelt: The Lion and the Fox* (New York: Harcourt, Brace, 1956); Arthur M. Schlesinger's trilogy, *The Age of Roosevelt* (Boston: Houghton Mifflin, 1956–1960); William E. Leuchtenburg, *Franklin D. Roosevelt and the New Deal* (New York: Harper Torch Books, 1963); idem, *In the Shadow of FDR: from Harry Truman to Ronald Reagan* (Ithaca, N.Y.: Cornell University Press, 1983); idem, *The National Experience* in two parts, contributors John M. Blum, Edmund S. Morgan, Willie Lee Rose, Arthur M. Schlesinger, Kenneth M. Stampp, and C. Vann Woodward, 5th ed. (New York: Harcourt Brace Jovanovich, 1981), particularly the second volume; Richard E. Neustadt, *Presidential Power* (6th printing, New York: New American Library, 1964); and Clinton Rossiter, *The American Presidency* (New York: New American Library, 1956).

Spanish–American War, are seen as morally desirable actions. Though the Vietnam War occasioned doubts for at least some of these historians, who have never been as anticommunist as they are antifascist and Teutonophobic, the story line has stayed largely the same. International involvement is mandated by morality and our global position, and only those who suffer from Richard Hofstadter's "paranoid style of politics" or Gregory Fossedal's isolationist impulse reject America's rendezvous with destiny.[2] In Schlesinger's scenario, the U.S., as fashioned by Wilson, Franklin Roosevelt, and Truman, defines and upholds a "vital center" positioned between two ominous extremes: communism and what is a kind of generic "Right." The latter is a sufficiently sweeping category to take in a medley of evils, from anti-New Deal Republicans to Francisco Franco and the shattered remnants of Nazi Europe.[3]

It would be tedious to dwell on this characterization of presidential America for an obvious reason: We all know it well. Most of us have had it drummed into our heads by middle- and high-brow cultures and by American educational institutions. One does not have to visit Mount Rushmore or look at our coins to get the point: The U.S. is a land of morally driven, energetic presidents who have made us into the envy and dread of the world. They have nudged and sometimes pushed us into assuming international leadership while moving the furnishings around in our own national home. In the extreme example of this thesis put forth by Harry Jaffa and Gary Wills, our greatest president—the *sanctus omnium sanctorum* Abraham Lincoln— had to reconstruct our regime and national purpose to provide us with a "second birth in freedom." That is the way these historians understand the Civil War: as a bloody rite of passage into a new America dedicated to democratic equality.[4]

---

[2]See Gregory Fossedal, *Exporting the Democratic Revolution* (New York: Basic Books, 1989).

[3]Arthur M. Schlesinger, Jr., *The Vital Center: The Politics of Freedom* (reprint, New York: Da Capo Press, 1988).

[4]Cf., for example, Harry Jaffa, *Crisis of the House Divided* (Chicago: University of Chicago Press, 1982) and *Equality and Liberty* (New York: Oxford University Press, 1965), particularly pp. 82–84; and Gary Wills, *Lincoln at Gettysburg: The Words that Remade America* (New York: Touchstone Books, 1993).

Such arguments about a presidential America prevailed despite a very different founding, one that mavericks M.E. Bradford, Murray Rothbard, George W. Carey, and Forrest McDonald all have focused on.[5] These and other scholars bring up the embarrassing fact that the authors of the Constitution and *The Federalist Papers* assumed they were establishing a legislative republic. This republic would be dominated at the federal level by Congress, not by the president, and certainly not by what Alexander Hamilton called the "weakest of the three branches," the Supreme Court. The preeminence of the legislature seemed inevitable in a republic, and the Founders devoted more attention to that body than to other branches of government, discussing its powers and limits in Article I. The assignment of a presidential veto, in Article Two, was not intended to allow the president to push around Congress but, as indicated in *Federalist* No. 5, was thought necessary "to allow him to defend himself."[6] The need for such a defense, explained Publius, is undeniable in "purely republican regimes" in which "the tendency of the legislature" to overwhelm the other branches is "almost irresistible." In such situations, representatives "appear disposed to assert an imperious control over the other departments; and as they commonly have the people on their side, they always act with such momentum as to make it very difficult for the other members of the government to maintain the balance of the Constitution." Not belief in a necessary and salutary executive supremacy, but a different assumption—namely, that presidents would be irreparably weak in republican government—caused

---

[5]See, for example, George W. Carey, *The Federalist: Design for a Constitutional Republic* (Urbana: University of Illinois Press, 1990), esp. pp. 154–73; Murray Rothbard, *Conceived in Liberty*, vol. 4, *The Revolutionary War: 1775–1784* (Auburn, Ala.: Mises Institute, 1999); and for me the most compelling indictment of the Wilsonian experiment in presidential dictatorship, "War Collectivism in World War I," in *A New History of Leviathan*, Ronald Radosh and Murray N. Rothbard (New York: G.P. Dutton, 1972). See also Forrest McDonald, *The Presidency of George Washington* (Lawrence: University of Kansas Press, 1974); and M.E. Bradford, *A Worthy Company: Brief Lives of the Framers of the United States Constitution* (Marlborough, N.H.: Plymouth Rock Foundation, 1982); *Original Intentions: On the Making and Ratification of the United States Constitution* (Athens: University of Georgia Press, 1993).

[6]Roy P. Fairchild, ed., *The Federalist Papers*, 2nd ed. (Baltimore, Md.: The Johns Hopkins University Press, 1981), pp. 322–23.

the Founders to assign countervailing powers to the executive in dealing with Congress.

A more considered defense of American executive power, made by Straussian authors Martin Diamond and Harvey Mansfield, is that presidential government, though not mandated by the American Revolution or Constitution, came along in the course of time, and that, these authors say, was a happy turn of events.[7] That turn has contributed to a more just society and to a more peaceful and democratic world, where American influence has been brought to bear. Such a defense typically cites all the happy outcomes attributable to presidential energy: the emancipation of slaves, the victory of democracy in the two world wars, civil rights enforcement, and New Deal initiatives. Without strong executives at the right moments, they tell us, American democracy and democracy in general would not have survived.

It is fairly predictable what old republican critics of such a view would say in response. In fact, the tracts of Murray N. Rothbard, Llewellyn H. Rockwell, Jr., Justin Raimondo, Albert J. Nock, and H.L. Mencken all serve as illustrations. To wit, that overreaching executive power has made a mockery of the rule of law; that socialism by any other name tramples on republican liberty; and that if the U.S. had stayed out of World War I and had not lied its way into it, the European powers might have been forced to make a peace without conquests. Moreover, continues this rejoinder, Lincoln's war against the South's constitutionally defensible (albeit imprudent) secession cost the American people more than six hundred thousand lives as well as the end of the old republic. Although these respondents would differ in their judgments from the promoters of executive energy, they would all agree on the general picture of what has happened. Both sides look at the rise of presidential power as the major political change since the Progressive Era. Both stress that the consolidation of presidential power took place at the expense of Congress, after a long struggle for federal control between

---

[7]Cf. Martin Diamond, "Challenge to the Court," *National Review* 19 (June 13, 1967): 642–44; Harry Jaffa, "The Case for a Stronger National Government," in *A Nation of States: Essays on the American Federal System*, Robert A. Goldwin, ed. (Chicago: University of Chicago Press, 1963), pp. 106–25; and Harvey Mansfield, *Taming the Prince: The Ambivalence of Modern Executive Power* (New York: Free Press, 1989).

these two branches. One might also perceive an overlap in the way the two sides trace presidential ascendancy, from Hamilton's establishment of a central state with centralized banking and a monarchical president to Lincoln's seizure of dictatorial power to the activist, interventionist executives of this century. Though most would disagree with the triumphalist depiction of this process, they would accept the evolutionary course it highlights, from a congressional republic to a presidential empire. The same process is the object of study in James Burnham's postwar monograph on American congressional government. In the late '40s Burnham celebrated the legislative branch as "the one major curb on the expanding executive and unleashed bureaucracy. If Congress ceases to be an active, functioning political institution, then political liberty in the United States will soon come to an end." While Burnham ultimately opted for the imperial presidency as a corollary of the American empire that he thought necessary to oppose Soviet expansion, he nonetheless recognized its Caesarist, anticonstitutionalist feature: "Caesar is the symbolic solution—and the only possible solution—for the problem of realizing the general will, that is, for the central problem of democratist ideology." Furthermore, once the "structure of government" in the modern world, including the U.S., moves away from "the rule of law," the only alternative by the "soaring executive" is Caesarism. For the rule of law represented by an effective Congress to be restored, "individual members of Congress [must] have the courage to say no against the tidal pressures from the executive bureaucracy and the opinion-molders so often allied with them."[8]

This author has no problem with Burnham's strictures about presidential power or with his distinction between a republican rule of law vested in Congress and the ensuing presidential Caesarism. It is equally reasonable to treat early American history as belonging predominantly to the first and most of our more recent history as betokening the second. In fact, it may be argued that down to the present century, even vehement assertions of presidential power, e.g., by John Adams in the Alien and Sedition Acts, by Andrew Jackson during the Nullification Controversy

[8] James Burnham, *Congress and the American Tradition* (Chicago: Henry Regnery, 1959), p. 344. See also Frank S. Meyer, "The Revolt Against Congress," *National Review* 1 (May 30, 1956): 9–10.

and by Abraham Lincoln, far more cataclysmically, during the Civil War, did not exhaust the republican framework of our government entirely. Movement back in the direction of congressional authority, shared sovereignty with the states, and effective limits on federal overreach usually followed extraordinary assertions of presidential will.

After the Civil War, when a largely Republican Supreme Court struck down Reconstructionist legislation, brakes were put on the central state, by the central state itself. From the Civil War down to the Progressive Era, with the possible and useful exception of the old Democrat Grover Cleveland, presidential power was at least as restrained as it was in the early republic. It is only in the twentieth century that, save for the Harding–Coolidge anomaly, the presidential momentum has seemed unstoppable. Presidential bureaucracy has reached the density of a middle-sized municipality; presidents initiate war basically at will; and a national media and its academic adjunct advocate even further extensions of presidential prerogative, providing they fit progressive models of social reconstruction. Despite these developments, This writer would suggest a modification of the received conservative view of presidential power. The apparent enhancement of executive authority points to something else. Indeed by now it is principally something else, the expansion of the managerial state.

The American intellectuals and journalists who drool over bumptious executives have no scruples about running down and even unseating presidents when it suits their ends. They will turn around, as Schlesinger and other "liberals" did, and decry the imperial presidency—even when associated with liberal presidents Johnson and Nixon—if they decide they want someone else in the White House. Most of our opponents are no more pro-presidential than the Earl of Warwick was pro-monarchical. They support executives whom they and their friends can jerk around or whom they happen to fancy. It is unfitting to compare such devious opportunists or mere agenda-pushers to divine-right monarchists or to those who, like the German legal scholar Carl Schmitt, believed honestly in executive dictatorship.

Moreover, the executive democracy that our opponents talk up has less and less to do with presidential energy. It does not require willful presidents but demands figureheads who allow the right sorts of strategists to take charge. Those who extolled Clinton's policies would likely have turned on him if he had issued executive orders ending federal antidiscrimination enforcement. What has happened is that most federal adminis- trations are now tied to the executive, so the chattering class prize that branch as the one especially concerned about human rights as opposed to mere republican liberty. This contention is not gainsaid by the fact that President Clinton saved his political neck and enhanced his popularity by exaggerating the size and ferocity of the Religious Right. The relevant question is whether President Clinton would have remained a powerful political force if he had decided to act in a way that offended the media and other parts of the political class. Would he still have enjoyed his level of support inside and outside of the government if, say, he had embarked on the restoration of a constitutionally limited republic, i.e., one that took the Tenth Amendment seriously?

Such rhetorical questions must be asked if we are talking about a plebiscitary caesar of the kind described by James Burn- ham. Such a leader must have real scope for his actions and is the same as someone who merely presides over a managerial empire. This is not to deny that presidents in the past con- tributed to the unmaking of constitutional government, but such is no longer the case because of frantically energetic execu- tives. Our presidents are becoming Scandinavian monarchs, photogenic front men for a managerial dictatorship. While Dan- ish and Swedish kings in the past crushed local liberties and instilled servile habits, their descendants function as decorative art for socialist governments. They make public appearances and dutifully read speeches that are prepared for them by unfail- ingly leftist administrations. In a way, that prefigures the cur- rent American presidency: place-holding monarchs reign while administrators rule.

But our executive may be more problematic. After almost a century of constitutional derailment bringing cumulative power to the office of president, both the possibility and the temptation to abuse that office exist. If the abuser cultivates journalists and the permanent administrative state, he should be able to get away with considerable mischief. Each time the president steps forth to call for collective atonement for racism, sexism, and homophobia, he encounters diminishing public objection and resonant media approval. Today most Americans do not care if the same president who inflicts quotas and sexual harassment suits on other white males takes gross liberties with female employees. What for others is a public disgrace and a costly crime is for him a private matter. For tens of millions of Americans (mostly black and female), it is outrageous that one dares even to judge the current political correct occupant of the Oval Office. Whatever else may have caused this suspension of ethical judgment, it is related to our cult of the president. The German president, who is a largely powerless windbag given to preaching on the burden of German history, does not have the resources to become a Clinton-like deity. He is a proper figurehead intended to be little more. We would do well to imitate this practice and not to allow our executives their present cultic status.

The most that can be said in favor of energetic presidents is that they resemble willful monarchs of centuries past. Because of their unfettered energies and contempt for constitutional restraints, they have increased not only their own influence but the imperial sway of their country. This does not justify adulation for the presidency in general or for its recent depraved place-holder, any more than, say, admiration for William of Orange should predispose one to empower Prince Charles to invade other countries or to punish the sexism of his subjects. An argument can be made that presidents should be forced to accept the original limits on their power. To this the response from Charles Krauthammer and the *Weekly Standard* would be that an emasculated presidency leaves the U.S. vulnerable.[9] This of course begs the question, "vulnerable to what?" Are we speaking of an invasion from Latin America or the incursion of Middle-Eastern terrorists? Both are now happening with presidential support and partly because of the immigration policies endorsed by the conservative opposition. Besides, lamenting a weakened executive branch is a bit like worrying about the future barrenness of teenage recipients of welfare if we discourage underclass fertility. Let's worry about present excesses and not conjure up hypothetical alternative ones! All the same, any attempt to control the presidential mystique will surely fail unless sufficient actions are taken to rein in the federal bureaucracy. Administrative tyranny will continue to rage no matter under what branch of the federal government. It can thrive as easily behind a congressional shield as a presidential one, and it can behave arbitrarily in either case.

---

[9]See, for example, William Kristol, "On the Future of Conservatism," *Commentary* 103 (February, 1997): 32–33; and Charles Krauthammer's "The Lonely Superpower," *The New Republic*, July 29, 1991, pp. 23–27.

One of the most cloying tributes to presidential arrogance ever devised is the deprecation of Dwight Eisenhower in the revised edition of Clinton Rossiter's *The American Presidency*. According to Rossiter, Eisenhower

> came to the office with practically no thoughts about its powers and purposes. . . . He had swallowed a good deal of the propaganda directed at Roosevelt and Truman, and the result was a first year in office during which his view of his powers was not much different from that announced long ago by William Howard Taft.

Rossiter scolds Eisenhower "for asking congressional approval in 1955 for the authority to defend Formosa and the Pescadores." Because of his quaint belief that the president was "under a stern moral obligation" to ask congressional support for the deployment of troops abroad, Eisenhower was willing to "cripple the striking power of the presidency in a sudden crisis." Rossiter believes that "history will likely judge Mr. Eisenhower's leadership to have been the most disappointing of all" because of his failure to expand executive power in two areas: "his abdication of both moral and political leadership in the crisis of integration in the South and his refusal to push steadily for solutions of the crisis of education throughout the union."[10]

Rossiter despises Eisenhower for not going far enough both to impose federal control over learning and to reconfigure the social life of the American South. But what he blames on Eisenhower's "modest conception of the presidency"—the failure to engage in grandiose social engineering—no longer hinges on the person of the chief executive. Rossiter's plans for the American presidency can now go forward at an accelerated rate, because it has been turned over to bureaucrats, judges, and opinion-wrenchers. The presidency has at last been turned into a bureaucracy under Caesar's banner, with a debauched chief of state cast into a mock imperial role.[11]

---

[10]Clinton Rossiter, *The American Presidency*, p. 124.

[11]For a study of the managerial ascendancy in American government and its effects on the presidency, see my *After Liberalism: Mass Democracy in the Managerial State* (Princeton, N.J.: Princeton University Press, 1999), esp. pp. 49–71.

21

THE PRESIDENT AS SOCIAL ENGINEER

MICHAEL LEVIN

In America's tripartite system of government, only Congress is authorized to make social policy. "The will of the people" is to be expressed in laws passed by the people's representatives, thus ensuring that rules are imposed only when a majority, at least, wants them. The application of the law to particular cases will sometimes be unclear; then, the task of interpreting it falls to the judiciary. For its part, the executive branch, headed by the president, exists to enforce the law and ensure that the people's will is realized. There are, of course, limits, too often ignored, to what even democratically elected legislators may do, and a federal system such as ours is supposed to keep most rulemaking local. The point is, such rules as there are, are fixed by legislation.

As American society has become more regulation-ridden, however, the executive has acquired increasing power, so much so that the lines between implementing, influencing, and initiating policy have blurred. By manipulation of the many levers that now lie readily accessible to his hand, a president, with relative ease, can affect aspects of society that should not be under his—or indeed anyone's—control. This state of affairs is especially visible in the area of social engineering, particularly of racial and gender equality.

It is useful to begin by defining "social engineering." For that, it is necessary to distinguish social relations from political relations. Political relations are those involving power, legitimate authority, and subordination. They are not expected to engage the emotions or, except in the case of the individuals exercising power, to afford personal gratification. The relations of policeman to citizen, politician to voter, and, in a metaphorical sense, boss to employee, are political. (That is why we speak of office politics.) Social relations, by contrast, do not involve power, are consensual, are often based upon emotions, and are expected to be a source of satisfaction. Friendship is the standard example. The informal rules governing social relations rest not on law but in great part on mutual expectations—expectations that are held because everyone knows everyone else expects them to be held. Men once doffed their hats to women because everyone expected them to, men knew that everyone expected them to, and everyone knew that men knew this. Social engineering, then, may be defined as the attempt to shape social relations by political means, generally in the service of what is thought to be a higher good. Sex education in public schools, supposedly to discourage extramarital pregnancy, is one example. Another is the war on "sex stereotypes" that requires the presence of women in occupations previously thought unsuitable. Yet another, which is discussed later, is the attempt to normalize homosexuality by upgrading its place in the military. A final example is school integration ordered by the courts in the hope of making children of different races see how similar they are. As the latter examples illustrate, a common government strategy is to constrain behavior so as to alter expectations and thereby change the social rules.

Just as bridge-building requires knowledge of mechanics, all forms of engineering rest on theoretical foundations. Since behavioral science—sociology and psychology—is a creature of the twentieth century, social engineering was virtually unknown before then.[1] Presidential policies of previous eras in particular, whatever their merits, were politically driven. In buying the Louisiana Territory, Jefferson was seeking to enlarge the country, not to work the effects on the American psyche that the westward expansion allegedly had. Even such a Rooseveltian initiative as Social Security seems to have been intended economically, to keep people from destitution in old age, rather than to change how they get along with each other.

The first clear-cut social engineering project undertaken by an American president was Harry Truman's integration of the armed forces after World War II. This action, of course, had its antecedents. The civil rights movement was already well under way. During World War II, Roosevelt's Executive Order (EO) 8801

---

[1]Virtually every recommendation in Plato's utopian *Republic* is social engineering. Historically, Jacobin hopes of creating equality by renaming the months fit the definition; the first serious bid to reengineer society was Soviet efforts to make the New Socialist Man.

had prohibited discrimination by government contractors. That order, however, does not appear to have been intended as an attack on basic racial attitudes, and the War Department seldom disciplined the many contractors who ignored it. Truman's goal was more ambitious. In a June 1947 speech to the NAACP on the steps of the Lincoln Memorial, he had already committed to using federal power against not only lynching and the poll tax but the whole "racial caste system." In doing so, Truman crossed an important line. Lynching, a form of violence against persons, is a proper concern of government, as is the franchise— although, arguably, neither is a federal matter. However, "caste systems," insofar as they are extra-statutory arrangements not based on force, are quite a different matter. They reflect voluntary associations and expectations built thereon. They would appear to fall outside the purview of government and certainly of the presidency.

Truman's Executive Order 8991, issued in 1948, integrated the military. (At the same time, he integrated the federal Civil Service and created the Civil Rights Commission.) Although more than a half-century later it is difficult to know precisely why he did so, the question is an important one. As commander-in-chief of the U.S. Armed Forces, the president bears the ultimate responsibility for their morale and efficiency, but improving morale and combat readiness clearly was not Truman's motive. The military was not happy with Truman's edict, with some officers complaining that the military is not a vehicle for social change. It may be relevant that in the aftermath of the war, the Carnegie Foundation was preparing a study, ultimately published as *The American Soldier*, in which sociologist authors urged the integration of the army in the interests of justice and smoother race relations.[2] Although there apparently were no references to this study in any of Truman's speeches or communications to Congress concerning civil rights, it is quite possible that some of the president's advisers were influenced by it.

In any case, Truman's own characterization of his actions qualify them as "social engineering." While he often represented his integration policy as a limited moral and constitutional duty, he equally often expressed a wish for the end of a social system in which "Negroes have been preyed upon by all types of

[2]Samuel Stauffer, et al., *The American Soldier* (Manhattan, Kans.: Sunflower University Press, 1949), vols. 1 and 2.

exploiters, from the installment salesman of clothing, pianos and furniture to the vendors of vice."[3,4] Here he is describing voluntary economic interactions and tastes, matters beyond equality before the law. One can understand Truman's dismay at black addiction to "vice," but taking steps to end it exceeded his constitutional obligations.

Fifteen years after EO 8991 the Department of Defense took two further noteworthy steps: It forbade soldiers to use segregated bus or rail facilities, and it instructed the discipline boards of military bases to declare all segregated businesses off limits. These measures, unnecessary for integrating the military itself, could only have been intended to advance integration in civil society by means of the Defense Department's economic clout. During this period—which included the demobilization after World War II, the Korean War, and the cold war military build-up—millions of military personnel were traveling across the country, making it financially suicidal for any carrier to remain segregated. Likewise, the many bars and restaurants near military bases faced failure if soldiers were denied access to them. Incidentally, the new regulations governing local businesses violated the spirit of the "off-limits" concept, originally a protective device designed, for instance, to keep soldiers from being victimized by bars known to make a practice of rolling drunks. Given this purpose, off-limit orders were usually issued on an ad hoc basis. The new measure was intended solely to end practices founded on customer preference.

The effectiveness of these tactics depended on the size of the military. When in the 1930s the U.S. had fewer than 150,000 men under arms, carriers more easily could have absorbed the loss of military contracts. Few bars, restaurants, and shops needed military custom. It was only because the postwar military commanded many more resources that resistance to it was impossible. This illustrates how the power of the president to influence social behavior is a function of the resources at his disposal. The more he controls, the juicier the carrots he can dangle, and the higher the supplicants for his largesse will jump.

[3]See for example, David McCullough, *Truman* (New York: Simon and Schuster, 1992), p. 587.

[4]From a 1940 speech in Sedalia, Missouri; quoted in William Helm, *Harry Truman* (New York: Duell, Sloan and Pearce, 1947).

An important question is whether federal carrots are genuinely coercive. After all, it will be argued, the government (at least before the Civil Rights Act) was not forcing businesses to integrate; a bar could choose to remain segregated and risk going under, just as it could risk alienating customers by not serving certain brands of beer. But this analogy ignores a difference in the ways in which civilian and military customers pay for services. A civilian who won't patronize a bar that won't serve Blatz is holding back resources acquired consensually. The money is originally his, or was earned in an exchange with its previous owner. But the money held back by the Department of Defense was and is acquired coercively, from taxpayers. The difference is all the more significant as the government's agents circa 1955, largely draftees, were forced into government service. The state must raise its revenues coercively, whether by taxing, collecting tariffs, or some other means, and insofar as its activities are legitimate, so is the coercion needed to finance them. But it is misleading to describe compliance with government regulations to get government business as fully voluntary.

The second exercise of presidential power is affirmative action, and it contains no lingering ambiguity. It cannot be interpreted as enforcing any law or neglected provision of the Constitution. It was meant, rather, to bring about, by the use of public revenue as bait, a racial and eventually sexual equality in wealth and status that had never existed previously—on the apparent assumption that forcing this equality would somehow make it voluntary and permanent.

The flood of litigation, referenda, and contention that affirmative action has produced tends to obscure its virtual lack of a statutory basis. To be sure, numerous federal and state laws reserve some proportion of specific public works contracting for firms owned by blacks or females, set hiring quotas for public employment, or provide start-up aid for "minority" businesses, but no legislature would dare tell private firms across the board to hire fixed numbers of blacks. Hubert Humphrey famously promised in 1964 to eat his hat if the pending Civil Rights Act sanctioned quotas. Likewise, while court-ordered quotas in specific cases are common enough, no judge has ever ordered societywide preferences for nonwhites and women. The entire extant structure rests principally on executive orders issued during the 1960s and 1970s.

The phrase "affirmative action," first used during the Kennedy administration, came to wide public attention under Lyndon Johnson. Speaking in June 1965 at Howard University, Johnson called for racial equality "not just as a right and a theory but . . . as a fact and a result."[5] He memorably compared blacks to a recently shackled runner: "You do not take a person who for years has been hobbled by chains and liberate him, and bring him up to the starting line, and then say, 'You are free to compete with all the others.'" (Those words were actually written, it is said, by Daniel Moynihan.)[6]

Johnson followed up on September 24 of that year with Executive Order 11246, requiring all federal contractors and subcontractors to take "affirmative action to ensure that applicants are employed, and [insure] that employees are treated during employment, without regard to their race, creed, color or national origin."[7] Enforcement fell to the Office of Federal Contract Compliance Programs of the Labor Department. In 1967, Johnson issued EO 11375, extending the forbidden grounds to sex:. In one stroke of the pen, the coverage of affirmative action expanded from 12 percent of the population to 50 percent. Section 202(3) of Subpart A of EO 11246 read: "The contractor will, in all solicitations or advertisements for employees placed by or on behalf of the contractor, state that all qualified applicants will receive consideration for employment without regard to race, creed, color, or national origin," with "sex" added in EO 11375. This provision seems clearly to violate First Amendment protections of freedom of speech and the press. The requirements on federal contractors were soon made more stringent. In 1971, under the so-called Philadelphia Plan, Richard Nixon's Labor Department's Order Number 4 required federal contractors with

---

[5]Clint Bolick, in *The Affirmative Action Fraud* (Washington, D.C.: Cato Institute, 1996), p. 53, gives 1969 as the year in which the labor Department adopted numerical goals and timetables. However, his reference is an article in the *Los Angeles Times* of February 22, 1995.

[6]A useful collection of early affirmative action documents is K. Greenawalt, *Discrimination and Reverse Discrimination* (New York: Knopf, 1983). Greenawalt's introductory essays are useful, but he tends to declare without argument that one or another aspect of the "problem" of race "is national in scope," begging the question of the federal role.

[7]Michael Levin, *Feminism and Freedom* (Transaction: New Brunswick, N.J., 1987), p. 206.

more than fifty employees and $50,000 in federal contracts to set "goals and timetables" for the proper "utilization" of blacks, defined to obtain when "the rates of minority applicants recruited . . . approximate or equal the rate of minorities in the population of each location."[8] Shortly thereafter, Revised Order Number 4 extended "goals and timetables" to women.

Little noticed at the time—and now hardly ever mentioned in histories of the period—the step from EO 11246 to EO 11375 was perhaps Johnson's most momentous. For the first time in human history, throughout which men had supported the women who, in turn, had raised the next generation, the state was actively seeking to replace men by women in the breadwinner role. Where quotas for blacks have been an intense irritant to the sense of justice, quotas for women became part of a reversal of sex roles whose adverse consequences—including a below-replacement birthrate among the white population—are just beginning to be felt. The phrase "social engineering" is almost too modest for this seismic change.

The next extension of the quota reach occurred in 1977, when regulation 45 CFR 80 (1977) of the then-Department of Health, Education, and Welfare prohibited racial or sexual discrimination by any recipient of federal financial assistance. It not only required that any recipient "must take affirmative action to overcome the effects of prior discrimination," but added that

> even in the absence of such prior discrimination, a recipient in administering a program may take affirmative action to overcome the effects of conditions which resulted in limiting participation by persons of a particular race, color, or national origin.[9]

---

[8]Clint Bolick, in *The Affirmative Action Fraud* (Washington, D.C.: Cato Institute, 1996), p. 53, gives 1969 as the year in which the Labor Department adopted numerical goals and timetables. Bolick's reference is to an article in the *Los Angeles Times* of February 22, 1995.

[9]A useful collection of early affirmative action documents is Kent Greenawalt, *Discrimination and Reverse Discrimination* (New York: Alfred A. Knopf, 1983). Greenawalt's introductory essays are useful, but he tends to declare without argument that one or another aspect of the "problem" of race "is national in scope," begging the question of the federal role.

Affirmative action now applied to higher education, and not merely to universities funded directly for, say, government-sponsored research, but those merely enrolling recipients of federal student loans. In 1987, the coverage of the OFCCP regulations was estimated to lie between 16 million and 25 million workers—a figure considerably greater by now; the DHEW regulations added the approximately 12 million students enrolled in American colleges, along with the 400,000 faculty who teach them and supporting staff.[10]

The aftermath of the regulations affecting the university shows how executive initiatives reverberate throughout society. Most conspicuously, getting federal grants and enrolling students receiving federal aid now depended on a university's hiring more blacks and women. Blacks tend to go into Black Studies and newly-invented black subgenres of recognized academic subjects; women, likewise head disproportionately for "Women's Studies" or metastatic feminist growths on normal subjects, like "Gender Politics in Art History." As a result, universities have been forced to hire incompetents to teach rubbish, giving students the impression that what goes on in Black Studies and Women's Studies has something to do with scholarship. Thus is the well of knowledge polluted.

Johnson almost certainly did not have in mind a changed pattern of medical care, but this is now touted as another welcome result of affirmative action. The idea is that black doctors are more inclined than white to practice in slums, so admitting more blacks into medical school enhances the health of blacks generally. Looked at another way, quotas are intended to decrease the number of white doctors, degrading medical care for whites or, equivalently, increasing its cost. There is in fact no evidence that black doctors do prefer black patients, but this is the kind of broad effect affirmative action is intended to have.

Despite appearances, the DHEW's allowance of quotas in the absence of discrimination did not exceed Lyndon Johnson's original rationale, at least as expressed in his chained-runner analogy.[11] After all, the other runners in Johnson's hypothetical race were not the ones who did the shackling, but they were being

---

[10]Michael Levin, *Feminism and Freedom* (New Brunswick, N.J.: Transaction Publishers, 1987), p. 206.

[11]The Nixon Department of Labor Order No. 4 was officially issued to counteract documented labor-union discrimination.

asked to give an opponent a head start. In fact, much of the criticism of affirmative action has centered on this very point: its cost to the innocent. As restitution normally requires that the tortfeasor alone give up what his wrongful act cost his victim, placing the other runners—that is, typical white males—at a relative disadvantage is unjust. It is unjust to give blacks an advantage over whites who never harmed them.

But Johnson's analogy failed in a more serious respect. Whether the traditional, narrow notion of compensation is retained or the concept is so stretched that even the innocent must pay for past wrongdoing, Johnson obscured a key distinction. Like that of every civil-rights advocate of the past fifty years, his rhetoric implicitly conflated private discrimination with discriminatory laws, such as those ordering separate seating by race on public or private conveyances. Whether such laws actually harmed blacks and how, in general, governments should rectify their own past misdeeds are questions that may be debated, but at least Jim Crow laws were state actions, whose bad consequences, whatever they were, can be laid at the feet of the individual states. Private discrimination, sanctioned by freedom of association, is another matter. It is not a harm at all, let alone a compensable harm, but in any case private discrimination is not government action; it implicates the state only in that the state allows it, and if that is enough for the state to step in, the state has a right—indeed, a duty—to rectify any misuse of freedom whatever.

In other words, even if affirmative action retains the fig leaf of restitution, the restitution at which Johnson aimed exceeded anything that government at any level is supposed to pursue. EO 11246 was not meant to return to blacks what had been taken from them or to restore them to a position from which they had been wrongly dislodged, but to penalize and thereby extinguish longstanding patterns of consensual behavior. This is clear even from Johnson's Howard University speech, in which he deplored the fact that fewer than half of black children lived to age eighteen with both parents—a figure that now, thirty-five years after the civil rights revolution Johnson welcomed, is below 20 percent. He blamed that squarely on whites: for "the breakdown of Negro family structure, most of all, white America must accept responsibility," he said.[12] (Apparently no white

---

[12]Quoted in Joseph Califano, *The Triumph and Tragedy of Lyndon Johnson* (New York: Simon and Schuster, 1991), p. 57.

public figure challenged this ignorant canard.) Johnson was out to stabilize marriage and decrease illegitimacy, a goal light-years beyond the faithful execution of the laws.[13]

Affirmative action was not Lyndon Johnson's only effort to remake his society. His symbolic actions were many, including dispatch of Army troops to protect the 1964 Selma, Alabama, civil rights march. The Civil Rights Act of 1964 cannot be held to Johnson's account, as it was an act of Congress, but it would not have passed if not for his extraordinary efforts. During and just prior to Johnson's presidency, executive orders and legislation had placed a wide array of agencies with civil rights responsibilities under the executive branch: the Civil Rights Division of the Justice Department, the U.S. Commission on Civil Rights, the President's Committee on Equal Opportunity in Housing, the President's Committee on Equal Employment Opportunity, the Equal Employment Opportunity Commission, the Community Relations Service in the Commerce Department, and the President's Council on Equal Opportunity. Johnson used them all.

Complementing the bad-cop pressure these agencies brought were good-cop incentive programs, like the National Alliance of Businessmen, a jobs-training program set up in January 1968 in response to the black riots of 1967. Nominally a voluntary effort, businessmen who participated in the NAB were promised government reimbursement for "extraordinary" costs, including those for health services, teaching reading and writing, and counseling in basic work and life skills. No wonder the Ford Motor Company could afford to let one of its executives work full time for the NAB. This tidbit is reported in Joseph Califano's highly sympathetic *The Triumph and Tragedy of Lyndon Johnson*, which also frankly characterizes Johnson's use of the billion-dollar congressional appropriation under the Elementary and Secondary Education Act as a "carrot [and] a sizable stick" to "encourage" compliance with school desegregation.[14]

---

[13]We see a tension, if not an inconsistency, here. Affirmative action for women knowingly weakens the mutual dependence of the sexes, hence the family; yet affirmative action for black women, and much of the rest of the Great Society programs, were intended somehow to strengthen the black family. As things turned out, the centrifugal forces exerted by these programs proved far stronger than the centripetal.

[14]Califano, *The Triumph and Tragedy of Lyndon Johnson*, p. 226, and pp. 70 and 72.

Of the individuals mentioned so far, Truman's motives were the clearest. While he personally regarded some separation of the races as appropriate and natural, his belief that he was obligated as president to pursue integration was, based on the evidence, sincere.[15] Nixon's extension of affirmative action is more opaque. Perhaps he sought to disarm his critics on the Left; perhaps his Labor Secretary George Shultz became convinced that blacks could not prosper on their own. Yet in 1971, the feminist bracketing of women with blacks as victims of oppression was accepted only by intellectuals, who despised Nixon no matter what he did, and Nixon's "silent majority" constituency hardly wanted to smash patriarchy. It appears that his administration slid down the slippery slope of consistency: Once one group's baseless claims to special treatment are accepted, so must be the claims of any other.

It was Johnson's zeal that was most enigmatic. His dealings with black, Mexican, and other ethnic voting blocks in his native Texas were exceptionally corrupt and cynical during his political ascendancy in the 1930s and 1940s.[16] As a congressman in 1947 and a senatorial candidate in 1948, he denounced Truman's civil rights program as "an effort to set up a police state in the guise of liberty."[17] He criticized proposed antilynching laws "because the federal government has no more business enacting a law against one form of murder than against another," and he opposed the creation of a permanent Fair Employment Practices Commission—a step incomparably more modest than quotas—on grounds that "if a man can tell you whom you must hire, he can tell you whom he [sic] cannot employ."[18] Yet Johnson waxed euphoric the day before signing the 1965 Voting Rights Act, telling an aide, "Get a table so people can say . . . This is the table on which LBJ signed the Voting Rights Bill." Afterward he urged

every Negro in this country: You must register. You must vote. [T]he vote is the most powerful instrument ever devised by

---

[15]Rick Hampson, "Private Letters Reveal Truman's Racist Attitudes," *Washington Times*, October 25, 1991.

[16]They are recounted in Robert A. Caro, *The Path to Power* (New York: Vintage, 1983), and *Means of Ascent* (New York: Vintage, 1990).

[17]Caro, *Means*, p. 125.

[18]Ibid., pp. 125 and 196.

man for breaking down injustice and destroying the terrible walls which imprison men because they are different from other men.[19]

Equally strange was Johnson's embrace of feminism, which was even more precocious than Nixon's. His actions remain a puzzle for future psychohistorians.

Where Nixon and Johnson were complex men and Truman was a straightforward one thrown into a world made complex by the A-bomb and the rise of communism, Bill Clinton was simplicity itself, at once devious and transparent.

Clinton's attempt to allow homosexuals to serve openly in the military was a break not only with centuries of military policy but with Judeo-Christian ethics.

There was no mystery here about motives. Clinton had supported homosexuals, and they, in turn, supported him. Among his most prominent backers, for instance, was David Geffen, a wealthy, flamboyantly "out" Hollywood mover. Despite media attempts to portray Clinton as a "centrist" and a "new Democrat," only 39 percent of the white electorate voted for him in 1992, and 43 percent in 1996. He was the first president whose core constituency was minority groups and deviants: blacks, Hispanics, Jews, feminists, lesbians, and, as the activists among them prefer to call themselves, gay men.

Among Clinton's 1992 campaign promises was an executive order forbidding the military to ask applicants about their sexual orientation or to expel servicemen discovered to be homosexual. He assured traditionalists that homosexuals would still be held to all other standards of military conduct, but the operative effect of the proposed order would have been to raise homosexuality to the status of heterosexuality by erasing any distinction in the treatment of the two. If one soldier were allowed to brag in the barracks of seducing a young lady, another could with equal impunity brag about same-sex promiscuity.

Upon election, Clinton moved quickly to keep his promise. At a press conference on January 29, 1993, only nine days after his inauguration, he reported that the issue had been under discussion "over the last few days." In other words, ending the

---

[19]Califano, *The Triumph and Tragedy of Lyndon Johnson*, p. 57.

homosexuality exclusion policy topped Clinton's agenda, a point of great symbolic value to homosexual activists. But what Clinton found in these discussions were career military men so perturbed and congressmen so infuriated by his proposal, that a congressional override of his proposed order seemed inevitable. Eventually, in September 1993, the House and Senate did arrest Clinton's ambitions. In response to this setback, he apologetically announced a six-month delay for further negotiations, the upshot was his "don't ask, don't tell" policy: a homosexual enlistee need not declare his homosexuality and his superiors may initiate no steps to investigate him, but he subjects himself to discharge by declaring his homosexuality or performing certain other acts, such as attempting to marry a person of the same sex.

To gauge more finely what Clinton was up to, we should note that the reasons he gave for his initiative were so obviously flawed as to amount to a wink to homosexual activists that he didn't mean them. These reasons were stated most fully in his January 29, 1993, press conference, and in a speech on July 16 of that year to the joint chiefs of staff.

The press conference began with a non sequitur of head-spinning abruptness: "The issue is not whether there should be homosexuals in the military. Everyone concedes that there are. The issue is whether men and women . . . should be excluded from military service solely on the basis of their status." Compare: "The issue is not whether there should be stock fraud. Everyone concedes that it occurs," or "The issue is not whether there should be racial discrimination. Everyone concedes that it exists." Or, for that matter, "The issue is not whether we should excise that tumor in your pancreas. All your doctors concede it is there. The issue is whether a biological entity ought to be removed solely on the basis of its status."

Clinton muddied the rhetorical waters further by lamenting antihomosexual "witch hunts." This term has become a surprisingly popular device for dismissing any inconvenient inquiry as hysteria—surprising, given that the whole reason the witch hunts of old made no sense was that there weren't any witches, and the belief that there were was completely irrational. Homosexuals, by Clinton's own insistence, are very much in evidence.

After this start, Clinton added that the military spent $50 million in the 1980s to separate about 17,000 homosexuals from the service, a sum he also raised in his July speech. Now, it ill-becomes a president presiding over an annual $1.7 trillion budget to bemoan a yearly expenditure of $50 million. Clinton never complained of the billions spent refitting warships so that women could be deployed on them, redesigning aircraft cockpits and ejection seats to accommodate women, and arranging virtually all facilities to provide the "privacy" women would not need in the sex-blind military that egalitarians said they wanted. The real question was one Clinton begged: If an all-heterosexual military is a good idea, isn't a relatively modest expenditure to keep it so also a good one?

The positive considerations Clinton offered for admitting open homosexuals into the armed services were that everyone otherwise qualified has a right to join the military and that closeted homosexuals have "served with distinction." The question remains how military service can be a right when throughout history it has been viewed as at best an onerous duty and sacrifice. And the necessarily unsystematic record of homosexuals to date fails to reflect the critical fact that they were closeted, assumed by fellow soldiers and superior officers to be heterosexual. Any effects their orientation, were it known, might have had on morale or unit cohesion, were suppressed. Indeed, since homosexuals are already free to enlist so long as they stay in the closet, the contributions they might make—Clinton's ace in the hole—provide no serious reason to alter the status quo. They are free to make those contributions anyway.

Since Clinton was offering homosexuals nothing material that they lacked, his real point must have been to offer them something symbolic—namely, validation. In this man's army, a homosexual would not so much be able to serve, but be able to serve and tell everyone within earshot that he's gay. The only point there could be to allowing this openness was relief of the stigma that taints homosexuality. Clinton wished to confer on homosexuals the gift of legitimacy, not just in the military but absolutely.

Indeed, stigma-relief was the point of prioritizing the exclusion issue in the first place: It gratuitously rammed into the public's face a subject, homosexuality, that in the normal course of events most people never think about, but which homosexual activists want everyone to take as seriously as they do. The sheer fact of constant, unavoidable discussion of a subject such as homosexuality tends to inure people to it, dulling their instinctive, visceral aversion. (L'affair Monica, of course, desensitized the American public about sexual matters once considered unfit for public airing.) One might call this symbolic social engineering.

This was not the only way the Clinton presidency entered the age of symbolism. Clinton conspicuously flouted old precedents and set new ones. Social relations, as was earlier noted, depends on what we think others expect of us, and people have always determined this, in part, by watching salient figures—leaders—whose behavior is considered a reference point to the acceptable. This cuing was once local, for the most part, its effects slowly spreading. But that has changed in the present century. The trendsetting movie star bears witness to the media's immense acceleration of the process, and no one achieved greater celebrity than President Clinton during his tenure in the White House. This happened almost insensibly. One hundred years ago, boys might have wished to model themselves on George Washington's probity, but one can hardly imagine Washington, or, say, James Garfield, being admired for their chicness. But newsreels made people aware of Eisenhower's eponymous jacket, and TV showcased the famous Kennedy style. Now a president's image is inescapable, everywhere.

Clinton exploited this circumstance eagerly. In the interest of egalitarianism, he and the first lady almost never let themselves be photographed in a group without blacks or other minorities. The sole finding of Clinton's highly publicized "Commission on Race" was the perfidy of whites. His favorite author was black, or so he said. He ostentatiously displayed his black best friend. His "spiritual adviser," Jesse Jackson, was black. With great show he appointed women and nonwhites so government would "look like America." By making second-class citizenship for white males less unthinkable, this drumbeat of gestures both instructed white males to prepare for lower status and helped to bring this new condition about.

A president can now influence the broad structure of society because of his power. Did Clinton not oversee a vast federal work force and armed force and did he not control the disbursement of hundreds of billions of dollars, the private sector could have more easily ignored him. His celebrity also would also have shrunk, and, along with it, his capacity to legitimize social deviance.

There is a Bill of Rights to protect certain activities from all government intervention, but this sphere of autonomy has imploded under pressure from federal alphabet agencies issuing regulations where Congress would fear to tread with laws. Most of what these agencies do, from the FDA to the EEOC, should not be done by government at all, by any branch at any level. Indeed, this bureaucracy has grown so large that, as many political scientists have pointed out, it has to some extent captured the presidency itself. Staffed with idealists, that is, ideologies, committed to the mission, these agencies are hard even for the chief executive to control.

Eliminating the regulatory monster would leave a much reduced, much less intrusive presidency. In the penultimate analysis, that job falls to Congress; but in the last analysis, it falls, as it always does in a democracy, to the people.

22

ON THE IMPOSSIBILITY OF LIMITED GOVERNMENT AND THE PROSPECTS FOR A SECOND AMERICAN REVOLUTION

HANS-HERMANN HOPPE

In a recent survey, people of different nationalities were asked how proud they were to be American, German, French, etc., and whether or not they believed that the world would be a better place if other countries were just like their own. The countries ranking highest in terms of national pride were the United States and Austria. As interesting as it would be to consider the case of Austria, we shall concentrate here on the U.S. and the question of whether and to what extent the American claim can be justified.

In the following, we will identify three main sources of American national pride, the first two of which are justified sources of pride, while the third actually represents a fateful error. Finally, we will look at how this error might be repaired.

I

The first source of national pride is the memory of America's not-so-distant colonial past as a country of pioneers.

In fact, the English settlers coming to North America were the last example of the glorious achievements of what Adam Smith referred to as "a system of natural liberty": the ability of men to create a free and prosperous commonwealth from scratch. Contrary to the Hobbesian account of human nature—*homo homini lupus est*—the English settlers demonstrated not just the viability but also the vibrancy and attractiveness of a stateless, anarcho-capitalist social order. They demonstrated how, in accordance with the views of John Locke, private property originated naturally through a person's original appropriation—his purposeful use and transformation—of previously unused land (wilderness). Furthermore, they demonstrated that, based on the recognition of private property, division of labor, and contractual exchange, men were capable of protecting themselves effectively against antisocial aggressors—first and foremost by means of self-defense (less crime existed then than exists now), and as society grew increasingly prosperous and complex, by means of specialization, i.e., by institutions and agencies such as property registries, notaries, lawyers, judges, courts, juries, sheriffs, mutual defense associations, and popular militias.[1] Moreover, the American colonists demonstrated the fundamental sociological importance of the institution of covenants: of associations of linguistically, ethnically, religiously, and culturally homogeneous settlers led by and subject to the internal jurisdiction of a popular leader–founder to ensure peaceful human cooperation and maintain law and order.[2]

[1]On the influence of Locke and Lockean political philosophy on America, see Edmund S. Morgan, *The Birth of the Republic: 1763–89* (Chicago: University of Chicago Press, 1992), pp. 73–74:

> When Locke described his state of nature, he could explain it most vividly by saying that "in the beginning all the World was America." And indeed many Americans had had the actual experience of applying labor to wild land and turning it into their own. Some had even participated in social compacts, setting up new governments in wilderness areas where none had previously existed. (p. 74)

On crime, protection, and defense in particular, see Terry Anderson and P.J. Hill, "The American Experiment in Anarcho-Capitalism: The Not So Wild, Wild West," *Journal of Libertarian Studies* 3, no. 1 (1979); and Roger D. McGrath, *Gunfighters, Highwaymen, and Vigilantes: Violence on the Frontier* (Berkeley: University of California Press, 1984).

[2]Contrary to currently popular multicultural myths, America was decidedly not a cultural "melting pot." Rather, the settlement of the North American continent confirmed the elementary sociological insight that all human societies are the outgrowth of families and kinship systems and hence are characterized by a high degree of internal homogeneity, i.e., that "likes" typically associate with "likes" and distance and separate themselves from "unlikes." Thus, for instance, in accordance with this general tendency, Puritans preferably settled in New England, Dutch Calvinists in New York, Quakers in Pennsylvania and the southern parts of New Jersey, Catholics in Maryland, and Anglicans as well as French Huguenots in the Southern colonies. See further on this David Hackett Fisher, *Albion's Seed: Four British Folkways in America* (New York: Oxford University Press, 1989).

II

The second source of national pride is the American Revolution.

In Europe there had been no open frontiers for centuries, and the intra-European colonization experience lay in the distant past. With the growth of the population, societies had assumed an increasingly hierarchical structure: of free men (freeholders) and servants, lords and vassals, overlords, and kings. While distinctly more stratified and aristocratic than colonial America, the so-called feudal societies of medieval Europe were also typically stateless social orders. A state, in accordance with generally accepted terminology, is defined as a compulsory territorial monopolist of law and order (an ultimate decision-maker). Feudal lords and kings did not typically fulfill the requirements of a state; they could only "tax" with the consent of the taxed, and on his own land every free man was as much a sovereign (ultimate decision-maker) as the feudal king was on his.[3] However,

---

[3]See Fritz Kern, *Kingship and Law in the Middle Ages* (Oxford: Blackwell, 1948); Bertrand de Jouvenel, *Sovereignty: An Inquiry into the Political Good* (Chicago: University of Chicago Press, 1957), esp. chap. 10; idem, *On Power: The Natural History of its Growth* (New York: Viking, 1949); and Robert Nisbet, *Community and Power* (New York: Oxford University Press, 1962).

"Feudalism," Nisbet sums up elsewhere (idem, *Prejudices. A Philosophical Dictionary* [Cambridge, Mass.: Harvard University Press, 1982], pp. 125–31),

> has been a word of invective, of vehement abuse and vituperation, for the past two centuries. . . . [especially] by intellectuals in spiritual service to the modern, absolute state, whether monarchical, republican, or democratic. [In fact,] feudalism is an extension and adaptation of the kinship tie with a protective affiliation with the war band or knighthood. . . . Contrary to the modern political state with its principle of territorial sovereignty, for most of a thousand-year period in the West protection, rights, welfare, authority, and devotion inhered in a personal, not a territorial, tie. To be the "man" of another man, in turn the "man" of still another man, and so on up to the very top of the feudal pyramid, each owing the other either service or protection, is to be in a feudal relationship. The feudal bond has much in it of the relation between warrior and commander, but it has even more of the relation between son and father, kinsman and patriarch. . . . [That is, feudal ties are essentially] private, personal, and contractual relationships. . . . The subordination

in the course of many centuries, these originally stateless societies had gradually transformed into absolute—statist—monarchies. While they had initially been acknowledged voluntarily as protectors and judges, European kings had at long last succeeded in establishing themselves as hereditary heads of state. Resisted by the aristocracy but helped along by the "common people," they had become absolute monarchs with the power to tax without consent and to make ultimate decisions regarding the property of free men.

These European developments had a twofold effect on America. On the one hand, England was also ruled by an absolute king, at least until 1688, and when the English settlers arrived on the new continent, the king's rule was extended to America. Unlike the settlers' founding of private property and their private—voluntary and cooperative—production of security and administration of justice, however, the establishment of the royal colonies and administrations was not the result of original appropriation (homesteading) and contract—in fact, no English king had ever set foot on the American continent—but of usurpation (declaration) and imposition.

On the other hand, the settlers brought something else with them from Europe. There, the development from feudalism to royal absolutism had not only been resisted by the aristocracy but it was also opposed theoretically with recourse to the theory of natural rights as it originated within Scholastic philosophy. According to this doctrine, government was supposed to be contractual, and every government agent, including the king, was subject to the same universal rights and laws as everyone else. While this may have been the case in earlier times, it was certainly no longer true for modern absolute kings. Absolute kings were usurpers of human rights and thus illegitimate. Hence, insurrection was not only permitted but became a duty sanctioned by natural law.[4]

---

of king to law was one of the most important of principles under feudalism.

See also notes 8, 9, and 10 below.

[4]See Lord Acton, "The History of Freedom in Christianity," in idem, *Essays in the History of Liberty* (Indianapolis, Ind.: Liberty Classics, 1985), esp. p. 36.

The American colonists were familiar with the doctrine of natural rights. In fact, in light of their own personal experience with the achievements and effects of natural liberty and as religious dissenters who had left their mother country in disagreement with the king and the Church of England, they were particularly receptive to this doctrine.[5]

Steeped in the doctrine of natural rights, encouraged by the distance of the English king, and stimulated further by the puritanical censure of royal idleness, luxury and pomp, the American colonists rose up to free themselves of British rule. As Thomas Jefferson wrote in the Declaration of Independence, government was instituted to protect life, property, and the pursuit of happiness. It drew its legitimacy from the consent of the governed. In contrast, the royal British government claimed that it could tax the colonists without their consent. If a government failed to do what it was designed to do, Jefferson declared, "it is the right of the people to alter or abolish it, and to institute new government, laying its foundation on such principles, and organizing its powers in such form, as to them shall seem most likely to effect their safety and happiness."

III

But what was the next step once independence from Britain had been won? This question leads to the third source of national pride—the American Constitution—and the explanation as to why this Constitution, rather than being a legitimate source of pride, represents a fateful error.

Thanks to the great advances in economic and political theory since the late 1700s, in particular at the hands of Ludwig von Mises and Murray N. Rothbard, we are now able to give a precise answer to this question. According to Mises and Rothbard, once there is no longer free entry into the business of the production of protection and adjudication, the price of protection and justice will rise and their quality will fall. Rather than being a protector and judge, a compulsory monopolist will

---

[5]On the liberal-libertarian ideological heritage of the American settlers see Murray N. Rothbard, *For A New Liberty* (New York: Collier, 1978), chap. 1; idem, *Conceived in Liberty*, 4 vols. (New Rochelle, N.Y.: Arlington House, 1975); and Bernard Bailyn, *The Ideological Origins of the American Revolution* (Cambridge, Mass.: Harvard University Press, 1967).

become a protection racketeer—the destroyer and invader of the people and property that he is supposed to protect, a warmonger, and an imperialist.[6] Indeed, the inflated price of protection and the perversion of the ancient law by the English king, both of which had led the American colonists to revolt, were the inevitable result of compulsory monopoly. Having successfully seceded and thrown out the British occupiers, it would only have been necessary for the American colonists to let the existing homegrown institutions of self-defense and private (voluntary and cooperative) protection and adjudication by specialized agents and agencies take care of law and order.

This did not happen, however. The Americans not only did not let the inherited royal institutions of colonies and colonial governments wither away into oblivion; they reconstituted them within the old political borders in the form of independent states, each equipped with its own coercive (unilateral) taxing and legislative powers.[7] While this would have been bad enough,

---

[6]This fundamental insight was first clearly stated by the French–Belgian economist Gustave de Molinari in an article published in 1849 (*The Production of Security* [New York: Center for Libertarian Studies, 1977]). De Molinari reasoned:

> That in all cases, for all commodities that serve to provide for the tangible or intangible needs of the consumer, it is in the consumer's best interest that labor and trade remain free, because freedom of labor and trade have as their necessary and permanent result the maximum reduction of price. . . . Whence it follows: That no government should have the right to prevent another government from going into competition with it, or to require consumers of security to come exclusively to it for this commodity (p. 3). . . . If, on the contrary, the consumer is not free to buy security wherever he pleases, you forthwith see open up a large profession dedicated to arbitrariness and bad management. Justice becomes slow and costly, the police vexatious, individual liberty is no longer respected, the price of security is abusively inflated and inequitably apportioned, according to the power and influence of this or that class of consumers. (pp. 13–14)

[7]Furthermore, in accordance with their original royal charter, the newly independent states of Georgia, the Carolinas, Virginia, Connecticut, and Massachusetts, for instance, claimed the Pacific Ocean as their western boundary; and based on such obviously unfounded, usurped ownership claims, they—and subsequently as their "legal" heir the Continental Congress and the United States—proceeded to sell western territories to private

the new Americans made matters worse by adopting the American Constitution and replacing a loose confederation of independent states with the central (federal) government of the United States.

This Constitution provided for the substitution of a popularly elected parliament and president for an unelected king, but it changed nothing regarding their power to tax and legislate. To the contrary, while the English king's power to tax without consent had only been assumed rather than explicitly granted and was thus in dispute,[8] the Constitution explicitly granted this very power to Congress. Furthermore, while kings—in theory, even absolute kings—had not been considered the makers but only the interpreters and executors of preexisting and immutable law, i.e., as judges rather than legislators,[9] the Constitution

---

homesteaders and developers in order to pay off their debt and/or fund current government operations.

[8]See Bruno Leoni, *Freedom and the Law* (Indianapolis, Ind.: Liberty Classics, 1991), p. 118. Leoni here notes that several scholarly commentators on the Magna Charta, for instance, have pointed out that

> an early medieval version of the principle "no taxation without representation" was intended as "no taxation without the consent of the individual taxed," and we are told that in 1221, the Bishop of Winchester, "summoned to consent to a scutage tax, refused to pay, after the council had made the grant, on the ground that he dissented, and the Exchequer upheld his plea."

[9]See Kern, *Kingship and Law in the Middle Ages,* who writes that

> there is, in the Middle Ages, no such thing as the "first application of a legal rule." Law is old; new law is a contradiction in terms; for either new law is derived explicitly or implicitly from the old, or it conflicts with the old, in which case it is not lawful. The fundamental idea remains the same; the old law is the true law, and the true law is the old law. According to medieval ideas, therefore, the enactment of new law is not possible at all; and all legislation and legal reform is conceived of as the restoration of the good old law which has been violated. (p. 151)

Similar views concerning the permanency of law and the impermissibility of legislation were still held by the eighteenth-century French physiocrats such as, for instance, Mercier de la Rivière, author of a book on *L'Ordre Naturel* and one time governor of Martinique. Called upon for advice on how to govern by the Russian Czarina Catherine the Great, de la Rivière is reported to have replied that law must be based

> on one [thing] alone, Madame, the nature of things and man. . . .
> To give or make laws, Madame, is a task which God has left to

explicitly vested Congress with the power of legislating, and the president and the Supreme Court with the powers of executing and interpreting such legislated law.[10]

In effect, what the American Constitution did was only this: Instead of a king who regarded colonial America as his private property and the colonists as his tenants, the Constitution put temporary and interchangeable caretakers in charge of the

---

no one. Ah! What is man, to think of himself capable of dictating laws to beings whom he knows not? The science of government is to study and recognize the laws which God has so evidently engraved in the very organization of man, when He gave him existence. To seek to go beyond this would be a great misfortune and a destructive undertaking. (Quoted in Murray N. Rothbard, *Economic Thought Before Adam Smith: An Austrian Perspective on the History of Economic Thought* [Cheltenham, U.K.: Edward Elgar, 1995], vol. 1, p. 371)

See also de Jouvenel, *Sovereignty*, pp. 172–73 and 189.

[10]The much cherished modern view, according to which the adoption of "constitutional government" represents a major civilizational advance from arbitrary government to the rule of law and which attributes to the United States a prominent or even preeminent role in this historical breakthrough, then, must be considered seriously flawed. This view is not only obviously contradicted by documents such as the Magna Charta (1215) or the Golden Bull (1356) but more important, it misrepresents the nature of pre-modern governments. Such governments either entirely lacked the most arbitrary and tyrannical of all powers, i.e., the power to tax and legislate without consent, or even if they did possess these powers, governments were severely restricted in exercising them because such powers were widely regarded as illegitimate, i.e., as usurped rather than justly acquired. In distinct contrast, modern governments are defined by the fact that the powers to tax and legislate are recognized explicitly as legitimate; that is, all "constitutional" governments, whether in the U.S. or anywhere else, constitute *state*-governments. Robert Nisbet is thus correct in noting that a pre-modern

king may have ruled at times with a degree of irresponsibility that few modern governmental officials can enjoy, but it is doubtful whether, in terms of effective powers and services, any king of even the seventeenth-century "absolute monarchies" wielded the kind of authority that now inheres in the office of many high-ranking officials in the democracies. There were then too many social barriers between the claimed power of the monarch and the effective execution of this power over individuals. The very prestige and functional importance of church, country's monopoly of justice and protection. These caretakers did not own the country, but as long as they were in office, they could make use of it and its residents to their own and their protéges' advantage. However, as elementary economic theory predicts, this institutional setup will not eliminate the self-interest-driven tendency of a monopolist of law and order toward increased exploitation. To the contrary, it only tends to make his exploitation less calculating, more shortsighted, and wasteful. As Rothbard explained:

> while a private owner, secure in his property and owning its capital value, plans the use of his resource over a long period of time, the government official must milk the property as quickly as he can, since he has no security of ownership. . . . government officials own the use of resources but not their capital value (except in the case of the "private property" of a hereditary monarch). When only the current use can be owned, but not the resource itself, there will quickly ensue uneconomic exhaustion of the resources, since it will be to no one's benefit to conserve it over a period of time and to every owner's advantage to use it up as quickly as possible. . . . The private individual, secure in his property and in his capital resource, can take the long view, for he wants to maintain the capital value of his resource. It is the government official who must take and run, who must plunder the property while he is still in command.[11]

---

family, gild, and local community as allegiances limited the absoluteness of the State's power. (*Community and Power*, pp. 103–04)

[11]Murray N. Rothbard, *Power and Market: Government and the Economy* (Kansas City: Sheed Andrews and McMeel, 1977), pp. 188–89. See further on this chaps. 1–3. In light of these considerations—and in contrast to common wisdom on the matter—one reaches the same conclusion regarding the ultimate "success" of the American revolution as H.L. Mencken, *A Mencken Chrestomathy* (New York: Vintage Books, 1982):

> Political revolutions do not often accomplish anything of genuine value; their one undoubted effect is simply to throw out one gang of thieves and put in another. . . . Even the American colonies gained little by their revolt in 1776. For twenty-five years after the Revolution they were in far worse condition as free states than they would have been as colonies. Their government was more expensive, more inefficient, more dishonest, and

Moreover, because the Constitution provided explicitly for "open entry" into state-government—anyone could become a member of Congress, president, or a Supreme Court judge—resistance against state property invasions declined; and as the result of "open political competition" the entire character structure of society became distorted, and more and more bad characters rose to the top.[12] Free entry and competition is not always good. Competition in the production of goods is good, but competition in the production of bads is not. Free competition in killing, stealing, counterfeiting, or swindling, for instance, is not good; it is worse than bad. Yet this is precisely what is instituted by open political competition, i.e., democracy.

In every society, people who covet another man's property exist, but in most cases people learn not to act on this desire or even feel ashamed for entertaining it.[13] In an anarcho-capitalist society in particular, anyone acting on such a desire is considered a criminal and is suppressed by physical violence. Under monarchical rule, by contrast, only one person—the king—can act on his desire for another man's property, and it is this that makes him a potential threat. However, because only he can expropriate while everyone else is forbidden to do likewise, a king's every action will be regarded with utmost suspicion.[14] Moreover, the selection of a king is by accident of his noble birth. His only characteristic qualification is his upbringing as a future king and preserver of the dynasty and its possessions. This does not assure that he will not be evil, of course; at the same time, however, it does not preclude that a king might actually be a harmless dilettante or even a decent person.

---

more tyrannical. It was only the gradual material progress of the country that saved them from starvation and collapse, and that material progress was due, not to the virtues of their new government, but to the lavishness of nature. Under the British hoof they would have got on as well, and probably a great deal better. (pp. 145–46)

[12]See on the following Hans-Hermann Hoppe, *Eigentum, Anarchie und Staat. Studien zur Theorie des Kapitalismus* (Opladen: Westdeutscher Verlag, 1987), pp. 182ff.

[13]See Helmut Schoeck, *Envy: A Theory of Social Behavior* (New York: Harcourt, Brace and World, 1970).

[14]See de Jouvenel, *On Power*, pp. 9–10.

In distinct contrast, by freeing up entry into government, the Constitution permitted anyone to openly express his desire for other men's property; indeed, owing to the constitutional guarantee of "freedom of speech," everyone is protected in so doing. Moreover, everyone is permitted to act on this desire, provided that he gains entry into government; hence, under the Constitution, everyone becomes a potential threat.

To be sure, there are people who are unafflicted by the desire to enrich themselves at the expense of others and to lord it over them; that is, there are people who wish only to work, produce, and enjoy the fruits of their labor. However, if politics—the acquisition of goods by political means (taxation and legislation)—is permitted, even these harmless people will be profoundly affected. In order to defend themselves against attacks on their liberty and property by those who have fewer moral scruples, even these honest, hardworking people must become "political animals" and spend more and more time and energy developing their political skills. Given that the characteristics and talents required for political success—good looks, sociability, oratorical power, charisma, etc.—are distributed unequally among men, then those with these particular characteristics and skills will have a sound advantage in the competition for scarce resources (economic success) as compared with those without them.

Worse still, given that, in every society, more "have-nots" of everything worth having exist than "haves," the politically talented who have little or no inhibition against taking property and lording it over others will have a clear advantage over those with such scruples. That is, open political competition favors aggressive, hence dangerous, rather than defensive, hence harmless, political talents and will thus lead to the cultivation and perfection of the peculiar skills of demagoguery, deception, lying, opportunism, corruption, and bribery. Therefore, entrance into and success within government will become increasingly impossible for anyone hampered by moral scruples against lying and stealing. Unlike kings then, congressmen, presidents, and Supreme Court judges do not and cannot acquire their positions accidentally. Rather, they reach their position because of their proficiency as morally uninhibited demagogues. Moreover, even outside the orbit of government, within civil society, individuals will increasingly rise to the top of economic and financial success, not on account of their productive or entrepreneurial talents or even their superior defensive political talents, but rather because of their superior skills as unscrupulous political entrepreneurs and lobbyists. Thus, the Constitution virtually assures that exclusively dangerous men will rise to the pinnacle of government power and that moral behavior and ethical standards will tend to decline and deteriorate overall.

Moreover, the constitutionally provided "separation of powers" makes no difference in this regard. Two or even three wrongs do not make a right. To the contrary, they lead to the proliferation, accumulation, reinforcement, and aggravation of error. Legislators cannot impose their will on their hapless subjects without the cooperation of the president as the head of the executive branch of government, and the president in turn will use his position and the resources at his disposal to influence legislators and legislation. And although the Supreme Court may disagree with particular acts of Congress or the president, Supreme Court judges are nominated by the president and confirmed by the Senate and remain dependent on them for funding. As an integral part of the institution of government, they have no interest in limiting but every interest in expanding the government's, and hence their own, power.[15]

---

[15]See on this the brilliant and indeed prophetic analysis by John C. Calhoun, *A Disquisition on Government* (New York: Liberal Arts Press, 1953), esp. pp. 25–27. There Calhoun notes that a

> written constitution certainly has many advantages, but it is a great mistake to suppose that the mere insertion of provisions to restrict and limit the powers of the government, without investing those for whose protection they are inserted with the means of enforcing their observance, will be sufficient to prevent the major and dominant party from abusing its powers. Being the party in possession of the government, they will . . . be in favor of the powers granted by the constitution and opposed to the restrictions intended to limit them. As the major and dominant parties, they will have no need of these restrictions for their protection. . . . The minor or weaker party, on the other contrary, would take the opposite direction and regard them as essential to their protection against the dominant party. . . . But where there are no means by which they could compel the major party to observe these restrictions, the only resort left them would be a strict construction of the constitution. . . . To which the major party would oppose a liberal construction—one which would

IV

After more than two centuries of "constitutionally limited government," the results are clear and incontrovertible. At the outset of the American "experiment," the tax burden imposed on Americans was light, indeed almost negligible. Money consisted of fixed quantities of gold and silver. The definition of private property was clear and seemingly immutable, and the right to self-defense was regarded as sacrosanct. No standing army existed, and, as expressed in George Washington's *Farewell Address*, a firm

---

give to the words of the grant the broadest meaning of which they were susceptible. It would then be construction against construction—the one to contract and the other to enlarge the powers of the government to the utmost. But of what possible avail could the strict construction of the minor party be, against the liberal interpretation of the major, when the one would have all the powers of the government to carry its construction into effect and the other be deprived of all means of enforcing its construction? In a contest so unequal, the result would not be doubtful. The party in favor of restrictions would be overpowered. . . . The end of the contest would be the subversion of the constitution . . . the restrictions would ultimately be annulled and the government be converted into one of unlimited powers. . . . Nor would the division of government into separate and, as it regards each other, independent departments prevent this result . . . as each and all the departments—and, of course, the entire government—would be under the control of the numerical majority, it is too clear to require explanation that a mere distribution of its powers among its agents or representatives could do little or nothing to counteract its tendency to oppression and abuse of power.

In sum, then, Rothbard has commented on this analysis,

the Constitution has proved to be an instrument for ratifying the expansion of State power rather than the opposite. As Calhoun saw, any written limits that leave it to government to interpret its own powers are bound to be interpreted as sanctions for expanding and not binding those powers. In a profound sense, the idea of binding down power with the chains of a written constitution has proved to be a noble experiment that failed. The idea of a strictly limited government has proved to be utopian; some other, more radical means must be found to prevent the growth of the aggressive State. (*For A New Liberty*, p. 67)

See also Anthony de Jasay, *Against Politics: On Government, Anarchy, and Order* (London: Routledge, 1997), esp. chap. 2.

commitment to free trade and a noninterventionist foreign policy appeared to be in place. Two hundred years later, matters have changed dramatically.[16] Now, year in and year out, the American government expropriates more than 40 percent of the incomes of private producers, making even the economic burden imposed on slaves and serfs seem moderate in comparison. Gold and silver have been replaced by government-manufactured paper money, and Americans are being robbed continually through money inflation. The meaning of private property, once seemingly clear and fixed, has become obscure, flexible, and fluid. In fact, every detail of private life, property, trade, and contract is regulated and reregulated by ever higher mountains of paper laws (legislation). With increasing legislation, ever more legal uncertainty and moral hazards have been created, and lawlessness has replaced law and order. Last but not least, the commitment to free trade and noninterventionism has given way to a policy of protectionism, militarism, and imperialism. In fact, almost since its beginnings the U.S. government has engaged in relentless aggressive expansionism and, starting with

---

[16]Robert Higgs, *Crisis and Leviathan: Critical Episodes in the Growth of American Government* (New York: Oxford University Press 1987), p. ix, contrasts the early American experience to the present:

> There was a time, long ago, when the average American could go about his daily business hardly aware of the government—especially the federal government. As a farmer, merchant, or manufacturer, he could decide what, how, when, and where to produce and sell his goods, constrained by little more than market forces. Just think: no farm subsidies, price supports, or acreage controls; no Federal Trade Commission; no antitrust laws; no Interstate Commerce Commission. As an employer, employee, consumer, investor, lender, borrower, student, or teacher, he could proceed largely according to his own lights. Just think: no National Labor Relations Board; no federal consumer "protection" laws; no Security and Exchange Commission; no Equal Employment Opportunity Commission; no Department of Health and Human Services. Lacking a central bank to issue national paper currency, people commonly used gold coins to make purchases. There were no general sales taxes, no Social Security taxes, no income taxes. Though governmental officials were as corrupt then as now—maybe more so—they had vastly less to be corrupt with. Private citizens spent about fifteen times more than all governments combined. Those days, alas, are long gone.

the Spanish–American War and continuing past World War I and World War II to the present, the U.S. has become entangled in hundreds of foreign conflicts and risen to the rank of the world's foremost warmonger and imperialist power. In addition, while American citizens have become increasingly more defenseless, insecure, and impoverished, and foreigners all over the globe have become ever more threatened and bullied by U.S. military power, American presidents, members of Congress, and Supreme Court judges have become ever more arrogant, morally corrupt, and dangerous.[17]

What can possibly be done about this state of affairs? First, the American Constitution must be recognized for what it is—an error. As the Declaration of Independence noted, government is supposed to protect life, property, and the pursuit of happiness. Yet in granting government the power to tax and legislate without consent, the Constitution cannot possibly assure this goal but is instead the very instrument for invading and destroying the right to life, property, and liberty. It is absurd to believe that an agency which may tax without consent can be a property protector. Likewise, it is absurd to believe that an agency with legislative powers can preserve law and order. Rather, it must be recognized that the Constitution is itself unconstitutional, i.e., incompatible with the very doctrine of natural human rights that inspired the American Revolution.[18] Indeed, no one in his right mind would agree to a contract that allowed one's alleged protector to determine unilaterally, without one's consent, and irrevocably, without the possibility of exit, how much to charge for protection; and no one in his right mind would agree to an irrevocable contract which granted one's

---

[17]On the growth of U.S. government, and in particular the role of war in this development, see John V. Denson, ed., *The Costs of War: America's Pyrrhic Victories* (New Brunswick, N.J.: Transaction Publishers, 1997); Higgs, *Crisis and Leviathan*; Eckehart Krippendorff, *Staat und Krieg* (Frankfurt/M.: Suhrkamp, 1985), esp. pp. 90–116; Ronald Radosh and Murray N. Rothbard, eds., *A New History of Leviathan* (New York: Dutton, 1972); Arthur A. Ekirch, *The Decline of American Liberalism* (New York: Atheneum, 1967).

[18]For the most forceful statement to this effect see Lysander Spooner, *No Treason: The Constitution of No Authority* (Colorado Springs, Colo.: Ralph Myles, 1973); also Murray N. Rothbard, *The Ethics of Liberty* (New York: New York University Press, 1998), esp. chaps. 22 and 23.

alleged protector the right to ultimate decision-making regarding ones own person and property, i.e., of unilateral law*making*.[19]

Second, it is necessary to offer a positive and inspiring alternative to the present system.

While it is important that the memory of America's past as a land of pioneers and an effective *anarcho-capitalist* system based on self-defense and popular militias be kept alive, we cannot return to the feudal past or the time of the American Revolution. Yet the situation is not hopeless. Despite the relentless growth of statism over the course of the past two centuries, economic development has continued, and our living standards have reached spectacular new heights. Under these circumstances a completely new option has become viable: the provision

---

[19]In fact, any such protection-contract is not only empirically unlikely, but logically praxeologically impossible. By "agreeing-to-be-taxed-and-legislated-in-order-to-be-protected," a person would in effect surrender, or alienate, all of his property to the taxing authority and submit himself into permanent slavery to the legislative agency. Yet any such contract is from the outset impermissible and hence null and void, because it contradicts the very nature of protection-contracts, namely the self-ownership of someone to be protected and the existence of something owned by the protected (rather than his protector), i.e., private—separate—property.

Interestingly, despite the fact that no known state constitution has ever been agreed upon by everyone falling under its jurisdiction, and despite the apparent impossibility that this fact could ever be different, political philosophy, from Hobbes over Locke on down to the present, abounds with attempts to provide a contractual justification for the state. The reason for these seemingly endless endeavors is obvious: either a state can be justified as the outcome of contracts, or it cannot be justified at all. Unsurprisingly, however, this search, much like that for a square circle or a perpetuum mobile, has come up empty and was merely generated a long list of disingenuous, if not fraudulent, pseudo-justifications by means of semantic fiat: "no contract" is really an "implicit," or "tacit," or "conceptual" contract. In short, "no" really means "yes." For a prominent modern example of this Orwellian "newspeak," see James M. Buchanan and Gordon Tullock, *The Calculus of Consent* (Ann Arbor: University of Michigan Press, 1962); James M. Buchanan, *The Limits of Liberty* (Chicago: University of Chicago Press, 1975); and idem, *Freedom in Constitutional Contract* (College Station: Texas A&M University Press, 1977). For a critique of Buchanan and the so-called Public Choice School, see Murray N. Rothbard, *The Logic of Action Two* (Cheltenham, U.K.: Edward Elgar, 1997), chaps. 4 and 17; and Hans-Hermann Hoppe, *The Economics and Ethics of Private Property* (Boston: Kluwer, 1993), chap. 1.

of law and order by freely competing private (profit and loss) insurance agencies.[20]

Even though hampered by the state, insurance agencies protect private property owners upon payment of a premium against a multitude of natural and social disasters, from floods and hurricanes to theft and fraud. Thus, it would seem that the production of security and protection is the very purpose of insurance. Moreover, people would not turn to just anyone for a service as essential as that of protection. Rather, as de Molinari noted,

> before striking a bargain with (a) producer of security, . . . they will check if he is really strong enough to protect them. . . . (and) whether his character is such that they will not have to worry about his instigating the very aggressions he is supposed to suppress.[21]

In this regard insurance agencies also seem to fit the bill. They are big and in command of the resources—physical and human—necessary to accomplish the task of dealing with the dangers, actual or imagined, of the real world. Indeed, insurers operate on a national or even international scale. They own substantial property holdings dispersed over wide territories and beyond the borders of single states and thus have a manifest self-interest in effective protection. Furthermore, all insurance companies are connected through a complex network of contractual agreements on mutual assistance and arbitration as well as a system of international reinsurance agencies representing a combined economic power that dwarfs most if not all contemporary governments. They have acquired this position because of their reputation as effective, reliable, and honest businesses.

While this may suffice to establish insurance agencies as a possible alternative to the role currently performed by states as providers of law and order, a more detailed examination is needed to demonstrate the principal superiority of such an alternative to the status quo. In order to do this, it is only necessary to recognize that insurance agencies can neither tax nor legislate;

---

[20]See on the following also chap. 12; Morris and Linda Tannehill, *The Market for Liberty* (New York: Laissez Faire Books, 1984), esp. chap. 8.

[21]De Molinari, *The Production of Security*, p. 12.

that is, the relationship between the insurer and the insured is consensual. Both are free to cooperate or not to cooperate, and this fact has momentous implications. In this regard, insurance agencies are categorically different from states.

The advantages of having insurance agencies provide security and protection are as follows. First, competition among insurers for paying clients will bring about a tendency toward a continuous fall in the price of protection per insured value, thus rendering protection more affordable. In contrast, a monopolistic protector who may tax the protected will charge ever higher prices for his services.[22]

Second, insurers will have to indemnify their clients in the case of actual damage; hence, they must operate efficiently. Regarding social disasters—crime—in particular, this means that the insurer must be concerned above all with effective prevention, for unless he can prevent a crime, he will have to pay up. Further, if a criminal act cannot be prevented, an insurer will still want to recover the loot, apprehend the offender, and bring him to justice, because in so doing the insurer can reduce his costs and force the criminal—rather than the victim and his

---

[22]As Rothbard has explained, even

> if government is to be limited to "protection" of person and property, and taxation is to be "limited" to providing that service only, then how is the government to decide how much protection to provide and how much taxes to levy? For, contrary to the limited government theory, "protection" is no more a collective, one-lump "thing" than any other good or service in society. . . . Indeed, "protection" could conceivably imply anything from one policeman for an entire country, to supplying an armed bodyguard and a tank for every citizen—a proposition which would bankrupt the society posthaste. But who is to decide on how much protection, since it is undeniable that every person would be better protected from theft and assault if provided with an armed bodyguard than if he is not? On the free market, decisions on how much and what quality of any good or service should be supplied to each person are made by means of voluntary purchases by each individual; but what criterion can be applied when the decision is made by government? The answer is none at all, and such governmental decisions can only be purely arbitrary. (*The Ethics of Liberty*, pp. 180–81)

See also Murray N. Rothbard, *For A New Liberty: The Libertarian Manifesto*, rev. ed. (New York: Collier, 1978), pp. 215ff.

insurer—to pay for the damages and cost of indemnification. In distinct contrast, because compulsory monopolists states do not indemnify victims and because they can resort to taxation as a source of funding, they have little or no incentive to prevent crime or to recover loot and capture criminals. If they do manage to apprehend a criminal, they typically force the victim to pay for the criminal's incarceration, thus adding insult to injury.[23]

Third and most important, because the relationship between insurers and their clients is voluntary, insurers must accept private property as an ultimate given and private property rights as immutable law. That is, in order to attract or retain paying clients, insurers will have to offer contracts with specified property and property damage descriptions, rules of procedure, evidence, compensation, restitution, and punishment, as well as intra- and interagency conflict resolution and arbitration procedures. Moreover, out of the steady cooperation between different insurers in mutual interagency arbitration proceedings, a tendency toward the unification of law—of a truly universal or international law—will emerge. Everyone, by virtue of being insured, would thus become tied into a global competitive effort to minimize conflict and aggression. Every single conflict and damage claim, regardless of where and by or against whom, would fall into the jurisdiction of exactly one or more specific and enumerable insurance agencies and their contractually

---

[23]Comments Rothbard:

> The idea of primacy for restitution to the victim has great precedent in law; indeed, it is an ancient principle of law which has been allowed to wither away as the State has aggrandized and monopolized the institutions of justice. . . . In fact, in the Middle Ages generally, restitution to the victim was the dominant concept of punishment; only as the State grew more powerful . . . the emphasis shifted from restitution to the victim, . . . to punishment for alleged crimes committed "against the State." . . . What happens nowadays is the following absurdity: *A* steals $15,000 from *B*. The government tracks down, tries, and convicts *A*, all at the expense of *B*, as one of the numerous taxpayers victimized in this process. Then, the government, instead of forcing *A* to repay *B* or work at forced labor until that debt is paid, forces *B*, the victim, to pay taxes to support the criminal in prison for ten or twenty years' time. Where in the world is the justice here? (*The Ethics of Liberty*, pp. 86–87)

agreed-to arbitration procedures, thereby creating "perfect" legal certainty. In striking contrast, as tax-funded monopoly protectors, states do not offer the consumers of protection anything even faintly resembling a service contract. Instead, they operate in a contractual void that allows them to make up and change the rules of the game as they go along. Most remarkably, whereas insurers must submit themselves to independent third-party arbitrators and arbitration proceedings in order to attract voluntary paying clients, states, insofar as they allow for arbitration at all, assign this task to another state-funded and state-dependent judge.[24]

[24]Insurance agencies, insofar as they enter into a bilateral contract with each of their clients, fully satisfy the ancient and original desideratum of "representative" government of which Bruno Leoni has noted that "political representation was closely connected in its origin with the idea that the representatives act as agents of other people and according to the latter's will" (*Freedom and the Law*, pp. 118–19 [see also note 8 above]. In distinct contrast, modern democratic government involves the complete perversion—indeed, the nullification—of the original idea of representative government. Today, a person is deemed to be politically "represented" no matter what, i.e., regardless of his own will and actions or that of his representative. A person is considered represented if he votes, but also if he does not vote. He is considered represented if the candidate he has voted for is elected, but also if another candidate is elected. He is represented, whether the candidate he voted or did not vote for does or does not do what he wished him to do. And he is considered politically represented, whether "his" representative's will finds majority support among all elected representatives or not. "In truth," as Lysander Spooner has pointed out,

> voting is not to be taken as proof of consent. . . . On the contrary, it is to be considered that, without his consent having even been asked a man finds himself environed by a government that he cannot resist; a government that forces him to pay money, render service, and forego the exercise of many of his natural rights, under peril of weighty punishments. He sees, too, that other men practice this tyranny over him by use of the ballot. He sees further, that, if he will but use the ballot himself, he has some chance of relieving himself from this tyranny of others, by subjecting them to his own. In short, he finds himself, without his consent, so situated that, if he uses the ballot, he may become a master, if he does not use it, he must become a slave. And he has no other alternative than these two. In self-defense, he attempts the former. His case is analogous to that of a man who has been forced into battle, where he must either kill

Further implications of this fundamental contrast between insurers as contractual versus states as noncontractual providers of security deserve special attention.

Because they are not subject to and bound by contracts, states typically outlaw the ownership of weapons by their "clients," thus increasing their own security at the expense of rendering their alleged clients defenseless. In contrast, no voluntary buyer of protection insurance would agree to a contract that required him to surrender his right to self-defense and be unarmed or otherwise defenseless. To the contrary, insurance agencies would encourage the ownership of guns and other protective devices among their clients by means of selective price cuts, because the better the private protection of their clients, the lower the insurers' protection and indemnification costs would be.

Moreover, because they operate in a contractual void and are independent of voluntary payment, states arbitrarily define and redefine what is and what is not a punishable "aggression" and what does and does not require compensation. By imposing a proportional or progressive income tax and redistributing income from the rich to the poor, for instance, states in effect define the rich as aggressors and the poor as their victims. (Otherwise, if the rich were not aggressors and the poor not their

---

others, or be killed himself. Because, to save his own life in battle, a man attempts to take the lives of his opponents, it is not to be inferred that the battle is one of his own choosing. . . .(15) [Consequently, the elected government officials] are neither our servants, agents, attorneys, nor representatives . . . [for] we do not make ourselves responsible for their acts. If a man is my servant, agent, or attorney, I necessarily make myself responsible for all his acts done within the limits of the power that I have entrusted to him. If I have entrusted him, as my agent, with either absolute power, or any power at all, over the persons or properties of other men than myself, I thereby necessarily make myself responsible to those other persons for any injuries he may do them, so long as he acts within the limits of the power I have granted him. But no individual who may be injured in his person or property, by acts of Congress, can come to the individual electors, and hold them responsible for these acts of their so-called agents or representatives. This fact proves that these pretended agents of the people, of everybody, are really the agents of nobody (29). (Spooner, *No Treason*, pp. 15 and 29)

victims, how could taking something from the former and giving it to the latter be justified?) Or by passing affirmative action
laws, states effectively define whites and males as aggressors
and blacks and women as their victims. For insurance agencies,
any such business conduct would be impossible for two fundamental reasons.[25]

First, every insurance involves the pooling of particular risks
into risk classes. It implies that to some of the insured, more will
be paid out than what they paid in, and to others, less. However,
and this is decisive, no one knows in advance who the "winners"
and who the "losers" will be. Winners and losers—and any
income redistribution among them—will be randomly distributed. Otherwise, if winners and losers could be systematically
predicted, losers would not want to pool their risk with winners
but only with other losers because this would lower their insurance premium.

Second, it is not possible to insure oneself against any conceivable risk. Rather, it is only possible to insure oneself against
accidents, i.e., risks over whose outcome the insured has no control whatsoever and to which he contributes nothing. Thus, it is
possible to insure oneself against the risk of death or fire, for
instance, but it is not possible to insure oneself against the risk
of committing suicide or setting one's own house on fire. Similarly, it is impossible to insure oneself against the risk of business failure, of unemployment, of not becoming rich, of not
feeling like getting up and out of bed in the morning, or of dis-
liking one's neighbors, fellows or superiors, because in each of
these cases one has either full or partial control over the event in
question. That is, an individual can affect the likelihood of the
risk. By their very nature, the avoidance of risks such as these
falls into the realm of individual responsibility, and any agency
that undertook their insurance would be slated for immediate
bankruptcy. Most significantly for the subject under discussion, the uninsurability of individual actions and sentiments (in

---

[25]On the "logic" of insurance, see Ludwig von Mises, *Human Action: A Trea-
tise on Economics*, Scholar's Edition (Auburn, Ala.: Ludwig von Mises Insti-
tute, 1998), chap. 6; Murray N. Rothbard, *Man, Economy, and State*, 2 vols.
(Auburn, Ala.: Ludwig von Mises Institute, 1993), pp. 498ff; and Hans-
Hermann Hoppe, "On Certainty and Uncertainty, Or: How Rational Can
Our Expectations Be?" *Review of Austrian Economics* 10, no. 1 (1997).

contradistinction to accidents) implies that it is also impossible to insure oneself against the risk of damages that are the result of one's prior aggression or provocation. Rather, every insurer must restrict the actions of its clients so as to exclude all aggression and provocation on their part. That is, any insurance against social disasters such as crime must be contingent on the insured submitting themselves to specified norms of nonaggressive, civilized, conduct.

Accordingly, while states as monopolistic protectors can engage in redistributive policies benefitting one group of people at the expense of another, and while as tax-supported agencies they can even "insure" uninsurable risks and protect provocateurs and aggressors, voluntarily funded insurers would be systematically prevented from doing any such thing. Competition among insurers would preclude any form of income and wealth redistribution among various groups of insured, for a company engaging in such practices would lose clients to others refraining from them. Rather, every client would pay exclusively for his own risk, respectively that of people with the same (homogeneous) risk-exposure that he faces.[26] Nor would voluntarily funded insurers be able to "protect" any person from the consequences of his own erroneous, foolish, risky, or aggressive conduct or sentiment. Competition between insurers would instead systematically encourage individual responsibility, and any known provocateur and aggressor would be excluded as a bad insurance risk from any insurance coverage whatsoever and be rendered an economically isolated, weak, and vulnerable outcast.

---

[26]In being compelled, on the one hand, to place individuals with the same or similar risk-exposure into the same risk group and to charge each of them the same price per insured value; and in being compelled, on the other hand, to distinguish accurately between various classes of individuals with objectively (factually) different group risks and to charge a different price per insured value for members of different risk groups (with the price differentials accurately reflecting the degree of heterogeneity between the members of such different groups), insurance companies would systematically promote the above-mentioned natural human tendency (see note 2 above) of "like people" to associate and to discriminate against and physically separate themselves from "unlikes." On the tendency of states to break up and destroy homogeneous groups and associations through a policy of forced integration, see chaps. 7, 9, and 10.

Finally, with regard to foreign relations, because states can externalize the costs of their own actions onto hapless taxpayers, they are permanently prone to becoming aggressors and warmongers. Accordingly, they tend to fund and develop weapons of aggression and mass destruction. In distinct contrast, insurers will be prevented from engaging in any form of external aggression because any aggression is costly and requires higher insurance premiums, implying the loss of clients to other, nonaggressive competitors. Insurers will engage exclusively in defensive violence, and instead of acquiring weapons of aggression and mass destruction, they will tend to invest in the development of weapons of defense and of targeted retaliation.[27]

V

Even though all of this is clear, how can we ever succeed in implementing such a fundamental constitutional reform? Insurance agencies are presently restricted by countless regulations that prevent them from doing what they could and naturally would do. How can they be freed from these regulations?

Essentially, the answer to this question is the same as that given by the American revolutionaries more than two hundred years ago: through the creation of free territories and by means of secession.

In fact, under today's democratic conditions, this answer is even truer than it was in the days of kings. For then, under monarchical conditions, the advocates of an antistatist liberal-libertarian social revolution still had an option that has since been lost. Liberal-libertarians in the old days could—and frequently did—believe in the possibility of simply converting the king to their view, thereby initiating a "revolution from the top." No mass support was necessary for this—just the insight of an enlightened prince.[28] However realistic this might have been then, this top-down strategy of social revolution would be impossible today. Political leaders are selected nowadays according to their demagogic talents and proven records as habitual

---

[27]See also chap. 12; and Tannehill and Tannehill, *The Market for Liberty*, chaps. 11, 13, and 14.

[28]See on this Murray N. Rothbard, "Concepts of the Role of Intellectuals in Social Change Toward Laissez-Faire," *Journal of Libertarian Studies* 9, no. 2 (1990).

immoralists, as has been explained above; consequently, the chance of converting them to liberal-libertarian views must be considered even lower than that of converting a king who simply inherited his position. Moreover, the state's protection monopoly is now considered public rather than private property, and government rule is no longer tied to a particular individual but to specified functions exercised by anonymous functionaries. Hence, the one-or-few-men-conversion strategy can no longer work. It does not matter if one converts a few top government officials—the president and some leading senators or judges, for instance—because within the rules of democratic government no single individual has the power to abdicate the government's monopoly of protection. Kings had this power, but presidents do not. The president can resign from his position, of course, only to have it taken over by someone else. He cannot dissolve the governmental protection monopoly because according to the rules of democracy, "the people," not their elected representatives, are considered the "owners" of government.

Thus, rather than by means of a top-down reform, under the current conditions, one's strategy must be one of a bottom-up revolution. At first, the realization of this insight would seem to make the task of a liberal-libertarian social revolution impossible, for does this not imply that one would have to persuade a majority of the public to vote for the abolition of democracy and an end to all taxes and legislation? And is this not sheer fantasy, given that the masses are always dull and indolent, and even more so given that democracy, as explained above, promotes moral and intellectual degeneration? How in the world can anyone expect that a majority of an increasingly degenerate people accustomed to the "right" to vote should ever voluntarily renounce the opportunity of looting other people's property? Put this way, one must admit that the prospect of a social revolution must indeed be regarded as virtually nil. Rather, it is only on second thought, upon regarding secession as an integral part of any bottom-up strategy, that the task of a liberal-libertarian revolution appears less than impossible, even if it still remains a daunting one.

How does secession fit into a bottom-up strategy of social revolution? More important, how can a secessionist movement escape the Southern Confederacy's fate of being crushed by a tyrannical and dangerously armed central government?

In response to these questions, it is first necessary to remember that neither the original American Revolution nor the American Constitution was the result of the will of the majority of the population. A third of the American colonists were actually Tories, and another third were occupied with daily routines and did not care either way. No more than a third of the colonists were actually committed to and supportive of the revolution, yet they carried the day. And as far as the Constitution is concerned, the overwhelming majority of the American public was opposed to its adoption, and its ratification represented more of a coup d'etat by a tiny minority than the general will. All revolutions, whether good or bad, are started by minorities; and the secessionist route toward social revolution, which necessarily involves the breaking-away of a smaller number of people from a larger one, takes explicit cognizance of this important fact.

Second, it is necessary to recognize that the ultimate power of every government—whether of kings or caretakers—rests solely on opinion and not on physical force. The agents of government are never more than a small proportion of the total population under their control. This implies that no government can possibly enforce its will upon the entire population unless it finds widespread support and voluntary cooperation within the nongovernmental public. It implies likewise that every government can be brought down by a mere change in public opinion, i.e., by the withdrawal of the public's consent and cooperation.[29]

---

[29]On the fundamental importance of public opinion for government power see Etienne de la Boétie, *The Politics of Obedience: The Discourse of Voluntary Servitude* (New York: Free Life Editions, 1975), with an introduction by Murray N. Rothbard; David Hume, "On the First Principles of Government," in idem, *Essays: Moral, Political and Literary* (Oxford: Oxford University Press, 1971); and Mises, *Human Action*, chap. 9 sect. 3. Mises there (p. 189) notes:

> He who wants to apply violence needs the voluntary cooperation of some people. . . . The tyrant must have a retinue of partisans who obey his orders of their own accord. Their spontaneous obedience provides him with the apparatus he needs for the conquest of other people. Whether or not he succeeds in making his sway last depends on the numerical relation of the groups, those who support him voluntarily and those whom he beats into submission. Though a tyrant may temporarily rule through a minority if this minority is armed and the majority is not, in the long run a minority cannot keep a majority in subservience.

And while it is undeniably true that after more than two centuries of democracy the American public has become so degenerate, morally and intellectually, that any such withdrawal must be considered impossible on a nationwide scale, it would not seem insurmountably difficult to win a secessionist-minded majority in sufficiently small districts or regions of the country. In fact, given an energetic minority of intellectual elites inspired by the vision of a free society in which law and order is provided by competitive insurers, and given furthermore that—certainly in the U.S., which owes its very existence to a secessionist act—secession is still held to be legitimate and in accordance with the "original" democratic ideal of *self-determination* (rather than majority rule)[30] by a substantial number of people, there seems to be nothing unrealistic about assuming that such secessionist majorities exist or can be created at hundreds of locations all over the country. In fact, under the rather realistic assumption that the U.S. central government as well as the social-democratic states of the West in general are bound for economic bankruptcy (much like the socialist people's democracies of the East collapsed economically some ten years ago), present tendencies toward political disintegration will likely be strengthened in the future. Accordingly, the number of potential secessionist regions will continue to rise, even beyond its current level.

Finally, the insight into the widespread and growing secessionist potential also permits an answer to the last question regarding the dangers of a central government crackdown.

While it is important in this regard that the memory of the secessionist past of the U.S. be kept alive, it is even more important for the success of a liberal-libertarian revolution to avoid

---

[30]See on this "old" liberal conception of democracy, for instance, von Mises, *Liberalism: In the Classical Tradition* (Irvington-on-Hudson, N.Y.: Foundation for Economic Education, 1985). "The right to self-determination in regard to the question of membership in a state," writes Mises,

> thus means: whenever the inhabitants of a particular territory, whether it be a single village, a whole district, or a series of adjacent districts, make it known, by a freely conducted plebiscite, that they no longer wish to remain united to the state to which they belong at the time, but wish either to form an independent state or to attach themselves to some other state, their wishes are to be respected and complied with. This is the only feasible and effective way of preventing revolutions and civil and international wars. (p. 109)

the mistakes of the second failed attempt at secession. Fortunately, the issue of slavery, which complicated and obscured the situation in 1861,[31] has been resolved. However, another important lesson must be learned by comparing the failed second American experiment with secession to the successful first one.

The first American secession was facilitated significantly by the fact that at the center of power in Britain, public opinion concerning the secessionists was hardly unified. In fact, many prominent British figures such as Edmund Burke and Adam Smith openly sympathized with the secessionists. Apart from purely ideological reasons, which rarely affect more than a handful of philosophical minds, this lack of a unified opposition to the American secessionists in British public opinion can be attributed to two complementary factors. On the one hand, a multitude of regional and cultural-religious affiliations as well as of personal and family ties between Britain and the American colonists existed. On the other hand, the American events were considered far from home and the potential loss of the colonies as economically insignificant. In both regards, the situation in 1861 was distinctly different. To be sure, at the center of political power, which had shifted to the northern states of the U.S. by then, opposition to the secessionist Southern Confederacy was not unified, and the Confederate cause also had supporters in the North. However, fewer cultural bonds and kinship ties existed between the American North and South than had existed between Britain and the American colonists, and the secession of the Southern Confederacy involved about half the territory and a third of the entire population of the U.S. and thus struck Northerners as close to home and as a significant economic loss. Therefore, it was comparatively easier for the Northern power elite to mold a unified front of "progressive" Yankee culture versus a culturally backward and "reactionary" Dixieland.

In light of these considerations, then, it appears strategically advisable not to attempt again what in 1861 failed so painfully— for contiguous states or even the entire South trying to break away from the tyranny of Washington, D.C. Rather, a modern

---

[31]For a careful analysis of the issues involved in the War of Southern Independence see Thomas J. DiLorenzo, "The Great Centralizer. Abraham Lincoln and the War Between the States," *Independent Review* 3, no. 2 (1998).

liberal-libertarian strategy of secession should take its cues from the European Middle Ages when, from about the twelfth until well into the seventeenth century (with the emergence of the modern central state), Europe was characterized by the existence of hundreds of free and independent cities, interspersed into a predominantly feudal social structure.[32] By choosing this model and striving to create a U.S. punctuated by a large and increasing number of territorially disconnected free cities—a multitude of Hong Kongs, Singapores, Monacos, and Liechtensteins strewn out over the entire continent—two otherwise unattainable but central objectives can be accomplished. First, besides recognizing the fact that the liberal-libertarian potential is distributed highly unevenly across the country, such a strategy of piecemeal withdrawal renders secession less threatening politically, socially, and economically. Second, by pursuing this strategy simultaneously at a great number of locations all over the country, it becomes exceedingly difficult for the central state to create the unified opposition in public opinion to the secessionists that would secure the level of popular support and voluntary cooperation necessary for a successful crackdown.[33]

---

[32]On the importance of the free cities of medieval Europe on the subsequent development of the uniquely European tradition of (classical) liberalism, see Charles Tilly and Wim P. Blockmans, eds., *Cities and The Rise of States in Europe, A.D. 1000 to 1800* (Boulder, Colo.: Westview Press, 1994).

[33]The danger of a government crackdown is greatest during the initial stage of this secessionist scenario, i.e., while the number of free city territories is still small. Hence, during this phase it is advisable to avoid any direct confrontation with the central government. Rather than renouncing its legitimacy altogether, it would seem prudent, for instance, to guarantee the government's "property" of federal buildings, etc. within the free territory, and "only" deny its right to future taxation and legislation concerning anyone and anything within this territory. Provided that this is done with the appropriate diplomatic tact and given the necessity of a substantial level of support in public opinion, it is difficult to imagine how the central government would dare to invade a territory and crush a group of people who had committed no other sin than trying to mind their own business. Subsequently, once the number of secessionist territories reached a critical mass—and every success in one location promoted imitation by other localities—the difficulties of crushing the secessionists would increase exponentially, and the central government would quickly be rendered impotent and implode under its own weight.

If we succeed in this endeavor, if we then proceed to return all public property into appropriate private hands and adopt a new "constitution" that declares all taxation and legislation henceforth unlawful, and if we then finally allow insurance agencies to do what they are destined to do, we truly can be proud again and America will be justified in claiming to provide an example to the rest of the world.

23

THE AMERICAN PRESIDENT: FROM CINCINNATUS TO CAESAR

CLYDE N. WILSON

The great body of the nation has no real interest in party.

—James Fenimore Cooper
The American Democrat, 1838

The American presidency offers many fascinating questions for historical exploration. Here, historical exploration does not mean the all-too-common form of pseudohistory that puts the presidential office at the center of our experience as a people. In that scenario, presidential Lone Rangers—Abraham Lincoln, Woodrow Wilson, Theodore and Franklin Roosevelt, John Kennedy, Ronald Reagan—gallop in to save us from dark forces that threaten divinely ordained progress toward the universal triumph of "American democracy." (The dark forces are often discovered to be ourselves: The American people must be saved by presidential heroes from their ignorant prejudices against such things as foreign wars, affirmative action, and unlimited immigration.)

That scenario is not history at all but a part of the mythology of empire. Its origins can be traced to nineteenth-century Massachusetts when Calvinists lost their theology but none of their aggressive belief in their own chosenness, when the godly City upon a Hill was replaced by "American democracy" (that is, Bostonian arrogance) as the end goal of the universe.

No, we mean real historical questions to be explored. How did the chief magistrate of a confederacy of republican states evolve into the leader of the world? Historians of the remote future, should there be any such after the disintegration of Western civilization, will see this as a central factor in the rise and fall of the American empire.

But here let us take a more limited and manageable question. How did we come to the present system of choosing our elective monarch? Of determining what citizen has the qualifications necessary for an office which surely requires patriotism, intelligence, and character of a high order? Or to put it another way, what could possibly cause an apparently normal person to stand on a chair and cheer at the prospect of an Al Gore or a George W. Bush assuming such grave responsibilities, as many did in the most recent election?

Part of the answer lies in the invention of the two-party political system—something utterly unknown to the framers of the Constitution, and particularly to the invention in the early nineteenth century of the diabolically-devised political nominating convention. The intent of this nominating convention was to take the choice of candidates away from the people and ensure control by professional politicians; that is, persons who seek profit and place by the pursuit of power rather than by honest, productive work.

There was a time when candidates for high office were expected to show their achievements and services for the commonwealth—successful leadership in arms, wise executive administration that met public necessities while relieving the burden of taxes, forethought, and eloquence in the legislative hall in dealing with hard issues. Compare recent occupants and aspirants of the presidential office with this standard. What does the absence of this or any other standard from our electoral discourse tell us about our state as a people? In fact, presidential candidacy is and for some time has been a factor, not of achievement or service but of celebrity, or what patriots who decried the emergence of this phenomenon in the nineteenth century called "availability."

One of those patriots, James Fenimore Cooper, wrote in his *American Democrat*:

> Party is an instrument of error, by pledging men to support its policy, instead of supporting the [true] policy of the state. . . . Party leads to vicious, corrupt and unprofitable legislation, for the sole purpose of defeating party.
>
> The discipline and organization of party, are expedients to defeat the intention of the institutions, by putting managers in the place of the people; it being of little avail that a majority elect, when the nomination rests in the hands of a few.
>
> Party is the cause of many corrupt and incompetent men being preferred to power, as the elector, who, in his own person, is disposed to resist a bad nomination, yields to the influence and a dread of factions.

Party pledges the representative to the support of the executive, right or wrong, when the institutions intend that he shall be pledged only to justice, expediency and the right, under the restrictions of the Constitution.

When party rules, the people do not rule, but merely such a portion of the people as can manage to get control of party.
. . .

The effect of party is always to supplant established power. In a monarchy it checks the king; in a democracy it controls the people.

Party, by feeding the passions and exciting personal interests, overshadows truth, justice, patriotism, and every other public virtue, completely reversing the order of a democracy, by putting unworthy motives in the place of reason.

It is a very different thing to be a democrat, and to be a member of what is called a democratic party.[1]

Cooper's hope was for a Washingtonian president who would be above party—an Andrew Jackson. It was not an unreasonable hope in the beginning. But there were two problems with this appeal to a noble executive such as the Constitution had designed the office to be. By the time anyone achieved the distinction necessary, he had more than likely reached the stage of declining mental powers. This was true of Jackson, as it was of George Washington. Though not in the same category as Washington and Jackson, it is likely that some of the worst mistakes of Wilson, FDR, and Reagan can be traced to this fact of life. Those who hope to manipulate a powerful officeholder for their own ends are many, wily, and adept at raising plausible public clamor for their goals.

An even greater problem was the hope for a president above party, which both Washington and Jackson erroneously believed themselves to be. No sooner had the government been founded than Alexander Hamilton and his northeastern friends began to force through an agenda that boldly disregarded all the understandings that had been reached at Philadelphia, in the ratifying conventions, and in the first ten amendments—under the cover of Washington's prestige. The Jeffersonians managed to halt this initiative in mid-course

---

[1]James Fenimore Cooper, *The American Democrat* (Baltimore, Md.: Penguin Books, 1969), pp. 226–27.

and hold it in abeyance for a quarter century. But Thomas Jefferson should not be regarded as a player in the leftist scenario of presidential Lone Rangers. He did not regard the presidential office in that way, but as a consensual and restraining force. He walked to his inauguration rather than riding, like "plain" John Adams did in a carriage with white horses; he sent his messages to Congress in writing rather than delivering them from the throne; and he established Virginia country pell-mell as etiquette in the executive mansion. But he could not help being the leader of a party, however he wished otherwise.

For a time, Jeffersonians did establish the dominance, at least rhetorically, of a limited collegial presidency, and more important, the dominance, at least rhetorically, of a confederal central authority restricted in its jurisdiction. This was the bedrock public feeling when Jackson was elected president. The majority was disgusted with John Quincy Adams's efforts at neo-Hamiltonian expansion of the government and regarded Jackson as honorable and safe. But, as Washington had his Hamilton, so Jackson had his Martin Van Buren, the American solon of party.

One may interpret Van Buren's motives in constructing the American party system in two different ways: He was a devotee of Jeffersonian principles who realized that under the conditions of mass democracy only a strong party organization could defend them; or, as most observers at the time and later have believed, he was a shrewd pursuer of political preferment for its own sake, troubled no more by principles than was necessary to keep the hayseeds in line. Motive really does not matter. The effects were the same either way.[2]

These effects were the substitution of party machinery and patronage for public opinion and the transformation of electoral contests into trials of celebrity rather than of issues. As an 1829 newspaper commented:

> Mr. Van Buren seems disposed to take a conciliatory course. He looks forward to a higher station in the General Government,

---

[2]My interpretation of this period of presidential history differs greatly from that in this volume by Jeffrey Rogers Hummel, a very fine historian. Good historians, as honest men, may disagree, and that is all to the good. The reader may have his consciousness expanded in more than one direction and consider the options for himself.

and his whole air and manners evince it. He desires, therefore, to make as many friends, and as few enemies, as possible.[3]

It would be hard to find a better description of the way our aspirants to the highest office have been addressing the issues most of the time since. Perhaps the most important issue of the late 1820s and early 1830s was that of free trade versus tariff protection. President Jackson took a bold and decided stand for "a judicious tariff." The Jeffersonian principle of free trade had become a party trick. One could be for or against free trade as long as one supported the party. Though it was assumed that Jackson's party leaned toward free trade, his supporters among Mr. Van Buren's friends in the northeast were free to vote for all the tariffs they wanted.

The key, of course, was organization. New York, because it had more patronage than other states, because political contests were close, and because Hamilton and Burr had left a legacy of competing organizations, provided the model for the nation. And federal patronage grew with the phenomenal expansion of the country in every measurable dimension. One need not be troubled with public opinion or issues. All you needed was to control the meetings. So appeared the party convention, which was actually thought of as an advance in popular control over the legislative caucuses that previously had nominated candidates and that now were decried as aristocratic evils.

So, if enough postmasters and pensioners and contractors and their friends and relatives, and those who expect to be postmasters, contractors, etc., when their ticket wins, and their friends and relatives show up, that settles the matter. Whatever resolutions and platforms and nominations emerge from the meetings, already carefully designed by the managers, are, by definition, public opinion. The people have spoken. If you don't believe it, just ask the newspapers (who are getting most of their profits from public printing).

Meanwhile, you have been busy putting into place all those nice, new devices to better express the will of the people (that is, to make the managers' job easier). Let us suppose that 20 percent of the electorate of Massachusetts and 80 percent of that of Mississippi are Democrats. But in the convention, states are represented by population. Your Massachusetts Democratic voter is going to have several times the power per capita of my Mississippi

3Charleston, South Carolina *Courier*, April 14, 1829.

voter writing the platform and choosing the candidate. The real effect, of course, is to allow a well-organized minority of a minority to choose the president. As Cooper pointed out: It is "of little avail that a majority elect, when the nomination rests in the hands of a few." And the minority that controls is a stealth minority, with a vested interest in disguising its agenda and avoiding any real public debate and decision of issues, since controversy might scare off voters. And have you noticed those new laws, unknown and unanticipated by the Constitution, which mandate that the party that wins New York by 51 percent or, by even less in a three-way race, gets 100 percent of New York's votes in the electoral college? Thus do our leaders labor ceaselessly to bring us ever and ever greater democracy.

Despite historians' endless blather about "Jacksonian democracy," pro or con, there was now a president and party ruling by patronage and popularity with no principle in sight. True, there was much talk in the air about the common man, which meant that the party managers had learned to get his vote, after the options had been carefully culled down to the safest ones. (Rather, there were two Jacksonian principles in sight: an insistence on maximum presidential prerogative, and one the historians never mention in this context—firm opposition to abolitionism.) Even the vaunted war against the national bank—put forward as a campaign for hard money—actually resulted and probably was intended by the president's managers to result in a host of government-protected banks, inflating the currency happily for private profit.

It is true that Van Buren opposed this, as he did anything so decisive as to make enemies. As he reported unblushingly in his autobiography, he once missed a key vote because he had promised to accompany a friend on a cemetery visit. This method failed him at last when he lost the 1844 nomination by attempting not to take a stand either way on Texas annexation. Still, it made him president for a term. When elected in 1836, he was a veteran officeholder, but he had no real achievements to rank with Adams, Jackson, Clay, Calhoun, Webster, and many others. Cincinnatus had been called from the plow and turned out to look a lot like Uriah Heap rather than the natural aristocrat for whom the presidential office had been designed.

But the game was not over. Two could play. The Whigs, on the outs while Jackson was popular, had learned a few tricks from Van Buren. In 1840 their managers, who had been busy building up their own patronage network, devised a new strategy. They found another quondam military hero, General William Henry Harrison, who was completely unburdened by any political opinions or record. They adopted no platform, thus reducing the chance of offending any potential voter. Instead of a platform, there was a campaign: torchlight parades carrying log cabins, coonskin caps, and jugs of cider, to symbolize their candidate's identity with the common people, and whooping it up for "Tippecanoe and Tyler Too."[4]

A traveling circus had been sent to find Cincinnatus and had come back with his distinguished-looking but rather dimwitted cousin who did not have a clue as to what he had been called for. This was just what the managers had in mind. The real leader of the party, Clay, announced that the electoral victory had been a mandate for the party's policies (which had hardly been mentioned in the campaign)—a national bank, a high protective tariff, and distribution of tax money for internal improvements. For the moment, the agenda stalled because Cincinnatus's cousin ungraciously died and was succeeded by a junior member of the electoral coalition, a "states' righter" who had opposed Van Buren without going for the Whig program.[5]

But the party men had managed to co-opt the process by which the people were to find their Cincinnatus and corrupt it beyond repair. The Whigs, soon to be Republicans, had designed a formula that they have clung to since. Never address a real issue if you can help it, and if you have to, redefine it till it's harmless. Serve big business—that is, safe, as opposed to entrepreneurial, capital but never mention it. Always be the party of the respectable middle class, a sure vote-getter everywhere outside the South. In pursuit of this goal the party has for more than a century and a half, with very rare interruptions of talent, produced a succession of presidential and vice-presidential candidates who have astonished the world with their mediocrity.

Calhoun, who shared Cooper's distaste for party and his preference for an independent presidency, and who was in a much better position to assess the real state of affairs, described it thus:

[4]Harrison actually had been born in one of the best plantation houses in Tidewater, Virginia, a fact lost on Northern voters.

[5] For years I hoped vainly I would be important enough to be asked to participate in one of those surveys where historians are asked to rate presidents, so I could nominate John Tyler as one of the greats.

the existing party organization[s] look only to plunder. The sole object of strife is to elect a president, in order to obtain the control through him of the powers of the government. The only material difference between the two parties is, that the Democraticks [sic] look more exclusively to plundering through the finances and the treasury, while the Whigs look more to plundering by wholesale, through partial legislation, Banks, Protection and other means of monopoly. The one rely for support on capital and the other on the masses; and the one tends more to aristocracy and the other to the power of a single man, or monarchy. Both have entirely forgot the principles, which originally gave rise to their existence; and are equally proscriptive and devoted to party machinery. To preserve party machinery and to keep up party union are paramount to all other considerations; to truth, justice and the constitution. Every thing is studiously suppressed by both sides calculated to destroy party harmony. . . .

It is impossible for anyone, who has not been an eyewitness, to realize the rapid corruption and degeneracy of the Government in the last few years. So callous has the sensibility of the community become, that things are now not only tolerated, but are scarcely noticed, which, at any other period, would have prostrated the Administration of Washington himself. . . . It is time for the people to reflect.[6]

Calhoun's description of the end effect could serve as an epitaph for the late-twentieth-century presidency:

When it comes to be once understood that politics is a game; that those who are engaged in it but act a part; that they make this or that profession, not from honest conviction or intent to fulfill it, but as the means of deluding the people, and through that delusion to acquire power; when such professions are to be entirely forgotten, the people will lose all confidence in public men. All will be regarded as mere jugglers—the honest and patriotic as well as the cunning and the profligate—and the people will become indifferent and passive to the grossest abuses of power, on the ground that those whom they may elevate, under whatever pledges, instead of reforming, will but imitate the example of those whom they have expelled.[7]

---

[6]Clyde Wilson, ed., *The Essential Calhoun* (New Brunswick, N.J.: Transaction Publishers, 1992), pp. 341, 353.

[7]Ibid., p. 101.

Remember George H.W. Bush and "Read my lips." In some quarters there has been much emphasis on the disgrace brought on the presidential office by Bill Clinton and his obvious sleaziness. So what else is new? In fact, the Bush deception of the people is by far the worse of the two. Clinton's lies were mostly to cover up his misdeeds. Bush's lie was a deliberate deception of the people made publicly in presenting himself as an aspirant to their highest office, a corruption of the democratic process at its very root. But, of course, our sensibilities have become so callous that neither the deceiver nor the deceived thought much of it.

It is in fact possible to praise what Calhoun decried, to glory in the fact that American political parties present the people with no real alternatives. Freedom from ideological strife can be seen as a great boon when compared to the havoc wrought in Europe by struggles over irreconcilable visions of the political good. This has been a basic theme of left and right democratic capitalist penmen, such as Arthur Schlesinger in *The Vital Center* and Daniel Boorstin in *The Genius of American Politics*.[8] Instead of wasting themselves on class struggle, Americans have been busy manufacturing more refrigerators and automobiles for everyone. There is indeed much to be said for a nonideological regime that promotes peace and prosperity. One may wonder, however, if that accurately describes a country that killed six hundred thousand of its men in a civil war. Or if any number of fridges, or even of guided missiles, can save a people with a leadership unable or unwilling to address honestly its real necessities.

Can a lack of principle—a refusal to contest real issues—be covered by an appeal to the evils of ideology? Would not a more accurate description suggest that since the Progressive Era of the late nineteenth century the driving force of American history has been a quasi-socialist ideology, whether it is called progressivism, liberalism, or neoconservatism? There has not been an absence of ideology but rather a two-party agreement on one. For those who believe in Clinton's worldview, mistaken though they are, a vote for Clinton or Gore is a rational choice. In the

[8]Boorstin was the original neoconservative, beginning as a communist and ending as a spokesman for respectable conservatism (appointed director of the Smithsonian by President Ford). However, unlike Schlesinger and the giant minds that took up the cause of democratic capitalism after him, Boorstin was too good a historian not to see some of the ironies in such a position, as in his *The Image: A Guide to Pseudo-Events in America* (New York: Atheneum, 1975).

same circumstances, a vote for a George Bush (junior or senior) is a vote for "Tippecanoe and Tyler Too" if it is thought of as a vote for an alternative.

The Whig frustration after 1840 was compounded by Calhoun's eloquent and intransigent stand for free trade, free banking, and strict construction, which had rallied the latent Jeffersonianism of the people. The Democratic Party, after the breaking of Van Buren's power in 1844, returned to principle and held to it until principle was rendered irrelevant by blood and iron.

The economic centralists, whose drive since the time of Hamilton had been presented as a moral imperative, needed other cards to play. The American presidency required two more steps to Caesarism. First, the party men must learn how to combine predatory patronage and predatory policy—which separated the Democrats and Whigs—into one power, something best accomplished in crisis. Lincoln was able to lay the groundwork for this in the midst of war, though the final consummation would not come until a century later when the Great Society discovered how to buy both sides by shifting the costs to posterity.

Ronald Reagan came to power, like Jackson, on a wave of protest over what the party men had done to the people's property and principles. He spoke like, and perhaps even believed himself to be, the Jeffersonian who would turn back to states' rights and limited government. But as Jackson had his Van Buren, Reagan had a phalanx of handlers ready to reinterpret the revolution into a Hamiltonian form. The patronage thrown up by the Great Society was too great a temptation to be spurned. The bakery would not be closed; the cake would just be sliced a little differently. In order for the Reagan revolt to have worked, there would have to have been a real opposition party determined to take wealth and power from the federal government and give it back to the people.

The war allowed Lincoln to combine patronage and policy by eliminating effective political opposition. But a second step was needed before the presidential office metamorphosed from CEO to Caesar. This was the establishment of American history as a salvation drama. The groundwork for this had to be religious and cultural. It required a country in which superficial education emanating from New England schoolmarms had replaced, in a substantial part of the population, tradition and common sense.

Since the War of 1812, New England had declined severely in prestige and power. Its intellectuals had lost their religion but had retained their sense of themselves as The Elect. The Calvinist mentality, even without its theology, reasoned diabolically. That which stood in its way was by definition evil. By the time this impulse got to the hustings in the greater New England of the Burnt Over District of New York and the upper Midwest, it took on strange forms.

The New England clergy had preached rabidly that Jefferson was a tool of the Bavarian *Illuminati* who would set up the guillotine, kill Christians and declare women common property. A generation later came the belief that the harmless fraternal order of Masons was conspiring to subvert the country—a fantasy that was soon transferred to the Catholics. In the meantime, the religious dissolution of New England spun off many strange subcults, including vegetarianism, feminism, communalism, Mormonism, and Adventism. The underside edge of this great age of reform was the psychopathic gang of John Brown, in the same way that Charles Manson was the underside of the great sexual liberation of the sixties. (Late bloomers of the latter include the Unabomber and Timothy McVeigh, whose crimes have been blamed by the intelligentsia on the "right-wing Southern gun culture.")

The more respectable side of this phenomenon was a conflation of Christianity and Americanism, America as the fulfillment of God's plan for mankind, a seductive bit of blasphemy that has remained a strong motif in our national consciousness ever since. Out of this matrix came a thirst for vanquishing the devils that stood in the way, a thirst satisfied perfectly by the idea of the "slave power." The South, which stood in the way of Northern progress, economic and moral, was not simply a region defending its own interests within a federal system; it was a diabolic conspiracy by degenerate and imperious slaveholders to spread their evil ways to the North, threatening all things good and decent. Since domestic slavery had been a feature of American society from its first days, and since all American law and tradition forbade interference by one section with the internal affairs of another, this strategy could only work politically by the fantasy that the "slave power" was the aggressor, a convenient forgetting of the fact that most of the most stalwart founders and defenders of American liberty and the American Union had been Southern slaveholders.

It was the combination of economic agenda and cultural hysteria that brought Lincoln to power, thanks to the tricks that the party managers had played with the electoral college. Lincoln was far too shrewd to really believe the conspiracy theory, but he was willing to allow it to benefit himself and his party. As long as the South remained a large, prestigious, and skillfully-led minority, there was an irreducible body of opposition to both economic nationalism and the cult of Americanism.

The trauma of war followed by Lincoln's assassination provided the final missing ingredient in the drama of presidential salvation. The president had begun as the CEO of a federal republic, expected to have extraordinary republican virtue in the exercise of his powers. He was now the martyred savior in the world historical drama of American uniqueness. The Northern clergy and their business lobbyist allies were not slow to use the opportunity for all it was worth. A huge literature developed in which Lincoln was literally a Christ figure who died for our sins. (They had tried this out on a limited scale with John Brown before the war, but it had not flown.) To read the Lincoln hagiography is to understand easily how the Romans came to grant divinity to their emperors, the difference being that those Romans did not claim to be Christians.

The conflation of America with God's plan for the perfection of human history was complete. And the president as savior was essential to the drama. It could not, of course, be used every day. But it would ever after be there as a potential to clothe dubious objectives with sacredness. And there would always be a portion of the people ready to follow. So Wilson could lead the country into the insane mayhem of the European war, kill and be killed in order to end killing, and make the world safe for democracy. Many would believe that Franklin Roosevelt had personally saved us from depression and fascism.

Perhaps the strangest eruption of all of the salvation drama occurred after the dramatic assassination of the youthful President Kennedy. This dubiously elected, questionably competent, and somewhat churlish power seeker became in death a sacrificed god. You have to be old enough to have been there to really remember what an orgy of adulatory hysteria was whipped up for that occasion.

It was that emotional eruption that provided the fuel for the Great Society, a salvation drama against the sins of poverty and discrimination, the chief result of which was to engross for the presidency ever more of the power and wealth of the country. That could not have happened, however, if there had been a real opposition party. The Great Society did not create the moral breakdown of the sixties. Rather it was a product of moral breakdown in which the intelligentsia, through the grace bestowed upon them by the martyred president and their paternal egalitarianism, liberated themselves from morality and into irresponsible power and privilege to remake the world.

What was new about this was that the president no longer had to be even a dim copy of Cincinnatus. By the time we get to Clinton, the imperial office itself had become the object of worship. It does not matter how tainted the credentials of its occupant. In the drama of salvation, a sleazy prevaricator can be the savior of the oppressed. It does not matter if this requires the murder of innocent women and children at home or abroad. The emperor can do no wrong.

This was in part because the presidency had become enmeshed in the public relations, advertising, and mass entertainment culture. It was no longer a debate on the business of the public, but a popularity contest. So the Republicans of this writer's state were treated, during the 1996 presidential campaign, not to a declaration of Mr. Dole's principles and policies, but to a visit from his daughter who regaled us with the assurances of what a wonderful fellow he was.

As an undergraduate student, this writer repeatedly heard that the American press was owned by big business, and therefore, could always be expected to support the reactionary side in American politics. It was up to the working stiffs of the media to correct this terrible imbalance as best they could. A prime example of the corruption of American politics by public relations instructors was the fact that Eisenhower had taken elocution lessons from a Hollywood actor. In a remarkably short time, the brave crusaders of the media became slavish lickspittles of the imperial Kennedys, who had pretended to regard them as wise and important.

The Federalists who designed the presidency at Philadelphia wanted a vigorous and independent power that could preserve the honor of the Union against all foes. In constructing the office, they violated all the wisdom of American experience. The American Revolution had been in essence a struggle of the representative bodies of the thirteen colonies against the executive power, the monarchical prerogatives represented by the royal governor and his placemen. Because of these struggles, the colonies emerged from the revolution with weak executive power, a governor elected annually by the legislature, a magistrate with very limited initiative in the vital matters of purse and sword.

The prevailing element at Philadelphia designed an office unlike any other in the world—a monarch, with more than monarchical powers—in all respects except the requirement for election by the people of the states. (The electoral college was designed not so much to take the decision out of the hands of the people as to guarantee weight to the states. If there was no majority, as might happen often, the House would choose, with each state having an equal vote. Party management once more triumphs over the intent of the Constitution in selecting the president.) Theory prevailed over experience.[9]

All three branches of the federal government, and thus the people too, are guilty in the transformation of America from a constitutional federal union to an empire. But it was the president who was meant to check evil tendencies in the body politic. This is why he was given the power to negate acts of Congress and to appoint the judges and generals. He was to be the hero of republican virtue who would represent all the people as a historic community of freedom rather than a coalition of interest groups and ideological agendas.

At the beginning of the new millennium, we see only too well how misplaced was the hope. From Cincinnatus to Caesar was a long road. From Caesar to Caligula is but a few short and easy steps.

---

[9]This is why the theoretician James Madison is revered by every fake and superficial political philosopher in the land, because he provides a vehicle to translate the American regime from historical experience to the rationalization of power.

APPENDIX A

EXECUTIVE USURPATION: A SPEECH BY
THE HONORABLE CLEMENT L. VALLANDIGHAM,
CONGRESSMAN FROM OHIO

INTRODUCTION

One of the greatest speeches in American history on behalf of individual freedom and against despotism, especially relating to the unconstitutional usurpation of executive powers by the president of the United States, was made by Clement Vallandigham, a Democrat congressman from Ohio. It was a reply to President Lincoln's address to Congress on July 4, 1861, and it was also an assault upon the tyrannical conduct of this new administration. The speech was delivered in the chambers of the House of Representatives on July 10, 1861, and it eventually led to Vallandigham's illegal arrest, unlawful imprisonment, mock trial before a military commission, conviction on the charge of "declaring disloyal sentiment and opinions" in violation of a military order, and banishment from the United States of America by the Lincoln administration.[1]

Clement Vallandigham was a prominent Ohio lawyer who had served with distinction in the Ohio state legislature and was first elected to Congress in 1858. He made his last speech in Congress on February 23, 1863, against the Conscription Bill. After he completed his last term in Congress, he returned to his home in Dayton, Ohio, to resume his law practice. The speech he delivered in Congress entitled "Executive Usurpation" caused him to be designated by President Lincoln as a person to be silenced by legal prosecution if necessary. However, he continued to speak out against the tyranny of President Lincoln after he returned to Dayton, and at 2:30 A.M. on the morning of May 4, 1863, armed military troops under the command of Union General

---

[1]The forced exile or banishment of Vallandigham by President Lincoln was undoubtedly the model and inspiration for the fictional character Phillip Nolan in the famous book *The Man Without a Country* published in December 1863. The author was a Puritan preacher from Boston, Edward Everett Hale, who was the nephew of Edward Everett who delivered the principal oration at the Gettysburg battlefield on the same day President Lincoln spoke. In the story, Nolan was convicted by a military commission and banished for life from his own country.

Ambrose E. Burnside broke into his home by knocking down the back door and two interior doors, and arrested him without a civil warrant, merely upon the order of General Burnside. He was forcibly removed to a military prison in Cincinnati. Realizing that his arrest and imprisonment were not only punishment for his opinions expressed against President Lincoln and his administration for its unconstitutional usurpation of power, but also to set an example for others who might oppose such tyrannical behavior, Vallandigham wrote a letter to his fellow Democrats on May 5, 1863, from his prison cell, to explain why he was arrested and imprisoned:

> To the Democracy of Ohio:
>
> I am here in a military bastille for no other offense than my political opinions, and the defense of them and of the rights of the people, and of your constitutional liberties. Speeches made in the hearing of thousands of you in denunciation of the usurpation of power, infractions of the Constitution and laws, and of military despotism, were the sole cause of my arrest and imprisonment.[2]

The next day, he was brought to trial before a military commission for "publicly . . . declaring disloyal sentiments and opinions," in violation of Military Order Number 9, which prohibited any criticism of the civil or military policies of the Lincoln administration. He objected to the jurisdiction of the commission to try him and objected to the unconstitutional methods of his arrest and confinement.[3] He represented himself at the trial and protested the right of a military commission to try him since he was not in the armed services; also, the courts of Ohio were completely available for legal process, and the State of Ohio was not in rebellion against the United States. He further stated that there was no proper warrant for his arrest and that his home had been illegally broken into, all in violation of his constitutional rights. The military commission convicted him

---

[2]John A. Marshall, *American Bastille: A History of the Illegal Arrests and Imprisonment of American Citizens in the Northern and Border States, on Account of Their Political Opinions, During the Late Civil War* (Wiggins, Miss.: Crown Rights, [1881] 1998), p. 727.

[3]Ibid., pp. 712–51, for the details of this tragic demonstration of despotism in American history.

and sentenced him to a military prison for the remainder of the war, but the Lincoln administration later changed this sentence to banishment from the United States. Vallandigham petitioned for a writ of habeas corpus, which was denied, and he was placed aboard a ship and forcibly exiled. Thousands of other American citizens were also made victims of similar tyrannical procedures that would be declared unconstitutional by the United States Supreme Court after the Civil War, in the famous case of *Ex parte Milligan*.[4]

The Democrats of Ohio were so enraged by this unconstitutional action and tyranny on the part of the Lincoln administration that they nominated Vallandigham for the office of governor of Ohio by a large majority vote in the next election, even though he was still exiled from the United States. The Vallandigham case still stands as one of the most horrible examples of tyrannical government and shows that President Lincoln and his administration were the worst offenders of the constitutional protections for individual liberty in all of American history.

The Speech

The House was in session as a Committee of the Whole, and the subject under consideration was *The State of the Union*. Congressman Vallandigham's long speech, entitled *Executive Usurpation* was delivered on July 10, 1861, and the most pertinent excerpts are as follows:

> Mr. Chairman, in the *Constitution* of the United States, which the other day we swore to support, and by the authority of which we are here assembled now, it is written, "All legislative powers herein granted shall be vested in a Congress of the United States." It is further written, also, that the Congress to which all legislative powers granted, are thus committed "Shall make no law abridging the freedom of speech or of the press."

---

[4]Ibid., pp. 71–91; *Ex parte Milligan*, 71 U.S. 2; see also Mark E. Neely, Jr., *The Fate of Liberty: Abraham Lincoln and Civil Liberties* (New York: Oxford University Press, 1991). Here, the director of the Lincoln Museum unsuccessfully defends Lincoln for his usurpation of power and tyrannical behavior.

And, it is yet further written, in protection of Senators and Representatives, in that freedom of debate here, without which there can be no liberty, that: "For any speech or debate in either House they shall not be questioned in any other place."

Holding up the shield of the *Constitution*, and standing here in the place, and with the manhood of a Representative of the people, I propose to myself, to-day, the ancient freedom of speech used within these walls, though with somewhat more, I trust, of decency and discretion than have sometimes been exhibited here. Sir, I do not propose to discuss the direct question of this civil war in which we are engaged. Its present prosecution is a foregone conclusion; and a wise man never wastes his strength on a fruitless enterprise. My position shall, at present, for the most part, be indicated by my votes, and by the resolutions and motions which I may submit. But there are many questions incident to the war and to its prosecution, about which I have somewhat to say now.

Mr. Chairman, the President, in the message before us, demands the extraordinary loan of $400,000,000—an amount nearly ten times greater than the entire public debt, State and Federal, at the close of the Revolution, in 1783, and four times as much as the total expenditures during the three years' war with Great Britain, in 1812.

Sir, that same *Constitution* which I again hold up, and to which I give my whole heart, and my utmost loyalty, commits to Congress alone the power to borrow money, and to fix the purposes to which it shall be applied, and expressly limits army appropriations to the term of two years. Each Senator and Representative, therefore, must judge for himself, upon his conscience and his oath, and before God and the country, of the justice and wisdom and policy of the President's demand; and whenever this House shall have become but a mere office wherein to register the decrees of the Executive, it will be high time to abolish it. But I have a right, I believe, sir, to say that, however gentlemen upon this side of the Chamber may differ finally as to the war, we are yet firmly and inexorably united in one thing, at least, and that is in the determination that our own rights and dignities and privileges, as the Representatives of the people, shall be maintained in their spirit, and to the very letter. And, be this as it may, I do know that there are some here present who are resolved to assert, and to exercise these rights with becoming decency and moderation, certainly, but, at the same time, fully, freely, and at every hazard.

Sir, it is an ancient and wise practice of the English Commons, to precede all votes of supplies by an inquiry into abuses and grievances, and especially into any infractions of the *Constitution* and the laws by the Executive. Let us follow this safe practice. We are now in Committee of the Whole *on the State of the Union*; and in the exercise of my right and my duty as a Representative, and availing myself of the latitude of debate allowed here, I propose to consider the present State of the Union, and supply, also, some few of the many omissions of the President in the message before us. Sir, he has undertaken to give us information of the state of the Union, as the *Constitution* requires him to do; and it was his duty, as an honest Executive, to make that information full, impartial, and complete instead of spreading before us a labored and lawyerly vindication of his own course of policy—a policy which has precipitated us into a terrible and bloody revolution. He admits the fact; he admits that, to-day, we are in the midst of a general civil war, not now a mere petty insurrection, to be suppressed in twenty days by a proclamation and a *posse comitatus* of three months' militia.

Sir, it has been the misfortune of the President, from the beginning, that he has totally and wholly under-estimated the magnitude and character of the Revolution with which he had to deal, or surely he never would have ventured upon the wicked and hazardous experiment of calling thirty millions of people to arms among themselves, without the counsel and authority of Congress. But when, at last, he found himself hemmed in by the revolution, and this city in danger, as he declares, and waked up thus, as the proclamation of the 15th of April proves him to have waked up, to the reality and significance of the movement, why did he not forthwith assemble Congress, and throw himself upon the wisdom and patriotism of the Representatives of the States and of the people, instead of usurping powers which the *Constitution* has expressly conferred upon us? Ay, sir, and powers which Congress had but a little while before, repeatedly and emphatically refused to exercise, or to permit him to exercise? But I shall recur to this point again.

Sir, the President, in this message, has undertaken also to give us a summary of the causes which have led to the present revolution. He has made out a case—he might, in my judgment, have made out a much stronger case—against the secessionists and disunionists of the South. All this, sir, is very well, as far as it goes. But the President does not go back far enough, nor in the right direction. He forgets the still stronger case against the abolitionists and disunionists of the North and West. He omits to tell us the secession and disunion had a New England origin, and began in Massachusetts, in 1804, at the time of the Louisiana purchase; were revived by the Hartford convention, in 1814, and culminated, during the war with Great Britain, in sending commissioners to Washington to settle the terms for a peaceable separation of New England from the other States of the Union. He forgets to remind us and the country, that this present revolution began forty years ago, in the vehement, persistent, offensive, most irritating and unprovoked agitation of the slavery question in the North and West, from the time of the Missouri controversy, with some short intervals, down to the present hour. Sir, if his statement of the case be the whole truth, and wholly correct, then the Democratic Party, and every member of it, and the Whig Party, too, and its predecessors, have been guilty, for sixty years, of an unjust, unconstitutional, and most wicked policy in administering the affairs of the Government. . . .

Did he not know—how could he be ignorant—that, at the last session of Congress, every substantive proposition for adjustment and compromise, except that offered by the gentleman from Illinois [Mr. Kellegg]—and we all know, how it was received—came from the South? Stop a moment, and let us see.

The Committee of Thirty-three was moved for in this House by a gentleman from Virginia, the second day of the session, and received the vote of every Southern Representative present, except only the members from South Carolina, who declined to vote. In the Senate, the committee of thirteen was proposed by a Senator from Kentucky [Mr. Powell], and received the silent acquiescence of every Southern Senator present. The Crittenden propositions, too, were submitted also by another Senator from Kentucky [Mr. Crittenden], now a member of this House; a man, venerable for his years, loved for his virtues, distinguished for his services, honored for his patriotism; for four and forty years a Senator, or in other public office; devoted from the first hour of his manhood to the Union of these States; and who, though he himself proved his courage fifty years ago, upon the battlefield against the foreign enemies of his country, is now, thank God, still for compromise at home, to-day. Fortunate in a long and well-spent life of public service and private worth, he is unfortunate only that he has survived a Union, and, I fear, a *Constitution*, younger than himself.

The border States propositions, also, were projected by a gentleman from Maryland, not now a member of this House, and presented by a gentleman from Tennessee [Mr. Etheridge], now the Clerk of this House. And yet all these propositions, coming thus from the South, were severally and repeatedly rejected by the almost united vote of the Republican Party in the Senate and the House. The Crittenden propositions, with which Mr. Davis, now President of the Confederate States, and Mr. Toombs, his Secretary of State, both declared, in the Senate, that they would be satisfied, and for which every Southern Senator and Representative voted—never, on any occasion, received one solitary vote from the Republican Party in either House.

The Adams or Corwin amendment, so-called—reported from the Committee of Thirty-three, and the only substantive amendment proposed from the Republican side—was but a bare promise that Congress should never be authorized to do what no sane man ever believed Congress would attempt to do—abolish slavery in the States where it exists; and yet, even this proposition, moderate as it was, and for which every Southern member present voted—except one—was carried through this House by but one majority, after long and tedious delay, and with the utmost difficulty—sixty-five Republican members, with the resolute and determined gentleman from Pennsylvania [Mr. Hickman] at their head, having voted against it and fought against it to the very last.

And not this only, but, as a part of the history of the last session, let me remind you that bills were introduced into this House, proposing to abolish and close up certain Southern ports of entry; to authorize the President to blockade the Southern coast, and to call out the militia, and accept the services of volunteers—not for three years merely—but without any limit as to either numbers or time, for the very purpose of enforcing the laws, collecting the revenue, and protecting the public property—and were passed, vehemently and earnestly, in this House, *prior to the arrival of the President in this city*, and were then—though seven States had seceded, and set up a government of their own—voted down, postponed, thrust aside, or in some other way disposed of, sometimes by large majorities in this House, till, at last, Congress adjourned without any action at all. Peace, then, seemed to be the policy of all parties.

Thus, sir, the case stood, at twelve o'clock on the 4th of March last, when, from the eastern portico of this capitol, and in the presence of twenty thousand of his countrymen, but enveloped in a cloud of soldiery, which no other American

President ever saw, Abraham Lincoln took the oath of office to support the *Constitution*, and delivered his inaugural—a message, I regret to say, not written in the direct and straightforward language which becomes an American President and an American statesman, and which was expected from the plain, blunt, honest man of the North-west—but with the forked tongue and crooked counsel of the New York politician leaving thirty millions of people in doubt whether it meant peace or war. But, whatever may have been the secret purpose and meaning of the inaugural, practically, for six weeks, the policy of peace prevailed; and they were weeks of happiness to the patriot, and prosperity to the country. Business revived; trade returned; commerce flourished. Never was there a fairer prospect before any people. Secession in the past, languished, and was spiritless, and harmless; secession in the future, was arrested, and perished. By overwhelming majorities, Virginia, Kentucky, North Carolina, Tennessee, and Missouri—all declared for the old Union, and every heart beat high with hope that, in due course of time, and through faith and patience and peace, and by ultimate and adequate compromise, every State could be restored to it. It is true, indeed, sir, that the Republican Party, with great unanimity, and great earnestness and determination, had resolved against all conciliation and compromise. But, on the other hand, the whole Democratic Party, and the whole Constitutional-Union Party, were equally resolved that there should be no civil war, upon any pretext: and both sides prepared for an appeal to that great and final arbiter of all disputes in a free country—the people.

Sir, I do not propose to inquire, now, whether the President and his Cabinet were sincere and in earnest, and meant, really, to persevere to the end in the policy of peace; or whether, from the first, they meant civil war, and only waited to gain time till they were fairly seated in power, and had disposed, too, of that prodigious horde of spoilsmen and office-seekers which came down, at the first, like an avalanche upon them. But I do know that the people believed them sincere, and cordially ratified and approved of the policy of peace—not as they subsequently responded to the policy of war, in a whirlwind of passion and madness—but calmly and soberly, and as the result of their deliberate and most solemn judgment; and believing that civil war was absolute and eternal disunion, while secession was but partial and temporary, they cordially endorsed, also, the proposed evacuation of Sumter, and the other forts and public property within the seceded States. Nor, sir, will I stop, now, to explore the several causes which either led to a change in the apparent policy, or an early development of the original and real purposes of the Administration. But there are two which I can not pass by. And the first of these was party necessity, or the clamor of politicians, and especially of certain wicked, reckless, and unprincipled conductors of a partisan press. The peace policy was crushing out the Republican Party. Under that policy, sir, it was melting away like snow before the sun. The general election in Rhode Island and Connecticut, and municipal elections in New York and in the western States, gave abundant evidence that the people were resolved upon the most ample and satisfactory Constitutional guarantees to the South, as the price of a restoration of the Union. And then it was, sir, that the long and agonizing howl of defeated and disappointed politicians came up before the Administration. The newspaper press teemed with appeals and threats to the President. The mails groaned under the weight of letters demanding a change of policy; while a secret conclave of the Governors of Massachusetts, New York, Ohio, and other States, assembled here, promised men and money to support the President in the irrepressible conflict which they now invoked. And thus it was, sir, that the necessities of a party in the pangs of dissolution, in the very hour and article of death, demanding vigorous measures, which could result in nothing but civil war, renewed secession, and absolute and eternal disunion were preferred and hearkened to before the peace and harmony and prosperity of the whole country.

But there was another and yet stronger impelling cause, without which this horrid calamity of civil war might have been postponed, and, perhaps, finally averted. One of the last and worst acts of a Congress which, born in bitterness and nurtured in convulsion, literally did those things which it ought not to have done, and left undone those things which it ought to have done, was the passage of an obscure, ill-considered, ill-digested, and unstatesmanlike high protective tariff act, commonly known as "The Morrill Tariff." Just about the same time, too, the Confederate Congress, at Montgomery, adopted our old tariff of 1857, which we had rejected to make way for the Morrill act, fixing their rate of duties at five, fifteen, and twenty per cent lower than ours. The result was as inevitable as the laws of trade are inexorable. Trade and commerce—and especially the trade and commerce of the West—began to look to the South. Turned out of their natural course, years ago, by the canals and railroads of Pennsylvania and New York, and diverted eastward at a heavy cost to the West, they threatened now to resume their ancient and accustomed channels—the water-courses—the Ohio and the Mississippi.

And political association and union, it was well known, must soon follow the direction of trade and interest. The city of New York, the great commercial emporium of the Union, and the North-west, the chief granary of the Union, began to clamor now, loudly, for a repeal of the pernicious and ruinous tariff. Threatened thus with the loss of both political power and wealth, or the repeal of the tariff, and, at last, of both, New England—and Pennsylvania, too, the land of Penn, cradled in peace—demanded, now, coercion and civil war, with all its horrors, as the price of preserving either from destruction. Ay, sir, Pennsylvania, the great key-stone of the arch of the Union, was willing to lay the whole weight of her iron upon that sacred arch, and crush it beneath the load. The subjugation of the South—ay, sir, the *subjugation* of the South!—I am not talking to children or fools; for there is not a man in this House fit to be a Representative here, who does not know that the South can not be forced to yield obedience to your laws and authority again, until you have conquered and subjugated her—the subjugation of the South, and the closing up of her ports—first, by force, in war, and afterward, by tariff laws, in peace—was deliberately resolved upon by the East. And, sir, when once this policy was begun, these self-same motives of waning commerce, and threatened loss of trade, impelled the great city of New York, and her merchants and her politicians and her press—with here and there an honorable exception—to place herself in a very front rank among the worshippers of Moloch. Much, indeed, of that outburst and uprising in the North, which followed the proclamation of the 15th of April, as well, perhaps, as the proclamation itself, was called forth, not so much by the fall of Sumter—an event long anticipated—as by the notion that the "insurrection," as it was called, might be crushed out in a few weeks, if not by the display, certainly, at least, by the presence of an overwhelming force.

These, sir, were the chief causes which, along with others, led to a change in the policy of the Administration, and, instead of peace, forced us, headlong, into civil war, with all its accumulated horrors.

But, whatever may have been the causes or the motives of the act, it is certain that there was a change in the policy which the Administration meant to adopt, or which, at least, they led the country to believe they intended to pursue. I will not venture, now, to assert, what may yet, some day, be made to appear, that the subsequent acts of the Administration, and its enormous and persistent infractions of the *Constitution*, its high-minded usurpations of power, formed any part of a deliberate conspiracy to overthrow the present form of Federal-republican government, and to establish a strong centralized Government in its stead. No, sir, whatever their purposes now, I rather think that, in the beginning, they rushed, heedlessly and headlong into the gulf, believing that, as the seat of war was then far distant and difficult of access, the display of vigor in re-enforcing Sumter and Pickens, and in calling out seventy-five thousand militia upon, the firing of the first gun, and above all, in that exceedingly happy and original conceit of commanding the insurgent States to "disperse in twenty days," would not, on the one hand, precipitate a crisis, while, upon the other, it would satisfy its own violent partisans, and thus revive and restore the failing fortunes of the Republican Party.

I can hardly conceive, sir, that the President and his advisors could be guilty of the exceeding folly of expecting to carry on a general civil war by a mere *posse comitatus* of three-months militia. It may be, indeed, that, with wicked and most desperate cunning, the President meant all this as a mere entering-wedge to that which was to rive the oak asunder; or, possibly, as a test, to learn the public sentiment of the North and West. But however that may be, the rapid secession and movements of Virginia, North Carolina, Arkansas, and Tennessee, taking with them, as I have said, elsewhere, four millions and a half of people, immense wealth, inexhaustible resources, five hundred thousand fighting men, and *the graves of Washington and Jackson*, and bringing up, too, in one single day, the frontier from the Gulf to the Ohio and the Potomac, together with the abandonment, by the one side, and the occupation, by the other, of Harper's Ferry and the Norfolk navy-yard; and the fierce gust and whirlwind of passion in the North, compelled either a sudden waking-up of the President and his advisors to the frightful significancy of the act which they had committed, in heedlessly breaking the vase which imprisoned the slumbering demon of civil war, or else a premature but most rapid development of the daring plot to foster and promote secession, and then to set up a new and strong form of government in the States which might remain in the Union.

But, whatever may have been the purpose, I assert here, to-day, as a Representative, that every principal act of the Administration since has been a glaring usurpation of power, and a palpable and dangerous violation of that very *Constitution* which this civil war is professedly waged to support. . . . Every other principal act of the Administration might well have been post-poned, and ought to have been postponed, until the meeting of

Congress; or, if the exigencies of the occasion demanded it, Congress should forthwith have been assembled. What if two or three States should not have been represented, although even this need not have happened; but better this, a thousand times, than that the *Constitution* should be repeatedly and flagrantly violated, and public liberty and private right trampled under foot. As for Harper's Ferry and the Norfolk navy-yard, they rather needed protection against the Administration, by whose orders millions of property were wantonly destroyed, which was not in the slightest danger from any quarter, at the date of the proclamation.

But, sir, Congress was not assembled at once, as Congress should have been, and the great question of civil war submitted to their deliberations. The Representatives of the States and of the people were not allowed the slightest voice in this, the most momentous question ever presented to any government. The entire responsibility of the whole work was boldly assumed by the Executive, and all the powers required for the purposes in hand were boldly usurped from either the States or the people, or from the legislative department; while the voice of the judiciary, that last refuge and hope of liberty, was turned away from with contempt.

Sir, the right of blockade—and I begin with it—is a belligerent right, incident to a state of war, and it can not be exercised until war has been declared or recognized; and Congress alone can declare or recognize war. But Congress had not declared or recognized war. On the contrary, they had, but a little while before, expressly refused to declare it, or to arm the President with the power to make it. And thus the President, in declaring a blockade of certain ports in the States of the South, and in applying to it the rules governing blockades as between independent powers, violated the *Constitution*.

But if, on the other hand, he meant to deal with these States as still in the Union, and subject to Federal authority, then he usurped a power which belongs to Congress alone—the power to abolish and close up ports of entry; a power, too, which Congress had, also, but a few weeks before, refused to exercise. And yet, without the repeal or abolition of ports of entry, any attempt, by either Congress or the President, to blockade these ports, is a violation of the spirit, if not of the letter, of that clause of the *Constitution* which declares that "no preference shall be given, by any regulation of commerce or revenue, to the ports of one State over those of another."

Sir, upon this point I do not speak without the highest authority. In the very midst of the South Carolina nullification controversy, it was suggested, that in the recess of Congress, and without a law to govern him, the President, Andrew Jackson, meant to send down a fleet to Charleston and blockade the port. But the bare suggestion called forth the indignant protest of Daniel Webster, himself the arch enemy of nullification, and whose brightest laurels were won in the three years' conflict in the Senate Chamber, with its ablest champions. In an address, in October, 1832, at Worcester, Massachusetts, to a National Republican convention—it was before the birth, or christening, at least, of the Whig Party—the great expounder of the Constitution, said:

> We are told, sir, that the President will immediately employ the military force, and at once blockade Charleston. A military remedy—a remedy by direct belligerent operation, has thus been suggested, and nothing else has been suggested, as the intended means of preserving the Union. Sir, there is no little reason to think that this suggestion is true. We can not be altogether unmindful of the past, and, therefore, we can not be altogether unapprehensive for the future. For one, sir, I raise my voice, beforehand, against the unauthorized employment of military power, and against superseding the authority of the laws, by an armed force, under pretense of putting down nullification. *The President has no authority to blockade Charleston.*

Jackson! Jackson, sir! the great Jackson! did not dare to do it without authority of Congress; but our Jackson of to-day, the little Jackson at the other end of the avenue, and the mimic Jacksons around him, do blockade, not only Charleston harbor, but the whole Southern coast, three thousand miles in extent, by a single stroke of the pen.

"The President has no authority to employ military force till he shall be duly required"—mark the word: "*required* so to do by law and the civil authorities. His duty is to cause the laws to be executed. His duty is to support *the civil authority.*"

As in the Merryman case, forsooth; but I shall recur to that hereafter:

> His duty is, if the laws be resisted, to employ the military force of the country, if necessary, for their support and execution; *but to do all this in compliance only with law and with decisions of the tribunals.* If, by any ingenious devices, those who resist the laws escape from the

reach of judicial authority, as it is now provided to be exercised, it is entirely competent to *Congress* to make such new provisions as the exigency of the case may demand.

Treason, sir, rank treason, all this to-day. And, yet, thirty years ago, it was true Union patriotism and sound constitutional law! Sir, I prefer the wisdom and stern fidelity to principle of the fathers.

Such was the voice of Webster, and such too, let me add, the voice, in his last great speech in the Senate, of the Douglas whose death the land now mourns.

Next after the blockade, sir, in the catalogue of daring executive usurpations, comes the proclamation of the 3d of May, and the orders of the War and Navy Departments in pursuance of it—a proclamation and usurpation which would have cost any English sovereign his head at any time within the last two hundred years. Sir, the *Constitution* not only confines to Congress the right to declare war, but expressly provides that "Congress" (not the President) shall have power to raise and support armies;" and to "provide and maintain a navy." In pursuance of this authority, Congress, years ago, had fixed the number of officers, and of the regiments of the different kinds of service; and also, the number of ships, officers, marines, and seamen which should compose the navy. Not only that, but Congress has repeatedly, within the last five years, refused to increase the regular army. More than that still: in February and March last, the House, upon several test votes, repeatedly and expressly refused to authorize the President to accept the service of volunteers for the very purpose of protecting the public property, enforcing the laws, and collecting the revenue. And, yet, the President, of his own mere will and authority, and without the shadow of right, has proceeded to increase, and has increased, the standing army by twenty-five thousand men; the navy by eighteen thousand; and has called for, and accepted the services of, forty regiments of volunteers for three years, numbering forty-two thousand men, and making thus a grand army, or military force, raised by executive proclamation alone, without the sanction of Congress, without warrant of law, and in direct violation of the *Constitution*, and of his oath of office, of eighty-five thousand soldiers enlisted for three and five years, and already in the field. And, yet, the President now asks us to support the army which he has thus raised, to ratify his usurpations by a law *ex post facto*, and thus to make ourselves parties to our own degradation, and to his infractions of the Constitution. Meanwhile, however, he has taken good care not only to enlist the men, organize the regiments, and muster them into service, but to provide, in advance, for a horde of forlorn, worn-out, and broken-down politicians of his own party, by appointing, either by himself, or through the Governors of the States, major-generals, brigadier-generals, colonels, lieutenant-colonels, majors, captains, lieutenants, adjutants, quarter-masters, and surgeons, without any limit as to numbers, and without so much as once saying to Congress, "By your leave, gentlemen."

Beginning with this wide breach of the *Constitution*, this enormous usurpation of the most dangerous of all powers—the power of the sword—other infractions and assumptions were easy; and after public liberty, private right soon fell. The privacy of the telegraph was invaded in the search after treason and traitors; although it turns out, significantly enough, that the only victim, so far, is one of the appointees and especial pets of the Administration. The telegraphic dispatches, preserved under every pledge of secrecy for the protection and safety of the telegraph companies, were seized and carried away without search-warrant, without probable cause, without oath, and without description of the places to be searched, or of the things to be seized, and in plain violation of the right of the people to be secure in their houses, persons, *papers*, and effects, against unreasonable searches and seizures. One step more, sir, will bring upon us search and seizure of the public mails; and, finally, as in the worst days of English oppression—as in the times of the Russells and the Sydneys of English martyrdom—of the drawers and secretaries of the private citizen; though even then tyrants had the grace to look to the forms of the law, and the execution was judicial murder, not military slaughter. But who shall say that the future Tiberius of America shall have the modesty of his Roman predecessor, in extenuation of whose character it is written by the great historian, *avertit, occulos, jussitque scelera non spectavit.*

Sir, the rights of property having been thus wantonly violated, it needed but a little stretch of usurpation to invade the sanctity of the person; and a victim was not long wanting. A private citizen of Maryland, not subject to the rules and articles of war—not in a case arising in the land or naval forces, nor in the militia, when in actual service—is seized in his own house, in the dead hour of night, not by any civil officer, nor upon any civil process, but by a band of armed soldiers, under the verbal orders of a military chief, and is ruthlessly torn from his wife and his children, and hurried off to a fortress of the United States—and that fortress, as if in mockery, the very one over whose ramparts had floated that star-spangled banner immortalized in song by the patriot prisoner, who, "By the dawn's early light," saw its folds gleaming amid the wreck of battle, and invoked the blessings of heaven upon it, and prayed that it might long wave "o'er the *land of the free*, and the home of the brave."

And, sir, when the highest judicial officer of the land, the Chief Justice of the Supreme Court, upon whose shoulders, "when the judicial ermine fell, it touched nothing not as spotless as itself," the aged, the venerable, the gentle, and pure-minded Taney, who, but a little while before, had administered to the President the oath to support the *Constitution*, and to execute the laws, issued, as by law it was his sworn duty to issue, the high prerogative writ of *habeas corpus*—that great writ of right, that main bulwark of personal liberty, commanding the body of the accused to be brought before him, that justice and right might be done by due course of law, and without denial or delay, the gates of the fortress, its cannon turned towards, and in plain sight of the city, where the court sat, and frowning from the ramparts, were closed against the officer of the law, and the answer returned that the officer in command has, by the authority of the President, *suspended* the writ of *habeas corpus*. And thus it is, sir, that the accused has ever since been held a prisoner without due process of law; without bail; without presentment by a grand jury; without speedy, or public trial by a petit jury, of his own State or district, or any trial at all; without information of the nature and cause of the accusation; without being confronted with the witnesses against him; without compulsory process to obtain witnesses in his favor; and without the assistance of counsel for his defense. And this is our boasted American liberty? And thus it is, too, sir, that here, here, in America, in the seventy-third year of the Republic, that great writ and security of personal freedom, which it cost the patriots and freemen of England six hundred years of labor and toil and blood to extort and to hold fast from venal judges and tyrant kings; written in the great character at Runnymede by the iron barons, who made the simple Latin and uncouth words of the times, *nullus liber homo*, in the language of Chatham, worth all the classics; recovered and confirmed a hundred times afterward, as often as violated and stolen away, and finally, and firmly secured at last by the great act of Charles II, and transferred thence to our own *Constitution* and laws, has been wantonly and ruthlessly trampled in the dust. Ay, sir, that great writ, bearing by

726

a special command of Parliament, those other uncouth, but magic words, *per statutum tricessimo primo Caroli secundi regis*, which no English judge, no English minister, no king or queen of England, dare disobey; that writ, brought over by our fathers, and cherished by them, as a priceless inheritance of liberty, an American President has contemptuously set at defiance. Nay, more, he has ordered his subordinate military chiefs to suspend it at their discretion! And, yet, after all this, he coolly comes before this House and the Senate and the country, and pleads that he is only preserving and protecting the *Constitution*; and demands and expects of this House and of the Senate and the country their thanks for his usurpations; while, outside of this capitol, his myrmidons are clamoring for impeachment of the Chief Justice, as engaged in a conspiracy to break down the Federal Government.

Sir, however much necessity—the tyrant's plea—may be urged in extenuation of the usurpations and infractions of the President in regard to public liberty, there can be no such apology or defense for his invasions of private right. What overruling necessity required the violation of the sanctity of private property and private confidence? What great public danger demanded the arrest and imprisonment, without trial by common law, of one single private citizen, for an act done weeks before, openly, and by authority of his State? If guilty of treason, was not the judicial power ample enough and strong enough for his conviction and punishment? What, then, was needed in his case, but the precedent under which other men, in other places, might become the victims of executive suspicion and displeasure?

As to the pretense, sir, that the President has the Constitutional right to suspend the writ of *habeas corpus*, I will not waste time in arguing it. The case is as plain as words can make it. It is a legislative power; it is found only in the legislative article; it belongs to Congress only to do it. Subordinate officers have disobeyed it; General Wilkinson disobeyed it; but he sent his prisoners on for judicial trial; General Jackson disobeyed it, and was reprimanded by James Madison; but no President, nobody but Congress, ever before assumed the right to suspend it. And, sir, that other pretense of necessity, I repeat, can not be allowed. It had no existence in fact. The *Constitution* can not be preserved by violating it. It is an offense to the intelligence of this House, and of the country, to pretend that all this, and the other gross and multiplied infractions of the *Constitution* and usurpations of power were done by the President and his advisors out of pure love and devotion to the *Constitution*. But if so, sir, then they have but one step further to take, and declare, in the language of Sir Boyle Roche, in the Irish House of Commons, that such is the depth of their attachment to it, that they are prepared to give up, not merely a part, but the whole of the Constitution, to preserve the remainder. And yet, if indeed this pretext of necessity be well founded, then let me say, that a cause which demands the sacrifice of the *Constitution* and of the dearest securities of property, liberty, and life, can not be just; at least, it is not worth the sacrifice.

Sir, I am obliged to pass by for want of time, other grave and dangerous infractions and usurpations of the President since the 4th of March. I only allude casually to the quartering of soldiers in private houses without the consent of the owners, and without any manner having been prescribed by law; to the subversion in a part, at least, of Maryland of her own State Government and of the authorities under it; to the censorship over the telegraph, and the infringement, repeatedly, in one or more of the States, of the right of the people to keep and to bear arms for their defense. But if all these things, I ask, have been done in the first two months after the commencement of this war, and by men not military chieftains, and unused to arbitrary power, what may we not expect to see in three years, and by the successful heroes of the fight? Sir, the power and rights of the States and the people, and of their Representatives, have been usurped; the sanctity of the private house and of private property has been invaded; and the liberty of the person wantonly and wickedly stricken down; free speech, too, has been repeatedly denied; and all this under the plea of necessity. Sir, the right of petition will follow next— nay, it has already been shaken; the freedom of the press will soon fall after it; and let me whisper in your ear, that there will be few to mourn over its loss, unless, indeed, its ancient high and honorable character shall be rescued and redeemed from its present reckless mendacity and degradation. Freedom of religion will yield too, at last, amid the exultant shouts of millions, who have seen its holy temples defiled, and its white robes of a former innocency trampled now under the polluting hoofs of an ambitious and faithless or fanatical clergy. Meantime national banks, bankrupt laws, a vast and permanent public debt, high tariffs, heavy direct taxation, enormous expenditure, gigantic and stupendous peculation, anarchy first, and a strong government afterward—no more State lines, no more State governments, and a consolidated monarchy or vast centralized military despotism must all follow in the history of the future, as in the history of the past they have, centuries ago, been written. Sir, I have said nothing, and have time to say nothing now, of the immense indebtedness and the vast expenditures which have already accrued, nor of the folly and mismanagement of the war so far, nor of the atrocious and shameless peculations and frauds which have disgraced it in the State governments and the Federal Government from the beginning. The avenging hour for all these will come hereafter, and I pass by them now.

I have finished now, Mr. Chairman, what I proposed to say at this time upon the message of the President. As to my own position in regard to this most unhappy civil war, I have only to say that I stand to-day just where I stood upon the 4th of March last; where the whole Democratic Party, and the whole Constitutional Union Party, and a vast majority, as I believe, of the people of the United States stood too. I am for *peace*, speedy, immediate, honorable *peace*, with all its blessings. Others may have changed—I have not. I question not their motives nor quarrel with their course. It is vain and futile for them to question or to quarrel with me. My duty shall be discharged—calmly, firmly, quietly, and regardless of consequences. The approving voice of a conscience void of offense, and the approving judgment which shall follow "after some time be past," these, God help me, are my trust and my support.

Sir, I have spoken freely and fearlessly to-day, as became an American Representative and an American citizen; one firmly resolved, come what may, not to lose his own Constitutional liberties, nor to surrender his own Constitutional rights in the vain effort to impose these rights and liberties upon ten millions of unwilling people. I have spoken earnestly, too, but yet not as one unmindful of the solemnity of the scenes which surround us upon every side to-day. Sir, when the Congress of the United States assembled here on the 3rd of December, 1860, just seven months ago, the Senate was composed of sixty-six Senators, representing the thirty-three States of the Union, and this House of two hundred and thirty-seven members—every State being present. It was a grand and solemn spectacle—the ambassadors of three and thirty sovereignties and thirty-one millions of people, the mightiest republic on earth, in general Congress assembled. In the Senate, too, and this House, were some of the ablest and most distinguished statesmen of the country; men whose names were familiar to the whole country—some of them destined to pass into history. The new wings of the capitol had then but just recently been finished, in all their gorgeous magnificence, and, except a hundred marines at the navy-yard, not a soldier was within forty miles of Washington.

Sir, the Congress of the United States meets here again to-day; but how changed the scene! Instead of thirty-four States, twenty-three only, one less than the number forty years ago, are here, or in the other wing of the capitol. Forty-six Senators and a hundred and seventy-three Representatives constitute the Congress of the now United States. And of these, eight Senators and twenty-four Representatives, from four States only, linger here yet as deputies from that great South which, from the beginning of the Government, contributed so much to mold its policy, to build up its greatness, and to control its destinies. All the other States of that South are gone. Twenty-two Senators and sixty-five representatives no longer answer to their names. The vacant seats are, indeed, still here; and the escutcheons of their respective States look down now solemnly and sadly from these vaulted ceilings. But the Virginia of Washington and Henry and Madison, of Marshall and Jefferson, of Randolph and Monroe, the birthplace of Clay, the mother of States and of Presidents; the Carolinas of Pinckney and Sumter and Marion, of Calhoun and Macon; and Tennessee, the home and burial-place of Jackson; and other States, too, once most loyal and true, are no longer here. The voices and the footsteps of the great dead of the past two ages of the Republic linger still—it may be in echo—along the stately corridors of this capitol; but their descendants, from nearly one-half of the States of the Republic, will meet with us no more within these marble halls. But in the parks and lawns, and upon the broad avenues of this spacious city, seventy thousand soldiers have supplied their places; and the morning drum-beat from a score of encampments, within sight of this beleaguered capitol, give melancholy warning to the Representatives of the States and of the people, that *amid arms laws are silent*.

Sir, some years hence—I would fain hope some months hence, if I dare—the present generation will demand to know the cause of all this; and, some ages hereafter, the grand and impartial tribunal of history will make solemn and diligent inquest of the authors of this terrible revolution.[5]

---

[5]Clement L. Vallandigham, *Abolition, The Union, and the Civil War* (Cincinnati: J. Walter and Company (1863, Wiggins, Miss.: Crown Rights, 1998), pp. 94–109.

Conclusion

If Americans are to reclaim the liberty and freedom created by our Founders, we must cut through the propaganda of the court historians and see the real causes and effects of the Civil War. Congressman Clement L. Vallandigham stated the true facts of both the causes and the effects of the war, and he paid a terrible price. However, if we can learn the lessons history taught by his speech, then his brave stand will not have been in vain.

APPENDIX B

SPEECH ON THE DECLARATION OF WAR AGAINST GERMANY BY THE HONORABLE ROBERT M. LA FOLLETTE, SR., U.S. SENATOR FROM WISCONSIN, OPPOSING PRESIDENT WOODROW WILSON'S REQUEST FOR A DECLARATION OF WAR FROM CONGRESS FOR WORLD WAR I

INTRODUCTION

Senator Robert M. La Follette, Sr. (1855–1925) was one of the most courageous U.S. senators in American history. He earned the nickname "Battling Bob" for his vigorous political tactics. He was born in Primrose, Wisconsin, and worked his way through the University of Wisconsin. He became a lawyer and within a year was elected district attorney of Dane County, Wisconsin. Four years later, he was elected to the United States House of Representatives. He was the youngest congressman to be sworn in to the House in 1885.

La Follette was defeated in the election of 1890 and returned home to Wisconsin to practice law in Madison for ten years. He continued to take an active role in Republican Party politics and became the leader of a group which was opposed to the state administration. This particular group became influential enough to elect him governor in 1900. He immediately began to make governmental reforms, which included direct primaries, equalization of taxation, and control of railroad rates. He resigned in 1905 to become one of the United States senators from Wisconsin and was reelected in 1910, 1916, and finally again in 1922.

While in the U.S. Senate, La Follette became the leader of a group of progressive Republicans called the "Insurgents," and he continued to work for reform legislation. He established everlasting fame, however, as a result of his opposition to President Wilson in regard to the declaration of war for World War I by voting against American entry into that ill-advised and unnecessary war.

Probably the most important provision of the Constitution for the protection of individual liberty is the clause which grants Congress the exclusive power to declare war. The Founders recognized that the executive could not be trusted with the warmaking power, since war always enhanced the power and prestige of that

733

office. The clause granting the exclusive warmaking power to Congress has been ignored by American presidents for the second half of the twentieth century. Presidents have plotted numerous ways to place pressure on Congress to declare war, such as provoking the enemy to fire the first shot. However, a few courageous and patriotic members of Congress who have understood the Constitution and the reasons for the separation of powers have braved the outrage of the public and the press to oppose the president of the United States regarding his request for a declaration of war.

La Follette not only stood against President Wilson regarding the declaration of war, but he later opposed the United States's membership in the League of Nations and signing of the Treaty of Versailles. Wilson's alleged purpose of fighting the war to "make the world safe for democracy"—participating in the "war to end all wars"—instead produced the fraudulent and vindictive Versailles treaty, which virtually made another war in Europe inevitable and set the stage for continuous warfare throughout the twentieth century. This was the prelude to America's role as world policeman today. Americans who love individual freedom should always revere La Follette for his courageous stands.[1]

---

[1]Two other U.S. senators spoke out against the war. Senator George W. Norris warned:

> "[W]e are going into war upon the command of gold." He argued that munitions makers and bankers were instrumental in taking the country toward war. "I would like to say to this war god," he exclaimed, "You shall not coin into gold the lifeblood of my brethren." Then he told his colleagues, "I feel that we are about to put the dollar sign upon the American flag." (H.C. Peterson and Gilbert C. Fite, *Opponents of War, 1917–1918* [West Point, Conn.: Greenwood Press, 1957], p. 5)

Senator James K. Vardaman spoke against the declaration of war as follows:

> The President . . . suggested that if the people who are now engaged in this war in Europe had been consulted there would have been no war. If I may be permitted to indulge in a little speculation I will say, Mr. President, that if the people of the United States—I mean the plain, honest people, the masses who are to bear the burden of taxation and fight the Nation's battles, were consulted—the United States would not make a declaration of war against Germany to-day. . . .

The Senate passed the war resolution on April 4, 1917, by a vote of 82 to 6; two days later, the House adopted it by a vote of 373 to 50.[2] President Wilson then proceeded to bring a "reign of terror" down upon American citizens who objected to the war. Not since the excesses of Abraham Lincoln and his administration had there been such violations of the constitutional rights of individuals. The French Revolution had come to America and dissent was to be stamped out.[3] Much of the criticism and dissent related to the fact that this was a war between capitalist countries for a determination of whether Germany or England would be the superior economic force. It was widely recognized that J.P. Morgan and his banking interests were supporting England and thereby making a fortune.[4]

> If it is wrong for a king to plunge his subjects into the vortex of war without their consent it can not be less reprehensible for the President of the United States and the Congress to involve their constituents in a war without their consent. (Ibid., p. 6)

[2]Ibid., p. 8.

[3]Tom Watson, the Georgia politician and prominent objector to the war declared:

> Upon the pretext of waging war against Prussianism in Europe, the purpose of Prussianizing this country has been avowed in Congress, with brutal frankness, by a spokesman of the administration.
>
> On the pretext of sending armies to Europe, to crush militarism there, we first enthrone it here.
>
> On the pretext of carrying to all the nations of the world the liberties won by the heroic lifeblood of our forefathers, we first deprive our own people of liberties they inherited as a birthright.
>
> On the pretext of unchaining the enslaved people of other lands, we first chain our own people with preposterous and unprecedented measures, knowing full well that usurpations of power, once submitted to, will never hereafter be voluntarily restored to the people. (Ibid., p. 155)

[4]The following poem was read into the *Congressional Record* on November 10, 1919. (Ibid., p. 157):

> "And how goes the battle today, J.P.?
>
> How many thousands were slain?
>
> How many blind eyes lifted up to the skies
>
> In pitiful pleading and pain?
>
> And how many curses of hate, J.P.,

In 1924, La Follette broke with the Republican Party when Calvin Coolidge was nominated for president. A group of Republicans met in Cleveland, Ohio, and formed the Progressive Party. La Follette ran as an Independent candidate for the presidency but carried only the state of Wisconsin. Upon his death in 1925, his son Robert M. La Follette, Jr. was appointed to fill his senate seat and subsequently was elected in 1928 and reelected in 1934 and 1940. Bob La Follette, Jr., continued to lead the Progressives in Wisconsin until 1946, when the party rejoined the Republicans under his leadership. He was finally defeated for renomination in 1946.

The following speech was delivered by Robert M. La Follette, Sr., on the floor of the Senate on April 4, 1917, and forever established him as one of the great U.S. senators of all time.

THE SPEECH

Mr. President, I had supposed until recently that it was the duty of Senators and Representatives in Congress to vote and act according to their convictions on all public matters that came before them for consideration and decision.

Quite another doctrine has recently been promulgated by certain newspapers, which unfortunately seems to have found considerable support elsewhere, and that is the doctrine of "standing back of the President," without inquiring whether the President is right or wrong. For myself I have never subscribed to that doctrine and never shall. I shall support the President in the measures he proposes when I believe them to be right. I shall oppose measures proposed by the President when I believe them to be wrong. The fact that the matter which the President submits for consideration is of the greatest importance is only an additional reason why we should be sure that we are right and not to be swerved from that

---

And how many agonized groans?
And how many dollars were lent today,
    At how many per cent for the loans? . . .
But what is our life or our death, J.P.,
    And what are our tears and our moans—
The grief-stricken mother, the life without light—
    As compared with a great banker's loans?

conviction or intimidated in its expression by any influence of power whatsoever. If it is important for us to speak and vote our convictions in matters of internal policy, though we may unfortunately be in disagreement with the President, it is infinitely more important for us to speak and vote our convictions when the question is one of peace or war, certain to involve the lives and fortunes of many of our people and, it may be, the destiny of all of them and of the civilized world as well. If, unhappily, on such momentous questions the most patient research and conscientious consideration we could give to them leave us in disagreement with the President, I know of no course to take except to oppose, regretfully but not the less firmly, the demands of the Executive.

On the second of this month the President addressed a communication to the Senate and House in which he advised that the Congress declare war against Germany and that this Government "assert all its powers and employ all its resources to bring the Government of the German Empire to terms and end the war."

On February 26, 1917, the President addressed the Senate and the House upon the conditions existing between this Government and the German Empire, and at that time said, "I am not now proposing or contemplating war or any steps that needs lead to it. . . . I request that you will authorize me to supply our merchant ships with defensive arms, should that become necessary, and with the means of using them" against what he characterized as the unlawful attacks of German submarines.

A bill was introduced, and it was attempted to rush it through the closing hours of the last session of Congress, to give the President the powers requested, namely, to arm our merchant ships, and to place upon them guns and gunners from our Navy, to be used against German submarines, and to employ such other instrumentalities and methods as might in his judgment and discretion seem necessary and adequate to protect such vessels. That measure did not pass.

It is common knowledge that the President, acting without authority from Congress, did arm our merchant ships with guns and gunners from our Navy, and sent them into the prohibited "war zone." At the time the President addressed us on the second of April there was absolutely no change in the conditions between this Government and Germany. The effect of arming merchant ships had not been tested as a defensive measure. Late press reports indicate, however, that the *Aztec*, a United States armed merchant man, has been sunk in the prohibited zone, whether with mines or a torpedo, I believe, has not been established, so the responsibility for this sinking can not, so far as I know at this time, be placed.

When the request was made by the President on February Twenty-sixth for authority to arm merchant ships, the granting of such authority was opposed by certain Members of the House and by certain Senators, of which I was one. I made at that time a careful investigation of the subject, and became convinced that arming our merchant ships was wholly futile and its only purpose and effect would be to lure our merchantmen to danger, and probably result in the destruction of the vessels and in the loss of the lives of those on board. The representatives of the President on this floor then having that bill in charge saw fit, by methods I do not care to characterize, to prevent my speaking upon the measure and giving to the Senate and to the country such information as I had upon the subject.

Under the circumstances, I did the only thing that seemed practical to me, and that was to give such publicity as I was able through the press to the fact that the proposition to arm merchant ships would be wholly futile, and could only result in loss of the lives and property of our own people, without accomplishing the results intended. I regret to say that the President, according to statements in the public press purporting to emanate from him, and which have never been denied, saw fit to characterize as "willful" the conduct of the Senators who, in obedience to their consciences and their oaths of office, opposed the armed-ship bill, and to charge that in so doing they were not representing the people by whose suffrages they are here. I know of no graver charge that could be made against the official conduct of any Member of this body than that his official action was the result of a "willful"—that is, an unreasoned and perverse—purpose.

Mr. President, many of my colleagues on both sides of this floor have from day to day offered for publication in the RECORD messages and letters received from their constituents. I have received some 15,000 letters and telegrams. They have come from 44 States in the Union. They have been assorted according to whether they speak in criticism or commendation of my course in opposing war.

Assorting the 15,000 letters and telegrams by States in that way, nine out of ten are an unqualified endorsement of my course in opposing war with Germany on the issue presented. . . .

Mr. President, let me make another suggestion. It is this: That a minority in one Congress—mayhap a small minority in one Congress—protesting, exercising the rights which the Constitution confers upon a minority, may really be representing the majority opinion of the country, and if, exercising the right that the Constitution gives them, they succeed in defeating for the time being the will of the majority, they are but carrying out what was in the mind of the framers of the Constitution; that you may have from time to time in a legislative body a majority in numbers that really does not represent the principle of democracy; and that if the question could be deferred and carried to the people it would be found that a minority was the real representative of the public opinion. So, Mr. President, it was that they wrote into the Constitution that a President—that one man—may put his judgment against the will of a majority not only in one branch of the Congress but in both branches of the Congress; that he may defeat the measure that they have agreed upon and may set his one single judgment above the majority judgment of the Congress. That seems, when you look at it nakedly, to be in violation of the principle that the majority shall rule; and so it is. Why is that power given? It is one of the checks provided by the wisdom of the fathers to prevent the majority from abusing the power that they chance to have, when they do not reflect the real judgment, the opinion, the will of the majority of the people that constitute the sovereign power of the democracy. . . .

We need not disturb ourselves because of what a minority may do. There is always lodged, and always will be, thank the God above us, power in the people supreme. Sometimes it sleeps, sometimes it seems the sleep of the death; but, sir, the sovereign power of the people never dies. It may be suppressed for a time, it may be misled, be fooled, silenced. I think, Mr. President, that it is being denied expression now. I think there will come a day when it will have expression.

The poor, sir, who are the ones called upon to rot in the trenches, have no organized power, have no press to voice their will upon this question of peace or war; but, oh, Mr. President, at some time they will be heard. I hope and I believe they will be heard in an orderly and a peaceful way. I think they may be heard from before long. I think, sir, if we take this step, when the people today who are staggering under the burden of supporting families at the present prices of the necessaries of life find those prices multiplied, when they are raised a hundred per cent, or 200 per cent, as they will be quickly, aye, sir, when beyond that those who pay taxes come to have their taxes doubled and again doubled to pay the interest on the nontaxable bonds held by Morgan and his combinations, which have been issued to meet this war, there will come in awakening; they will have their day and they will be heard. It will be as certain and as inevitable as the return of the tides, and as resistless, too.

I promise my colleagues that I will not be tempted again to turn aside from the thread of my discussion as I have outlined it here, and I will hasten with all possible speed.

Now that the President has in his message to us of April second admitted the very charge against the armed-ship bill which we made, I trust that he is fully convinced that the conduct of the Senators on the occasion in question was not unreasoned and obstinate, but that it was inspired by quite as high purposes and motives as can inspire the action of any public official.

I would not, however, have made this personal reference did not the question it suggests go to the very heart of the matter now under consideration. If the President was wrong when he proposed arming the ships; if that policy was, as he now says, "certain to draw us into the war without either the rights or the effectiveness of belligerents," is it so certain he is right now when he demands an unqualified declaration of war against Germany? If those Members of Congress who were supporting the President then were wrong, as it appears from the President's statement now they were, should not that fact prompt them to inquire carefully whether they are right in supporting the proposed declaration of war? If the armed-ship bill involved a course of action that was hasty and ill advised, may it not well be that this proposed declaration of war, which is being so hotly pressed, is also ill advised? . . .

The President in his message of April second says:

"The present German warfare against commerce is a warfare against mankind. It is a war against all nations."

Again referring to Germany's warfare he says:

"There has been no discrimination. The challenge is to all mankind."

It is not a little peculiar that if Germany's warfare is against all nations the United States is the only nation that regards it necessary to declare war on that account? If it is true, as the President says, that "there has been no discrimination," that Germany has treated every neutral as she has treated us, is it not peculiar that no other of the great nations of the earth seem to regard Germany's conduct in this war as a cause for entering into it? Are we the only nation jealous of our rights? Are we the only nation insisting upon the protection of our citizens? Does not the strict neutrality maintained on the part of all the other nations of the earth suggest that possibly there is a reason for their action, and that that reason is that Germany's conduct under the circumstances does not merit from any nation which is determined to preserve its neutrality a declaration of war?

Norway, Sweden, the Netherlands, Switzerland, Denmark, Spain, and all the great Republics of South America are quite as interested in this subject as we are, and yet they have refused to join with us in a combination against Germany. I venture to suggest also that the nations named, and probably others, have a somewhat better right to be heard than we, for by refusing to sell war materiel and munitions to any of the belligerents they have placed themselves in a position where the suspicion which attaches to us of a desire for war profits can not attach to them.

On August 4, 1914, the Republic of Brazil declared the exportation of war materiel from Brazilian ports to any of these powers at war to be strictly forbidden, whether such exports be under the Brazilian flag or that of any other country.

In that connection I note the following dispatch from Buenos Aires, appearing in the Washington papers of yesterday:

> "President Wilson's war address was received here with interest, but no particular enthusiasm. . . . Government officials and politicians have adopted a cold shoulder toward the United States policy—an attitude apparently based on apprehension lest South American interests suffer."

The newspaper *Razon*'s view was illustrative of this. "Does not the United States consider this an opportune time to consolidate the imperialistic policy everywhere north of Panama?" it said.

This is the question that neutral nations the world over are asking. Are we seizing upon this war to consolidate and extend an imperialistic policy? We complain also because Mexico has turned the cold shoulder to us, and are wont to look for sinister reasons for her attitude. Is it any wonder that she should also turn the cold shoulder when she sees us unite with Great Britain, an empire founded upon her conquests and subjugation of weaker nations. There is no doubt that the sympathy of Norway, Sweden, and other countries close to the scene of war is already with Germany. It is apparent that they view with alarm the entrance into the European struggle of the stranger from across the sea. It is suggested by some that our entrance into the war will shorten it. It is my firm belief, based upon such information as I have, that our entrance into the war will not only prolong it, but that it will vastly extend its area by drawing in other nations. . . .

Just a word of comment more upon one of the points in the President's address. He says that this is a war "for the things which we have always carried nearest to our hearts—for democracy, for the right of those who submit to authority to have a voice in their own government." In many places throughout the address is this exalted sentiment given expression.

It is a sentiment peculiarly calculated to appeal to American hearts and, when accompanied by acts consistent with it, is certain to receive our support; but in this same connection, and strangely enough, the President says that we have become convinced that the German Government as it now exists— "Prussian autocracy" he calls it—can never again maintain friendly relations with us. His expression is that "Prussian autocracy was not and could never be our friend," and repeatedly throughout the address the suggestion is made that if the German people would overturn their Government it would probably be the way to peace. So true is this that the dispatches from London all hailed the message of the President as sounding the death knell of Germany's Government.

But the President proposes alliance with Great Britain, which, however liberty-loving its people, is a hereditary monarchy, with a hereditary ruler, with a hereditary House of Lords, with a hereditary landed system, with a limited and restricted suffrage for one class and a multiplied suffrage power for another, and with grinding industrial conditions for all the wage-workers. The President has not suggested that we make our support of Great Britain conditional to her granting home rule to Ireland, or Egypt, or India. We rejoice in the establishment of a democracy in Russia, but it will hardly be contended that if Russia was still an autocratic Government, we would not be asked to enter this alliance with her just the same. Italy and the lesser powers of Europe, Japan in the Orient; in fact, all of the countries with whom we are to enter into alliance, except France and newly revolutionalized Russia, are still of the older order—and it will be generally conceded that no one of them has done as much for its people in the solution of municipal problems and in securing social and industrial reforms as Germany.

Is it not a remarkable democracy which leagues itself with allies already far overmatching in strength the German nation and holds out to such beleaguered nation the hope of peace only at the price of giving up their Government? I am not talk-ing now of the merits or demerits of any government, but I am speaking of a profession of democracy that is linked in action with the most brutal and domineering use of autocratic power. Are the people of this country being so well represented in this war movement that we need to go abroad to give other people control of their governments? Will the President and the supporters of this war bill submit it to a vote of the people before the declaration of war goes into effect? Until we are willing to do that, it illy becomes us to offer as an excuse for our entry into the war the unsupported claim that this war was forced upon the German people by their Government "without their previous knowledge or approval."

Who has registered the knowledge or approval of the American people of the course this Congress is called upon to take in declaring war upon Germany? Submit the question to the people, you who support it. You who support it dare not do it, for you know that by a vote of more than ten to one the American people as a body would register their declaration against it.

In the sense that this war is being forced upon our people without their knowing why and without their approval, and that wars are usually forced upon all peoples in the same way, there is some truth in the statement; but I venture to say that the response which the German people have made to the demands of this war shows that it has a degree of popular support which the war upon which we are entering has not and never will have among our people. The espionage bills, the conscription bills, and other forcible military measures which we understand are being ground out of the war machine in this country is the complete proof that those responsible for this war fear that it has no popular support and that armies sufficient to satisfy the demand of the entente allies can not be recruited by voluntary enlistments. . . .

Jefferson asserted that we could not permit one warring nation to curtail our neutral rights if we were not ready to allow her enemy the same privileges, and that any other course entailed the sacrifice of our neutrality.

That is the sensible, that is the logical position. No neutrality could ever have commanded respect if it was not based on that equitable and just proposition; and we from early in the war threw our neutrality to the winds by permitting England to make a mockery of it to her advantage against her chief enemy. Then we expect to say to that enemy, "You have got to respect my rights as a neutral." What is the answer? I say Germany has been patient with us. Standing strictly on her rights, her answer would be, "Maintain your neutrality; treat those other Governments warring against me as you treat me if you want your neutral rights respected."

I say again that when two nations are at war any neutral nation, in order to preserve its character as a neutral nation, must exact the same conduct from both warring nations; both must equally obey the principles of international law. If a neutral nation fails in that, then its rights upon the high seas—to adopt the President's phrase—are relative and not absolute. There can be no greater violation of our neutrality than the requirement that one of two belligerents shall adhere to the settled principles of law and that the other shall have the advantage of not doing so. The respect that German naval authorities were required to pay to the rights of our people upon the high seas would depend upon the question whether we had exacted the same rights from Germany's enemies. If we had not done so we lost our character as a neutral nation, and our people unfortunately had lost the protection that belongs to neutrals. . . .

Had the plain principle of international law accounted by Jefferson been followed by us, we would not be called on today to declare war upon any of the belligerents. The failure to treat the belligerent nations of Europe alike, the failure to reject the unlawful "war zones" of both Germany and Great Britain, is wholly accountable for our present dilemma. We should not seek to hide our blunder behind the smoke of battle, to inflame the mind of our people by half truths into the frenzy of war in order that they may never appreciate the real cause of it until it is too late. I do not believe that our national honor is served by such a course. The right way is the honorable way.

One alternative is to admit our initial blunder to enforce our rights against Great Britain as we have enforced our rights against Germany; demand that both those nations shall respect our neutral rights upon the high seas to the letter; and give notice that we will enforce those rights from that time forth against both belligerents and then live up to that notice.

The other alternative is to withdraw our commerce from both. The mere suggestion that food supplies would be withheld from both sides impartially would compel belligerents to observe the principle of freedom of the seas for neutral commerce.[5]

[5]Arthur A. Ekrich, Jr., ed., *Voices in Dissent: An Anthology of Individualist Thought in the United States* (New York: The Citadel Press, 1964), pp. 211–22. See also Robert M. La Follette, "Speech on the Declaration of War Against Germany," from the *Congressional Record*, Sixty-fifth Congress, First Session (April 4, 1917), pp. 222.

(Prepared by Marilyn Tenney)

CONTRIBUTORS

- JOHN V. DENSON is editor of *The Costs of War: America's Pyrrhic Victories.*

- GEORGE BITTLINGMAYER is professor of economics at the University of Kansas.

- MARSHALL L. DEROSA is professor of history at Florida Atlantic University.

- THOMAS J. DILORENZO is professor of economics at Loyola College.

- LOWELL GALLAWAY is professor of economics at Ohio University.

- RICHARD M. GAMBLE is associate professor of history at Palm Beach Atlantic College.

- DAVID GORDON is editor of *The Mises Review.*

- PAUL GOTTFRIED is professor of political philosophy at Elizabethtown College.

- RANDALL G. HOLCOMBE is professor of economics at Florida State University.

- HANS-HERMANN HOPPE is professor of economics at the University of Nevada, Las Vegas.

- JEFFREY ROGERS HUMMEL is adjunct associate professor of history at Golden Gate University.

- MICHAEL LEVIN is professor of philosophy at the City University of New York.

- YURI N. MALTSEV is professor of economics at Carthage College.

- WILLIAM MARINA is professor of history at Florida Atlantic University.

- RALPH RAICO is professor of history at Buffalo State College.

- CAREY ROBERTS is assistant professor of history at Arkansas Tech University.

- JOSEPH T. SALERNO is professor of economics at Pace University.

- BARRY DEAN SIMPSON is a doctoral candidate in economics at Auburn University.

- JOSEPH R. STROMBERG is the JoAnn B. Rothbard historian in residence at the Mises Institute.

- H. ARTHUR SCOTT TRASK is a Peg Rowley fellow in history at the Mises Institute.

- RICHARD VEDDER is professor of economics at Ohio University.

- CLYDE N. WILSON is professor of history at the University of South Carolina.

- THOMAS E. WOODS, JR., is instructor of history at Suffolk County Community College.